The Russian Adoption

The Russian Adoption Handbook

How to Adopt from Russia, Ukraine, Kazakhstan,
Bulgaria, Belarus, Georgia, Azerbaijan and Moldova

John H. Maclean

iUniverse Star
New York Lincoln Shanghai

The Russian Adoption Handbook
How to Adopt from Russia, Ukraine, Kazakhstan,
Bulgaria, Belarus, Georgia, Azerbaijan and Moldova

iUniverse Star
an iUniverse, Inc. imprint

For information address:
iUniverse, Inc.
2021 Pine Lake Road, Suite 100
Lincoln, NE 68512
www.iuniverse.com

John Maclean and his wife Brigitte have adopted twice from Russia.
He is an attorney and can be reached at wassaw2@email.com.
He is also the author of *The Chinese Adoption Handbook: How to Adopt from
China and Korea.*

ISBN: 0-595-30115-0

Printed in the United States of America

For my two wonderful Leaps of Faith
Alexander and Catherine

CONTENTS

INTRODUCTION

This handbook is written to assist those who have decided to adopt from Russia and its former Republics. Some of the comments and discussion are relevant to adopting internationally in general, however the focus is on Eastern Europe and Central Asia. Americans are now adopting over 7,000 children a year from those countries.

The main reason foreign adoption has become so popular is simple. Compared to the United States, the paperwork and process is easier. If you go through the steps, you have a very good chance of adding to your family within 8 months. This is not to say that the process does not have its bumps in the road, and notice I did not use the word "easy," but "easier."

Why adoption in the United States is so hard is beyond the scope of this book. However, if you have gone through the fertility nightmare and then the long wait for a domestic child, you will find the Russian, Ukrainian or Kazakhstani adoption process to be wonderful, just for its straightforwardness, if nothing else.

My wife and I have adopted twice from Russia and as a lawyer I have made it a point to study the laws of the US and foreign countries in regard to adoption. The purpose in writing this handbook is simply to provide a roadmap and to give you more control over the process. You will not find the answers to all of your questions in this book. But it will cover most of them. As to the remainder, between your agency and the Internet, you should be able to find the rest. Opinions expressed in this book all come with the caveat that they apply *generally* to situations. Exceptions will always exist.

The best way to use this book is to read all of the chapters, even if you are not adopting from Russia. Most of the procedures in the other countries are derived from the Russian process. Chapters on packing, traveling, and medical conditions also apply universally. In the chapters on the other countries, I have tried to highlight the differences from the Russian experience rather than simply repeat applicable chapters. Adoption rules, both official and unofficial, have a tendency to change from year to year so you can expect some variations.

Finally, adopting is an art, not a science. Whether your experience in Russia or in any country is a happy one depends in some part on your expectations, comfort level and demeanor. Further, your adoption is full of important choices that are yours, and yours alone. No one has the right to second-guess you. This includes your choice of whether to hire an agency or adopt independently, your choice of whether to adopt this particular child or whether you should pay an "expedite" fee or not. The decisions and consequences are yours alone.

You will find that there is no such thing as a stress free adoption. The Chinese have a saying that progress is two steps forward and one step back. You should expect that in adopting from Eastern Europe, there might be a few bumps in the road, but there is nothing that you cannot handle with a good attitude. You might not like the food. It might be colder than you thought. The Judge might ask you a question you didn't anticipate. Your homestay host doesn't speak English. The INS (now known as the BCIS) or Judge wants yet another piece of paper. In comparison to having and loving your child, it's all small stuff.

Now for the usual disclaimer. All opinions expressed in this book are those of the author. The information contained within these pages is intended to educate and not to serve as legal or medical advice on a particular problem. Discussions and links relating to web sites, medical conditions and tax aspects of adoption are not intended to be endorsements or professional advice whether in this book or on the aforementioned web sites. The companies and products referred to in this book maintain their trademarks and copyrights, and no infringement is intended. They are simply mentioned for information only.

CHAPTER I

OVERVIEW OF INTERNATIONAL ADOPTION

Adoptions of Russian orphans first occurred in 1921 after the United States withdrew from its invasion of northern Russia. When the soldiers (primarily from Michigan) returned, they also brought with them about 20 orphans. International adoption though really began as a response to the growing number of orphans (Displaced Persons) in Europe after World War II, which was followed by the Korean wave beginning in the mid-1950s, after the Korean War. Currently, there are more than 100,000 Korean adoptees in the United States.

The third wave of internationally adopted children came from Latin and Central America and really began to grow in 1973, peaking at 2,500 children in 1991. The last wave began with the fall of the Iron Curtain. Russia and Romania became the primary sending countries. At the same time, China began to allow intercountry adoption of infants.

Below are some of the adoption statistics since 1995.

IMMIGRANT VISAS ISSUED
TO ORPHANS COMING TO THE U.S.

TOP COUNTRIES OF ORIGIN

	FY 1995	FY 1996	FY 1997
1	2,130.......CHINA	3,333.......CHINA	3,816......RUSSIA
2	1,896.......RUSSIA	2,454.......RUSSIA	3,597......CHINA
3	1,666.......KOREA	1,516.......KOREA	1,654.....S. KOREA
4	449........GUATEMALA	427........GUATEMALA	788.......GUATEMALA
5	371.........INDIA	555.........ROMANIA	621.........ROMANIA
6	351........PARAGUAY	380.........INDIA	425........VIETNAM
7	350........COLOMBIA	354.........VIETNAM	352.........INDIA
8	318.........VIETNAM	258........PARAGUAY	233.......COLOMBIA
9	298........PHILIPPINES	255........COLOMBIA	163.......PHILIPPINES
10	275.........ROMANIA	229.........PHILIPPINES	152........MEXICO

	FY 1998	FY 1999	FY 2000
1	4,491......RUSSIA	4,348.......RUSSIA	5,053........CHINA
2	4,206......CHINA	4,101.......CHINA	4,269........RUSSIA
3	1,829.....S. KOREA	2,008......S. KOREA	1,794.......S. KOREA
4	911.......GUATEMALA	1,002......GUATEMALA	1,518.......GUATEMALA
5	603........VIETNAM	895.........ROMANIA	1,122.......ROMANIA
6	478........INDIA	712.........VIETNAM	724.........VIETNAM
7	406........ROMANIA	500.........INDIA	659.........UKRAINE
8	351........COLOMBIA	323.........UKRAINE	503.........INDIA
9	249........CAMBODIA	248.........CAMBODIA	402.........CAMBODIA
10	200.......PHILIPPINES	231.........COLOMBIA	399.........KAZAKHSTAN

	FY 2001	FY 2002
1	4,681........CHINA (mainland born)	5,053........CHINA (mainland)
2	4,279.........RUSSIA	4,939........RUSSIA
3	1,870.........S. KOREA	2,219........GUATEMALA
4	1,609.......GUATEMALA	1,779........S. KOREA
5	1,246........UKRAINE	1,106........UKRAINE
6	782..........ROMANIA	819..........KAZAKHSTAN
7	737...........VIETNAM	766..........VIETNAM
8	672...........KAZAKHSTAN	466..........INDIA
9	543............INDIA	334..........COLOMBIA
10	407..........CAMBODIA	260...........BULGARIA
11	297...........BULGARIA	254...........CAMBODIA
12	266...........COLOMBIA	221...........PHILIPPINES
13	219...........PHILIPPINES	187..........HAITI
14	192..........HAITI	169..........BELARUS
15	158...........ETHIOPIA	168..........ROMANIA
16	129...........BELARUS	105...........ETHIOPIA
17	86............POLAND	101...........POLAND
18	74............THAILAND	67............THAILAND
19	73............MEXICO	65............PERU
20	51............JAMAICA and LIBERIA (both 51)	61............MEXICO

A country's numbers that are missing or very low from one year to the next usually reflect a change in the sending country's laws or the imposition of a moratorium.

In FY 2002 the US Consulate in Moscow issued 5,836 IR3 visas and 50 IR4s. These numbers may include adoptions from other countries like Kasakhstan.

Two kinds of visas are issued by the Department of State for children who have been or will be adopted, and thus qualify for an "immediate relative" visa. One is the visa for the "orphan" (as defined by the Immigration and Nationality Act) who is to be adopted abroad by a U.S. citizen, the "IR-3." There were 13,803 IR-3 visas issued in FY 2001. The other is for the "orphan" who is to be adopted in the U.S. by a citizen, the "IR-4." There were 5,334 IR-4 visas issued in FY 2001. The main distinction is that an IR-3 is given when a single parent or both married parents have seen the child prior to adopting abroad. An IR-4 is given when only one married parent has seen the child or the child is escorted to the US before anyone has met the child. The IR-4 visa means that in the eyes of the State Department the adoption is "not final" for purposes of immigration even though it may be "final" under the laws of the foreign country Instead, the child is considered in guardianship status or if one parent has seen the child then it is a "proxy" or "simple" adoption. Both parents do not have to attend court, but they both have to have seen the child before or at the court hearing before an IR-3 can be issued. The importance is that children with an IR-3 visa obtain automatic citizenship once they reach the United States. A child with an IR-4 visa must await re-adoption or adoption if in guardianship status, or must be in a state like Michigan that recognizes foreign adoption decrees regardless of the visa type. You can read more on this distinction at: *http://travel.state.gov/state105804.html.*

CHAPTER II

RUSSIA TODAY

The Russian Federation is twice the geographic size of the United States and is a country of 145 million people. It used to have more, but Ukraine with 55 million is now a separate country. Kazakhstan also is a separate country and has 17 million people. While Russia seems to be exotic, it really is not. The flight to Moscow is just a little over 9 hours from New York. It takes the same amount of time as if you drove from Atlanta to Tampa.

Metropolitan Moscow contains about 20 million people, almost 15% of the population. The country is far larger than the United States. Once you leave the major urban areas, the population is quite thinly spread out. Both Moscow and St. Petersburg have about two months in the summer when the heat is unbearable. The winters are pretty rough on the other end of the scale. Welcome to Russia.

Notwithstanding the thinly spread population, Russia is an incredible melting pot of people. Generally speaking, pure Russians have a strong Viking/Finnish ethnicity. Yet in the central regions, there is a strong Tatar mix. In the south and across the Urals, a more Asian background is prevalent. Yet all of this has been mixed together for a thousand years to produce a melting pot like no other. Generally, the Ural Mountains mark the boundary between European Russia to the west and Asian Russia to the east. The official breakdown of ethnicity is Russian 81.5%, Tatar 3.8%, Ukrainian 3%, Chuvash 1.2%, Bashkir 0.9%, Byelorussian 0.8%, Moldavian 0.7%, Other 8.1%.

The recent history of Russia follows a path no fictional book could tell. Gorbachev succeeded Chernenko in 1985. In 1988, he began to loosen the reins on the various Soviet Republics, leading to their eventual independence, beginning with the Baltic countries. In August 1991, the old timers and hardliners staged a coup. It appeared to be a close run thing at the time, although comical afterwards. The coup was defeated when the military refused to participate in a bloodbath of their own people. Yeltsin was the hero of the moment and became President of the Russian Federation. Russia and eleven of the former Soviet Republics joined together to form the Commonwealth of Independent States ("CIS") in 1991. Yeltsin then ran the country into the ground. Putin, succeeding Yeltsin, became President in 2000.

Vast forbidden areas, once marked in red on official maps of the Soviet Union, were suddenly open for travel in 1992 when the United States and Russia signed the "Open Lands" agreement which allowed free travel throughout both countries.

Economically Russia is still a mess. It had a brief period of prosperity in 1993-4 but has undergone two severe devaluations. The nascent middle class has had its hopes and expectations, generated by the short lived economic boom, replaced by a feeling of hopelessness that things will ever get better. The middle class was seriously damaged in the 1998 bank meltdown. Nowadays, Russians forgo any thought of saving as that just sets them up for another government crisis, but rather "saves" by buying something as soon as they have the funds. Thus, a typical Russian will spend 95% of their income. Internal saving leading to internal capital investment just doesn't happen. That part of capitalistic theory doesn't function in Russia. If the Russians have any savings, it is in U.S. $100 bills, hidden somewhere in their apartment or in offshore accounts in Malta.

The national minimum monthly wage is $22, but millions earn less than that. Russians have one official job and 5 unofficial ones. In the first quarter of 2001, there were 54.4 million Russians (one in three!) earning less than $100 a month. About 73 percent of Russians grow some or all of their food. Fifty-five percent grow half of the food they eat. What saves them is that the government gave the population the apartments they live in and currently provides large subsidies for electricity, gas and transportation.

Russia imports almost all of its consumer goods. Russia has few exports other than natural resources such as gas, oil and heavy metals. Oil accounts for 40% of Russia's exports. Russia is the largest oil producer in the world, having surpassed Saudi Arabia. Oil exports are set to increase even more as two new pipeline systems opened additional routes to the Baltic Sea and Black Sea in 2001, and a new extension links a Ukrainian port to Russia's main pipeline.

Whenever the Sakhalin Island joint venture finally begins to bear fruit, that field's production will likely change the entire oil dynamics in Asia. Oil exports from Russia and Kazakhstan will increase as much as 45 percent by 2005, according to some estimates. Russia is now in a position where it can almost dictate to OPEC.

As the commodity markets go, so does Russia's economy. Since the oil price increases of 1999-2001, Russia has been more prosperous from a governmental perspective. However, there has only been a trickle down effect in the major cities and not in the countryside. Further, this trickle down effect has only marginally improved the quality of life of the middle class.

The retail industry has expanded to soak up this oil-based income. Sales are climbing for everything from beer to hair coloring. Analysts tracking the fortunes of Danish brewer Carlsberg watch the ruble exchange rate as a profit indicator for the company. Carlsberg owns 50% of Baltic Beverages Holding, maker of the popular Baltika beer. Last year, Baltika sales soared 60% to $537 million. While Russian men guzzle more beer, women are snapping up cosmetics. Last year, L'Oréal's sales in Russia jumped 52%.

Yet any real increase in the people's wealth is a mirage. A bigger mirage has been any great increase in actual Russian based production or industry. There simply hasn't been any. Without a foundation of legal and cultural respect for private property and contracts, local capital investment in Russian manufacturing is still a very risky proposition and one that is only undertaken by the largest multinationals.

High global oil prices have provided funding for the armed forces in Chechnya and helped to pay the salaries of government employees who still make up what might be counted as the middle class. They have—even more importantly—allowed payments to be made on the country's staggering, multi-billion-dollar debt. In all, revenues from the oil and gas industry account for about half of the budget.

For the best and the brightest who do not want to struggle through the two generations it might take to create a viable economy, emigration is a siren's call that some resist, but many do not. Over a million have gone to Israel and thousands to the United States. Since the era of the czars, Russia has placed the interests of the state above those of the individual. That has not changed.Yet despite all of this adversity, Russians persevere and are a very warm and generous people.

History of Russian Adoptions

The Russian Ministry of Education and Ministry of Health have jurisdiction over children's homes. The Ministry of Education has more to do with foreign adoptions. While foreign adoptions in Russia began in 1991 with 12 adoptions, it really began to take off in 1992 when the Russian Education Ministry established a separate division, "The Rights of the Child," that had access to the federal computerized database on children and dealt exclusively with adoption by foreigners. This division was responsible for selecting children for adoption, getting their papers ready, investigating the adoptive parents, and arranging for the children's departures abroad.

At that time, Russian law held that foreigners could only adopt children with documented health problems. As a result, Russian doctors often exaggerated concerns on health reports, knowing that it would mean a chance at a good life for that child. It also meant valuable income to the Ministry. This process was changed with the institution of the "data bank restriction" in 1995, which is nothing more than a period of time within which only Russians can adopt a child. When the exclusive period ends, the child is cleared for international adoption.

1995 was a watershed year for Russian adoptions. The new laws passed by the Duma in late 1994 were implemented, and a six-month moratorium on foreign adoptions was put into place to give the officials time to create the new system. This system eliminated the medical basis for foreign adoptions and created the database registry instead. The proposal for licensing (accreditation) of foreign agencies and elimination of "middlemen" was not implemented but would come back into play 3 years later. Instead of licensing agencies, the Russians just accepted licenses issued to adoption agencies from the countries of origin with the main requirement being the agencies prove they are non-profit organizations.

Since setting up a licensing agency was the point of the moratorium, all the moratorium did is delay adoptions for hundreds of children and create heartbreak for their foreign families. Nor did Russia really get rid of the "middleman," since parents were allowed to execute a power of attorney to a representative or facilitator. A constant pattern in Russia is that even when a new law is actually followed, the result may be described as two steps forward and one step back, and sometimes the reverse. The western concept of progress as a linear progression doesn't necessarily apply. Another theme in Russian jurisprudence is the power of local authorities to overrule the central authority by simply electing not to follow it. During the moratorium, the mayors of St.

Petersburg, Sobchak (Putin's mentor who was later run out of the country but seems like a decent guy) and of Moscow, Luzhkov, (who has his own agenda and is almost as powerful as Putin) ignored the moratorium and allowed many children to be adopted. In Russia, following the law is like taking a college elective. Their culture does not yet make it a required course.

The Education Ministry's division no longer exists, and in its place is the current system of adoption agencies in the adoptive country working with facilitators in Russia. Some of the facilitators are actually employees of the adoption agency, and the agency may even have an office in Russia. Yet most work is done through independent facilitators. Facilitators are Russians who have good connections and good will with the federal and regional Ministries and the children's home directors and who shepherd you along through your Russian experience in country. They will arrange for the driver, translator, and homestay. They will assist you on your travel around Russia, whether by plane or train. They will take you to the children's home, work with the home's director and attend the court hearing with you.

Your agency probably began its adoptions in Russia in one of four ways. First, it may be an experienced international adoption agency, and Russia is just another country in its long list of countries with which it works. Second, it may be an agency founded by people who did missionary work or gave medical help to Russia in the early 1990's and who returned to the States with the idea of helping the children. Third, Russian émigrés may have founded the agency. Fourth, persons who have adopted internationally may have founded the agency.

Today the United States probably adopts the largest number of Russian children, although Italy, France and Germany also adopt from Russia. For example, in St. Petersburg in 1991, foreigners adopted 529 children. While the majority, 262, went to homes in the United States, many of the children were placed with families in other countries—including 126 in Italy, 36 in France, 34 in Israel and 33 in Finland.

In fiscal year (ends September 30th) 1992, the US Embassy's Visa Unit in Moscow issued 324 visas to adopted children. In 1993 the figure doubled to 746. In 1994, the number was 1087. In 1995, it jumped to 2178. In late 1995, Russia issued a moratorium on adoptions as it was revising its laws. In 1996, the United States Embassy in Moscow issued 2,454 immigrant visas to adopted children. In 1997, 3,816 visas were issued, in 1998, 4,491, in 1999,4,348, in 2000, 4,269 and in 2001, 4,279.

Adoption Today

Russia allows adoption when it is in the best interests of the child. Russian officials do not like to have sibling groups split up, however, they will allow it when it is best for the children. To adopt a child, who has reached ten years of age, it is necessary to have the child's permission. While there is no law to this effect, the general rule is that parents must be under 55 years of age, and there should be no more than 45 years separating the mother's and the child's ages (some regions say 52). This "unwritten" rule is not strictly applied and is barely a rule at all. Singles of either gender are permitted to adopt, although men seem limited to boys only. Regions can also have their own "rules." One region does not allow you to adopt a second child within a year of the first adoption, if the two children are unrelated. Another region has no limit for couples, but won't let a single parent adopt unrelated children at all. Some judges frown at single fathers. In Irkutsk a single father has no chance at all, but in Tyumen they do.

There are very few young sibling sets available for adoption in Russia. Sibling groups under the age of 3 are rare. Russians prefer to space their children about 5 years apart. Most of the available kids are given up at birth by an unwed mother and adopted before the age of 1 1/2. That's usually not time enough for a sibling or, more likely, a half sibling to be born and identified as being related to the first child. Most families who wish to adopt an infant and a toddler find that it's easiest to adopt unrelated children to achieve this goal.

Cases where young siblings are available would be where there is a birth of twins, or where parental rights were terminated because of abuse or neglect, or the parents have died. These are a minority of cases. Yet if your heart is set on adopting twins, and you are willing to wait, then there is always a chance that twins can become available. Most sibling groups are ages 5 and older. Because of this, most people who want to adopt young children adopt unrelated children.

For unknown reasons, more boys than girls appear to be available for adoption. This does vary by Region, however it generally is true. The wait time for a girl can be longer. One reason that is given for there being more boys is that Russian women think that a daughter will more likely take care of them in their old age. Also, Russian men still have a problem with the idea of raising another man's son.

The earliest an infant can be adopted in Russia seems to be around 6 months. Most infants are adopted between 8 months and a year. The age difference depends on how quickly your agency receives the referral from the Region's inspector and how quickly American families are "paper ready."

For the most part, the children are healthy. By this I mean that once brought over to the United States and given proper vitamin enriched foods, medical attention, and love, Russian children respond like any American child. Many do have developmental and speech delays and some have mild attachment issues, but with speech therapy and stimulation they respond favorably. The severe attachment problems that were seen in some of the early Romanian adoptions do exist, but only a minority of children have these issues.

During the first 7 months of 1999, 2,272 children were adopted. It was almost evenly divided between girls and boys with girls holding a slight edge. Couples adopted 89% of the children, single mothers 10%, and single fathers 1%. The largest numbers were in the 2-year-old range with the 1 and 3 year olds the second largest. Past the age of 3 and the adoption numbers are in the teens until the 9 year olds when they begin to drop below 10. The last age group is age 13. The total number of American adoptions from Russia in 1999 was 4,470 and in 2000 4,677. In contrast, domestic adoptions by Russians totaled 15,000 in 2000.

Russia's Children's Homes

The number of children in Russia's orphanages is usually listed at 600,000 (about the same number as in America's foster care system), but that figure is misleading, as many of these are not eligible for adoption. Only about 10% or 60,000 of the children can be adopted. Most of these children are in the homes because the poor economic conditions of the country have made it hard for parents to support their children. Others are there because their parents have privatized their apartment and sold it to pay for the parent's alcohol habit, leaving the children homeless. There is also neglect and abuse because of alcoholism. There is also the plight of the grandmother who took in her grandchild because her daughter was an alcoholic and has died. Economic circumstances might then later force the grandmother to place the child in a home.

In Russia there are several types of orphanages for different children. It is estimated that there are 252 baby homes for the youngest children. Because most of the children are not real "orphans" in the sense that we use that word in America, I will refer to the institutions as "children's homes". The reason they are not real "orphans" is because a great many of the children are placed with the state because their family is simply too poor to support them at that time. This is not necessarily a permanent condition and the child may return to the family later. Also, the mother may have relinquished the child, but other family members, like a grandmother, may periodically visit. If a family member shows an interest, then the child is not eligible for adoption at that time.

Some of the children have parents who are in prison and are simply waiting for their parent's term to end. These children are part of the 600,000, yet are obviously not eligible for adoption. Of course, others are abandoned or relinquished without any family visitation or have had their parents' rights terminated because of abuse or neglect. These are the children who are eligible.

The reasons children are relinquished to the children's home are as varied as snowflakes. Yet at the core, economics drives the majority. It is very hard to raise a large family in Russia under the current economic environment, and if a surprise fourth or fifth child comes along, the best alternative can be to relinquish the child. This is especially true if the woman is a single parent. It also cuts across classes and education levels. You can find birth mothers that are homeless, blue collar or college educated. About 95% are social orphans which means their parents are alive, but either relinquished their child to an orphanage or have had their parental rights revoked which is the case for 40% of social orphans. Usually parental rights are revoked due to alcoholism or jail sentences. Only 5% are true orphans.On average, every 100th child born is sent to an orphanage directly from the maternity hospital. Doctors have historically encouraged mothers to give up their child if there is the slightest indication that the child might not be considered normal.This was also a common medical practice in the United States until the 1960's.

Russians consider being raised in a children's home a stigma. You would not be a happy Russian parent if you learned your son or daughter was marrying one. That label stays with you forever when you are looking for a job, housing, or school.

Sometimes you may find that your child is under some sort of quarantine. The disease season runs from October through March in a children's home. You may have heard the expression, "As fast as a cold through a day care." That is certainly the case in children's homes as well. Russian orphanages use quarantine to help prevent the spread of chicken pox, flu, measles, and other communicable diseases. It is a rather common measure. Sick children are hospitalized when they need more care than is available from the staff. They are often hospitalized for much less serious illnesses, such as bronchitis, than we would hospitalize our kids. The difference is that a parent can provide one on one attention and round the clock care for a sick child, but this is not available in a Russian children's home.

What follows is a general description of the types of children's homes in urban Russia. You will find that exceptions exist. In Russia, they always do. Uniformity may be preached, but it is rarely achieved.

In the past adoption was rarely considered by Russian families. It was frowned upon. Russians went to great lengths to hide the adoption. Mothers would wear pillows under their skirts. They would change the birth date and birthplace of the child. That is now changing a little. Certain regions are even experimenting with family children's homes (like foster care) and adoption incentives. Foster care has not become a widespread solution because of problems with the Russian bureacracy and the lack of funding. Legally, the family children's homes fall under government jurisdiction, but functionally the families are on their own. Many of these families did receive large houses (as opposed to apartments) and large cars or minivans as a form of assistance, but government regulation and follow-on support never materialized. The foster parents receive a monthly stipend for each child but inflation has made the stipend almost worthless.

Financing of baby orphanages is the responsibility of the local government. It has been argued that the cost to sustain one child in an orphanage is 20-40% higher than in a family children's home and is much higher than the average Russian family spends per child. Since the children's home's money comes from the local governmental budget, their financial status is by definition unstable. Most orphanages don't receive all the money allotted, and they may receive nothing. Money is budgeted only for food, medicines and salaries, so there is little investment in development, continuing education of staff, or even toys. This is why foreign donations are so important.

Interestingly enough, the distribution of aid roughly follows a geographic guideline by donor country. The basic principle at work is that the aid recipient and donor country are located near each other. For example, in the Russian Far East, Japan leads in aid giving, in Northern Russia, Sweden is the main aid-giver, International aid organizations focus on the major cities, notably Moscow and St. Petersburg. For Germany and the United States, there is no regional preference, although Germany is more involved in Kalingrad. Aid from New Zealand comes in the form of help to certain orphanages, which have been involved in adoptions through one particular agency.

The orphanage system is divided into three sections depending on the age of the child and according to disabilities, if any. A child who becomes an orphan from birth goes through a minimum of three separate orphanage facilities, each answering to a separate Ministry under the government. First a baby orphanage, then a children's home and finally a school-internat. If a child is disabled, he or she is usually sent to a special orphanage and segregated according to disability. The system is based on segregation and doesn't consider the basic rights of children as set down by the United Nations, which Russia has agreed to on paper. Imagine this scenario: Four siblings separated in age by 2 to 5 years, one of whom has Cerebral Palsy. In this situation the kids would each live in different institutions. Within a single institution children are also segregated by age group. The child with CP would be sent to a special orphanage only for kids with CP.

Children from birth to the age of 4 years live in a "dom rebyonka" (house of the child). These homes belong to the (federal) Ministry of Health, so the director is often a pediatrician. They are normally better equipped and are in a better condition than the other types of homes. There are approximately 252 of these homes in Russia, housing 18-20,000 children.

After their fourth birthday, the children are evaluated in order to decide where they should continue to live. If the child has no delays or only minor developmental delays, he will go to a home from the educational system. They are called "dyetski dom" (children's house).

For school age children, there are two different types of homes: those with an internal school (called "internat") and those without, which means, that the children living there visit external state/public schools. These schools (internal as well as external) could be regular schools or "vospomogatelnye schkoly" ("schools for backward children", or schools for children with learning disabilities). Usually children are moved to an "internat" school around the age of 7 and stay there until they are about 17. Because there is a mixture of ages, it can be a tough place to grow up.

A child could live there until their 18th birthday. But normally they will change to a PTU ("Prof-Tekh-Uchilishche", vocational school) at the age of about 15 or 16. Notwithstanding, when a child graduates from the boarding school they are given about one month's wage and sent on their way. They have no support mechanism to help them adjust to society or living on their own. Most don't know how to budget, cook, or even wash their socks.

Homes for blind, deaf or physically impaired children also belong to the educational system. They are nearly all "internaty". Often the children living in the homes of the educational system are labeled as "umstvenni otstali" (children with learning disabilities).

Children with severe mental handicaps or with multiple handicaps live in homes of the social welfare system from their fourth birthday on. In these homes, called "dyetski dom/internat", the children are living in several different sections, according to their problems. The more problems a child has and the more severe they are, the less help the child gets. These are the homes you may have seen pictured in magazines and on television. There are also homes that have groups of about 15-20 children living in one room. These children are fed (more or less) and cleaned (better or worse), but they do not get any attention, occupation, education and only most basic medical therapy. The situation of these last children is terrible. The more severe the problems of the children are, the younger they die. Normally, no adoptions are allowed from these homes. There are a few homes that are based on a German model. They are a "village" made up of several houses. Each house has a "den mother" and 5 or 6 kids. They function as a family, each having their chores with older kids looking after the younger. The "mother" gets one weekend off each month, and an "aunt" comes in for that time. These types are very few, but as expected, the children are emotionally much better off.

You have to be careful when discussing "special" schools. The word "special' in Russia can be applied to anything. A "special school" might be one where children learn English starting in the second grade and is for "specially advanced" kids. It can mean a "special labour" school which focuses on vocational opportunities. It can also be a school for say Down Syndrome children, which is also called "special".

While many countries no longer separate orphaned siblings, Russia's adoption system cannot always prevent their separation. Legal regulations state that siblings should be kept together as much as possible, but there are many factors—age, gender and the mental and physical health of the siblings, as well as lack of space in orphanages that can conspire to separate siblings.

There are several organizations that offer help for older kids. One organization is Maria's Children; their web site is *http://www.mariaschildren.org/*. Another is MiraMed Independent Living; their web site is *http://www.miramedinstitute.org/*. These programs offer some hope for these older children, teaching them some basic life and job skills. Some US companies, such as Cisco, have also pitched in to help.You can see a list of other helping organizations at *http://www.russianadoption.org/charity.htm*. What I have described are the basic "types" of homes. Now as to "conditions," it is impossible to generalize about Russia's children's homes simply because there is one or more in every town. You can find good ones and bad ones and everything in between. The infants might have their diapers removed at the age of 1 and allowed to stay in soiled clothes all day. Sometimes a rural home will be better than an urban one simply because food is more plentiful. Sometimes an urban one is better because it receives more money. Some homes are actually cottages where the children live in family-like groups. In others, the caregivers have not been paid and are uncaring. You simply cannot generalize. No television show, no magazine story or newspaper is able to capture the true picture. You would actually have to visit many of the homes in a particular region to receive a generalized view.

Nevertheless, let me do a little generalizing, knowing that I will be inaccurate. Most of the homes do lack money. They do lack food (those that have food are primarily on a starch based diet). They do lack vitamins and medicine. They lack love. Because you might only have four caregivers to 30 children, life is regimented. The children go to potty at the same time and eat at the same time. They sleep in a dorm or barracks-like room. Beds are made up and tidy. The older children help with the younger ones. Their clothing and linen are well worn. The children do not receive as much stimulation as they need. Playground equipment is limited. The caregivers only have time to care for the children's basic needs, and little time is left over for stimulation. They do not have kid spoons so the children have difficulty eating their food, as they have to use large adult spoons. Mashed potatoes, soup, bread, kasha and tea are the usual diet. Most children do not see fruits or vegetables with any regularity, no matter what the director may tell you. Many children in orphanages have a diet heavy in the popular Russian drink kefir, but it contains relatively few nutrients, lacks vitamin D and has very little calcium or phosphates that are necessary for healthy bones.

Some children do not recover from this environment, but many, the "resilient rascals" as they are called do rebound successfully.

The addresses and phone numbers of most Russian orphanages can be found at *http://www.fireflykids.org/engl/*. Just type in your town or region in the search box. Also, you can find them at *http://www.karensadoptionlinks.com/orphanage.html*

If you have a strong stomach, you can read the Human Rights Watch's 1998 report on Russian orphanages at *http://www.hrw.org/reports98/russia2/*. When you read it, remember that this report focused on abuses.

Descriptions of Children's Homes

Here are descriptions of a few homes by people who have actually been there. This is for illustrative purposes only and is not intended to describe a typical children's home. There is no such thing. You can find descriptions of children's homes in Glazov, Izshevsk and Votkinsk in the Sept/Oct 1999 issue, Vol 32, No. 5. of "Adoptive Families."

Rostov Region

Our daughter was adopted from the Rostov Region of Russia in June of '97. Most of the buildings in the area were tired looking, mostly brick. We turned down what looked like an alley, which was the entrance to a dirt compound the orphanage was built around. There were a couple big trees and lots of weeds and piles of junk. No playground equipment... just a bunch of kids running around in their underwear because it was so hot. The compound side of the orphanage was white stucco walls with dull green trim (green was the color of choice for all the buildings it seems). Inside we were led down a hall (another shade of green) past a kitchen and through what was our child's play/eat/sleep area. One end of it had small tables and chairs where they ate their meals of mostly soup for the entire time we were there...and on the other end the wall was covered with a huge outdoor mural. There was a couch and a desk that separated the beds from the table area...and the beds were nothing but mattresses on the floor. There was one small nightstand. Through a set of tall double doors we were led to the "waiting room," which faced the street with a wall of windows, covered with lace curtains. There were tables, couches, and a TV and piano. The floor was a wood parquet pattern, which must have been beautiful in its time. The facilities were clean, if sparsely furnished and worn with time. We saw two toys in the place but there may have been more—we were only allowed in these two rooms. One was a ragged bear and a doll missing its nose.

Komi Republic, Syktyvkar Region

When we adopted our son in December of '97 his orphanage was a stark contrast. Again we were only allowed in the playroom where we were introduced to him. There was another playroom for younger children where they dressed him when we were ready to leave. The director's office had huge built in shelves stocked with dolls and toys of all kinds that didn't look like they had been used much. This region of Russia operates in the black because of natural resources. It was dark outside about 18-20 hours of each day and the ground was covered with a deep layer of snow and it was very cold, minus 40 degrees. There was a nice playground outside equipped with a sandbox and things like that (you could only see the outlines of them in the snow though). The rooms we were allowed in inside were well equipped with mats and bars and balance beans and all kinds of sensory stimulating activities. The walls were painted with beautiful murals of cartoon characters, fairies, flowers and the like. When they got our son ready to leave, the room they dressed him in had a huge built in playpen and the kind of equipment one would see in most daycare centers here in the states.

Krasnodar Territory

In the city of Novorossiysk which is located some 2,000 miles south of Moscow on the Black Sea.

Baby Home

The Baby Home was a two-story building that looked very old and decrepit from the outside. There were rusty-looking grates on the windows, chipped and broken stone stairs and railings, and peeling paint all over. The outside yard was overgrown and the "playground" looked unsafe for children. It had 2 or 3 climbing things made of splintered wood and a few other rusty pieces of equipment.

Upon entering the Baby Home, the inside felt very gloomy—almost spooky. The place was cool, dark and damp, and the entry door led into a poorly lit corridor that had 4 locked doors off of it. One door led to the director's office and one led to the first children's group facility. One led to a stairway and another led to a corridor that went to other sections that housed other groups of kids and staff.

Inside one group's section the look and feel improved. We entered a large 20' x 20' recreation-type room which had hardwood floors, most of which was covered with a red tapestry rug. The ceilings were very high. There were several dark wood display cases with glass fronts and they contained a myriad of toys. The windowsills were covered with dolls and stuffed animals and there were white lace curtains on the very tall windows. There were several playpens full of toys. On one side of the room there was living room-type furniture—a sofa, two chairs, a table and lamp. Caregivers often sat and held, read to, and played with the children here. Another section of the room had little tables and chairs for the kids to sit at, along with doll beds and high chairs, and a few of those walking/seats for those babies beginning to move around. There was a desk and a television set in this room, too. In the back section of the room were a freestanding divider and another sofa and table. It looked like the place the caregivers might sleep.

There was a back door that led to the kids' sleeping room—approximately 12' x 15'—that was very dark, even with sunlight coming through the tall windows on the side wall. The room was a pale green with a few storybook characters painted on the walls. There was a print carpet on the floor and the only furniture in the room were the dozen or so toddler beds lined up on the two sides of the room. Each had matching blankets and pillows, and there was a tiny chair at the end of each bed. The remaining wall had a built-in closet-type structure with a dozen narrow cubbies with hooks for clothing.

A second door off of the main room led to the eating and kitchen facility. This room had three small tables with four chairs at each, and a counter, sink and stove with overhead cabinets in the other section. It was a very tiny food preparation area. Everything was very rundown but very clean. A dozen bibs were hanging below the cabinets. The last room in this group's facility was a tiny anteroom (maybe 6' x 8') off the kitchen that contained a single large, deep sink, wall hooks with towels, and cubby shelves containing the kids' potty seats.

When we arrived at the scheduled time, the main room was brightly lit, fresh smelling, and the kids were all tidy, and busy at play. On days when we arrived unannounced, it was a lot darker—most lights were off or curtains drawn, and the place didn't feel as fresh or cheery at all.

As for the care the children received, it appeared to be excellent. The care-givers were all very warm, affectionate women who clearly had established loving relationships with the children. The kids were held, played with, attended to when they cried or sought assistance, and kept very tidy and clean. One group had 9 or 10 kids and there were three caregivers on duty at all times, working shifts that consisted of 3 days on for 24 hours and 3 days off for 24 hours. They lived there, ate there, and slept there on their assigned workdays. There were about 80 kids in this Baby Home.

I was there for mealtime, naptime, potty-time, and playtime and was impressed with it all. Certainly everything was regimented—like clockwork—and the kids followed the routine like little robots. Meals were well balanced and sizable and the kids appeared to be well nourished. All the same, it was a sad place to be—a day-to-day existence of limited and repeated activity, limited and shared toys and clothing, and nothing to be excited or enthusiastic about. Most of the kids were not eligible for adoption because of visits or inquiries from family members as little as one time per year.

The staff had become very attached to my child in the months they had cared for her. Outside the orphanage in the entry courtyard, each of her care-givers, including the orphanage doctor and director, held her and spoke with her individually, ending their goodbye with a teary hug and kiss on each cheek.

Older Children's Home

The children's home was also old and decrepit looking from the outside, and very similar inside. My time there was limited. I did have access to the main recreation room, the corridors and sitting areas between the group living quarters, and the director's office. As with the Baby Home, the inside was very dark and gloomy most of the time, with a few brightly lit rooms where visitors were present or expected. The walls all had storybook characters similar to the children's section of a public library, but appearing in dimly lit foyers and corridors they were a bit eerie. The facility did appear to be very clean. The atmosphere here was very different than in the Baby Home. The director was much more business-like and did not seem to have any emotional attachment to the children. The few caregivers I met were very brusque and seemed to run the place in a "colder", more military manner. After their departure from the orphanage (and subsequent to their return to the U.S.) some older children indicated that there were some tough disciplinarians among them and beatings were not uncommon.

The children seemed to have some degree of independence, coming and going in and out of rooms on their own. But they, too, were on a very regimented schedule of meals, playtime, and sleep.

Republic of Mari-El

In the city of Yoshkar-Ola, which is a 17-hour train, ride east of Moscow.

Baby Home.

The facility was new, modern, bright, and well equipped both inside and out. In addition to the group living spaces, which consisted of recreation rooms, eating rooms, sleeping rooms and bathrooms, the facility also housed an infirmary, a chapel, and even a swimming pool—all of which were used regularly. There were also small classroom-type rooms where speech therapy and other individual care were given.

The kids ate at the little tables in their little chairs, with their plastic bibs tucked under their big bowls of food. They collectively and uniformly would wash their hands, sit on the pots, and go sleep at naptime. The children received loving care from the Baby Home staff. My child was always being showered with hugs and kisses, cuddled and rocked to reassure her that everything would be fine. She received a lot of love and attention from these caregivers. The departure from this Baby Home was emotional for everyone involved. One of the caregivers had access to email and she asked for my email address to stay in touch. Upon my return, we began weekly online correspondence and I have sent photos and letters to the staff to keep them up to date on my child's new life. We even had a visit in our home from one of her caregivers that was traveling in this area!

Perm Region

In the city of Solikamsk which is located three hours north of Perm. Perm is 800 miles east of Moscow near the Ural Mountains.

Baby Home

We adopted our son in 1997 from Solikamsk. The home was a two story concrete rectangular building on a dirt street. It was painted and not worn looking. The front door was made of very heavy wood in contrast to the painted concrete building. The home was very clean although not well lit. We were led into a large room on the first floor containing a mural of forest scenes and a piano. There were many toys on a cabinet against one wall. We were not sure if these were for show or if the children played with them. The room seemed to double as both the music room and the visitor's reception area. The room was about 30 feet long by 15 feet wide and had a set of windows along one side overlooking the road below and the forested land outside the town. The home director was a doctor and there were about 5 caregivers for 40 children. The children seemed to be from infant to age 4. The children had drawn pictures and these lined the wall as you went up the stairs.

On the second floor were little cots in neat rows against the wall. It was like a barracks type dorm room. It was very clean and tidy. No blankets just sheets as they kept the home warm. The cots were all made up. We saw a small play area next to the infant crib room. The play area was clean but only had a few toys in it. The crib room had old wooden cribs against the walls on either side. There were 4 on each side. There were no bumper pads or much in the way of toys. One room had a large playpen, but with no toys in it.

On the first floor we saw a small square pool about the size of a hot tub where the children would swim for therapy for 20 minutes. There was also a gravel box in which the children walked back and forth for a few minutes a day in order to stimulate their feet to help them walk. We saw no playground equipment outside.

The caregivers appeared very loving toward the children and the facility appeared clean although somewhat bare.

Chapter III

RESEARCH

To complete a Russian adoption, parents must fulfill the requirements of their State, the Bureau of Citizenship and Immigration Services (BCIS) and Russia. This may appear to be an endless paperchase and quite overwhelming at first. However, if you break down the process to its component parts, then it becomes just another manageable checklist. The checklist can be divided into three parts: Home Study, BCIS, and Foreign Country requirements. If possible, you will find your stress reduced if you work on the home study and BCIS contemporaneously before choosing an adoption agency. The reason is that an agency may refer a child to you, and you will then have the significant added stress of deciding whether to accept the referral while you are undergoing the paperchase. Choosing an agency should be the last step you take, not the first.

Do not just jump in to the adoption process. Understand the process and some of the issues. Thanks to the Internet, there are hundreds of web sites devoted to foreign adoptions. Just type in "Chinese adoption" or "Korean Adoption" on your search engine and you will be inundated with sites. The BCIS regulations governing international adoption can be found at 8 CFR 204.3, which can be found at this web site: *http://www.access.gpo.gov/nara/cfr/waisidx_99/8cfr204_99.html.* The US Department of State has good overviews of the adoption process for each country. These overviews or flyers are on the State Department's web site and provide a good starting point. They cannot be relied upon too much as they are usually out of date or don't reflect the practical realities. You should read

BCIS publication M-249, <u>The Immigration of Adopted and Prospective</u> <u>Adoptive Children</u>, at *http://www.immigration.gov/graphics/lawsregs/handbook/adopt_book.pdf* as well as the Department of State publication, <u>International Adoptions</u>. Another good outline of the process can be found at *http://www.foia.state.gov/masterdocs/09fam/0942021N.pdf.*

Remember too that each state will have its owns rules. Some, like Georgia, are relatively painless and are handled within the home study process. Others, like Arizona, require several fingerprint checks and a Court Resolution. Here is a web site listing the state's laws: *http://www.calib.com/naic/laws/index.cfm*

The following are some very helpful web sites. This is by no means an exhaustive list. Your first stop might be to *http://eeadopt.org/*. It is one of the best sites to visit. Its listserv is exceptional in the amount of information exchanged. It even has an English translation of the Russian Family Law as of 1995. There have been some changes since then, but reading the actual law is a good beginning. It is at *http://eeadopt.org/home//preparing/paperwork/laws/ countries/russia/russian_excerpts_1996.htm.*

A terrific site is *http://mywebpage.netscape.com/RhouseKaren/index.htm.* This site contains a lot of links to international adoption stories and links to specific city and region e-groups. There are also many, many web sites where families tell their adoption stories. I recommend reading a few of these just to get a feel for the process. Here is one such story at *http://www.furman.edu/~treu/sasha/.* A great diary of one family's journey is at *http://www.wilmothlatitude.com/diary.html.*

The survey results at *http://education.umn.edu/icd/IAP/* provide the best snapshot of life after an international adoption. You can also purchase an inexpensive video showing one family's adoption journey to Siberia at *http://www.adoptlaw.org/tiac_htm/5stories.htm* by scrolling down to the video "Adopting a New Life."

Here are some other informative sites:
http://www.adoptingfromrussia.com
http://www.ins.usdoj.gov/graphics/services/advproc.htm
http://www.jcics.org/
http://www.iaradopt.com/toc.shtml
http://www.frua.org/index.html
http://travel.state.gov/adoption_russia.html
http://www.russianadoption.org/
http://adoption.about.com/msub_russia.htm

http://www.geocities.com/PicketFence/1045/adopt_bk.htm
http://www.ftia.org/russia/paperwork.htm
http://www.ftia.org/resources/ins.htm
http://www.rainbowkids.com/
http://www.calib.com/naic/
http://www.roofnet.org/about/life-en.html

http://www.adopt-sense.com/fees&forms.htm is an excellent Ukrainian adoption site and has good information on the American and Ukrainian paperchase. A good Canadian site that has information is *http://familyhelper.net/*.

If you need BCIS forms or information you can retrieve them at *http://www.immigration.gov*. A good number of helpful forms and tips can be found at *http://groups.yahoo.com/group/Ind_Russian_Adopt/files/*.

If you want to compare countries, the January-February 2002 issue of Adoption Medical News contains a survey by medical professionals relating the health of the children adopted from different countries. You can obtain back issues at 814-364-2449 for $10.00. You can also go to *www.adoption-news.org* for more information on obtaining back issues.

The I-600A and I-600 forms are of a particular color, orange and blue respectively. You can download those forms from the BCIS website, or call them at 1-800-870-3676 or pick them up from a BCIS office. Your agency should also be able to send them to you. The BCIS and Visa Units in the various Embassies will now accept downloaded copies of forms on white paper. The BCIS has a general explanation of the adoption process at
http://www.ins.usdoj.gov/graphics/howdoi/fororphan.htm.

A strong reality check, which is a must read is at
http://www.pnpic.org/jcics.htm. It is an article by Dr. Jenista on the lack of safeguards for parents. Dr. Jenista also has a good discussion of her view of the Russian adoption process at *http://eeadopt.org/home/jenista_hague.htm*. While her testimony illustrates some of the problems with international adoption, just remember that her conclusion is that "[t]he vast majority of intercountry adoptions have been tremendously successful, building happy 'forever' families."

The National Adoption Information Clearinghouse has a brief summary of each state's requirements at *http://www.calib.com/naic/pubs/l_review.htm* and a link to state laws at *http://www.calib.com/naic/pubs/l_states.htm*.

Many adoption organizations have lending libraries where you can borrow tapes and books on adopting. In Massachusetts, one such organization is ODS Adoption Community of New England at *http://www.odsacone.org*. An interesting CD is "With Eyes Wide Open". It talks about what it will feel like for the prospective parents and child to adjust to the adoption. Each chapter has homework that asks you what the potential problems and solutions could for different areas of life. For example, could a newly adopted child have issues with sleeping and what could a parent do to help? You can also buy it from *http://www.tapestrybooks.com/.*

An interesting research technique is to look at videos of adoption trips so as to get a feel for the experience. You can look at a Perm trip adoption video called "A Passage to Parenthood." It is a 15-minute travelogue that follows an adoptive couple as they fly to Perm, meet their two babies with the Russian social worker, and then travel to Filatov medical clinic and US Embassy in Moscow. The Ural Hotel, shops, orphanage, history, and the children of the Perm region are shown. Contact Linda Brownlee at *lindbrownl@aol.com* of the Adoption Center of Washington. Another video is from a Siberian trip at *http://www.adoptlaw.org/tiac_htm/5stories.htm*; scroll down to the video "Adopting a New Life." There is also a Khabarovsk video available. It was made by one if the Khab families, and shows some hotels, and some city sites. It gives a nice overview of the area. Go to the Khabarovsk adoption website for ordering info. *http://68.33.177.103/.*

Finally, and you probably have already done this, do not fall in love with a picture of a child posted on the web. That child may not be available for adoption or might not be 6 months later when you are ready to travel. Someone else might adopt that child. It just adds to your stress in addition to all of the paperwork. Of course, it is a great motivator, and many people have adopted children that they first saw posted on the web. Just be careful. Protect your heart.

Also, remember that everything about the adoption is your responsibility. You have to educate yourself. You have to ask questions and get involved. You have to make decisions. If you decide that you really just want to pay money to an agency and have them deliver a child to you without much involvement on your part, then you need to look deeper within yourself. Adoption is just a prequel to parenting. You have to be *involved* when you adopt or parent.

Research on Adoptive Children and Families

Since the large numbers of Eastern European adoptions are a fairly recent phenomena, it has really been too soon for any long-term studies to be completed.

Most of the currently published books and studies are based on the early Romanian adoptions where the institutional life was horrendous. However, you cannot simply say that all children's homes are alike no matter where they are located. Certain issues may have a commonality, yet each child's story is by its very nature an individualized event with its own peculiar history. Know that history and you will know that child. So much is dependent on such factors as whether your child was abused, or neglected, in a good children's home or a bad one, his age, the presence of loving caregivers or not, and length of stay in the home, that it is hard to compare your child with a study.

If you read a study, check its relevance by first checking for the country of origin of the study group, then for the ages of the children and finally for whether it is a self selective group. For example, a specialist that treats attachment may say that all Eastern European children have an attachment issue because that is the only population of children that she sees.

One recent study by Michael Rutter (Institute of Psychiatry, King's College London) compared behavioral dysfunction in 165 children adopted from Romania before the age of 42 months, with that of 52 non-deprived UK children adopted in infancy. At four and six years of age, dysfunction was assessed according to seven domains: attachment problems, inattention/over activity, emotional difficulties, autistic features, cognitive impairment, peer difficulties, and conduct problems. Among the Romanian children, between a fifth and a quarter showed normal functioning in all seven domains. This even included children who were aged over two years when they left Romania. However, the researchers note that the chances of normal social functioning were substantially less the older the child was at the time of leaving the institution. The only psychological functions that were associated with institutional privation, either alone or in combination, were attachment disorder behaviors, inattention/over activity, quasi-autistic behavior, and cognitive impairment. Surprisingly, there was no increase in either emotional or conduct problems. Rutter's team comments that the "degree of resilience was remarkable." The study was published in the *British Journal of Psychiatry* in 2001.

Other studies of adopted children in general have demonstrated that under normal circumstances, while early experience may confer a temporary advantage, ultimately IQ is strongly determined by genetic factors. In essence, a good environment can help, but only if the genetic groundwork is first present. Environment cannot create intelligence. Michael Rutter has also concluded in another study that "...[e]nvironmental effects on IQ are relatively modest within the normal range of environments, but that the effects in markedly disadvantageous circumstances are very substantial." My analogy is that you have no control over the genetic potential of the seed you take home from the greenhouse, but whether it flourishes to its potential depends on the soil.

One recent study by Dr. Laurie Miller of the Floating Hospital was published in *Pediatrics* in June 2000. You can find it at *http://www. pediatrics.org/content/vol105/issue6/index.shtml#ELECTRONIC_ARTICLE*   by scrolling down to the article. This study surveyed 452 adopted children from China. They were adopted between 1991 and 1998. The findings were similar to those found in other international adoption populations. 39% of the children were delayed by 2 standard deviations for height, 18% for weight, and 24% for head circumference. The duration of orphanage life was inversely proportional to the linear height lag, with a loss of 1 month of height age for every 2.86 months in the orphanage. Of the children, 75% had significant developmental delay in at least 1 domain: gross motor in 55%, fine motor in 49%, cognitive in 32%, language in 43%, and social-emotional in 28%. Elevated lead levels were found in 14%, anemia in 35%, abnormal thyroid function tests in 10%, hepatitis B surface antigen in 6%, hepatitis B surface antibody in 22%, intestinal parasites (usually *Giardia*) in 9%, and positive skin test results for tuberculosis in 3.5%, none seriously ill. One child each had hepatitis C exposure and congenital syphilis. No child had HIV. Unsuspected significant medical diagnoses, including hearing loss, strabismus, hip dysplasia, orthopedic problems, and congenital anomalies, were found in 18% (81/452) of the children.

One clear finding is that the percent of high lead levels in adopted Chinese children is greater than in other international adoption populations and you should insist that your pediatrician test for lead when you bring your child home. It is an easily correctable condition, if known. This survey also shows that you must also insist that your pediatrician conduct the entire list of recommended tests for adoptive children in order to catch unsuspected problems.

As might be expected, scores for height, weight, and head circumference were lower in children with developmental delays as compared with developmentally normal children. Dr. Miller made an interesting finding that delays in language and activities of daily living skills tended to increase with duration of orphanage confinement, whereas delays in other domains did not show this pattern.

Also, there are other studies listed in Dr. Boris Gindis' articles in the Communique (a professional journal for school psychologists) at: *http://bgcenter.com/communique-article.htm*. You can also read some in the "Pediatric Annals" issue on international adoption in Volume 29, Number 4, April 2000. Back issues can be ordered at 856-848-1000.

In order to remedy this paucity of research, in 2001 the NIH funded a Minnesota study under the auspices of Dr. Dana Johnson of the University of Minnesota's International Adoption Clinic. The project has provided a wonderful snapshot of adoptive parents and their children. The website for the International Adoption Project is at *http://education.umn.edu/icd/IAP/*. Findings from the survey are on this web site.

In February of 2001, surveys were sent to the Minnesota parents of 3,751 children adopted internationally between 1990-1998. Parents sent back 2,299 surveys, a response rate of 61%. The 2,299 children live in 1,857 families. About 50% of the families filled out surveys for more than one child. As of 2001, the moms were approximately 45 years of age (plus or minus 5 years and dads were 46, give or take 6 years. Most parents were between 35 and 40 years old when they adopted. The children were eight years of age (plus or minus 3 years). Eighty-eight percent of the children live in two parent families (86% married; 2% in a committed partnership). Seven percent live in homes with one parent who has never been married and less than 3% of the children live in divorced or separated families. Ninety-three percent of the fathers were employed full time, and 60% of the mothers stayed at home or worked part-time. The parents were generally very well educated. Over 70% have graduated from college. Over 30% have masters, doctorates, or professional degrees.

Moms and dads/partners were very similar in their educational. The household incomes varied considerably with15% having incomes below $50,000, 27% over $125,000 per year; and 58% of the families with incomes between $50,000 and $125,000.

An interesting finding from the surveys was that parents who did not have the referral reviewed by a medical professional were more likely to say the child had more medical problems than they were led to expect, compared to those who had the referral reviewed by a medical professional (23% vs.17%). 67% of parents reported that bonding occurred within a few days, and only 3% were still struggling after one year. (Even if you assume that the first number is high due to parental bias, this shows that bonding eventually occurs for most adoptions within the first year.)

Of the surveyed children, 7 countries accounted for 79%. These are South Korea (32%), Colombia (11%), China (10%), Russia (7.6%), India (7%), Guatemala (6%), and Romania (5.2%). The lowest instances of illness occurred in Korean children, and the highest were from Colombia, followed by China, Russia, Romania, Guatemala and India. Chronic ear infections were the largest medical problem, followed by vision, speech, behavior, anemia, and Hepatitis B and Hepatitis C difficulties. Immediately after adoption to six months later, most problems occurred in sleeping, with children experiencing nightmares, followed by withdrawal, tantrums, hoarding, feeding difficulties, aggression, and crying.

The age of the child at adoption and the care-taking environment prior to adoption had a major affect on school outcome. Children adopted at 2 years of age or older or who received poor or very poor care prior to adoption were 3 to 4 times more likely to be falling behind in some or all classes. If children were adopted at less than six months of age and were well cared for, they did better in school. Thirty-three percent of parents of the 1,483 school-aged children said they were excelling in most or all of their classroom subjects. Forty-four percent of the teenagers had at some time received an award for academic excellence, 20% had received awards for artistic endeavors, and 25% had received awards for athletics. 16% of the children are in gifted classes.

School performance seemed to decline as the children became older and were more academically challenged. It has been noted in other studies that complex abstract thinking in the higher grades is more difficult for adoptive kids coming from an institutional environment and that sometimes tutoring or other special services are needed. These findings also show that children who spent less than 6 months in institutionalized care prior to adoption look similar to children who have lived in foster/family settings.

Dr. Johnson makes the salient point that a child's condition does not depend on the country, but on the care. Thus, a blanket statement that Chinese or Korean adoptive children are better or healthier does not really mean anything per se. If you adopt a child from a terrible Chinese institution, then that child will need additional attention. It is the care that matters, not the country. If the children are being placed in foster care at an early age, if they are not being neglected in the orphanage or if there is no exposure to alcohol, that is what is important, not the country. He gave the example of a Russian child who is placed in foster care (and there are a few) as compared to a Korean child who may have FAE. While you can make generalizations, you have to also realize that it is child specific care that is critical.

Dr Johnson broke down the risk factors into seven main areas. The risk factors were 1) a birthmother who was malnourished during the prenatal period, 2) prenatal exposure to alcohol or other drug exposure, 3) premature birth less than 37 weeks, 4) neglect of basic physical needs such as food, clothing or medical care, 5) neglect of basic social needs such as lack of love, affection, attention and cuddling, 6) physical abuse and 7) a child who was in an orphanage, baby home, or hospital for more than 6 months.

He summarized the results as follows:

	Europe	Latin America	Asia
Prenatal Alcohol/Drug Exposure	44%	15%	9%
Prenatal Malnutrition	50%	41%	24%
Premature Birth	30%	14%	28%
Physically Neglected	45%	26%	12%
Socially Neglected	57%	22%	13%
Physically Abused	13%	6%	3%
6 months or more in an Orphanage, Baby home or Hospital	79%	17%	13%

He did find that children adopted over 24 months of age with a lot of risk factors did have significant behavioral and emotional problems and difficulties in school. The parents of these children will have a different parenting experience that those parenting a child without a lot of risk factors. They can still have a successful adoption, just that it is more work. These parents will have to learn to be advocates for their child and educate themselves on the special education system and how it works. Their child may need attachment therapy and may have more medical issues. Nevertheless, parents that are forewarned and forearmed do much better. They can set a level of expectations that is reasonable for their child and this in turn increases their chances of a successful adoption.

The problem with even this large study is that generalizations must be made carefully. There is no way to compare an adoption of a Romanian or Columbian child in 1990 with one in 1998, as the early care of these children has improved. Nor can you compare a 1 year-old Russian child with a 12-year-old Russian child. So all generalizations naturally must come with plenty of caveats and footnotes.

Other surveys can be found here:

Multi-Agency Survey 1998
http://www.cradlehope.org/surv.html

Rainbow House Agency 1997
http://www.rhi.org/ANews/SurveyResults1997.html

Children Adopted from FSU 1998
http://www.adoption-research.org/parent.html

EEAC also has some research
http://www.eeadopt.org/home/services/research/index.html

Disabled Parents

Russia and the FSU are culturally behind the West when it comes to integrating people with disabilities into mainstream life and accepting them as just another flavor of the human experience. Their viewpoint is that of the US in the 1950's or West Germany in the 1970's. Acceptance is coming, but it waits for this generation of children to become adults. During the Soviet era, people with disabilities were segregated from society and kept out of public view. For example, in the Soviet Union there was a city of the blind, which was an entire city where only blind or sight-impaired people could live. The idea that people with disabilities need to be segregated away from society continues to exist in Russia and the FSU with "specialized" orphanages and with parents encouraged to give up their disabled child to an institution. Ordinary Russians do not go to those institutions nor are foreigners allowed to see the really bad ones. Even today, a disabled Russian or Ukrainian will be stared at or teased.

There is a limitation in the adoption law in Russia connected with the health of the adopting parents. The Russians classify the disabled (Russians, Americans, doesn't matter) using three degrees of "invalidization" based on a sort of functionality index. The 3d degree is when a person can't perform his usual work after a disease or trauma (say, lost finger of a pianist)—the person CAN work, but he is not capable of playing a piano. If he has to change jobs, he should be paid extra for being an invalid. 2d degree is when a person can't work at all but he can take care of himself, do routine things. He is given a social pension. 1st degree is when he can't work and needs help of a second person. In Communist times when needs could be easily calculated and there were funds for social support such a person used to get a pension and money to hire a somebody to meet his needs.

If you think about how the Soviet system and its medical profession viewed people, this system makes sense. Their view was to look at people in a negative sense. It is "what can't they do" versus our approach of "what can they do." The current Russian medical profession still has some of this.

In Russian adoptions this disabled scenario might be played out in several ways. For example, it might just be ignored. Even as late as 1998, a husband's disability would just slide by without a whole lot of comment. Now in a region where they go by the book then the local court and medical specialists (in

Russia there is no such thing as just a doctor, everyone is a specialist) would be consulted as to the husband and his lifestyle functionality i.e. there is a whole lot of room to argue the case that the husband is just fine. It is not cut and dry. Nothing is ever cut and dry in Russia.

For example, a husband with an amputation of both legs might be classified as invalidity of 2d degree under certain circumstances based on whether the man can take care of himself. If it is proved that he has sufficient income to have a family and provide kids AND has a wife that is not crippled, the husband might be approved.

Technically, the judge cannot just waive the disability limitation although if the problem is explained from the functional point of view he can CLASSIFY the problem in a different way (different from Russian classification) with the help of local medical specialists. As you might expect, the medical system in Russia has so called "Medical expertise of disability" which can classify the state of the man as a lesser degree of invalidity than the same state of a man living in Russia. Then the court can make a decision based on a lesser degree of disability and in full compliance with adoption laws.

Of course, the only result of a "disabled" husband not being able to adopt is that the wife will be the initial adoptive parent until the child is home in the United States. The child will need to be re-adopted in the US and will not be a US citizen until that is completed as the child would have entered the US on an IR4 visa.

Out of the 19,000 international adoptions each year, many are to parents that have some sort of disability. Finding the right country therefore becomes just a little trickier as you must find one that not only is one from which you want to adopt, but also one that will allow you to do so. The general rule in Russia and the FSU is that the husband's condition will not prevent an adoption. Adoptions have occurred in cases where the husband was a dwarf, in a wheelchair, or used crutches extensively. In all cases, the wife was not disabled, and since she is viewed as the primary caregiver, the adoption was completed without any problems.

The sticking point is when the wife is disabled or has some illness. The Eastern European mindset still views disabilities and illnesses with suspicion. The general rule is that if the wife can show that the illness is under control with medication and produce a doctor's letter stating that the illness is being successfully managed and that she'll have a normal life span, then it is likely the adoption can go forward. Successful adoptions have occurred where a wife was on medication for arthritis but showed no visible signs of the illness. Remission of cancer has also not prevented adoption. You just need a good letter about treatment and prognosis. There is a web site to help parents with cancer at *http://groups.yahoo.com/group/adoption-after-cancer/*.

Taking anti-depressants, as long as it is downplayed, is fine in many regions of Russia. See the home study section for advice on whether to disclose depression medication. Taking estrogen falls into the same category. The Russian judges simply have no clue. Some Moms with rheumatoid arthritis, for example, have had their doctor carefully word the medical clearance in such a way that says the condition does not affect their ability to work, parent, lead a full life, etc. The social worker needs to carefully write the homestudy in the same way. Also, limit the medications you list. Once in Russia, do not go into great detail about your illness or medications if asked by the Judge. Keep it bland and general.

In addition to "good" doctor letters (these you write or suggest yourself, of course), an agency has to know which regions are friendly to disabled parents. In this case, it may make more sense to look to a larger agency that works in several regions and countries rather than to a smaller one.

Now there is another option if the disability is not an obvious one and that involves nondisclosure. This option is outlined in the home study chapter and involves either not telling your home study agency at all or producing two home studies. One home study goes to the BCIS and details everything while the second is submitted to the foreign country and omits the disability. You can also have a doctor that is not treating you for the disease sign the medical clearance form, thereby producing a clean letter. This option is also one that parents have taken.

Currently, Russia is not too friendly toward moms in wheelchairs. They used to allow the nondisabled husband to travel and attend court, but even then they seemed to limit the parents to adopting a special needs child. Again, this is typical of the segregationist thinking that prevails in Eastern Europe. India and Guatemala seem to be better choices. In India, the right judge is the key, and in Guatemala, a massaged home study helps. Guatemala has also allowed sight-impaired moms to adopt. Of course, the US Embassy in Guatemala is not wheelchair accessible so they have to bring the visa papers out to you (but the Marriott is).

Finding the right agency with experience in working with a disability is not easy. You have to keep searching and asking, but they are out there.

For information and tips on a disabled parent raising a child, see *http://www.lookingglass.org/*. For an adoption story by a disabled parent see *http://www.oifamily.com/main/main.htm*. For a disabled adopter group see *http://groups.yahoo.com/group/disabledadoptiveparents/*.

Transracial Issues

Eastern Europe is full of nationalities. The children may be part Finnish, Turkic, Chuvash, Tatar, Kazak, Rom (Gypsy), and on and on. It is certainly possible that your children will look like you, but it is also very possible they might not, in which case welcome to the world of the transracial family!

Only a handful of studies have been done on the success of transracial adoptions, but most show that the adopted children generally are well adjusted and comfortable with their families. In a recent study, the Search Institute found that a sample of 199 Korean-born adolescents scored as well as same-race adopted counterparts on 4 measures of mental health, and were more likely to be highly-attached to both adoptive parents. Sharma said 80% of Korean adoptees said they get along equally well with people of their own and different racial backgrounds, though 42% said they're occasionally ashamed of their race.

Older studies of Korean adoptees focused on the adaptation of the child to the American family. Smoothness of adaptation equaled success. A positive outcome was the child's identification as an American, not as a Korean. No one ever asked how well the family adapted to its new identity as one with a diverse membership and diverse cultural connections.

There is no doubt that transracial adoption introduces a layer of complexity into the child's life, but so does illness, divorce, and everything else that goes with living. Sharma also noted that any family that adopts transracially "becomes inherently a transracial family, not a white family with a child of color."

For most adoptive parents, the important information is that these studies on intercountry adoptees paint an optimistic picture. The general impression from reading the studies of specifically Korean adoptions is that of good outcome based on positive indicators such as educational achievement, good relationships with families and peers, and a general feeling of positive self-worth and confidence enjoyed by the adoptees.

The question of connection with cultural heritage and racial identity is considered in all the studies. The commonly held position is that "pride in cultural identity is essential to reducing the crisis of adolescent identity and resolving role conflict." Studies describe parents eagerly providing cross-cultural experiences for children until adolescence. At that point, the children's interests seem to naturally wane as they become involve in teenage pursuits that require "fitting in" to their mostly Caucasian peer group. A group of Korean adult adoptees cautioned parents to be sensitive during this period. They advise parents to be responsive to their children's reactions to cultural activities native to the child. Interactions with Asian Americans may be awkward for children of this age, as the thoroughly American behavior of the adoptee may perplex and disappoint the Asian American. Other studies emphasized that such factors as self-esteem are more important than cultural identity for successful adoption results.

While growing up, adoptees do not want to be differentiated by other children in the society. They want to have blue eyes, blond hair, and fair skin. When they reach college age, they begin to appreciate their ethnic background. On one survey of Korean adoptees 45% of the male respondents considered themselves Caucasian and 34% of the female respondents viewed themselves Caucasian while growing up. Once adoptees go to college, they are exposed to a diversity of races on campus and this gives them the opportunity to seriously consider their ethnic identity.

The positive outcome from intercountry adoptions surprises some researchers, though probably not adoptive parents. Why does intercountry adoption work as well as it does? Some researchers' explanations build on David Kirk's belief that adoption works best when there is openness about the adoption and acceptance of the difference between parenting biological and adopted children. The researchers suggest that parents of ethnically different children approach the inherent difficulties of adoption in an open and accepting fashion.

Some suggestions on achieving this openness are interacting with people of your child's race; finding mentors or role models for your teenager that are of her race; confronting racism openly and discussing it with your child; creating a positive cultural environment at home. There is no formula for success. The most you can do as a parent is try hard and hope it all turns out.

The vast majority of Korean adoptees show positive self-esteem, and a good sense of integration into their nuclear and extended family. Most intercountry adoptive parents said they would definitely "do it again" if given the choice.

Chapter IV

AMERICAN PAPERCHASE

An important tip is that if there is an opportunity to walk a document through then by all means do it. Each time you can have some gatekeeper take care of a document in front of you, the more time you will save. You can literally save months if you push hard enough.

BCIS Overview

In 2003, the INS was merged into the new Department of Homeland Security. The INS' immigration benefits function, which includes processing I-600As, was renamed the Bureau of Citizenship and Immigration Services (BCIS). Nothing has changed except for the name. Now there has been a great amount of disruption in regard to the border security side of the INS, with many employees leaving the Service, but this has not been the case with the immigration benefits side.

Whenever you deal with the BCIS you must remember that although you have paid your taxes, and your family may have come over on the Mayflower, you will not receive any special treatment from the BCIS just because you are an American. The BCIS does process the I-600A on an expedited basis, but do not expect them to answer any of your questions. There is no hotline or ombudsman. You will have to wait in line like everyone else.

You truly begin your international adoption journey when you file for pre-approval to adopt with the BCIS. This is actually pre-approval of the parents since you may not have accepted a child yet. The form is called the I-600A, the Application for Advance Processing of an Orphan Petition. It used to be orange. It is to be contrasted with the I-600, the Petition to Classify an Orphan as an Immediate Relative, which is the approval of the adopted child for a visa and which is filed at the time of your child's visa request at the US Embassy in Moscow. The I-600 used to be blue. The BCIS offices and the various Embassy visa units will now accept downloaded copies of these forms on regular white paper. The filing fee for the I-600A is $460. You will also need to include an additional $50 per person for fingerprinting. This fee is charged for each person living in your house over the age of 18. Therefore, if it is just you and your spouse living in the house, include an extra $50. If you are only adopting one child or a sibling group, then no additional fee is required when you file the I-600 in Moscow, other than the $335 visa fee.

You can now download all of your forms from the BCIS and they should be accepted, even if they are not on the correct colored paper. You can download them at *http://www.immigration.gov/graphics/formsfee/forms/index.htm.* The BCIS web site states that…" [i] n an October 17, 2000 revised rule, these printing requirements were loosened to facilitate printing from the Internet. As a result, all BCIS forms may now be printed from the BCIS Website *without* any special printing requirements (such as head-to-foot, using specially-colored paper, etc.). However, using a dot matrix printer is not advised." The BCIS forms for the I-600A, I-600 and N-643 are in Acrobat and are in "fillable" mode, which should make life easier. The I-864 form is not yet fillable. Except for the N-643, these forms cannot be filed electronically.

In March 2003 the BCIS changed the way they handled approving the I-600A by issuing a policy memo stating that you would not get your fingerprint appointment until after you filed your home study. This was such a ludicrous policy that the BCIS withdrew it in May and issued another policy memo saying that each of the dozens of field offices could make their own policy as to when they issued fingerprint appointments. By delegating authority, the Washington office was able to avoid any responsibility and any criticism. This means that the good field offices will go back to the way they did things and will fingerprint you sooner, while the bad offices will continue to jerk you around by delaying your fingerprint appointment until the last moment. The May 2003 policy memo is at *http://www.immigration.gov/graphics/lawsregs/handbook/FprntChks051303.pdf*

If the BCIS field office tells you that it can not give you a fingerprint appointment until your home study is filed, remind them that you are adopting from

Russia or other FSU country and that unlike China the adoption occurs in less than 15 months from when you file your I-600A. This is the discretion the policy memorandum gave to the offices. They should understand it and tailor their fingerprint policies accordingly. With a country like China, where the adoption can take 18 months after the I-600A is filed, then it may make sense to delay the fingerprint appointment until the last moment. But it does not make sense when adopting from a country where you are not going to run out of time.

Within four weeks of filing your I-600A (and home study if the office wouldn't give it without it), and sooner if you are lucky, you will be notified of where and when to go to be fingerprinted. An "official" BCIS fingerprint person will take your fingerprints. The BCIS used to allow you to submit them from your local police department, but no longer. They claim they had too many bad prints. You no longer bring fingerprint cards with you. The BCIS provides these cards to you when you are fingerprinted. Do not use hand lotion on the day you are fingerprinted as this may cause a problem. Some offices, such as the Philadelphia BCIS, now use optical machines that take your fingerprints and send them out upon completion of your prints. No cards are needed.

On the I-600A at line 17 it asks you for the number of children you are adopting. You should put a number greater than you are currently considering. The same goes for your home study. The BCIS will actually go by the figure in your home study. Even so, both figures should be consistent. The reason for the higher figure is that many times people returning from Russia decide to increase their families by adopting again the following year. By already being approved for the higher number, you may be able to cut out a few steps the next year. Further, sometimes you find out late (as in while you are in Russia) that your child has a sibling that you want or need to adopt. Being already approved for more will certainly make the sibling adoption easier.

A perplexing problem in dealing with the BCIS can occur when you wish to adopt more than one child and they are unrelated. The rule should be that since the I-600A is for the parents, then only one form and fee is required at the time you file. However, some BCIS offices require you to file separate I-600As for each child and to pay separate fees. Other offices will only require one fee. Some offices make a distinction between filing one form for siblings versus separate I-600As for unrelated children. Other offices allow only one form if the children are in the same children's home or region. There appears to be little consistency between offices. Just do whatever your BCIS office tells you. Make sure you receive some sort of receipt or other evidence of having paid the second child's $460 or else the US Embassy will make you pay it again.

Perhaps enclose a stamped return address envelope and ask that a receipt be mailed to you.

Even if you have filed only one form, but are adopting two unrelated children, be prepared for the likelihood that you may have to pay an additional $460 for the other child when you obtain their visas at the US Embassy in Moscow. The reason for this is that the I-600 states that only one fee per sibling group is required as that is considered one adoption. However, since an I-600 must be filed for each unrelated child in order that they each obtain a visa, a separate fee logically follows. It really is all a question of whether you pay the fee up front or at the back end. If given a preference, I would go with the back end.

An even more confusing issue appears when you have filed an I-600A requesting approval for the adoption of more than one child but have used the approval to only adopt one. By the way, approvals are good for 18 months. Now you want to go back the following year and adopt another. Do you have to go through the whole BCIS process again? The answer is that it differs in each BCIS office and in each state. In North Carolina and in most BCIS offices all you have to do is file a brief amendment updating your home study and as long as the adoption is within the 18 months, you should be fine. You still may need to be refingerprinted, since they are only valid for 15 months. However, in states such as Georgia and Florida, you have to do the whole thing all over again, from start to finish.

You may file the I-600A and complete the home study later. Your home study agency will then get the state to approve the study and that agency will then file it with the BCIS.

After the BCIS has received your I-600A, your home study and your FBI fingerprint clearance, you will, barring some home study agency brain drop or a crime against humanity on your record, receive official United States government approval that you are eligible to adopt a child. That approval arrives in your mailbox on a form known as the I-171H. At the same time, the BCIS will send a cable to the appropriate Consulate/Embassy notifying them of this approval. If you receive another form called a 797-C, this is a Notice of Action, and does not equate to an I-171H. It is the I-171H you need. Like with all government documents make sure you double-check your I-171H for typos.

After you receive your I-171H you will need to verify with the US Embassy that they have received a cable (VISAS Cable 37) from the BCIS indicating that you are approved. You can do this through email at one of the following addresses (sometimes one works and the others don't):

MoscowConsularR@state.gov; ConsularM1@state.gov, consulmo@state.gov,

ConsularM4@state.gov or by fax at: 011-7-095-728-5247.If you send a fax or email, be sure to direct it to the "Adoption Unit." The Moscow Embassy's phone numbers are: 011-7-095-728-5058 (direct line) or 728-5000 (switchboard ask for ext: 5804). Do not call them except as a last resort and only between noon and 3 p.m. Russian time (4a.m to 7a.m EST). Email and fax are the best methods, as you will then receive a paper confirmation, which you should take with you to Russia. Sometimes your I-171H will have the number of children for which you are approved marked at the top. Don't worry if it does not. You are approved for the number stated in your home study and you can check this when you email the US Consulate for verification of the Visas Cable 37.

The reason for taking the confirmation with you is that sometimes when your facilitator calls the Embassy to set up the visa appointment, the Embassy cannot locate your file. The paper confirmation will help overcome that little problem. After receiving BCIS approval of your adoption, the Embassy should mail you a several page letter giving some information regarding the Russian adoption experience. The Embassy only mails out this little packet of information half the time so do not be surprised if you do not receive it.

After your experience with your local BCIS, you may be surprised to learn that the Adoption Unit at the US Embassy in Moscow has been recognized as one of most well run organizations in the entire United States government. Under Michelle Bond it won the highest award such an organization can receive. Eric Myers who continued the high quality of service later succeeded her. He has now moved on, but Anna Malkova and Marina Tikhonova are also well regarded. Indeed, the persons working in that unit, both American and Russian, regularly go far beyond the call of duty in helping parents get home with their bundle of joy. The Warsaw Consulate probably gets top honors for Eastern Europe. They are usually on top of any recent changes, but the Almaty Consulate is also well run. The US Embassy in Kyiv will likely begin to process adoption visas in 2004. They are currently thinking about it. That Embassy has been very helpful about interacting with the NAC and relaying changes to the adoption community.

Assuming you filed your I-600A then proceeded to complete a home study and fingerprints, the time to approval is around 6 months. If you have already completed a domestic home study and just need it amended to authorize adopting internationally, then the approval time should be shorter. Of course, delays can crop up. The FBI might lose your fingerprints. The BCIS might have a stack of applications and the only person handling them in that office gets sick or goes on vacation. Your home study might need corrections or be delayed because of the need for a document like a certified marriage certificate from Timbuktu. Or you might have to deal with the Gruesome Twosome, two BCIS offices from hell, San Jose and Denver. Now this time line may change, since as of 2003 the BCIS will not even begin to look at your file until they receive your home study. This means there is little point in filing the I-600A until your home study is close to completion.

When you receive I-171H notice of approval letter, it should have box #3 checked that "Your advance processing application has been forward to the Consulate at (Moscow Almaty, Warsaw etc)." Beneath it should be typed, "Notice of approval has been cabled to (same)." This is done in accordance with your designation of the Embassy at Moscow at question 16 on the I-600A petition. So, in other words, if you designated the Consulate in Moscow on the I-600A, the cable will go there, if Almaty it will go there etc.

This is how it works, except in Illinois. In Illinois there is an additional bit of red tape. In Illinois, DCFS has to approve all foreign adoptions, and you will receive TWO I-171Hs. The second one is the one with "box 3" checked and it is only after these additional steps that your cable can be sent to Moscow as outlined.

In Illinois the additional steps appear to be that after you accept a referral you need to notify BOTH your home study social worker (through which you got your DCFS Foster Care license) AND Ms. Muriel Shaennan at DCFS in Springfield, IL. Her phone is 217-785-2692. You MUST provide her the following information after you accept a referral: Child's name (Russian and new adoptive name), country of birth, and birth date of child.

After reviewing your DCFS file, she will fax BCIS that they can release your final I-171H. BCIS will send you a second updated I-171H form with box 3 checked. Then you should e-mail or fax the Moscow Embassy after you get your second I-171H to confirm receipt of your Cable.

If you happen to have a picture of the child you are adopting, you may find that you receive quicker service from the BCIS if you attach a copy of child's picture to whatever document you need them to approve. It is surprising, but people tend to care more once they see that an actual living child is involved. This also works for state offices when you are looking for a quick turnaround on an apostille or other document.

BCIS Offices

The following is a list of some of the BCIS offices and a description of the kind of experience you can expect. The description is based on how fast you can expect to obtain your I-171H approval and how you are treated. This is not a scientific poll.

It is helpful if you understand how these offices generally operate. Usually there is no more than one person in each office that handles adoption petitions. This is called the Orphan Officer. The person may change every year or so, with the result that an office can be great for a while then suddenly go bad. This happens frequently. Then you have some where the office stays bad decade after decade. San Jose and San Francisco are prime examples.

Each field office now has the discretion to fingerprint you before your home study is filed or afterwards. If a field office does not send out fingerprint appointments until your home study is filed, that will significantly delay you in receiving your I-171H.

Arlington, VA takes 6-8 weeks to send out the I-171H once everything is in.

Atlanta is rated as being in the middle of the pack. Not very fast, but not bad either. Takes about 3-4 week for approval of I-600A, once your home study and fingerprints are in.

Baltimore has generally been a terrific office. It has had some recent problems lately with losing files and fingerprints, but hopefully it will get back on track.

Boston has had a terrible reputation. They are difficult to talk to. Yet, their time for approval is not too bad. The best that can be said is that they receive mixed reviews. If you have a question, the social worker has to call. They don't take calls from families. Boston only accepts money orders, not checks.

Buffalo seems very much on the ball. Your fingerprints are optically scanned and take only 24 hrs for FBI clearance.

Charlotte takes 4 to 12 weeks after everything is in. They do not take calls.

Chicago is not bad. They have a pretty good reputation.

Cincinnati and Cleveland are not far behind Chicago.

Dallas used to be very fast, but they have been having problems lately and losing files and applications. You may need to involve your Congressman. Part of their problems is that they have a new orphan officer who is trying to dig out from the backlog. She is also new on the job, so has a learning curve. The backlog was 3 months as of May 2003. The number is 214-905-5700, X5789.

Denver is next to last at giving poor service.

Detroit did have a reputation for being slow, but recently they seem to have become more helpful and friendly.

El Paso is not very fast at all.

Ft. Smith, Ark. office is rude to parents.

Houston, Texas is just great. Mary Chavez is just one of the nicest and most professional people you will ever meet. The BCIS is lucky to have her. She deserves an award and a raise!

Jacksonville seems to be giving Baltimore a run for its money and is an outstanding office.

Kansas City, MO is pretty fast as is Wichita, KS. It may be that fewer people in the Mid-West adopt internationally so the BCIS offices are not as overwhelmed as others.

Los Angeles is not very good. The wait for your fingerprint date is long. The I-171H can take as long as 10 weeks and you may have to go in person and plead your case.If you need help, you can call the Adoption/Orphan room at (213) 830-5122 and ask to speak to Marty, the Director. Be nice. It is really hard to get through.

Los Vegas is not very fast.

Louisville is very quick and gets high marks.

Manchester, NH is good and friendly.

Memphis is very good. Rated much higher than Atlanta. If you want to check on your status, the office phone numbers are 901-344-2300 and 901-544-0264. A human being always answers the phone. Officers Miller and Dockery are in charge of orphan petitions, so they're the ones that can help you. Under the old policy, Memphis would fingerprint you the day you turned in your I-600A, if you asked. They are very courteous and helpful. In Tennessee, your home study first has to be submitted to the state ICPC, then the BCIS. It can take as long as 3 weeks to go through the ICPC, and then 4 weeks to get your I-171H once the home study is received at the BCIS.

Michigan's office for I-171Hs is in Sault Ste. Marie. The examiner is Ms. Gladys Teske at 906-632-8822. The office gets decent marks.

Minneapolis is fast.

New Jersey is in the middle although Newark has a tendency to lose documents, and fingerprints. The NJ BCIS adoption unit phone number is 973-645-6309. Like all BCIS offices they receive lots of calls from people that have no idea what they are doing so they may be rather gruff sometimes, but you will get your questions answered. Call between 2 and 4 PM. Fingerprints are taken electronically in Newark, Philadelphia and Hackensack so their status is available to the New Jersey BCIS within 5 days. Once the file is complete (I-600A, home study and fingerprints) New Jersey has been known to issue the I-171H within 2 weeks.

New York gets pretty high marks. There is only one person in BCIS NYC that reviews adoptions, Mrs. Troupe. You can call her once a week on Wednesday mornings to find out the status of your home study or fingerprint approval. Mrs. Troupe's number is 212-264-3905.

New Orleans is not bad.

Philadelphia is fast.

Pittsburgh is fast and friendly. They will even talk to you.

Portland, Or. is dreadful. Almost dead last.

Oklahoma has poor customer service.

Orlando BCIS office is fast and efficient. Once they have your home study they turn the I-171H around very quickly.

St. Louis office seems to have nice people working there and is fast.

The Salt Lake City office can be difficult. If you have to wait any longer than 2 months for approval, call Senator Hatch's office.

San Antonio used to have problems, but it seems there has been a change as it is now very quick about arranging fingerprint dates and about sending out your I-171H after it receives your home study. It used to be possible to be fingerprinted the same day if you hand-carried your I-600A with the required documents and a money order. The line is shorter after 3pm.

San Diego is also poor.

San Francisco is a nightmare. Horrendous lines (you must be in line by 5 a.m.) If you have to visit, there is no one to speak to that has a clue about international adoptions. The Congressional offices don't want to get involved unless it is truly urgent since the San Francisco office is so bad. Most parents end up having to involve their Congressman.

San Jose is dead last as far as service is concerned. It has been dead last for years and years and this appears likely to continue. If you must use San Jose, then establish a relationship with Senator Feinstein's office. She is VERY responsive and her office cares about adopting parents. Forget about Senator Boxer—her office NEVER responds. A suggestion in filing your I-600A with San Jose is not to leave any information blank. List your home study agency name where it asks "which agency" and as far as a travel date, you can write, "to be determined"—that will be an acceptable answer. If you leave anything blank, your documents will get shoved in a drawer or put in a box in an old restroom (yes, this is their filing system), and you'll never see them again. Another suggestion is to use a home study agency that has a good relationship with the BCIS office or orphan petition processing officer. You have to ask around, but it is well worth the effort. I have heard from parents that BAAS or Adopt International have "good" relationships with San Jose BCIS. Regardless of which home study agency you use, try to make them work the San Jose office rather than you.

Always, send your documents by certified mail or by FedEx or UPS, local delivery, since that is same day and much faster and is easier to track if it goes missing. (This is good advice for sending documents to any BCIS office). Watch to see when San Jose cashes your check. They almost always do that first, even if they have a "problem" with your documents. If they haven't cashed your check within 8 weeks, then you might want to consider sending them a certified letter inquiring about the status of your documents, along with a copy of your certified mail postcard. Not that they will ever answer you, but you have created a paper trail to make it easier for the congressional liaison's office to intervene on your behalf (which you most probably will have to do at some point).

For those who have the heartache of having to use the San Jose office, it is simply an abomination. Contacting the BCIS by phone in San Jose is impossible, instead one must stand in line from 5 a.m. to 9 a.m., hearing that the numbers of the day are gone and be told to come back tomorrow. IF (and only if) you are actually lucky enough to actually get *into* the building (your lucky outdoor lotto number is actually allowed in) you will enter the "inner sanctum" only to see 2 windows open, and 200-300 people crammed into the building waiting to actually speak to one of the 2 people at the windows (not to mention the 50-100+ people you have been standing with OUTSIDE). Most times, unless you are incredibly lucky to actually GET to the window, you are told the office is closing, and that you will have to "come back again tomorrow" to stand in line OUTSIDE again, and pray that you get another try at getting into the inner sanctum.

Finally, good luck!

Seattle and St. Louis are pretty good.

Spokane takes about 6 weeks to issue the I-171H after receiving your home study.

Washington, DC is poor.

The BCIS field offices also all have their own peculiar procedures.

For example, Denver does not like personal checks, but will only accept money orders and certified checks. They also want in the home study the size of the child's room in your home and the distance to the nearest bathroom.

Atlanta, on the other hand, will take personal checks and doesn't care about bathrooms. It will take the downloaded white form.

Baltimore will accept a copy of the I-600A downloaded onto white paper. They don't care that it is not salmon colored (orange) They will not accept a personal check but prefer separate money orders for the $460 fee and for the $50 fingerprint fee.

Buffalo has gotten high praise for being very friendly. They answer questions and let you do your fingerprints at the same time as filing the I-600A.

The DC office in Arlington VA accepts the downloaded version with one personal check including the fee and fingerprints.

In the Jacksonville, Florida office they do accept the form on downloaded white paper, but they don't accept personal checks. You can combine the form fee and fingerprint fees on one money order.

Here is one tip when dealing with the BCIS. If you have to go to an actual office, go as early in the morning as you can. If the doors open at 8 am, then get there no later than 6:30 am. The line will grow exponentially.

I-600A Instructions

Several documents must be included with your I-600A form. You need to include proof of US citizenship and the best example is to copy the photo pages from your passport. This can be black and white copies, not color. You will need a passport to travel so you might as well use the one you have or obtain one. (This is a good time to check on whether your passport needs to be updated.) The passport must be unexpired and valid for five years. If you do not have a passport you can submit a copy of your birth certificate. If married, also submit a copy of your marriage certificate. If divorced, then they need a copy of the final decree. If the home study is not ready, explain in a cover letter that it will be provided at a later date. The $460 fee and $50 per person fingerprint fee can each be paid by regular check. (Write separate checks for these fees and do not use abbreviations such as BCIS, but the whole name.) Indeed, this will give you a receipt that it was paid. You can pay by certified check, but that will not really speed the process along, as the BCIS must still wait for your home study and FBI fingerprint check before issuing the I-171H.

These document copies do not have to be certified, however, you will need to obtain certified copies of your birth and marriage certificates for your dossier and home study, so if you have an extra one, just send it with your I-600A. If you are adopting a second time, also include a copy of your previous I-171H. This will show them that you were approved before so they don't have to do any real checking on you. You should put in your cover letter that "Copies of documents submitted are exact photocopies of unaltered documents and I understand that I may be required to submit original documents to an Immigration or Consular officer at a later date." Sign, print your name and date it.

The form may say that the filing fee is $120 or even $405. Ignore this. It is an old form. The correct filing fee is $ 460 plus fingerprinting fee of $50 per person (over 18 years of age) Filling out the I-600A is not difficult and should only take a few minutes.

If married, then one of you becomes the petitioner. Don't fight over it! Make sure the petitioner is a US citizen. Questions 1-9 are self-explanatory. As to question 10, regarding the name of your agency. You may not know at the time of filing the I-600A in which case just put "unknown at this time, will supplement." You can also leave it blank and include in your cover letter that you will supplement this information later. Those going independently just put down 'independent.'

One result of the I-600A is a determination by the BCIS as to whether your child will be issued an IR3 or an IR4 visa upon entering the United States. An IR3 visa means that both parents traveled over to Russia and saw the child before the actual Court hearing. An IR4 means that only one parent saw the child and that re-adoption in the United States is necessary before the child can be eligible for citizenship. So the I-600A asks you at question 11 whether both parents are traveling. BCIS will confirm this at the time that you visit the US Consulate. The general law in Russia is that both parents must travel to adopt. In the early 1990's this was not the case, but it is now. Thus questions 11 and 12 on the I-600A should be answered in the affirmative, 14, in the negative and 15 in the affirmative. The answer to question 16 is "Moscow, Russia" if adopting from Russia, "Almaty" if from Kazakhstan, "Tblisi" from Georgia or Azerbaijan. If adopting from Ukraine or Belarus, then the answer is "Warsaw, Poland."

On question 13, just put down "unknown" for all three parts. You can also just take a guess at the month and year and the city in Russia you intend to visit. The BCIS does not hold you to these dates.

As to question 17, always put down one more than you expect and make sure you are consistent with your home study. If you decide to increase the number after you have received your I-171H then you will need to send in a revised home study or amendment to your local BCIS office with the approval paragraph noting that you are now approved for "whatever# of children". That's what the BCIS uses to decide how many you are approved for, not what you put on a BCIS form. You then fill out form EOIR-29 changing the number and send that to the BCIS for a check for $110 along with a copy of your original I-171.The BCIS will then you a new I-171. This new I-171 does not change the original 18-month window.

Express mail the package to the BCIS so you can have a trace receipt of its having gotten there. You must submit it to the office that serves your location. If you live in a large urban city this is easy to determine. Otherwise ask your home study agency or your adoption agency to which office it should be submitted. This information is also located on the BCIS' web site. Put on the envelope, "ATTN: I-600A/Orphan Petition Section."

The result of filing the I-600A is that once you have submitted your home study and fingerprints, you will eventually receive approval from the BCIS. This approval comes in the mail in the form of a document known as an I-171H. It is valid for 18 months. It cannot be extended.

I-600

The I-600 is the *Petition to Classify Orphan as an Immediate Relative* a/k/a the blue form. You file this form with the overseas US Consulate when you are over there in order to obtain your child's US immigrant visa. The same petitioner on the I-600A does not have to be the petitioner on the I-600, as long as both are US citizens. Both parents must sign it, although only needs to before a consular officer. You will need to file one for each child you are adopting. Some fill out the form before leaving the States and then fill in those blanks for which they did not have the information once they are in Russia. Others wait to complete the form in Russia. Bring an extra blank form in case you need to make a change. You **must** file your I-600 with the Consulate before your I-171H has expired. If the I-171H will expire before you are able to file, then you have to begin the process anew. The BCIS does not grant extensions. An explanation of the I-600 is at *http://www. immigration.gov/graphics/formsfee/forms/i-600.htm*.

If you both saw the child before the adoption and the child is now with you, the form is easy to fill out. Questions 1-9 are the same as on the I-600A. You should ask your adoption agency regarding the answers to questions 16 and 17. Question 17 b and c should be answered with "no."

Here are some other suggested answers. Question 20 should be "no" unless there is something obvious. The answer to question 21 is you, and to 22 and 23 none. Question 24 is your US address. Question 25 is Moscow (or Warsaw, Almaty etc). Ignore the second 25 and for 26 give your name. The answer to question 28 is Moscow, Russia (or Warsaw, Almaty etc).

The U.S. citizen petitioner must sign the completed Form I-600 in the presence of the consular officer. If the petitioner is married, the other spouse must also sign the petition once it has been completed, although he and/or she does not/not have to sign before the consular officer. A third party may not sign the petition on behalf of the petitioner and/or spouse, even with a power of attorney. In the event that only one spouse travels abroad to file the Form I-600 petition at post, the consular officer is supposed to verify that the non-traveling spouse did not sign the petition before all of the information relating to the child had been entered onto the form. If a Form I-600A, *Application for Advance Processing of Orphan Petition*, has been approved on behalf of a married couple, either spouse may sign and file the Form I-600—it does not have to be the same spouse who obtained the Form I-600A approval. The only exception is when the married couple consists of one U.S. citizen and one alien, since only a U.S. citizen may file the Form I-600 and the Form I-600A.

I-864

Beginning in 1997, the BCIS began to require immigrants to file Form I-864, called the *Affidavit of Support*, in order to comply with the new federal law making it more difficult to bring immigrants into the United States. There is no exception for Americans adopting children overseas, unless your child will be receiving an IR-3 visa from the US. Most children from Eastern Europe receive the IR-3, but not all. In FY 2002, the Moscow Consulate issued 5800 IR3s and 50 IR4s. If your child will be receiving an IR-4 visa, then you have to file this form. The difference is that an IR-3 means that both parents saw the child before the Court hearing. Usually an IR-4 is reserved for those adoptions in countries where the child was escorted to the United States or where only one married parent saw the child. Unfortunately, not having to file the I-864 is not as wonderful as it sounds. Even though the BCIS has decided there is no logic behind the I-864 where a child automatically becomes a citizen once the plane touches down in the USA, the State Department has decided that they will still apply the requirements of Section 212(a)(4) of the INA. This section just says that the immigrant must have some financial means and cannot be a "public charge." The State Department is interpreting that section as still requiring the parents to show some financial documents. There is no list of required documents. (See the section on **Tax Returns** for more information on this requirement.)

If you do have to file the I-864 then by signing the *Affidavit of Support* a sponsor (parent) is agreeing to repay the federal government for any means-tested benefits paid to your child. Your obligation ends as soon as your child becomes a citizen. You can get the form from the BCIS website or call 800-870-3676. To qualify as a sponsor, you must be at least 18 years old and a U.S. citizen or a legal permanent resident. The sponsor must have a domicile in the United States or a territory or possession of the United States. The form is not difficult to fill out. Where it asks for the name of your child, use the name she will have after the adoption.

Form I-864, Affidavit of Support, should be completed and notarized before you travel. I would sign shortly before you travel, although the signature is good for 6 months. Gather copies of your last three years of filed personal federal tax returns, including schedules. Your state return is not involved, only your 1040. If you have not yet filed for the previous year, then bring the 3 years before that. If you have filed for an extension, you will need to bring a copy of that with that year's W-2s, in addition to the previous 3 years of filed returns. Make copies of all of this. The tax returns do not need to be notarized, just the signed Form. Notarize it before you leave for Russia. Apostilling is not necessary, as this is a document for the US Embassy Visa Unit, not for any Russian official. If you can't find your last three years of tax returns, you can call the IRS at 1-800-829-1040. They will likely give you a one page summary transcript of your tax return or a letter called a 1722. Both of these are acceptable to the Embassy. They take about 10 days to get and are free. If you filed electronically, then just print out the return and sign it. The I-864 serves as verification to the BCIS that you will be able to support your adopted child by demonstrating that your income is at least 125% of poverty guidelines (100% if in the military). As an example, 125% of the poverty guidelines for 2003, except for Alaska and Hawaii, would require a family of four to have income of $23,000.You can find the most recent poverty guidelines at *http://www.immigration.gov/graphics/formsfee/forms/files/I-864p.pdf*

Be sure to bring along a notarized verification of your employment and salary. If you are basing your Affidavit on documents other than tax returns, make sure you take those. Pack all of this in your carryon, not your checked luggage.

If you rely on the income of your spouse in order to reach the minimum income requirement, your spouse must complete and sign a Form I-864A; *Contract Between Sponsor and Household Member.* If the spouse did not file jointly, but separately, then that separate tax return must also be attached to the sponsor's Affidavit along with the spouse's employment verification. If you are not using the income of your spouse, but filed a joint return, then you must include your W-2s to prove that your income alone qualifies you. The W-2s are not necessary if you filed jointly and are using both incomes to qualify. However, I would take them along if you have them, just in case. The 1722 is a substitute for your tax return so the rules regarding W-2s are the same. If you are missing your W-2s, ask your employer. By law they have to keep them for a few years. When filing the documentation with the US Consulate, place the I-864 on top, followed by the sponsor's tax returns, evidence of employment, and then evidence of assets, if these are used to qualify.

If you are adopting more than one child, then you will need to file a second notarized I-864 accompanied by another (non-notarized) copy of your tax returns.

For information and forms see
http://www.travel.state.gov/checklist.html
http://www.immigration.gov/graphics/formsfee/forms/i-864.htm

Tax Returns

When you visit the US Consulate overseas to receive your child's US visa you are required by Section 212(a)(4) of the Immigration and Naturalization Act (INA) to provide information showing that your child will not be a "public charge."

The question of what sort of financial documents a parent is **required** to bring to satisfy the public charge section of the INA is a matter of law and procedure. It is not a matter of opinion, it is not a matter of what a Russian or Ukrainian facilitator may believe, or what some US agency thinks. It is a matter of law and procedure.

A Consular officer will certainly take your envelope of tax returns. He'll take 3 years worth, 5 years worth, 100 years worth. But the question is—what is required.

If your child will be receiving an IR4 visa, then you must file an I-864 and bring the usual 3 years of tax returns and schedules. However, since there were only 50 of these issued by Moscow in FY 2002 and 5800 or so IR3 Visas, most children will receive an IR3.

Prior to February 27, 2001, this distinction did not matter at all. However, on that date the Child Citizenship Act went into effect. The INS then did something very smart and they deserve credit for it. They realized that because of this new law, an IR3 child became a citizen the second the plane landed in the US and the child received an IR (Immediate Relative) number stamped in his foreign passport. That had the effect of rendering the sponsorship responsibilities represented by the I-864 null and void, since those responsibilities do not apply to citizens.

On June 17, 2001, the INS issued a memorandum stating that the I-864 was no longer required for IR3 children since it would only apply for the time it took you to fly from Moscow to the US.

Foreign adoption is governed by at least five government agencies. One of these is the State Department. The State Department is the agency that actually issues the Visa to your child, not the INS. The State Department was a little slow in understanding the ramifications of the Child Citizenship Act. They pretty quickly agreed that the INS had made a good policy decision on the I-864, but were not going to give up completely.

The problem the State Department had was with INA 212 (a) (4). This section of the Immigration Act says that the State Department Consular officers must make sure that the immigrant (your child) does not become a "public charge." No guidance is given in the Act as to what evidence needs to be produced. Before February 27, 2001, it was not a problem. The State Department just looked at your I-864 and supporting documents. But now they had to come up with a policy.

So they issued a policy memorandum, which became part of their FAM (Foreign Affairs Manual). This policy memo, while leaving the public charge issue still in the discretion of the consular officers around the world, stressed that because of the Child Citizenship Act and because the INS in issuing the I-171 looks at the financial capability of the applicant, Officers needed to only review minimal documentation.

In response to my question regarding this issue, in July, 2001, the Moscow Adoption Unit said…"(s)uch document may include tax returns for the most recent tax year, W-2s, letter from your employer indicating the current salary, bank statements, etc"

They had given up the I-864 requirement and gone to just the most recent tax return.

By 2002, the State Department had clarified the issue further. In March, 2002 at 9 FAM 42.2 they issued a policy memorandum stating "…[a]n approved Form I-600A serves as proof that the underlying requirements of INA 212(a)(4) have been met. Additional financial evidence should only be required if the child has an illness or defect not addressed by the approved I-600A, which would entail significant financial outlay or if other unusual circumstances prevail." At 9 FAM 40.41, also issued March 2002, the State Department specifically told its Consular officers that the I-864 was not required for IR3 children.

Just to clarify the point in even further, the State Department's latest guidelines at 9 FAM 42. 21 (issued January 23, 2003) for necessary documents to process the I-600 states "c. Documents Not Required: The consular officer need not verify the adoptive parents' marriage, citizenship status, and ability to support the adopted child or children. INS addresses these issues in the I-600A approval."

The above procedural manual memo is what all consular officers are supposed to follow. In a perfect world, that is what they would do, but as one Consular Officer told me "…[t]here was fairly clear guidance from the State Department, but some posts ignored it." Ignore may be too strong a word as we live in a world where humans are reluctant to give up "the way things have always been done." The result is that each Consulate has its own way of handling the public charge requirement, but the underlying feature is that at the most all you need is the most recent tax year.

Here is a survey of some of the Consulates. Again, this is only for IR3s.

1. **China**-Guangzhou Consulate wants no documents. In my opinion, this is one of the best run Consulates for adoptive families. They said "…if both parents will participate the adoption and register with Chinese government, neither I-864 nor tax returns is not required for IR3 visa."

2. **Poland**-Warsaw Consulate only wants "…[a] copy of the last year's federal tax return and/or 2-3 recent pay stubs." This is from an email and off their web site.

3. **Kazakhstan**-Almaty Consulate-no documentation. I like this Consulate also. "IR3s will not usually need to submit any financial documentation unless there are questions regarding the petitioner's (i.e. adoptive family's) ability to provide financial support."

4. **Georgia**-Tiblisi Consulate. They are just starting up with issuing children's visas. They are trying to catch up. They have a real learning curve ahead of them. They also have the most difficult I-604 job of all the Consulates in Eastern Europe. They basically told me they are flexible on documents.Here is their take on the tax return question "…will require to see at the very least the last year's tax return, preferably the last three years' tax returns (including W2's)." They followed that with an email saying they are flexible.

5. **Bulgaria**-Sofia Consulate. "If the child falls into the IR-3 visa category we do not require an Affidavit of Support and tax returns."

6. **Russia**-Moscow Consulate. As you can see from the July 2001 email, all they want is the most recent tax return. Their web site used to have the old 3-year requirement, but if you notice now, they have deleted it entirely (except for IR4s). In an email to me in 2003 they reiterated the "most recent tax return" rule stating "...if the family's income is beyond the poverty level then we can accept tax returns only for one recent year. We don't require pay stubs or any other financial documents to process a visa. The adoptive parents can bring for the interview the 1040 or IRS transcripts."

Conclusion: Take the most recent year's tax return. If you have more, they'll accept them, but you don't need to. A better approach is to take the transcript. It is free, it is less paper, and it is acceptable at all Consulates. The phone number to get a transcript at the IRS is 800-829-1040.

FBI and Fingerprints

Under the new Homeland Security Act, your fingerprints are only good for 15 months. The FBI keeps your fingerprints in their computer in West Virginia for at least 18 months and probably unofficially for years.

After you have your fingerprints taken by the BCIS, they will travel to the BCIS Service Center in Nebraska. Then they are sent to the FBI's fingerprint office in West Virginia. Once the fingerprints are logged in with the FBI, it takes them a very short time to actually run a check. Some offices are using digital fingerprinting (optical), which theoretically should speed up the process. I believe this is the case in New York. After the FBI has processed your prints they send the results back to Nebraska, which sends them back to your local BCIS office. (Don't even begin to ask why they have to go to Nebraska.)

The U.S. Immigration office in Lincoln, Nebraska is a regional processing office and does not deal directly with the public. They have two public phone numbers: (402) 323-7830 and (402) 437-5218. Be aware that BCIS phone numbers change frequently.

Approximately 2 weeks after the fingerprint appointment, you can call the FBI and ask them to check whether the fingerprints have gone through. To check on your fingerprint status, phone the FBI Liaison Unit at 304-625-5590.

Hours are from 7pm to 11pm EST. You could also try (304) 347-5769. Voice mail is available from 7am to 11pm EST. It is easier to get through later in the evening. They are now scanning in all fingerprints they receive on cards to make searches faster.

Just tell the liaison the date and city in which you had your fingerprints done and ask if he can give you a status. If they have been approved, then you can ask him to fax a copy of the approval to your BCIS office. It's most helpful if you can give him your BCIS assigned application number so he can put that on the fax. I believe this is called a LIN number. You can also call your local congressman's office and ask to speak to his BCIS liaison. His liaison can do some checking for you on your status.

Sometimes the FBI will tell you they can't locate your fingerprints and the next day you will receive BCIS approval. There is a certain amount of randomness in this process that defies understanding.

Sometimes fingerprints are rejected because your finger swirls are too light or they have damage from rough work or some other reason. One suggestion is NOT to use any hand lotion the day you are fingerprinted and if possible wash your hands right before being printed. Some have suggested using corn huskers oil. The BCIS has gone to optical scanning in many offices. This was supposed to be more efficient, but instead it has caused more fingerprints to be rejected, delaying the process even more. Try to have the operator check your fingerprints while you are there in case there are any obvious imperfections.

If they are rejected twice, the BCIS is likely to ask you to go to your local police and obtain a record check and a letter saying you have no record. Now most home studies require this anyway. You then give this letter to the BCIS. If you've lived in more than one place over the last 5 years, you'll need a letter from each jurisdiction. Just send a written request, the proper check, and a copy of your driver's license or passport for ID.

Now asking what might show up in the FBI fingerprint check is like Geraldo asking what it is Al Capone's vault. You don't know unless you peek. Now peeking is really not allowed. Generally speaking, the FBI runs an NCIC on you during the background investigation. However, any police department can (and frequently does) run them also. It is a nationalized reporting system. What that means is if you have been arrested in Iowa, assuming Iowa reports your arrest into the NCIC system, then it will appear on an NCIC report generated by the New York City Police Department (for example). Some states are horrendous for not reporting, Arkansas is a good example. The system is used by practically all city and county law enforcement agencies in the U.S. with a sizable population. If your local police department runs the report, it will be identical to the FBI report. The problem is getting your hands on it. If you need to know what will be in the report before you complete your home study, then you need to have someone local do you a big, big favor. In most states it is a criminal offense for that person to provide you an NCIC report if you're not in law enforcement. They are required to enter their own name, the subject's name, and the recipient's name on each report.

An NCIC report should show juvenile felony arrests. Yet your state may or may not report them at all to the national database. The same goes for first offender dispositions. The state should not report those, but sometimes they do. Each state is different. If an item does appear, then you will know that you must disclose it in your home study and deal with it. If it does not appear, then you may want to consider not mentioning it. Just remember that even if an old (more than 10 years) arrest is out there, it will not likely disqualify you from adopting, but rather you will have to provide additional paperwork to the BCIS. As to Russia and the rest of the FSU (Former Soviet Union), some regions are bothered by it and some are not. All it means is that you adopt from the ones that don't have a problem.

If you are pretty sure an old arrest will show up, then you should confess during the home study. The worst thing you can do is know it will appear and let the BCIS find out from the FBI and not from your social worker. Your social worker won't be happy either.

In a rule enacted in 2002, the BCIS now makes parents get re-fingerprinted, if their prints will expire 15 months after approval without an I-600 having been filed. In typical BCIS fashion, there is no consistent rule as to when the 15 months begins. Some offices use the date when the prints are first taken and others the date when the FBI cleared the prints. Whichever way your local office does it, it will be typed on your I-171H. If you are in Moscow or Sofia or any Consulate and your fingerprints have expired prior to filing your I-600, the Consulate will make you get refingerprinted there. Then you have to wait (days?) before they will give your child his US Visa. This is when you call your Congressman.

To complicate matters further, when the new policy came out the BCIS provided no direction, no form and no semblance of guidance as to how parents were to obtain a new FBI fingerprint check, other than just say they must. A month after the rule was announced, the BCIS finally came out with a procedure. The procedure makes absolutely no sense, so you have to do a work around.

The procedure says you are to visit your local BCIS office within 30 days of traveling and pay the fingerprint fee again and take a copy of your I-171H. There are three fatal flaws to this procedure. One, no one can actually visit a field office. You mail everything in. Everyone knows that except for the person in Washington that wrote this procedural memo. Second, with most countries you don't know when you are going to travel. You might get a phone call about your court date and have 3 days to get here. Finally, it can take a lot longer than thirty days to get a fingerprint appointment, FBI clearance and receive a new I-171H with the new expiration date on it. Indeed, it usually takes at least 45 to 60 days the first time. Some people have waited months.

So here is the work around. Unless you know you will be traveling soon, when your fingerprint date is 12 months old, you mail in a copy of your I-171H with the requisite finger print fee and a cover letter explaining that you need a new fingerprint check. Now it is possible that they will send it all back saying you have to wait until the 14th month.

If you have to travel before re-fingerprinting is complete, then go without it. First, this is your child and you need to get him out of the orphanage as soon as possible for his health and the next court date could be months away. Secondly, the fingerprints might clear while you are still meeting your child and going to court. Third, the consulate might just ignore the requirement and give your child a Visa. Fourth, even if you have to be re-fingerprinted over there, if you call your Congressman immediately, the prints will probably clear within hours or maybe a day. Take the phone number of your local newspaper as well. One thing the Cambodia fiasco has taught the BCIS is to never, ever get in the way of parents who are stuck overseas with their child. Fifth, even if your fingerprints may take a few days to clear over there, you can play with your child and bond with him or leave him with your facilitator/agency representative and return to carry him home when the prints have cleared or have him escorted.

Some Consulates will accept FBI clearance letters that are direct between the parent and FBI. You just have to check with them ahead of time. Indeed, no one has figured out why the BCIS wants to play the middleman anyway. For those Consulates that will accept FBI direct clearance, then to update your fingerprints, go to your local police station, and obtain 2 sets of fingerprint cards and get fingerprinted. You mail the cards to West Virginia for a federal background check (with a check for $18 made out to the FBI) to this address:

FBI
CJIS Division, Attn: SCU
1000 Custer Hollow Rd.
Clarksburg, WV 26306

They will mail the results directly back to you. If you go to the FBI web site, there is a detailed description of the process, the mailing address and how to get the blank fingerprint cards. Do *not* use this process for the intial fingerprinting required for the I-171H, but only if the BCIS is simply too slow and you have a court date that you must attend.

Home Study

A home study is a document created by a social worker giving a snapshot summary of your life. This summary is based on interviews with you and from documents you provide. A home study is required by your state, the BCIS and the foreign country, so there is no getting around it. It should take about two months to complete. It must be submitted to the BCIS within one year from when you filed the I-600A and must not be more than 6 months old at the time of submission. The home study should be 20% screening and 80% education. Sometimes it may feel that it is the reverse. There are very few absolutes in this world, but if you can have your adoption agency also write your home study, then you should have few problems. One of the most time consuming aspects of adoption is completing the home study. If you have completed a domestic home study then all you have to do is pay a little more money and get an addendum saying you are approved for international adoption. Unlike international adoption agencies, a home study agency usually must be licensed by your state. There are some states that allow independent social workers to conduct these studies, however, you need to check with your state if this is allowed before hiring one. Also, some regions in Russia will not accept an independent social worker home study.

When hiring a home study agency, make sure that the agency and the social worker have some experience with international adoptions. If they don't, then don't hire them. A social worker that has adopted internationally can really be helpful to you. Also make sure that their state license will not need an extension any time soon. The Russians do not like expired licenses. The home study agency should tell you the cost up front; approximately how long it will take, how many visits and if the price includes post placement visits or if they are extra. They should have a working relationship with the BCIS and know who to talk with there. If you have a first meeting with the social worker and she makes offensive comments or you are not comfortable with her, just fire her and hire another home study agency. It's completely your decision. Your goal is just to get the document and move on. The cost is generally $1200+, but it can be less.

In Utah it can cost as low as $400 and in California, as high as $2,200. Do shop around.

If you want to do anything "out of the ordinary" (adopting out of birth order, adopting a large sibling group with no prior parenting experience, adopting two unrelated children at once) or if you are very young, or older, have multiple divorces, then talk to the social worker about this before you pay the agency any money. Some agencies rarely approve certain types of people to do certain types of adoptions, and if they have any "secret guidelines" it is better to find out about them before you waste your time and money. Some parents have found that home study agencies have a problem if a parent had an arrest years ago. Others find that their social worker demands some special number of months between adoptive children. So if you were to spend all this money, get to Russia and find two unrelated children, but they miss the social worker's magic number of months, then you are out a child and the child is out a life. It is one thing for the social worker to emphasize that she believes spacing to be important; it is another to impose an artificial time frame. She has no basis for doing so. These are the sorts of things you want to cover both with the home study agency and your placing agency before you spend lots of money.

Home studies by independent social workers are not acceptable in all regions in Russia. Some regions want the home study on agency letterhead. In addition, there are statements of sponsorship and a commitment to post placement reporting that they require comes from a licensed home study agency. Generally, Russian home studies must be completed by a licensed social worker. The home study must be on agency letterhead and signed by the Executive Director (not the placement supervisor or any other person) and the agency's license must accompany the home study. Home studies for independent adoptions Russia must also be accompanied by a post placement letter and registration letter. Without these, the home study is worthless. If you are adopting independently, make sure the home study agency agrees to provide these letters before paying them any money.

The foreign country does not really want to know about your extended family and their troubles. They do not really want to read about your entire emotional life story. They do not care about your relationship with your mother, father, brother, or Uncle. Nor do they care about the trauma caused when your childhood dog "Skippy" was run over by a submarine. So why are you asked these sorts of questions? It is certainly invasive. Just remember that it is up to you how much information you want to give beyond the basics. No one forces you to tell your entire life story. It is entirely up to you how much information you wish to disclose. The best policy is not to offer more than what is asked.

Keep explanations brief. The home study is just another document to check off on your list of things to do. It is not a therapy session, but a learning exercise.

This advice is especially important if you are asked to write your "autobiography." Be careful about what you spill on paper. You don't want to write anything that could be used against you. Use positive language. Think about the questions and do not put down anything negative that could be unfavorably misinterpreted. Stick to factual information, do not write a novel and leave your doubts and problems for your verbal discussions with the social worker or your day on Oprah.

One negative item that should be openly discussed (but not put into writing) with your adoption agency and home study agency is if there are any problems with an ex-spouse. If the divorce was a bad one and the relationship is polar, then it isn't rare that the ex-whatever will write a letter or call your agencies and bad-mouth the other spouse. So be upfront with the agencies in case this happens. You want them to be prepared, not surprised.

Now the BCIS in their regulations at 8 CFR 204.3 (e) requires some of these questions. The Service requires at least one personal interview of the couple and one home visit. They want the home study preparer to check your physical, mental, and emotional health. They want an assessment of your finances and whether you have a history of sexual or child abuse, substance abuse or domestic violence. You will need to disclose any history of arrest or conviction. They want a detailed description of your house or apartment. The home study must include the specific number of children you may adopt. If you are adopting a special needs child, then the home study must include a discussion about your preparation, ability and willingness to properly care for the child. Your state may also require some of the questions asked by the social worker.

There are two immgration cases that outline some of the information the BCIS can consider when passing judgment on your ability to care for an orphan. In *Matter of Suh, 10 I&N Dec. 624*, it was held that the BCIS is allowed to consider the employment record, financial status, military record, and arrest and conviction record of the petitioner. In *Matter of T-E-C, 10 I&N Dec. 691*, it was held that the BCIS was authorized to see if all preadoption requirements of the state of intended residence of the orphan were met. According to this case, the petitioner's financial status, work record, receipt of welfare, and current number of dependents are items properly considered.

A good social worker can be of great help to you. She can ask questions that relate to parenting and cause you to think things through. For example, questions dealing with disciplining your child. You and your spouse may have generally talked about it, but this question can focus you on the issue. Now the discipline issue is one where the social worker will eventually require you and your spouse to agree never to spank your child. You may even have to sign a piece of paper to that effect. Just do it and move on.

Yes, the corporal punishment police are out in force and you must give them what they want. They want to hear that when you discipline your child you will use time outs, logical consequences, thinking chairs, grounding, holding time, taking away toys, or canceling play dates, but you would never ever spank your child. The reality is that all decent parents try very hard to use anything but corporal punishment, but sometimes, under certain circumstances, your child will do something serious where a swat on the rear is the only educational tool that may work. A child who puts their finger in the light socket or their head in the microwave or runs out into the street to bite tires, may need more than a time out to prevent him from becoming an early Darwin Award winner. Contrary to what is taught in academia, a tap on the leg or diaper bottom does not immediately turn your child into a psychopath. A 1996 special conference by the American Academy of Pediatrics concluded that there was no evidence to suggest that spankings per se are harmful. Just know the answer the social worker is looking for and give it to her. Now the truth is that producing a well-behaved child probably results more from a parent's consistency in meting out consequences than in the punishment itself.

Now each state has it owns rules about the corporal punishment issue. In Virginia, adoptive families are required to sign a statement saying that corporal punishment will not be used, although there seems to be some discussion on ending this requirement. One of the reasons the corporal punishment statement exists is primarily due to foster care laws. In cases where children have been physically abused by their bio parents and subsequently removed from the home, it is rightfully felt that the foster parents should not be allowed to use corporal punishment. After all, that was the reason why the children were removed from their parents in the first place. However, as most of us can agree, there is a big difference between swatting a child's behind every now and then, versus severely beating him with a belt. Children have died from that kind of abuse, and in two cases, one in 2001 and another in 2002 young Russian children adopted by Americans became such victims. The law does not really distinguish between those two extremes, though, and so we are left with the poor social worker having to throw out common sense in order to satisfy what is required of her.

The other problem with the corporal punishment statement, at least in Virginia, is that it is only "valid" until a Final Order of Adoption is issued. So in other words, you cannot use corporal punishment on your child until after he is officially adopted. So what is the point of having parents adopting internationally make such a statement?

Finally, depending on how things were handled in the children's home your child may not be so different from the kids in the U.S. foster care system. A child who has been physically abused often cannot distinguish between different kinds of hitting, and this is why corporal punishment is so ineffective. The reality is that you will be like all parents and have to undergo trial and error in determining what action on your part conveys to the child the message and lesson that the behavior was improper or unsafe and will not be tolerated. If authority of the parent and consequences are not understood early on, it is much more difficult to gain that authority later. Again, consistency of consequences, not the type of punishment, is the key.

Because of there can be a transracial aspect to adopting from Eastern Europe, some time might be spent exploring your attitudes and beliefs about parenting a child of another race and the affects of becoming a multiracial family on your extended family. Russian has over 100 nationalities. Kazakhstan is a Kazak, German and Russian melting pot. Bulgaria has a lot of Rom children in their orphanages.

Your social worker may also ask about lead paint, fire extinguishers, guns, fire alarms, child proof locks, prescription medicines, insecticides, cleaners, pets, and other potential hazards in the home. She will ask where the child will sleep and want to see the room. If you live in an older home, she may ask about updated electricity and plumbing. She may want to see if you are using an older crib where the slats are too far apart, or have older window blind cords that still have loops. Since 1995 window blind cords have been manufactured without loops, which can strangle a young child. She may ask about guns in the house and how they are stored. All of these questions are not necessarily bad questions to ask. These questions may have little to do with adopting a child, but they have a lot to do with creating a safe environment in which to parent that child.

Other ideas regarding baby proofing your home are to take electrical cords and tack them to walls and not just place them under the rug. Place bumpers on sharp edges like the fireplace and coffee table before the baby can pull up Your fireplace will need a hearth gate and a strong screen. Place nonskid pads underneath rugs. Look out for dangling appliance cords. Put plastic covers over electrical outlets. Safety gates at top and bottom of stairs. Secure your entertainment unit and bookcase to the wall so the child cannot pull it over. Place smoke and carbon monoxide detectors in hall. Put safety latches or locks in the kitchen where dangerous utensils or chemicals or poisons or stored. Use the back burners on the stove whenever possible and turn the pot handles toward the back Lower hot water heater to no more than 120 degrees or perhaps install anti-scalding devices on faucets. Use a toilet lock to prevent drowning When bathing your child, bring the cordless phone in with you so you do not feel the need to run out to answer the phone. Put a bath mat in the tub to prevent your child from slipping and slamming his head back in the tub. (This one happens a lot!)

Parents sometimes become very nervous when the home study social worker makes her required visit to the home. They clean, they make cookies, and they watch re-runs of the Beaver to see how Mrs.Cleaver did it. It is not necessary. This is not a white-glove test for dirt under the refrigerator. It is not unusual to have the house look like a Tonka construction zone as you might be remodeling a room into the baby's room. All the social worker works to see is that the house looks like a safe and normal place to raise a child. That's all. There is a funny story about a single parent whose neighbor had the flu. His buddies were not letting him get any sleep at his house so she let him come over and sleep at her house in the morning. That afternoon she forgot he was still there and the social worker came over for her visit. She flicked on her bedroom light to show off the room and there he was sitting on the side of her bed without any clothes! She was able to explain it all and received an approved home study the following week.

BCIS regulations require that a home study amendment be submitted if there has been a "significant change in family circumstances." This generally means that people have moved, and it doesn't matter whether it is next door or many countries away. The reality is that if the move will take place after the adoption or close in time, then just leave everything alone and don't volunteer anything. If it will take place while you are still waiting for a referral, then you should made the change, which is usually accomplished by a one page amendment from your home study social worker.

One exercise, that only a few home study agencies require, but which would be the best help to you in preparing for your international adoption, is to meet at least two families who have adopted from the country in which you are interested. You will learn far more from them than from reading or listening to a social worker. You will learn first hand about adoption language, grieving, medical issues, the process, parenting, etc.

After the home study is completed, the home study agency will obtain your state's seal of approval. Then it will be sent on to the BCIS by your home study agency. This is generally how it works. Do not be afraid to call your home study agency and follow up as to when the study was sent to the BCIS. Your social worker should allow you to see a copy before she sends it, in order for you to review it for minor errors like names, birth dates and matching the number of children with the figure placed on your I-600A. You should also receive a final copy of the home study once it is signed, sealed and delivered. If the home study agency does not agree to give you a final copy, don't hire them. The reason your state must give approval to the home study is that the BCIS is not allowed to issue a visa to your child unless you meet state pre-adoption requirements.

Make sure you put in your home study that you wish to adopt one child more than you really mean too. As previously mentioned, it is very common for a family to adopt one child then go back the next year to adopt a second. By already having the approval in your home study for more children, you may be able to shorten the process. If you find your child has a sibling and you need to increase the number of children then have your home study amended and write a letter to the BCIS amending your answer to line 17. You may have to change the number of approved children by paying the BCIS a fee of $110.00 and file a "Motion to Reopen" in order to increase the number of children you want reflected in your I-171H approval. Also, make sure you add a couple of years to your expected child's age. For example, if you want to adopt a child under 2, then put that you are looking for 0-4. The reason is that during the process of adopting that 2 year old, he may turn 3. Also, you may find yourself in a children's home in Russia or Ukraine and you suddenly find yourself bonding to a 5 year old of a different gender. Thus, having some cushion on the age and gender means you do not have to amend the home study and the BCIS approval at the last minute. Now this has no bearing on how specific you actually tell your adoption agency and what referral you accept from the foreign country. This only has to do with the problem of showing up at the Consulate with a child outside the age for which the BCIS approved you. At the Warsaw Embassy it is not a major problem and all they do is ask why you went outside your age preference.

The social worker will likely want the following documents from you so begin collecting them:

1.   Certified copy of your marriage license and birth certificate

2.   Copy of the deed to your house or apartment lease

3.   Copy of your passport and copy of your latest tax return or W-2.

4.   A fingerprint clearance letter from your State or County

5.   Medical form to be filled out by your doctor

6.   Criminal record clearance letter

7.   Some States require a child abuse clearance letter

8.   Letters from friends saying that you will make great parents.

She will likely ask you the following questions so prepare your answers. Remember that the questions are her problem, but the answers and what follows are yours. Elaborate answers just lead to more questions.

1. Why do you wish to adopt a child?
2. How do you feel about adopting a child of a different race?
3. What do you consider to be acceptable methods of disciplining a child?
4. How might you facilitate your child's learning about her birth culture?
5. What values would you like to pass on to your child?
6. What are your hopes and dreams for your child?
7. What was it like growing up in your family?
8. What are the strengths and weaknesses in your marriage?
9. How do you and your spouse resolve disagreements?
10. If you are single, what extra challenges do you anticipate facing as a single parent? (the Dad (or Mom) question)

If you have been arrested in the past like for an old DUI, it will likely show up on the FBI fingerprint check. Although it is possible that if it occurred in a small town, then it might not have been reported, the odds are against you. The BCIS may send you a "J" letter asking you to submit original or certified copies of any court dispositions and proof of completion of court requirements. The BCIS is now looking for any criminal record, no matter how small. There is no reasonable test. They may also ask you to supply an affidavit explaining the situation and any extenuating circumstances. If documents are not available, the BCIS will want the police station or court to sign a letter stating that no records exist. If you know an arrest is going to turn up, you might as well begin to collect these documents and submit them with your home study. The BCIS and your home study agency will be very, very unhappy if the arrest shows up on the FBI check, but not in the home study so be careful if you decide not to disclose. The good news is that unless it is recent and was a charge involving violence, you will most likely be approved.

A description of the BCIS attitude toward criminal checks can be found in their memorandum on N-400 applicants at *http://www.immigration.gov/graphics/lawsregs/handbook/natznq2.pdf.* I can not locate a memorandum on the I-600A process and criminal checks, but this one gives you the general idea.

If there was full disclosure of the criminal record, full consideration by the home study preparer, and full compliance with regs at 8 CFR § 204.3(e), BCIS can accept the recommendation of the home study preparer and, if State review is required, of the State authorities. However, if BCIS believes that the prospective adoptive parent is a danger to the child, further information can be sought so that either the home study preparer withdraws the favorable recommendation or reconfirms its favorable recommendation. BCIS must still decide whether it is satisfied that proper care will be given. The good news is you have appeal rights if BCIS acts arbitrarily.

Some other issues that might arise include multiple marriages or depression due to infertility stress. Multiple marriages should not be a problem unless they were recent. However, occasionally you will run into a social worker whose bias and inexperience causes them to give you a hard time. If you have settled down into a long relationship, then your ancient history should be just that and no more. You will not likely run into a judgmental social worker if you find one that has some years of experience. Stay away from the less experienced ones, who are fresh out of school.

Now many people have taken anti-depressants to cope with infertility. However, there are two schools of thought about whether to disclose it to your social worker. The first school says they will find out anyway and if they find out and you haven't told them then you will look bad. That school of thought is nonsense. This isn't nursery school and the social worker is not your mother. If you do not tell them, it is unlikely they will find out. It will not show up on any medical report or test, unless your doctor hates you. If the social worker sees a bottle on the home visit, then maybe she will find out, but that is about it. Now actually taking an anti-depressant will not likely affect the home study. Depending on your social worker, it will be glossed over or discussed then dismissed. For example, your social worker might put, "well controlled with medication." Now the Russians do have a problem. They will see it as a real psychiatric issue. They don't understand that most functioning Americans take hordes of drugs every week, such as vitamins, 11 herbs and spices, Aspirin, headache pills, arthritis pills, pills for Monday, pills for Thursday and anti-depressants. Even veterinarians give anti-depressants to dogs. So what usually happens is that your social worker will minimize the issue or issue two home studies, one for the BCIS containing everything and one for the Russians that is sanitized. This is another reason to use a home study agency that is used to doing reports for international adoptions. You don't want an inexperienced social worker making a big deal about it.

If you are unsure from which country you will adopt, all you have to put in your home study is "Eastern Europe." BCIS will issue the I-171H without a specific country. Now you will have to return to your social worker to get some added paragraphs to comply with the specific country and even region requirements when you do decide. Also, the BCIS will have to be notified so they can send the Visa 37 Cable to the correct Embassy, but meanwhile you will have received your I-171H. If you decide after receiving your I-171H, then you will have to pay $140 and file Form I-824. If you decide before receiving the I-1717H, then when you send in your home study just add a short note on top of the submission telling the BCIS from which country you intend to adopt.

The full BCIS checklist is as follows:

<u>Home Study Checklist</u>

1. <u>Personal interviews and home visits</u>
- conduct at least one interview in person
- conduct at least one home visit
- state number of interviews conducted
- state number of home visits
- interview in person with any other adult member
- discuss whether post adoption counseling is offered

2. <u>Assessment of ability to properly parent the orphan</u>
- initial assessment of physical, mental, and emotional
- assessment of potential problem areas
- referral to licensed professional, if appropriate
- copies of any outside evaluations
- any recommended restrictions
- apply all to any adult members of household

3. <u>Assessment of the finances of the prospective adoptive parent(s).</u>
- description of the income, financial resources, debts and expenses
- describe evidence that was considered in the assessment

4. <u>Screening for abuse and violence</u>
- statement regarding results of appropriate checks

5.   Inquiring about abuse and violence

- response from each prospective adoptive parent regarding history of substance abuse, sexual or child abuse, or domestic violence, even if it did not result in an arrest or conviction

- response from any additional adult members of the household regarding history of substance abuse, sexual or child abuse, or domestic violence, even if it did not result in an arrest or conviction

6.   Information concerning history of abuse and/or violence and/or criminal record

- information concerning all arrrests or convictions for substance abuse, sexual or child abuse, and/or domestic violence and the date of each occurrence

- certified copy of the documentation showing final disposition of each incident, which resulted in arrest,indictment, conviction, and/or any other judicial judgement or administrative action

- signed statement from the prospective adoptive parent giving details including mitigating circumstances, if any, about each incident

- apply all to any additional adult members of household

7.   Evidence of rehabilitation

- discussion of rehabilitation

- evaluation of the seriousness of the arrest(s), conviction(s), or history of abuse

- number of such incidents

- length of time since the last incident

- any counseling or rehabilitation programs which have been successfully completed

- evidence of rehabilitation by an appropriate licensed professional

- all facts and circumstances which were considered

- reasons for favorable home study

- apply to any additional adult members of the household

8.   Previous rejection for adoption or prior unfavorable home study

- adoptive parent's response to whether rejected or a previous unfavorable home study
- if rejected or unfavorable, the reason for such findings
- copy of previous rejection and/or unfavorable home study
- must be applied to any additional adult members of household

9. <u>Living accommodations</u>
- detailed description of the living accommodations
- assessment of the suitability of accommodations
- determination whether space meets applicable state requirements, if any

10. <u>Handicapped or special needs orphan</u>
- discussion of preparation, willingness, and ability to provide proper care

11. <u>Summary of the counseling given and plans for post-placement counseling</u>
- statement that there was a discussion of the processing expenses, difficulties and delays associated with international adoptions
- any plans for post-placement counseling

12. <u>Specific approval of the prospective adoptive parent(s) for adoption</u>
- favorable recommendation for proposed adoption
- reasons for approval
- number of orphans that may be adopted
- any specific restrictions such as, nationality, age or gender of orphan
- approval for a handicapped or special needs adoption, if any

13. <u>Home study preparer's certification and statement of authority to conduct home studies.</u>
- statement certifying authorization to conduct home studies
- for parents residing in the U.S., a statement should include authorization under state of orphan's proposed residence, license or authorization number and expiration date of such authorization

- if prospective adoptive parent(s) reside abroad, and the orphan's adoption is finalized abroad, a statement identifying the authorization by the adoption authorities of the foreign country where the child will reside or the authorization by any state in the U.S., including authorization or license number if any, and expiration date of such authorization, if any.

14. Review of homestudy

- review by state authorities if prospective adoptive parents reside in a state which requires such review.

- if prospective adoptive parents reside abroad, appropriate public or private adoption agency licensed or otherwise authorized by any state to place children for adoption, must review and recommend.

15. Home study updates

- must accompany a home study that is more than six months old or

  if at any time, there have been any significant changes including, but not limited to:

- residence of prospective adoptive parent(s)

- marital status

- criminal history, substance abuse and/or history of abuse or violence

- financial resources

- addition of one or more children or other dependents

One last coment on homestudies.Some social workers in small towns feel under pressure to approve international families as they believe they will not receive work if they turn a family down. Yet there are many families who do not read the materials, do not prepare for an international child as if it was a special needs adoption, and simply give lip service to the professionals. Balancing against the family's lack of parenting preparation is that there is a child that is literally languishing to death in some institution. This balancing act is what can make a social worker's life very stressful.

More information on the BCIS' home study requirements can be found at *http://www.immigration.gov/graphics/services/bopreq.htm and http://www.immigration.gov/graphics/services/homestud.htm.*

CHAPTER V

RUSSIAN PAPERCHASE

Russian Adoption Law

Russian adoption policy is based on making a clean break between the child's old and new family. Open adoption is not an accepted concept. Russians are much more organized about adoptions than the United States. All children who are eligible for adoption are placed on the Federal Ministry of Education's Central Data Bank also known as the registry. While the child is on the registry, only Russian families may adopt the child. However, once the child is listed for the required amount of time then the regional education department will ask Moscow for permission to allow a foreigner to adopt. Notwithstanding, a Russian family always has priority over a foreign one up to the time of the actual court hearing.

According to Article 126 of the Family Code of the Russian Federation, Regional Ministry officials enter data into the federal database by electronic mail or use the "Atlas" network. The child's biographical form must contain the following:

* Date of filling out the form by the children's home
* Date of entering the above data into the regional database

*   Data on each of the parents and the date of issue of the document serving as the basis for placement (death certificate; parents' consent to adoption; court decision on the deprivation of parental rights, court decision stating the parents are unknown, incapable etc., certificate #24 on the absence of father)

*   Data on all brothers and sisters (including half-brothers and half-sisters), with their place of residence, if possible

The original photo (or its electronic copy) of the child, taken at the time of filling out the form should be attached to the biographical form. Prior to allowing a foreign adoption, the Regional Ministry of Education must describe the efforts that were made to place the child with Russian Federation families.

Under the old laws children were only listed on the registry for 3 months and after that foreigners could adopt the child. However, in 1998 the Federal Minister of Education issued a regulation that any child who was put on the registry after July 1, 1998 must be on the registry for 4 months instead of 3. The actual timeline is 1 month for the local database, 1 month for the regional database and 3 months on the national or federal database. This law can be found in Article 122 of the Family Code of the Russian Federation.

Commonly though the local and regional database is the same so that is why it is normally just 4 months. Your agency should know whether your child has been on the required amount of time and the child's status.

In addition to this change there was a change in the "abandonment" provision. A child whose mother (and father if married) have signed "relinquishment papers" will only have to wait the 4 months time on the registry before being eligible for foreign adoption. However, if no "relinquishment papers" have been signed then Russian law concerning "abandonment" says that the child must be abandoned for 6 months before adoption can be considered. In order to be deemed "abandoned", 6 months must pass from the time of the court order making the child a ward of the state without any family member appealing the decision. This is not actually the same as being on the database. An appeal period of 6 months is also the same amount of time in cases where parents' rights are "terminated" through court action because of problems with the home situation. Fortunately, this 6 months time can run concurrently with the listing on the database. At the end of 6 months the child will have the legal status of "orphan" as required by the United States for the child to be issued an immigrant visa by the US Embassy.

To summarize the registry timeline, a child must be on the registry for 4 months regardless. If the child is going under the designation of "abandoned" or "parental rights terminated" then a concurrent appeal period of 6 months must also pass. A child remains on the registry database until adopted. The required time in the database to become eligible elapses, but the child is not 'removed' until adopted or reunited with their family of birth. Once a family has petitioned to adopt a particular child, Moscow will issue a "release or clearance letter" releasing the child from the database. If a child is 10 or older, the law also requires his/her consent.

In most regions there is a Department of Social Protection. This department has authority over the regional Department of Health (baby homes) and regional Department of Education (older children's homes). The Regional ("Oblast") inspector for the Protection of Children's Rights is in charge of receiving and processing adoption applications. She works within the regional Department of Education. If your agency has a good relationship with her then she will allow your agency to work with a children's home. The inspector is basically the social worker who represents the child. The inspector is with you when you meet the child and in court to testify. She has seen your file, knows the child's background and will give her opinion in court that the child is available and that you will be good parents. When you meet the child, she is there to watch you interact so she can feel comfortable that you are happy with the child. The inspector is a good source of information. If you ask her politely about the background of the birth family she often has useful information that you may wish you had in the future. She is often the only source for this.

If your agency has a good relationship with the children's home director, then she will allow your agency to place some of "her" children. Once the child has cleared the federal data bank and your dossier documents collected, the inspector will send the application to the central federal office at the Ministry of Education in Moscow for final approval. She will send a formal letter asking that the child be removed from the Federal Data Bank and naming you as the adoptive parents. The Federal Ministry of Education will then reply with a formal letter (federal clearance letter) stating that the child has been on the registry for the required time and is now available for adoption by the named adoptive parents. After all of this, a court date can be set.

In addition to these other changes in the law that occurred in 1998, the law also required Regional Courts, rather than District or City Courts, to hear adoption cases. In 1992 when Russian adoptions were really first starting the process was very informal and the "hearing" was nothing more than an administrative proceeding without any court involvement. Since the natural order of bureaucracy (no matter what country) is to make things more complicated without adding value, the process has progressed from administrative to a city or district court and now all the way to the regional appellate courts. The regional courts have always been where serious criminal matters were heard. Therefore, imagine the regional judges' surprise in 1998 when they found out they were to also hear adoption cases. It was a whole new area of law and there has been a learning curve.

Each Region has slightly different documents and adoption procedures that they require. Indeed, some calculate the necessary time a child must stay on the national data bank differently than others. Some regions will waive the 10-day period of appeal and some won't. There are even slight differences depending on which regional judge is responsible for your case. Things are still very regionalized in Russia. Some regions are very independent and move at a slower pace in their reaction to edicts from the federal government, while others fall right in line and adopt changes very quickly.

One interesting aspect of Russian law is that if the father is not married to the child's mother, he has no rights towards the child. No marriage equals zero parental rights. When this is the case, a "Form 4" or "Form 25" is issued by local ZAGS (the bureau of vital statistics), which confirms the absence of marriage and thus absence of a legal father.

The Form 4 can also indicate that the mother simply gave the name of a man as the father and that she really does not know. Since she was not married to the man (whoever he was), he has no rights as father unless he establishes those rights in court. You may also see wording, which says, "father's name based on the testimony of the mother." This also means the birth mother was not married and that the name of the birth father on the paperwork was most likely false. This form can also just be one the facilitator gets to solve some problems. It's easier to get this form than have to deal with the judge's questions about the father. In reality "no information about father" can mean one of three things:

(1). The father really is unknown to the birthmother, (2). the birthmother decided not to put his name in the birth certificate for reasons only she knows, or (3) the facilitator decided to go this way rather then find a father and try to obtain his written consent for adoption.

In the Russian judicial system the judge has a wide degree of discretion. Judges can waive the ten-day appeal period if they want. They can ask for more documents from you or less. They can require the child's third cousin be located and give consent to the adoption (like in Omsk) or not require anything more than relinquishment and consent by the birthmother. As another example, normally under Russian law, both parents must attend court. However, if this is difficult, you can petition the judge to allow only one to attend (Rostov). It would be rare that it is granted, but it is within the judge's discretion.

Changes in Russian Adoption Law

On March 28, 2000, the President of Russia, Vladimir Putin, signed a series of decrees aimed at tightening control on adoptions. Some of these new regulations had been in the works since 1998 and some were new.

The decrees outlawed the use of "middlemen" but did not define who is considered to be a middleman. This rule was actually discussed some years before, but there was no real consensus on what it really meant and so business went on as before using facilitators or "middlemen." Russian government officials have often alleged that intermediaries facilitate adoptions for foreigners by paying bribes to orphanages and bureaucrats. There has also been a perceived conflict of interest issue with persons who are in charge of the children actually being facilitators. Therefore, adoption agencies can now not employ people who also work for Russian State educational, medical, social service establishments or similar organizations that work with the children. Additionally, employees of Russian State adoption services, their spouses and close relatives are also prohibited from working for foreigners. The decree also established an "accreditation" process whereby foreign adoption agencies had to be "accredited" by the Russian government in order to work in Russia. The thrust of the new laws was asserting control over the process by the Russian federal government.

A special government commission oversees foreign adoptions and the accreditation procedure. Accredited adoption agencies are responsible for reporting back to the Education Ministry about the welfare of the children they have helped place in homes abroad. Since all adoptions must have post-placement reports anyway, this was not any real change. There are about 50 accredited US agencies and it appears that number will not change for a few years. The list of accredited agencies can be found at the Russian Ministry of Education site at *http://www.informika.ru/eng/Ministry/Accred.html*. The Russian Embassy site also has a list.

The new rules also seemed to restrict sending any medical, video or other background information on any particular child to a prospective parent in the US. Different regions have interpreted this rule in different ways. Some regions have allowed this sort of information to be sent to prospective parents as in the past. Others have prohibited the practice. At first, agencies that became accredited were able to continue receiving pre-identification material, however, the trend now is toward not allowing any pre-identification information regardless of whether you use an accredited or unaccredited agency or go independent. It really varies by region. The rules also required that you register your child with the Russian Embassy upon returning to the States.

The result of the limitation on pre-identification material is that families have to make two trips to Russia. The first trip is to choose a child and the second to attend court. You do not need to have your I-171H from the BCIS before making the first trip, but you better have it for the second. Some agencies require you to have it for the first trip, but most regions do not. You do not have to make two trips of course, just that the wait for a court date can be as long as 4 weeks to three months. This limitation on pre-identification material is not an absolute rule, just an option for the regions to adopt. With 89 regions in Russia (and with their various degrees of independence from Moscow), there has been a wide variation in practices. In the majority of regions parents go over twice.

To illustrate how the adoption process varies between regions, some regions have not changed anything and everything is proceeding as before including referrals, videos and medical information. In these regions, one trip is all that is needed. Even in those regions where there is a two-trip process, there is variation. One region may send you several children's photographs and brief medical histories while you are in the States. You then travel to the children's home to meet them and choose. In others, you have no information until you arrive at the regional Department of Education.

There are also some new documents to add to your dossier. The first is the Commitment to Register the Child with the Russian Consulate or Embassy upon your return and the second is an agreement to allow your agency to conduct post-placement follow-up. Your agency will also have to make a commitment. These documents seem to be required by all of the regions. The agency commitment to file post-placement reports can be just a letter from them containing your name and address, and stating that the agency agrees to monitor the upbringing and living conditions of your adopted child and will provide post-placement reports to the appropriate Russian Departments, within the required time frames, and for as long as is required by Russian Law which is usually 3 years.

Some regions have asked for other documents. You may be asked to file a document officially asking for the exact date your child came off the registry. Some regions also have asked for a medical report on any child that you have in your home, vaccination record of your dog, or a document showing you live in a house or an apartment. These documents have to be notarized and apostilled.

The requirement of registering the child may give you pause. However, other countries such as Ukraine and Kazakhstan have this requirement as well. All it means is that when you return to the States you send the Russian

Embassy in Washington, D.C., a registration form with your address on it and the name of your child and their Russian passport. It doesn't change your child's status as your child or even as an American citizen once they obtain citizenship. If you think about it, the Russians already have this information from all of the dossier papers you had to file so this is just duplicative information.

Apostilles and Authentications

The United States is a signatory to the Hague Convention on legalization of foreign public documents. By this Convention, the Russians and other countries will accept as authentic, documents that have been "Apostilled." An Apostille is a form of certification by a participant country verifying the authenticity of the signatures, the authority of the persons signing, and the authenticity of the seals and stamps. The Apostille is a stamp established by the Hague Convention, entered in documents by a competent authority of the country in which the document was issued. In the US, your state's Secretary of State enters the Apostille. Be sure to tell them from which country you are adopting so the Secretary of State will apply the proper seal.

Now some countries, like Ukraine, only accept documents that have been "Authenticated." This is a different procedure than "Apostilled." In the "Authentication" procedure the notarized document is taken to that State's Secretary of State where the notary's signature and stamp are essentially certified by the State. Make sure they do a "regular certification" not an apostille certification. Tell them it is for Ukraine. If you have documents notarized in a different state, then it will have to be certified in that particular state. For example, if you live in Georgia, but were born in Arizona, then your certified birth certificate will have to be authenticated by the Arizona Secretary of State. In some States, like New York, the notary is first certified at the county level then the New York Secretary of State. After your documents are authenticated at the state level, they go to the State Department in the Washington, D.C for authentication and then over to the respective foreign consulate for final authentication.

Ukraine has a hard time accepting a parent's signature that the I-171 is a true and correct copy. Sometimes a social worker can attest, and then have it notarized. If you run into a real problem you can authenticate an I-171H by asking the BCIS for the "red ribbon and seal". Once the document is certified, it should be submitted to the State Department for authentication.

Some families have used a dossier courier group to make the rounds called Pata Group. Their address is: 617 K Street NW Washington, DC 20001 and their telephone number is: 202-789-1330. Another one is Jeff Doyle, P.O. Box 3239, Arlington, Virginia 22203-6134; phone is 703-298-2382; *jaydoy@starpower.net*. A courier that some families have used is Patti Urban at *http://www.Legal-Eaze.com*. Her email address is *Patti@Legal-Eaze.com* and her phone is 914.362.4630; fax: 914.362.4637. Another courier service is Laura Morrison, also an adoptive mom. Her email address is *laura@asststork.com* and she has a great website at *http://www.asststork.com*. The Plachtas (also adoptive parents) are at *http://www.special-deliveries.net* and finally Denise Hope at *www.theres-always-hope.com* has a good handle on the procedures at the Chicago Consulate. Laura Morrison's web site has a lot of good information on the authentication process. The couriers keep a pretty good eye on your dossier and can help you if there are mistakes. Usually they can tell you where your dossier is at any given time

States vary as to how much they charge for apostilles. It can range from $3 per apostille (Georgia and Massachusetts) to $15 for Pennsylvania to $20 for Florida. In Michigan it is a $1, Wisconsin $10, Colorado $2, Ohio $5, California $20 plus $6 to authenticate the signatures, and in Indiana free. A lot of California parents simply take their non-state specific documents over to Arizona to be notarized and apostilled for $3. Make sure you call first in case these fees have changed. It is recommended that you use the same notary as much as possible as that will eliminate the State's need to look up different notary's licenses. California has a website that describes its procedure at *http://www.ss.ca.gov/business/notary/notary_authentication.htm*

You can find a list of each state's Secretary of State at *http://www.corban-consulting.com/adoption/states.html*, Here is a sample of some states' addresses:

VIRGINIA:
Secretary of the Commonwealth
Capitol Square
Old Finance Building
Richmond, VA 23219
Tel 804-786-2441
$10 per apostille

NEW YORK:
(New York City)

Department of State
Certification Unit
123 William Street, 19th Floor
New York, New York 10038
Hours: 9:00 a.m. to 3:30 p.m.
Phone #: (212) 417-5684
The closest subway station is Fulton on the green line.
$10 per apostille

Note that in New York State, after you have your signature notarized, the county in which he is registered as a notary must certify the notary's signature. It is only after completing that process that you then go to the Secretary of State for the Apostilles. The cost for certification of the notary's signature is $3.00 per document. When having all of this done, make sure that all of the seals are raised. Do not remove an apostille to make copies and then try to re-staple.

NEW JERSEY
State of New Jersey
Business Services Bureau—Notary Division
225 West State Street, 3rd Floor
Trenton, NJ 08608-1001
Main #: 609-292-9292

Or
State of New Jersey—Dept of Treasury
Business Services Bureau—Notary Division
PO Box 452
Trenton, NJ 08625
Ph: 609-633-8258 or 609-633-8257

For expedited service, you must deliver your package by hand or use a commercial carrier like FedEx. You can't use USPS Express Mail because they don't deliver to the West State Street address.

MASSACHUSETTS
Secretary of the Commonwealth
McCormick Building
Public Records Division/Commissions Section

Room 1719
(17th floor)
One Ashburton Place
Boston, MA 02108.
Phone (617) 727-2832

You can walk in without an appointment or obtain them by mail. Either way, they are processed on the same day. The fee is $3 per apostille. If you have more than 10 documents, they may ask you to return later to pick them up, or the next morning if you drop them off in the afternoon. They can do them in 5 minutes. There is never a line and there are several clerks. If you send by mail, include a check and return envelope with postage. The McCormick Building is the gray building a block behind the statehouse, just up the little hill from Government Center metro. Additional info is available at *www.state.ma.us/sec/pre/precom*

A general recommendation is that you express mail your document with a return prepaid express and indicate your name, address, phone number. In your cover letter you should tell them that it is for an adoption. One way to avoid high fees is to take your documents to a nearby state that has lower fees and have them notarized and apostilled. This does not apply to state specific documents such as a birth certificate or marriage certificate. If you get into difficulty with apostilling a document, ask your agency if you can simply get a copy of the document, type that it is a correct copy on a cover page, staple the two together and have your cover page notarized and apostilled where you live. Only if you get into a real jam should you try this for official documents like marriage licenses and birth certificates. Another method of cutting costs is to determine if the region or country from which you are adopting will allow bundling of documents. Some will. If it does, then you must see if your Secretary of State will allow bundling. Some do not. Bundling will allow you to use just one apostille for a whole set of documents. There is a website with all of the addresses of the offices of vital records in all 50 states at *http://www.asststork.com/pages/myvitalrec.html*

A trick with state specific documents that are not located near you is to ask the clerk to send the certified document on to the state's Secretary of States' office to be apostilled. This will save time. In order to do this you need to enclose a stamped pre-addressed envelope to the state and then a second one that the state can use to send the document back to you. You will need to include all fees of course and the usual cover letters. Sometimes the state's

Bureau of Vital Statistics will simply send you an apostilled version for an additional fee. South Carolina is one such state. In some states, like Georgia, the apostille process has been delegated to another office rather than the State's Secretary of State.

Like everything in life, always call ahead to make sure of the correct procedure and fee. Always double-check your notary before and after she signs the documents. Make sure the expiration of her license shown on her stamp is at least a year away. Make sure she signs using the exact name on her seal and stamp and puts the county name on the document. No abbreviations are allowed. Some states, like Tennessee and Maryland, also require the county clerk to certify the notary's signature before the Secretary of State will apostille. Different states have different rules. One tip is that AAA members can use their local AAA office's notorial service. There is usually a notary on staff.

A good tip is to open your own FedEx account. It only takes a few minutes and does not cost anything. You can do this over the phone or if you live close enough to a FedEx branch you can also do this in person. This allows the return express mail to be billed to your account, saving much time.

Dossier

What is a dossier? It is all your paperwork that you have gathered in the States. It is your home study, your birth certificate, marriage certificate, form for this, and form for that. It is all of those documents, notarized and apostilled. Your agency compiles all of this into your "dossier" and has it translated. It is sent to Russia and reviewed by the local and regional Ministry of Education departments. If the child is under 4 years of age, the Ministry of Health also must approve it. Also, the baby home director must give approval. Once approved by the Ministries it can then be submitted to the Court and the Court is under a timeline to schedule a court date. The Ministry departments may delay the process by its employees going on vacation, getting sick, or not making it a priority. They are also overworked and underpaid.

This is also true with the courts. While your agency can not control the timing of the Ministries' approval, in some Regions they may have a little more control over the setting of the Court date. Even so, a good working relationship between your agency's people and the Ministry officials can be of great importance in speeding the process along.

The dossier will likely contain some of the following documents accompanied by a certified Russian translation:

1. Your home study

2. Copy of marriage license

3. Copy of birth certificate (a quick way to get a certified copy of your birth certificate is through vitalchek at *http://www.vitalchek.com*

4. Medical report on the parents

5. Employer verification of employment

6. Proof of home ownership or proof of housing. Some Regions are happy with just a copy of your deed or lease with a notary stamp on a cover sheet saying, "this is a true and correct copy" and then an apostille. Other Regions also want a notarized and apostilled copy of your tax bill. You can get copies of anything at the county courthouse and then just have a notary on a cover sheet.

7. The facilitator should provide the Ministries with a form letter from the US Embassy stating that if the correct documents are submitted then a visa will be issued to the child. This form letter has no form number, but is on the computers at the Embassy.

8. Your I-171-H form from the BCIS

9. Copy of your Home Study Agency's license

10. A post-placement agreement letter

11. Copy of your State's law on adoption

12. Some Regions ask for a letter from your pediatrician stating that he will be the child's doctor and the date of the first visit.

13. Copy of your Passport. You make a copy of the signature and picture page for each of you (all on one page). Then put a cover page and you will both attest to it being an original, true, unaltered copy and have it notarized.

If you are self-employed, you will likely be asked for a letter from your accountant stating that you are self-employed, description of job or position, the length of time self-employed, some W-2 information over past three years and the number of years the accountant has been doing your taxes. The letter needs to be notarized.

Now there are some additional documents that are peculiar to certain regions and even certain Judges. Some regions (Chelyabinsk) require a letter from your home study agency promising that the agency will file post placement reports in accordance with Russian law. Other regions just require it from your placing agency. Also, some regions require that the home study social worker submit a letter stating that the photos of your home submitted with your dossier are actually of your primary residence. These "extra" documents are just that, extra. Just roll with it and get them notarized and apostilled. Also, many regions require two dossiers (Ivanovo, Magadan, and several others) so you probably need to collect at least two of everything and have it all apostilled. Previously, when you completed your dossier it only had to go to a regional Department of Education. Now, they want one filed with the regional court as well.

All of your dossier documents have to be notarized and apostilled (or authenticated), unless bundling is allowed. Usually the notary statement above the notary's signature should say, "This is a true and correct copy of the original" or some variation of that. You should ask your adoption agency if there is any particular wording that they like. Of course, official documents such as birth certificates and marriage certificates will already be certified and will just need the apostille.

For some regions of Russia, a copy of the I-171H must be part of your dossier and must be apostilled. To do this, you make a copy of the 171-H and put the statement on the bottom or the back of the copy (but not on a separate page): "This is a true and accurate copy of an original." You take this copy to the notary public and have them witness YOUR signature and have it notarized. The state is then able to apostille this notary signature. If you live in New York State, you first have to have the county clerk's office verify the notary's signature and then the state will apostille the county clerk personnel's signature, and it becomes part of your dossier.

In addition, the local Russian child welfare representatives will provide to the Court:

1) Evidence that the child was registered for the requisite amount of time on the data bank and that no Russian family has shown an interest in adopting the child.

2) They also have to show that no family member has shown an interest as well.

3) A statement that the adoption is in the child's best interest.

4) Child's birth certificate

5) Medical report on the child

6) If child is over 10 year of age, his consent.

7) Consent of the children's home director

If you are single, some regions may ask you to provide a letter from a family member or friend saying that they agree to raise the child in the event of your death.

If you were born overseas as a United States citizen, then you can either get someone over there to obtain your certified birth certificate or you can order a certified copy of your Certification of Report of Birth (Form DS-1350) from: Correspondence Branch, Passport Services, Department of State, 1111-19th St. NW, Suite 510, Washington, DC 20522-1705. Phone number is 202-955-0308. Call them first to determine the correct procedure and fee.

If born in the United States, your birth certificate is likely located at some division or bureau of vital statistics that may be connected to the Department of Health of your birth state. They will send you a certified and apostilled birth certificate upon payment of the usual fee.

Photos for your dossier should not be just mug shots of your home or you with a zip code taped across your chest. Relax! They should reflect your lifestyle and your community. For example, you could show pictures of you at work, on vacation, doing something with friends or at church. You can include pictures of relatives even if they don't live nearby. Include the room the child will occupy even though not completed. You can include photos of your area, such as a park, recreation center, or elementary school. You can include your pets. A photo can show you doing something you enjoy, such as gardening, playing sports, or a musical instrument. Russians are not impressed with how many cars you have or how wealthy you are. They are more interested in seeing that their children will grow up in a supportive and educational environment. So take a picture of that piano in the corner, even if the keys are covered in dust!

Some regions want a notarized copy of your doctor's license. Doctor's are sometimes hesitant to provide this as they feel the license could be used for improper purposes. One way to get around those fears is to have your agency director write a letter to the doctor explaining the situation and suggesting they send the license directly to her (so that it's not in several hands, but just goes straight to the agency).

Health Form

Generally, regions in Russia require a health form on each spouse to be filled out by a doctor. This is a different form than the one your home study agency wants. Most people go to their usual GP or to a doctor that is a family friend. A specialist is not normally required. The form usually needs to be notarized which can be a slight problem if the doctor does not have a notary in her office. You can either hope the doctor's office has a notary, or take a notary with you or have a notary sign after the fact, if they will do so. The health forms vary according to the region. Therefore, you should not anticipate the tests or medical review that might be required until you have signed with an agency as that agency is likely to work in only one or two regions and have the required form. Another reason not to have the medical review completed before signing with an agency is that some regions require the review within 6 months of the adoption, and therefore you may find yourself repeating the process if you do it too soon.

Don't expect your doctor or your doctor's staff to have a clue about filling out these forms. Make sure they understand that if the question is on the form, then that means your agency wants a test result or a definitive answer like "no." The words "Not tested" are not enough. You may want to fill out as much of the form as you can before giving it to the staff or have the doctor fill it out in front of you."

Usually the form requires a blood test for syphilis, HIV, and HEP. It might ask if you have TB. It also will likely have a line for the doctor to sign to the effect that she knows of no health reason that would interfere with your ability to raise a child.

The form is usually just one or two pages and is very simple. It does not ask for everything that might be wrong or that every blood test in the world be taken.

Some insurance companies might not pay for the exam or tests. If you have doubts, you might check beforehand. Alternatives that might be cheaper could be your county health clinic.

Some regions in Russia now require that the form not be any older than 3 months prior to the submission of your dossier. Other regions allow for 6 months. Because of this short timeline, you may find yourself having to go back to your doctor. Ask your agency, but sometimes simply a notarized cover sheet stating that nothing has changed will be all that is necessary. You could write up something for your doctor to type on his letterhead stating that the information documented on the physical/medical forms are still complete and accurate and that nothing has changed in your medical condition to preclude you from being parents to adopted children. It is likely that you will have to be involved in obtaining this doctor's letter or form, in order to get his office to do it correctly.

Holidays

Holidays can interfere with the process of having your dossier approved and setting up a court date. Embassies are closed on American and country holidays. This can delay the visa appointment at the Embassy and your return. Knowing when these holidays occur can help you plan. Also, Eastern Europeans, like most Europeans take a month off during the summer to vacation. Each Judge is different so you are likely to find a certain slow down occurring in obtaining court dates during the summer months. This can particularly happen in August and can extend into September. Keep this in mind if your agency tells you there is a delay in late summer. No doubt this will be the reason. Typically August is THE popular month for vacations. This is true all across Europe. Government employees in Russia get at least 5 weeks (not counting weekends) of paid vacation each year and there is a liberal holiday schedule also. Many regions have no court that month at all. You must also factor in that the U.S. Embassy's Immigrant Visa Unit is also closed on the last Monday of every month for administrative duties. It is also closed on Saturdays and Sundays.

Ukrainian and Russian Eastern Orthodox congregations celebrate New Year's Day on January 14 because they continue to follow the Julian calendar. The Julian preceded the Gregorian calendar that is used in most Western countries. The Julian calendar dates from 46 B.C. The Gregorian is named for Pope Gregory XIII and first came into use in 1582. It wasn't adopted in the American Colonies until 150 years later. (And you thought you wouldn't learn anything by reading this book.)

Listed below are the official American and Russian holidays. The Embassy in Moscow is closed on all of these holidays. The actual date may be slightly different each year. The countries also have "bridge" holiday dates such as a Friday, if the holiday is on a Thursday. Each US Embassy web site has a list of holidays. Here is a web site listing all of the holidays in Russia: *http://www.usembassy.ru/mission/holidays.htm*

January 1 R/US New Year's Day	January 2 R New Year's	January R Orthodox Christmas	January US Birthday of Martin Luther King
February US President's Day R National Defender's Day	March 8 R International Women's Day	May 1 R International Labor Day	May 2 R Spring Day
May 9 R Victory Day	May US Memorial Day	June 12 R Independence Day	July 4 US Independence Day
September Monday US Labor Day	October Monday US Columbus Day	Nov. 7 R Day of Consent and Reconciliation	Nov. US Veterans Day
Nov. US Thanksgiving Day	Dec. R Constitution Day	Dec. 25 US Christmas Day	

CHAPTER VI

AGENCY OR INDEPENDENT

Agencies

Using an adoption agency for a Russian adoption is no longer a family's only option. Since the changes in 2000, many families have opted to adopt independently using their own facilitator and applying directly to the region's Department of Education and the federal Ministry of Education. However, adopting independently from Russia is not all that easy and for most families, the agency route works best for them.

As I have mentioned, Russia has 89 regions with over 200 baby homes (257 in 1996) spread across a country twice the size of the United States. Therefore, it should not come as any surprise that the way agencies operate differs from region to region and home to home.

Some agencies share the same Russian personnel. For example, families might use the same drivers, translators and facilitator, but belong to different US agencies. To add to the confusion, the fees charged these families for these same services might all be different. This scenario seems to occur more often around Moscow, where agencies appear to face more control from official or unofficial authorities.

It is important that your agency be on good terms with the regional Department of Education inspector. She is the social worker liaison between the children's home and the regional offices. She also attends court and will testify regarding your meeting with your child and possibly your dossier documents. She may help track down a missing document or signature. Since everything in life is based on relationships, it should come as no surprise that the better the relationship your agency has with the children's home director and the regional Department of Education personnel, the smoother things will go for you. Cultivation of this relationship can be as simple as giving small gifts, to paying for a trip to the United States to see how the adopted children are doing, to something a little larger.

You should interview Russian adoption agencies just like interviewing for a pediatrician or a home study agency. Although you may feel intimidated, remember that they work for you. Your agency should give you references of families who have adopted and who have agreed to be references. They should (but not all do) include some families that have not had a great experience. All agencies, no matter how wonderful, will have situations that did not turn out where everyone is happy. It may have been just one of those things, or something beyond the agency's control, or the agency may have dropped the ball. But you are entitled to hear it all before making your choice. After all, this is your life and family you are talking about. Remember that you should never have to pay an agency anything but a small registration fee before reviewing their contract and set of program fees.

Most agencies have web sites where you can find a lot of information about their various programs. Here are two web sites with a list of agencies that work in Russia:*http://www.russianadoption.org/adoption_agency_list.htm* and *http://www.eeadopt.org/home/services/agency/agencies_list.htm.* Some of the agencies listed are not accredited or are just facilitation companies and work in a joint venture capacity.

One factor that is usually not very important is your geographic location to the agency. Phone, fax, mail, and e-mail work fine. Your agency does not have to be in your state for you to use them. Of course, if you feel more comfortable with actually seeing their offices and people then by all means make that a consideration. Another issue that is not too important is the actual size of the agency. A larger agency will likely have a permanent staff in Russia and everything over there will go like clockwork. However, the size of the agency has no bearing on how fast your American BCIS paperwork is processed and no bearing on the ultimate outcome of bringing a loving child into your family. You might think that a bigger agency means more referrals and it does; yet it also means more clients for those referrals. In the end, size of the agency's operation is just not that important. Now the longer an agency has worked in a country then the more established should be its organization and track record.

You can always do some general searches for information on an agency that you are investigating. You can search using paid services like Lexis/Nexis, *www.knowx.com* or Westlaw. These may be available at your local library.

Some questions you might ask:

1. Does the agency have an 800 number? You don't want to pay for your calls.

2. Will the agency allow you to call the children's home and speak to the doctors? This is very important since then you can get the information and answers direct. The interpretation of the answers is why you have your medical expert on the line.

3. Will the agency tell you how many other "customers" they have? You want to know where you will be in the "line" and how many children are they currently referring. This will help you figure out how long you will have to wait.

4. Will the agency give you a referral before your entire dossier is completed? This can be both good and bad. Good, because it shortens the process, but bad because it adds to your emotional stress and strain. (Of course, this assumes that the region in which your agency works allows pre-adoption information to be transmitted.)

5. What regions does the agency work with and how do these regions apply the 10-day waiver request. You would like to avoid the 10-day appeal period if you could.

6. Will the agency help you with the paperwork, or do they expect you to do it all?

7. How knowledgeable is the office staff? How long have they been with the agency? Can the person who will be assigned to your case answer questions about Russia, or do you have to wait until they get back to you?

8. When was their last Russian adoption? (If it was more than 2 months ago, then you have to wonder how well run is their program.)

9. How many referrals have been "lost"? Ask the reference families regarding the agency's "lost referral" experience. If an agency has Russian contacts that are close to the children's home director and the Ministry, there should be few "lost" referrals.

10. Do their Russian facilitators work with other US agencies or agencies in other countries? The more a facilitator works with multiple agencies,

the higher the risk that your child is the subject of multiple referrals and that you could lose the child to another family. How long have they worked with this facilitator? Any problems?

11. Does the agency refer children when they are coming off the registry or that still have a way to go? You want an agency to refer children who are close to coming off the registry or are off. If they were just placed on the registry, then you run a higher risk of having the child, if an infant, adopted by a Russian family.

12. Does the agency refer mostly infants, toddlers or older children? You may find that an agency refers more from an age group other than the one in which you are interested. What is the average wait time for a boy, girl, infant? Don't let them put you off on this question. They may give the answer with a lot of caveats, but at least you will have an idea. Of course, this is also a question to ask their references.

13. Does the agency always provide a video of the child?

14. They should also give you a good explanation for where your money goes.

15. How long, and in what detail will the videotape be of the prospective child?

16. What medical records and family history will I receive?

17. Who pays for the translations?

18. Does the children's home have any objection to a doctor visiting and examining the child? Sometimes Dr. Downing, and there may be others, are able to visit a children's home if not too far from Moscow and conduct an examination of the child. It depends really on the children's home director. After all, it is her home.

19. What are the exact costs and what do the payments go to for the adoption?

20. If you give me a referral, and I do not accept, when will I receive the next referral? In other words, do I lose my place in line?

21. How many successful adoptions has your agency performed in the past year? In the age group that I am interested in?

22. If there is a facilitating agency or individual in Russia with whom you work, how long have you worked with him/her? The longer the agency has worked with a facilitator the better. You want someone who is reliable.

23. Where will I stay while in (adoption city) and in Moscow?

24. Will I travel with a group or will we travel by ourselves?

25. What support will I receive while in Moscow? a guide and driver?

26. What if I decide not to continue with your agency, for whatever reason, what will it cost me? What is your refund policy (it is very important to see this in writing)?

27. Who obtains the visa invitation and the visa itself?

28. Does the facilitator live in the same city as the children's home? If the agency works in Siberia, yet the facilitator lives in Moscow, and travels back and forth, then when you have a question or seek further information on a child, it may take longer to receive that information if they live thousands of miles away. Now a lot of facilitators have email access so that if they regularly travel to the outlying region they can just email you from there.

29. Does the agency require your health insurance company to sign a letter stating they will cover the adopted child? Some agencies and Regions, but not all by any means, require such a letter. If you have an individual policy versus a group policy, obtaining this letter may prove difficult.

30. In the Region in which this agency works, do you have to make two trips? (Once to meet the child in person and the second to attend court.) What support from the agency's translator/facilitator will you have at the Regional Department of Education and children's home? Who will help you file the request for a court date and for the Federal Registry clearance letter (databank release letter)? What medical review can you have i.e. photos, questioning of the home doctor, translation of medical records? How long will you have to visit and observe the child and make your decision?

31. Does the agency have rules about how long you have to be married, or the age of the child you can adopt, or do they restrict you from choosing the gender? Some agencies have such rules. Most do not.

32. Are post placement reports free or do they charge you for processing? They should be free or included in the cost.

33. Does the agency have rules about adopting while pregnant (some don't allow it) or adopting within a year of adopting the first child?

34. How long has the agency worked in that region? How long has the facilitator worked in that region? How many families have come home

with children from that region through the agency? You want to avoid being the first family in a new region. It is better to stick with a region in which the agency has experience and good contacts, rather than you becoming part of some experimental expansion plan of the agency.

35. If there is dissolution or disruption of the adoption, how will the agency help?

36. If things go wrong when you are in the foreign country, what resources and commitment does the agency have to getting the adoption back on track?

37. If you plan on taking other family members with you to Russia, such as a child or parent, make sure the agency agrees to allow that before you pay them any serious money. Get them to confirm that in writing. You do not want any surprises immediately before traveling.

38. Does anyone in the agency speak and read Russian? Some agencies have no one who knows Russian and completely rely and then blame everything on the Russian facilitator. This is wrong. The agency should have stateside employees who can communicate in Russian with the facilitator, Orphanage Director or Orphanage doctor. They have to take some responsibility for the Russian side, as that is the most important part of the adoption puzzle.

39. Does the agency do any screening of the children (assuming you are under the old referral process)? If so, how? If they say they have doctors who review these children, are these Russian doctors? Russian doctors have a propensity to say that the child is fine. He'll catch-up. While that may be true, it is also true that many times there are medical and developmental issues and you would like a little notice. Rely on your own IA doctor and just add the agency doctor's opinion to your growing pile of medical information. I am not suggesting you dismiss the agency's medical opinion; just weigh its credibility along with the doctor's training and incentive.

Ask about the wait from the time you submit a dossier until the time you should be receiving referrals or told to travel for your first trip. This time will vary depending on the region and the agency. But it will also vary depending on whether you are asking for a boy or girl, infant or older. Some agencies are more aggressive in tracking down birth mothers to get final signatures or fill in blanks left off of original relinquishment paperwork. Some agencies also seem quicker to get translations of documents and dossier approval by local adoption officials.

Then ask the agency about the time to expect to wait for a court date after you have accepted a referral or after meeting the child on the first trip. This will vary by region and by agency, too.

You can find out which regions an agency works in from this unofficial source: *http://www.geocities.com/mgummere/index.html*. This site has many links to helpful resources. You can also search for agencies by region using the Inter-Country Adoption Registry (ICAR) Website, *www.adoptachild.org*. You can scan the list for the region and hit the tab for list by agency and you will see at least a partial list of the agencies serving a particular region. Agencies discontinue working in regions, too.

You may run into the Professor Harold Hill syndrome as I call it. Beware of the following salesman's pitches:

1. *We have many infants and toddlers available for immediate placement*
    This is simply a marketing pitch, pure and simple. "Immediate" may mean a month or a year or it may mean they have no infants available at all.

2. *Our agency is a Christian agency.* Your idea of a Christian might be different than their idea. Further, it makes no difference to the foreign country. What does make a difference to the foreign country is whether the agency participates in real humanitarian efforts with the children. These are efforts toward providing clothes, medicines, shelter etc. You are paying for a service, not a religion. If you are adopting solely because of religious motivation, then just make a donation. You should adopt because you want to parent a child and make him part of your family.

3. *Part of your foreign fee goes to support the orphanage.* Maybe yes, maybe no. Maybe a dollar, maybe $10, and you will know the minute you see the children's home if your agency's statement was the truth or if they were just blowing smoke.

4. *Our representatives/facilitators in Russia/Bulgaria/wherever are reputable and well respected.* By who? There is no one grading these people. You need to ask the agency as to the length of time these folks have worked for them and to ask the reference families for their experience with a particular facilitator.

5. *We are available 24 hours a day! We are here to hold your hand throughout the adoption process!* First, this is not rocket science. Doing the paperwork is not that hard, just time consuming. This is your adoption, not theirs. They won't be with you for the next 18 years. You have to take some responsibility for the adoption, as you will have 100% of it afterwards. You want service, not warm and fuzzy feelings.

6. *All our babies are healthy.* And there is no swamp land in Florida and the Cubs win the World Series every year. All the children are delayed in some regard. I tell all parents to at least budget for speech therapy. Do they change for the better after you bring them home, most do. Not all. The poor children with FAS or FAE take a lot of work and they and their families have a difficult time. If the majority of orphanage children from Eastern Europe received minimal pre-natal care, poor nutrition, poor medical care, poor stimulation, poor love and affection, then how can any agency makes this salesman's claim with a straight face? This is also where your idea of "healthy" needs a reality check. The children are healthy, depending on your definition. My definition is rather expansive, but yours may not be. My healthy definition includes speech delay, cleft/palate, heart murmur, one limb shorter than another, dwarfism, etc. If I see a twinkle in the eye, that child is healthy. But that is me, not you, and who knows what your agency thinks.

7. *We have a beautiful child right here who desperately needs a family! S/he's a real cutie!"* Why are they tossing a child at you before you have signed up? She's not a puppy. Refuse to be sold.

There is also the Ostrich syndrome known as "Don't blame Us!"

1. **No agency can please everybody.** Actually this one is true. You wouldn't believe the things parents do or don't do. Parents get so focused on adopting a child they lose their sense of responsibility and perspective. The real question is quantity. Having a few parents unhappy over a large number of years is one thing, but having lots of unhappy parents over a short time is another.

2. **Every adoption is different.** This is also true. One person's independent adoption in Ukraine will be different than another's independent

adoption. But one person's agency directed adoption using the same facilitator in the same region with the same Judge should be pretty close to being the same experience.

3. **Tanya had that and she's ok.** This phrase has flashing red lights all over it. Your agency is not responsible for the health of your child. If you don't believe it, re-read your contract. They are not medical specialists. Not only have they not personally examined your child, taken blood work, run DNA tests, investigated the pre-natal background or the family genetic history, but also they are not trained to do so. You must do your own independent medical review as best as you can. This phrase belongs with the Professor Harold Hill lines above. It's salesman's talk.

4. **You can't believe most of what you read on the Internet.** I suppose that applies to agency web sites as well. You can believe some, but not all of what you read on the Internet. You can believe some, but not all of what you hear over the telephone from your agency. Use your normal common sense and always double check information.

5. **It's the Russians, Bulgarians, Ukrainians, Georgians, etc. It's the weather.** All of that is meaningless. Exactly what is the glitch? Did the facilitator forget to file a particular piece of paper? Is there an investigation going on? Is the coordinator/facilitator too busy working for other families or agencies? If so, where are you in line? If there was a holiday, you can check holidays on the Internet and except for needing something from an official foreign or US government agency, your facilitator should be working around the holidays. Granted, the Judge's 6-week summer vacation is a different story. **The Russian government won't let you see that.** Why not? How did Joe Bob with this other agency get that information? **No other parents want that information.** If it's medical or related to terminating parental rights, you bet they did. Besides, adoption is not cookie cutter. Each one involves a child and this one involves you—for a lifetime. **There are no police or judicial records.** Parental rights, even in Russia, do not get terminated without a court hearing. There is a transcript somewhere. **There are no medical records on the mother.** If she was registered at a clinic for drug or alcohol, there are very likely to be. She has to be registered though. **The medical records at the orphanage are all there are.** The

orphanage doctor has only a summary of the child's medicals. If the child was born a preemie and had to stay in a baby hospital, there are a whole lot of records. (sometimes handwritten and hard to get I'll admit.)

We are adults, not mushrooms. Demand specifics not generalities.

Finally, believe that the waiting time you hear at a seminar is only a very general statement based on everything going perfectly. Recent returned families have the real information on waiting times. It is not even a case of being just marketing language, it is the fact that circumstances change in country and what used to be a 6 months wait is now 9 months.

An agency's refund policy is very important. It may be triggered by a "stalled adoption." This term is rarely defined. You should ask for the agency's policy as explicitly as possible, including dates. If you have to wait six months or a year from the date the dossier was submitted, does that trigger the refund clause? If you are shown boys, when you wanted a girl during that time, does that prevent the triggering of the clause? You don't have to be Perry Mason, just be aware that the ability to walk away, with your money and your dossier, becomes increasingly important the longer you have to wait and the longer you are not getting straight answers from your agency.

The underlying thrust in an international adoption is that you are ultimately responsible for the adoption, even if your control is limited. You have to understand that principle or allow yourself to be surprised. The BCIS is not responsible, the State Department is not responsible, your state children's department is not responsible and your agency is not responsible. Just to make that last point even clearer, agencies have been including exculpatory clauses in their contracts and even gag clauses. These exculpatory clauses have been litigated with results in favor of the agency. See Ferenc v. World Child, Inc. 977 F. Supp. 56 (D.D.C.1997); Sherman v. Adoption Center of Washington, Inc. 741 A. 2d 1035 (D.C. 1999) and Regensburger v. China Adoption Consultants, Ltd., 138 F.3d 1201 (7th Cir. 1998). A more recent case is discussed at *http://adoption.about.com/library/weekly/uc031102a.htm.* Contrast these cases with Commonwealth v. Stephen R. Walker, 653 N.E. 2d 1104 (Mass. 1995) and you have to ask whether parents who adopt internationally are being treated differently from domestic adoptions.

Some agencies include gag clauses in their contracts. They want to deny you the right to post questions (and criticisms) on the Internet. One choice is to agree and then simply post anonymously on the listservs or email privately to other listserv members. It is difficult to respect these sorts of adhesion clauses or the agencies that have them. Another choice is simply to ask for changes in the contract before you sign it. Again, the refund and return of the dossier is the place where most changes are requested.

Since it is now more likely than not in Russia that you will be in a region that uses the no referral/two trip system, you should ask your agency (and the reference families), how long is the average wait for a court date between the identification trip and the court date trip? Also, how are they going to help you maintain connection with the child you've identified during this waiting time?

Some of these questions may not matter to you. You must decide which questions are important to you. Other questions to ask can be found at this web site: http://www.adopting.org/choosagn.html

You can also review a non-profit agency's balance sheets (including assets, revenues, operating expenses) at http://www.guidestar.org. You can call the International Concerns for Children office at (303) 494-8333. Ask them for whatever information they might have on the agency. Call the Department of State at (202) 647-4000 and talk with the "desk officer" for the country you wish to adopt from. What do they know about the agency or facilitator you are working with or wish to work with? Call the Office of Children's Issues at the Department of State at (202) 647-2688. What do they know about the agency? Call the Consular Officer at the U.S. Embassy in the country you are interested in adopting from. What do they know about the organization? Your state's Better Business Bureau is next to useless as is your state's children services department.

Some things that some agencies do that are positive is telling clients beforehand what kind of post-placement support services they offer, telling clients that the agency will call them when they are settled in and for the client to definitely call if they have any post-adoption questions. Good agencies send information on re-adoption, applying for citizenship, and requirements for post-placement reports.

As an example of how parents can differ on what is important is that some parents feel that a good agency is one that does not provide a referral until their dossier is in and deemed complete (or at least very close to being complete.) This is deemed important, as they do not want to lose a referral because the dossier is not ready. Another important factor for some parents is that they not receive a referral of a child who is not already cleared through the registry. This eliminates some of the chance for a lost referral. At the same time, other parents have no problem with having their dossier incomplete before a referral or receiving a referral, which is not yet off the registry.

Since most agencies only work in certain regions of Russia (and certain regions will only work with certain agencies—interesting), you should find out if in their regions you will need to make one trip to Russia or two. One way to reduce the risk of an unpleasant surprise is to pick an agency with a track record of placing a lot of children through the specific court that you will go through. If the judge, the prosecutor, the representative of the Department of Education, and the social worker are comfortable working with your agency and trust the information the agency provides about you, then you probably won't have a problem. When you are picking an agency, ask how many children they have placed with the courts in the region where your referral will come from. Ask how many have been denied and why. When you are checking the agency's family references, ask how their court appearance went.

How the process works is what many people ask. It works in as many ways as the human mind can imagine. Under the old referral process, in some regions, agencies were assigned children by the DoE. Or more precisely, they were assigned to a facilitator based on relationships and other factors. Until parents accepted all of the children assigned to that facilitator, the DoE made no further assignments to that facilitator, thus causing a "wave" effect in referrals with a bunch of referrals then a trough then another bunch. This method was by no means the way it is done in all regions or even the majority. It is just one method. There is also evidence that in the larger cities a few agencies may have exclusive relationships with the baby houses for infants. This leaves smaller agencies and those that do not want to play that game to adopt children over 12 months in age that may not be subject to this "exclusive" arrangement.

A few agencies are very large and many are very small. A large agency will obtain many referrals (if on the referral system) since it works in more regions. A smaller one may not. A smaller one may be able to do things faster, since there are not that many families on its list. Yet a larger one can send you another referral immediately, if you turn down a previous referral. A smaller agency will return your calls quickly, while a larger agency may be too busy. For every argument in favor of one type of agency over another, there is a counter argument.

The cost of adopting varies with each agency. However, the general rule of thumb is that an agency directed adoption should cost between $15,000 and $22,000, not including an additional $4000 for traveling and staying in Russia. There should be a reduced fee for adopting a special needs child. Adopting siblings or two children at the same time should cost you more than one, but should not be double. Adopting from Moscow may be a little more expensive than from the outlying regions.

Now some agencies will have you pay a $250 registration fee then afterwards tell you that you will receive no referrals unless you pay an additional $3000. Make sure that before you pay an agency a single dime, they fully disclose to you at what stage of the game you will receive referral information (assuming it is not a two-trip region). There are other agencies that use a lottery method for referrals and pressure you by saying that the first family that sends in the fee will be sent the referral information. This isn't right. You should not have to pay thousands of dollars upfront. There are many agencies that only require an application fee before entering you into their program. Large fee payments should come at the time you accept a referral, or prior to traveling.

Some agencies charge more to adopt infants as they are in high demand. Not all agencies do this and this isn't right. Sometimes it is tied to the higher donation the agency gives to the children's home. If so, then it is a palatable reason. Similarly, not all agencies charge thousands more to adopt a second child at the same time you adopt the first. Find your comfort zone and know that if you think an agency's practice doesn't sound right, then be confident in your decision that the agency isn't for you.

Ask for your child's Russian medical records and have them **independently translated**. The same for any court records dealing with parental termination of rights. I cannot emphasize that point strongly enough. Sometimes things appear that would not necessarily show up on an agency translation. If you are not able to get them until your adoption is completed, still have them translated. If you find important items were missing from the agency provided translation, then go back to the agency and demand more information. One area where an agency cannot limit their liability, no matter what is in the contract, is where they intentionally withhold information. You have to view an adoption like a consumer. Adopting is not a commercial transaction, but it is for the rest of your life and the rest of this child's life.

You will eventually wonder where all the money goes that you pay. That is not an easy question. Generally, agencies are not open about how the money is applied and it also differs from agency to agency. It is particularly hard to understand since the Russian government does not really charge anything for adoptions. Your facilitator may receive between $1000 and $2000. The children's home will probably receive no more than a $1000, and then only if you are there to see it happens. Yet to illustrate the lack of standardization, some agencies give a lot more to a children's home than just a $1000, and some give less. You will be able to judge for yourself whether a children's home is actually getting any real donations from foreign adoptions by just seeing the condition of the home itself. A home that is receiving a lot of support will have lots of toys that the children _actually play with_, televisions, murals on the walls, low staff to child ratio, food, decent clothing etc.

Don't forget that an agency has real expenses. Some of the money goes to an agency's overhead such as office expenses, salaries, large bills for express mail to Russia, domestic phone calls, international phone calls, travel expenses, advertising, licensing, insurance, accreditation expenses and translations. The agency may have "relationship costs" and have Russian Ministry personnel and Judges visit the United States to see how the children are doing. This "relationship cost" benefits everyone, not just the agency's clients. An agency may put on "free" educational seminars, which certainly cost the agency. Any cost that a small business has, an agency will have. Some agencies have large staffs overseas and are adept at handling any problem. Certainly if you go with an agency that has such a staff, you will pay more. Some agencies just have one or two people working for them. In that case, their cost will be lower, but then again, you are paying for less handholding and problem solving as well.

In the end, the question of where the money goes never gets answered very satisfactorily. Agencies have developed interesting category names such as "program fees," "agency fees," or "country fees." These category names do not really describe anything. Rather, they are like Humpty Dumpty's response to Alice, "a word means what I wish it to mean." There is no fee by any country per se. Russia doesn't charge one neither does the NAC in Ukraine. You have the right to ask what part of the fee is a payment to the facilitator. If they say part is a donation, then suggest that you hand that directly to the orphanage director yourself. Some agencies do break down their fees so you will see real expenses such as "translation fees." However, translating documents overseas is very inexpensive. It would not be unusual for a translator to make $20 a day and a driver (with car) $30 a day. In the same vein, a homestay should not cost more than $50 outside of Moscow and not even $75 in Moscow. You must be on your guard against getting charged under the double pricing system overseas. Russians pay a much lower price for the same goods and services than they will charge a foreigner. You have a legitimate right to argue against it. You may not succeed, but you've sent them a message that you do not like it.

Some agencies may give a large amount of the funds to the facilitator, also sometimes referred to as the "coordinator". The facilitator is the one that maintains the relationship with the Ministry of Education, Ministry of Health, and children's home director. He files your dossier and follows the paper trail. He sets up the court date and guides you through your journey in-country, children's home visit, and Court appearance. He answers all your questions when you are in-country and is responsible for you. Having a good facilitator is the linchpin of a good adoption as the real work is in-country, not the United States. For example, a good facilitator will know exactly which Judges are adoption friendly and which are not. He might even delay your court date for the very reason that he wants a friendlier Judge, yet you will likely never know this was the reason. In many instances a good facilitator supplies the elbow grease that turns the bureaucratic wheels. A director might have the responsibility for the care, feeding and education of some 60 to 200 children. Trying to track down little Sasha's mother to sign one more relinquishment paper does not often make it to the top of the priority list. A motivated facilitator might help find the mother, get the paper signed, or even send in the paperwork to put a child on the database and get that clock ticking. If the facilitator's reward is that he is "assigned" that child for adoption purposes, what of it? There can be no worse alternative than leaving a potential adoptable child in an institution for the rest of his life, which if he has a medical condition, might be short indeed.

Exactly what the facilitator does with the money given to him is unknown and will certainly vary from agency to agency and region to region. It can truthfully be said that adopting from overseas has gotten more complicated, not less. Judges require more documents and more signatures. On the other hand, there are some agencies that do not give large sums to their facilitator.

The fee paid to the agency does not cover your out of pocket expenses while in-country. The better agencies will give you an estimated, but itemized list of expenses. You will pay all of your travel expenses including your homestay visit and hotel. You will pay for your driver. Your facilitator may have another person working with him in Moscow or in the Region. You will pay for that. You will pay for a translator.

Your agency will help you with some of the paperwork (although the apostille legwork is more often than not on you) and serves as a liaison with the facilitator. It retrieves the photographs and videotapes from Russia and sends them to you. You are responsible for having a medical review of the video and dealing with the BCIS.

Now in the "old days" of Russian adoptions, fees were much, much lower and the process less complicated. It then became a victim of its own success. As more and more agencies and facilitators decided to place children from Russia, fees started to rise. There were those agencies/facilitators who went into a city and promised large amounts of money to be able to work with the homes and facilitate adoption. This caused all the other agencies working in that city to raise their fees, too, or else be unable to place children from there. So fees have gone up and up over the years. But this is not an uncommon economic spiral in many countries involved with foreign adoption and Russia is certainly not unique in this respect.

There are also exceptions. Some agencies have such good relationships that they can still work in a city even though they are not matching the higher priced agency. Indeed, in some places, if an unknown facilitator offers large amounts of cash so they can work there, officials become fearful and refuse to work with them. The general rule, if there is one, is that fees vary by region and agencies have some flexibility depending on special needs, age of the child, or if you are adopting several children.

One thing to remember when researching agencies is that not all fee quotes are alike. One agency's fee may be less than another, but it also may not include some services that another agency includes in its "higher" fee. Indeed, you can easily find yourself paying more "a la carte," than for a flat rate arrangement. Some parents have found setting up a spreadsheet helpful in order to make true comparisons.

You may wonder if you really need an agency or if you can adopt independently. It certainly is less expensive. An independent adoption from Russia should cost no more than $8000 to $12,000 including travel expenses. It can be more, or less stressful than an agency directed adoption. Do remember that not all regions allow independent adoptions. Adopting independently might be for you if you were confident about your ability to handle all the paperwork on the American side, and if you had a reliable Russian speaking facilitator or attorney in Russia. You must have someone in Russia who works with the Ministries and children's home director and who will translate and file your paperwork. This person must be reliable, honest and knowledgeable. It is the difficulty of finding such a person on your own which is the agency's real service to you.

The difficulty in writing about agencies is that there are some very good ones and some very bad ones and a lot in between. It is wrong to generalize and say that everyone in the FSU is corrupt or that all US agencies do nothing for the money they charge. There are many people in both the FSU and America who work for children's homes and agencies who have dedicated their lives to helping children who have little hope. Just keep asking questions and you should discover, at the very least, the agencies to avoid.

My final advice is to know what risks you are willing to assume and which you are not. Do not be afraid to speak candidly with your agency. The better they know you, the better they can match your referral request. Remember too, hiring an agency is no guarantee that your adoption will go smoothly. It might, it might not.

Accredited or Unaccredited Agency

The accreditation process created by the Russians in 2000 was a nightmare for US agencies. The good news is that no other Eastern European country has established such a process, although Bulgaria is thinking about it. The Russians stopped the official adoption process for 8 months in 2000 forcing everyone into an unofficial limbo where adoptions continued, but there were no standard rules. By the end of 2001, Russia had accredited about 52 US agencies. Russia has pretty much ended accrediting any new ones. The actual fact that an agency is accredited does not have any impact on your adoption. Just because the Russian government accredits an US agency does not mean that you will have a better or worse adoption experience. It does not mean that you will receive more or less medical information on a child or that you will be referred a healthier child than a non-accredited agency. It does give the Russians some control over an agency if post-placement reports are not filed or if some other transgression is publicized in the press. That really was the whole purpose.

Accreditation means that an agency can represent you and be open about it. That is about it. If you use an unaccredited agency, then the facilitator and translators simply cannot advertise that they are working for a particular agency, however, it is perfectly legal for them to work for you and do the same things facilitators and translators do that work for accredited agencies. Indeed, sometimes the same people work for both! In the beginning of 2001 it appeared that accredited agencies might be allowed to go back to obtaining pre-identification material on a child (i.e. video and medicals), but the trend now in many regions is to deny all agencies this information.

The fact that in many regions it doesn't make any difference has been very frustrating for agencies that hired Russian lawyers and filed mountains of paperwork to be accredited. The process was not only time consuming, but costly. Further, there are some pure facilitation companies with which agencies contract to handle the overseas aspect. These are not necessarily accredited, but simply have people and connections in-country. Some regions have implemented a policy of not working with any agency that is not accredited. Certainly the trend toward making two trips regardless of whether you use an accredited or unaccredited agency or go independent will continue.

A few regions are having unaccredited agencies and independents make three trips! In this scenario the purpose of the first trip would just be to file the papers at the Department of Education. Then in a week or so (or perhaps longer) you receive an invitation to visit the regional Department of Education. A region that makes the independent parent personally file the papers is taking the Russian adoption procedures to their illogical extreme. Russian laws are really suggestions or guidelines. They are not "laws" like we think of them. Judges and regional DoEs have wide discretion. Normally a parent would be able to give a power of attorney to a translator/facilitator who files the papers. The Kurgan region is one where there has been some talk of going to 3 trips for unaccredited agencies. Of course, you do not have to make three trips or even two. If you have no job and just like staying in foreign countries, you can wait out the time in Russia.

Some agencies who did not want to go through the trouble of becoming accredited because they did not do many Russian adoptions or because they did not want to go through the expense or did not feel they had the connections, have opted to joint venture (sometimes call umbrella) with an accredited agency. There is nothing really wrong with this as long as your non-accredited agency discloses to you who the other agency is and their responsibilities to you. The federal Ministry of Education has put out a policy statement saying they disapproved of joint ventures, however it has no effect in the US and does not really control the actions by the regions. For some unaccredited agencies the referrals of children still do not come from anyone other than their own employees, just as before. For these "unaccredited agencies," working under an umbrella merely means that the accredited agency gets the databank letter and puts their "seal of approval" on the unaccredited agency's client's dossier before it is presented to the court. Judges in some regions, but not others permit this practice. In the regions where it is permitted, everyone knows about it. Remember that the staff at the regional Departments of Education and the judges all know which facilitators work for which agencies. They know perfectly well at the Department of Education when an unaccredited agency's employee walks in with a client to get permission to visit an orphanage. The judge knows perfectly well when their employee walks into the courtroom with a client to present the dossier and request a court date. That is simply the way Russian law and culture is…the laws are inexact and the regions interpret them any way they want.

Independent Adoption

Notwithstanding what many agencies say, independent adoptions are alive and well in many regions of Russia. They are legal for Americans although they have been suspended for Spanish and German citizens. In Ukraine, independent adoptions easily account for half of all adoptions. In Bulgaria and Georgia they also can be done.

The law in Russia expressly permits a parent to directly apply to a regional Department of Education (DoE). If that DoE does not give an acceptable referral to that parent after three referrals, then the parent has the right to request that the federal Ministry of Education (MoE) in

Moscow give them a referral in that region or another region. Some regions in Russia do not encourage independent adoptions and in those regions it is best to just move on to another one. It doesn't really pay to spend time fighting the system. You can obtain a rough idea of which regions are freindly by looking at

http://www.geocities.com/mgummere/RussianIndependent

In a few regions accredited agencies are still able to obtain advance referrals for their clients. If that is your preferred method of referral, then that is a good reason to choose an accredited agency. With an independent adoption you will not have a referral until you visit Russia on your first trip. Of course, this is how it is now commonly done regardless of whether you adopt independently, or with an accredited agency or unaccredited one. You do not need to have your I-171H from BCIS before making the first trip although agencies have their own rules and might not allow you to travel until you do. However, it is not a Russian requirement.

The experience of independent adopters in Russia is no different than using an agency. Some have had quick, easy and especially cheaper adoptions. Others have had more difficult experiences. Parents adopting independently have felt much more in control of the process and timing. They don't have to ask the agency why the travel date or court date is taking so long. They can just ask their trusted facilitator themselves. Of course, that is the rub. How do you find such a person? You have to research and talk to people on the Internet and in your local adoption group. Look for a recommended Russian lawyer among the local émigré community. There is an independent adopters group at http://groups.yahoo.com/group/Ind_Russian_Adopt that has some information as well as this web site:

http://www.facesofsiberia.org/Independent%20Adoption.htm.

Facilitators for independents act little differently than facilitators working for agencies. They help parents send in their dossier to the regional Department of Education (DoE) and then go with them to the DoE to receive the referral. Each region has its own requirements. There are some regions that will only work with certain chosen agencies (for whatever reason) and in those, independents must simply move on to another region unless they want an expensive legal fight. The parents' request will describe the age, gender, and physical characteristics of the child the parents desire. In certain circumstances, this referral might be pre-arranged by unofficial agreement between a facilitator and the DoE person. Or your facilitator may have some inside knowledge about which children are available. While this is not likely to be the case, one cannot ignore that it sometimes occurs. Some regions make the independent adopter travel 3 times with the first visit just to file the papers. Other regions will still allow you to give a power of attorney to a facilitator to do it for you.

The main concern by the Russians is that they feel they lack control over independent adopters in regard to registration and post placement reports. They feel that with accredited agencies they can use that accreditation process to pressure an agency in ensuring that both are completed. It has been claimed that this concern has been fueled by comments to the MoE from accredited agencies. Regardless, there is pressure by the MoE on regions to limit independent adoptions because of this problem. What is interesting is that the Russians now require that both independent adopters and accredited agencies provide the same commitment letter from the parents' home study agency agreeing to conduct post-placement reports. In a negative development, there has been a discussion by the federal Ministry of Education to require all independent adopters to join up with an accredited agency prior to a child's databank release letter being sent to the court. If all regions adopt this course, then independent adoptions may very well cease.

Reference Families

When interviewing reference families for an adoption agency you should ask them some of the same questions asked of the agency. This way you can compare answers. Be sure to inquire as to the year they adopted since significant procedural changes have occurred in Russia since April 2000, and the region (since not all programs in all regions are the same). The EEAC web site has a registry of reference families at
http://www.eeadopt.org/home/services/agency/agency_registry/index.html
as does ICAR (Inter-Country Adoption Registry) at
http://www.adoptachild.org and also *http://adoptingfromrussia.com/*.
Some questions to ask are as follows:

1. Does the agency have good contacts in Russia? Find out everything you can about an agency's contacts in Russia. Was the process in Russia smooth and quick? Any hitches? Were they able to overcome any obstacles? Do they help you through the entire adoption process? What are the arrangements for housing and travel while you are in Russia?

2. How long did the agency give you to decide on a referral?

3. What is the health and developmental condition of the children placed (with the families you talk with)? Be specific as to which children's home and age of child.

4. If a family was uncomfortable with a referral, was the agency cooperative in finding another child within a reasonable amount of time or did they try to pressure you?

5. Did the process work as the agency said it would?

6. Was the agency supportive and helpful during the process?

7. Were you informed, in advance, of all the costs involved in the adoption, including travel and incidentals?

8. What is the agency's policy about returning a portion of what you paid if the adoption doesn't work out? For example, if a country closes or has a moratorium, you withdraw because of a long wait; the agency encounters problems, etc.

9. Did the agency seem to be familiar to the children's home director and other officials? (If the agency has hosted the local Judge and the director in the United States, then you can assume that they have a good working relationship.)

10. When they asked questions of the children's home director or doctor did the translator give them a verbatim translation or just a few words? Some facilitators/translators have a tendency to think they know what is best for you and will give you only the information they believe is necessary. While it may turn out that you did not need the other information, there is a trust issue involved and it should be explored with the reference families.

11. Did the family think the agency was more an advocate for the child rather than your family? A few agencies are such advocates for these children (whether for humanitarian or monetary reasons) that they forget that it is really your family's well being that comes first. This issue should be explored with the reference families.

12. Make sure you compare apples to apples. Do not compare the same agency's program in Belarus with its program in Ukraine. So when you speak with families make sure you categorize the country program and the year of adoption.

13. If a reference family had a bad curve thrown at them in the foreign country, find out how the agency handled it. Some agencies will move Heaven and Earth for you and others will leave you high and dry.

14. Ask the families if you should talk to anyone else. You may find that a family that is not on anyone's list has some interesting information.

15. What services do the adoption agency offer after the adoption? A lot of agencies feel that once you return, you are on your own. While post-adoption services are not necessary for the majority of adoptions, if you run into an issue, it would nice to know what help is available from your agency.

16. How long did they get to stay at the children's home to see the child? At some homes the Director is strict and might allow you to see the child for no more than an hour. This is unacceptable. The problem is that agencies (through their facilitators) are very unwilling to rock the boat with these Directors. You end up being the one that pushes for more time. So ask these families if they had enough time to adequately assess the child.

17. Ask about the waiting time. A family that has just recently adopted from your region will give you more accurate information than an agency with its rosy view.

18. Ask about the age of the children referred by the Department of Education. If they are referring only older children to your agency when a family has requested a younger child, then it could be a case of: a) no infants were available at that time, or b) another US agency has moved into the region and made an "arrangement" with the DoE for the younger children.

Sometimes when you hear from a reference family that there was a problem with an adoption, keep in mind that it may not have been the fault of the adoption agency. Because of client confidentiality, agencies are limited in the information they can release that might either explain the situation or make it very clear that the accusation is unfounded. Nor can you always say that the fees are too high when there are many dedicated people working long hours trying to put you from Little Town, USA together with your Siberian child 10,000 miles away. They worry about the children (that is why they work at an agency) and the delays (which they have no control over) to which they can give you no rational reason. This is not a defense of all agencies; just a desire to see the debate is kept fair.

Chapter VII

ASSESSING CHILDREN'S INFORMATION

Pre-Identified Referrals

The Russian law on adoptions is always undergoing some changes. These can be minor ones like adding a new document to the dossier list or major ones, such as the accreditation change in 2000. Therefore, this chapter on how the pre-identified referral process works and the chapters on the video and medical review are not relevant in those regions which now require the two trip process and a direct referral from the regional Department of Education. However, some regions in Russia continue to allow the single trip and pre-identification referral procedure as well as such countries as Kazakhstan.

After choosing an agency and giving them your paperwork and a portion of their fee, you then wait for a referral of a child. Good agencies will refer you a child that is within the parameters you have set. They will also give you some time in which to decide and should not rush you. By the same token, this child is waiting for a "forever" family and a family is possibly waiting for this child, so time is of the essence.

You may wonder how an agency receives permission to refer a child. Each region and country operates differently. However, if an agency has been working in an area for several years then it probably has built up relationships with the children's home director and Department of Education (DoE) officials. It may give a lot of humanitarian aid, or sponsor officials on trips to the United States to see how the children are doing. It may also have a great track record of adoptions so that a positive spiral is in place and they obtain more and more referrals. Some agencies work by contract with the region's government's officials in the Health Department and the Education Department. The Health Department is over the baby hospitals and baby homes and the Education Department is over the children's homes, preschool homes, and internats (boarding schools). The agency will be assigned babies and children each month who then make the referral to their clients. A child may initially be represented by Agency A, and later be transferred by the state government to Agency B, if "A" cannot find adoptive parents in a reasonable amount of time.

In Russia, it is technically possible for an adoptable infant to be as young as 4 months old, but by the time a family considers and accepts a referral, and receives a court date, the baby is likely to be 7 months or older at time of placement.

The children's home director's permission to adopt is one of the required court documents. While officially it is a function of the state government to decide who adopts which child, the home director has some input, as does your agency. It varies from region to region as to who has "matching" authority. If it is your agency's decision, there are many factors that go into the "matching" of a referral to a family. It might be simply that the child has dark hair and so do you, or the child's personality and how they think she might fit in your family, given what they know about you. Possibly one child is in a region likely to provide a quicker court date and one family has been waiting longer; possibly there are children in 3 regions and one waiting family has an age limit or other aspect that would eliminate them from working in one of the regions. Possibly one family desires to return to a region where their other child was born. There are lots and lots of reasons matches happen. (Of course, in a region that does not provide pre-identified referrals, the agency has little ability to match.)

The referral comes by way of a phone call from the agency saying that a video and medical summary of the child is on its way to you. They will describe the child over the phone. The video that you receive will only be a few minutes long and the medical summary will probably not be very detailed. However, if you decide to pursue this child, you should be able to get additional videos and additional medical information. The Russians do not give you much information unless you ask. But when you ask, they do seem willing to answer most medical questions that you have. Be persistent. If something doesn't sound quite right, then try to obtain the actual medical report on which the agency is basing its English translation. Sometimes when you have it translated you find other things on it.

Sometimes an agency will send a referral to you that is outside your parameters. Give the agency the benefit of the doubt in this regard. Many times a child whose age or gender is different than what you initially requested will captivate you. Now if the referrals you see are far outside your parameters and you ask the agency to stop sending those kinds of referrals to you, then the agency should honor your request.

Always ask if your child is in a "specialized" orphanage and is so, is it special as in gifted or special as in special needs? The Russians tend to label children at a young age and shunt them off to different homes based on the Russian's perception of the child's cognitive skills. If a child has been labeled "debil," then you know the child has had few opportunities for an education. It doesn't mean that the evaluation is correct, just that the educational opportunities are less and that you need to ask more questions regarding the diagnosis and specialized home.

A referral can be lost even though you have accepted the referral and accepted the child in your heart. It is a very difficult thing to have happen. Losing a referral is not a common occurrence and happens mostly with very young infants. The most common reason is that a Russian family has chosen to adopt the child. Usually this happens only in large metropolitan areas. Russian families have priority up to the date of the court hearing.

Your feelings after losing a referral are analogous to a miscarriage with the loss of dreams and attachment to a child whose only manifestation might have been a short video and a photo. However, it is a loss nevertheless, and it takes the wind out of you. It takes time to regroup and feel "normal" again. Adoption is difficult, and full of hurdles, and most people who have not had anything to do with this process are totally oblivious to your pain because it's not a type that they know anything about.

Other reasons for a lost referral might be where a regional judge suspends all adoptions temporarily due to problems with other adoptions. Also, a child's grandmother or other family member might visit the child, in which case the child is no longer eligible for adoption at that time. Some Courts will require that older siblings or other related family members approve of the foreign adoption and this can cause an adoption to fail. This is rare and your agency should know if this is a requirement in your region. Also, some facilitators or children's home directors might allow the child to be referred to more than one agency at a time. You might then be told that a Russian family adopted the child when the fact is that it was a family from another agency. This is unlikely to happen now with the advent of the two-trip process.

A referral could fail because of an unexpected paper glitch. For example, after 1998 the Russian courts were required to have the birthmother execute a second relinquishment specifically authorizing foreign adoption. Many times the birthmother cannot be found. Usually judges will allow an alternate paper stating that the birthmother cannot be found, but sometimes they are sticklers and the child cannot be adopted. Also, there are a few foster care programs in some areas. For example, in Kaliningrad the Germans established a foster program and some children that were otherwise adoptable were placed into it. (Remember that Kalingrad really belongs to Germany.) Also, in some regions of Russia judges have taken a hard line and have gone way out of their way to find some extended family member to agree to raise the child. The fact that the family member doesn't actually show up makes no difference.

Families also turn down referrals. It may be the child has issues that the family does not think it can handle successfully. These issues may be medical for which the family has no insurance coverage or simply the family is not in position to deal with certain issues. Your agency should not try to pressure you. It is your decision and your marriage and your family. Instead, the agency should try to obtain another referral. Quite often what is a medical problem to one family is perfectly acceptable to another. Indeed, it is the unknown that causes the most fear.

Some families turn down a referral because they decide they want to adopt a girl rather than a boy or vice versa. Or perhaps they started out adopting two and instead decided on just one. Or the referral is of an older child or a sibling group and they want a younger child or not as many children. There are many reasons for turning down a referral that may have nothing to do with the child.

You really need to look at your family and decide what you can handle. If you are a young couple with no children, then maybe adopting a child under 3 is best. If you are a couple with 3 teenagers (let's say 13, 15 and 17), then an older child could work for you. Families wanting an older child who already have a 10 month old, 3 year old and a five year old, need to stop and think some more. Older children take a lot of work initially (new language to learn, educational delays, learning to live in a family, etc.). Dealing with all of this will take a lot of your time and energy away from your other children. You must choose the right child for your family and be realistic about what you want. Your first priority is your existing family and not an image of a child you saw on the Web late one night. There is no shame in admitting that you do not have the resources to deal with a particular issue or that you are not the right family for a specific child. Not every family is right for every child. If because of your personal schedule or personal health issues you will not be able to give the necessary attention to a certain special needs child, admit it without guilt, and choose a child that will be a better fit.

Once you are reviewing a referral, you may want to contact those reference families who adopted in the region you are now considering. By checking with those who have adopted from your region, you can gain a precise knowledge of your agency's program in that region.

You may wonder if you have been given all the information that there is. Russian privacy laws prohibit sharing every single note in a child's full medical report the instant some adoptive family shows an interest. That doesn't happen in the United States either. If the child was a preemie, then he probably has a rather full report at the children's hospital. Just remember that this report is in Russian, is handwritten, there are no copy machines, and the children's home does not have a copy. The children's home doctor will have a summary of medical information and from that he prepares a summary and releases it to the state government, which is then released to the agency or the facilitator, who shares it with the family. The agency does not have unlimited access to the child's records or to visit the child. To visit, photograph, or videotape the child requires permission from the state government and the home director. The fact is, you will never know everything about your child's history. You just have to do as much research as you can, and then take that leap of faith. But it should be faith based on the knowledge that comes out of doing your homework first.

Information you would like to have with the referral is anything pertaining to maternal history, the child's birth history (prenatal care if any, birth weight, height, and head circumference, gestational age, Apgar scores), medical examinations, tests, and hospitalizations. Ongoing measurements over time are extremely helpful to assess growth. Current developmental milestones (vocalizing, sitting alone, eating semisolid food, strong eye contact) are also helpful. Sometimes statements are available from the caregivers about the child's personality, demeanor, and skills. It's very helpful if the orphanage doctors give an opinion about whether the child has any signs of fetal alcohol syndrome. Descriptions of the child's verbal abilities and determination of the child's ability to hear are also extremely valuable.

It is not unusual for parents to turn to their agency and ask, "What should we do?" Be careful if you do this. Look out for responses like "that's just something they write to make the kid eligible for adoption. If they said he was healthy, he couldn't leave Russia." Or "we've had lots of kids adopted with that diagnosis. They're all fine," or "he just needs good nourishment and love. You're just what he needs to thrive'" and "many other people have adopted children in worse shape and they've turned around with proper attention and care." Agencies have even said to parents who were struggling with the decision that "you should decide to adopt the child soon or risk losing him" and "if I were into gambling, he's a good one."

If you wanted to gamble, you'd go to Vegas. What you want is to make an informed decision knowing that adoption comes with risk. You want advice from professionals like the international adoption doctors and information from your preparation classes and materials. There is always the chance that what you receive from an agency is marketing, not reliable advice. On the other hand, by you asking them that question you have placed them in a difficult position. Do not use the agency as a substitute for your research and preparation. You have to put in the time. There are no short cuts. Remember that the credibility of any information is affected by its source.

At some point you will have all the medical information and all the medical expert reviews you can obtain. There will come a time when you must decide whether to accept this child or not. You will still have doubts. You will not have answers to all of your questions. You will have plenty of facts about this child but not the answer to the ultimate question of "what should I do?" Yet, it is time to either take that "leap of faith" or decide against. Only you can make that decision. Just remember that when a child is born to you it comes with both good and bad. As a parent you just accept them and love them. Make the same conscious choice in your adoption and make the best of this wonderful gift of this child that you will care for and love.

Finally, fight against the natural desire of wanting "the perfect child" or the "Gerber baby." Parents sometimes forget that life doesn't give guarantees and the child whose referral they tuned down because she was a little short or had an ear infection, might have become a loving child and a concert pianist in contrast to the "perfect" child they adopted that ran off with the rock band. Have realistic expectations. Raising children, whether adopted or biological, is not a fantasy experience. It's real and it's a lot of work.

Video

A video is important to a medical evaluation. If you read the one or two page medical form it will have the usual scary Russian medical terms on it, which can be difficult for a non-international pediatrician to understand. However, any pediatrician can understand a video. Just remember that because of the video's limitations, you should use the video as just another piece of information to be placed along side all the others and not as the sole determinant. Most of the following discussion pertains to infant videos.

You should ask the agency for the approximate dates of the videos. It is important in order to evaluate the child's development. Indeed do not hesitate to ask for another video prior to accepting the referral. The videos are not very long which can make them difficult to evaluate. Further, a lot of infants are wrapped to keep them warm, so that when they are shown unclothed on the video they really are not use to moving around and may just lay there. If the child is an infant, you will want to see the child unclothed if possible. This way you can see all the fingers, toes, hands, arms and legs. Here are some of the things to look for:

1. How does the child respond to people in the room? Usually the child's primary caregiver will be in the room. It will be interesting if the child responds to the caregiver only. While this indicates attachment, which is good, you may need to follow up because it is even better if the child also responds to other caregivers.

2. Does the child move and bend her arms and legs in a normal fashion? Normal movement can indicate that cerebral palsy is not a concern. You might look to see if the muscle mass and fat on the arms and legs is approximately equal and symmetrical indicating the baby is equally coordinated and developed on both sides. Also, when the baby moves, is there any expression of discomfort?

3. Do her eyes follow the camera or some other toy? This indicates responsiveness and is a slight indication of the condition of her eyes. Does she track sound in the room?

4. Does she roll over, sit up, play with toys and move them from hand to hand? These are milestones to look for. Does she show emotions? Even crying is a good sign.

These are questions the international adoption (IA) doctors would like answered

One caveat with videos is that a lot of times when you return with the child and look at the video at home, the child and the video just do not match up. The reason is that to produce the video the child may have been woken from her nap and suddenly thrust into a situation with bright lights and strangers touching her and moving her around. This is likely to produce a withdrawn response and the child is simply scared and not sure of what is going on. The bright lights and attention from all these people can confuse a child. It may have been taken around mealtime, which might change how a child reacts. Sometimes the children are fed prior to their taping session because the caregivers do not want the children to cry or appear unhappy. They feel that this is not appealing to prospective adoptive parents. So that if the child seems slow, it could just be a result of the usual slowdown that occurs from eating. Also, her hair may seem sparse and red on the tape. This is from poor nutrition and will change dramatically once you have brought her home.

Also, caretakers love to offer different toys to the child. These might be toys that they take off the shelves of a large wall unit and you wonder if the kids ever get to play with them or if they are just decorations. They like to repeatedly offer toys, and not even give the child enough time to do much with the item. Another common theme in referral videos is that the child is often not verbalizing. Yet, once the camera is put away he won't quit talking. The difference is that when the video is taken, the child is out of his normal environment. Often there are no other kids in the room and there are extra adults—strangers, with strange equipment. It's intimidating to be the center of attention like that.

A funny thing that could happen is that you might hear Russian being spoken in the background of the tape. You might get curious as to what is being said and have the tape translated. Don't be surprised if you find that all that is being discussed by the caretakers is their boyfriends! I have also heard of a parent whose occupational therapist looked at the tape and thought there might be a problem with the baby's tongue because he kept sticking it out during the video. When the tape was translated, the parent found that the reason the baby kept sticking his tongue out was because the caretakers were telling him in Russian to do it!

Sometimes the child may seem to have an ear that sticks out somewhat. The usual condition ranges from a slightly protuberant ear on one side to protuberance combined with elongation in the vertical axis and actual thinning of the ear. While you should certainly ask the medical experts about this condition, generally it is not a congenital condition, but develops in the maternity home prior to orphanage admission from infants always being positioned on the same side in their cribs. Incidence in some regions is very high, almost one in three.

Medical Review

What drives the desire for better medical records and knowledge about children's health is the fact that international adoption works best when prospective adoptive parents know as clearly as possible what sorts of challenges a specific child may bring to the family. Some parents believe they care for a child with many medical challenges. Other parents, including some who already have children with special needs in their families, believe they can only cope with an additional child if the child has minimal health problems. Good preparation before making the decision to adopt internationally includes understanding and accepting that no child, whether born in a family, adopted domestically, or adopted internationally, comes with any "guarantees" or "warranties." Just look around your neighborhood. All children have challenges and gifts that cannot be anticipated.

Listed below are some of the medical specialists available to provide pre-adoption and post-adoption assessments to adoptive parents and children. This is by no means an exhaustive list. The procedure is that you mail a copy of the video (if you have one) and the medical report to the physician, and after she reviews the material, you speak with the doctor by phone. The doctor will likely call you within a few days of receiving the video and probably in the evening or at night. You should have a list of questions prepared ahead of time so the maximum amount of information is exchanged. You may wish to ask the doctor if you can record the conversation in case a spouse is unavailable or you want to keep better record of what was said. These doctors all have jobs, families and receive many videos a week, so take that into account if you pressure them to expedite a review. Most of these doctors are adoptive parents themselves, which is how they got into the field.

Generally if you request the review of pre-adoptive medicals and videos, you should include a donation. The figure of $100 to $350 is customary, but always inquire as to the suggested donation amount. The information you receive is far more valuable.

Dr. Jerri Ann Jenista, M.D.
551 Second Street
Ann Arbor, Michigan 48103
Phone: 734-668-0419
Fax: 734-668-9492
Web site: *http://www.comeunity.com/adoption/health/jenista.html*

She was the editor of Adoption Medical News and has a long history in the international adoption medical field. She knows a lot about which regions take care of their children.

International Adoption Clinic
University of Minnesota
Dr. Dana Johnson, M.D.
420 Delaware Street SE
Minneapolis, Minnesota 55455
Phone: 612-626-2928; Fax (612) 624-8176
Donation: $200

Dr. Johnson is one of the founders of the international adoption medical field and runs a very well known clinic. His web site is at *http://www.peds.umn.edu/IAC/*

Dr. Andrew Adesman, M.D.
Schneider Children's Hospital
Division of Developmental and Behavioral Pediatrics
269-01 76th Ave.
New Hyde Park, N.Y. 11040
Phone: 718-470-4000 Fax: 718-343-3578

Dr. Adesman takes a direct approach and concentrates solely on the child he is reviewing. He is a night owl and likes to schedule phone conferences late at night (after 11 pm). This can be helpful for people who have a lot of other commitments during the day or who do not live on the East Coast. He is very thorough and nice. Like a lot of these doctors, he really cares about you and the children.

Dr. Julia Bledsoe, M.D.
Pediatric Care Center
University of Washington, Roosevelt Site
4245 Roosevelt Way N.E.
Seattle, WA 98105
Phone: 206-598-3000, 3006 Fax: 206-598-3040

If you have a child who you think might have the signs of FAS, Dr. Bledsoe has a real expertise in that area and you may want to consult with her for an opinion.

She is head of Adoption Medicine at University of Washington and charges $260-350 for a video and medical review. The person to contact is Cyndi Musar, Dr. Bledsoe's scheduler/coordinator at *CMusar@u.washington.edu*. She will be able to get back to you much quicker than Dr. Bledsoe. The fax number I have is (206) 598-3040. Here is a web site connected to the clinic: *http://depts.washington.edu/fasdpn/*

International Adoption Clinic
The Floating Hospital for Children at New England Medical Center
Dr. Laurie Miller, M.D.
750 Washington Street Box 286
Boston, Massachusetts 02111
Phone: 617-636-8121 or 617-636-7285; Fax: 617-636-8388
This clinic is associated with Tufts University Medical School.

She charges $150-250 for a video and medical review. She has a great manner. Some call her the Marcus Welby of adoption medicine. Her web site is *http://www.nemc.org/adoption/*

Dr. Aronson can be reached at:
151 East 62nd Street Suite 1A
New York, New York 10021
orphandoctor@aol.com
Phone: 212-207-6666
Fax: 212-207-6665

Dr. Aronson charges $350 to review a video and medical information. Her web site is at *http://www.orphandoctor.com/*.

The Rainbow Center for International Child Health
Adoption Health Service
11100 Euclid Avenue, Mail Stop 6038
Cleveland, OH 44106-6038
Contact: Adele, Center Coordinator
Phone: 216-844-3224
Rainbow Center's web site is
http://www.uhrainbow.com/International_Health/page14.html

Rainbow's approach is to spend time determining what you know about the process and then to conduct an educational session. It is child specific, but it also encompasses more. Many families like Rainbow's approach. The review costs about $265.

Dr. Eric Downing
Moscow, Russia
http://www.russianadoption.org or http://209.79.114.199
tel (7) (095) 799 3452 or (7) (095) 262 4079 or 954-2627
Fax (212) 214 0873; cell number is (7) 095) 799 3452

($100 donation. Up to $650 plus expenses to visit a child)

If the children's home director allows it, Dr. Downing is able to visit a child in a home and give you a report or travel with you. He is a Canadian and has lived in Moscow for several years. You can contact him through his assistant Olga at *ofilina@hotmail.com*. His colleague, Natalia Belova, also does medical reviews. She is a professor at the Medical School in Moscow and is well versed in the field of genetics. She's Russian, so she can communicate with the child, read and understand the medical records. Her email is *belova@comtv.ru* or *natbelova@yandex.ru*.

Dr. Sunitha Narayanan, with the SOS International Clinic in Moscow, at *drvsn@yahoo.com* also will visit a child. She is fluent in Russian and English.

Dr. Oleg Togoev can visit children as well. He is at *togo@online.ru*. Dr Togoev trained in the US and speaks English well. He is based in Moscow and can fly out to the region.

Dr Olga Bazhenova may be able to get your child's medical records for you, even after the adoption. She is at
http://www.geocities.com/ob_k2002/RussPed.html. She's a Russian pediatrician living in the States. You can also have her call your orphanage pediatrician directly and get more information. She will also translate reports. She does not have a license to practice medicine in the States. There is a modest fee plus phone charges for calling overseas.

Dr. Elizabeth Galkina, a Russian and English speaker can also visit. She has been to some of the Perm orphanages.

Dr. Alexei Khoukhrev
He is affiliated with the American Medical Center in Moscow
His cell phone in Moscow: is 7 095 7203600; his e-mail address is:
huhorka@hotmail.com

Dr. Basham from St. Petersburg can also visit your child.
British American Family Practice
St Petersburg Russia
Tel: (+7 812) 327 6030
Fax: (+7 812) 327 6040
http://www.british-americanclinic.com/adoption.php

Another doctor in St. Petersburg recommended by parents is Dr. Alexander
Abdin at the EuroMed Clinic. The clinic can do blood tests and give the Denver
developmental screening test. It is very modern. It can also help you, if you get
sick.

www.euromed.ru
email: *euromed@euromed.ru*
60 Suvorosvsky Ave
St. Petersburg
Phone number in Russia 7-812 327-03-01

One way to reduce the visiting fees is to share the cost with another family
adopting from the same region.

Dr. Ira Chasnoff
Chicago, Illinois
Tel: 312-362-1940

Dr. Chasnoff has an $8 developmental booklet he sells called "Across the Seas."
You can buy it at *http://www.childstudy.org/crtstore.cgi/bkt-002.html.* "Across the
Seas" is a booklet checklist designed to be completed in country and then used to
consult with Dr Chasnoff or any IA specialist. The guidebook provides a struc-
tured assessment parents can perform while at the orphanage with the child. This
assessment helps parents appraise the child's growth, development and attachment status.

Alla Gordina, MD
Global Pediatrics
International Adoption Medical Support Services
7 Auer Ct,
East Brunswick, NJ 08816
Tel 732-432-7777; Fax 732-432-9030
You can contact her at *drgordina@netzero.net or
drgordina@GLOBALPEDIATRICS.NET*
www.globalpediatrics.net

Dr.Gordina speaks and reads Russian. She can read untranslated medical reports and make calls to the orphanage doctors. As with some of the other IA doctors, you can call her from Russia with questions about your referrals. She also has a good sense of humor and a lot of patience.

Texas Children's Hospital International Adoption
Dr. Heidi Schwarzwald is the Director
6621 Fannin St.
Houston,Texas
832-824-1038
Toll free: 866-824-5437
Fax: 832-825-1281
Email: *internationaladoptions@texaschildrenshospital.org*
Website: *http://www.txchildrens.org/CntExe/IntAdopt/IntlAdoption.pdf*

This Texas IA program charges $250 to review a video. They will also write a letter supporting your request for the 10-day waiver (no guarantee that your request will be granted, of course.)

Dr. Boris Skurkovich
Hasbro Children's Hospital
Providence, RI.
http://www.lifespan.org/Services/ChildHealth/Adoption/contactus.htm
Phone: 401-444-8360; Fax: 401-444-5650
Email: bskurkovich@netscape.net
http://www.lifespan.org/services/infectious/hch/adoption/default.htm

Dr Skurkovich speaks Russian, which can be helpful if you are allowed to call the children's home doctor and ask follow up questions.

If you adopt in St. Petersburg and Moscow, some agencies offer the service of having your child undergo Western style medical testing at the St Petersburg offices of the American Medical Clinic or Filatov before you adopt. Not all children's homes allow it and not all agencies offer the service. There is an additional fee involved of around $350.00.They can do blood tests and X-rays. The AMC pre-adoption services can be found here: http://www.amcenters.com/services_06.htm

You really should try to read an article written by Dr. Jenista on "Russian Children and Medical Records" published in the July/August 1997 edition of "Adoption Medical News." It is very helpful. The phone number for back issues is 407-724-0815. It should also be in your local medical school library. Another informative article is in the November 1995 issue of "Adopted Child." Call 202-882-1794 for back issues. You should definitely read Dr. Downing's web site on medical terminology. Also, this web site has some very helpful information on what a specialist looks for in a video and in the records. http://members.aol.com/jaronmink/russvid.htm. Another good website for medical conditions and IA doctors is at http://www.comeunity.com/adoption/health/clinics.html

In general, the older the child, the easier it is for an expert to identify potential problems. Also, doctors are going to err on the side of caution since they are not able to examine the child or run any tests so expect cautious optimism at best. I would also talk to other parents who have adopted children of the same age as the referral and also from the same children's home. Do not discount other parents' experiences.

Finally, there are lots of things you and the doctors cannot see such as learning disabilities, developmental delays, speech delays, sensory integration issues, and so on. I remember a doctor who said that premature children from an institution would always have to pay some price. By that she meant that in school the child will likely be delayed in an area, you just do not know which one. Look around your neighborhood though, there are plenty of children who are physically healthy and are wonderful kids, but who have one or more of the above issues. Many of the conditions are ones you cannot see for years.

When you begin this adoption journey you have to ask yourself, "Am I prepared to deal with the unknown?" This is a question that most biological parents do not have the chance to ponder; it is just thrust upon them. Just because a child has rickets, or a cleft palate, or some other "identifiable" physical ailment doesn't mean that this child will be more of a health risk than that supposedly perfectly healthy child who comes home and has attachment issues.

Finally, there is a limit to the information that any doctor can give you, based upon a child's health records and a few pictures. You can only be prepared up to a certain point. You can guide your agency about what you think you are capable of handling, study all the medical information, read all the books, but in the end you must accept that there are no guarantees in life nor in international adoption. Sometimes, you just have to follow your intuition and your heart. A doctor's opinion is good thing to have, but it is you in the end that must make the decision.

Children's Home Medical Questions

In 1992, when Russian adoptions began, medical information barely existed. The adoptive parents may have had only a single photograph and no more than a one-page summary of medical information. The normal leap of faith that exists with any adoption was more like a long jump. By 1996 the process had become more organized. The standard (until the recent year 2000 changes) was that you received a video of the referral, plus some still shots and some medical information. Some agencies only gave you the one page medical summary and left it to you to follow up with questions to which they tried to discover the answers.

The better practice was for the agency not to wait for your obvious questions but to give you as much of the medical history as possible and to anticipate your questions. Some agencies try to fend off medical inquiries by saying that it was difficult to obtain information from the Region, children's home or facilitator. Yet, some facilitators have access to email and can give you the phone number of the children's home. You can then set up a three way phone call with your medical specialist and a translator and call the children's home doctor yourself. This is not too difficult. Both MCI and AT&T will provide a translator if you cannot find one. It is very helpful to make the call to Russia with a medical professional on the line, preferably one that has dealt with international children. Here is one list of Baby Homes in Russia and their phone numbers: *http://www.iespana.es/adoptaenrusia/OrfRusia.xls*.

Here are some of the questions that you might ask if you are able to call. They are also good ones to ask if you under the two trip process and meeting your child for the first time. You can also use these if calling Kazakhstan.

1. Current information: current head circumference, height, weight; developmental milestones appropriate for the child's age, rolling over, sitting, crawling (what can the child do); You really want to get a range of measurements over time in order to gauge the velocity of growth.

Don't accept just one set of measurements taken at just one point in time.

2. Emotional development of the child (attachment evidence);

3. History of illnesses, fevers, hospitalization, surgery, etc., and outcomes.

4. What do you know about his birth parents? Their medical history and medical history of siblings. Any history of alcohol use by the birth mother? How many pregnancies?

5. What was the prenatal history (less relevant for older children)

6. Why was the child put in the orphanage?

7. Does the child have a favorite caretaker?

8. Does your child have any special friends?

9. What are the child's likes and dislikes?

10. What seems to comfort the child?

11. What kinds of foods will he eat?

12. What is the routine at the orphanage?

13. What is the child's ethnic background?

14. Does the child smile or laugh?

15. What should I know in caring for this child?

16. How is he doing health wise?

17. What do they know about the birth mother? age? number of pregnancies? Physical description? Birth father information?

18. What are the lab results for HIV, HEP, and syphilis?

19. How does the doctor think he compares to other babies his age at the orphanage?

20. Child's Apgar scores and at what minute intervals?

21. What inoculations has the child had?

22. How many children are in the home, in his sleep area, how many caregivers?

23. What toys does he play with?

24. Does he use a spoon or bottle?

25. Does he use both hands?

26. Does he pass a toy from hand to hand?

27. Will he be able to go to a normal school?

28. What is his age of development?

29. Results of any eye examination and hearing exam?

30. Result of any ultrasound of the brain?

31. What antibiotics has he been given? (Certain ones given to preemies may cause deafness)

32. What future help might this child need based on the doctor's experience, i.e. physical therapy, speech or developmental help?

33. Does the child have floppy muscles or stiffened limbs?

34. Has the child had any convulsions? If there is a notation in the medical record of the child being given barbiturates, you will want to know what these are for and if they are related to a seizure condition?

35. Is there anything else the doctor would like to add about the baby or give advice about? How does this child compare with other children the doctor has seen?

36. What does the orphanage need us to bring? clothes? shoes? Medicine toys?

The number of pregnancies and age of the birth mother is just one indicator of the sort of lifestyle the birth mother might lead. The older the woman and the higher the number of pregnancies then you can extrapolate that the birth mother had a lifestyle of frequent sex partners with its associative risks, possibly higher risk of alcohol, with malnutrition and poor prenatal care. Remember though that it is only an indicator and nothing more.

You may wish to review the **normal** developmental milestone timeline of a child in order to gauge how delayed your child may be. One set of guidelines can be found at *http://www.health.state.ny.us/nysdoh/eip/earlydif.htm* Another good site is at *www.kidsgrowth.com*. This site goes beyond just plotting on charts. It gives information on daily, weekly, monthly, and yearly growth. The What to Expect books are good as well. Just remember, these children are delayed by a month for every 3 months in the children's home, so you must consider that in your analysis of what is normal for these children.

Generally a 6-month-old infant not in a children's home should be able to:

Follow moving objects with their eyes
Turn toward the source of normal sound

Reach for objects and pick them up
Switch toys from one hand to the other
Play with their toes
Help holding the bottle
Babble

A 12 month old should:

Sit without support
Pull to a standing position
Crawl
Drink from a cup
Play peek-a-boo
Wave bye-bye
Put objects in a container
Stack two blocks
Know five words

An 18 month old should:

Like to pull, push, and dump things
Follow simple directions
Pull off shoes, sock and mittens
Like to look at pictures
Feed themselves
Make crayon marks on paper
Walk without help

A 2 year old should:

Use two to three word sentences
Say names of toys
Recognize familiar pictures
Feed themselves with a spoon
Identify hair, eyes, ears and nose by pointing
Build a tower of 4 blocks

A 3 year old should:

Walk up steps alternating feet
Put on shoes
Open door
Turn one page at a time
Repeat common rhymes
Use three to five word sentences
Name at least one color correctly

Older Children

Adopting older children is a great experience. Older children bring their culture, their language, and their history with them. They are interesting and fun right out of the box. Their medical reports are probably more accurate than an infant's, simply because most symptoms will already have appeared and be present. The psychological issues are a little more risky. With an infant, the risk is reversed. Like everything else, you need to do your research and talk to parents who have adopted older children. If you are older, it may be that parenting an older child is better. You don't have to go through the whole diaper and baby experience, but can jump right in with children who will interact with you. You also don't have to wait 18 years until they go off the college to reclaim your life!

Some keys to assessing older children is to find out how long they have been in the children's home, did they ever live with a family, and are they attached to a particular caretaker now. These questions relate to attachment. You need to find out about siblings and where they are located. Siblings who are attached to each other are more likely to be able to attach to their new family. A good predictor of being able to attach to someone new is being attached to someone already. In addition, siblings give each other a lot of comfort and support. These are just a couple of the good reasons to consider adopting siblings if you want more than one child. Find out as much as you can about their life before she was placed in the children's home. The most important factor in assessing attachment isn't how long a child was in an institution, but the care received before and after entering. A child who was in an institution for a long period of time but was cared for, loved and had stability will be better prepared than a child who was in for a much shorter time but who was abused, neglected, unloved and moved from place to place (like in the US foster care system).

Also, talk to other parents who have adopted older children or from foster parents. You will learn more from them than from any book.

If you discover that parental rights were terminated, push your facilitator and the regional officials to discover the real reasons. You may not be able to do this until you are in Russia and even so they may not open the records to you, but finding out the reasons for the termination of rights can greatly help in any post-adoptive therapy that the child may undergo. Push to get the child's medical records translated and sent to you ahead of time, including a translated parental termination of rights document. This is one reason why waiving the 10 days may not actually be a good idea with an older child. During those 10 days you will likely be able to observe your child as he really is.

Some older children may have sensory integration issues such as Central Auditory Processing Disorder (CAPD). CAPD is sort of like dyslexia, but it's about what you hear getting mixed up rather than what you see. Many times what happens it that in a classroom for example, there are so many auditory stimuli that the child cannot focus on the teacher's words and therefore misses the lessons and the homework, This condition may arise if they spent several years in the institution. This can take a toll as they may be deprived of the stimulation that comes from normal nurturing and loving. You may have to help him reclaim his right to parental love. There are professional language programs such as Fast Forward or Earobics that are available. Then there are those older children that will suffer no ill effects from institutionalization. It may be that they were in a family for a while and had normal attachment experiences. They may not have been in the institution for very long or were a favorite of a caretaker. If you do accept a referral of an older child, send him a photo album of his forever family, future friends and pets. This will allow him to become accustom to his new life while you both wait for a court date and will give him a reason to believe that a new and happier life is just around the corner.

Older children (and younger ones as well) are likely to have siblings in other children's homes. Press your agency to discover if there are other siblings and if they are close. They may be in different homes, but travel to see each other. Adopting siblings, who are close, gives you and the children a great head start and an advantage in integrating them into your family.

There are many questions that surround adopting older children. Indeed, by the time you wade through all of the medical and family advice, you are guaranteed to be thoroughly confused. Just remember that there are plenty of stories of very happy older child adoptions. Good stories are just not news. Still, being prepared through education is the best medicine, even if painful. Gain the knowledge, file it away, and hope you never have to use it. There is an older child support list on EEadopt called PEP and an interesting website regarding adopting older children at *www.hannahandhermama.com/*.

One of the risks adoptive parents take when adopting a child that comes from a background of abuse is that the child will perpetuate the abuse. Thus younger siblings may be at risk. This is one reason that when an older child is placed, it may be better for her to become the youngest in an established family or be an only child. The other reason is that an oldest child has a firm sense of identity, based on birth order, and it is often traumatic to him to be displaced. Sometimes families with several children adopt a child who becomes the 3rd or successive number because the youngest children aren't affected as much by having one more older sibling. It is the first 2 children in the family who have the strongest sense of their position.

Now some believe this birth order issue is an artificial one created by academics just looking for a problem where none exists. In many families adopting out of birth order is not a problem at all, although the US social worker will be against it. You could look it as the oldest has a special place since she is oldest; the youngest has a special place since she is the baby; and your middle child is special because maybe she was the first. Definitely do some research before deciding if this is right for your family.

If adopting an older child, three or older, you should ask additional questions of the children's home, particularly if the child will be older than existing children in your house:

1. How does she treat the other children in the orphanage in her age group?
2. How easily is she disciplined?
3. What is her temperament like?
4. Does she show aggression?
5. What is her personality like?
6. Has she bonded with a caretaker in the home?
7. What do they know of her background?
8. Why is the child in the home? The Russians do not view child abuse as we do. They will discuss a parent's rights being terminated for alcohol abuse, but for some reason they do not recognize the long-term damage of child abuse, either physically and sexually and thus do not place much emphasis on it in a child's records. They are more willing to assign "neglect" as the reason.

9. Height and weight. If the child is in the 5th percentile that means that of all American children who have been charted for height vs. weight at that particular age over a certain period of time your child fell in the 5th percent, meaning that your child is on the low side. If he is at 50% (percentile), then he is at the bell curve, where most American children of that age fall. If he were in the 95%, then he would be much large than most children that age.

When you are at the children's home, watch her around the other children in her group and how she plays with them and how she treats them. If she is very loving, and helpful while playing with them then she is likely to be loving and helpful to her new siblings. You do have to ask a lot of questions about their mental state and what you can get about their past and do your homework. Compare what your agency and the children's home has told you with what you actually observe.

When you travel to Russia and arrive at the children's home you will receive current medical information and be able to talk with the director and home physician. If the child was placed in the children's home because parental rights were terminated and not because the child was relinquished, then you may receive sealed court records revealing the history and basis for the termination. You may have to press to receive these records, but do so. The records will likely reveal abuse or neglect. There will always be abuse or neglect or the government cannot terminate parental rights. In many ways, their system and ours is similar. The problem with being given this information when you are in Russia is that you are not given much time to change your mind and changing your mind, after all the expense and time you have put in, takes great courage. Remember though that in the time between the first and second trip you can have a US doctor look at your pictures and read your observations and *you can change your mind*. The adoption is not final until your court hearing.

Now don't misunderstand. Not all older children were abused and there are many, many happy "forever" families with adoptive older children, but you do have to be careful and get as much information as you can about the child's past and mental state. Before you travel you should look inside yourself and be prepared to have the courage to walk away. Do not overestimate your parenting skills. Make an accurate assessment of your support network. Love and good food are not cures for everything.

Infants and Wobblers

The general rule is that children are delayed a month of development for every 3 months in the children's home. The children tend to run on the small side as well. The reason for this is that in addition to factors such as prematurity, undernourishment and sickness, a child's development, both physical and mental, depends in large part on how much affection they receive. It is a common story that when the children are brought into a loving home with lots of cuddling, they suddenly grow like weeds. So it is important not to overemphasize the weight or size of a child, as the child could very well be perfectly healthy, just small. This is not to say that when the higher cognitive abilities like abstract thinking are accessed in the third or fourth grade the child might not need some extra help. But that is true with any child.

Now the Russian method of measuring head circumference is to measure a circumference that is parallel to the floor, whereas the method in the States is to find the largest circumference, which is usually not parallel to the floor. The measurement in the States is taken at the largest area of the head, above the eyebrows and ears and around the back of the head. Finding the largest circumference often means adjusting the tape and taking two or three reads. This is what happens in a US pediatrician's office, but is unlikely to happen in most children's homes. This might explain why you are told your child's head circumference is one figure but when you bring her home, your pediatrician has another.

A small head circumference that is not proportional to the body may be a red flag as it could indicate that the brain is not growing. On the other hand, a small head circumference that is proportional may not be cause for alarm. If the child is born with a head circumference below the charts then you begin to look for problems in utero that caused growth retardation and those can often be more serious. (birthmother's drinking, drugs, poor pre-natal care). Of course you can also just have a baby that is tiny because of genetics or because she was premature. After looking at the birth statistics you will want to see a 'curve' on the chart with growth in head circumference, height and weight. You may be less concerned with a small head circumference if the rest of the child is small also. If you see height and weight gains, but no head growth, then that is a problem. The head only grows if the brain is growing. Remember that microcephaly (which has many negative associations) is a small head size compared to the rest of the body and is different than simply being low on the charts. Not all doctors make that distinction so if they use the word; make sure you are all discussing the same condition.

One mitigating factor is if the child comes from a poor region where a lack of food is a real possibility. This can cause small growth all the way around. Also, if the child has a cleft palate, then it is possible she is having difficulty getting enough food. If malnutrition is a factor, then you should see weight and height gains fall off first, but head circumference continues to increase. This means that the body is sending what nutrients it has to the brain for growth. Do not base a whole referral on head circumference alone, but look at the whole picture and see if the rest of the child is small, talk with others who have adopted from this orphanage/region, and check where the child is developmentally, and see if there are other contributing factors to the small head circumference like small birth parents, lack of food at the orphanage, etc. This is one advantage the two-trip system has over the referral method.

Most international specialists focus on the head circumference measurement, as that can be indicative of mental development. The average head circumference for a full term infant is 35cm.Doctors worry about full term children born under 31cm.The general theory is that big heads equal big brains. The larger the head the greater the number of neurons and the more neurons you have the larger the bandwidth. Heads grow because the brain grows, and this mostly occurs in the first few years of life. Be aware that some of the experts are now saying that many Russian children are demolishing the medical community expectations and heads are growing when adopted after the age of 3 years. While head size may be an objective medical evaluative tool, it should not be the only factor to take into consideration when assessing a child's cognitive potential. Indeed, Dr. Keenan of Harvard Medical School has questioned the connection between overall birth size and higher cognitive ability. He believes a family's expectations about a child's intelligence and ability has more of an impact than birth weight. Dr. Aronson has written about what she has found in regard to head circumference in Russian children at *http://members.aol.com/jaronmink/russvid.htm*. Dr. Dana Johnson has written an excellent article regarding HC and risk profiles which can be found at *http://www.russianadoption.org/Headcircumferencedj.htm*. One of the more recent studies is published in JAMA at volume. 289 No. 6, February 12, 2003. *http://jama.ama-assn.org/cgi/content/abstract/289/6/705*. This study seems to say that many preemies will gain cognitive ability over time and will end up as normal average kids. The truth is that you won't *really* know, until a few months after your bring your child home, whether she is "bounce back" baby.

Usually the head circumference is plotted on an old 1979 American growth chart developed by the National Center for Health Statistics. The CDC has recently published an updated one, which is available on their web site at *CDC.gov* then click on National Center for Health Statistics. For older children, the Nelhouse curves are commonly used and these were published in 1968 and were based on a compilation of 14 studies of head growth published in the 1940's, 50's and early 60's. This is widely accepted by pediatricians. Nelhouse in his original paper said that these curves should be applicable to all children regardless of ethnicity and geographical location. However, in looking into the basis for the curves it was found that they rely primarily on studies of American Caucasian children so there is a question about whether the curves are really applicable for children from other countries.

There have been many studies of head circumference in children and what it means. None have specifically targeted adoptive children. Head circumference studies of large groups of children were published in the 1960's and 1970's using already at-risk populations of children. Using children that have other issues puts a question mark on the credibility of the findings. The findings from these studies were that children with a head circumference 2 standard deviations and greater below the mean are of lower intelligence. You might call this the generic finding. In 1977, 1000 children in the Seattle school system were studied. No difference in IQ between small heads and big heads was found, but there was a difference in truly microcephalic kids.

Two standard deviations below the mean is the 3rd percentile. The mean is the 50th percentile. Think of the mean, or the 50th percentile, as the top of a bell curve where half the people fall on one side and half on the other. Standard deviation (SD) is how far one travels along the bell curve away from the top peak, or how far away one deviates from the 50th percentile. One SD from the 50% is the 16th percentile on one side and the 84th percentile on the other side. Two SD from the 50% is the 3% and the 97%. A growth percentile ranking represents the percentage of all same-age children larger or smaller than the child in question. So a 12month child who measures at the 10th percentile for height would be taller than 10 percent of all 12month-old children and shorter than 90%. For whatever reason, many growth charts show a "normal" range as 5% to 95%. Most experts prefer a "normal" range of 3% to 97%, or 2 standard deviations. The experts see the risk going up below the 3rd percentile. There is a further differentiation between those children that are within the normal range at birth (3%-97%) and fall below this over time versus those that are consistently below the 3rd percentile (the latter group carrying a higher risk of long term neuralgic problems).

The conclusions about head circumference are truly mixed, as there are no definitive studies concerning adoptive children. There are some general findings that head circumference tends to drift down the longer a child is in the children's home, even where head circumference was normal at birth. This is not at all unexpected, due to factors such as malnutrition and lack of love and stimulation. Children in general (not just adoptees) who have suffered an early brain insult because of these factors, tend to show residual effects even where the insult is resolved such as where nutrition is improved (the Barbados study). The residual effects that appear later at school age may be language delay, impaired sensory inputs, and higher incidence of ADD. Notwithstanding, a supportive new environment greatly improves the outcome for an adoptive child underlying the importance of early intervention, whether it is speech therapy, occupational therapy or simply love, good nutrition, and lots of parent-child interaction. A clear finding by the adoption medical community is that there can be a remarkable recovery in head growth in adoptive children. What they are reluctant to conclude, without a proper study, is that some sort of residual effect will not appear in a child later during the school years.

In summary, cognitive abilities are mainly determined by genetic factors therefore the effect of a low head circumference in adoptive children cannot be interpreted in isolation. The IA doctors will want to know the gestational age of the child and other risk factors. The longer the insult to the brain the more profound the deficit, yet a healthy post-adoption environment has a profound positive influence on outcome, yet a residual effect cannot be ruled out. Keep in mind that head circumference is but one data point to consider, albeit an important one. There are many other factors to consider that might either minimize or increase the risk profile of a child. If you want to read more about the bell curve and deviations see

http://www.wrightslaw.com/advoc/articles/tests_measurements.html.

Here are some issues to investigate in regard to infants.

1) If the head circumference is proportional to her body, then the growth rate may be proportional as well. In other words, if the body were growing slowly then it would not be surprising to find that the head was likewise. If the body and head do not match then that may be a concern. Try to have the measurements taken in metric form and taken over several months.

2) How is the child developmentally? Is she close to her milestones after deducting for the usual institutional caused delays? Does she crawl, walk, babble and have good social interactions? Is there evidence of early handedness? Infants usually do not choose which will be the dominant hand until they enter toddler stage and begin to use tools,

such as a spoon or crayon. Early handedness may be an indication that one side of his body isn't functioning properly.

Dr. Downing, *www.russianadoption.org* and Dr. Aronson, *www.orphandoctor.com*, have developmental checklists on their sites that you can print out. Another developmental list is at the site *http://www.kidsgrowth.com/stages/guide/index.cfm*. Some parents also like the lists in the "What to Expect" books. Just remember that generally these children lose one month for every three months in an orphanage.

3) Was her mother young and was it a first pregnancy? There seems to be a correlation between alcoholism and a mother who is older and has had numerous pregnancies.

Small head circumference means that you need to look at the total picture in order to assess the risk.

The World Health Organization defines low birth weight as less than 2,500 grams or 5 pounds, 8 ounces. 10% of infants born in the United States are low birth weight. Infants have low birth weight if they are born premature before 37 weeks, or because they failed to grow inside the uterus (IUGR). In the United States IUGR is closely associated with maternal hypertension. A problem with assigning an adoptive child to one of these categories is that the birth weight may not be accurate, the gestational age may not be accurate, and prenatal history of the presence or absence of alcohol may not be available.

There are two types of intrauterine growth retardation (IUGR): one is asymmetric and the other symmetric. Asymmetric as its name suggests is where the effect on the three measurements (height, weight, head) is not the same. The weight is affected the most, followed by the height some and the head little. This occurs in a situation where the fetus must make a choice and starves the rest of the body saving the most important parts the brain and heart. It is typically seen in mild malnutrition situations. In symmetric cases the insult is even across all three factors. The head is not spared. It is thought it comes from an early insult as from an infection in the first trimester or severe malnutrition. Where the head circumference is the most affected of the three factors, then serious pre-natal alcohol abuse or early infection is generally the cause. Other toxins like lead and mercury can also affect fetal growth. Maternal smoking does affect weight, although not brain development.

A smaller than normal infant is always a concern, but there are studies supporting catch-up growth. There was a study published in the Journal of

Pediatrics in June 1998.It described adolescent growth of 32 extremely premature children from birth through 12-18 years of age. All weighed less than 1000 grams at birth (<2.2lbs) The study found that by 12-18 years of age, only 6% of the children were below the normal range for height, and these children had mothers who were short themselves. This study did not discuss the ages at which small children landed on the growth chart, but did state that 45% of all children grew faster than normal between 8 years and 12-18 years. The conclusion was that catch-up growth continues well into adolescence. Here is a web site that discusses growth and the premature infant in more detail: *http://www.comeunity.com/premature/child/growth/catchup.html*

You may also notice that some infants have their hands clenched. While it can be a sign of cerebral palsy, most times it is not. They clench their hands because it provides stimulation and touch. If they had had a lot of toys to play with, they probably wouldn't do this. It goes away after a month or so. Just give them toys to hold and massage the fingers.

You might also see some rocking back and forth by an infant or toddler. It can be mild or severe. Rocking is a pretty typical comfort behavior. They rock for comfort or when they are upset or under stress. It is probably better to just let it be. In most children it will eventually diminish after a few months and then stop.

If you receive a videotape and it shows the child at less than 2 months, see if the child has a Moro reflex reaction to something going on in the room. A very young infant when startled will throw his hands out to the sides and his feet in the air and open his eyes wide. This Moro reflex indicates the nervous system is on target. The problem is that you rarely see a videotape of a child that young and even if you do he will be so swaddled in clothes that he can't even move, much less react.

Medical Measurements

Russia uses the metric system, which means that all road signs are in kilometers and speed limits in kilometers per hour. Drinks come by the liter (mostly 0.5 or 0.3) or in hundreds of milliliters (usually 330 ml for a can of soda). The exception is shots of vodka (and other liquors), which are generally served in 50- or 100-gram measures. Food is weighed in grams or kilograms. There are 10 millimeters in a centimeter, 100 centimeters in a meter and 1,000 meters in a kilometer. You can type in a child's head circumference, length and weight and find

out what percentile they fell in at
http://www.babycenter.com/live/growthchart.html

In order to read the medical summary you will need to have a metric conversion table handy. To convert kilograms to pounds, multiply by 2.2:
2.8 kg x 2.2 lb/ = 6.16 lb

If the weight is in grams, convert it first to kg by moving the decimal point:
2800 gm = 2.8 kg

Length will be given in centimeters. Some conversions are as follows:

30 cm =11.81 inches
35 cm = 13.7
40 cm =15.7
50 cm =19.7
70 cm =27.5

The actual formula is to multiply the cm figure by 0.3937. Therefore 45 cm would be equal to: 45 x 0.3937 = 17.7 inches

And you thought you were through with 7th grade math!

CHAPTER VIII

MEDICAL CONDITIONS

Medical Terminology

As I mentioned in the previous "Medical Review" section, I encourage you to read both Dr. Jenista's article and Dr. Downing's Russian medical articles at his website. These articles will provide you with some background as to what the terms in the medical summary mean. Dr Gindis also has an excellent article at http://www.bgcenter.com/adoptionPublication.htm on Russian medical terminology. If you are following the two-trip process, you should take at least one of these articles with you.

Russian and American medical terms coincide when they are describing actual physical features, but not when they are in the subjective realm. For example, inevitably the medical summary will include the words "perinatal encephalopathy." This is a Humpty Dumpty word. It means whatever the Russian doctor wants it to mean. It is used to describe a baby who might be equally fussy, hungry, irritable, or brain impaired. Because it means everything, it means nothing. Then there is "hyperexcitability syndrome." This term is used to describe a baby who might be crying or fussy for perfectly normal reasons. It's a nonsense word like "oligophrenia" which is translated as feeble mindedness. How can you tell a child has problems if you do not describe the objective observations through testing? Rather than relying on these subjective labels given by someone who only saw the newborn child for a few minutes,

142

your medical reviewer will focus on specific milestone developments such as does the child cry, roll over, sit up, crawl, stand, walk, play with toys, move hands and legs.

Even so, some Russian diagnoses are accurate and cannot be ignored. In this chapter I would like to touch on just a few of those conditions. I also provide a brief description as to what an APGAR score means. Most doctors do not rely on the score. You will see why when you read the description. Yet it is a factor that is listed on the medical summary for infants and which always leads to further questions.

In reviewing a child's medical summary, just keep in mind the limitations of the Russian pediatric medical establishment. Their training is not western based, it's not very modern, and they generally do not have access to advanced technology such as a MRI machine. If you ask how his hearing is, you will get that "he can hear sounds." You will not get a print out from an actual hearing test. They don't have that kind of machine. Russian doctors tend to specialize, but not after having gone through the same quality of training that the West requires. A good explanation of the Russian approach to medicine is at this site: *http://www.russianadoption.org/adoptionfaq.htm.* The *Rainbowkids* web site also has many articles on various aspects of Russian medicine and adopted children.

The Russian medical approach to pediatrics is to analyze a patient using the idea sometimes described as "defectology." They focus on the shortcomings, disabilities and inabilities of a child, even those that have not developed, but which they think might happen in the future. They emphasize what a child cannot do. In contrast, the West looks at rehabilitation of the child and the possibility of overcoming obstacles. You could almost simplify it by saying that one approach is a more negative view of the world while the other, more positive and hopeful. A typical example is the over diagnosis of "perinatal encephalopathy." The majority of children in a home will likely have it on their records. The diagnosis could be from the birthmother being a drug addict; an alcoholic or perhaps she did not have proper nutrition during the prenatal period or had an overcrowded home life. The factors causing the diagnosis are endless. The diagnosis is also made from the consequences i.e. a child who has a speech delay or a delay in walking must have "perinatal encephalopathy." In the Russian medical view, the defect was always there. This diagnosis is also applied to children who are in a children's home simply because the birth parents could not take care of them due to economic circumstances. Even these children are viewed as defective from birth.

Now Russian doctors will take a sonogram or ultrasound at the drop of a hat. Those are routine tests that are given to all infants. Indeed, because they routinely do sonograms and ultrasounds there are a lot of false positives. Typical scenario is an ultrasound performed which was not indicated in the first place leading to a diagnosis in a patient who feels quite well. Of course, the doctor will recommend a follow up ultrasound in 6 months. Russian patients and physicians have an inordinately high regard for ultrasound studies. Sometimes they will diagnose a condition, like hepatitis, by ultrasound that would normally require a tissue specimen and a microscope. Ultrasounds are also available in Moscow without physician referral.

Another interesting aspect of Russian medicine is that a lot of prescriptions are for mixing chemicals. People will travel from store to store then go home to brew their own, such as for penicillin.

Good resource web sites can be found at *http://www.russianadoption.org/* If you scroll down the site, on the right hand side you will see links to medical papers that discuss Hepatitis, FAS/FAE, parasites and post-institutional issues. Another good resource on medical issues is at: *http://www.childrensdisabili-ties.info/* and for "oligophrenia," see *www.bgcenter.com/oligophren.htm.*

APGAR

APGAR is merely the evaluation of the baby's condition at the time of birth. A.P.G.A.R. stands for Appearance, Pulse rate, Grimace, Activity and Respiratory effort. This score enables medical personnel to identify babies that need routine care and babies who may need further assistance. The baby is evaluated and scored at one minute after birth and then again in 5 minutes. The second score is more important than the first one, as many infants may have a brief period of being "stunned" and need help initially adjusting to life. The APGAR is important to identify babies *at the time of birth* who need help and to observe whether the help that has been given has had the desired effect.

There are several examinations that are made for an APGAR score:

Heart Rate
Respiratory Effort
Muscle Tone
Reflex
Response to Stimulation
Color

The scoring is as follows
HEART RATE/PULSE: 0 points for absent heart rate, 1 point for heart rate below 100, 2 points for heart rate over 100.
RESPIRATORY EFFORT: 0 points for absent, 1 point for weak cry and hypoventilation, 2 points for good crying.
MUSCLE TONE/ACTIVITY: 0 points for limp, 1 point for some flexion of extremities, 2 points for well flexed.
REFLEX/RESPONSE TO STIMULATION/GRIMACE: 0 points for no response, 1 point for grimace, 2 points for coughs, sneezes or cries.
COLOR/APPEARANCE: 0 points for blue or pale, 1 point for body pink, extremities blue, 2 points for completely pink.

An APGAR score will typically be stated in the form of two numbers with a slash between. The first is the one-minute score; the second is the 5-minute score. The scoring ranges for the APGAR are:

1. 7-10: Active, vigorous infant routine care

2. 4-6: Moderately depressed infant requires stimulation to breathe and oxygen

3. 0-3: Severely depressed infant, immediate ventilatory assistance required

Because the APGAR score is subjective and only taken at birth, its importance after birth should not be overemphasized. It will only tell you that your child had a stressful birth or a non-stressful one.

It is just a snapshot of how the baby was one minute and five minutes after birth. Don't accept or reject a referral on that alone. Indeed, most children with developmental disabilities have excellent APGAR scores when born and most children with poor APGAR scores do well. How the child is today and what your medical reviewer says regarding the video and any conversation you have with the orphanage doctors is far more important in evaluating your child.

Fetal Alcohol Syndrome

One of the issues usually discussed in relation to intercountry adoptions is the risk of your child having Fetal Alcohol Syndrome and Fetal Alcohol Effect. In

Russia, with its high rate of alcoholism, children are always at risk. However, remember that the high alcoholism rate is generally found among men. In Russian women, age is an indicator, with an older woman more likely to drink than a younger one.

Fetal Alcohol Syndrome (FAS) is always a risk in any child where the birth mother drank alcohol. Its effects vary widely. Some birth mothers can drink heavily and there can be no effect. In others, just a few glasses can cause damage. FAS occurs in every country including the United States. It is almost impossible to detect with certainty before the age of two. If you believe your referral might be affected, have one of the adoption medical specialists give you an opinion. Of course, remember that a brief video and a few still shots make any precise diagnosis of any medical condition difficult at best.

An FAS diagnosis usually is made based on impairment of growth and development plus a characteristic pattern of facial features including short eye openings (palpebral fissures-small width of the eye), short upturned nose, low nasal bridge (sometimes noticed as a broad nasal bridge), flat vertical groove (almost absent) between upper lip and nose (philtrum), and thin upper lip and simply formed external ears. Another minor facial anomaly is epicanthal folds (which can be either unilateral or bilateral) and which are also representative of certain ethnic groups, just to make things harder. Other anomalies are ptsosis-muscle drooping of the eyes; clown eyebrows-eyebrows, which are laterally arched; hyperterlorism; and flat mid-face. Since an infant may have some of these characteristics by just being a baby, it is very hard to make any diagnosis at a young age. Dr. Bledsoe has also suggested that an isolated cleft is more worrisome than a cleft/palate combination.

Since so many young children have developmental delays and poor growth due to neglect and malnutrition, many children will have some of the features of FAS or FAE. It is difficult to figure out when a child is delayed because of just general children's home experience or due to alcohol. Also, some children with an Asian background like Chuvash, Kazak or Bashkir can appear to have some slight FAS facial characteristics when in fact it is just the way they may look. For example, children from the Chuvash region, which has a mix of Mongol genetics, tend to have the "epicanthal folds" on their eyelids and the relatively flat philtrum (ridges between lips and nose).

Another example of how difficult a diagnosis can be is that some young toddlers will not have well developed earlobes and this can be as a result of FAE. But, if the child has no sucking instinct then her facial muscles will be very underdeveloped. Once home and actively sucking, earlobes will begin to grow. Of course, you won't know that until after the fact. This is another reason to look at the whole picture. Webbing between the 2nd and 3rd toes is also a trait, but this too can occur naturally.

A good article written by Dr. Aronson on FAS and international adoption can be found at: *http://www.russianadoption.org/fas.htm*. She writes that children born to women who drank alcohol excessively during pregnancy can appear to be at increased risk for ADD with hyperactivity, fine motor impairment, and clumsiness as well as more subtle delays in motor performance and speech disorders. In the absence of physical features and abnormalities, this is called Fetal Alcohol Effects, or Alcohol Related Neurodevelopmental Effects. FAE is usually not apparent until children are school age. Behavioral issues will surface in pre-school and cognitive difficulties around third or fourth grade. The term "Fetal Alcohol Effects (FAE)" has been used to describe conditions that are presumed to be caused by prenatal alcohol exposure but do not follow the exact configuration of the three characteristics used to identify FAS. Typically children with FAE are of normal size and have some but not all of the facial anomalies and central nervous systems (CNS) dysfunction associated with FAS. Family history is important. Without the telltale facial features, identification of CNS damage as a result of prenatal alcohol exposure can be difficult. Dr. Bledsoe's clinic has specialized in FAS/FAE and if you suspect that your referral may be subject to the condition, you may wish to contact her for a second opinion.

Dr. Bledsoe is a primary care pediatrician who practices pediatrics at the University of Washington's pediatric center and has an emphasis on adoption. The University of Washington is one of the top centers on Fetal Alcohol Syndrome. According to Dr. Bledsoe, FAS is a birth defect expressed by a child having four characteristics: 1) below 10% for height, weight and head circumference; 2) specific set of facial anomalies; 3) structural or functional evidence of brain damage-very small head or abnormal results from neuropyschometric testing; 4) history of alcohol exposure in utero. True diagnosis of the syndrome requires careful measurement in each of these areas. In the United States about 5000 infants a year are born with FAS. Infants are most vulnerable in the first trimester. Alcohol exposure is dose dependent. The higher the level of exposure the more damage to the brain. Damage lasts a lifetime. Pre-natal alcohol exposure does not always result in FAS. There are factors both in the individual and maternal such as placenta blood flow that can influence the amount of alcohol exposed to the brain. Dr. Bledsoe now believes that infants below the age of 2 can be evaluated for FAS by doing a "computer mapping" of a child's face and then comparing this child to their database of FAS characteristics.

The behavioral consequences of a child having FAS/FAE can be hyperactivity, ADD, lack of inhibition, learning disabilities or mental retardation. They have trouble with habituation. They can't tune out stimuli and are easily over-whelmed and distracted. They demonstrate inappropriate perseverance in that they will continue maladaptive behavior despite negative consequences, as they do not absorb normal cause and effect lessons. The detrimental cognitive effects can include lower IQs, lower achievement test scores, poor comprehension of words and grammar, poor word recall, and lower math skills.

Children with FAE are routinely misdiagnosed as being rebellious, uncooperative, lazy or stubborn rather than as disabled. They have difficulty learning from experience, lack remorse, and are vulnerable to peer influence. They can be emotionally volatile. Doctors are reluctant to diagnose FAE for various reasons. Toddlers and young children with FAE are described as requiring high maintenance, being manipulative, being very loving, a danger to self and others as they do not understand cause and effect, unable to engage in normal sequential learning so they lack proper reasoning, judgment and memory, being difficult to manage in public, having no fear of danger, and commonly misdiagnosed as their IQs appear normal. Pre-adolescents are impulsive, manipulative, have no sense of fairness or empathy, need a lot of stimulation, have mood swings, are isolated and lonely. Adolescents are described as having no moral compass, still a safety concern to themselves and others, obsessed by basic primal instincts like fires and sexual activity, very vulnerable to peer structures like gangs, impaired judgment and reasoning, vulnerable to ideas in movies, music, and on television, mood swings, and are unable to take responsibility. Young adults with FAE are described as being without a moral center, vulnerable to anti-social behavior, not following safety rules, unable to manage money, emotionally volatile, and being vulnerable to mental problems. While some of these traits occur in non-FAS/FAE people, in these children the behaviors are exaggerated and do not respond to normal modification techniques.

Intervention with FAS/FAE kids should begin as early as possible and continue throughout their lives. The keys to appropriate early intervention are developing and maintaining realistic expectations, thinking long-term, learning to reframe child behaviors, and keeping an open mind about goals and strategies. Early intervention is necessary in order to prevent or lessen secondary consequences. These consequences are problems such as depression, disruptive school experiences and problems with the law. Lack of inhibition controls lead to inappropriate sexual behavior. Jobs are difficult to keep. Alcohol and substance abuse is also higher. To an outsider FAS children seem slow and are criticized for just nor "getting it" when the truth is that they are trying as hard as they can but their body is letting them down. Expectations must be realistic and may need to be reset at a lower level. These children can learn, just in a different manner. They benefit from early specific motor and mental stimulation, loads and loads of structure, classrooms with minimal stimuli, and concrete learning methods. Abstract thinking is very difficult for these children. They learn through seeing, feeling or touching. Instruction should be given one task at a time. Change should be kept to a minimum and advanced warning of what is to come next should be given. Focus on teaching them vocational and life skills.

These children benefit from living in a stable and nurturing home, not having frequent changes of household, not being a victim of violence, receiving developmental disability services, and receiving a diagnosis before age 6. They benefit from moderate stimulation rather than over stimulation and concrete instructions and consistent limited rules. They need structure both at home and at school.

Life with a fetal alcohol child can be very difficult. Respite care to prevent caregiver burnout may be necessary. Get as much knowledge as you can, and decide what you can honestly handle. The outcome cannot be guaranteed, but if your referral is suspected of having FAS/FAE, the probability of a lifelong involvement with these issues is great. You might read Ann Streissguth's book, *Fetal Alcohol Syndrome: A Guide For Families and Communities* (1997). She gives a lot of very good, detailed information based on 25 years of research. She even includes pictures, which is helpful. There is a parent's group with a lot of information at *www. fetalalcoholsyndrome.org*. A site with some pretty graphic, but very good color pictures of some of the facial and physical deformities associated with FAS, including "railroad track ears" is at *http://w3.ouhsc.edu/fas/*.

Strabismus

Strabismus is a vision problem in which the eyes are misaligned, meaning they do not look at the same point at the same time. For example, while one eye looks straight ahead, the other may look up, down, in, or out (deviate). Strabismus is sometimes called cross-eyes, walleye, or squint. Strabismus may also be called "lazy eye," but this term is more commonly associated with poor vision resulting from amblyopia.

Normally the six muscles surrounding each eye work together to move both eyes in the same direction at the same time. An infant's brain learns how to control the eyes' movement with these muscles by 3 or 4 months of age. The brain then merges what the two eyes see into a single image. When the eye muscles do not work right, the eyes may become misaligned. Because misaligned eyes look at different points in space, they send two different images to the brain. The brain cannot merge what the misaligned eyes see into a single image.

In a young child with strabismus, the brain is able to avoid the confusion of two images by ignoring (suppressing) the image from one eye. Before age 7 to 10 years, the visual system is still developing and the brain is still learning to use both eyes to see, so it is easy for it to ignore the image from one eye. Once the visual system in the brain has completed its development, however, it cannot ignore the image from one eye. A person who gets strabismus after this development is complete will therefore have double vision (diplopia).

A newborn's eyes may be misaligned, but the eyes should become aligned by 3 to 4 months of age. Any child older than 4 months whose eyes are not aligned all of the time should have an eye exam by an ophthalmologist. A child will rarely "outgrow" strabismus once it has developed. Without treatment, strabismus can cause permanent vision problems. For example, if the child is not using one eye because it is misaligned, it can lead to poor vision in that eye ("lazy eye" or amblyopia). Also, seeing with only one eye instead of two limits how well a person can perceive depth and distance.

Strabismus may affect vision all of the time (constant) or some of the time (latent or intermittent). The eye may turn the wrong way (deviate) only when the person is looking in a certain direction, or it may deviate the same amount no matter which way the person is looking. The eyes may become more misaligned when the person is tired or in bright sunlight. Without treatment, strabismus that initially comes and goes may become more constant.

Usually the cause of strabismus is benign, such as a muscle imbalance or uncorrected farsightedness. Rarely, is the cause more serious, such as an underlying neurological condition. In some cases, children with signs of FAS or CP will also have strabismus, which is why you should always evaluate the whole child and not just an individual condition.

Children with strabismus can appear clumsy, as they have limited depth perception. Double vision is not uncommon. Depending on the case, the solution is glasses, patching or surgery. If left untreated, it can cause developmental delays. Surgery is usually done before the age of 7 and is generally a 45 minute out patient procedure. The surgery "relaxes" certain muscles so they can orient in unison. It is not painful. The eyes heal very quickly and the child should be able to go back to school in a day or so. Toddlers may need to wear arm splints for a few days to keep them from rubbing their eyes.

Will's Eye Hospital in Philadelphia has a good reputation, but the surgery is done everywhere. The most serious issue with this surgery is the anesthesia. You should research and find out who is a good pediatric anesthesiologist. In a small percentage of children the pre-medication causes a reaction and the child is miserable when he wakes up. Try to stay with your child as long as possible, even through the pre-medication stage. Adoptive children tend to react to separation very strongly as you might expect so try to be with him when he wakes up. Don't let the hospital treat this as just another case. Explain to them that unless they want a possible hysterical child in the recovery room they should allow you to go to him as soon as he awakes. Now your child probably won't have any of these reactions, but if it is his first surgery you do not know.

There are many articles on treating strabismus. One is in the American Orthoptic Journal, Volume 48, 1998.

Syphilis

If your child's medical information states that the birthmother had "Lues," that is syphilis. It might also say "D registered" which means "dispanser", a treatment facility of veneral diseases and alcohol abuse. Sometimes a child will test positive for syphilis at birth because of the mother's umbilical chord blood. Syphilis is treatable, and Russian doctors have plenty of experience treating it, and penicillin is cheap and widely available in Russia. Usually the child will be tested again and the test will come back negative, however, you will see the positive test in the history. No Russian couple will consider adopting a baby with this history; so one benefit is that you are protected from having the child adopted domestically before you arrive for the court hearing.

You can ask for another test if that makes you more comfortable or wait until you are back in the States and have it done by your pediatrician. Dr. Aronson has reported on a study of 478 adopted children from various countries. Of this number eleven children were positive with nine from Russia, one from Moldova and one from Vietnam. None had an acute infection. This is good news.

Here's a good web link: *http://www.orphandoctor.com/medical/4_2_1_6.html*

HIV

HIV-1 and HIV-2 are zoonotic infections thought to have originally crossed over in the 1930's. HIV-1's primary primate reservoir is the chimpanzee subspecies *P.t.troglodytes* and for HIV-2, the *sooty mangabey*. HIV was first recorded in Russia in 1987. It developed into a real epidemic in the mid-1990s as drug addiction spread. It mainly exists in the larger cities. Most Russian children do not have HIV. It is not widespread in that population. It is also almost impossible to accurately test a newborn for HIV, however many Russian birth clinics try to do so. Many of the babies that test positive do so because they are carrying some of the HIV antibodies from their (HIV+) mothers. As the baby gets older, the mother's antibodies die off allowing for an accurate HIV test. Thus, the presence of HIV antibodies at birth usually only reveals the mother's status. This is similar to Hepatitis. There is not much done in Russia prenatally to stop the vertical transmission. (from mother to the child) of those viruses.

So if the Russians tell you that a child has tested positive for HIV, try to find out exactly when the test was done and what type of test, ask for a re-test and always consult with an IA doctor. Since children under 18 months may still have maternal antibodies, HIV ELISA, Western Blot, PCR, p24 antigen, and HIV cultures are needed. Note that the Western Blot (WB) is a more specific test that allows one to visualize antibodies directed against each viral protein and is a confirmatory test for a positive HIV. ELISA. PCR, or polymerase chain reaction, extends the capacity to identify, manipulate and reproduce DNA, while the p24 antigen is not a very sensitive test. It will only appear as positive if there is a huge amount of viral replication going on.

Now this is not to say that there are not some HIV-positive babies in Russia. There are bound to be. For example the AIDS virus has even come to Siberia. In 1998 there were 26 reported cases of HIV-positive people in Irkutsk, a large city in southern Siberia and a hot spot for drug trafficking rings from Uzbekistan, Tajikistan and Mongolia. In 2001 Irkutsk reported 10,406 confirmed cases, including some HIV positive babies. No one in this city of 600,000 was prepared for this sort of epidemic, but the cause was simple. Until 1999, heroin had not been available in Irkutsk. Where you find heroin in Russia, you will find HIV-positive unemployed young people. It is a sad, but simple truth. But to illustrate the point in the first paragraph, some of these Irkutsk babies have later tested negative, meaning the first test was done too soon.

Russia has the second largest immunity to HIV in the world. 13% of the population is estimated to have the Delta 32 gene. Sweden has the highest immunity at 14%. If a child has a copy of the gene from his birthmother and another from his birthfather, then he will not get HIV (or Bubonic plague for that matter for those parents living in the plague states of Arizona and New Mexico). The delta 32 mutation in the CCR5 coreceptor for HIV significantly slows disease progression in heterozygous children born to seropositive mothers, although it does not protect completely against maternofetal HIV-1 transmission.

Russia currently has 180,000 registered HIV patients, but reportedly over one million or 1% of adults are infected due to drugs. More than 82 of the Russian Federation's 89 regions have now reported HIV cases. Ukraine recorded 240,000 cases at the end of l999. In Belarus, 14,000 were living with HIV/AIDS at the end of 1999.

Anecdotally I have heard of 3 adopted children from Russia that were HIV positive. I do not know if this is a reliable figure. If it is, it is 3 out of 25,000 adopted Russian children over a ten-year span. Dr. Aronson has reported a study of 490 adopted children with only two Chinese children HIV ELISA positive and these were PCR negative so they were not actually infected. In the May-June 2002 issue of Adoption Medical News it was reported that out of 7,299 children tested in 17 centers in the U.S. upon their arrival since the early 1990's, only 12 children were found with the HIV infection (0.16%); four cases each from Cambodia and Romania, two from Vietnam, and one each from Russia and Panama. Excellent information can be found at *www.thebody.com* on infant HIV.

Cleft Palate/Lip

Some children have a condition called cleft palate and/or cleft lip. You will likely see at least one child in the Embassy waiting room with this condition. It is entirely treatable. A cleft lip is a separation of the two sides of the lip. The separation often includes the bones of the upper jaw and/or upper gum. A cleft palate is an opening in the roof of the mouth in which the two sides of the palate did not join together, as the unborn baby was developing. Cleft lip and cleft palate can occur on one side or on both sides. Because the lip and the palate develop separately, it is possible for the child to have a cleft lip, a cleft palate, or both cleft lip and cleft palate. Dr. Bledsoe has suggested that an isolated cleft is more worrisome for FAS/FAE than a cleft combination.

Generally surgery corrects the condition and is done in stages. As a general rule you can expect to have one surgery to repair the lip and a second surgery to repair the palate during their first year home. Both surgeries generally involve a 1-2 night stay in the hospital. Sometimes the lip and palate can be repaired together in one surgery if the cleft is not that wide. You want the palate fixed sooner so you can start on speech therapy. You might have a third surgery (bone graft) when your child is 7-10 years old to 'fix' the gum line so permanent teeth have a place in which to anchor themselves. Almost any other surgeries are outpatient cosmetic. There is some postoperative pain, like with tonsils, but it is of short duration. The end result is just a small scar on the lip. Before this or any surgery, make sure the child (if an infant) does not have an oval opening in their heart.

There is an organization called Operation Smile. They help children all over the world that are born with facial defects. Operation Smile will assist families whose insurance will not cover the entire surgery. If you have a referral of a child with a cleft palate or lip, you should contact them for more information. Their website is at *http://www.operationsmile.org/*. Another is at *www.widesmiles.org*. A web site that contains a lot of personal information about cleft surgery is at *http://www.bylerbunch.com/*.

Cerebral Palsy

Cerebral Palsy (CP) is the general term used to describe the motor impairment resulting from brain damage in a young child. The more severe the case, the earlier a diagnosis can be made. Severe cases can be diagnosed in the first few weeks or months of age. If a child is able to walk normally at 14-18 months, it is quite unlikely that the child has CP. The problem is that for most children, CP cannot be diagnosed until a child is at least 18 months old. The etiology of CP is still not well understood. It seems derived from a prenatal condition and preceded by a perinatal inflammatory condition.

Many of the normal developmental milestones, such as reaching for toys, sitting, and walking, are based on motor function. If these are delayed, then CP might be a reason. Indeed, your reviewing doctor will be looking for just these sorts of milestones. Yet, developmental delays are expected in these children because of the institutional environment, which makes the diagnosis difficult. A delay in walking or a problem with limbs by a child in a Russian children's home can occur for many reasons such as malnutrition and not just because of CP.

A diagnosis of cerebral palsy cannot be made on the basis of an x-ray or blood test. An APGAR score of less than 3 at the 5 minute mark is one of the few possible indicators, but even this is not always so and can not be relied upon. The most meaningful review of cerebral palsy is examining the physical evidence of abnormal motor function. An abnormal motor function may be spasticity, which is the inability of a muscle to relax, or athetosis, which refers to the inability to control the movement of a muscle. Infants who at first are hypotonic wherein they are very floppy may later develop spasticity. In reviewing a videotape a doctor will be looking for normal movement of the limbs and will be concerned if floppiness or a stiff limb is indicated.

Of course, the problem is that a one minute videotape cannot substitute for a physical medical exam. And an observation of delayed motor skills, which could simply be based on poor nutrition and environmental factors, is hardly an adequate basis for a CP diagnosis.

Hip Dysplasia

Hip Dysplasia is sometimes caused by asymmetrical hip ball joints. In most cases hip dysplasia is corrected by either wearing extra diapers or a brace for a limited time. It is considered a mild special needs attribute, if everything else looks good. Ultrasound of the hip is the most important imaging study and will demonstrate hip deformity. A hip X-ray (joint X-ray) is helpful in older infants and children. If the dysplasia is picked up in the first few months of life, it can almost always be treated successfully with bracing. In a few cases surgery is necessary to put the hip back in joint. The older the age at diagnosis, the worse the outcome and the bigger the surgery needed to repair the problem.

Many Russian children are diagnosed with this in the first month, usually by a clicking sound, or because they lean to one side when stood up in their crib (which is ridiculous at one month of age!). In Russia, once a child is given a diagnosis, there is a common tendency by Russian medicine not to later review the diagnosis to see if it is still applicable.

Post-Institutional Issues

Research on children adopted from Eastern European countries is now just starting to emerge; the earliest studies (the 90-91 ones, like the Ames study) were done on kids from the terrible Romanian orphanages who came out in the first flood. You have to keep in mind that Russian, Ukrainian, Bulgarian, and Romanian institutions (to name a few) are not all the same. However, that doesn't mean you should discard the early studies. Just that you should not automatically assume that the conclusions are equally valid in regard to your child in his particular children's home.

It is your child's particular situation in his particular children's home that is far more important in judging whether your child is at risk for post-institutional issues. First, the majority of adoptions from Eastern Europe turn out just fine. Even among older children adoptions you will find many happy families and many situations that defy the general view. Yet there are some children who will have serious psychological issues. I am not talking about developmental or speech delays. Almost all of the children have at least a mild case and it is to be expected. Rather, serious issues such as reactive attachment disorder (RAD), posttraumatic stress disorder (PTSD), and sensory processing disorder are always a possibility, although found in only a minority of Eastern European adoptions. Here is an article on RAD: *http://www.olderchildadoption.com/rad/*.

Age of a child at adoption is not directly linked to attachment issues although the roots are always in the early years. The key factor is quality of care. You can have a 24 month old who lived in an orphanage where there was a low child/staff ratio and a loving, nurturing environment. Likewise, you can have a 10 month old who had little contact with caregivers beyond being fed and changed. This child is at far greater risk for attachment issues than the 24 month old in a loving orphanage. As long as a child has learned how to bond and attach, he can do it again. It is when a child has never learned to attach and bond that attachment issues arise. Most therapists use a RADQ assessment test and can tell by the child's score how severe their attachment issues are.

Also, realize that layering is a common practice in cold climates due to the lack of adequate heat. Because of this, a child's limbs might not be able to extend and flex because of the bundling. If a child is unable to bring her hands and fingers to her mouth, she will not learn to get pleasure sucking her fingers and hands like most newborns, resulting in an inability to move her tongue, make noises, put food in her mouth, or chew. She will be very quiet. Without the experience of sucking/chewing on her finger and hands, a child has no reason to move her tongue much, resulting in the delayed speech. However, with simple exercises from a specialist, a child can soon discover the joy of babbling, chewing and putting food and other things in her mouth. Each child's circumstances reflect the specific delays that might result—most of which can be easily treated with the help of skilled professionals. This is why it is important to request a referral to an early intervention program if you have concerns about you child's development.

In addition to focusing on the care in the children's home rather than just the length of time, there is the benefit of a sibling relationship. In a study of internationally adopted children in the Netherlands, 399 children placed with one or more siblings were followed up approximately ten years after placement. A comparison of problem behavior in this group with that of 1,749 children placed alone shows that the adoption of sibling groups was relatively successful. Attachment issues when siblings are placed are low.

You are, at a minimum, the child's third placement after the birthmother and the children's home. If the child was with a grandmother or other relative, then it is like a foster situation and you may be the fourth or fifth placement.

CHAPTER IX

WAITING AND WAITING

While You Wait

You may be waiting for the day when you can travel for your first trip to Russia to choose a child. Or your agency might be delaying your departure so as to bundle several families together (it's more convenient for them). Or you are waiting to fit into your facilitator's schedule. Or your facilitator knows of a child that meets your requirements, but the child hasn't come off the registry yet. There are lots of reasons for delay.

You also may have already accepted a referral and that child is now yours. But you can't have him yet; you must wait for a court date. Waiting for a court date can be very stressful. Usually the reason for the delay is not because your paperwork is incomplete, but because some crucial Russian piece to the puzzle is sick or on vacation. Remember the officials are very underpaid. The court date could be delayed because the Federal clearance letter (a/k/a orphan data bank letter or release letter) from the Ministry of Education in Moscow has not reached the court officials in the region. This letter states that the adoptive child has been in the Ministry's data bank for the required amount of time (three months for the Federal database). It used to be that a facilitator could simply pick up the letter in Moscow and hand-carry it to the Regional Court or have it couriered, but was a change in 2000 and now these letters must travel by regular Russian post. This can take anywhere from 3 to 7 weeks. Also, the

Deputy Minister of Education must now sign this letter. This obviously adds to the delay. The court date cannot be set until this letter is received. This change in procedure has probably more to do with the Ministry of Education taking a closer look at babies that are being adopted and not just rubberstamping the clearance letters.

Any delay is as frustrating for your agency and facilitator as it is for you. Your agency should be able to tell you where the kink is in the chain. Still, everything is really out of your hands, you have done all you can do and YOUR child is there and you are here. Here are some suggestions as what you can do while you wait:

If you are close to the holidays, go to the Salvation Army or some other organization and support a family with a child around the age you are adopting and give that child a gift.

Learn child CPR while you are waiting.
Gather social security and citizenship application forms
Study up on the federal adoption tax credit rules
Interview pediatricians
Begin your Hepatitis vaccine shots and any other shots you need
Begin to pack your suitcase, your child's and your donations
Check into the school system or day care centers in your area. Ask your neighbors.
Write your will so it includes your adoptive child
Discuss with spouse about parenting styles, discipline styles and which relatives get to raise the child in case you both have an accident.
Learn about your State's re-adoption requirements.
Baby proof your house. Have friends with kids come over to review.
Install plug protectors, edge protectors, cabinet locks, toilet locks.
Practice with the Diaper Genie. (I was beyond clueless)
Diaper your dog, neighbor's child or a furry doll for practice.
Do lots of things nice for yourself. It will be your last time. Go away for a long weekend with your spouse.

You should also investigate with your agency exactly which children's home your child is located. Keep pressing them until you are sure they have given you the correct information. Some agencies will just tell you the major city like Rostov-on-the-Don or Perm. Yet Rostov has 4 children's homes and its outlying towns like Novoshakhtinsk, Novocherkassk, and Shakhti also have one. Perm is the same way with at least 6 children's homes and several more in the outlying towns. With this specific information you can then post on the Internet and find someone else who has traveled to the same home and who can tell you exactly what to expect. Also check out travel tips for your particular city at *http://www.virtualtourist.com/vt/38a/*. (A great travel site.)

Study some Russian phrases
Start your child's Lifebook.
Fix up the baby's room
Buy the crib, car seat and the usual baby books. Read the books.
Post poison control and children's hospital phone numbers on the fridge

Begin thinking about what kind of adoption notices you want to send out, if any.

Write a letter to your child telling them how you are feeling while you wait for them. Give it to them when they turn 18 or some other special time.

File an application for Title IV non-recurring money if your state allows it.
Get your passport ready
Check out your county's early intervention programs if appropriate. Ask your pediatrician for some recommended evaluators.
Clean your house like its never been cleaned before.
Take a parenting class
Find out the dates for children's consignment sales and plan to attend.
Make an effort to go out with your friends, as you will not have time later.
Take that swing dancing class you've always wanted to take.

Nest, Nest, Nest—it's your time! This waiting will be the slowest weeks of your life. Just fill your days.

Choosing a Pediatrician

Most parents choose a pediatrician based on recommendations from friends and family. Find out if the doctor has worked with international children and has any as clients. If she has not, then you can expect to have to educate the pediatrician. Indeed, if the doctor just works in a middle class community, you are likely to find that he is not knowledgeable regarding the issues faced by an international child.

Is she willing to review the referral video? Since this child might be a patient of hers soon, she should be. On the other hand, if you are not used to giving a medical conclusion based on a skimpy medical report and skimpy video, then giving such a conclusion is against a pediatrician's standard training. Also, remember that any local pediatrician review is in addition to the adoption specialists' review and not in place of it. Bringing the local pediatrician into the referral review will process allows you to lean on that doctor for advice as to what medicines you should take over to your child.

The pediatrician should allow you to make an emergency appointment as soon as you return from Russia. You should not have to wait a week to have a thorough examination and screening. You should emphasize to the doctor that the examination needs to be thorough and longer than the usual visit. If you can, you should try to make the appointment for your child before you leave for Russia.

You should raise the issue of reimmunization of your child. Even if your child has been immunized in Russia, the vaccines may have been out of date, not given the same dosage as in the States or not refrigerated. You should not accept any resistance regarding your desire to reimmunize.

Is she familiar with Hepatitis B and C in children? What about parasites such as giardia and other international medical issues? Middle class doctors do not have patients with parasites and may be resistant to testing for them. Any resistance is unacceptable.

Standard questions would be to find out if the doctor has a particular area of pediatric interest, the hours of the office, and the hospitals in which the doctor practices. Check out the waiting room, as you will likely spend quite a bit of time there over the next year. Are there things to keep the child occupied? Toys, books, fish tank, that sort of thing. Do you like the nurses and staff?

Lifebook

Some families create what is called a "Lifebook" for their child. It is an illustration of the adoption journey and can serve as the baby book they never had. The Book might include a section on the history of your life before the child such as where you grew up, lived, work, went to school, etc.

You might have a section on the adoption process itself including pictures of the agency people and the referral picture. Then a section on your child's life showing where she was born and lived and why you chose her name and what it means to you. Copies of her social security card court petition and decree and citizenship certificate could be included. Then add a section on your home and fixing it up for her arrival. Pictures of her room.

A section on traveling to Russia including copies of receipts and ticket stubs. Pictures of the plane, hotel, tourist spots, homestay families. Include maps, money and brochures. You could even include a small vial of dirt or a rock from the children's home. Some families have their children's caregivers write a letter to the child, which you can have her open at whatever age you see fit. This letter could be part of the book.

If there is a baby shower then you could include the invitation, photos of baby shower, and a piece of the gift paper. You could have a section regarding your return with ticket stubs, description of the travel with the child, and passport photos. If people met you at the airport then pictures of the celebration and pictures of your house when you returned. Include the adoption announcement. Include your child's own section with her favorite toy and book. Include what you found out about her immediately such as her sleep and nap patterns, favorite foods, and bathing and nighttime rituals. You may (or may not) have a medical section with information from the children's home, report from your pediatrician when you returned, hand and foot imprints, birth statistics (height and weight)

You could have a section on what was happening in Russia and the United States at the time. (This is a good reason to buy some English language newspapers while you are there.) You could include movies and songs that were playing in the United States.

The White House will also send you a welcome card for your child if you ask them. (It's a little hokey, but cute) Better yet is the flag they will fly over the Capitol the day your child is a citizen. Just ask your Congresswoman.

If you adopt an older child, then you might consider sending a copy of the "Lifebook" to her, in order for her to get used to the idea of joining your family and leaving Russia. It should be a picture book, which might include actual photographs of the child, your family, your dog or cat, home, her new school, extended family, friends, the city she will live in and the places you and she will go. It might include magazine cutouts and notes from family members. If possible, the book might include both English and Russian captions/translations. This book is particularly helpful in the two-trip process, as you will want to leave your child something tangible to remember you by while you both wait for a court date.

Here is a sample outline:

1. Introduction: including the child's picture and how you and your family feel about her.

2. An explanation of things to come: This portion can include a lot of magazine cutouts. Include pictures to indicate a judge will give her a new name; we'll take a train to Moscow (pictures of Russia from a tourist guide); acknowledge her feelings—understand she'll be sad to leave her friends; see a doctor; get her picture taken; take an airplane ride to the US; pictures of friends and the house.

3. An explanation of the first few weeks home and the normal routine for both weekdays and weekends. Include an explanation of her being taken to the doctor and dentist visits. Pictures of her classroom, explaining the purpose of each area; the playground; daily routine (get up, brush teeth, get dressed, drive to work/school; eat breakfast/lunch at school; come home cook dinner; a large variety of after-school/dinner activities; take a bath; brush teeth; set out clothes for next day; say prayers; give hugs and kisses; go to sleep); our weekend routine (clean house, other chores like laundry/shopping, go to church. List potential activities and sports.

4. Spring/Summer events: pictures of friends who she will meet; pictures of family who will be visiting; magazine cutouts of the beach and pool, Fourth of July fireworks, etc.

Some families create an audio "Lifebook" for their older child. They make the tape in Russian before leaving the States or in Russia with the help of their translator. The tape explains what a hotel is and that they will fly on several large planes to get home; what a city is; that there will be lots of cars and people in the larger cities they will be stopping at on their way home; that their new mama and papa love them and it will take time for everyone to get use to being a family; all about the household pets; all about his new home and that he would have his own bed; who his new relatives would be; school; routines and house rules. This kind of tape can really help an older child understand the whirlwind adjustments to his life that he is undergoing. It can become his story.

An adoption oriented Lifebook or "Keepsake" book can be found at *http://www.adoptshoppe.com/holdontight.htm*. It has removable pages, and appropriate sections for you to fill in, such as "Tell me about the day you adopted me" and "Tell me about the first time you held me", etc. Tapestry Books also has one at *www.tapestrybooks.com*, called "This Is Me: Memories To Gather And Keep." Other places sell them as well.

Learn Some Russian

You do not have to learn any Russian for your adoption. It will go just as well if you do not know any of the language. However, it is like traveling in any foreign country, knowing the native language broadens the experience. Also, it is not all that difficult. A couple of months of listening to tapes in a car while you are commuting to work will give you enough pidgin tourist Russian to get by. A background in the Greek language is certainly helpful as the two are based on a similar alphabet. Further, Russians are like any other people (except the French), they appreciate you trying to learn their language. Just preface your remarks with "Excuse me please, I speak Russian poorly, can you help me find....?" and you will see a tremendous difference in your relationship. About the only benefit from the existence of the Soviet Union was the use of Russian across Eastern Europe and Central Asia as the *lingua franca*. It will work wherever you go, from Latvia to Uzbekistan.

Now if you are adopting an older child or even one as young as 4, you should consider learning some basic Russian, just to help with the bonding process and to make the trip less stressful. Even infants under 1 can recognize when you speak a few Russian words to them. You can use the Pimsleur audiocassettes, which are expensive or *Childspeak: 99 Ways to Speak to Your Child in Russian*, which is available from the Adoption Center of Washington at 1-800-452-3878. It's an audio language tape and booklet with Russian pronunciations. It helps you learn how to greet your child, has words and phrases for eating, sleeping, soothing, and playing. It is phonetically based. The cost is $29.95 plus $4.00 shipping and handling (price includes donation). Some have also used *Russian In Three Months* (with a cassette), Nicholas J. Brown, Michael Jenner (less than $30). Also, parents have used Baron's 2-cassette and book kit *Getting By in Russian* for $20. These may also be available at your local library. There is also Russian-English Dictionary by Kenneth Katzner.

Many adoptive parents recommend an adoption language book by Teresa Kelleher. This book gives English-equivalent pronunciations that are quite

good. The tape is easy to follow and well paced. The book and tape are $42.95. The book is 67 pages and is called "A Language and Parenting Guide." The book includes 20 pages of phrases you will need in each of your adoption travel and adjustment situations. Also included are travel tips, bonding stages and expectations, enhancing bonding and parenting pointers. The booklet covers the basics like "Do you need to go to the bathroom?" "Time to go to sleep." "Time to brush your teeth." To contact Teresa, email her at *Adopttlc@aol.com* or write to Tender Loving Communications, P.O. Box 90 Taylor, AZ 85939-0090. Her web site is
http://WorkNotes.com/AZ/AdoptingFromRussia/Kelleher

Here is a sample of some simple words and phrases that might come in handy when speaking with your child.

Meeting your child

Hi!	Draws-vee
I'm your mama	Ya teh-voy mama
I'm your papa	Ya teh-voy papa
You're my son	Tee moy seen
You're our daughter	Tee nash dochka
my sweet daughter	MY-yah DO-chen-kah
Our home is in America	Nosh dome America.
I love you	Ya loo-blue tibya
Everything is okay	Beh-see-yo = Nee-chee-voo
It's ok, don't worry	nee-chee voo
We're going home:	Pie Dome
Let's go	Posh Lee
You are very great, good, etc.	Tee ocean hah-roe-she
Good boy	hah-roe-she mal-check
Good girl	hah-roe-she de-vooch-ka
You are mine forever	Tee my-oh = nahf-seeg-dah, nahf-seeg-dah
You are my sunshine	Tee my-oh = sole-neeshka
This is our house	Eta nahsh dome
This is our car	Eta nahsh mah-chee-nah
This is our church	Eta nosh ser-cuff

Eating phrases

Do you want a drink?	Teh = hoe-chiss peet? (Or teh boo-dish peet?)
Do you want to eat?	teh hoe-chis yest? (Or: teh boo-dish yest?)
Simple—eat?	Yest?
Simple—drink?	Peet?
bread	kleb
juice	soak
apple	yah-blick-ka
banana	banan
candy	cone-fee-yeh-tee
water	vada
soup	soup
cookie	bisquit-tee
tea	chie (pronounced ch-eye)

Bathroom and nap time

Toilet?	Too-ah-lyet?
Pee	peet-zit
BM	Kah-kits
toilet paper	boom-ah-gah
soap	meel-lah
a nap	spot
Go to sleep	spee
goodnight	spah-koy-nih noche
Stay (in bed, in stroller, etc)	stoy
good morning	doe-breh oo-trah

Family

grandma	babooska
grandpa	dyah-dooshka
dear father	PAH-poo-shkah
dear grandmother	BAH-booshka)
dear grandfather	Dyed-OO-SHKA
my brother	mean-ya braht
my sister	mean-ya see-estra
friend	droog

friends	droog-ee
dog	sibaka
cat	kotka
our dog (cat)	nahsh sibaka (kotka)
God	bog (rhymes with 'vogue')

The stern parent!

No!	Nyet! Or: neel-zah
Yes	Dah
Wait!	Pah-stoy
Poison	eta yat
Come here!	Eedeesh-hoo-dah
Get down	ah-zheesh
Be careful	asta-roe-zhna
Stop	stope
Stay	stoy
Stay by me	stoy ree-add-em
Don't touch	nee troe-gee
It's not safe	eta ah-pahs-nah
Please share	nah-bee dih-leetza
Hush!	Tee-haa
Listen!	Slew-shit
That's not allowed	eta nee zyah
Calm down	oo spakoysa
Go to your room	ee-deet svie-ya komnetta
THAT'S BAD!	Ploe-haa!

The nice parent

Mama's here	Mama zz-dees
It's yours	eta tib-ya
I'm sorry	prass-tee minya
I forgive you	ya prahshoy tibya
Does it hurt?	Bah-leet?
Where is the hurt?	Koodah bahleet
Afraid?	Tib-yeh sh-seeya?
Good girl	Ha-RO-shai-ya Dye-VATCH-ka
Good boy	Ha-RO-shee MAHL-chick

Good!	Haa-rah-show! Or = Mall-lah-dee-ets
Are you OK	Kak tee—?
It will be OK	Fsyor boo dehit ha ra shore
Don't cry	Nee platch
Dear	Me la
I'll be back soon	Ya score ra veer noose—

Stressed syllables are capitalized:

Mah-Lah-DYETZ—'Good Job!' to a child; it's a generic praise word only for children when they do something you like.

OOM-nee-tsah—Smart little one
Krah-SEE-vih-tsa—Little Beauty (girl)

Be sure to ask you coordinator, for the diminutives for your child's name. If you use the formal name, they may think you are formal and not close to them.

Recommended is taking a set of the adoptive traveler cards, which can be purchased for $15 at this web site: *http://www.chinaconnectiononline.com/rusvocab.htm*. There are online translators of varying ability.

There are also language lists for the adopting parent on the EEadopt web site at: http://eeadopt.com/home/heritage/russia/language.htm, *http://eeadopt.com/home/heritage/russia/language.htm* and a downloadable phrasebook at *http://www.kidsave.org/resources.htm*.

Leaving Your Child At Home

Many families have other children at home and leave them with family members or friends while they are overseas. Some families also take their other children with them as it can be an enriching experience. The general consensus is that any child under 4 should be left behind. There simply isn't any point to taking a child as young as that.

You should provide the caretaker with a power of attorney to cover ordinary things as well as a specific medical power to allow for medical treatment of your child if it becomes necessary. A local hospital should be able to show you the form they use.

You should also give the caretaker your pediatrician's name and phone number, any medical conditions, medications or allergies, of your children and the name, policy number and phone number of your health insurance company. The caretaker should be given the health insurance card showing coverage for your child. The caretaker should be given a list of phone numbers of friends and relatives they can call if they have questions.

A map showing where the doctor office is located and the nearest hospital should also be given to the caretaker. Phone numbers of your local car dealer, plumber, electrician and heating and air guy should also be given. Another authorization is one to allow the caretaker to drive your car and to have it repaired.

Now in a real life saving emergency the hospital will treat your child, but it makes things go smoothly if your caretaker can show them all of this information and it is critical for non-emergency situations.

A sample form is as follows:

To whom it may concern:
As the parents of _____, we hereby authorize_____ to approve any and all necessary medical treatment for our child.

Our child is covered by _____Insurance Company, policy number_____, phone number _____. This is a PPO(HMO). The employee member is_____.

Our child's date of birth is_____. She is allergic to - _____. Her pediatrician is _____, at_____, phone number_____. Our child's blood type is _____. Her last hospitalization was on _____for _____.

Our home address is_____. Our home phone number is _____.

Signed (<u>both parents</u>)

Notary

A problem is explaining the trip to young children who may not fully comprehend why you are leaving, but just know Mommy and Daddy will be gone. You might buy a book called *Seeds of Love* and read it to him. Other things you can do include making a map and calendar showing when you plan to leave and when you will return. Give him stars to put on the calendar to mark out the days when you will be home.

Some parents have audiotaped or videotaped several tapes showing them reading stories to the kids, singing favorite poems, songs, and rhymes and telling funny stories. They have also taken brown lunch bags, and for each day away they have written a note on each one for each child. Inside they placed a small toy, treat, or craft activity. Here is an interesting web site on the issue of leaving your child behind: *http://www.adoptiontravel.com/articles/art2.htm*

Employer Benefits

You may wish to use this time to investigate what adoption benefit programs your employer may offer. One of the best is derived from the federal Family Medical Leave Act (FMLA). As always consult with your employer's human resources department or an attorney for specifics, however the law is generally as follows. The FMLA applies to all:

1) Public agencies, including state, local and federal employers, schools, and

2) Private-sector employers who employ 50 or more employees in 20 or more workweeks in the current or preceding calendar year.

To be eligible for FMLA benefits, an employee must:

(1) work for a covered employer;

(2) have worked for the employer for a total of 12 months;

(3) have worked at least 1,250 hours over the previous 12 months;

The 12 months need not be consecutive. The 12 months include any time off spent on workers' compensation, military leave or court leave The 1,250 hours must be actual work hours, not including any type of leave.

A covered employer must grant an eligible employee up to a total of 12 workweeks of unpaid leave during any 12-month period for placement with the employee of a son or daughter for adoption or foster care. Leave for placement for adoption must conclude within 12 months of the placement.

Under some circumstances, employees may take FMLA leave for placement of adoption intermittently—which means taking leave in blocks of time, or by reducing their normal weekly or daily work schedule. This is in the discretion of the employer.

Before (or after) an adopted child is placed, the employee may take FMLA leave for making required arrangements for the placement—to attend counseling sessions, appear in court, consult with an attorney or submit to a physical examination. A father or mother may take FMLA leave for these reasons.

Whether the child arrives by birth or by placement, a mother or father is entitled to FMLA leave to care for the child during the first year. No medical justification is needed—the FMLA leave is guaranteed simply to care for the new child. This particular right to FMLA leave terminates on the first anniversary of the child's birth or placement.

Federal employees can also investigate using sick leave for certain aspects of the adoption process. Check your OPM regulations on the specifics.

Here are some resources:

Employers with Adoption Benefits
http://www.holtintl.org/benefits.shtml

Employers with Adoption Benefits
http://www.adopt.org/workplace/

Adoption Benefits for Fed. Employees
http://www.opm.gov/wrkfam/html/adoption.htm

Military Families
http://www.nmfa.org/FactSheets/Adoption.pdf

Title IV-E

Adoptions are not inexpensive. In addition to sources of funds such as employers, state and federal adoption tax credits, the federal government also provides in all 50 states a reimbursement program called Title IV-E. This program was established to encourage the adoption of children who are otherwise considered hard to adopt. The Federal government pays 60% and the state the remainder. The state controls the program for the most part, subject to certain federal requirements.

The program was originally established for domestic adoptions. At this time, the states have applied the program unevenly to foreign adoptions. Some do and some do not. The program has two types of funds. One type gives recurring funds, which is means tested, and is an ongoing program. More importantly for foreign adoptions, it also gives non-recurring or a one-time payment up to $2000 for expense reimbursement. This part of the program is not means tested. Some states give the whole $2000 and others a smaller amount like $400. Every little bit helps. Many people have obtained nonrecurring funds for their foreign adoption. Check with your accountant, but the $2000 should not be taxable, as it is a welfare benefit.

First check with your state's adoption services unit to see if they apply Title IV to foreign adoptions. At this time it appears that Georgia, South Carolina, Kansas, Alaska, Massachusetts, and Ohio do apply the program to Russian adoptions, but that New York, Michigan and Texas may not. Maryland will also apply it to foreign adoptions, but they throw obstacles at you. Be persistent and file before you adopt. In Maryland call Mrs. Kirby and ask for an adoption reimbursement packet. Her number is 410-767-7625. Don't leave a message, but talk to her in person. Maryland makes it hard for parents, but just persist and make sure you file prior to adopting in Russia. The County Human Services Department or County Children Services Board administers Ohio's program. The initial application must be filed prior to the adoption being finalized and the $2000 reimbursement is issued after the finalization. In Ohio the application should be made in advance of travel, but after the child to be adopted is identified. In Georgia, the county DFACS office intakes the application, but the State DFACS office makes the decision. It should also be filed prior to travel. In Alaska, the filing can be made after travel, but before any re-adoption decree. If you miss the deadline of filing before traveling to Russia, then try the Alaska method of filing before the re-adoption decree and argue that that decree is the final decree.

Remember that you are the only advocate your child has. The state adoption units normally have no idea what an international adoption is or what you have had to go through. If they reject your application, do not give up but appeal and continue to push using all of your resources. Treat this as "found" money, but also money your child deserves. Usually the local country intake person thinks that because maintenance payments do not apply to international adoptions, that nonrecurring payments do not as well. This is completely wrong. Further, the federal agency that runs the program has told the states that they can not change the legibility requirements. Remind them that your child is now a US citizen and a resident of your state and has needs like any other adopted child.Don't let them get away with treating your child as second class. You've fought through infertility, BCIS nonsense, a homestudy, and a foreign country's requirements, so fighting your state should be a piece a cake!

A good explanation can be found at *http://cb1.acf.dhhs.gov/programs/cb/laws/cwpm/policy_dsp.jsp?citID=175.* In this discussion Human Health says that international children may qualify for non-recurring funds as distinquished from maintenance payments.The agency says:

> "Although it is highly improbable that children adopted through an intercountry adoption will meet the title IV-E adoption assistance requirements, States cannot in policy categorically exclude these children from consideration since the statute does not authorize such an exclusion. In the case of reimbursement of nonrecurring expenses of adoption, the State need only to determine that the child is a child with special needs, consistent with section 473(c) of the Act. Accordingly, if a child who is adopted from abroad meets the three criteria for special needs, the State must pay for the nonrecurring adoption expenses for these children, consistent with 45 CFR 1356.41, if requested by the parents prior to the finalization of the adoption."

Section 473 (c) describes special needs as:

> (2) the State had first determined
> (A) that there exists with respect to the child a specific factor or condition (such as his ethnic background, age, or membership in a minority or sibling group, or the presence of factors such as medical conditions or physical, mental, or emotional handicaps) because of which it is reasonable to conclude that such child cannot be placed with adoptive parents without providing adoption assistance under this section or medical assistance under title XIX,

Assuming your state does allow Title IV-E to apply to foreign adoptions then in most states it is necessary to file the application prior to adopting. If you are using the two-trip method then you need to file between the first and second trip. There should be no filing fee involved and the application should not be difficult. After returning from Russia your state will require some documentation explaining your child's health condition and the background of the adoption. This documentation may include a letter from your child's pediatrician and a summary from your agency regarding the adoption, and a copy of the adoption decree. Your agency's letter should include information on how your child was hard to place and efforts in Russia to place the child with a Russian family.(Usually the Databank Release letter will say that or a section in the Court Decree.). This is the purpose of the Title IV program so include how long your child was on the database and available for adoption in Russia, or was with your agency or if your child was specifically referred to any Russian families who may have declined to adopt. You won't have all of this information when you first apply, so just send them the application and few tidbits and stall them until you return.

Generally the process for applying for the non-recurring funds is as follows:

Step 1 is to file the application before leaving for Russia, if you already have a referral or before leaving for the second trip in the event you are under the two-trip process.

Step 2 is for your pediatrician to write up a post adoption medical report (or you can do it and have your pediatrician sign it on his letterhead). Your goal is for the State to recognize that your child has medical or special needs relating to developmental delays, medical issues, nutritional and failure to thrive issues.

Step 3 is that your county sends all of this information to the State's department, which is in charge of the Title IV program. This department will evaluate the information and decide if you have proven your case. You should have administrative appeal rights.

You may need to give the county copies of a few receipts showing that costs greatly exceeded the $2000 non-recurring reimbursement. Most counties also have an early intervention/baby's first program that provides a free evaluation of your child. Sometimes using this evaluation to substantiate your application can be helpful.

Here is a website with a list of each state and how much money they will reimburse for adoptions. *http://www.calib.com/naic/pubs/reim_tab.htm*

Here are some other websites that may be useful:

http://www.fpsol.com/adoption/checklist.html#four-e

http://www.acf.dhhs.gov/programs/cb/laws/fed_reg/fr012500.pdf

Airfares

One thing you can do while you are waiting for a court date is to check on air-fares and airlines. Most people traveling to Moscow will land at Sheremetyevo Airport. This airport serves 82 scheduled airlines—42 international, 34 domestic and six from the Commonwealth of Independent States. The airport is planning to spend $8 million redoing the interior of the 40-year-old, includ-ing the introduction of air conditioning. However, you will likely land at, the international terminal, built for the 1980 Olympics. There are discussions about Aeroflot building its own Sheremetyevo-3.

Most people fly into Russia on either Aeroflot or Delta. There are other air-lines such as Swissair and Lufthansa. I do not recommend Air France. There are many stories from parents of Air France's inability to place bags on the flight to Moscow, if there is just an hour or so connection time in Paris. Czech Airlines from Prague is also not a bad airline. It is part of the Star Alliance Group and has very reasonable prices into Moscow.

Swissair (now just Swiss) always gets very high marks for service, although its bankruptcy, which left thousands of passengers stranded, is unforgivable. There is a nursery run by Swiss in the Zurich Airport that is a wonderful place to go between the two flights and it has changing stations, cribs, loungers, playpens, toys, showers, and someone who will help you with your child while you shower or use the toilet. If you do fly Swiss, tell them in advance when you book about your child and there is the possibility of getting your child a crib on the plane if he/she is less than six months old and you sit in a bulkhead seat. On any flight they will board baby food for you as well. Unlike Delta, there are usually just one or two to other adoptive children on board so it is quieter. You board first and they will help you stow your stuff. They help in other ways as well. This is a good airline if you are a single Mom. If the flight arrives at JFK before the Delta "baby" flight, there will be little waiting at BCIS for IR-3 visa processing since you have so many agents warming up for the Delta rush.

Lufthansa has several adoption benefits including waiving weight limits and change of ticket fees. Just tell them it is for an adoption and see what they can do for you. If you want to transfer, do it in Europe rather than in the US. Flying into JFK for a transfer, just wastes your time.

Generally, airfares are higher from April 1 through October 1 with coach fares around $600 roundtrip in the winter and $900 in the spring and summer. However, specials are not unusual. Sometimes, due to short notice, your fare will be very high such as $1200. One problem in buying tickets is that usually you do not receive a lot of notice prior to traveling. It is rare that someone can actually buy a 21-day advance ticket. There are travel agencies that specialize in Russian travel or you can buy the ticket yourself. Check a lot of places to get a range of prices.

The debate over whether it is better to fly Aeroflot or Delta is similar to the stroller versus Snugglie argument. Whether you did the right thing will only be known after the fact. Delta usually has a flight that leaves at 6pm in the evening from JFK in New York and arrives in Moscow at 11:30am in the morning. The actual flight takes about10 hours. This can help with jet lag. You will also need to buy a ticket for your child. It is usually 10% of the fare and is cheaper to buy it in the States rather than in Moscow. Ask your agent about buying the child a round trip ticket originating in Moscow and when you return to the States just throw the JFK-SVO portion of the ticket away. This is usually far cheaper than buying the ticket from the States. If you do it originating from JFK, the airline may label the child a no-show and cancel the return. If you book coach, you might check on using your frequent flyer miles to upgrade to first class for your return. Unlike Aeroflot, Delta's return flights are always very crowded.

In addition to flying from JFK, Aeroflot also flies from Washington, San Francisco, Seattle and Chicago. Aeroflot usually charges just a nominal fee to change tickets. This can be important as a delay of a day or two on the return is not unusual and indeed you should give yourself a cushion of an extra day when planning your return. Aeroflot's web site is *www.aeroflot.com*. At the moment, Aeroflot's fleet consists of 27 Boeing 737s, 767s, 777s and Airbus 310s, along with more than 100 Russian aircraft, some of which are grounded. By December 2005, it will comprise 18 Airbus 319/320s and nine Boeing 767s through different leasing arrangements. Around 50 Russian planes will remain. Aeroflot's choice to buy or lease Airbus planes was reciprocated by France's decision to support Russia's illogical Kalingrad plans. There were other *quid pro quos* as well.

Swiss Air sometimes has less expensive fares and fewer charges if you change tickets, but it does land in Moscow later in the afternoon. It always gets high marks for service. Swissair also will give you their lowest fare without restrictions if you tell them you are adopting from Russia. Sometimes airlines, such as Northwest or British Air, will advertise an adoption discount. The problem is that the discount is off the full refundable fare and can be more than a regular economy ticket with restrictions. So don't just go for the "discount" before checking other fares.

Aeroflot flies the same Boeing type airplanes, as does Delta. A lot of people fly Aeroflot and sit in business class. It is more expensive but comfortable. May even be cheaper than Delta. If you fly business class in Aeroflot, there is a First Class lounge in the Moscow airport that is very nice. The flight attendants speak English and the service is fine. Aeroflot has been criticized for allowing smoking and drinking on its planes. Smoking used to be allowed in the last 6 seats in the back of the plane and not up front. However, Aeroflot is now taking the position that no smoking is allowed on its flights from the US. The FAA also has enacted a rule to that effect. Still, the smoking culture is very engrained in Russia and it may be a while before the practice of not smoking is universally followed. One benefit to having the smokers in the back though is that they can be very helpful in opening the bathroom door and pulling down the diaper changing shelf! If smoke is really a problem then try to sit in business class or in the front of coach.

Another benefit in flying Aeroflot, in addition to it usually being cheaper than Delta, is that it is less crowded going over and returning. Veteran travelers will wait until the plane levels off then immediately find an empty 3 seat row in the middle to lie down in as their bed for the night. It can be akin to musical chairs soon after takeoff. Aeroflot is probably better if you are adopting older children, as they may feel more comfortable surrounded by Russian speaking passengers. The flight attendants are also willing to talk with your child.

Check the airlines' policy on changing tickets. Some allow a change with a fee and some charge no fee. The odds of having to change your return ticket by a day or two are fairly high due to the vagaries of traveling abroad and the unexpected that sometimes occurs in the adoption process. Delta used to allow you to change tickets without penalty. However, Delta has instituted a "no waivers, no favors" policy and strictly applies its penalty charges. In this regard, it is not adoption friendly. Delta does have an "adoption discount." As with all such discounts, it may not last. Delta will charge the restricted fare for an unrestricted ticket. They sometimes require you to show a copy of your 171H at the ticket counter. All ticket agents do not know about it. Keep insisting. If you run into a roadblock, have the agent call the Delta Promotions desk at 800-325-7441. In order to get the Delta adoption discount, call between regular working hours Monday through Friday. That is when the most knowledgeable call center people are working. If the adoption rate seems outrageous, then ask the Delta person to look for "GRS topic 10, at page 48," where at one time a very friendly adoption rate used to be located.

Always ask anyone, whether it be an airline or hotel, if they have an adoption discount or waiver, when faced with an expensive charge. Of course, many times the airlines "adoption rate" far exceeds their regular excursion fare so beware. Sometimes the discounted "adoption rate" is just hype. Another tip when buying a ticket is that it is usually cheaper to fly roundtrip from the same city rather than different cities. Also, taking a train which is part of the Trans-Siberian system is not a bad way to travel domestically and can be cheaper (and safer) than flying as well as giving you time to recover from jet lag.

Some airlines stop over in Amsterdam. If you spend the night in Amsterdam on your return from Russia, you will need an overnight visa for your child from the immigration office in the Amsterdam airport before you go through passport control to leave the airport. As Americans, you do not need a visa. The visa does not cost anything and will take 20-45 minutes to get. You turn in the overnight visa at the passport checking station at the airport when you fly out. Do not waste time and money getting the transit visa from the Dutch Embassy in Moscow. The temporary visa office in the airport is located just before passport control. You will see off to the side a counter with a sign for immigration. The officer is helpful and your child will receive a transit visa good for 24 hours. You just show them your passport, your child's passport and your airline ticket confirming your departure. It only takes a few minutes. Now the passport control person is not very forthcoming with the idea that all you have to do is step over to the immigration desk to get this visa. Just ignore him and go to the immigration window. After passport control, you can pick up your luggage. Frankfurt works the same way. If you are merely changing planes or staying at the **Mercure** in the Amsterdam airport, you do not have to go through passport control or have an overnight visa for your Russian born child. If you are staying at the **Mecure** hotel in the airport and have any checked baggage, you will have to pass through passport control to get the baggage.

Amsterdam airport has nice baby care centers with sinks, changing tables, cribs and playpens. You should definitely ask where these rooms are located, as they are clean and quiet. Amsterdam airport also has an attached mall that stays open almost all night.

For those flying to Perm or Ekaterinburg, Lufthansa has a flight on Monday and Thursday from Frankfurt that is direct. This flight allows you to skip Moscow. They also have a direct one to Nizhny Novogrod. Of course, you will still have to fly out of Moscow on your return from the court trip. Now this is not true if you are adopting from Vladivostok. You don't have to go out of Moscow if your agency employs a courier service. Magadan Airlines used to fly direct from Seattle to Vladivostok. Some families prefer taking Singapore Air from San Francisco to Seoul then Seoul Airlines to Vladivostok.

If you have the time, you can also fly to some of the Scandinavian cities and spend the night, then continue with a short hop to Moscow the next day. Many people also like to stop over in Amsterdam on the return. It breaks up the trip and allows you to get about 8 hours of sleep in a hotel before making the next leg back to the States. Your child will need an overnight visa, which should be easy to get at the airport.

If your travel agency has the right connections, it can get you into the VIP lounge at the Sheremetyevo-2 Airport in Moscow. The cost is about $175 per person. If you have the budget, this is the first class way of flying into and out of Russia. When you arrive at the Moscow airport, someone will meet you as you get off the plane. She'll take you to a nice lounge. You'll wait 15 minutes or so, and she will take care of everything. Then you will be on your way and out of the Moscow airport.

There are actually two kinds of VIP services at SVO International airport in Moscow—regular VIP where you are picked up at the exit from the airplane and taken to the VIP lounge to wait while your passports/visa are stamped and your baggage is delivered to you and there is so-called "VIP-light" or "Fast Track" where you are picked up at the exit from the airplane and taken to the baggage claim area without waiting in "line" for passport clearance. The second option is cheaper. Check the *aerotour.ru* website for details but it usually runs about $60 per person on arrival and $50 on departure. They meet you at the arrival with your names on a sign and take you to the front of the line. You are in and out in less than 10 minutes, rather than 1-2 hours. On departure from Moscow, you can use the same service or use a skycap. You can find more about the VIP service at *http://www.go-russia.com/vinnetou.htm* and *http://www.awintl.com/travel/vip.html.*

If you give your bags to a skycap, make sure you negotiate the price before you hand him a single bag. It should be around $20.He will also take you to the front of the lines.

On your return flight, you may wish to ask for a bulkhead seat, as that will give you more room. If adopting an infant, ask for a bassinet. Returning Delta flights are usually jammed with people. If you have an infant, you will be holding her on your lap during the entire flight. If you use Delta, you may wish to consider buying a seat for your child so as to be able to lie her down. On Aeroflot, there is more room. Also, Delta no longer will allow you to walk the aisles with your child. This can be a major inconvenience.

Now flying domestically is a different story. If leaving from Moscow, you will fly out from a different airport than from the international airport you flew into. You will have to buy tickets once you reach Russia or your facilitator can buy them ahead of time. You should buy a first class ticket or business class, not coach or economy. Make sure your travel agency or facilitator understands this. The domestic airlines range from terrific to frightening. A good one seems to be TransAero. There are 20 or so domestic airlines in Russia and Aeroflot is just one of them. But it is the biggest and the safest. Among Russian airlines, Domodedovo, which has a fleet of 24 aircraft, ranks No. 4 for domestic routes by the number of passengers carried and No. 9 for international routes. The company is the internal freight route leader. If you are feeling fatalistic, then go to this web site and read the history of Russian airline safety: *http://www.airsafe.com/events/airlines/fsu.htm*

If you are taken to Vnukovo a/k/a VKO (one of the domestic airports in Moscow) for your flight to Rostov or anywhere else and are going to be at Vnukovo for at least an hour, tell your coordinator you want to be placed in the business lounge. The business lounge costs about $8 per person and is well worth it. They pre-check your bags, and the lounge is safe, clean, air conditioned, and comfortable. The remainder of Vnukovo is downright strange, loud, dirty and very hot and stuffy in the summer. You can even check-in through the business lounge as early as you want, unlike regular check-in which is and hour and thirty minutes prior to departure, not a second earlier. The business lounge at any of the domestic airports is a nice place to wait. They also make sure you do not miss your flight! That is particularly important if you do not speak a word of Russian. Another place to wait in VKO airport, which is even a lot better than the business lounge, is the VIP lounge that is attached to the international part of the airport. If you pay the extra $45, you will be treated like a king. They even feed you there (included in the cost)— snacks, coffee, etc. Then they take you to your plane. When you arrive back to Moscow the service is free of charge. They even send a minivan right to the airplane and take you to the VIP lounge.

Domodedevo (DME) is another domestic airport, although several European airlines (Swiss, and Lufthansa) now fly directly into it. As a result it has been transformed from a Soviet airport with no English spoken, to a real international airport. Signs are now in English and it is easy to find your check-in desk and boarding gate. Customs and visa check take much less time than at SVO. At SVO it can take 30 minutes and very often, up to 2 hrs. DME is very clean and bright while Sheremetyevo is drab. Rather than flying into SVO, consider the advantages of DME. You need to allow yourself at least an hour and fifteen minutes for a taxi between DME and SVO. The Swiss flight is usually never full and the seats are nice. Customs and passport control is really short as compared with SVO.

Most Russian domestic airlines have reserved seats. You reserve it when you purchase the tickets. Always ask your facilitator to get the most desired seats, and don't mind if it costs a little extra, it is worth it. Aeroflot assigns seats upon check-in. The earlier you arrive at the airport for check-in—the better chance you have to get the seat you like.

There are four domestic airports located outside Moscow. They are fly east, west, north and south. Do not be surprised if the pilot helps with loading the baggage and if all the passengers begin to smoke and drink as soon as the plane takes off. The domestic airport's bathrooms are just a hole in the floor. Be prepared! At the domestic airport you will hear the sound of hundreds of bags having tape or a saran type of material wrapped around them. It can be a bit startling. You first carry your bags to the weigh in where they will assess you an overweight charge. They do not seem to care that the overweight is because of donations. This is another reason the train is better. They will want to weigh your carryon as well. The domestic airports strictly enforce (as a revenue measure) the weight limits. The weight limit is around 40 kilos per person and is less than is allowed for international flights. The overweight charge is paid in rubles so be sure to have changed some money before leaving for the domestic airport. The overweight charge usual comes to about 1% of the ticket price per kilo. So if your ticket is $100, you might pay $1 per overweight kilo. One tip is that if you have already met your Moscow homestay host, then leave some items with her that you will not need until your return. This will save some space and weight.

Unless you have paid for business or VIP service, when your flight is called you will walk out on the tarmac and climb aboard the plane. If you don't speak Russian, while you are checking in, look around you. The people checking in with you will be on your flight and you will feel better and know you are on the right plane if you remember one person and look for them when you are boarding the plane. Drinking is very prevalent on the domestic planes and if you are taking one of those frightening kinds of airlines, you will start drinking too! Now there are some domestic airlines that are just fine and you will think you are back in the States. You just have to find one of those and hope it flies to your destination. When you land you will bless your driver and coordinator as you have made it! The usual arrival at a region's airport will have you stepping off the plane onto the middle of the tarmac and then crammed into a small bus that takes you to the terminal. It may remind you of flying into Dulles.

Even if you did not sign up for VIP service flying out of Moscow, when you fly back, if VIP service is offered, take it! VIP service means that your bags are checked by people who care, that you get to stay in a relatively clean and quiet waiting room, and you get on the plane before most people. It is definitely worth the couple of extra dollars. The airport in Perm offers a great VIP service for $12, which includes breakfast.

It is difficult to get the best deal to Russia without using a travel agent. You can research the fares yourself, but a travel agent can sometimes get you special adoption rates and have the ticket changing charge waived. There some travel agencies that specialize in adoption travel to Russia such as Rainier World Travel, Inc. in Renton, WA. 1-800-432-4456, All Ways International in New York, (212) 947-0505, *http://www.awintl.com*, Federal Travel in Florida 1-800-551-8666, John Nairn at Far Horizons Travel (formerly Global Travel) in California at 1-800-574-0875 (use John only). Also, Red Star Travel in Seattle at 206-522-5995 (*www.travel2russia.com*, Peace Travel Service at *http://www.go-russia.com* and see *http://www.etn.nl/*

If you have confidence in an airline consolidator, you can try booking through them. Some people have used Airfare Busters at 713-961-5109 or 407-391-9560. Just remember that if you use discount tickets or "buddy passes" you may have a difficult time flying out the day you want or getting your ticket changed. With "buddy passes" in particular you may have to wait several days in Moscow before being able to get on the plane and the additional hotel cost may eat up any savings you gained from using the passes.

The National Council for Adoption sometimes has information about special fares and can be reached at 202-328-1200.

Visas

In order to go to Russia, or to any of the FSU countries you will need a visa. You receive a Russian one from the Russian Consulates such as in San Francisco or New York or the Embassy in Washington. Go to the FSU's consulates for theirs. You will need a visa for each person over the age of 16 traveling to Russia from the United States. Visas can be single entry or double entry, tourist or business. Single entry just means that the person will be entering Russia one time.

There is no official federal law forbidding you to come on tourist visas to adopt children. Many families have. However, each region has different rules some of which are "unpublished." If there were a federal law about it there would not be such confusion. Your agency will tell you whether the region in which you are adopting requires the parents to travel on a double entry business visa or single entry tourist. St Petersburg seems to allow tourist visas for adoption, but Rostov and Moscow apparently do not.

Visas are $100 for a single entry or double. This does not include what you may have to pay for an "invitation" and for expedited service. It is not unusual to pay $150 for complete visa service. Families used to travel on tourist visas, as they were good for up to three months. However, now they are only good for one month, so families have been turning more toward 3-month business visas. This may change since it now takes a lot longer to obtain a business visa.

Notwithstanding, in many regions parents can travel on tourist visas both times. Tourist visa invitations are very easy to get. Ask your agency if tourist visas are accepted in your region and if you will have time to get them. You need letters of invitation for tourist visas. Two papers are required for tourist visa; a "voucher" and a "confirmation".

Some agencies will arrange for the visa and others leave it up to the families to obtain them. There are also companies that specialize in obtaining such visas and for a small fee will assist families. These are very helpful when you have only a short notice to travel. The rules on visas have increased in complexity. The San Francisco Russian Consulate has a very good outline of the requirements.

All business visa invitations now have to go through OVIRs. It takes a lot longer. There is no 1 or 3 day service as it was before with the Ministry of Foreign Affairs. All business visa applicants are checked by FSB (branch of former KGB) prior to approval. Normal processing times for visa invitations in Moscow are 20 to 25 days for single and double entry business visas for a 1 or 3-month stay. It is about 35 days for multiple entry business visa invitations. The visa is obtained from the Consulate. This is probably diplomatic reciprocity for the US making the Russians go through US Homeland Security for theirs. Tit for tat. This extra step has slowed down the issuance of a business visa so do not wait to the last minute to apply.

You should put "adoption" down on the application as the reason for travel. Always check first with the Russian Consulate or Embassy regarding the latest requirements. Do not worry about any medical insurance question on the application; none is required of US citizens unless they age staying longer than 6 months.

If you are obtaining the visa yourself, call the Consulate or Embassy to verify the information required. There are different rules as to what's required depending on which Russian Consulate you apply through. Most Consulates now require you to submit your original passport, although Seattle appears to still allow you to just submit a copy. Call before applying if you have any questions. The Consulate in San Francisco used to be faster at processing visa applications than the Embassy in Washington, however recently the Russians have tried to standardize the process at two weeks. Expedited service is still available, but at a higher price. If possible, try to obtain your visa from the San Francisco or Seattle Consulates before using the ones in New York and Washington.

As soon as you receive the visa, proofread it very carefully to make sure the names and dates are accurate. You can see what a visa looks like and where certain information is written at *http://www.waytorussia.net/RussianVisa/Info.html.*

All male US citizens aged 16-45 in addition to the standard visa question-naire form 95 also need to submit a 2-page supplement. This supplement form asks the same questions that the US asks Russians who want a visa to the US. Indeed, the Russians simply scanned in the US form and changed the heading. There is always a reciprocity issue with the Russians. Call it national pride or tit for tat. This supplement form can be downloaded from the embassy and consulate sites and asks the same silly questions that the US does. These questions asks about military service, participation in military conflicts, college or university degrees, full name of your mother and father, your two previous employers, all professional, social, and charitable organizations you belong to and a list of countries visited in the last 10 years. It is questionable whether either country has any intention if actually checking this information. Rumor has it that the same US bureaucrat that thought up these questions also wants to know who you kissed in the second grade. But that is just a rumor.

Recently the United States has begun to require the citizens of Russia and other countries to have face-to-face interviews when applying for nonimmigrant visas.This will delay visas for these citizens by months as no additional funding for new personnel is being given to US Consulates to meet this mandate. No one wants to think about what might happen if Russia invokes its tit-for-tat policy in this instance.

You will need to keep the visa in your carry-on to show Russian immigration when you land in Moscow. You will also need to show it when you leave. Therefore, do not pack the visa document in your checked luggage.

The Seattle Russian Consulate has an excellent web site for visa information and down loading of the application form. The site is: http://www.russia-travel.com/visas.htm The San Francisco Consulate site is also very informative at *http://www.vldbros.com/consul/english/main.htm*. The Russian Embassy is at *http://www.russianembassy.org*. Another source of information regarding visas is at Peace Travel Service's website at *http://www.go-russia.com*. Peace is one of several companies offering a visa service.

If traveling to Ukraine, use the tourist visa application form and your reason for traveling is "adoption." You can use your passport number, rather than social security when filling out line 7.Line 9 with be U.S. Issuing Authority. Line 15 is "adoption." Line 16 can be "30-45 days." Line 17 is ballpark date, as it doesn't matter as far as the validity of the visa. Line 20 under "private person" should be your facilitator/translator and not your US Agency. Line 21 is "regional cities." Always check with the Ukrainian Consulate for the latest visa information.

Calling from Russia

You should also investigate how to call from Russia, as you are likely to want to tell someone back home your good news as well as the exact time you will be returning home.

You should be able to use all of your major phone company calling cards if you are in Moscow. Always check with your carrier prior to leaving for Russia on rates and access. In some Regions it is difficult to call the US. Unless you are on a special international plan you can expect it to cost about $3.20 a minute although some hotels like the Marriott will charge you about $8 a minute and the President $6 a minute from your room. Some of the hotels have business centers where you can buy a pre-paid card and call at a much less expensive rate. Parents at the Marriott have used the lobby phone along with the MCI international calling plan. You dial a local Moscow number and then call home to the U.S. for about 24 cents/minute.

The actual calling process is not very difficult, at least from Moscow. Be aware that some hotels use pulse dialing, rather than touch-tone. This may cause difficulty when trying to reach the access number. If so, turn the phone over and see if there is a little switch to change to tone or buy a "pocket pipper" from Radio Shack. By the way, the Marriott and President do not charge for local calls and the Ukraina charges just a penny or two.

Not all phones can make long-distance calls, but for those that do, dialing 8 will get you a long-distance line. Thus, to dial another region of Russia, dial 8, wait for the new dial tone, and then dial the rest of your number. For international dialing, dial 8, wait for the tone, then dial 10, then the country code and the rest of your number.

For example, to call the U.S. number (123)-456-7890 from Russia, you would dial 8-(**wait for dial done**)-10-1-123-456-7890.

When you are calling to Moscow or other regions of Russia where the area code starts with a "0", you do not omit this first zero when dialing from outside Russia. For example, to call the Moscow number (095)-123-4567 from U.S. you would dial 011-7-095-123-4567.

If you want to call from Moscow to United States using AT&T dial the local access number of 755-5042. To call from St. Petersburg dial 325-5042. You will hear an English voice prompt which will ask you for the number you are calling. Just dial the US area code and number. You will then be prompted for your calling card number and PIN. To call from outside Moscow dial 8 095 then the Moscow access code. If calling outside St. Petersburg, dial 8 812, then the St. Petersburg local access number. Since you are dialing long distance to Moscow or St. Petersburg, there will be additional charges. If calling from Yekaterinburg, Khabarovsk, Novosibirsk, Rostov-on-Don, or Samara dial 8, wait for a second dial tone then dial 10 800 110 1011.Whoever you call in America will hear an echo as you are connecting through a satellite. MCI's access number from Moscow if you are using Rostelcom is 747-3322. If using SovIntel then it is 960-2222.

A cheaper method to call is to buy a prepaid international calling card. These are available at most stores such as Walmart or Sams. Sam's Club 1000 minutes converts to about 112 minutes calling from Russia. Call for access instructions before leaving US. By using one of these, you know ahead of time what the cost will be. You won't get tagged for hidden charges when you return to the States. Check with the carrier in case you need to activate it before you go.

Some carriers like AT&T and MCI also have special international plans that you can sign up for before you go. They cost $3 a month but allow you to call your home for around $.70 a minute. However, if you call some place other than your home, then very high rates apply. After you return from Russia, you can always cancel the plan and the $3 monthly charge. If your folks live within your same local calling area, you can set your home phone to call forwarding and this way dial your parents at the low rate. Just an idea. When calling with your calling card it may be possible to save the connect fee by pushing # to end a call instead of hanging up. Then you can dial another number. Check with your carrier about this before you leave.

Since rates and programs change frequently, you should always verify the method you will use and the rate you will pay prior to leaving. You don't want any surprises on your phone bill when you return.

You can also buy an international phone card while in Russia such as a "Takso-phone" card. These cards are sold in kiosks (where newspapers and magazines are sold) and at metro stations. They come in different denominations and seem to work almost everywhere. It seems far cheaper buying a card in Russia than even using the prepaid cards bought in the US. You may be able to call the USA from Russia for 20 cents a minute (from Ukraine—25 cents) using Rinotel Phone cards. These appear to have access numbers in many of the larger cities. More information can be found at http://www.go-russia.com/rinotel.htm. Others are at http://www.ldpost.com and select Euromama phone card—4.5 cents a minute to Moscow, no connection charges, no monthly fee, and a toll free number. Or Pallada Telecom International phone card—http://www.call-o-call.com (6 cents a minute to Moscow, 14 cents to any other city in Russia). Just do some research.

You can also buy the card in the city you will be staying. If you stay in Rostov, then buy one when you get to Rostov rather than buying one in

Moscow. For the first call have your facilitator with you as the auto-instructions can be in Russian only. Get him to explain to you how to make a call.

Even cheaper than calling is to use the Internet cafes that have sprung up throughout Russia. Usually each city's main post office has Internet access. There is a cyber-café in the underground mall by the Kremlin. Just note that the FSB (former KGB) has forced most Russian ISPs to install surveillance software, just like the FBI has done here with their Carnivore program.

Some families have even rented a cell phone in Russia. They work in the larger cities like Moscow and Krasnador. Russia primarily uses GSM. Usually for incoming and outgoing local calls you pay $ 0.20 a minute. Outside of the major cities, you will pay a roaming charge of around $ 1 to $ 1.50 a minute. One such company that parent's have rented from is a company called Rent-a-Phone, which is based in the UK. The company's toll free number is 1.888.309.8560. Other parents have rented this type of phone through American Express Platinum Service. The price is $6 / day or $25 / week with 2 weeks of rental. You receive free shipping to and from your home and $25 free usage. The phone is rented out of the UK and there is someone available 24/7 to help. The Russian calls were $2.99/minute in and out to the States. If you rent these phones be sure to read all of the fine print. For example, the voice mail costs can get expensive and you may want to just turn off that function. These rented phones usually come with an extra battery and compatible charger. Buying a phone card in Russia is probably a lot cheaper. You might be surprised to learn that some of the cell phone systems are actually American owned partnered with a Russian landline company

Since Russia still has mostly rotary phones, you may want to buy a pipper if you need to use tones. You can buy a pocket pipper (to use with old rotary phones in Russia) at any Radio Shack.

Here are certain Moscow numbers you may want to bookmark:

American Express
21A Sadovaya-Kudrinskaya Ul.; Tel: 755-9024; Fax: 755-9004

Western Union
Tel: 797-2194

Internet Access

If you want to access the Internet in Russia or any FSU country from your laptop you will need a phone jack adapter as well as an electrical adapter. An interesting article on laptops and Russia can be found at *http://www.epinions.com/trvl-review-4654-AC20686-3A369E71-prod1.*

There are Internet or Cyber cafés in every medium to large city in Russia and in every main post office. In Moscow you can find it in an Internet café at the glitzy Manezh underground Mall near the Kremlin. The computer may be set up for Cyrillic, but you should be able to switch it to English fonts. Test your computer at home as to how to switch between languages. It should not be difficult. Another cyber café in Moscow is located below Planet Hollywood.

Most new Moscow hotels and refurbished hotels have business centers where you can access the Internet for between $7.50 and $9 per 15 minutes. It may pay to write offline first. In Rostov, the Internet cafés charge around $6 per hour. That is in both the Internet cafe and the business center at the Hotel Intourist.

If you will be using email, it is suggested that you set up a web email account at Yahoo or Hotmail rather than risk revealing your password to your regular account on AOL, Earthlink, or MSN.

A laptop is useful for watching DVDs and CDs and for writing email messages that you can take on a disk to the Internet café. It is a lot of trouble to lug around. You can always take a small DVD only player. Another argument against taking a laptop is that you can have your child's photos developed, then scanned at an Internet Café, then send them to your IA doctor for review. Record the make, model and serial number of each electronic item you bring so in the event anything is stolen you can make a claim with your homeowners insurance policy.

Of course, many people like taking their laptop. You can easily buy an Internet pre-paid card in Russia. It gives you a local phone number, user ID and password. The cost is around $12 for 50 hours. You may be able to then connect from your hotel room. You will need to have a phone jack adapter (*www.laptoptravel.com*) and may need to change your settings so you don't have to wait for a dial tone before dialing. Don't forget the phone cord! And don't forget an adapter!

Russia-on-Line (ROL) sells pre-paid cards and has local access numbers in many cities in Russia. You pay approximately $ 1 an hour for internet access from any place—hotel (beware of hotel charges for local calls!), or apartment or airport. You can buy pre-paid cards in many banks or magazine kiosks in Moscow or you can order them online.

Some parents take both a camcorder and a digital camera, so they have a back up in case one didn't work. Some digital cameras will also take short video clips. If you take a camcorder it needs to be one that can save MPEG files to what is called a memory stick (if it's a Sony). Other brands may use compact flash cards or some other removable media. A 256-megabyte card is enough memory to store 150 or more of the highest-quality images, or 400 or more at good quality. If your digital camera can shoot video clips onto a removable media (memory stick or compact flash card), that is probably the easiest way to go. Either way you will also need to take a "card reader" which is a small inexpensive ($30) device that hooks up to a computer's USB (Universal Serial Bus) interface. SanDisk is just one kind of card reader. There are others. If you take a laptop, you can download the files onto a CD and take that to an Internet Cafe. If you don't want to take a laptop, the computers at the Internet Cafes usually support USB and you can just plug the card reader directly into the computer at the Internet Cafe. The tech support person there can help you get the file off your card and attaché it as e-mail.

If you go to an Internet Café, make sure you take your card reader's CD driver disk. This is key. Copy the MPEG file off the card and attach it the e-mail. One thing to remember is that video files are large. A 1 minute 15 second video is over 1 megabyte. Some ISP accounts (Yahoo! and AOL) have size limitations. Try to get one that does not. You can also break up the video into separate emails. Transmission should not take very long and your IA doctor can then download the file. Definitely practice making and sending files before you go. This will allow you judge the size of the file. It is also suggested that you practice with Cyrillic fonts in case you run into a computer that has the regular Windows icons, but does not have English language versions. You can muddle your way through, but if you have a cheat sheet, it helps.

Finally, some cameras allow you to download pictures and a 5 second movie onto a floppy disk bypassing all the connection issues.

If sending video sounds complicated, don't worry. Your written observations of your child may be more valuable to the IA doctor. Also, many parents take an instamatic camera so they can print out pictures and have them scanned in at the Internet Café. This way they can have the ultimate back up in case none of this techie stuff works.

Money in Eastern Europe

Eastern Europeans will not accept American money that is dirty, torn, creased across the face, stamped in ink with a bank stamp, or marred in any way. The US Embassy will also not exchange any money that looks like that either. Their theory, right or wrong, is that dirty looking money is easier to forge.

It is recommended that you visit your local bank a few days before you travel and ask them for clean, brand new bills in 100s and 50s. You may also need a few 20s and 5s for tips. You need a $1 for the soda machine at the US Embassy. Emphasize that the bills need to be crisp. The bank will give you bills and allow you to proof them. Just give back the ones that don't meet your specification. Your bank should not give you any problems with this request. It is better to go in the morning and early in the week rather than late on a Friday afternoon. You can also iron your money and this makes them fairly crisp.

By the way, it is rumored that after the United States, Russia has more $20 and $100 bills floating through its economic system than any other country.

You can wire money to Russia through Western Union. You wire dollars but receive rubles on the other end. There use to be very few ATMs in Russia and even then only in St. Petersburg and Moscow. This has changed somewhat and the number of ATMs in St Petersburg and Moscow has increased greatly. The screens have a Russian/English option. Try to use ones inside a building for safety reasons. Be discrete. Just remember that you will not have much time to go running off to an ATM. You will be on the go from the moment your feet hit Russia. The ATMs do not allow you to withdraw in dollars, but in rubles.

Neither Travelers Checks nor credit cards are accepted in most places in Russia or the FSU. St. Petersburg and Moscow seem to be the only places that accept these and even then only by the largest hotels or banks. Visa is accepted in a few stores and hotels in Moscow, however you have to be careful to review the receipt before you sign in case they add something to it. You can also obtain cash advances in rubles from hotel money exchange places using Visa with your PIN number. You have to be careful that the exchange rate used by the stores and foreign currency exchange places is one with which you agree, but nevertheless it is a relatively painless way of obtaining additional funds. Do not use a direct debit card. You do not want to give anyone access to your checking account. Just use a regular visa card. You should never allow your credit card to be taken out of your sight by the cashier. Skimming the magnetic strip is a well-known practice. Before taking your card overseas, find out from your card issuer what the money conversion fee will be. It can add a tidy sum to your bill and be a surprise.

Since the Russian financial system is fickle. There may be times when you cannot receive any money using a credit card advance or a wire. The best advice is to still carry American cash along with your ATM and Visa card. There has been a problem with the ATM system in Russia so do not rely solely on that means of obtaining funds.

There is no point in trying to change some money into rubles before you go. First, not only is it quite difficult to find rubles, but secondly, you really don't need any until you land at the Moscow airport. At the airport there is an exchange booth on the second floor. The rate is not the best you could get, but we are only taking about a few dollars difference. Generally Moscow has a better exchange rate than in the regions. Here is a website with the current dollar/ruble exchange: *http://finance.yahoo.com/m5?a=1&s=USD&t=RUB*

Shots for Travel

Usually it is recommended to get the Hepatitis A and B shots, plus a tetanus/diphtheria and a polio booster. The Hepatitis vaccine is not cheap and you should check with your insurance company regarding coverage. Insurance companies may reimburse the vaccines if your doctor codes it for contact risk/exposure. If they deny coverage, appeal their decision and emphasize that you are adopting a child of unknown risks from a country with a high prevalence of hepatitis and that this is a small preventive cost compared with them paying to cure you. Also, tell them that the CDC recommends these shots. Push them on this. Your regular doctor or the foreign travel office of a hospital should be able to give these shots. Your local health department may also give them. Most health departments have these vaccines available at reduced cost. Shop around in order to get the lowest price. For more information on vaccines for adoption travel, see the January 2001 issue of Adoption Medical News.

The Hepatitis A vaccine is two shots and the Hepatitis B is three, although you obtain the majority of the Hepatitis B benefits with the first two shots. You should talk with your doctor before receiving these shots.

Hepatitis A is much more contagious than is Hepatitis B, and is spread through contaminated water, contaminated food, or the mouth or fecal excretions of a person/baby/toddler infected with this virus. Thus, it can be communicated by sharing food, drinking unsafe water (ice in drinks, as well as water that is not boiled or bottled), eating food washed in unsafe water (including lettuce, uncooked vegetables and unpeeled fruits), and even by changing the diaper of an infected infant without using good hand washing.

This vaccine is effective for a short term if given one month prior to travel abroad. If multiple trips are planned, it is suggested that an individual have a booster 6 to 12 months after the initial dose, as this will avoid the need for a repeat booster prior to all future trips. This vaccine should not be given to children less than two years of age. The Hepatitis A vaccine has replaced the need for the gamma-globulin shot, which was formerly given to most adults prior to international travel.

The Hepatitis B vaccine is given three times, the second one at one month after the first dose, and the third shot four to six months after the first dose. Although the risk of exposure for families while traveling is probably low, this is an important vaccine that should be given in the event of an accidental exposure to an adult or child with Hepatitis B, especially if that child becomes a member of your family (since it may take more than four months for an adult to become immune from the vaccine). At the very least, the primary caregiver should receive these shots.

Although wild polio has been eradicated in North America (some vaccine-acquired polio has been seen from the polio vaccine that is given by mouth in individuals who have a compromised immune system), polio is still seen in developing nations. It is recommended that all adults traveling to a developing nation receive an inactivated polio vaccine (IPV) to lessen the risk of acquiring polio abroad. This should be done even if the polio vaccine was given during childhood, as it will serve as a booster dose. The oral polio vaccine (OPV) should not be given to adults because of the risk of acquiring polio from the vaccine itself in individuals whose immunity may have waned. If children are traveling abroad for the adoption, they should also receive an additional dose of the polio vaccine, preferably as IPV. This means that they should have a total of five doses of polio vaccine by age 4 rather than the recommended four doses. Adults that receive a booster before travel do not routinely need a dose before each trip. Ask your doctor about polio boosters.

Diphtheria and tetanus are still seen in other countries. Adults should have a Td booster every ten years to give continuing protection against these diseases. Since none of us can predict what injuries may occur while we are abroad, it is recommended that adults have a tetanus shot booster if it has been more than five years since the last shot. This lessens the chance that a tetanus shot may be needed while overseas.

Measles, mumps and rubella are childhood illnesses that were once common, and have lessened in frequency due to the MMR vaccine, now given during childhood. All adults born in or after 1957 should have a booster shot for these illnesses, unless one is absolutely sure that they had all three of these illnesses. If the history is unclear about a past history of these diseases, it is not harmful to repeat this vaccine. Most adults born prior to 1957 had these three diseases during childhood, so it is unlikely that they need the vaccine.

There is now an effective shot to protect against chicken pox, which can cause significant illness in adults. The shot, given in two doses (the second 6 weeks after the first), is thought to be fairly protective against this disease, lessening the illness if an individual does acquire chicken pox. A blood test can be done if an adult's history is unclear, although the shot is not harmful if given in someone who had the disease and did not know it. This shot, as well as the MMR, should not be given to pregnant women.

For individuals traveling during the fall and winter months, it is recommended that they have the influenza vaccine.

Always consult your doctor prior to taking any of these shots. See these helpful websites for additional information:
http://www.cdc.gov/travel/easteurp.htm and
http://members.aol.com/jaronmink/immunize.htm For more information on vaccines for adoption travel, see the January 2001 issue of Adoption Medical News. Check with *http://www.adoptionnews.org/pub3.html* on how to order back issues.

If you have a medical condition or are simply nervous about being sick in a foreign country, then you might investigate buying overseas medical insurance. This is available at AEA/SOS for around $55. Their phone number is 800-523-8930. They have a website at *http://www.intsos.com/* Also, for AAA+ members, there is evacuation insurance at little or no charge. Check with AAA on the specifics. The only caveat is that you have to have already been an AAA+ member for 3+ years to qualify for the coverage. You cannot simply purchase or upgrade to AAA+ just to get the medivac coverage. Last year, the AAA+ coverage included $25,000 per person for evacuation. AAA has a special international number to call if you need that service in an emergency. You must call your regional office to get the customer service number for medivac, your local AAA office usually doesn't have the information. It is also VERY important to check with your own health insurance coverage company before you go to find out where in Europe your health insurance is valid.

For more information on medical services abroad see
http://travel.state.gov/medical.html

Packing for Adults

1. Documents

You should be able to get both parents' clothes in one suitcase and your child's in another. Any more luggage than that and you have over packed. If you have packed more than 2 bags for yourself, you have over packed. Take older luggage that is plain in color. Never take luggage that does not have wheels. Don't take the cheap portable wheels, but luggage in which the wheels are already built in.

If you are taking documents, then pack these in your carryon. Do not pack these in your checked suitcase. These documents are worth more than all your clothes. You should place them in a large zipper case or in individual plastic sleeves or an expandable file folder. These can be found at an office supply store. You might need to pack an I-864, if your child is getting an IR-4 visa, a duplicate dossier, a tax return, your 171-H, a copy of your home study, your confirmation that the US Embassy received the Visas 37 cable and any other documents your agency may think is important. A copy of your passport and visa should be taken. Of course your original passport and visa need to be accessible, as you will be showing those as soon as you land.

Also, you need your airplane tickets and lots of American cash. You should also carry your agency's phone number and the US Embassy's as well, in case you run into a problem at the airport when you land. One problem that could happen is that your facilitator fails to meet you at the airport. It should not happen and it probably will not, but anything is possible. Some people put all of these documents in a three ring binder, but that can be bulky.

Here are some organizational tips for your documents.

1. Print out all the phone numbers of your contacts such as facilitator, host family, agency in the States, agency office in the foreign country, US Embassy, phone numbers and email address of your Congressional representatives in case you run into serious BCIS/State Department trouble and anyone else you can think of. Give a copy to your spouse as well.

2. Timeline and instructions from your agency.

3. Plastic sleeve holding plane tickets and airline or travel agent phone numbers

4. Calling card and access number

5. Plastic sleeve holding passports (and copies of same), visas (and copies), and customs declaration forms.

6. Plastic sleeve holding copies of birth and marriage certificates if needed.

7. Plastic sleeve to hold expense receipts for adoption credit documentation

8. Plastic sleeve to hold extra pictures of your home life and photo of your child.

9. Type up tip sheets on traveling including tourist sights

10. Plastic sleeve for I-171H plus US Embassy confirmation

11. Questions to ask at the children's home and copy of all medical information on your child to use in conjunction with the questions.

12. Plastic sleeve for blue I-600.

13. Plastic sleeve for I-864 and all supporting documents (necessary for IR4 visa).

14. Extra plastic sleeve for your child's new Russian passport and any other documents of his you have like new birth certificate, court decree etc.

15. Plastic sleeve for extra dossier and supporting documents if your agency feels it necessary.

16. Copy of map showing the capital city and the region where the children's home is located. (Not a full size, a reduced copy) You can find this on the Internet.

17. Same kind of map of showing tourist sites and streets.

18. Sheets of notebook paper to be used for notes

19. Cheat sheet for converting foreign currency, centimeters and kilograms. Temperature conversions are easy. Just double the Celsius number and add 32, then subtract 4. This is within one or two degrees of the right answer.

20. A regular diaper bag will eat at your shoulder after a while. Some parents have taken a backpack instead. You don't need a special purpose diaper bag backpack. Just a lightweight internal frame backpack with a belt and vertical side pockets. The belt will keep it from coming apart and the side pockets for bottled water and formula.

21. If you go in the summer, take cotton not linen. Linen takes forever to dry and is hot.

22. Phone number of your pediatrician or IA specialist back home in case you need to do an overseas consult. Set this up ahead of time and only use it if necessary. (Make sure you understand the time difference.)

Sometimes after the court hearing, one parent unexpectedly must return to the United States. Thus you should take two executed notarized powers of attorney giving one another permission to represent the other in all adoption proceedings.

Also have your translator give you a piece of paper on which is written the name and address of your hotel. If you get lost, you can simply show someone this card or paper.

2. Clothes and Sundries

The first rule, second rule and only rule is to pack light. You will have to carry everything by yourself, including a wiggly child, through a number of airports, train stations and hotel lobbies, usually with no help at all. It is the ultimate planes, trains and automobiles. You will need to get luggage and child in and out of taxis, buses and vans along the trip. Make sure that everything is on wheels or can easily be attached to something wheeled. Think carefully about each item, and try to figure out if you can do without it, or do double duty with something else.

Some suggest using hard sided luggage with good locks. Do not lock it for the international trip. Luggage takes quite a beating on a trip like this. Cloth bags will work and are lighter, so it is a tradeoff. Start your packing plan early. You'll be astonished how time disappears once you get your referral. Set aside a place at home to collect stuff for the trip—shampoo and toothpaste samples, power converters, Ziplocs, etc. Put your packing list in there, and make a note every time you think of something.

Leave your vanity behind. Forget lugging the hairdryers, makeup, and jewelry. Get a short, easy care, run-a-comb-through-it-and-you're-done haircut.

Each airline has their own baggage policies and these are undergoing changes all the time. You need to check with your airline for its specific rules. Most people go over to Russia with bags that exceed the weight limit. You just can't help it if you are taking donations over. The official luggage limits are 110 pounds per person. Delta divides it as 70 pounds for checked (2 bags) and 40 pounds for carryons. The carryon limit is 1 bag plus a personal bag like a pocketbook, purse, camera case or computer case. May travelers wear a coat on to the plane and stuff the pockets with books, water bottles, candy bars, a 56 Chevy etc. Aeroflot is 100 pounds per person with 88 pounds for checked (2 bags) and 12 pounds for a carryon. They weigh everything together so don't worry about having the carry on a little heavy. Purses (very large purses, hint, hint) do not count. Some parents have taken two hardsided suitcases with wheels and two carry-on backpacks, which fit under the seat, along with a large diaper bag and camera bag. If you don't do anything to attract attention to your luggage in the States or in Moscow then the airline and customs officials would prefer a "don't tell me, I don't want to know" policy. If one of the Russian customs people does decide to get technical, the penalty is $5.00 per kilo over weight charge. This is not to say that occasionally a customs person might not decide to get technical. It happens. Just don't worry about it too much. By the way, Lufthansa reportedly never charges anything for overweight bags if you tell them they are donations to an orphanage.

Now these rules do not apply to Russian domestic flights. The Russians will charge you for overweight bags; they just won't take them off the plane. They also do not seem to care that the overweight is children's home donations. Overweight charges are simply a revenue stream. If you buy a first class domestic ticket, one benefit is a higher weight limit.

Some Russians used plastic or duct tape to completely wrap their luggage. If you travel through the domestic airport in Moscow all you will hear is the sound of tape being wrapped around luggage. You might want to consider this, as then your luggage will look Russian rather than American, and possibly a less likely target for theft. Of course, if your luggage makes it out of JFK in one piece, you might consider that a victory in itself.

Here are some suggested tips on packing. The key is to pack light. You will not need a lot of outfits. One sweater, two pairs of pants that sort of thing. Of course, if you are not traveling outside Moscow then you might be able to get away with packing more. But it is really not necessary. One nice outfit for court is all that is needed and the other outfits can be jeans or slacks. Everything should be of the "no iron" variety. Since there is always the possibility that your luggage gets lost, pack some clothes in your carryon. Some people have used a vacuum cleaner to remove the air from the suitcase. This will reduce the size and weight of the bag. Do not take any jewelry with you. Just a simple watch. This isn't a cruise. Why tempt fate. Pack snacks like breakfast bars—your days may be long and meals delayed. Carry something to munch on.

Pack lots of small packages of Kleenex to be used in the bathrooms. Also small rolls of toilet paper for the same reason. One tip is to use a roll at home until it's about 2/3 used. Then remove the cardboard center and collapse it. You easily can store these mini rolls in a small Ziploc bag. Baby wipes work as well.

Take a few disposable cameras. If for any reason yours quits, you can still take some pictures. Also, take a spare battery for your camera and a European converter for your recharger. If you use a video camera, replace the film cassette prior to using it all up in case one of the cassettes turns out to be defective.

Keep a journal or a small tape player so you can remember all the things that happen. Take some pens to write with and maybe a crossword book to pass the time. Do not take a lot of books or books on tape. You simply will not have the time to use them. Take items you can leave behind.

Take a list of your medical allergies. If you are at risk for a medical emergency, you may wish to consider purchasing medical insurance and investigating what sort of medical arrangements would be available to you in Moscow. The two best medical clinics are the Filatov and the American Medical Clinic. Both are of equal quality. If you get car sick, take some Dramamine. Car rides over Russia's roads are very bouncy. Also, take the airplane sickness bags with you when you get off the plane. They may come in handy for you or your child.

Take good photos of your home for the judge on your court date, the prosecutor and the orphanage director. They are very interested in America and interested in what will be the home life of this Russian child. Show books, maybe a piano in the photos. Bring picture postcards of your hometown to share with host family. They do not want to see your fancy car or fancy clothes. That does not impress them. They understand that real success has nothing to do with money, but family and how you live.

Pack KaoPectate KaoLectrolyte Rehydration Solution that comes in dry packets that you mix as needed. This saves trying to take pedialyte, as it would be too much liquid volume and weight. You could take a small bag of powdered Gatorade to replace electrolytes in case you get diarrhea. Just mix it in bottled water.

You might take Pepto Bismol chewables to eat with each meal to coat the stomach and help prevent traveler's diarrhea and to carry artificially sweetened Kool-Aid mix to use as a rehydration fluid, which can be mixed with electrolyte solutions to improve the taste.

If you are taking prescription medications with you, you may want to take a letter from your doctor describing why you need them. You will probably get away without needing it, but sometimes the customs guy can get picky. Most of the time all you have to do really is carry them in their containers. Same with over the counter meds. Take Immodium for diarrhea, Cipro for anything that comes along (including diarrhea), Bactrim or Septra (trimethoprim-sulfa) for urinary tract infections. Check with your doctor, of course.

Take a list of useful Russian words and phrases or even a Russian/English dictionary. Bring a cheat sheet with Russian letters on them. Once you can decipher the letters you have half a chance you can understand the words. There is even an electronic Russian/English translator but it is a little pricey.

If traveling in the summer, take some bug repellant, as the windows have no screens. You should also take some hydrocortisone for bites and a spritzer fan to keep you cool. You might also take an antibiotic ointment like Neosporin for cuts, scrapes and infected mosquito bites. Most children's homes do not have screens on their windows so that during the summer, mosquitos are prevalent.

If traveling in colder weather then you should have some very warm clothes in your carryons in case you deplane in extremely cold weather. It can be -25 in parts of Siberia like Magadan, and Moscow in February 1999 was no picnic. Pack really warm boots and hand and toe warmer packs. In cold weather take a nylon blouse with a high neck and collar. You can wear this under sweaters.

Take 400 or at least 200 film. You'll miss fewer shots due to low light. It is impossible to take too many pictures or too much video. You will always wish you had taken more. There is conflicting advice on what to do with your film now that the airports have machines that could radiate a ham sandwich on Mars. Some say put all film in a leaded bag and others say put your film and camera in a clear bag and hand it to the machine guy. The only safe thing to do is ask parents who have just returned how their film survived. Here is a good article on taking film through airports and the problems people have with TSA personnel.

http://www.magellans.com/content/art_t.jsp?ruleID=86&itemID=64&itemType =ICArticle

If you go in the winter, make sure you have thick (warm) waterproof boots and very warm gloves and scarf and (preferably dark) hat. You will be glad you did. If you own fur—here is your chance to wear it or buy it. Black stretch pants (like for cross-country skiing) come in very handy with baggy black jeans over them. When it is really cold, jeans are insubstantial. Take layers. Either don't wash anything or take some soap packs and wash when you have to. Most Russians wear the same outfit everyday and so can you. The key is to take enough clothes, but not too much. Go light but warm.

If you are going to tourist sites you may want to pack a purse, as you do not have to check it when going to museums or the Bolshoi. This will allow you to have things with you. Any other kind of bag will have to be checked.

Take the usual toiletries such as a small bar of soap, toothbrushes with paste, brush/comb, shaving cream, a razor, shampoo, deodorant, hair spray/gel, alcohol wipes, antibiotic ointment, small scissors, contact lens stuff, makeup, extra pair of glasses allergy/sinus, headache stuff, prescriptions if any, Imodium, bottle opener, Swiss army knife etc, etc. You may decide that you will listen to a portable tape or CD player. Quite frankly, you should be sleeping on the plane over and you won't have time to do any listening on the way back, and if you are on the train you should be looking out the window. On the hand, I do remember that on a 3-hour drive on a very bumpy road in the middle of nowhere I found some reggae music to be quite soothing.

Take a few books, preferably about Russia. Leave these with your translator or homestay host after you finish. They will enjoy them. News or fashion magazines also are good items to take and leave behind. Also take some playing cards and maybe a Game Boy or something small with games on it. If your appeal period is waived, you will only have time to read one book. Once you have your child, there is no such thing as personal time for the next 18 years.

Since you might eat a little in your room, you might take a few paper plates and plastic knives and forks.

It doesn't really matter if you lock your suitcase or not. If someone at JFK or Russia wants in, it is easy to pop. Also, the security types will pop your lock if they see something they don't understand, like a shoe or underwear.

If you take a long distance calling card, make sure you bring the access number with you. (I recommend a prepaid card.) Take the number of your adoption medical specialist in America. Also take the phone numbers of your agency. Your agency will be notified by the facilitator that you have arrived in Moscow. Arrange for the agency to then phone or email your family to that effect as well.

Here are some other ideas:

Plastic Shoes to wear in the shower as the floors can be wet and grungy.
Comfortable shoes to walk around in.
Take a few bottles of water for the plane as well as a few for traveling in Russia. Be careful that you don't take too many, as the weight can be heavy. Bottled water is available in all urban cities and is sold by both Coca-Cola and the Russian Church.
Take a plug for the sink, as many Russian sinks do not have them.
Duct tape is always handy. Large freezer Ziplocs or some other poopy diaper container. (With Ziplocs and Duct tape, man can go to Mars)
Laundry detergent for washing of clothes in the sink.
Maybe a fanny pack. Small travel alarm clock and small flashlight. The flashlight comes in handy on the plane and train so put it in your carryon.

Pack an empty film canister so you can put a little dirt in it from your child's home.

Hot pot

Small dual-voltage travel hair dryer

Adult vitamins. You will get stressed and you will get tired.

TravelSmith clothesline (if you pack light, you might need to do a little laundry)

Jet lag medicine such as Melatonin or a homeopathic one called No Jet Lag, but consult with your doctor.

Waterless hand cleaner

Take plastic bags. Zip-loc and garbage kind.

Pack washing soap packets.

European converter for your electronics

Take Shout wipes for fast clean up of stains, burp spots etc.

Some people take paper towels. If you do, take out the middle for easy packing.

Some coffee singles

3. Money

Your agency should not just give you a lump sum figure of how much money you should bring with you for in-country expenses. Rather, they should give you an itemized list of the estimated cost of traveling such as room and board, escort fees, interpreter, document translation fees, drivers, domestic air, domestic train, donations to orphanage, gifts to officials and host families, hotel cost, home stay cost and visas. This list will still be an estimate, however, it will give you some feel for where the money will be spent. Make sure the money is in crisp, brand new bills. Most should be in $100s although a few ones, $5s and $20s also come in handy, but majority should be in $100s.

Take money belts for you and your spouse. Some go around the neck, others the waist or you can even get the leg passport/money holder. Take whatever is most comfortable and easily accessible. If you take a purse, take the kind that goes over your head and hangs across your chest. It is square and flat.

You will want to divide the money between you. If you have been instructed to give some to your facilitator, have the correct amount segregated in an envelope in your money belt. Some like the belts that go around the neck and others the ones around the waist. When you change money, be careful that you do not just open up your money belt for the world to see. There are many eyes at the Moscow airport and on the street. There are very few places in Russia where credit cards can be used. Some of the larger hotels and restaurants in

Moscow do take them. It is not really worth taking them except that you can get cash advances from the money exchangers using a Visa card. Make sure you take your PIN number with you, as that is necessary. Also, do not bother with traveler's checks, as they are not accepted in most of Russia. Except in St. Petersburg and Moscow, ATM machines are non-existent. The ATM network in Russia is sometimes compromised. If you do plan to use an ATM machine, then set up a sub account at your bank with a separate PIN, and put in a few hundred dollars. Use this account from which to access funds while in Russia. This way no one can get the PIN and drain your entire bank account. If you plan on using a credit card in Moscow, call your credit card company beforehand. Many banks find the use of a credit card in Moscow suspicious and will put a hold on your card.

4. Electrical Adapters/Converters

Russia uses the European style of electrical outlets (two round pins a little further apart than our plugs) with 220 volt/50 Hertz service. Assuming your equipment is 220 capable (and most modern electronics are, but check) all you will need is an adapter plug and not a converter as well.

If you have a 110-volt only item (the US is on a 110 volt/60 Hertz system), you will need a converter. Note that there are two converter options: Inverters and transformers. Inverters can handle high power devices (hair dryers, hot plates etc.) but should not be used more than short periods of time (NEVER overnight). These are in the $20 range and can be found at your local Radio Shack or Brookstone. Transformers are more expensive ($50+) and heavier, but can be used continuously, but transformers are for lower power devices (<100 watts typically) such as for PDAs, cassette/CD players and shavers. You can purchase an RCA "Foreign Voltage Adapter" kit from Radio Shack. Inside, there is a large dual wattage converter with 5 color-coded plugs plus a chart indicating which plugs to use in various countries.

All of this is further explained in great detail on the EEadopt web site under travel and at these web sites:
http://www.walkabouttravelgear.com/wwelect.htm#text and
http://www.magellans.com/content/art_t.jsp?ruleID=86&itemID=95&itemType=I
CArticle

Child Packing Tips

Generally your child's size will be smaller than his age. This is due to his being raised in an institution and nutritional issues. The rule of thumb is to deduct a month of development for every 3 months a child has been in an orphanage. Thus if your child is 18 months old then he will probably fit into 12 month old clothes. But every child is different so you should take a range of sizes. Be aware that as soon as your child begins to get proper food and medical attention at your house, he will likely begin sprouting like a weed. So assume that he will fit the initial size clothes for only a short time. Take clothes that you won't grieve over if they get lost, soiled or are so nasty after a week in Russia that you just throw them away. Sometimes after being with a child in close quarters with food spills, vomit, and the usual diaper action, it just isn't worth bringing his or your clothes back as they now qualify as a Superfund site.

You may have heard that old rule of thumb that when buying clothes for infants and toddlers you take their age and double that for their size. For example, if your child is 12 months old double that to 24 months and that is the size you should look for. This rule applies to American born children. This "doubling" rule does not apply with children in Eastern Europe, especially those in institutional settings. These children usually are of a smaller stature anyway, and then add in the lack of nutrition and/or stimulation and they are just not as large as American children. One idea for Russian children that seems to work is that for every month the child is in age that is what they will weigh. For example, if the child is 16 months old, buy clothes for a 16-pound child.

If you are in Moscow or in a large city and you run out of items, you will be able to find replacements. Such items like diapers can be found in most large towns. However, it is not like going down to the corner store and will be an effort to get. Thus, try to bring most of what you will need.

For a baby:

Take several travel bottles and nipples of assorted sizes and shapes. Your child will experiment until she chooses the size nipple that works best for her. Do take a tri cut "toddler" nipple, as one of the problems is that the American small baby nipples simply do not provide nourishment faster enough for these kids. The holes in the Russian bottles are much larger and the children will get frustrated with the smaller American nipples. Many parents use scissors or small knife to make the holes larger and then transition back to a medium flow when they return home. Take 8 oz and 4 oz bottles. If you take the Playtex kind with the disposable liners, then also take a few regular Gerber bottles. Some children just will not drink out of the disposable liner type. The Avent brand works well.

Some parents take soy formula with extra iron. Check with your pediatrician first. You can find it in individual packets of powder, as well as in individual serving pre-mixed cans making them easy to take with you.

Here are some more ideas:

Take a few small blankets (3) that you don't plan to return with
8-12 onesies, 2-4 pj's, 10 pair socks (tubes), 2-4 t-shirts
Jacket, a hat, gloves
9-12 outfits
If your child is not walking, then you do not need shoes. If you need them, take one pair and just buy them there once you know her size.
Disposable diapers (10-12 per day, thin style)
Garbage bags or large freezer Ziplocs for dirty diapers & laundry (Ziplocs are wonderful when you are traveling.)
Large diaper bag, unscented baby wipes (200-300)
Cheerios (at least half a box); goldfish
Instant oatmeal in individual packets.
Rice cereal
Several orthodontic pacifiers with clip attachments
Anti-bacterial soap
Baby shampoo, baby wash, Baby lotion, powder, toothbrush, toothpaste, hairbrush, comb, nail clipper, thermometer
Liquid baby decongestant (baby Dimetapp)
Liquid baby acetaminophen (baby Tylenol, Motrin)
Small plastic bowls, sippy cups, spoons (plastic coating on the scoop) and 2 plastic bibs
Toys: rattle, teething rings, small stuffed animal, small blocks, keys
Don't forget that to a child anything can be a toy. They love stickers.
Small towels or cloth diapers for burping or sitting on your lap while eating
Elimite (in case of scabies); Nix shampoo (in case of lice, but ask your pediatrician as it may be too strong for small children)
Diaper rash ointment for regular diaper rash (Lotrimin, Desitin). If it is a fungal diaper rash (yeast), then try Nystatin cream (a prescription).
Baby wipes, a few band-aids
A few band-aids

Pedialyte packets, Infant Mylicon (for gas). Infants get so much gas, you could drill a well. Cornstarch baby powder for baby and mommy, especially if it is hot where you are going. Take one 4 oz. container.
Skin lotion, as your child's skin may be dry, especially after a bath. Good for you too. Coming out of the orphanage environment, a child's skin is incredibly dry.

Dirty diapers go in the regular trash in your hotel room. Therefore bring a good supply of quart size plastic bags that can be sealed airtight such as freezer Ziplocs or equivalent. You do not want to share your room with a smelly diaper overnight. An alternative is the scented diaper disposal bags with a twist tie. And please, please wash your hands after changing your baby's diaper. Your child (like all carbon based life forms) has bacteria in her stomach, which will travel from her diaper to you quicker than you can say The Cherry Orchard, so, please wash.

Take several packages of baby wipes. You will go through 400 of them without breaking a sweat. Do not take the hard containers, but rather the refill packages that you can put in a Ziploc

Take some of the infant suppositories along. Sometimes when the babies change from the formula that they have been on to yours, they really get constipated. Ask your pediatrician about a formula that will be easy on their tummys. Maybe one with not so much iron in it, of course then you run into the anemia question.

The Playtex bottles with drop in liners are nice. They are handy, as you don't have to worry about sterilizing the bottles. You can also take a lot of nipples already sterilized in a Ziploc bag and just kept using clean ones.

Take some small bubble bottles. They pack well, and are by far the most delightful toy you can take with you. Kids love them. Take bubbles for your child and as presents for the other children in the home.

If the child's scalp appears red in areas, or brownish-yellow then cradle cap may be present. If so, take some T-Gel shampoo by Neutrogena. It helps remove the scales and oil until the scalp looks cleaner.

Make sure you have some baby food for when you find yourself traveling with the baby and on the plane. You might not be able to find baby food in the store when needed although any large town will have it. It is good to have food with you in case of a delay at mealtime. Respect your child's feeding time and don't always trust that you can get baby food when you need it.

Take some lollipops, raisins or M&Ms. Bonding can begin with bribery. It's ok. She will likely share them with her children's "group."

Take powdered formula: 1 can per 1-½ days. The kids are hungry. This should be soy based, as the child may be lactose intolerant. You might even take one that is milk based as the soy is usually of the low iron variety and in some children this can also be a problem. The Russians use Kefir, which I believe is from Germany. It is milk based. It tastes awful, but then so does any formula. If the child doesn't take to the soy, then just go back to the Kefir. It won't hurt for the week you are in Russia. Just use the hot water from the sink to mix the formula and shake it to eliminate "hot spots." The children are use to the Russian water so it won't bother them.

There is a Nestle/Carnation plant in Moscow that makes baby formula. Pretty much the same stuff that is available in the US, sometimes under the same name, sometimes different. It is widely available in Moscow and in the larger cities of Russia and Belarus. It costs $3-5 for a can that would cost $8-10 in the States. The special Preemie milk is only $6.50. So you might go light on bringing over formula if you will be in a large city.

Changing pads should be taken, as it is a challenge to change your child in anything like a clean environment when you are traveling. Some parents take a cheap vinyl picnic tablecloth, which they then leave in the foreign country.

Since it is very common for your child to have an ear infection or other respiratory problem, take some infant Motrin or infant Tylenol to bring the fever down and some pain drops for the ears. It is rare indeed that a child does not have such an infection, particularly during the fall and winter months. Ask your doctor if you can take an antibiotic that doesn't need refrigeration like Zithromax. Zithromax should be packed in powdered form when traveling and just reconstituted when needed. Doctors like it as it can work on both ear and respiratory infections. Of course, never, ever give a young child aspirin. You have to be careful for allergic reactions if you use penicillin. Remember too if you are given Russian medicines, most Moscow hotels have a house doctor who can help you mix them. While the FSU has a serious problem with resistant strains of bugs, it is likely your child has never had an antibiotic so this should not be too much of a factor.

Here are some suggestions for toddlers:

A hat. gloves, scarf
Cheerios, Goldfish, crackers (no hard candy or peanuts because of choking risk)
1-2 dozen small packs of fruit sacks
4-6 containers applesauce

2-3 picture books
Toys: ball, toy cars, doll or stuffed animal, Stacking cups, baby rattle, coloring books and a few crayons for the airplane, hand puppet
Sippy cups, bowls, spoons, forks, plastic bibs
Soothing cream for the skin if the child has a rash
Benadryl (Great for flying with kids. Make sure it is the clear kind and not the pink colored kind. The pink dye can cause hyperactivity in some kids. Just what you need!)
Actifed syrup-acts like Benadryl. Good for colds. Watch that dye!
Scented diaper sacks (box of 50 purchased at Wal-Mart). Great
for "poopy" diapers at the homestay. You can also use giant freezer Ziploc bags.

You might also take an antibiotic ointment like Neosporin for cuts, scrapes and infected mosquito bites. Most children's homes do not have screens on their windows so that during the summer, mosquitos are prevalent.

Toddlers may or may not be potty trained. Sometimes the so-called potty trained child just has very well trained adults around them. Accidents will happen while traveling. Talk to others who have adopted from this age group.

If adopting an older child remember that the child might be developmentally younger than her age and therefore you should plan on taking toys that are for a younger child. Remember also that you are not trying to bring America to your child, but rather just bring enough to tie you both over until you can get your child back to the States.

Bring some toys, books, picture flash cards, crayons and coloring books, a stuffed animal, things to take apart and put together again, little dinosaurs, etc. Try to avoid stuff that will fall on the floor and roll away under the airline seats. Don't spring the toys all at once. Keep some in reserve for those boring moments while traveling or waiting for the next thing to happen. Make a little photo album of your home, siblings, other family members, pets, your town, and talk about them.

You can buy a travel medical kit from *www.handsacrosstheocean.org* or make one up from their list.

Take a Walkman and buy some Russian children's songs when you are there. There are even tapes with children's songs that teach them English. The Teach Me Russian tapes also have songs. Listening to their native language while on the flight to the US can really help soothe a toddler or older child.

There is a book called My First 1000 Words in Russian. Some parents have just used the book in reverse. It has pictures of things like the home, the doctor's office, the park, etc. and labels everything in Russian so that you can help your child make the connection. It is a good communication tool. Sonia Baxter at Adoption CoordiNations also sells a 14-page set of adoption-specific sentences and phrases. It gives the English, then the Russian translation and then phonetic Russian. If you aren't successful using the phonetic guide, you can just point to the Russian sentence and get your point across. Contact Sonia at soniabee@aol.com or 412-781-7343.

Here is another web site resource:
http://members.aol.com/jaronmink/prep.htm

Suggestions from the Crowd

Here are also some last minute ideas to think about doing or bringing. Not all of these may be appropriate to your situation.

a)   Spend time with the other children in the home. You'll have the rest of your life to love on your children. Think about taking the time to affirm and love the children you will leave behind.

b)   Bring a wrist harness if adopting an active toddler and cannot communicate with him in Russian.

c)   Fly in a day early so you can see the sights in Moscow or Kyiv.

d)   After packing, throw half of it out, as it will probably be too much. Mantra: "Do I really, really need this stuff?" You can honestly get by with one suitcase for both spouses and two carryons. Pack essentials in carry-on, as bags sometimes don't make it.

e)   Take lots of small Kleenex boxes.

f)   Take lots and lots and lots of pictures of your child's children's home and caregivers. Then take lots more.

g)   Force yourself to journal each and every day. FORCE yourself.

h) If you know you will not have the appeal period waived, take a lot of books. You will have loads of down time. This is when a laptop with a DVD is not a bad idea.

i) If you will be in a large town, go light on packing diapers and baby food. They will have a store there where you can buy the stuff. But you might also look into ready to use pop-top formula cans to use on the plane home.

j) Look into those water filters and TravelSmith pants from Magellan and other stores.

k) If you like people, then stay in a homestay, but if you might be uncomfortable, don't hesitate to tell your agency that you want to be in a hotel.

l) Do not forget Immodium,Tums and children's gas stuff.

m) Make sure you have a hat for your child.

n) Don't forget to use frequent flyers to upgrade to business class and use your hotel points as well.

o) Bring blue jeans and comfy shoes. You will be doing a lot of walking. Don't be scared off by everyone saying the Russians are always dressed up. Who are you trying to impress?

p) If you go in December, bring foot warmer packs.

q) If you buy a digital camera for the trip, get the kind that uses disks so you don't have connection issues.

r) Take penlights that go around the neck. Useful for strange hotels and at night.

Stroller or Snugglie

The discussion regarding whether it is better to take an inexpensive umbrella stroller or a Snugglie is one in which there is no right answer. However, here are some thoughts:

In Russia, pedestrians do not have the right of way and the drivers drive like maniacs. Thus having a stroller can be a hazard as compared with fleeing with your life and Snugglie across a street. Also, sidewalks are uneven, particularly with all the construction going on. Russia is also stroller unfriendly in that it has steps everywhere and high speed escalators in the subway.

Of course, a stroller is very nice when you are going out for a walk around the Kremlin in the spring or summer. If your child weighs 15 or more pounds, a Snugglie just will not cut it. A stroller also gives a calming ride to the child. They get to sit and watch the world go by! If you are in Russia for awhile you may find that a Snugglie gets to be a little tiresome as you travel around to tourist spots such as the Kremlin, Victory Park, the Zoo, TV tower, and GUM. If you take a stroller, also pack a clear plastic rain shield for the stroller. It will not only keep out the rain but also cut down on the wind blowing on the stroller.

If your child was kept on his back, he may not be used to the upright position of the Snugglie. However, using a Snugglie does give you two free hands and a stroller can be awkward to carry. Of course, if you find you really do need a stroller you can certainly buy an inexpensive one in Russia and use it while you are there.

There are other alternatives such as the Over The Shoulder Baby Holder or Hip Hammock.

Children's Home Donations.

Many parents try to bring donations to the home. Before packing donations for the children's home, check with your agency as to what is needed and what is the routine. Some agencies try to discourage donations and say that out of the money you paid the agency, the agency makes a cash donation to the home. You can ignore this and just do what your heart tells you. However, it may be easier and better to wait until you are there and actually find out what the home really needs and then go out and buy it right then, rather than guess. Generally, items are available in Russia, just that the children's homes do not have the money with which to buy them. You may very well find that being able to purchase fresh fruit and coloring books for the children is better than taking clothes that will not be worn. Some directors may tell you that cash is preferred so that they can buy what is needed. You need to tread carefully if cash is requested. Some homes have a special bank account for donations. You might inquire about this.

One reason an agency may try to discourage donations is that your extra duffel bag of donations ends up weighing quite a lot and is bulky for the facilitators to get in and out of cars, trains and planes. Just leave the duffel bag or suitcase with the children's home. There is no need to drag an empty suitcase back to the States. Most homes need blankets, sleepers, warm clothes, socks, and gloves. You need to take quantities of an item as they may have some 25 children in a home. Err on bringing just a few items but in quantity and in different sizes. Make sure that the medicines you bring are of a major brand, not generic and not close to expiration. The medicines should be of a normal kind with which the Russian doctors will be familiar such as Children's Tylenol, Motrin or Dimetapp. Ask your agency if the children's home doctors will accept generic drugs. Some do and some don't. Any clothing should be new and preferably with the tags still on. Used clothing, even if clean, is generally frowned upon. However, ask your agency if the home director approves of good used clothing. If you take name brand clothing, cut off the brand tags so as to discourage any re-selling of the items. With donated brand name medicines, some suggest marking the outside with an indelible marker and unwrapping the extra outside wrapping in order to discourage any re-sale.

Some companies will even donate items if asked. Companies like Hanes and Fruit of the Loom have sent children's clothes. Avon has donated toys, mosquito repellent and shampoo, and L'Oreal contributed bottles of children's shampoo. John O. Butler Co. and Wisdom Toothbrush Co. have sent toothbrushes and dental floss, all desperately needed in the orphanage, where many of the older children may have poor teeth. 3-M has sent bandages and Warner-Lambert, antiseptic cream, Ace bandages from Becton Dickinson & Co. and soap from Dial. Ascent Pediatrics has sent over-the-counter cold medicine and Mead Johnson vitamins. These are just a few of the companies who may be willing to donate items for you to take over.

Some suggested donations are:

Children's Tylenol, Motrin, Dimetapp
Diaper rash ointment

Pediatric cough medicines
Neosporin ointment, antibiotic creams,
Anti-diarrhea medicine.
Toothbrushes, toothpaste, shampoo, bar soap
Bed sheets, towels, bibs, blankets,
Plastic baby bottles and nipples
Brand new children's clothing (with tags on, very important), shoes,
New children's underwear. Note that they generally wear sock type tights as
this makes the children easier to clean.
Developmental toys are especially needed.
School and art supplies—pens, scissors, colored pencils, regular pencils, note-
books, crayons and coloring books. You can buy some of these items when you
are there.
You might also take headbands or barrettes for the girls.
Leave any clothing that you brought which does not fit your child at the chil-
dren's home.

There are two schools of thought on vitamins. Some children's homes will
not accept American vitamins. The children sometimes get rashes because of
them. It may be that the children do not receive enough food or fluids to help
digest them properly. The better practice is to buy some there, they are cheaper
and you can get them the kinds that they like. This is just another reason to go
light on taking donations to Russia, but rather just ask the Director what she
needs and buy those items there.

Bringing a lot of toys is probably not the best use of your money. You can
buy perfectly good Russian toys there if you see they have the need. Otherwise,
the American toys will likely end up on a wall, unused.

I would really consider just buying donations and fresh fruit when you are
in the country. Your money will go a lot further. The children never get
bananas except as a very special treat. Their socks, shoes and underwear are all
worn.

Gifts

Small gifts for the people who help you are both a tradition in Russia and a
nice gesture. The list should include the director of your child's home, your
child's caregivers, your translator, driver, facilitator, and homestay host. Your
agency should be able to give you advice on gifts and to whom they should be

given. They do not have to be expensive, just of good quality. American made is preferred. Do not give gifts made in China. If they are, cut off the tags. The stores in Russia are now full of quality goods; just that no one has the money to buy them in quantity. Also, remember that the Russians you are likely to meet as part of your "Team Adoption" will be educated and sophisticated. (Our translator went to the Bolshoi twice a month!) They would really like American mementos, rather than consumables. Most Russians appreciate something from your hometown.

Here are some ideas:

Calendars with American scenes are nice as well as scenic postcards. Anything with a team logo on it such as a shirt, but no ball caps.
A kitchen towel/hotpad set.
Jewelry (coat pins, scarf clips) is always appreciated.
Coffee (Nescafe Instant), makeup (especially Revlon), solar calculators
Pen and pencil sets (although they may have seen lots of these), small flashlights, post it notes
Candy, leather goods
Books in English for your translator
Pantyhose (beige, large sizes), batteries, lipsticks, gloves, scarves.
Tabasco sauce
American Indian gifts
Postcards of your city
Cutlery kitchen knives
Computer CD games and music CDs such as for movie tracks.
Cotton flat sheets
Sweatshirt (American logos are popular)
American magazines like People, Vogue, Glamour, or Redbook
Tea and coffee bags
Cloth shopping bag, dark print is best
500 or 1000 piece jigsaw puzzle
Large scented candle in glass jar
Candy or anything else in a tin—they love the tins!
Decorative playing cards
Other games not language dependent
Anything depicting your city or state like a book, playing cards etc.
Decorative burner covers and pretty pot holders
Stay away from bath gel gifts

A nice gift is small bags of M&Ms to give to the children left behind. If you bring candy, Jelly Beans, Lifesavers, and suckers are treats the children probably have never had. Children also like raisins, crackers, butter or animal cookies, granola bars, instant oatmeal and lollipops. You can really start the bonding process with these sorts of bribes!

For the drivers, a small amount of money (unfolded) in a money card or given in addition with a gift is always appreciated. It also doesn't take up space in your suitcase

You should double check on the propriety of giving pantyhose. While that was a popular gift several years ago, there are indications that is no longer the case. Also, some women do not use makeup. So check with your agency on that item as well. Russians do not usually make a display when receiving a gift and will open it privately. That doesn't mean that they are not happy. When they really know you, then they are very expressive and kiss and hug and even jump up and down over the smallest of gifts.

Adoption Checklist

1. Expect some bumps in the road. Everyone runs into a few and you *will* get through them. Remember that your agency and the foreign country do want the adoption to succeed. (Notice I left out the BCIS.) If something goes wrong, try to concentrate on how to move forward and solve the problem. Let go of trying to figure out who is to blame and who will pay for the mistake. Don't waste energy on anything except getting and keeping your child happy, healthy and safe.

2. Expect to feel out of control. In a sense you are the director of a play and the BCIS, your agency, and the foreign country are all players set in motion by you. You control the really big decisions like do you adopt this child, but the little ones are out of your hands. What you cannot control, you must let go. (at least this is what Helga the Hun, a time management consultant once told me!)

3. Stay calm. You'd be surprised what a warm bath, a glass of wine and a piece of chocolate can accomplish.

4. Treat your hosts with respect and appreciation. You are an ambassador for the next couple.

5. Do not get mad at the officials. Chew on your agency instead. Their job is to be flak catchers. Do not expect your American adoption agency or guide to meet all your needs or to tell you everything. Yet, do not be afraid of requesting information and the help you need. Also, don't be afraid of making a scene or creating waves, if it is a serious matter. If it is a health matter dealing with your child, forget all that Ugly American nonsense and get what you need.

6. Try to ask all the questions you have about your child's history, but do not expect a whole lot of answers.

7. You may bond with your child immediately or you may not bond with your child for days or weeks, but you WILL bond with your child.

8. Do not worry if you wonder if this baby is the right baby. The idea that bells ring and angels sing when you meet your child is just a myth. Be calm, follow your instincts and do not condemn yourself for any doubts you may have.

9. Vent your fears and frustrations to your partner or close friend. Let it out.

10. If you have never been to Eastern Europe, expect it to be completely different from any place you have ever been. Dorothy, you're not in Kansas!

11. Keep your paperwork in one organized packet. Put all new documents and photos in this packet. Take the packet with you whenever you must accomplish any official function. Keep this packet with you as much as possible. Always keep all passports on your person. Make sure you have extra copies of your passport pages.

12. Don't lose your sense of humor.

13. Ask other parents of children from Eastern Europe about their experiences. Be sure to speak to families who traveled to the same city as you.

14. Expect this experience to be one of the most exciting of your life. The trip will change your life.

15. If you are single, <u>seriously</u> consider having someone accompany you. Anyone traveling with you, however, should understand that this is not a sightseeing trip. You and your baby will be the central focus and concern at all times.

16. Expect to be exhausted even before you receive your child. The physical, emotional and psychological strain on this trip is enormous. Expect to be even more exhausted once your receive your child.

17. Expect to play with your child and begin to establish your own routines with her from the very first minute you are together. Eating some meals in your hotel room makes life easier. Through trial and error make sure that the holes in your bottle nipples are large enough for a baby who is used to getting her formula rather quickly.

18. The home recipe for pedialyte (used to counteract dehydration) is one level teaspoon of sugar and one pinch of salt in eight ounces of water. Pack a few ounces of sugar and salt; carry a teaspoon and cup measure. This is very important. If any of the babies become dehydrated, this mixture will save the day

CHAPTER X

BACK IN THE USSR

Travel Guide

You've gotten the great "court date phone call," or "first trip call" and are ready to travel to Russia! First thing is to check the weather in the city to which you will be traveling. Russia's weather can be found at *http://www.weather.com/common/welcomepage/world.html?from=globalnav* or at *http://meteo.infospace.ru./cities/html/index.ssi* Just type in your city. One of the best travel sites is at *http://www.moscowtimes.ru/travel/*. It has links to maps of Moscow and the metro line. Also, read the Embassy's travel tips at *http://www.usembassy.ru/consular/wwwhca1.html#reg* and the American Chamber of Commerce at *http://www.amcham.ru/page.php?pageid=907966134649948*.

Although it is rarely within your control, try to travel when your agency has another family going. Having another family to "buddy" with can make the experience much more enjoyable. You share information, resources, equipment (clocks, food, diapers), and help with each other's kids. If you have to pass the time for a few days before a court date or going home, having another family can really help to fill the hours. It can also feel safer. The best advice is to just "go with the flow." Since you are not in control of your schedule or anything else, just flow along and don't let the little things bother you.

Remember that this trip is NOT a vacation. An international adoption journey is physically tiring, emotional and exhausting work. You will be dealing with major jet lag while running from city to city and office to office. Meeting your child for the first time is very emotionally draining. You will be changing your sleep and eating patterns. Prepare for the trip as if it were a competition. Because it is. It's you against your body and "your mind is writing checks that your body can't cash."

If you are flying out of JFK, make sure you leave yourself double the amount of time to make the connection. JFK is a madhouse, not very modern, and very spread out. Try to get a window seat and then look for 3 empty middle seats before the airplane takes off so you can claim them as soon as the plane levels off. Take some wooly warm socks for the over-the-ocean flights. As soon as you get to your seat take your shoes off and put these socks on (may be put on over the ones you're wearing if your feet tend to get cold easily). No matter what kind of feet you have they will very likely get cold before the flight is over. Also, carry a bottle of water on the plane. You will get dehydrated. As you board the plane try to locate an extra blanket in an overhead bin to take with you to your seat. It gets cold on these flights, especially if you sit next to the window. The blankets tend to be small so it's good to use one on your legs and one to wrap around your torso. Wear warm, loose and comfortable clothes on the plane. Even in the summer it's 50 below zero at 35,000 feet.

If you are in a region that follows the two-trip process, then this might be your schedule for the first trip:

Day 1—Leave US for Moscow

Day 2—Arrive in Moscow and leave for your Region's Department of Education

Day 3—Meet with a notary if you need to file some extra documents. Visit the Department and look through the database or photo album.

Day 4—Travel to the children's home and visit with your child and the home doctor

Day 5—Tell the Department you have accepted the child and file the acceptance form, court date application and request for clearance/release letter.

Day 6—Return to Moscow and leave for the US

This might be your second trip:

Day 1—Leave US for Moscow
Day 2—arrive in Moscow and leave for your Region
Day 3—meet your child
Day 4—Court hearing (assume 10 days is waived)
Day-5—Get child's amended birth certificate and passport from OVIR and
      ZAGS.
Day 6—Travel back to Moscow
Day 7—Child's pre-visa physical
Day 8—Visa trip to US Embassy
Day 9—Return to United States

The Moscow airport, which is called Sheremetyevo-2 after the family on whose estate it is located, has a web site containing a map showing you where everything is located such as passport control, baggage and customs. The home site address is *http://www.sheremetyevo-airport.ru*. If you are flying domestically you will not use this airport, but rather one of the domestic airports that are located about an hour outside the city. Sheremetyevo-2 is located about 50 minutes outside Moscow. It is 29 kilometers from Moscow. Sheremetyevo-1 is one of the domestic airports and is very close by Sheremetyevo-2.

If you fly Areoflot, your fellow passengers may begin to cheer and applaud. If you want to join in the fun, you shout "**Ya hachoo domoy**". This translates, roughly, as "How sweet it is!", though literally it means: "I want to go home!" Your words will produce an immediate reaction. While the plane is taxiing to the terminal, you'll hear the standard greeting, and the warning to stay in your seat until the plane has completely stopped. Note the way the locals completely ignore this injunction.

Coming off the plane, be sure to make the sign of the cross, but if you do, be sure to do it in the Russian Orthodox fashion, from right to left. Some have said that exiting the plane into Sheremetyevo airport is like that scene in *Saving Private Ryan* when the ramp drops on the beach. That is ridiculous. That's what it feels like when you get through customs. Leaving the plane is like entering the maze scene from *The Shining*.

You'll go down a flight of stairs, and find yourself in a badly lit hall in front of the passport control windows. If your flight is the only one arriving at the time, the line should be quite reasonable. Otherwise, get ready for a shock. Imagine a massive flock of strung-out, ill-tempered, cattle at then end of a

Dodge City cattle drive. Do not, under any circumstances, let anyone barge in line ahead of you. They'll pretend to step ahead just to read some sign and stay. They'll kick their bags ahead of you, and step boldly up to them when you aren't looking. Just growl at them and they should back off. Pretend you are fighting for a parking space at the Mall on Christmas Eve. Take no prisoners! At passport control, do not smile. Look blankly ahead as if drying paint is the most amazing thing in the universe. If you want to make the passport official happy, have a copy of your visa ready, and present it with your passport. That makes things easier for them, and gets you though to the next stage much quicker. If you arrive early in the morning, you do not spend much time at passport control and customs. For Delta flight # 30 from JFK the lines can be from 10 to 40 minutes at passport control, but for those arriving after 2 PM the lines can be as long as 2 hrs. Normally you do it in 1 hr or so. Leaving Moscow is easier than arriving.

Now it is time to pick up your bags. There are porters (sometimes wearing green vests) that charge about 50 rubles, which comes to $2 or $4 a bag or sometimes an outrageous flat rate like $20. Make sure you negotiate the price before you give them your business. That is important. Having a porter can help greatly accelerate the process of moving your bags through customs, which is the next step. Even if the price is $20, this is worth it. You can pay them in dollars. Those parents using porters seem to "glide" through customs. The custom officials sometimes ask families to open their bags upon entering the country. Usually if you are with a porter you will not be questioned and will pay no fine for overweight luggage. Also, in the back corner of the baggage claim area, there are carts for rent. Look for the cart rental desk (if you stand with your back to the baggage belts, the rental desk will be to the right of the customs corridors). If any luggage has not arrived, then proceed to the lost luggage counter.

You used to be able to pay for the carts in rubles or dollars, but I believe now you can only pay in rubles. At the end of 1999, the price was 50 rubles or $2. The porter in Moscow will stay with you until you find your driver. Keep some dollars handy out of your money belt. Otherwise you have to pull them out while people are looking at you, which defeats the point of keeping your money hidden.

You then drag your bags over to the red or green customs line or channel where they are placed on a small belt that takes your bags through an x-ray machine. The belt works, I'm not sure about the x-ray. Keep your eyes on your bags at all times. Never, ever take your eyes off your bags. You give the customs guy your declaration form and he stamps it and hands it back. Do not lose this form. Make sure he stamps it. On the form you list cash, jewelry, eyeglasses, and cameras. It is recommended that you go through the "red" line, not the "green" line. The green line is for those who have nothing to declare. It used to be that you could simply breeze through the green channel, but now that most people are carrying lots of cash, you do have something to declare and should go through the longer red channel. While it is not likely, if the customs guy starts to get serious with you, just play it cool, and don't offer unnecessary information and when he stares at you just stare back right at the middle of his forehead. There are many people behind you and the customs officer will crack first as his first motivation is to process the people. It takes about an hour and half on average to clear customs.

While you wait in line, look around for the bathroom. The airport has a pretty nice facility and if you have been drinking a lot of water on the plane, you will need it. The whole custom's line review can take an hour, and then it is another hour from the airport to your hotel. Trust me, you will not be able to hold it!

Sometimes (maybe when the Russian Customs Service misses a payroll), you may be told to weigh your bags and pay a "tax" (again, without receiving a receipt) based on the number of kilograms you are carrying into the country. Welcome to Russia!

On the other side of customs are screens shielding the area from the general airport area. But you will see facilitators and friends pop their heads in and out trying to find people. Look for your facilitator or host while you wait at customs.

One tip to remember is that when you return for your second adoption (don't be so surprised!), if you bring your first adoption along you can take advantage of his Russian citizenship by having your family enter the airport using the passport control line intended for Russians. That line is much shorter and moves about a lot faster than the non-citizen line. They allow all family members to enter via that line and you can save about an hour.

Once through customs you will drag your bags around the screens and into the general airport area. You will see a mass of people. Excited family members, taxi thugs, more luggage cart wiseguys, and brutal looking grandmas. They will not let you pass. Like Napoleon, no one simply marches into Moscow; you must fight all the way. If you haven't made eye contact with your facilitator, look for someone holding a sign with your name on it. Your facilitator and a driver will likely meet you.

Do not simply take a taxi into Moscow. This is usually a bad idea. Even Russians have someone meet them. If you are not being met, march to the kiosk window marked by the yellow "taxi" sign. Try not to make eye contact with the goombas who will be trailing you all the way and chanting "taxi, taxi" like a mantra. Since the August 1998 devaluation, prices have actually come down a bit and the going rate is actually $30 to city center, but you will have to fight for it. You might try to play out the following scene: Ask, **skolka?** (how much?) while looking straight into the kiosk man's eyes. He will probably reply, **sorok dollar** ($40). Wave your hand and start to walk away in disgust. There's an 80 percent chance you'll hear him call after you **skidka** (discount.) Go back, reestablish the steady eye contact and ask again, **skolka?** Chances are you'll hear **thretset** (30). It should cost no more than $30-40 to go from the airport to the center of town or from the airport to one of the four domestic airports. Native Russian speakers can bargain the price down to at least $15. Remember that none of the taxi drivers will speak English so make sure they understand the destination and the agreed upon price.

There are also a few taxi service windows on the ground floor, though they are more expensive. These work 24 hours without a prearranged pickup and could be your only alternative at night, when neither buses nor marshrutkas are running. Avtotrans offers a transfer to the city center for 1,200 rubles in a Russian car. Their Mercedes will set you back $70. Minibuses seating seven people go for $60, those seating 14 people for $80 to $90. A Goleks limousine to the city center or Baltschug or Renaissance hotels costs $200. Intourtrans charges $30 to the center.

There's no metro stop at the airport, but there is a regular marshrutnoye taksi, a minibus that runs along a fixed route for a fixed fare of 50 cents and allows passengers to get on or off wherever they want. It will take you to Rechnoi Vokzal and Planernaya metro stations. The minibus stand is just opposite the exit from the arrival area.

If you have to arrange your own transportation, then have the Marriott pick you up. It's about $60. Or go to the Intourist desk at the Moscow airport, and pay for a taxi ride to your hotel. Even if the taxis are controlled by the Xhimky mob, hiring one through Intourist provides some safety. Now there is a taxi desk in the center of the arrivals hall. The taxi ride to or from the city center should run about a half an hour to 45 minutes, depending on traffic.

The marshrutkas also will bring you back to the airport when you're ready for your next trip. They stand across from the row of regular buses at Rechnoi Vokzal. Don't mistake one for a green IKEA bus docked nearby.

For another way into town, catch the No. 851 bus, which stands next to the express parking lot. The bus goes to and from Rechnoy Vokzal for 8 rubles and takes about 40 minutes.

For those seeking the comfort of a car ride, the cheapest door-to-door option is to arrange for a taxi service to pick you up at the airport. Taxi Blues will pick you up or drop you off for 450 rubles ($16), plus a little extra if your plane is delayed. OTRA charges only 390 rubles for rides from town, but a heftier 585 rubles to meet your plane.

For your own set of wheels, you can rent a car at the Avis, Hertz or Mosrentservice desks on the ground floor. However, I wouldn't recommend driving in Moscow if you ever want to see your loved ones again. It is that crazy. Moscow makes Rome look like Driver's Ed.

To find your way around the airport or to your flight, ask at the information desk on either floor. They will also make an announcement if an arriving passenger cannot find people meeting him or her. They do not, however, all speak English, nor do they give city information. For such tourist information, try the Intourist window on the ground floor. They will also give you a metro map. Intourist charges $45 for transfer to the city center.

You can make hotel bookings at the Goleks window on the ground floor for the Baltschug and Renaissance hotels, at the Marriott window for the Marriott chain hotels. You can use the League Transportation Service for bookings at the Marriott, Baltschug and Renaissance hotels. The Novotel hotel desk gives a 50 percent discount for same-day bookings.

You'll probably only be able to find the business center at the airport if you speak Russian because there's no sign indicating it in English. It's called "mir uslug," or the world of services. Once you've found it, however, the staff can help you in English. There you can make a local or long-distance telephone call, send a fax, make a photo copy, take a photo, make a computer printout, buy a stamped envelop, make a business card or even pay a visit to a hairdresser. It also has a cafe where you can get chicken wings.

For ready cash, there's a MOST Bank office on the ground floor to the left of the entrance with a few ATMs. There is also a Sberbank office with a money exchange to the left of the entrance in the departure area that's open 24 hours. There's another exchange window by the Aeroflot reservation, but it's often closed.

The street on which you travel into town from the airport (Leningradsky Prospect) dead ends at Red Square's very entrance. Leningradsky at this point is called Tverskaya Street. It is Moscow's main drag.

If you are staying in a hotel, you will likely be asked for your passport and visa. Russia requires the visa to be registered within 3 days of arrival. The hotel will keep it for an hour or so. Make sure you get it all back. This is a hold over from Soviet days when all foreigners were tracked.

If you plan to use the famous Moscow Metro, check out this site for a great description:

http://www.friends-partners.org/partners/skipevans/atl/russia/metro.htm

You should keep your agency's phone number and their local contact number handy in case there is a glitch. The US Embassy number is 7-095-728-5000 (switchboard). The "7" and "095" do not need to be dialed in Moscow. The American Citizen Services Unit (telephone 7-095-728-5577) is open Monday through Thursday from 9:00 a.m. to 12:30 p.m. and 3:00 p.m. to 4:00 p.m., except on Russian and American legal holidays. In the event of an emergency, American citizens may telephone 7-095-728-5577 anytime from 9:00 a.m. to 6:00 p.m., Monday through Friday. After 6:00 p.m., call the Embassy duty officer at 7-095-728-5990. If you have an emergency you can dial "01" for fire, "02" for police, and "03" for an ambulance.

You should try to have a local contact in Moscow as a backup. If you ask around you should be able to come up with a friend of a friend who is currently living in Moscow. Arrange to bring some coffee to him, and you will have a contact for life. If you want to meet your contact, tell people to meet you at the fountain inside GUM or at the Tomb of the Unknown Soldier outside the Kremlin walls.

There are four domestic airports around Moscow. Many parents fly into Sheremetyevo-2 in the morning then fly out of one of these later the same day to their region. These are:

Sheremetyevo Terminal 1

Is located on the opposite site of the runway it shares with Sheremetevyo-2. Vans and buses running from the Rechnoi Vokzal metro station to Sheremetyevo Terminal 2 usually continue on to Terminal 1. Taxi and bus rides to Sheremetyevo-1 are 5 to 10 minutes longer than to Sheremetyevo 2. Prices are about the same.

Bykovo

Is connected to the center of Moscow by suburban trains that run to Kazansky Station. At the airport you can pick up the train at a station about 400 meters from the terminal. Leaving the city, trains headed to Vinogradovo, Shifernaya or Golutvin usually stop at Bykovo. Taxis to the center usually cost between $20 and $30.

Domodedevo

Vans run between Domodedevo and the Domodedovskaya metro station. The ride costs 50 cents and usually lasts about 30 minutes. Taxis to the center usually run from $20 to $30.

Vnukovo
Vnukovo Airport is connected to the Yugo-Zapadnaya metro by a 50-cent minivan ride. A taxi from Vnukovo to the city center runs between $20 and $30.

If you are flying domestically always get a business or first class ticket. Not only do you obtain marginally better accommodations but also your luggage weight limits are higher. You may want to duck tape your luggage as that will make it more like the locals or use one of the shrink-wrap machines. Again, you want to have your luggage blend in.

Customs Declaration Forms and Migration Cards

All of the airlines have these forms. When you are about an hour outside Moscow you will be given one of these forms. You and your spouse should each fill one out. They simply ask you for how much money you are bringing into the country and any other valuables. It is easy to fill out. The form asks for "Purpose of Visit" and some people put "tourism" and others "adoption". It doesn't really matter. You will give the form to customs at the airport in Moscow. They will stamp it and hand it back. Make sure they stamp it. DO NOT LOSE THIS FORM. You will need to show it to them when you make your return flight.

At times Aeroflot runs out of English forms and will only have the form in Russian. Do not panic. The form is easy and the flight attendant will certainly help you.

You may wish to obtain an extra English version of the form when flying into Russia, as you will also need to fill one out when you leave. If you have trouble obtaining the customs form in English when departing Moscow, use your first one as a guide and fill out the Russian, German or French form in English.

The reason that you need the form stamped is because a new law was passed by the Duma and signed by President Yeltsin on July 5th, 1999, whereby foreigners are no longer allowed to leave the country with an undeclared amount of more than $1,500.

Filling out the form. The first line asks for your name. Second line is your citizenship. Third line is the country from which you are arriving. Fourth line is your country of destination, which is Russia. Fifth line is the purpose of the visit. Just put "adoption." Sixth line asks for number of pieces of luggage including carryons. Then you have a list of four Roman numerals asking about weapons, narcotics, antiques and rubles. Just put none for all. Roman numeral V is a blocked area. One of the lines asks for the quantity of dollars first in figures then in the second cell, in words. The other lines are for other currencies. In the line below the blocked area at Roman numeral VI, it asks for amounts of rubles, just put none. Then date it and sign it.

The form was changed in August 1999 and adds some blocks to fill in later regarding the amount of currency purchased and the amount of rubles re-exchanged.

You may think that you should not declare all of your cash. This will only get you in trouble or at the very least create an additional worry that you do not need (like buying Cuban cigars and smuggling them into the States in your child's diaper—don't!). The Russians do not really care about the dollars coming into the country. It's the dollars going out that worries them. If you are carrying more than $10,000 in cash into Russia, you will likely be asked to go to another window and fill out a blue form. I recommend splitting the money so you and your spouse are both are under this figure, but if you are over, not to worry. Just fill out this other form. The main thing is to declare what you have honestly and don't lose your form. If they ask to see your cash, just show it to them. If they ask why you have so much, say that you might be staying a few weeks and were unsure about the use of credit cards. That's close enough to almost be the truth.

If you land in Moscow without the form do not panic. When deplaning in Moscow you will find the forms right inside the door you enter in the baggage claims area. The forms are located on a shelf/table that surrounds a pillar. If you walk around the pillar you will find the forms in English at some point. While waiting for your bags to appear simply fill out the forms.

If you are bringing in a laptop, software, radio, video camera or the like, declare them.

You may want to practice with the form. You can print out a copy at *http://www.moscowtimes.ru/travel/photos/arriving/byplane/custom14.gif* (front page) and at *http://www.moscowtimes.ru/travel/photos/arriving/byplane/custom24.gif* (back page)

There is also a migration card you must fill out. It is not too hard and if you don't receive one on the plane there should be some in the airport. It asks for some of the same information as the Customs Declaration. You can find an example of the card, (which you might print out and take with you), at *http://www.aeroflot.com.au/MigrationCard.pdf* and also on the Russian Embassy web site.

US Consulates

The United States has Consulates in St. Petersburg, Vladivostok, and Yekaterinburg, but immigrant visas are only issued by the US Consulate in Moscow.

You can reach the consulate in St. Petersburg at: Ulitsa Furshtadskaya 15; tel (7-812) 331-2600; fax (7-812) 331-2852; its emergency or after hours number is (7-812) 331-2888. 7 is the country code and 812 is the area code, so you do not have to dial those if you are calling in St. Petersburg. The e-mail address is: *usa.consulate@cltele.com* and web site is *http://www.usconsulate.spb.ru.*

You can reach the consulate in Vladivostok at: Ulitsa Pushkinskaya 32, tel (7-4232) 268-458 or 300-070; fax (7-501-4232) 300-091; after hours (7-4232) 471-644 and (7-4232) 287-290. The Consulate's website is at *http://vladivostok.usconsulate.gov/* and email contact at *conssect@gin.ru*

You can reach the consulate in Yekaterinburg at: Ulitsa Gogolya 15a, 4th Floor tel (7-3432) 79-30-01 or 7-3432-564-619/91; fax (7-3432) 564-515. The Consulate's website is at *http://www.uscgyekat.ur.ru* and email can be sent to. *consulyekat@state.gov.*

The US has also established about 20 virtual consulates, which mainly serve as promotional connections. They do not offer any services. The list is at *http://www.virtualconsulate.com/.*

Homestays

If you are traveling outside Moscow, I would follow the direction of your agency regarding where to stay. However, in Moscow you are likely to have some flexibility and will be able to stay in a homestay or hotel.

The homestay versus hotel debate is another one of those where there is no right or wrong. Homestays can be great. You get to actually live for a few days with a real Russian family. The cultural benefits will never be forgotten. Usually the Russian family will have at least one person that speaks some English. It could be the parent or one of the children. Homestay etiquette is that you don't wear your out door shoes inside. You take them off. Therefore, in the winter you may consider having boots or heavy shoes that are easy to put on and take off.

You will find that Russians are like everyone else. They like hot tea, although coffee is making inroads. They like sweets, think the western press doesn't understand Russian politics and do not like Gorbachev. They like to tell stories, have a party and watch soccer and hockey. The usual homestay host is very well educated and will have an advanced degree.

Usually the homestay is cheaper, although not always the case. Moscow hotels are generally closer to the Kremlin in case you want to get out and walk around. Moscow homestays will be in the suburbs and will be difficult, but not impossible to move around outside the apartment without guides.

A homestay provides you with an invaluable experience with a real Russian family. Unless the family has the luxury of having their own gas water heater, you might be faced with a hot water issue. Usually, the large basement boilers in these apartment complexes are not turned on until late October and could be off by April. That leaves a week or so in either direction when it is cold outside and you might be cold inside. Yet, I will never forget my host rising early to boil water on the stove so I could have a hot bath. The connection across cultures is what makes us human. A hotel is just the usual impersonal commercial experience. If you do plan to stay in a hotel deep in the birch woods of the Great White North, always ask when the hot water is turned on. I once took a bath at 7 am and came out a little multi-colored Popsicle (lips were blue, the rest was white). My wife took one at 7:30 am and was as warm as fresh baked bread. This is just one of many travel tips Russia will have you personally experience. All you can do is hope these are equally divided between you and your spouse!

In a Moscow hotel you can walk out to McDonalds or Pizza Hut, not so in a homestay. If you stay at one of the fancy American hotels like the Radisson or Marriott, you can use your credit card. If you stay at a hotel, your facilitator will have to come get you at the hotel whereas it might be easier to coordinate travel to the Embassy and airport from the homestay. A homestay in a town outside of Moscow may be in a location that is not within walking distance of shops, restaurants, or taxis.

A homestay may also provide you with baby-sitting service from the host, free or not, which may allow you to sleep, recover, and prepare for the Flight From Hell.

A hotel can offer you privacy that a homestay cannot and food choices beyond the usual heavy Russian meals. If you stay at one of the newer hotels in Moscow, you will feel like you are back at home.

A homestay can offer you a taste of real Russian food. Breakfast might be bliny (thin pancakes), yogurt and tea. Lunch could be pelmeni (dumplings); a vegetable soup like borscht and salads. Supper is more soup, salads and main courses like golubtsy (stuffed cabbage) and pierogi (dumplings filled with potato or cabbage).

Of course, a homestay experience could also be one filled with funky bathrooms shared with strangers, chain-smoking, no privacy, the Berlitz total immersion course every evening when you get home, and food that may be fabulous or horrible. People have ended up spending days at a homestay that was so far out of town that they were trapped with nothing to do. Agencies sometimes pressure their clients to stay at a homestay as it provides another method of feeding the food chain. The host, driver and translator all have some connecting thread to the agency. Ask your agency for the price of the homestay before you go to Russia and if they quote you a price approaching $75 a night then negotiate. Check with reference families if they've stayed at the same apartment and see what they say. You always have the power of staying at a hotel. Most Russian cities, even small ones, have Internet sites where hotels are listed. A travel agency that is used to Russia can also book you.

Finally, with adopting older children some parents believe that a hotel is best. First, if you stay with a host then the host will become involved with the child simply because the child can communicate with the host better than with you. This may not be a good thing as you will need to start bonding and teaching your child your family rules as soon as you can. For these parents, by not using a translator they force the older child to rely on them for their needs and for answers to all of their questions. This can help the bonding process. You can establish a bedtime routine, mealtime routine, bath time routine from the first day. The hotel is also a more predictable environment and allows the parent to better control events. You can focus all of your energies on the children and they on you.

Of course, some parents like the host speaking Russian to their child and letting her know what was to come such as the Embassy visit, plane ride home, your house etc. You may find that you have made a friend for life and your homestay host may become part of your extended family.

If you are asked to stay at a Moscow homestay during the summer you should check on the hot water situation before you agree to it. Every summer in Moscow and in other cities the hot water is turned off, district by district, block by block, for almost a month at a time. This allows workers to inspect the pipes. It is an annual tradition. Moscow's heat and hot water came on line in 1924. Few upgrades have been made since.

Moscow Hotels

Moscow's hotels used to have the reputation of being Sovietized. This meant that there was no customer service, no one spoke English, and the facilities had not been upgraded since the 1950's. Since about 1996, there has been a vast building and upgrading program. New hotels have sprung up and old ones refurbished. Times have changed. Many people stay at a less expensive hotel on the way into Russia, but a more expensive one on the way out. The theory is that the added amenities are worth it when you have a child in tow. Most foreign hotels are really just owned by local franchisees that simply pay for the right to use the international brand name. That way, the foreign company can make money off the name without any risk. Not surprisingly in Russia, sometimes the marriage doesn't quite work out and you have a divorce. As a result, several prominent hotels have left their international chains, including The Metropol, which left The Intercontinental chain, and the Iris Hotel, which parted ways with the Accor chain. One problem with Moscow is that there are few middle priced hotels. In recent years, not a single three-star hotel has been built in Moscow, as investors tend to put their money into top-class hotels, enticed by the potential for higher returns. A map showing the location of the hotels in Moscow can be found at *http://www.tourintel.ru/maps/e_ru_mow_maps.html* and in other parts of Russia and in Kyiv see *http://www.tourintel.ru/maps/index.html.*

Under the classification adopted in 1994, nine hotels in Moscow have been given five stars—Le Royal Meridien National, Hotel Baltschug Kempinski, Renaissance Moscow, Metropol, Marriott Grand Hotel, Mezhdunarodnaya, Marriott Aurora, Golden Ring and The President Hotel. The Sheraton says it is "high four-star, bordering on five."

Certification, however, is not mandatory in Russia, and many hotels in the lower segments of the market don't have any stars at all. Also, as many as 20 groups are empowered to issue star certificates and the criteria is not stringent. As a result, a three- or four-star hotel in Moscow bears little resemblance to a Western hotel of the same class. The Cosmos and Ukraina hotels, for example, despite having four-star certificates, hardly compare with The Marriott Grand Hotel in terms of the quality of services. In general, if you are staying at a western hotel like the Marriott, then you may do better just calling them direct. If you are staying at a Russian hotel like the Hotel President, then using a well-known travel agency might get you the best price. The old grand Soviet hotels are now coming down. They are demolishing the Intourist at the bottom of Tverskaya Street. City planners are debating the fate of the bulky Moskva hotel, an early example of Stalinist architecture, a drawing of which features on every bottle of Stolichnaya vodka. The Rossiya, a great beached whale of a hotel next to the Kremlin, may also go. These hotels used to have character, since they didn't have any service.

One of the best resources is *http://www.infoservices.com/moscow/index.html* This site has maps, lists of hotels and restaurants. Other informative sites are *http://www.moscow-guide.ru/, http://www.tourintel.ru/index.html, http://www.travlang.com/hotels, www.hotelsrussia.com,* and there are some nice reviews by adoptive parents at *http://adoptingfromrussia.com/Moscow.html#Hotels.*

Wherever you stay, always ask if there is an "adoption" discount. Many times you will be pleasantly surprised. This is especially so on the slow week-end nights but not so prevalent during the business weekdays. If you work for a large company, also check the "corporate" rate. Sometimes it is lower than the adoption discount. Cribs are not normally available in the older hotels. Most families use a variation of the suitcase, drawer or pushing the double beds together trick.

Marriott has several hotels in Moscow. The **Moscow Grand Marriott** is very nice but expensive. Use your Marriott or Reward points if you have them. The Radisson used to be the hotel of choice for US government travelers, but the newer Marriott is now the "in" hotel and even has a government rate. Former President Clinton stayed there when he was in town. The staff is helpful and most speak English. It is a block from Pushkin Square. The Marriott Grand is one of the few places that take American credit cards. The phone number for the Grand Marriott is 1-800-228-9290. You can also call directly during business hours (Moscow time) and talk directly to someone in reservations. Their number is 7 095 937 0000 or you might try email at *grand.marriott@cnt.ru.*

The rate has been quoted as $179 a night for a weekend and $199 and higher for a weekday stay, excluding tax. This includes breakfast. Deduct $20 if you don't want breakfast. Both of these rates are for a regular room with two double beds. This is called the Leisure Rate. As these rates are subject to change, always check before you go. They are also subject to a hefty tax. If you intend to pay by credit card, ask them ahead of time to verify their exchange rate as it can be a lot different than the official one causing your room rate to be higher. This is true for any payment you make using a credit card. If you need a nice break from Russia and a little taste of home, this may be the way to go. If you ask for the "adoption discount" and they cannot find it, ask them to check under "local promotions" or under the rate codes ADPK or ADKP (ATKD?). It is code A23 if using Marriott.com. Sometimes during the summer busy season Marriott gets restrictive with the discount. You may need to take a letter from your agency verifying that you are traveling for an adoption. Marriott also has a US government and a corporate rate. One of the "larger corner rooms" at the standard corporate rate is $155; including breakfast and excluding the hefty tax add on. The corner room is a large room with 2 double beds and is plenty large enough for four adults.

The Moscow Grand will also arrange to pick you up at the airport for a charge. They have king-size beds, good toilets (don't knock it), free bottled water, which they provide every day, and all the American food you, can eat. They have an ice machine and chocolates on the pillows! They also have an indoor pool and spa so bring your bathing suit. You can communicate with them through e-mail on their web site: *www.marriott.com/marriott/MOWGR*.

The Marriott has a Business Center that will allow you to have Internet access at $30 an hour. This is very high by Moscow standards. Just write offline then send it. Also, a one minute call from your room to the US is $ 9.00 without taxes! Using calling cards is only slightly better at a $1.00 for the first 3 minutes, then 30 cents per additional minute. If you are at Planet Hollywood one night, there is a cyber café below it that also provides Internet access.

Some parents staying at the Marriott Grand have ordered take-out from a restaurant called Jack's. They have menus in English and Russian. They deliver to your room (after calling from the lobby). The food is good, but slightly heavy.

As with any good hotel, the Marriott can help you hire drivers to get you to the medical clinics and embassy. They can also find you a tour guide and a van so you could take a driving tour of the city while you wait for your Embassy paperwork to be processed. Marriott Grande has more kids, more Americans and even toys and toy car-vehicles for kids to play with in a lower lobby. It is about 25 minutes by foot to Red Square. Red Square is about 6 blocks from the Grand and 10 blocks from the Marriott Tverskaya. The Metro is handy to both, so you do not have to walk if it is too cold.

Another **Marriott** is on Tverskaya Street (34 Tverskaya-Yamskaya), which is not as fancy as the Grand, but is also very nice. It is also quiet, clean and most of the staff speaks English. A nicely furnished regular room, with one king size bed, runs about $99 a night excluding breakfast. A very large suite, with sitting room, large bath and kitchenette goes for $149 a night, which includes a huge and delicious breakfast buffet. If you adopt two children, this is a great suite, but also consider upgrading to a suite even with one. Both Marriotts can book tickets at the Moscow Circus or Bolshoi, or confirm your plane reservations. Restaurants and the subway are close to both. You can also buy some staples at the local grocery and use the in room refrigerator to store the items. They also allow you to empty the room fridge so you can place your foods in it. This might save you on breakfast. Pizza places also deliver. The business center's Internet access is very reasonable. Even though you are not staying at the Grand, you can still use their pool. The best perk is the fourth floor lounge. Adoptive families gather there to let the kids play. It is nice to be able to let them run while having adult conversations with others. Think about getting a non-smoking room on the fourth floor. There is a pharmacy next door. The hotel restaurant has high chairs and will bring you a crib, although you may feel it is too upscale for kids.

The **Marriott Renaissance** used to be called the German Penta Renaissance and is located by the old Olympic Stadium built for the 1980 Olympics the US boycotted. It is not centrally located, but it is a nice hotel. The staff speaks flawless English. A metro entrance is not too far away. The breakfast buffet at the Renaissance reportedly surpasses that of the Grande. In addition, it is much quieter and the selection of TV channels is better at the Renaissance. The rooms are smaller than the President. Internet access is expensive. It has a nice pool and recreation room. It is fine for short stays of a day or two, but is not recommended for long stays and there are other hotels that are more child friendly. It really isn't the place to stay after you have adopted, but rather on your first trip when only adults are traveling. It has a more international clientele. The hotel also has a free shuttle bus that runs daily to Tverskaya Street. The shuttle leaves you off just a few blocks from a TGI Fridays, McDonald's, and Sbarro's Pizza. Some airline pilots stay there during their layover. Because it is not within Moscow's inner circle, the hotel tax is much lower than a lot of the other hotels—5% versus 20%. They have free coffee in the lobby.

The **Marriott Aurora Royal** is a five star hotel close to Red Square on Petrovka St. It is within walking distance to Red Square. It is on the expensive side. Be careful if you call the US from your room—you will really pay for it. This is a pricey hotel with rooms starting at $300, but ask for an adoption discount. The rooms have several telephones, satellite television, air conditioning, and minibar.

A real international one is **Hotel Mezhdunarodnaya** at the World Trade Center Moscow on 12 Krasnopresnenskaya nab; *www.wtcmoscow.ru*. The hotel is used to international guests and has an adoption rate. The breakfast buffet is large. There is a warm, children's pool with a water slide. Older children can play in it for hours. The pool area also has a bar. It also has lots of restaurants and a large shopping is in an attached mall. It is a 5 star hotel. The adoption rate is $115 per night. There is no charge for local calls. The room service menu is limited, but service is speedy. There is a business center within the complex and a passport photo shop. You can email home daily. If you visit the Kremlin and Red Square, you will need a taxi.

The **Radisson** is also very nice and has a business center where you can access the Internet. The Radisson, like the Marriott, has a great health club with a big pool, a gym with weight equipment, 4 treadmills, and even aerobics classes. The food prices in the hotel are a little high, but the rooms have refrigerators and there is a grocery store across the street. Also, the Radisson has a room-service special of a hamburger, fries and a Coke for $10. There is a Pizza place that delivers pretty good pizza to your room. The Radisson gained a certain reputation during Russia's "Wild West" days of the early 90's, but seems to have toned down its ways. United Airline frequent flyer points are sometimes accepted at Radissons, so check if you can use these. It has air conditioning, which not all Moscow hotels have. The rooms are clean and nicely sized with a refrigerator that the staff stocks each day with bottled water and canned soft drinks. The cribs are standard size wooden cribs and they fit nicely in the room. The staff is friendly and helpful and speaks English. There is a bank to exchange U.S. dollars to rubles. The first floor has several restaurants and shops, a newsstand, a fitness center with indoor pool, and an American movie theater. The hotel is adjacent to a train station and across the street from a McDonald's and grocery store. The Radisson also has a wonderful American style breakfast buffet with wonderful egg omelets and pancakes made to order.

The Radisson is near the Moscow River and within a short walk is a restaurant called "The Viking." (Remember that Russia was really founded by Vikings.) The boat has big Viking dragon heads on it. The Viking boat is sort of two separate restaurants, one side is Japanese the other serves European/Russian food. This other side also has two menus, one for European food and the other for Russian. The staff does not speak much English, but pointing works! You can pay with a credit card, but all tipping is in cash.

The **Metropole Hotel** is also nice, but more expensive. There is a terrific children's' store called Detsky Mir (Children's' World) across the street from the Metropole and down a block or so. It is like an FAO Schwarz. It has a 2-story carousel that kids can ride for free on the main floor. The main floor holds all the toys, beautifully displayed, and the upper floors are like kiosks selling practical items (of relatively poor quality but you can get shoes, etc).

The hotel **Belgrad** is near the Arbat (one of Russia's great shopping districts). It is one of Moscow's older hotels, but has been somewhat refurbished. The price is also right, between $80 and $100, including breakfast. The staff speaks some English and there are plenty of restaurants and shops nearby. An Italian restaurant is across the street and a Greek one is inside the hotel. The Greek restaurant will send meals up to your room. It is cheaper than the newer hotels.

It is not near the Kremlin but is near the Arbat. It is relatively clean and safe. The bathrooms are not as nice as the newer hotels. There are usually other adoptive couples staying there. You can eat breakfast in the hotel as they do make pretty good omelets or go across the street to a McDonalds. Parents have reported that they were cold in the winter, so you may want to stay elsewhere during the cold months. Space heaters are available.

It is a 5 block walk to the US Embassy which would be pleasant in the late spring and early fall. The babushka cleaning ladies in the hall will all talk to your baby in Russian and made sweet faces at her. Be sure to ask for the rooms with refrigerators. Also, ask for one of the renovated rooms. If you can, ask to see the room before you pay for it and always try to upgrade to a larger suite. Usually an upgrade will just cost a few dollars more. They do not offer cribs but do offer a taxi and sightseeing service. It is close to two grocery stores with baby food, diapers, and formula. Do not stay at the Belgrad during the summer months of June through August as it has no air conditioning and no screens on the windows.

The **Arbat Hotel** is a good choice for someone who wants a bit more local flavor than you can get at even the Ukraina. It's a small hotel in an older building on a back street. It's 2 blocks—all in the same direction—to the Arbat (great pedestrian shopping), Smolenskaya Metro station, and the Garden Ring Road, where you can catch a tram or bus. The Hotel Arabat has air conditioners in the rooms. A suite is comfortable although a single room is small. The hotel is clean and there is usually someone on staff who can speak a little English. You can use their laundry service and they will wash, dry, iron and fold everything. The cost is not unreasonable. It is about $150 per night for a two room suite, including breakfast and taxes (remember taxes are really high). You may have to pay an extra $10 per night for a crib. The suite rooms have a refrigerator, and you can get hot water from the floor ladies. They have one computer in the business center, and it is $5 per hour for internet access (as opposed to $30 at the Marriott).

Back in the old Soviet days, all foreigners were put up at the **Intourist** hotel. The Intourist was a huge hotel located just around the corner from the Kremlin. It was very centrally located. Before 1998, the Intourist was a drab, no service, Soviet type of place. But a lot of money was spent refurbishing and it was not bad at all and reasonably priced. It has now been closed and it is being demolished with plans to build a five star Hilton on the site.

Another very nice and expensive hotel is the **Kempinski Baltchug** in Moscow. It is German owned. They have an English speaking staff, great rooms (with view too), pool, and business center. Parents rave about the pool. The adoption rate is about $250 a night. Regular rates are between $225-$270. A suite is $500 a night. These rates are all before the hefty taxes, but they do include breakfast. It is pricey, but they have everything you need, including trustworthy taxis. Their Sunday Brunch (lunch/dinner 12-7) includes a playroom with a clown to keep the kids busy while you dine. Like any good New York hotel, they can arrange tickets to the Bolshoi, the Zoo, etc. It has the usual king size bed, television, and wonderful bathroom. It is directly across the river from the Kremlin and Red Square and comes with a terrific nighttime view of both. The Kempinski is a 5 star hotel, which is normally out of everyone's price range unless there is a special. Always inquire.

There is also the **Swiss Diamond/Golden Ring** hotel—which is located across the street from the McDonald's at the end of Old Arbat Street. This is obviously located well for shopping and is about a 30 minute walk from Red Square. It is across from the Belgrade. It is about $150-160 a night and has a good business center with Internet access.

An old soviet hotel is the "**Ukraina.**" It is a piece of Moscow's architectural history-like a Grand Old Lady. It is sometimes referred to as one of "Stalin's 7 Gothics." It is located across the river from the Russian White House, which was part of Russia's recent history. It is near the U.S. Embassy. It has been refurbished and has a business center where you can send and receive emails and faxes. Being near a fax machine can be important if some of your US documents need to be changed. It has large suites with lots of room, but is not as convenient to the Kremlin as the Moskva. It is priced from $100 to $150 a day, although a travel agency may be able to obtain a lower rate. Be careful about paying too little as the room will be less renovated. Also, be aware that they will charge quite a bit for a cot. It might just be better to get two rooms next to each other, if you have more people. Ask for a suite. Try to pay as you go and not prepay. Breakfast is included. The rooms are clean and some of the suites have gigantic, high ceilings and may even include a piano. There is a gift shop and money exchange in the hotel as well. The hotel has little soaps and shampoo just like in the USA. The tubs are very deep and there is plenty of hot water (don't laugh). There are restaurants in the hotel. Food at the downstairs breakfast buffet is not bad at all. You will see the usual assortment of rolls, tea, coffee, hot and cold cereal, and sliced cheeses. You can even have a pizza delivered to your suite. One little extra is that there is a hotel doctor, in case your child is sick or you are. Lots of tourists such as Japanese, Germans and Americans stay there. It is fairly safe. It used to not have air conditioning so if you are planning to stay there during the summer, check first to see if they have any air-conditioned rooms. This is good advice for any hotel during the short, but stifling hot summer months. It has a free shuttle that runs every hour or so to Red

Square. The staff is nice, and a few speak English. McDonalds is not too far away and there is a good baby store around the corner.

Near the "Ukraina" is a Quikmart type store within easy walking distance. It sells cheese, bread, juice, chocolate and feminine products. There is also a baby and kids store next door.

Many people like the **National** while in Moscow. It is an historic, (recently renovated) beautiful hotel. Members of the Russian Royal family used to stay there. It is reportedly in the same line as the Marriott hotels. It was built in 1903 and has 6 floors, 231 rooms, 3 restaurants, 3 bars, 12 conference rooms, fitness center, beauty salon, business center. Most rooms have air conditioning and a minibar. Because of the lack of air conditioning in some of the older hotels (like the Belgrade), the National is a good choice if you are traveling during the summer. Some rooms are small, so if you get one just ask for another. But all rooms are beautiful. The service is excellent. If you need an extra cot, they will gladly provide one. They have a buffet breakfast that goes with the room that is great and starts at 7 or 7:30 am. The kids will love the buffet as it has everything. There is a cafe that is almost always open. Most of staff speaks English. There is a place to exchange your money, get directions, and a little shop. They supply a hairdryer, shampoo, and conditioner in the room. It is like being at home. It is across the street from Red Square, the Kremlin, and the GUM shopping mall. McDonalds is nearby. Security is good as well. It even has a pool.

Some parents have stayed at the **Mir Hotel**. The cost is about $125 a night and includes a very generous breakfast buffet. The suite room has a bedroom and living room, refrigerator, table and desk. It also has regular size bath towels. It's a regular hotel. Nothing fancy. They have nice cribs They also have room service. It is about a five minute walk to the Embassy and there is a market just down the street from the Embassy. It is across from the Russian White House. The main dining room is expensive, but a little cafe on the 5th floor isn't too bad for the cost. The Mir is very security conscious and if this is a concern, then this may be a reason to stay here. It is not that kid friendly so it might be better on the trip in, but not going out.

Another old Soviet hotel is the "**Moskva**" at 2 Okhotny Ryad (095) 960-2020 Fax (095) 925-0155. This hotel overlooks Manezhnaya Square and is right next to the Kremlin and down the block from McDonalds. It is very convenient. It underwent renovation in 1997. In 1997 the price was $100 per night. The hotel is across from the State Duma and when the legislature is in session the "ladies of the night" patrol outside. The two wings of the hotel, on either side of its central core, are asymmetrical and in different architectural styles. The story is strange. The architect of the Moskva submitted his design for the hotel to Stalin in 1931. His blueprint had alternative versions for the wings and he imagined that Stalin would choose between the two. Unfortunately, when the architect received the blueprint back he discovered Stalin had simply signed in the middle of the page, apparently not realizing he was being offered a choice. The architect, reflecting on the possibly terminal consequences for him if he did not follow Stalin's instructions literally, then built the Moskva with two different wings.

It was finished in 1938 and, with an extension to the east built later, could accommodate 2,000 guests. It was considered the most luxurious hotel in the capital during the Second World War, and Guy Burgess, the Soviet spy in the British Foreign Office who defected, lived in the Moskva until his death in 1963. It also became well known to drinkers of vodka outside Russia because a picture of the hotel appears on the label of every bottle of Stolichnaya.

The Moscow City government, which is a country all to itself, is continuing to debate the fate of the Moskva. The latest news is that it will be torn down in late 2003 and in typical Russian tradition, rebuilt as a 5 star hotel in the same lopsided way.

Another former Soviet hotel next to Red Square is the **Rossiya Hotel**. This hotel is literally across the street from Red Square. It is very convenient plus you can get some excellent photos of Red Square from the higher floors of the hotel. It is a huge hotel like a labyrinth. Ask to stay in one of the newly renovated rooms that overlook Red Square. It costs about $70-90 per night and includes a huge breakfast. For an extra $10 you can get a room with a great view of Red Square and St Basil's. There are cafes on every corner of every floor. One floor, it may be the sixth, has everything in English. Room service is good and not expensive. Except for that floor, most of the staff is not fluent in English. It is hit or miss when you speak to the staff. If you call the front desk, they will transfer you to someone who speaks English so it isn't so bad. It has a bar/restaurant that serves great Pelmeni.There are no latches on the windows so make sure no one crawls out on the ledge. This hotel is not the one to use during the summer, as most rooms do not have air conditioning.

What people like most about the **Rossiya** are the location and the real Russian experience. The 9th Floor provides some spectacular views. It's not the oasis like the Marriott, but you can just walk outside and walk over to the Kremlin "mall" every evening to shop and eat as well as to GUM. St. Basil's Cathedral lights up every night right outside your window. Now your husband may get a few phone calls from inquiring "ladies of the night." Usually husbands think it is pretty funny, while wives have a different opinion. This usually happens when the Duma is in session. Wonder why. If you like adventure,this hotel is for you, but if you want a more normal atmosphere, try another.

The **Rossiya** also has a taxi stand in the lobby. You can arrange for a taxi to take you to Old Arbat Street (make sure you tell them OLD Arbat street) to shop or to anywhere. They will give you a business card in Russian and English that tells you how to call them for a return trip. You can just go into a restaurant and gave them the card and the restaurant will call for you and a short while later a taxi guy will come into the restaurant with a sign that says "Hotel Rossiya."

It is always much safer to take a taxi arranged by your hotel than to get one on your own. This is why most families walk, go by Metro or only get into a taxi with their facilitator or homestay host. In Moscow they also have gypsy taxis, which can be interesting if you are traveling with a Russian. These are large cars that wait by the curb until they are filled with people before they go. Everyone then chips in with the fare and the passenger in front collects the money for the driver. It works out fine and since Russians still have a community (collective) sense no one minds sharing the ride. Outside Moscow taxis are not expensive and should be no more than .50 cents to $2 an hour at the most, if you are paying the Russian rate. The rate charged you if your agency sets it up is a lot higher. Remember there is two tier fee system in Russia, a lower one for Russians and higher one for foreigners.

If you have a large entourage with you, such as a couple of kids and maybe a relative or two, then consider staying at the new refurbished **Slavyanka**. It is more like a suite hotel with kitchen facilities. You can buy groceries and simply eat in. This will save on the hassle and expense of going out to eat.

Another hotel is the **Hotel President**. A lot of businessmen use it. It is expensive, although the adoption discount rate is between $160-$170. The bedrooms are large, with two double beds, huge bathrooms, a desk, refrigerator and TV. It has a large breakfast buffet, which is included in the price. The hotel overlooks Gorky Park and most windows have excellent views. There is a business center with the usual computers, fax machines and Internet access at $6 per hour (compare Marriott's $30 per hour). Calling the US from your room can be very expensive so always check the rate before using the room phone to call home. (This is good advice for any phone you use.) It is reported that you can access the Internet from your room using your laptop. They do not charge for local calls from your room at all (Marriott does—30 cents a minute for all local calls). You can use your calling cards to call home. Also each room has direct phone number, so if your relatives and friends want to call you they do not have to go through an operator. Like most hotels there is a money exchange in the building. There are two supermarkets nearby, one

Russian style and one western and a children's clothing store. The gift shop in the hotel had great stuff at reasonable rates. You can even have pizza and subs delivered to your room from a local food place called Hot Smile. Security is very high and comforting, although some parents found it overbearing.The adoption rate includes the breakfast buffet. It has been described as being adoption friendly. Some parents like the fact they can take short walks with their new child to the nearby "Statue Park." Contrast this with the Marriott Grand, which is in a congested area. It is a 25 minute walk to Red Square. It has a swimming pool on one of the top floors. It is reportedly heavily chlorinated and only open certain hours.

There is also a **Holiday Inn** in Moscow. It is about 2 years old and costs around $120 plus a 5% sales tax and includes breakfast. The day rate is half of that. It is clean and nice. They have a small Casino, ping pong, a 4 lane bowling alley, a work out room, very small pool and nice rooms with CNN and air conditioning. They also have Internet access at $10 an hour and the computers have Windows in English. It is easy to hook your digital camera via USB and email pictures. Some of the staff speaks English. It is about 20 minutes from Sheremtyevo-2 and 40 minutes from Red Square. There is a free shuttle to both places. It is not near the center of the city, so if you need to be close to the US Embassy or Red Square, you may not want to stay there. The hotel is located in a village and out the front door are houses with little gardens. They have a little park pass to use the tennis courts. The park has a lake. It is not bad for a first trip and reasonably priced.

Near the Shermetyevo-2 airport, about a mile away, is the **Novotel.** It is literally right across the parking lot from the arrival gate. It is on the other side of a major highway though, which makes walking to it difficult. The hotel has a desk inside the airport, and there is a shuttle bus that travels between the hotel and the airport every 15 minutes. The hotel has 8 floors set around a central atrium. The Novotel is opulent downstairs and austere upstairs. There is a security officer in front of the elevators, and the elevators can only be operated by a room key. A typical room has a queen size bed and a sofa, which turns into a single bed. It comes with a small refrigerator and a TV that has cable (including CNN). Bottled water was in is in your room, and replacement bottles were for sale at the bar. The bathroom has a combination bath/shower and everything is very clean. As is often found in Europe, no facecloths are provided. The staff is very pleasant and speaks English. Many airline crews stay there, so the staff is multilingual. There is an excellent buffet breakfast, which is included in the room rate. Room service is available. The Novotel has a free shuttle to Red Square leaving every other hour with the last return leaving Red Square at 11pm. Travel time each way is 45 minutes. There is a small exercise room with a small pool. There is a bar and an "American" restaurant. Prices are from $155 to $185 a night. The Novotel also offers day rooms for about $70.00. They also have a late checkout for an additional $70. There is a small gift shop. Being right there at the airport can make it easy on your travel plans. You can purchase a video showing one family's adoption journey, including their stay at the Novotel, at *http://www.adoptlaw.org/tiac_htm/5stories.htm* by scrolling down to the video "Adopting a New Life."

There is a cheaper hotel near the international airport, across the road from the Novotel, called the **Sheremetyevo Hotel**. It is around $60 per night. It is not safe to stay there. Many report thefts from the rooms.

Remember that when you check in to any hotel, the staff will take your passport and visa for a few hours in order to register you. They will then return it. Make sure you remember that they need to return it. This is an old hold over procedure from Soviet days when all foreigners had to be registered. Eventually this procedure will disappear as has giving your key to the floor women each time you leave your room.

Remember also that if you are paying for something using a credit card, you might be told the price in US Dollars, but they then add tax (may not even mention it to you), and then they have you sign a credit card slip (amount is almost ALWAYS in Russian Rubles)—and you have absolutely no idea what are you signing. Always keep the exchange rate in your head or on your calculator and before you sign, convert the amount to dollars so you know how much you are being charged. Once you have signed the charge slip it is virtually impossible to dispute the charge when you find out back home it is much higher than you thought. For example, at one time the exchange rate used by Delta on a change of ticket charge was so different than the street rate as to make the charge in dollars almost double.

There is always tax on everything, but some agencies or companies give you the real price, including taxes, and some—to make things look attractive—do not even mention taxes unless you ask them.

Moscow Restaurants

Sometimes you just want a meal like home. You will find many adoptive parents congregate at McDonalds, Patio Pizza, Patio Pasta, Starlight Diner, American Bar and Grill, Pizza Hut, TGIFridays, and Il Pomodoro. These are all downtown near the large hotels like the Marriott Grand. There is also a Baskin Robbins very close to the Marriott Tverskaya. Check the restaurant review section on the web site for the Moscow Times before you go. If you plan to walk around, ask your hotel if they have a stroller loaner. And never cross a street, but use the underground passageways.

There is a large supermarket near both Marriotts. You come out of the Marriott onto Tverskaya, turn right and go one block to the next street. Turn right again, go about 2 blocks and you will come to a very large western style supermarket where you can buy pretty much anything except souvenirs. It has a very good bakery and deli section as well as all the usual stuff (fresh fruits and veggies, canned foods, baby food and diapers, etc.) It is a short 5 minute walk from the Marriott Grand and is about the same as any nice supermarket you will find here.

A good Mexican restaurant in Moscow is "Hola Mexico" (a/k/a Previt Mexico) near Detsky Mir. It is located at Pushechnaya Ulitsa 7/5. The phone number is 925-8251. You can also order pizza from Tulio's Pizza or Deli Meals at 978-5776 or 251-3338. They also have a great variety of salads and subs. They will deliver. This may be a good alternative to expensive hotel food.

There are several McDonalds in town. If you have been in-country for a few weeks, there is nothing better. There is also a Pizza Hut, which is usually crowded, and a TGIF. Both of these are located not far from the Marriott Grand. Patio Pizza is also a favorite with Americans and is near Pizza Hut. Also, right before you get to Patio Pizza is American Bar and Grill. They do a pretty good hamburger and have a good meatloaf, but they do not succeed so well on the Tex-Mex entrees. Their beer prices are most reasonable. There is a restaurant called Mongolian BBQ on Treveskya. It's about three blocks toward Red Square from the Marriott Grande. You can cook your own food so you know it's done right and the price is reasonable.

A subway stop from the US Embassy is an interesting Diner, the Starlight, which serves great hamburgers. It is a favorite with Expat business types. The story is that they brought in the Diner, lock, stock and barrel, from the United States. They use Baskins Robbins ice cream for all of their desserts and they make a mean chocolate shake.

Probably the best food in Russia is Georgian. Georgian food usually includes a good and somewhat spicy soup called kharcho, a warm bread called khachapuri which is stuffed with a feta type cheese, grilled meats, greens (raw) to be eaten with another type of bread, and good wine. There are two very good and reasonably priced Georgian restaurants. One is Diascuria located on a side street off of Novy Arbat. The Metro stop should be Arbat. The other is Guryia is on Komsomolski Prospekt, a ten minute walk from the Metro stop, Park Kultury. Not far from Gorky Park, is a very good Georgian restaurant,

Pectoral and even closer to the park is another Georgian restaurant, Rypya (Guria) that is a simple local restaurant with basic delicious food.

Another good restaurant is Scandinavia located on Maly Palashevsky Pereulok near the Grand. It is a splurge place at over $50 per person. But has truly outstanding fish dishes. And the place does feel Scandinavian. Another very good place is the City Grill located on Sadovaya Truimfalnaya (just a block from the Grand). It is an American style place with good grilled meats, salads and such, all with a semi California flair. Lots of ex pats eat there. The restaurant does have an English menu and the staff speaks some English.

For traditional cuisine with a family atmosphere, try "Yolki Palki." This is a kind of chain family restaurant with good food and reasonable prices. Near or on old Arbat Street are several good restaurants: MyMy (pronounced Moo Moo) has Russian food cafeteria style on old Arbat Street. A Ukrainian restaurant on old Arbat Street and Mexana Bancko (Bulgarian Restaurant) are nearby.

If you decide to go to a real upscale restaurant, and there are a few of those around, just be prepared to sit with the New Russians a/k/a/ Russian Mafia. They now drive Lincoln Navigators and Cadillac Escalades as opposed to their old stand-by of Range Rovers, which are now considered passe.

Russian Culture

Forget all that tourist stuff, here is the real scoop on when you know you are in Russia. All Russians wear black clothing and the Russian women are dressed up all the time. The women will out fashion you, just get use to it. All of the men wear black leather type jackets. (Now in truth, jeans have become far more universal than they were just a few years ago.)

Russians are very concerned with the dangers of sitting on cold concrete. They don't do it and they don't want us to do it. They believe it will make you very sick and cause sterility. So don't be surprised if a babushka yells at you for sitting on a concrete step. She is just looking out for your own welfare. If you see a Russian sitting on concrete, you can be sure that he or she is really sitting on something else and not directly on the concrete.

Every Russian is a member of the "hat police". If you are not wearing a hat, then something must be wrong with you. A ball cap is not a hat and no decent Russian would wear a ball cap. Be prepared to be lectured to if your child is not wearing the proper hat.

There is a substantial difference of opinion between Russians and Americans as to the wearing of clothes. We believe that clothes should fit the temperature and that if it is warm, then you do not need layers of clothing. Russians believe that the warmer you are, the healthier you are. Thus, they will insist that your child wear layers and layers of clothes when you think just one layer will do.

Russian men do not push baby strollers or change diapers. American men know better than to say no. Still, you may get a funny look as you stroll along. Deal with it. On the other hand, women do not carry suitcases when there is a man around.

If you have a cold you should put garlic or honey up your nose. Eastern Europeans have this idea that fresh air and breezes contribute to disease. It is a little like the early 18th Century idea in America that "bad air" or "vapors" caused malaria and other problems. So do not be surprised if you find yourself in a car or a house where the windows are rarely opened. Nor be surprised if in some orphanages the infants are not taken outside very much, if at all.

If you shake hands over a threshold you'll have bad luck. Whistle inside a building and you will lose your money. You can't swim in August because it's bad luck. Hand shaking is a common practice, but don't shake hands over a threshold as it also brings bad luck. If you give flowers, give only an odd number. An even number of flowers is usually put on the grave. Also because plastic flowers are mainly for the graves. Avoid giving them as a gift to older people. Younger people are more progressive in this respect and more accepting of artificial flowers.

Please remember to tip the bathroom attendant a few rubles. This is basic bathroom etiquette. This is not a Russian thing, but a European thing.

Russians live in buildings with central heat. By central heat I mean the boiler in the basement is cranked up on November 1 and runs nonstop until May 30. The only way to regulate the temperature is by cracking a window. You will either get use to the hot buildings or live by a window. Those are your choices. You will know you are in Russia when you have to hike up four long flights of stairs to your home stay apartment or talk to three different sales clerks (one counter to order the product and obtain a slip of paper, then to the cash desk to pay, and then to the pick-up desk to get it) to buy a diet coke. When you see turquoise, onion-domed minarets piercing the sky or hear the strains of balalaika music drifting from the shuttered door of a factory, you know you are in Russia.

Russians are a communal people by culture as well as by philosophy. In restaurants Russians will not hesitate to join a table with strangers rather than dine alone. Men kiss men and show affection, women hold hands while strolling. Recreation is often arranged in groups, often with colleagues with whom they work. They prefer organized sports with set teams. In a collective society, everybody's business is also everyone else's.

Russians do not stand with their hands in their pockets. Do not tell a Russian that you have to go to the restroom, just excuse yourself. Do not lounge or sit on the steps of a public building. Drinks are always served with something to eat, even if only a cookie.

Now let me give you a few stereotypes, all of which have a grain of truth in them. Russians are more likely to be cautious and to value stability, security, social order, and predictability. They avoid risk. The old is preferred over the new. Russian culture is very male-chauvinistic, even though the women are more responsible. Russian women are excellent naggers. Men retreat from this by hanging around together smoking and drinking vodka late into the night. (If they had a few sports bars, you could hardly tell us apart.)

Now, Americans stand out like a sore thumb. There is not much you can do about it, even if you dress all in black. We all tend to smile and look up a lot, whereas most Russians don't smile and usually look down. Smiling is deemed to be a sign of insincerity and/or mental illness unless you are with family and friends. Smile and they'll think you're the village idiot. What is interesting is that your facilitator is probably a hybrid. He will have characteristics of old Russia, but also of the new, entrepreneurial kind as well. Russians who have immigrated to the US and returned to visit are likely to be told, "*Prekrati uli-bat'sya. Ty ulibayesh'sya kak idiotka*", or "Stop smiling. You are smiling like an idiot." "*Chto lyudi podumayut?*" "What will people think?"

Russians view their laws as tools hanging on a belt. Pick one up and use it— if you like—is often the attitude. Enforcement of laws, rules, and procedures is often not uniform within one region or from one area to the next. This is because Russia used to be a land where the rules were contradictory and enforcement was not for the greater good of the many, but the greater good of the few. In order to just survive, you had no choice but ignore the law. When Americans hear of a new law we think about how we will comply, but the average Russian (or citizen of any FSU republic) thinks "…how can we get around this so we can live through the winter."

Russians love a good dip in a banya, Russia's version of a spa. As the modern world catches up to Russia, these are becoming anachronistic. The ritual is to steam yourself in the steam room, followed by a scrub down then a beating with birch branches and then perhaps a run in the snow and back to do it all over again. Downtown Moscow has the historic and architectural wonder Sandunovskaya Banya. Russian women sometimes bring their own beauty aids: coffee grounds to rub on the body, honey for the face and eggs for the hair.

Russians have a wicked sense of humor. Mostly it is about them. Even in Soviet days they would joke that "They pretend to pay us, and we pretend to work."

Here are a couple of other examples.

A Russian peasant's neighbor owns a cow. The peasant owns none. The peasant finds a bottle with a genie in it. The genie says you can have one wish, would you like a cow like your neighbor? No, replies the peasant, just kill my neighbor's cow.

Others in that vein:

God says to the peasant, "I will give you anything you ask, but remember I will give double to your neighbor. Ok, says the peasant, take the sight from one of my eyes."

These jokes are really a commentary on Soviet society. The Russian novelist Vladimir Voinovich once described his country's people as "...crabs in a basket. When one crab tries to climb out, the other ones pull him back."

Stalin, Khrushchev, Brezhnev and Yeltsin were on a train. The train broke down and stopped. Stalin said shoot all the engineers. Krushchev said send them to Siberia. Brezhnev said just close the curtains and pretend like we are moving, and Yeltsin said, "I'll drink to that."

A retired American intelligence agent is sitting on a bench with a Russian. The Russian asks him what he did. The agent says "I used to go to work every day and think of ways to destroy your country." The Russian thinks about this for a moment and then says, "well, the Communists beat you to it."

Chukcha bought a refrigerator.
Neighbor asks: "What do you need this 'fridge for? You live in Siberia."
Response: "To warm up during winter. Imagine the joy—it's -40 outside and +4 in a refrigerator."

A man showed some friends his apartment in Russia. One guest asked,
"What's that big brass basin for?"
That's the talking clock," answered the man. He gave it an ear-shattering pound with a hammer.
Suddenly, a voice on the other side of the wall screamed, "It's 2 a.m., you jerk!"

I like this one the best.

"I wish to propose a toast to the guest of honor, our deeply-cherished First Secretary, K.I. Kotenkov! I do not toast Comrade Kotenkov for his big, beautiful apartment that we've all seen, or for his lovely place in the country either! I do not toast Comrade Kotenkov for his German Audi automobile, for his fine Swiss watch, or his new Japanese stereo system! I do not even toast Comrade Kotenkov for his gorgeous young wife—or for all his girlfriends! No, brothers—tonight I raise my glass to our beloved Kiril Ivanovich for being a GOOD COMMUNIST!"

People individually are warm and generous, yet the overall lack of resources in Russia is astounding. It underlies any discussion about what can be done. There is a depression in Russia; people do not have the American attitude of "we can do anything". To the contrary, they are still dealing with the latent effects of Communism where the belief was "the state would take care of you no matter what", even though that is no longer true. People are learning a new way of thinking and that transition is difficult and painful. Indeed, after 70 years of de-humanization followed by 10 years of financial devaluations, chaos, and economic anarchy, the long suffering Russian is no longer just an image but a reality! What is worse is that Russians are accustomed to living in the present time, not planning for the long run, since in their experience, the future is always worse not better.

Life in Russia is unpredictable, but there are some things of which you can be sure:

1) It will always be freezing cold in the winter.
2) You will always be offered a glass of vodka with your cabbage soup.
3) The Russian traffic police will always be on the lookout for a backhander.

A good road cop can earn up to 20 times his paycheck in fine money—which is precisely why they are the bane of Russian drivers. You can be sure that at least once a week a cop will bring your driver's car to a screeching halt with a flash of his black and white poky stick. He'll approach the window, throw a brief salute and then it's down to business. Just let your driver handle it. It is all part of living and driving in Russia.

The Russian Duma or legislature is very much like any legislature in the US and Russian politicians can be described in the same terms as the Austin American-Statesman once described the Texas Legislature, "[s]ome are inspired geniuses mindful only of the greater good; some are connivers mindful only of personal good; most are wondering what's for lunch."

A good book to read which explains more about our cultural differences (and similarities) is Yale Richmond's From Nyet to Da. This book gives many more insights into Russian culture. Another interesting book is Red Tape, which gives insights (and has great stories) on doing business in Russia. An interesting web site on Russian customs is at http://www.infoservices.com/stpete/342.htm.

Safety Issues

Metropolitan Moscow has 22 million people. If you pretend you are in New York, you will do just fine in Moscow. In Moscow do not tell anyone where you are staying unless they are connected to your agency. Since you will be carrying around a lot of cash, you do not want to give anyone an invitation. Moscow is a lot like New York, except larger. The people move fast and are just as rude. A woman with a stroller is not cut any slack. Make sure you carry a piece of paper with the name and address of your homestay or hotel in case you get separated from your facilitator.

Russia has the usual begging and pickpocket scams: the girl with the fake baby asking for money; the groups of gypsy children that will crowd around you; the pickpocket behind you working with the man in front of you. These are all basic scams. Just be aware of your surroundings. If you feel trapped, create a scene. Of course, creating a scene doesn't always work. I once had a few gypsy children approach me on a Moscow street corner, so I danced around like I was doing a warpath dance. When I was done, they applauded!

Russians believe that everyone must eat, even bureaucrats. So it is possible a policeman might stop your car. Your driver will simply negotiate a fair price (fair to the policeman).

You may have heard of the Russian Mafia. They are not Siberian Sicilians. Rather they are Georgians, Chechens or even Russians. You can always tell who they are. They dress like Don Corelone, in black with wide lapels. They are the only ones who can afford a cell phone and a Mercedes. Some of them look like Odd Job from Goldfinger.Their basic business is protection. It is simple, bloody and right out of Godfather 101. They will leave you alone. You should leave them alone. You can pretty much assume that any factory or store in Russia in any large town is paying protection money to somebody. But it is not your concern. Indeed, the big corruption is by the former Communist Party aristocracy, the nomenclatura, and not by these jokers.

Notwithstanding that Russia has a murder rate three times that of the United States, Moscow, as a whole is very safe for tourists. Personal safety is not an issue, although property theft is. You should not leave any valuables in your hotel room and all suitcases should be zipped up when you leave your hotel room. Needless to say, you should maintain American safety rules and don't go out at night by yourself or to places you don't know. In Russia, you can contact the Fire Department by dialing 01, Police Department—by dialing 02, and Paramedics—by dialing 03.

During the adoptive process there is bound to be something going on in Russia that will give you pause. Just remember that your agency will not send you to Russia if there is a real safety concern. An example of a crisis is the financial collapse in August 1998. It seemed dire at the time and it did upset the normal wiring of funds. Families had to carry more cash than normal. Yet that was about the only effect the crisis had. Remember that the American press blows up every crisis in Russia as if it were the end of the world.

The NATO bombing of Belgrade was another crisis. Indeed, the Russians took a dim view of the United Sates' involvement in the bombing. Yet Russians were not upset with adoptive couples and differentiated between our government's actions and its people. In all but a few instances, the adoption process went on as before. In fact, the demonstrators outside the Embassy were actually a very small number and were outnumbered by the police. The demonstrations only lasted a few days and in all that time the Embassy's visa function went on as before. The only difference was that you went in the back door instead of the front.

The US invasion of Iraq was also a huge negative, but although the information flow in Russia is still limited and controlled, Russians are perfectly capable of separating what a government does from what its individual citizens may think. Occasionally, a Judge would ask parents what they think of US actions in Belgrade or Iraq. The best answer was to noncommittally say "I don't get involved in politics, and it is always sad when people are hurt." A court hearing on adoption is not the place to expound on your views of the world. Use discretion and common sense.

Next year there will be something else and the year after that. Just keep your head and when the time comes to travel, take your cue from your agency. After all, they should be in almost daily contact with the facilitator in Russia whose job it is to keep you safe.

Shopping

It may be that you find yourself with a little time to kill. The answer is to go shopping! Try to avoid the stores you can find in the United States like IKEA. This chain has proliferated throughout Moscow stoking the Muscovites desire to spend rather than save. It is a Swedish furniture and home accessories chain selling cheap chic. Just wait until one comes to your hometown.

If you travel near the end of the year you will have the opportunity to buy Russian holiday greeting cards. Look for New Year's cards in kiosks. They will display Father Frost, bells, winter scenes and churches. One good idea is to pick up books of postcards and newspapers or magazines while in Russia, these made interesting souvenirs for people and also are inexpensive and do not take up much room.

You may also find pretty but inexpensive baptism outfits for your child. They are sold in the old Arbat as well as in other places. Parents buy Russian dresses and headbands.and even traditional Russian costumes for their kids to wear on Christmas morning You can also purchase Christmas ornaments. (How you get them back to the United States without breaking them is beyond me.) There are also plenty of vendors who will want to sell you the usual Russian fur hat and St. Basil watercolor. There is a children's store called Dyetsky Mir next to the KGB at the Lubyanka Metro station. It's really close to the Kremlin.

Many people are interested in Matryoshka dolls (sometimes called Matrioshka). A good place to buy them is in the flea market (Vernisage market) across from Moscow State University in Izmailovski Park. and on Arbat street and in GUM. Prices vary quite a bit and are open to negotiation. Pick up the doll, turn it around and check for the quality of the lacquer job and the detail of the paint. Be sure to check if it is chipped at the center. Check the bottom to see if is signed and dated. Try to pack them so there is no rattle when you shake the doll. Try not to use newspaper to pack your dolls for transport.

The ink can rub off and if the shellac isn't all the way dry (this happens on occasion), then it will make black marks on the finish. Use toilet paper or paper towels or plain newsprint. Bubble wrap is nice to wrap the entire doll and if you bring them home in checked luggage, then protect them further with a rigid plastic container. If the dolls are hard to open, press gently on the seam, all around the doll, with your thumbs. If the fit is too tight, lubricate that joint with plain paraffin, a candle or soap.

Lomonosov cobalt net design porcelain is sometimes a good buy. You can buy it at Gostiny Dvor in St. Petersburg and in other places around Moscow. The only way to get the pieces home is by taking them as carryon items. Lacquer furniture for children is also a common buy. You will see these in all Russian homes. Samovars are available on the Arbat as are Russian costumes.

A good place to shop in Moscow is #27 Old Arbat. It is a shop with almost every souvenir you can imagine, at reasonable prices. The t-shirts that are sold in Russia are often made in India and they will shrink. You may be able to fins a few old style CCCP hockey jerseys from a few vendors on Arbat. Near the Bolshoi you can sometimes find vendors selling posters with the Russian alphabet. These have a nice, sturdy quality. Just beyond the Bolshoi there is a large children's store that has beautiful toys, books, posters and clothing, baby supplies, and even a Baskin Robbins.

North of Moscow are the villages Mysteria, Fedoskino and Palekh. These have the best lacquer artists. You want to buy boxes from them or find a store in Moscow which sells them. The boxes must be signed by the artist.

If you have never bargained overseas, ask a friend for the unwritten rules before you travel. Generally, you should not show the clerk that you are very interested in the item. Be prepared to walk away. Ask the price but don't look too anxious. Have a price in your head at which you are willing to buy. Don't be embarrassed to make a low ball offer. If you don't like the price quoted by the clerk, start walking away. Keep walking if the vendor does not reduce the price. If you want to buy several dolls or other items, demand a discount for a bulk purchase (think of presents for friends). Ask questions regarding any discounts. Be friendly throughout the process. Remember that if they say "no," that doesn't really mean "no". Be flexible on buying a less popular color or model. Check to see if there is even a slight scratch or other damage as you might be able to use that to get a slight discount at the higher end stores. Make sure the sales person knows you have adopted as they might give you a sympathy discount. Finally, you can always practice the famous "crunch", whereby you ask for an extra after you have made the deal but before paying the money. When packing dolls for travel, be careful to avoid having the paint chip during transit. Wrap each individual unit with cloth or paper.

You should obtain a receipt for all items of value purchased in Russia. Customs officials often consider articles, such as icons, samovars, rugs, paintings, coins, books, rugs, sculptures, musical instruments, medals and antiques, to be of cultural value. Under Russian law, such items require a certificate from the Russian Ministry of Culture indicating that it has no historical or cultural value and is exportable from Russia. Even if you purchased these sorts of items at an open-air market in Moscow, you may need a certificate. You may be able to also obtain this certificate from the store that sold the item. The certificates may be obtained from the Russian Ministry of Culture, at the Department of Preservation of Cultural Values, at 7 Kitaygorodskiy Pr., Rm. 103, tel. 095-928-5089.

Moscow Tourist Sights

Before you go, read one of the many books now published on Moscow and its history. In addition to the Lonely Planet and Fodor guides, there is also a pretty good travel guide by DK books called, "Moscow". It is a DK Eyewitness book. It covers everything from where to stay, eat, and shop and what to look for when picking a taxi (be very careful). It contains a survival guide with lots of practical info for traveling to Moscow and a phrase book in the back You can also hire a tour company If you are short on time go to this web site:
http://www.lonelyplanet.com/dest/eur/mos.htm.
One tip is to hire your translator or her mother to babysit your child for a few hours. This will give you the time to explore Moscow. It may be your last time.
In the evening many of Moscow's sights are beautifully lit with colored lights reflecting off the waters from the fountains. Here are some of the sights you might want to catch at night:

1. The new Historical museum has lighting emphasizing its beautiful architecture.
2. There are fountains on Poklonnaya Gora with colored shining lights
3. The bridge on the Neglinnaya River is lit at night.
4. See the Church of St. Nicola.
5. Pushkin Square

During the day you might go to see Novodevichy cloister (New Convent of the Maidens). This is where much palace intrigue took place in the 1600s. Nearby is a cemetery containing all the famous Russians like Chekhov, Khrushchev and the great composer Shostakovich. The anarchist Kropotkin is also buried here. Kropotkin was the Ozzy Osbourne of the 19th Century socialist/anarchist movement. You might also see Iverskaya chapel or Petrovskiy castle.

The Kremlin, St. Basils, GUM department store and Red Square are must things to see. The Kremlin is worth a half day itself. There is a great jewelry collection in the Armory Palace Museum including the Faberge Eggs. The rooms are stuffed full of gold plates and bible covers encrusted with rubies. Its real name is Moscow Kremlin State Museum-Preserve of History and Culture. It was founded 500 years ago as a royal treasure house. The Kremlin is just is a terrific place to walk around. The Kremlin has several churches on its grounds including the Archangel Cathedral and Assumption Cathedral. A row of Napoleon's cannon lines the wall when you first enter the grounds. Near them is the Tsar's Bell, which is huge but also very cracked. Near the bell is the huge, but not cracked Tsar's Cannon. On the outside of the Kremlin wall are many towers including the Tower of Secrets, which is the oldest, and Savior's Tower. Lenin's tomb is still on Red Square but its hours of operation are irregular. Across from the tomb is GUM, built in the 19th century and filled with hundreds of upscale stores.

Yeltsin wanted Lenin's Tomb to disappear and the poor guy finally buried. However, he still is in residence. You cannot take a camera or purse into the tomb. You walk into a long dark hall that gently slopes down for 50 feet or so and then turn 180 degrees and continue down further. Lenin lies there flat on his back, dead as a doornail, staring at the ceiling.

There is a huge, modern underground mall next to the Kremlin. In the food court is a Chinese restaurant and next to that is a large Internet café.

If you like shopping then check out the Arbat, new and old, and the flea market across from Sparrow Hill. The Tretayakov Gallery (icons and Russian art) near Gorky Park and the Pushkin Fine Arts Museum (western art) are two of the world's best art museums. The National War Museum is also of great interest to a WWII buff.

If you arrive near a weekend, you may see lots of brides around Red Square. There is a tradition that when you get married, you have your picture taken at the Tomb of the Unknown Soldier. The Tomb is a flame and lies next to the Kremlin wall. It is part of the monument to WWII, which contains markers with the names of the cities involved in the great battles. The story is that the young boy lying in the Unknown grave died where the big tank barrier symbol is located (looks like a giant's ball and jacks set) The brides also travel to Sparrow Hills near Moscow State to have their picture taken. Sparrow or Lenin Hills overlooks Moscow and the 1980 Olympic site.

You can also visit the houses of Tolstoy, Pushkin and Dostoevsky. If you hire a Russian tour guide, explain to her that you do not want every exhibit explained only the highlights. The tour guides are trained to say something about every little thing. It will drive you crazy. Also, don't be surprised if you are told there is an additional charge to take photos in the Museums. That seems to be the general rule.

There is an outstanding collection of Russian paintings at the Tretyakov Gallery. One of the most famous icons in Russia, Andrei Rublyov's Trinity, is kept here. The collection of Russian Impressionists is also worth seeing, as they are relatively unknown in the West. A separate gallery opposite Gorky Park holds the Tretyakov's 20th-century collection, which includes key works by Soviet Realist artists. The Pushkin Museum of Fine Arts is home to Italian and Greek sculpture and European paintings, including a whole gallery of Gauguins, Renoir's Bathing in the Seine and Manet's Dejeuner sur l'herbe. In the basement of the Pushkin is stored a great amount of "liberated" German art.

There are two Moscow Circuses and the Durov Animal Theatre with trained animals. There is also the Obraztsov puppet theatre, which is in Russian.

If you want to go to the Bolshoi, check the schedule on-line or through your hotel concierge. The Bolshoi does not perform every night. You can order tickets through them at about $80 a ticket for box seats or get them in front of the theatre for about $10. Remember that everything in Russia is marked up for non-Russians. If you are considering attending the ballet in Moscow, you should have no problems getting tickets. Just about any subway station entrance will have a booth where you can get tickets to many events. The prices will be much lower than trying to get them through your hotel.

Moscow Metro

The Moscow metro was completed in 1935 and each station is made of marble. It is world famous and is very easy to navigate. Even so, you may want to hire a translator to teach you how to use the metro and to show you the station in the immediate vicinity of your hotel. The metro escalators move very fast and so do the people. Just look for the big block "M." They are usually blue. Walk down the steps and look for the signs that point you to the Metro (Russian = metpopo). The subway is just like the subways in Rome, Florence, DC, etc. There is a bank of gates that let you enter with a subway entrance ticket or you can go to the first gate and pay the ticket person the 3 rubles. The easiest and fastest way is to find the ticket desk and give them 30 rubles (a dollar) and they will give you this white card that has a magnetic strip on it. It is good for 10 rides. You could ride the metro all day if you wanted and you would only pay for the entrance on to the subway. The card has a red arrow on it, which you put into the slot on the entrance gate…,wait a second or two and the card will pop out and on the back will be a print out of the date and time and a big "M" will appear on the same line. Make sure that you don't just put your card in and then walk through, as you need to grab your card. Also always put your metro card back into the same spot so that you can always find it easily. If your card gets wet it won't work. The good news is that as soon as it dries out it will.

The metro is made up of 9 subway lines. Each line is colored as in D.C. When you buy your metro card you can get a 5x5 map of the line to keep in your Russian language book. It is pretty much useless to buy an English map of the Russian metro routes, as all the signs down in the subway are Russian. If you have a straight shot to your destination then just follow the color-coded map and make your exit. If you have to do a transfer then you will probably have to go up an escalator or down one to get to the different colored line. The great thing about their subway system is that they have a circle around the maze of crisscrossing lines. The circle is the brown line and it gets you easily from one side of town to the other much faster then a driver and with no pollution and no traffic jams. You should never be in a hurry to make your connection because the beauty of their metro is that every 2 minutes there is another train—like clockwork. There are metro maps on the walls outside the metro, in the waiting area and on the subway car. A few stops have been added to the lines within the past year. Just follow the colors and the arrows. Also make sure that you know the Russian word for exit to the street so that you know how to get up to your destination. It really is easy and for $4 you can travel everywhere in Moscow. This beats the $10 an hour for a driver. Some of the most spectacular stations are on the circle line, but Arbatskaya on the dark blue line (there's a not-so-impressive Arbatskaya on the light blue line), Ploshchad Revolyutsii, Novoslobodskaya and Mayakovskaya are also worth a look.

When riding the Metro, it's important to know the name of the last stop on the line, in the direction in which you are traveling. This will keep you from getting confused and going in exactly the wrong direction. If you are looking to shop, Izmailovski Park is the name of the stop for the famous Izmailovski

Park Flea Market in the ENE part of the city, where you can buy some very good Russian souvenirs.

Trains

Moscow has nine major train stations. All are served by the Moscow Metro and located near the center of the city. Most stations are connected by the metro's circle line. Taxis are readily available outside most stations, but first negotiate the price, before giving them any of your bags.

1. **Belorussky Station** serves Kalliningrad, Lithuania, Belarus, Poland, Germany, the Czech Republic and some trains to Latvia. Address: 7 Tverskaya Zastava Ploshchad; Phone: 251-6093, 973-8191; Metro: Belorusskaya

2. **Kazansky Station** serves Central Asia, Ryzan, Ufa, Samara and Novorossiisk. Address: 2 Komsomolskaya Ploshchad; Phone: 264-6556; Metro: Komsomolskaya

3. **Kievsky Station** serves Western Ukraine and Southeastern Europe. Address: Ploshchad Kievskogo Vokzala; Phone: 240-1115/0415; Metro: Kievskaya

4. **Kursky Station** serves Southern Russia, Caucasus nations, Eastern Ukraine, and Crimea. Address: 29 Ul. Zemlyanoi Val; Phone: 916-2003, 917-3152; Metro: Kurskaya

5. **Leningradsky Station** serves Estonia, Finland, St. Petersburg and northwestern Russia. Address: 3 Komsomolskaya Ploshchad; Phone: 262-9143; Metro: Komsomolskaya

6. **Paveletsky Station** serves Voronezh, Tambov, Volgograd and Astrakhan. Address: 1 Paveletskaya Ploshchad; Phone: 235-0522/6807/1920/4109 Metro: Paveletskaya

7. **Rizhsky Station** serves some trains to Latvia. Address: 79/3 Rizhskaya Ploshchad; Phone: 971-1588; Metro: Rizhskaya

8. **Savyolovsky Station** serves Kostroma, Cherepovets and some trains to Vologda. Address: Ploshchad Savyolovskogo Vokzala; Phone: 285-9005; Metro: Savyolovskaya

9. **Yaroslavlsky Station** serves Siberia, the Russian Far East, Mongolia and China. Address: 5 Komsomolskaya Ploshchad; Phone: 921-5914/0817, 262-9271; Metro: Komsomolskaya This is the station for the Trans-Siberian's southern route.

Most Russian trains fall into one of three groups: firmeny, skorry or elektrichki. Firmeny trains are long distance trains run by a private company. They usually have a name and on the whole they are faster, cleaner, more comfortable and more expensive than other trains. The Rossia (Russia), connecting Moscow and Vladivostok, and the Krasnaya Strella (Red Arrow), connecting Moscow and Petersburg, are two of the more famous firmeny trains.

All other long distance trains are the not-so-aptly named skorry poyezdy (fast trains). These are generally not as comfortable and make more stops. For shorter trips a network of elektrichki, or suburban trains surrounds most sizable Russian cities. An elektrichka has no cabins or bunks and will usually stop everywhere, including those places when cows won't get off the tracks.

Most long distance trains have two different classes: platzcart and coupe. Coupe, the preferred option for most foreigners, is a private cabin with four bunk beds, two on each side of a small table. Some long distance firmeny trains include a deluxe coupe class where there are two bunks in a coupe cabin that normally holds four. Platzkart is transportation for that masses, an open train car that fits six bunks into the space the coupe uses for four. A platzkart car feels like it was made to transport troops and puts the sights, sounds, and smells of Russia right in your face.

In theory, foreigners are required to buy train tickets at a Central Railway Agency ticket window specifically designated for foreigners. Two of the most convenient are located at the Belorussky Station and the Leningrasky Station. If you find train station ticket offices daunting, it's possible to buy train tickets through travel agencies at slightly higher prices.

A good article on the Trans-Siberian Railroad can be found in the June 1998 issue of the National Geographic. The railroad begins in Moscow and runs for 5,770 miles through the breadth of the country. It is the longest in the world and has three lines: one to Vladivostok on the Pacific coast through Siberia, one to China and one to Mongolia. These are the best tracks and trains of the entire railroad system. In contrast, the purely local ones are very rustic in nature.

As soon as you know you know you are traveling on a train, ask your facilitator to buy you an entire first class cabin. You do not want to share. It will not cost a great deal and is worth every penny. If you take a local train the cars will not be so great. If you are on the Trans-Siberian, you will be in for a joy. The cost is about $100-$150.The cars are similar to European trains. The cabins are small with two padded bench seats that turn into beds. There are also bunks above these so that you can actually sleep four. But why do that if you don't have to. Use the extra room to spread out. Lift up the bench seats and you will find compartments to store your bags. There will be a small table by the window. You will likely be served a boxed lunch which is not too bad. But you may want to bring your own sacks. Each car has a uniformed female conductor that is responsible for the car and who has a samovar containing hot water. The conductor will provide you with tea bags with which to use the hot water to make tea. A samovar is basically a water heating urn. On top of it you put a teapot (CHAI-nik) with very strong tea (KRYEP-kee). When you serve a cup, you put in a little of the strong tea then mix it with the hot water. The great thing is, you can keep refreshing your tea over and over again with hot water and a little of the strong tea from the pot. Russians often use jam to sweeten their tea. Most Russians think US tea is very weak and has no flavor. Thirty years ago the samovars were kept hot with coal or wood fires; now they are mostly electric. Passengers are welcome to help themselves to the hot water at any time.

You will pour your tea in glasses, held in ornate metal holders. Your fellow Russians will break open their meal of smoked fish, vodka, bread, cucumbers, tomatoes and cheese. The view out of your window will be of miles of empty taiga with forests of pine and birch, occasional fields, flat or rolling country, interrupted by villages of small wood houses decorated with elaborate wood carving around the eaves, windows and doors. Close your eyes and you will be Lara and your husband, Dr. Zhivago. You will also see vacant houses and factories, fences fallen into disrepair, fields untilled and unplanted for want of manpower. The Russian countryside is economically in a deep depression. There still is hardly any real effort being made to privatize the farming sector and it shows. There is some statistic that 10% of the land which is held in private plots, generates 90% of the farm produce.

The train comes with a club car. If you go, leave one member behind to guard your stuff. Your facilitator may have a cabin near you so maybe he can watch your gear while you visit the club car. Do take a walk in the train from car to car. It will be a great experience. Be careful about ordering the Baltika (Baltic) beer, as the higher the number, the more powerful the kick. (Isn't that a great system!) A Baltic 3 is about right. If you drink a Baltic 9, you won't wake up until tomorrow.

There is a bathroom at the end of each car. It's functional and metallic. You will love the rocking and rolling of the train while you are in there. The toilet empties onto the tracks so the bathroom doors are locked 20 minutes before arriving and 20 minutes after leaving a town. There can be quite a line after leaving a town so you need to anticipate your trips. The fresh aroma of chlorine bleach awaits you. Safety is not a big issue on the Trans-Siberian. There used to be a problem on the St. Petersburg to Moscow run but that is no longer the case. Just take the usual precautions. Lock your door using the lock that is available. Some people tie a bungee cord on the door. The trains have heat but air conditioning is not guaranteed. During the day most people lounge in the hallways catching some air from the open window. There is nothing more fun than sitting by the window of your cabin watching the exotic Russian landscape go by and thinking about your child. As soon as you are outside Moscow, your view will change to a forested horizon of birch trees sprinkled with wooden cabins.

Whenever the train stops during the day there are townspeople selling produce. If you hear the train give a hiss that is the signal to get back on. You will notice broken down factories that are empty and the miles upon miles of woods containing pine and birch trees. You may even see gypsies living in teepees. There is no telling what you will see. But the best benefit of a train ride after arriving in Moscow is that you can sleep in semi-comfort and get over your jet lag and be fresh for the children's home.

In Western Europe the individual rails on nearly all rail lines are welded together, making a smoother and quieter ride. The Russians don't weld their rails, so one of the more noticeable features of long train-rides is the sound. Each car has sets of four giant wheels at each end, two pairs of two. As they roll over the small space between each rail, each pair of wheels makes a distinct "click." You will hear a steady, rhythmic beat: click-clack, pause, click-clack. When the train reaches its top speed (less than 60 miles an hour), the clicks and clacks come quickly one after the other at more typical, slower speeds, the clicks and clacks proceed more deliberately. Usually one spouse will think it soothing and go right to sleep and the other will stay up all night hating the sound of it.

One word of warning to the spouse that snores, don't sleep in the lower bunk. It makes it all too easy for the other spouse to whack you in the head with a pillow. Trust me on this.

Here are some interesting Trans-Siberian web sites:
http://www.istar.u-net.com/ru_tsr_1.htm,
http://www.ego.net/tlogue/xsib/plan.htm,
http://www.e-course.com/trek/train.htm
and *http://www.transsib.ru/Eng/.*

Regions and Cities

The best sources for information about the various oblasts (regions) and cities are from people who have adopted from there. Many of their stories are on this website: *http://www.karensadoptionlinks.com/regions.html.* She has a lot of cities and regions listed. You can also sign on to e-mail groups targeting these regions and cities. Just go to Yahoogroups.com. There are listserv groups there for many regions and cities including Kirov, Samara, Perm, Chelyabinsk, Vladivostok, Kurgan, Irkutsk and Borovichi, just to name a few. When you join one of these Yahoo! groups, always look at the "files" section for helpful archived information.

Here are just two of the many Yahoo! Groups:

Chelyabinsk—*http://groups.yahoo.com/group/chelyabinskadopt*;
Vladivostok—*http://groups.yahoo.com/group/vladadopt,*

One warning about the region specific adoption sites is that not all the information you read is necessarily true. There is continuous tension between agencies and independent adopters and this can lead to misinformation being posted. There is tension between parents who feel their agency has misled them and agencies who defend themselves using anonymous or fake names. These sites do offer wonderful region and city specific information for hotels, restaurants, travel, orphanage descriptions and the like. It is when you read something about a person, an agency, a Judge or the region's adoption process that you have to use your common sense and sift through everything before you decide something is really true.

Also, almost all regions and cities have web sites of some kind. You can see pictures of your city before you travel at this site: *http://www.friends-partners.org/friends/index.htmland* using its search feature. You may be able to see some orphanage homes by scrolling through *http://www.roofnet.org/about/life-en.html.*

A word of warning if you must drive out of the larger towns to an orphanage some distance away. There are no roadside restrooms and the driver does not often stop. So do not drink a lot of coffee or tea before setting out on a several hour journey.

AMUR

The main city in this region is Blagoveshensk, population 250,000. There is one non-stop flight from Moscow to Blagoveshenk. It leaves on Fridays from DME airport at 9 PM, arriving Blago at 10 AM. Non-stop flight is around $570 round trip economy class. There are also flights via Irkutsk (Sibir Airlines)— $535 round trip, or via Krasnoyarsk (Kras Air) at around $585 round trip. This is how most parents fly in there. At the airport in Krasnoyarsk there is a first class lounge you can wait in with a very clean bathroom, a real restaurant, and a lounge area with nice leather couches. If you enter the airport from the street it is toward the right, up the stairs, just to the right of the greasy-spoon type concession in the main part of the airport. You can take Siberia Air or Kras Air from Moscow. You can also fly in from Korea. Many parents say that Siberia Air is better than Kras Air.

Some families have stayed at the Churin Hotel or the less expensive Druzba. The Druzba is about 2 blocks to the east of the court and the Churin is about 3 blocks to the west. One full bed at the Druzba is $16 and two beds are $20 a night. The rooms at the Churin are roomy and the service is good. They serve you breakfast in a common gathering area and they will order other meals as well. The Churin has security cameras, a security guard and a police station in front of the hotel. The rooms have a lockbox, hair dryers, phone, and television. They have laundry service, a sauna and a pool.

It is very, very cold during the winter so dress warmly. They have a neat ice playground during the winter that you cannot miss. In December the temperature can get down to -15 degrees. It is a dry cold and there are not heavy snowfalls. The surface of the Amur River usually freezes by February and big trucks drive across it to and from China. Sidewalks are very slippery and beware the manhole covers and any outdoor steps. As usual, most buildings, including the orphanage are too warm. So dress in layers. Do try the coconut dipped ice cream while you are here.

Make sure you go to the church at the top of the hill to take a picture of the city for your child. Also, visit the local Folklore museum near the river. The Balkan Grill has good Serbian food. Downtown is wonderful. If you are there on Friday you will see all the weddings as everyone gets married on Friday.

This region and city allow independent adoptions. There are not many agencies involved in adoptions, as this area is hard to get to. There is one baby home in the city and then several in the surrounding towns. The baby home is called "Regional Specialized Dom Rebyonka." This is a pretty typical name. The word "specialized" does not denote anything regarding special needs or the like. It's just what the Russians call some of the orphanages. This home is for infants up to 3 years of age. There is a home for older children a few miles away from the city. As with any donation to a children's home, donations to this baby home, whether in cash or in kind, should be given directly to the Director of the home and not to any intermediary, including your facilitator.

The caregivers try hard at this baby home, but there is little money. The children are underweight and suffer from malnourishment. The kids have anemia, rickets and giardia. Get them to the US and the change is remarkable. The orphanage building is old but clean. The walls are painted with colorful murals of characters from children's books. The director's office has bookshelves full of well worn toys with which children actually are allowed to play. In the playrooms there are many worn toys in contrast to other homes where the toys are part of an untouched display. The children and caregivers played on the floor together.

This is generally a two-trip region with a month or so between trips. The court will try to make sure that the birth family has agreed to a foreign adoption and may go an extra step in that direction. Notwithstanding, the court will grant foreign adoptions.

An adoption stories from this region can be found at *http://www.jacksonkent.net/*

ARKHANGELSK

It is an 1 1/2 hour flight from Moscow. In 2001, this was a one-trip region. In the winter, Arkhangelsk is cold. Let me repeat that. It is really, really cold. Arkhangelsk's City Baby Home is about 3 years old and very nice. There are 7 children's homes. The baby home is fairly new with about a hundred children and lots of toys. The caregivers have their hands full. The Director is Dr. Pavlov and parents have praised him.

For more information about adopting from here, see *http://www.fastgraph.com/rita* and *http://www.jghaffari.com*. Also, here is a web site with pictures of baby home #1: *http://www.fororphans.org/ftrip2aono.htm*

Because there is very little sun in this region, and the milk is not fortified, you may find your child has rickets. This is pretty easily cured with Vitamin D milk, cheese and other types of dairy products.

BOROVICHI

Borovichi is a friendly region for foreign adoptions. It is 7 hours by car from Moscow and lies northwest. It required only one trip throughout 2001.

Because of the pressure from Moscow to go to two trips, it is not known how long, this or any region will remain one trip.

In Borovichi, the children to caretaker ratio is lower than in an urban areas like St. Petersburg. Here the children wake up to the same face on a daily basis, which adds to a child's day-to-day stability. Stimulation for the infants is good on a relative scale in that there are toys hanging above their cribs. They have gymnastics, music and art lessons. About 35% of the infants are below 5% on the growth charts for height and weight and only 23% are below 5% for head circumference, height and weight. These statistics bear out that the children appear healthier than some in other homes. Notwithstanding the stimulation, a great number of the children are developmentally delayed.

BRYANSK

Bryansk is about 7 hours from Moscow and is a pretty region with lots of forests and farmland. The city of Bryansk is very traditional and quite nice although depressed from a slowdown in the military business. There is one hotel where many adopters stay, but don't expect to see many Americans or tourists in the town. There is a restaurant in the hotel and another restaurant nearby. There is also a nice department store and a very large open-air market. There are plenty of shops to buy food.

Bryansk is very traditional. The Court goes by the book and does not waive the 10-day appeal process. The children's homes appear to be well run, but the region itself is undergoing hard times, so a lot of the infrastructure is in disrepair. This region seems to be friendly toward independent adoptions.

CHELYABINSK

Chelyabinsk is a huge city and the entire Chelyabinsk region is heavily populated. It is about a two and half hour plane ride east of Moscow. You can also take a Lufthansa flight up to Ekaterinburg and then drive 2 hours to Chelyabinsk by car.The region is just east of the Ural Mountains, south of Ekaterinburg and north of Kazakhstan.

This region appears to be a two-trip region with the court date set about 5 weeks from the date you accept your child. In general the children's homes seem in good condition. The serious environmental problems of the region do not seem to have affected the children's health in the homes. Do not be scared off from this or any other region just because of past environmental damage. It is the current health of the child that is important, not the region's radioactive legacy. That nexus simply isn't strong enough on which to make an adoption decision. This is not to downplay the radiation danger, if you were to live there for your entire life. Just that the question of whether to adopt an infant or toddler from Chelyabinsk is an entirely different issue.For a discussion on this issue see *http://www.peds.umn.edu/iac/for_families/ltissues/radiation.html*

Food and rent is not expensive. It is easy to get around without a car by using the bus system. It is not a high crime region. If you stay for a long period, you might rent an apartment. A furnished two bedroom apartment should run about $5 a day.

Court times were slow in this region in 2001, although previously they had not been. In 2000 it was reported that Destky Dom #1 was in good condition with warm, friendly caregivers. Parents were able to ask a lot of questions and talk to the home pediatrician. Medical information seemed to be more forthcoming. Destky Dom #2 also seems to be nice and a child adopted from there in 2002 had no parasites or other medical issues of that kind. The female judge and state prosecutor have stern demeanors and are strict, but fair. They ask a lot of questions, so parents should be prepared. The orphanage staff, the government people and judges seem to care very much about the children. They do not waive the 10 days unless the child is ill. Independent adoptions are fine, but single women may need to look to other regions.

There is an orphanage in the town of Miass. It is small, but reportedly the children are well cared for. Some children are even on the charts! The baby home in Magnitogorsk (3 hours from Chelyabinsk) is very well equipped.

This region asks for a copy of the license of your doctor who signs the medical form. Make sure the license is copied on the same letterhead as the medical form answers. There are many other documents that this region asks for which are not requested by other regions so be prepared to jump through some extra hoops.

There is no problem finding a place from which to email and fax information to your IA doctor. An interesting translation/tourist guide service can be found at *http://www.trema.ru/eng.html.*

CHUVASH

Chuvashia is about 350 miles east of Moscow. It is a 13 hour (overnight) train ride. Some parents can adopt with one trip and others two. The Judge in Cheboksary is pretty tough as is the prosecutor. They ask a lot of questions. At one time this region closed down foreign adoptions, as parents were not sending in their post-placement reports. It has since reopened. The 10-day appeal period is waived, but rarely.

The Alatyr Baby Home is in this region. It has limited funds but they do the best they can. It has about 120 kids organized into groups of 12.The home houses infants through about 3 years old.

There is a yahoo list of parents of children from Chuvash.

http://groups.yahoo.com/group/Chuvashfam/

Another resource is *http://www.cap.ru/cap/main.asp?id=103*. Here's another link to Chuvash background:

http://www.unpo.org/member/chuvash/chuvash.html

EKATERINBURG
(sometimes spelled YEKATERINBURG)

Ekaterinburg is in the Sverdlovsk Region. Indeed, the city was once known as Sverdlovsk. It is where the Tsar and his family were executed. It is at about the 56th parallel, Chicago is at the 42nd, so think Juneau, Alaska without the moderating ocean when you're thinking about weather (and about the number of hours of daylight!)

The world's deadliest outbreak of anthrax occurred in this city. At least 63 people died after a secret Soviet biological weapons testing facility accidentally released a plume of anthrax spores into the air in April 1979. There haven't been any further problems of this kind since. This is also the region where Boris Yeltsin was the Communist Party Chief before being tapped in the late 1980's by Gorbachev to come to Moscow. It is also where a UFO was once reported. (A KGB videotape of the autopsy of a little green man found in this region can sometimes be seen on the SciFi channel.)

Some families have flown Aeroflot from Ekaterinburg to Moscow and were highly complimentary. The food was good, and announcements were in Russian and English. Ural Air is a different story. Some families have called Ural Air, the Kiss Your A$$ Goodbye Airline. Just as an example, on one flight to Ekaterinburg on Ural Air, the plane had no overhead bins, only racks, seats were collapsing, seatbelts didn't work, and business class was separated from economy by a tacked up cloth. Aeroflot is by far the best airline to Ekaterinburg. Some families have also flown direct from Frankfurt on Lufthansa (its second stop is Perm). On the second trip they just return through Moscow. While this is a little more costly, it is certainly a lot easier on the body and soul than dealing with traveling to Moscow and then on to

Ekaterinburg. Lonely Planet's Russia travel book has a few pages on this city. You can also travel by train. It is only 27 hours!

The region is part of Siberia. It is the first large city on the Asian side of the Urals. The temperatures are a little chilly; 40 F in October for a high and 20 F for a low. Another month or so and it really drops. Yet, you will cook inside the buildings so wear layers. It is very large and polluted. The buildings and roads are in rough shape—potholes the size of small ponds. It has a lot of history and the museum and ballet are worth a visit. The outdoor "pubs" are fun for people watching. There is also a zoo to which you can take your new addition. They have lots of stores from which you can buy anything. The little stores on every corner are stocked with anything you need (baby food, diapers, wipes, etc.) You can shop at corner fruit stands everyday. The fruit is great and very inexpensive and makes a great gift for your child's orphanage (particularly bananas).

The Ekaterinburg region of Russia has about 6,000 children from infants to age 18 residing in eighteen state-run orphanages around the region. Judges do not normally waive the ten day appeal period in this city. They also have some rules different than other places. The prosecutor may require you to visit with your child at least three days prior to the Court date. The Judge may ask you to commit to giving post placement reports every year until the child turns 18 and to allow a Russian Embassy representative visit the child. Just say yes. After the first 3 years you should be able to just mail in a post placement letter yourself. Nor is anyone ever likely to visit. The Judges are also strict about the dates on documents such as the petition to adopt. The wait for a court date can be closer to 9 weeks than the usual 6 weeks. Independent adoptions areallowed.

Orphanage #2 takes pretty good care of the children. Parents have reported that their children are not significantly delayed. Donations of toys or clothes rarely make their way to the children. Unfortunately, throughout Russia this is more common than not. It is recommended that you either shop for the home while you are there, or bring vitamins or children's medicines.

Detsky Dom # 9 with older children 6 years olds and up gets pretty good. Reports. There is a full-time doctor on staff, a psychiatrist, and a reading specialist. The orphanage is clean and well stocked, and the children have their own clothes and (minimal) possessions.

A nice hotel is the **Atrium Palace**. It is beautiful and has a nice restaurant. It is expensive. With all fees and taxes, the rate can easily exceed $200 a night and you may not feel like you've gotten your money's worth. It does have air conditioning of some kind. The Atrium's breakfast buffet is very good as is dinner. Other parents have stayed at the **Central** and thought it worked out better. The rooms are large and the cost is about $70. A suite is $90. They only take rubles.

The rooms have television, but of course it is Russian dubbed American shows mostly. Some rooms have refrigerators. The hotel is simple, but clean and quiet. The location of the hotel is convenient and is close to some shops and not far from the airport. The downstairs cafe has simple, but good and inexpensive food. The Central staff is limited on English so you will need a translation book and just point out what you need. It is not too much of a problem. One other hotel that parents like is the Iset. The Iset is not fancy, but has a nice location. It is within walking distance to cafes, and English menu restaurants, department stores, bank machine, pharmacies, and grocery stores. A large room is about $100 and night with refrigerator and clean bathroom. Parents like it because you get more of the experience of living in Russia, yet it is still comfortable. The Iset serves a great pelmini.

If one spouse is planning to return to the States after the court hearing, be aware that this region has a peculiar rule that requires both parents to be present to sign the child's new birth certificate. This can cause a significant delay in leaving.

There is an Internet café in the main post office and in other places as well. The post office charges like $1 an hour for Internet time and it is a relatively fast connection. So if you have digital photographs of your child that you want an IA doctor to review, you might use the post office.

An interesting Ekaterinburg travel site (including web cam) is at *http://webcam.fondmira.ru/* and another interesting web site is at *http://www.friends-partners.org/oldfriends/mes/russia/ural/regions/ekaterinburg.html.*

There is an Ekaterinburg adoption group through Yahoo! at *http://groups.yahoo.com/group/Ekaterinburg_Adoption/* and also see *www.facesofsiberia.org.*

IRKUTSK

Irkutsk is in Siberia. It is one of the most beautiful and civilized places you will ever visit. It was the city to which the aristocratic, but reform minded Decembrists were banished in 1825 and they brought with them the culture of St Petersburg.

This region seems to require two trips for an adoption regardless of whether you use an accredited or unaccredited agency. One source of information is the e-group list at *groups.yahoo.com/group/Irkutsk.* The judge is very stringent in her requirements of adoptive parents and of the adoption authorities in Irkutsk. The adoption process can be strenuous and long. This is no reflection on the children, just on the process. You can obtain a video and medical information on a child before making the first trip. So in that respect it is more liberal. It is about a four month wait between the first trip and court date. In the later part of 2002 adoptions were flowing better than in 2001 and early 2002. As in all regions and countries, there is an ebb and flow to adoptions. Independent adoptions are allowed.

There is a baby home in Angarsk. The children seem well cared for, fed, clothed and even loved. There is even a special Music School for the Orphans in Irkutsk.

There is a beautiful photo book of this amazing city in Siberia: Irkutsk, By Alexandre Knyazev and Mark Sergeev, c. 1995.

You can purchase a video showing one family's adoption journey to this city in Siberia at *http://www.adoptlaw.org/tiac_htm/5stories.htm* by scrolling down to the video "Adopting a New Life." For more on adopting from Irkutsk see this website: *http://www.furman.edu/~treu/sasha/*

IVANAVO

Ivanovo is 175 miles northeast of Moscow. It takes about 4 hours by car to get there or you can take the train. The car ride is over some very bumpy roads but then the train is a local, with all that which goes along with being a local. The train takes about seven happy hours of riding the Russian version of Disney's Thunder Mountain Railroad, with about 40 stops. Ivanovo Oblast has a population of 1.3 million people.

Dr. Downing has visited the children's home in Ivanovo on several occasions. There is only one baby home. It is reported as very clean and the children seem to be well taken care of. Ivanovo #2 seems to take good care of the children. It is a relatively happy place (as happy as a baby home can be). It is clean. Caretaker to child ratio is 2 to 10-13 kids, though often there is only 1 caretaker. The staff makes many of the toys and decorations. The Head Doctor (director) is a wonderful woman who cares a great deal about her children. The Judge has even called her a "hero mother."

There is another baby home in Shuya. The home is poor, but the staff is kind and loving. The children are underweight, but seem happy.

The Court, if supported by the children's home Director, generally waives the ten-day appeal period. The process is fairly quick. There is about a two month wait for a court date. The Judge is a woman and is very nice, as is the prosecutor. The Judge will ask most of her questions of the wife and leave the husband alone.

Some parents have stayed at the Tourist Hotel, which is rather substandard. The Samoilov textile factory is one of the main sources of jobs in Ivanovo. It makes textiles, some in the design of the Kama Sutra and others in their best selling Teletubbies design.

A Yahoo! Group is at *http://groups.yahoo.com/group/Ivanovo_Adoption*

KALINGRAD

Kalingrad is north of Poland and was governed by Germany until WWII. The Germans call it Konigsberg or King's Mountain.Kalingrad is geographically separated from Russia and that has posed a recent problem for Russia and the EU. It is an hour and a half plane ride from Moscow. There are 4 daily flights from Moscow to Kaliningrad. The last flight, depending on the day of the week, is at 9-10 PM from DME. You need to allow yourself at least 1 hr 15 minutes for a taxi between SVO and DME. Kalingrad is surrounded by beautiful countryside and is only a 1/2-hour drive from the Baltic Sea. In the Kalingrad region most Russians dress in traditional dark colors. Unlike the large urban cities of Moscow and St. Petersburg, most men do not wear jeans. The women wear leather dress coats. President Putin's mother-in-law lives in Kalingrad.

In this region sometimes a facilitator can find out about children that generally fit a parent's description and obtain advance permission of the Department of Education for you visit that particular children's home. All he is doing is speeding up the process by not having you go to the DoE and do the same thing. There are three baby homes in the region with the one in Gusev being the furthest away. The Gusev baby home is said to be in good shape with a terrific Director.

This region is pro-adoption as well is the court. The Directors will allow you to spend a lot of time with your prospective child at the children's home. They also require you to spend a day or two with the child immediately before the court hearing. This region has also been very lenient about waiving the 10-day appeal period. The court date is scheduled very quickly after you have seen the child and filed your adoption petition.

It is reported that some children suffer from anemia. If you adopt from Kalingrad, be sure to have your pediatrician check for that.

Here is a web site with one family's story of adopting from Kalingrad: *http://www.vanthof.com/russia/* and a general support group can be found at *http://groups.yahoo.com/group/Kaliningrad_Adoption.*

KALUGA

Kaluga is about a 3 hour drive from Moscow. The city has seen better days.

Some parents have stayed at the **Hotel Priokskaya,** which is an old, but comfortable hotel. There is a 24 hour market where you can buy most anything.

It is a two-trip region. The DoE building is new. Dr Anna is the director of the baby home and it is described as being fairly nice. Getting the child's Russian passport can take as long as a week or it can be shorter.

There is a Kaluga Yahoo! Group.

KAZAN

Kazan has several things going for it. It is a one trip region and it has some pretty good restaurants. There is a fine Italian place called Guiseppes and even a McDonalds. **Guiseppes** is a hotel/restaurant owned by an Italian. They have excellent pizza, cappuccino, and Gelato! It is located in the heart of downtown and is the place to stay.The rooms are beautiful with a full size fridge, couch, full size table, 20 ft. ceilings, whirlpool bath, shower stall, tv/vcr, phone, and includes breakfast.

Other families have stayed at the **Safar.** It is nice except the heat is not the best so avoid it in the winter. Also, Safar is away from everything.

The judge can be a little strict, but overall is ok. Sometimes the ten day appeal period is waived and sometimes not.

I

KEMEROVO

There are two major cities—Kemerovo City where court takes place and Novokutznesk that is to the South. You fly into one of these cities depending on which the orphanage is closest to. Kemerovo is a pretty city with squares and colored buildings. It is a long flight from Moscow. Kemerovo is a very adoption friendly region and city with at least one very pro-adoption friendly Judge, a woman. Note that she does take a long vacation in August and September. The other Judge is fine as well. Both unaccredited and accredited agencies can work there, as well as independents. There is evidence that this region, as are all regions, are being pressured to only do adoptions with accredited agencies. It is not the law, but central in Moscow seems to be heading toward making independent adoptions more paper intensive than accredited ones. Don't be surprised if this region moves toward being a two-trip process with only accredited agencies allowed. Nevertheless, in this region the judge, prosecutor, and the inspector from the Department of Education are all on the same page. They want these kids to go to a good home and they all work to make the adoption go smoothly.

There two baby homes in Novokuznetsk. Baby House #2 has been only opened since August 2000 and the staff seems very caring, particularly the doctor. Because it is new it is very nice, clean, very bright with lots of windows and space for the children. They have plenty of toys and even had a with a ball pit, mats, slides, balance beam, etc. There is a music room with a piano and other instruments where the kids meet for music time. As usual they keep the place too hot. The children seem generally healthy and well cared for although the babies don't get held much. Baby Home #3 has a swimming pool, art and music classes.

Some parents have said that they thought the condition of the home in the city of Prokopyevsk was good. Prokopyevsk is a coal mining town about three hours drive from Kemerovo. (9 hours round trip from Kemerovo to Prokopyevsk to Novokuznesk back to Kemerovo.) The van ride to the home will show you a view of Siberia as desolate and cold. The road, as usual with Russian roads, is bumpy. The baby home is clean and apparently well run by Dr. Ludmilla. It has a music room. The children are well cared for. Some children appear well nourished and others are thin. There also was an outbreak of giardia in the children at some time in the past.

In Kemerovo, try to stay at the **Hotel Kuzbass**. This hotel is closer to your main sources of food—World Pizza and Golden Chicken. There is also a Greek restaurant that is just ok and an Irish pub called the Barg that is not bad. The food in the hotel is not bad if you can somehow communicate your wants and desires as no one speaks any English and if you look confused they will speak faster and louder—in Russian. The hotel does make a good omelet and soup. Speaking of wants and desires, the "floor ladies" will do just about anything to help you out for a small fee. They are very helpful and run a thriving prostitution business on the side. Be prepared to turn your phones off at night as the "call girls" will call you, over and over and over. You can rent a hot pot from the floor ladies for a nominal fee. Do NOT drink the tap water. Some parents have also stayed at the Tomsk.

The Kuzbass has a business center with an English-speaking staff. Internet use is two rubles per minute. You are limited to a 28.8 connection, but it's faster than smoke signals. There is a Department Store, a supermarket, any number of smaller markets and even a nice baby store within walking distance of the Kuzbass hotel. The Puppet Theatre is one block from the hotel—corny, but kids love it. Be prepared for the usual volcanic hot interiors. The thermostats have only one level—full blast...with your window the only regulator.

There is another hotel out by the river, the **Hotel Tomb** on the Tomb River. It is nice for quiet walks in the country, but it is not near the city. The Tomb has nice large rooms but no one speaks any English, so have your translator order your breakfast the night before. The rooms not facing the river are quieter. As with the Kuzbass, disconnect your phone at night. The "ladies" call rooms looking for customers.

If you have time, look for birch art. Artists paint the picture on the piece of birch. It may be unique to the Kemerovo region.

KHABOROVSK

You can reach Khaborovsk either by Moscow, which is an 8-hour plane ride or through Seoul, Korea. The flights out of Moscow are daily. You can also fly from the West Coast to Seoul and then to Khaborovsk. The planes fly from Seoul once a week on Asiana Air (a Korean run airlines) or Dal Avia twice a week. You can buy tickets for Dal Avia thru Aeroflot offices. Asiana is considered better than Dal Avia. See the section on Vladivostok for information on flying through Inchon Airport. You can also go by train, but it is a long trip. Some families have booked a day room at the Novotel Hotel at the Sheremetyevo (Moscow) airport after they arrive on the morning flight. They sleep at the Novotel, then go to the domestic airport for the 8:30 pm flight to Khabarovsk, and arrive in Khabarovsk the next morning ready to see their child. This is just one option.

It is generally hot and buggy during the summer. Bring some bug spray and a screen for the hotel window. Ask if the hotel has air conditioning, if you go during the summer.

Some families have stayed at the **Amethyst**. It is about $75 a night. It is comfortable, with a nice little restaurant downstairs. The Amethyst is located by an open market and the children's park. The Amethyst has an email address, and you can make reservations directly, which is a little cheaper than through a travel agency. They have Internet access through the computer at the front desk ($5 per hour). The Khabarovsk home page has links to hotels.

Others have stayed at the **Parus** and loved it. It is near the water. They felt very safe and well taken care of. The cost is about $120.00 a night for two people. The rooms are similar to US hotels. There is a computer in the lobby and you can get on the Internet and e-mail daily. It is within walking distance from just about everything. Others have stayed at the Intourist and it is about $70 a night. The rooms have a small refrigerator and plenty of hot water. It is comparable to a Best Western. There's an Aeroflot desk and a travel agency in the lobby. Everyone speaks English at the front desk. Another hotel is the **Sapporo** hotel at about $148 a night. You can also stay at the **Hotel Amur** for about $30 per night. Many adoptive families have stayed there. It's pretty basic, but livable and has clean, private baths, and hot showers most of the time. Others have stayed at the Central Hotel at about $50 a night. You can also stay at the Mar-Kuel Apartments at $70 per night for a suite with a full kitchen. It is nice, new and with great bathrooms, but it is a little off the beaten path.

There is a children's park in the center of town, and one called Mowgli, an indoor playground. There is also a park along the Amur River where there is a children's amusement park. Western style grocery stores are also available.

The baby home has recently moved to the location of a former kindergarten. It is surrounded by trees, and has a large play area. The home has lots of natural light. The 10 days is hardly ever waived, but when it has it was because the child was thought to have an illness that needed treatment he could not receive in Russia.

In children's home #2 (for 3-7 year olds), the kids look happy and healthy; there is a big play area in the back with swings, jungle gyms etc. The kids have a garden where they raise radishes and strawberries. The caregivers seem like they really care for the kids.

The baby home in Komsomolsk is spartan on the outside; clean, bright and cheery on the inside. The children are well cared for. They have daily music and dance for the toddlers. The caretakers spent a little one on one time with every child, but as usual it is not enough. The kids have adequate food, light on variety and protein, and a bit heavy on starch.

The adoption process is fairly straightforward in this region. The ten day appeal period is not usually waived. Some spouses go home during the ait with other family members coming over to help the one that remains. Some children's home Directors have allowed the children to stay with the adopting parents during this time.

A good resource is *http://www.khabarovskadoptions.homestead.com/index.html.* This site also has a Khabarovsk video available. It was made by one if the Khab families, and shows some hotels, and some city sites. It gives a nice overview of the area There is a helpful group at *listserv-KhabarovskAdoptions@comcast.net* (put subscribe in the subject line of your first email) and one family's journey at *http://www.garyrosenzweig.com/luna/.*

KHERSON

Kherson is near the Black Sea. It sometimes has problems with basic foodstuffs and infrastructure. Hot water and milk can sometimes be hard to find. The children's home staff is very friendly, and they seemed to love their children. The head physician is a wonderful man who takes pride in finding homes for the kids. They do not much, but the caretakers do love them. The Director has allowed some parents to take their children during the ten-day appeal wait, which is usually not waived.

The children's home is poor and has little heat. Some children have scabies so bring some cream. The usual respiratory illnesses are present.

KIROV

Kirov is a 13 hour train ride from Moscow.

Kirov will waive the ten days and there is a rumor it may allow just one trip. There is a Kirov group for parents at *Kirov@yahoogroups.com.*

KRASNODAR

Krasnodar is a small, industrial type city. Some families have taken Air Kuban to Krasnodar and have said it was short on legroom, but had good food and was a fairly new airplane. If you fly Kuban Air, be sure to pay the extra $15 to fly business class. It is worth it. Some parents have stayed at the **Intourist** hotel, which is just a short walk away from many "convenience" type stores or smaller eateries.

In 1999 Krasnodar was a good region from which to adopt. Since then it has become more difficult. In the spring of 2001, Krasnodar began to decline to hear foreign adoptions. This was due to Russia tightening up on post-placements and there was a problem in this region with families not sending them. This is another illustration of why it is so important for you to follow through with this obligation. Your actions really do affect other families. For several months during the spring and summer, families were kept from their children because of this delay in setting court dates. In the fall of 2001, the regional Department of Education had a change of personnel and the new person that came in is against foreign adoption even though it is clearly allowed by Russian law. She has made things difficult for families. Notwithstanding the road-blocks, foreign adoptions are occurring in this region. Indeed, there was an indication that by the summer of 2002 things had begun to get a little easier.

This is just another example of how things can change in Russia based on a change in personnel or a change in the law. Always give the opinion of the reference that just retuned higher credence than one from someone who retuned the year before. Independent adoptions are allowed.

Krasnodar is slow about responding to your follow up medical questions. You just have to be persistent. Some families are able to use the one trip referral method and others are going over using the two-trip system. Overall, the region is slow about setting adoption court dates. Several times court dates have been delayed for unknown reasons. The DoE is restrictive in the amount of videotaping you can do in the children's home.

Another troublesome development in this region used to be that relatives were been known to pop up out of the woodwork and say they would come and take the child, but then never show up at the children's home. This had the unfortunate result of taking the child out of the adoptability pool.

The children's homes seem to be in fairly good shape with malnourishment not as much of a problem. The Krasnodar Baby Home Director has been described as being nice and accommodating. She will let you see your child's playroom. The judge in Krasnodar is described as a woman, very fair, but by the book. Adoption judges change frequently throughout Russia so procedures can vary with each change. The court hearing takes 15 minutes with another 30 minutes for her to type out her decision, then you are off to the registration office to change his birth certificate and then to the orphanage.

Other families have adopted from Afipsk and raved about the orphanage and its Director.

KRASNOYARSK

Krasnoyarsk is an easy four or five hour flight from Moscow. It is a city of about a million people straddling the Yenisei River in the center of Siberia. Some parents have flown on Kras Air. The planes are big but old. The fare is around $325 per person round trip. The plane leaves late at night and arrives in Krasnoyarsk early in the morning. At the airport in Krasnoyarsk, you deplane onto the tarmac and have to wait outside for your luggage, so be prepared for the cold!!! The airport is a bit unusual. Your facilitator will most likely retrieve your luggage, as you never actually enter the terminal. Then it's a bit of a drive to the city. The city is gray and a little run down. Krasnoyarsk is right in the heart of Siberia. You may see more horses and carts than cars. People wear furs and felt, instead of clothes. Some feel like they are traveling back in time. Krasnoyarsk can also have a sort of Twilight Zone feel. The gangsters are known here as "the authorities" and in a bizarre tribal ritual they carve larger-than-life, granite reliefs of young Krasnoyarsk gangsters on their tombstones in the Badalukh Cemetery on the edge of town. But enough of the Elliot Ness local color.

Kranoyarsk in the past was a closed city as it was surrounded by top-secret military research centers and was the site of many defense industries. Now the city is accessible by plane from Moscow or on the Trans-Siberian Railroad. In the short summer with all of the fountains and outdoor cafes it can feel more like Rome than Moscow. Of course, with such a long winter, an enormous reserve of human energy is built up that seems to just explode during the late summer nights.

Kranoyarsk is actually a Krai, not a region, although many use the term synonymously. A Krai is a region that is a little less controlled from Moscow than a region. It is an historical anomaly and the difference in control is really just a matter of degree. The governor of Kranoyarsk used to be General Ledbed, who was not from the area or as they say in Charleston, "he was from off." Ledbed and Pimashkov did not see eye to eye, which made for some interesting politics. Overshadowing everyone is the Norilsk industrial complex, the world's largest producer of nickel, copper, palladium and other platinum metals. It was sold for a pittance to one of the oligarchs and there have been more machinations dealing with it, it's owners, and politicians galore including Putin, to make a best seller out of a dime store novel. The good news is that none of this will affect your adoption.

In addition to local children's homes, there is a baby home in Achinck, which is about 3 hours away by car, and also, one in Kansk. In 2001 the Judges would occasionally waive the ten-day appeal period.

The mayor, Pyotr Pimashkov, has taken the interesting tack of providing poor governance coupled with great looking fountains. Pimashkov just loves fountains, and Krasnoyarsk has 101 of them, including a giant one in the Yenisei itself that blows like Old Faithful some 60 feet into the air on the weekends.

The most elaborate fountains are a row of three in the square in front of the State Theater of Opera and Ballet. The theater's Soviet architecture some claim was copied a bit from the New York State Theater in Lincoln Center. The square in front of the theater is bounded by the ugly façade of the 8-story **Krasnoyarsk Hotel**. The square is huge and the three fountains produce a terrific show with dancing streams of water.

Some parents have stayed in the **Oktobrtysk Hotel**. The courthouse is across the street from the Oktobrtysk. The hotel has suites with a separate living room and bedroom. It is on the main street near grocery stores. The decor is soviet era with outdated furnishings. However, each room is really a small junior suite so there is an extra sitting room, which comes in handy when the new little one is sleeping. The bathroom has a tub and a hand held showerhead without a place to hang it. It also has a TV with lots of old American programs dubbed in Russian. There is a refrigerator. Laundry service is cheap and good. There is a small dining room on each floor where you can eat breakfast. The staff is not used to foreigners so do not expect great service. The hotel is not air-conditioned. If you go in the summer bring some mosquito repellent as you will most likely want to open the windows. There is a souvenir bookstore and "Baby store" downtown that is very inexpensive compared to Moscow. Here is a web site with information about Hotel Oktobraskaya: *http://tlcom.krs.ru/october/index.cgi?item=ch&lang=eng*

Some families have stayed in the **Krasnoyarsk Hotel**. They have suites of rooms and a Russian styled breakfast is included. You can find anything you need within walking distance of the hotel including baby food and diapers. The food is not so good, but edible. The staff is pleasant. A suite consists of 2 rooms, a nice bathroom, a small refrigerator, and a hot pot. They are clean and pleasant. Lots of adopting families have stayed there.

If you travel in the summer and your ten days is not waived, then you might consider visiting the Stolby Zapovednik, or nature preserve, just outside of town. Stolby is an urban park, an easy bus ride from town to its entrance. Then you have a two-hour uphill walk to the heart of the park, where its renowned rock formations can be found. You can try to wrangle a permit and drive to the lowest of the rocks. The park is big with the city's rock climbing crowd. The park is a Siberian mountain forest, its steep hillsides covered in Scotch pine, Fir and Birch. The rock formations are spectacular, rising 800 and 900 meters into the sky atop the Kusyumski Mountains.

When you leave and are at the airport in Krasnoyarsk, you will want to wait in the first class lounge. Either just walk in or gain entrance by paying a couple of dollars for VIP service. It has a very clean bathroom, a real restaurant, and a lounge area with nice leather couches. If you enter the airport from the street it is toward the right, up the stairs, just to the right of the greasy-spoon type concession in the main part of the airport.

KURGAN

It was about 2 1/2-hour plane ride from Moscow. Kurgan is a very industrial city.

There is a yahoo group of those who have adopted or are planning to adopt from Kurgan at *http://groups.yahoo.com/group/RussianAdoption-Kurgan*

KOSTROMA

Kostroma is a beautiful medieval city located around the middle Volga, 200 miles northeast of Moscow. It was founded in 1152.

Kostroma is adoption-friendly. Not too long ago it only required one trip of about 7 days and would waive the ten-day appeal period.

KURSK

Kursk is 8 hrs by overnight train from Moscow. You can drive it (also 8 hours), but it is not recommended. It is a very bumpy ride with nowhere to stop along the way. The train has the usual first class section with two bunks in a cabin and second class with four (two overhead). See the section on trains. The train is fairly clean. One of the biggest problems is getting luggage on and off the train. Sometimes your train stops on a platform several tracks over and then you have to go down a long flight of stairs, through a tunnel, and up another flight of stairs. Do not bring more than you can carry yourself. There are a few porters, but they charge too much. If you have a disability or are unable to carry all your luggage, then you should arrange for help ahead of time.

Kursk is a small industrial city that was fairly prosperous at one time. It has now fallen on harder times economically. Kursk is only about 300 miles from Moscow, but has a very remote, rural feeling. The area specializes in agro-industrials. There is some lovely architecture in the center of town. The people are friendly and well educated as there is a medical university and another university in the city. Kursk was utterly destroyed in World War II and was the site of the largest tank battle in history (Operation Zitadelle). Some historians credit the defensive battle in the Kursk salient for breaking the Germans on the Eastern Front and being the real turning point of the entire war. After Kursk, the Russians were always on the offensive and the Germans on the defensive.

Most parents stay in homestays rather than hotels. Supplies should be purchased in Moscow rather than relying on finding them in Kursk.

The Kursk baby home (Regional Orphanage-ages 0-5) is clean, caring and has many developmental toys for the children to play with. Food is limited. The home looks very stark from the outside, but inside there are folk murals on the wall. The staff in Kursk is friendly. Preschoolers are taken outside quite a bit for exercise and play time. There are music classes and a large bath area. Unlike in some homes, bath time is not a frightening experience. Giardia has been a problem with some of the toddlers so you will need to check this thoroughly and take precautions. There are quite a few bugs (roaches) in the home. Vaccinations are taken seriously and more often than not are accurate.

Court is simple but thorough. Know your dossier. The Ministry of Education representative is personable. The judges are known to be very thorough but fair. For some reason they are concerned about the possibility of you having biological children in the future and the relationship, even inheritance rights, between these unknown bio kids and the adopted children. Court lasts an hour. The 10-day appeal period is not waived. Evidence suggests that only accredited agencies can work in Kursk.

MAGADAN

The Magadan region is about 3,700 miles east of Moscow and its main products are gold mining and fishing. Magadan suffers from its former reputation as the most feared Gulag in all of Stalin's Soviet Union. Of the millions sent there, only a handful survived. It is a geological wonder with scores of volcanoes.

Two trips are usually required in this region, although there have been some one trip adoptions. The 10 days wait is usually waived. Flights to Magadan via Anchorage are the shortest route however; these are reduced to 2 per month during winter so you may need to take Korean Air via Vladivostok.

There is only one baby home in Magadan. The caregivers, social worker and medical director are very open, direct and caring. The home is in an old building but it appears very clean. The Director has allowed Dr. Downing to visit. There are Alaskan agencies that specialize in adopting from Magadan. The Courts are somewhat formal and believe in thoroughly going through your dossier. Court should take about an hour.

In 2002 Magadan was very difficult. Processing and paperwork moved very slowly. No one knew why there were problems. If you do have problems, you could try to call the head of the regional DoE. Her name is Caleria and her phone number is allegedly 0-11-7-4132-23221.

MOSCOW

The city of Moscow and Moscow Region are two separate programs. What happens in the city is not necessarily what happens in the rest of the region. It is sort of like comparing New York City with the rest of New York State. The city makes up its own rules that differ from the rest of the country. For example, they seem to be moving toward not allowing foreign adoptions until a child is 11 months old. This is similar to Orenburg. They do not encourage independent adoption. Sometimes they allow just one trip and sometimes it is the usual two.(This seems to vary by agency, so it might be a case of who-knows-who)

In the region it is a two-trip program with the court date about 6 weeks after the first trip. It is not unusual to have the 10 days waived in the region, unlike the city. Neither the city nor the region seems friendly toward independent adoptions. The bureaucracy in both the region and the city are very "political" as one might expect of the capital. The city will sometimes allow a one-trip process. It is not known why some adoptions in the city are one trip and others two trips.

The city has many children's homes so they all have numbers. Baby Home #2 in Moscow is a little old, but clean. The children are also clean and relatively healthy looking. It is somewhat like a school. The caregivers are nice. Orphanage #6 has a web page at *http://www.roofnet.org/progs/no06-en.html*. Baby Home #7 seems to take good care of the children. #13 is attached to the Filatov Children's Hospital and the director, Dr. Kurbatova, is an extremely competent doctor who runs a tight ship. It is clean, but worn, and the nurses care about the kids. The food is plentiful, but monotonous (lots of potato soup and what looks like oatmeal) and the medical care is decent. #12 has 100 children in the main building and 60 in the annex...#13 is also within walking distance from the Sheraton, Marriott Tverskaya and Marriott Grand. Number 14 is supported by the Lutheran Church and that has made a difference. It is located on the east side of Moscow as is #4. The director is Elenora and she seems to really care for the children. In children's home number 20, the children are malnourished and are generally not in as good a shape as in the other homes. This seems to be from intentional neglect. Why this home seems to be worse than many others in Moscow is unknown. The general rule in Russia is that except in the poorest of regions, the condition of the children is related to the degree of caring by the director. However, since only insiders know what is really going on, the only way a parent can tell that something is seriously wrong is by looking at the condition of the children. Children's Home #24 is a very good home. It is clean and the children do not seem to be malnourished. The staff is kind to the children who are relatively emotionally healthy. The children have the usual rickets and respiratory illnesses.

The orphanages at # 26, 50, and 62 have their own web pages at *http://www.roofnet.org/progs/no26-en.html,*
http://www.roofnet.org/progs/no50-en.html,
and *http://www.roofnet.org/progs/no62-en.html*

The city of Moscow is separate from the rest of the Russian Federation. By that I mean it is politically powerful enough so that it can follow its own rules. With some of these Moscow homes, the Director will limit the medical information provided to you even after you have filed the adoption petition and are waiting for a court date. This is contrary to Russian law, and completely unacceptable, but they do not seem to care.

If you do not have a digital camera and want to send pictures to your IA doctor, you can have them scanned onto a CD at *http://www.photocenter.ru/shop_en.html* then sent.

In the Moscow region there is a baby home called Kolomna Infant Home. It is about 2 hours south of Moscow. The baby home is clean and the staff caring. They will even allow a child to be evaluated at the Filatov or American Medical Clinic. This is something that a parent should request of any child in the city of Moscow as well. Parents like the home and it has a reputation as being pretty good. Food is plentiful although nutrition is not. This is fairly common throughout Russia. Children may get a lot of potato soup and oatmeal, but not fruits and vegetables.

Another town is Stupino, which is 1.5 hours from Moscow. The baby orphanage is described as clean and kept up. The caretakers seem to take good care of the children. The caregiver ratio is 1:8 and they have older girls living in the orphanage that help out. Babies are kept in the baby hospital until 12 months of age. The hospital is not so great.

The town of Sergiev Posad is about 2 hours from Moscow. Sergiev Posad has no facility for children under 2 so they remain in the District Hospital. The Hospital is the usual run down, poor looking facility. The children do not get nearly as much stimulation as they might in a children's home (and that's not all that much). The children are developmentally delayed but will generally show a quick increase in weight and height once adopted, although expect them to be on the small side.

A Yahoo! Group is at *http://groups.yahoo.com/group/Moscow_Adopt*

MURMANSK

This region has a long history with the British and American convoys in WWII. Many British and Americans merchantmen lost their lives delivering supplies to Russia through Murmansk. Just reading about PQ 17 will give you nightmares. It is the only port in northern Russia free of ice year-round.

Happily, those days are long past and the region enjoys a reputation for being adoption friendly and just plain having some of the nicest people. It is a one-trip region if you use an accredited agency. Some parents still receive videos and medical information like in the "old" days. Rickets seems to be a common ailment in the children, as you would expect in these northern climates that are low in sunlight. Parents have adopted from children's homes in Apatity and in Kandalaksha. Court can be long, but the judge is fair. The 10-day wait is sometimes waived. If you are under the two trip process, the time between trips is about 4 weeks.

You can fly into Apatity and Murmansk. They are both two hour flights from Moscow. Murmansk is the most populous city north of the Arctic Circle with approximately 300,000 people. Murmansk has everything you could possibly need such as baby food, diapers, and bottled water. There are only two tourist quality hotels in Murmanks. One is the Arktica and it is described as "ok" and the other is the Poliarnyezori Hotel (pronounced "Polyanna Zurie"). The food in the cafe is good and the hotel has cribs, pottys, and bathtubs, and a business center. The cost is around $90 a night.

Apatity is a medium sized city about 2 1/2 hrs by car south of Murmansk. It is fairly prosperous (by Russian standards). Its orphanage is pretty new and clean with nice grounds. This orphanage also has sections that take care of children who are not adoptable due to physical or mental disabilities. Apatity is also the overflow orphanage for the region. Some children in Murmansk have been transferred to this home because of space limitations.

The Murmansk region has 3 baby homes—for infants up to 3 yrs (Murmansk, Apatity, and Kandalaksha), 2 Detsky Doms—for children 3 or 4-6 (Monchegorsk, and maybe Murmansk), and then 1 boarding school for children in school ages 7-17 (Murmansk).

Kandalaksha is another 1 1/2 hours by car south of Apatity. It is on the White Sea. It is a very, very poor city. The only industry is fishing. The orphanage reflects the poverty of the city. It has concrete block walls, which need paint. The inside is old, but pretty clean. The caretakers care and do the best they can, but basically lack everything. Few adoptions happen from Kandalaksha. It is just too difficult to get to. Most agencies that go to the Murmansk region adopt children from Murmansk or Apatity. This is another reason to adopt from here.

NIZHNY TAGIL

Nizhny Tagil is in the same region as Ekaterinburg (Sverdlovsk Region). There are at least 2 baby homes in Nizhny Tagil (#1 and #3). #1 is small with about 40 children. #3 is newer and houses about 100 children. #3 is not bad, very clean and well organized.

At home #3, the kids are divided into "groupa's", self-contained rooms that include a bedroom, play area, kitchen, coat room, and bathroom. There are usually 8-10 other children in a "groupa". It goes according to age. The kids look well taken care of. There are two huge playrooms with riding toys, tunnels, balls and blocks, etc.

The car ride from Ekaterinburg to Nizhny Tagil is about 3 hours and is very rough. Since your court hearing will be in Ekaterinburg, read that section for a description of the judges.

If you do opt to stay in Nizhny Tagil, you will be pretty much on your own. You can stay at the Metallurg hotel for $20 a night. Bring a phrase book, as there are few locals that speak English.

NIZHNY NOVGOROD

Nizhny Novogorod is another old port on the Volga. The onion-shaped domes first appeared in this city in the 11th century.

Nizhny Novgorod has used the two-trip process for many years. It was probably the first to do so. In Nizhny you travel to Russia without any referral but rather receive a referral after visiting the regional Department of Education and finding out who is off the registry given the parameters of a child for which you are searching. After accepting a referral from the Department you travel to the children's home where the child is located and you hear the medical history and background. There are about 5 children's homes in this region. If you have a power of attorney from the other spouse then only one of you needs to make the first trip.

Court is not difficult and in 2000 at least, the 10-day appeal period was sometimes waived. The court date is scheduled approximately two months after the first visit.

The children's homes do not have much money. Last year in Baby Home #1, the heat was off for several days and it was freezing. The toddlers wore wearing winter coats and gloves indoors. The staff took shifts sleeping so they could boil water, watch space heaters, and constantly rotate water bottles in the cribs to keep the babies warm.

NOVOSIBIRSK

Novosibirsk has about one and half million people and is the third largest city of Russia (after Moscow and St.Petersburg) and the major city of Western Siberia. Founded in 1893 where the famous Trans-Siberian Railroad crosses the great Siberian river Ob, it officially became a town in 1903. It was renamed Novosibirsk, or New Siberia in 1926. It is due north of Pakistan.

The climate is sharply continental, with very severe, cold and snowy winters and hot and dry summers. Temperatures in summer range from 20 to 22°C, in winter -18 to -20°C, but can reach -35°C in winter and 35°C summer.

Novosibirsk has the biggest railway station along the trans-Siberian route, the biggest library in Siberia, and the biggest opera/ballet theater in all of Russia—even bigger than Moscow's Bolshoi.

Novosibirsk is the home of the formerly famous Science City with scientists from the world-renowned Siberian department of the Russian Academy of Sciences, comprising the country's biggest scientific contingent. It is no longer so famous and the more enterprising have emigrated or found work in the private sector.

The establishment of Science City was Nikita Khrushchev's idea and he enhanced Novosibirsk's status in the late 1950s when he decided to locate a new branch of the Soviet Academy of Sciences there. The center was called Akademgorodok. It was located in the woods about 20 miles from downtown Novosibirsk. It was a self-contained town consisting of research institutes and apartment blocks run by the Siberian branch of the Academy. At it's height it was home to some 65,000 scientiests. When the Soviet Union collapsed funding for the Academy of Sciences disappeared. Akademgorodok, the pride of Novosibirsk, became a ghost town. It has made a slight recovery in ten years time, but it will never be the kind of place it once was.

The city is doing relatively well by Russian standards. There are plenty of worn out streets and buildings, but then in downtown you may see new construction and commerce everywhere. There is even a Benetton store, and a Hugo Boss boutique. The restaurants have lots of customers. This prosperity separates the residents of Novosibirsk from the usual rural Siberian cities' depression and even from the only modest gains found in Irkutsk or Ulan-Ude. There are quite a lot of computer software firms in Novosibirsk doing programming work for American companies. They just send their finished product back to the States by the Internet.

Some parents have stayed at the **Hotel Siber**. It is clean and the staff helpful. The breakfast, which is included, is delicious. There is Internet access for about $1.50 an hour in their "business center", which is simply a room with a computer.

The place is very clean and the staff speaks a little English. The rooms are small and do not have cribs. There is another hotel called **Hotel Novosibirsk**. What a surprise! The hotel is in the very center near the main train station.

There is a very nice bookstore called "The Book Passage," located on Lenin Street downtown. The store has a main hall two-stories high, and is wrapped in bookshelves on the ground floor and on an upper level, reached by a staircase at the back of the main hall. The store is brightly lit and stocked with books. If you can, buy a picture book on the region to give to your child when she is older.

In Baby home #2 children are placed in their own quarters, separated by age. There are 2-3 caretakers per shift around the clock. The baby home is an older building, but well kept. It is clean and rooms are nicely decorated. The children seem well taken care of. The director is known to be at the home all the time and visits the children daily. There are approximately 100 children from infant to 4 years old in this home. Independent adoptions are allowed.

The judge and prosecutor are pro adoption. In 2003, the ten day appeal period was waived.

Here is an adoption group:
http://groups.yahoo.com/group/Novosibirsk_Adoption/

OMSK

Omsk is a wonderful city, but it can be a difficult region to complete an adoption from. The reason is that the judges are very "picky" in Omsk. Some require the dossier's apostilles to be "hand sewn" with threads and gold seals, some require birth parents to attend the adoption court hearing and justify why they can not care for the children themselves, and it can be very difficult to locate birth family members to attend court. They seem to have longer court date "waits" between trips.

PERM

Perm is 800 miles east of Moscow along the Trans-Siberian Railroad. Stretched out along the Kama and Chusovaya Rivers for almost sixty kilometers, Perm sits on the western edge of the Ural Mountains. It is at Perm, the last large city in Europe, that the Trans-Siberian Railroad crosses the Ural Mountains and enters Siberia and Asia.

The city of Perm was founded in 1723 and is divided into 7 Administrative Districts: Dzerzhinski, Leninski, Sverdlovski, Motovilikhinski,

Ordzhonikidzevski, Industrialni and Kirovski. It is a sister city to Louisville, Kentucky and there are many exchanges between the two cities. The Louisville/Perm web site is at *http://www.sclou.org/index.php?id=47.*

You can travel to Perm by taking the overnight Trans-Siberian from Moscow. It leaves about 5 pm from Moscow and arrives at 2 pm in Perm. While many prefer the convenience of air travel, taking the Kama train (#18 Moscow to Perm—#17 Perm to Moscow) is a really terrific experience It cost about $140-200 per person (round trip) and takes about 22 hours each way. This ride gives you plenty of time to get over your jet lag. You can also fly from Moscow, as it is just a 2-hour flight. Perm is two time zones away from Moscow so remember to change your clocks. Some parents have flown direct from Frankfurt. These flights are usually made twice a week and are more expensive. It does save on wear and tear though.

Perm (actually Solikamsk) was where the phrase "working in the salt mines" originated. Perm Region has for hundreds of years supplied Russia with vast quantities of salt, iron, and minerals of every kind. Entire cities have been built around these mines. Perm was also the home to about 36 gulags. Some of these have closed and some have converted over to regular prisons for criminals.

Infamous Perm 36, a Ural Mountains labor colony for political prisoners, is actually now a museum and opened for tourists, if you have the time and inclination. The political prisoners traveled in a rail car so tightly packed that they would all be infested with huge body lice by the time they arrived. The politicals slept in bare wooden rooms. The last prisoners arrived in 1985, soon after Gorbachev was elevated to Premier. You can also visit the Ice Caves and take the tour. They are beautiful and stay the same temperature year round. Be sure to wear a coat.

Just a few years ago Perm was a good place from which to adopt. Parents adopted from outlying towns like Solikamsk and from Perm itself. However, there has been a change of personnel in the Judiciary and prosecutor's office and there are longer waits for court dates (4 months or more), additional documents requested, and the ten-day appeal period is rarely waived. There are adoptable children in Perm, but parents should realize that Perm has, at least temporarily, become difficult. If you have adopted before, some of these problems may not manifest itself. There are currently two female adoption Judges, Ludmila Vasilovna and Lubov Ivanovna.The later is more difficult than the former. Ludmila's court sessions can run 3 hours.

There are many children's homes in towns throughout Perm Oblast. There is one in Solikamsk, Kungur and Breziniski.The baby home in Kungur is run by a wonderful director, Tatiana.

There is an odd requirement that parents complete a Perm specific medical form that is to be signed by 6 medical specialists with some sort of statement of a doctor's compentency. You have to just work around it. If you can not get all your doctors lined up before you go, consider going over a couple of days earlier and having Russian doctors complete the form. In Russia they do not have the concept of a "GP," but rather break down medical practice into a myriad of specialties, few of which equal the knowledge of a western GP. Be sure to take your own sterilized needles.

Here are some other paper requirements by Perm. These have to be notarized and apostilled.

1. An Adoption Petition to the Court, which include a list of all the documents in your dossier.

2. A copy of your state laws on international adoption, specifically regarding home studies and how post-placement reports will be handled.

3. A confirmation letter that your doctor(s) is competent to diagnose a list of 6 or 8 diseases provided by the court. Having any of them will negate your adoption

4. A medical report signed by a 1) oncologist, 2) physical therapist, 3) neurologist, 4) cardiologist, 5) internist, 6) radiologist, and 7) pharmacologist.

The children's homes, particularly in the city of Perm, do not seem well funded and this is reflected in the scarce resources the homes have and the malnourishment of the children. Perm could and should do better. Many of the children bounce back successfully, yet the region really could do better.

You can find web sites for all the hotels in Perm at *http://hotel.perm.ru/*. Just click on translate on the bottom right and the page will change to English. Many parents have stayed at the **Ural Hotel** in the city of Perm. The price can be as low as $30 a night. The Ural has good rooms and bad ones. Ask for a business one. Also, ask for an odd numbered room as the even numbered face the street, which has a noisy trolley running up and down. There are restaurants on the 1st, 3rd,

5th and 7th floors. The 5th floor restaurant does not have a menu in English. The 7th floor restaurant serves the best food for the money and if you don't like cigarette smoke, make sure you go for dinner there before 7:30 pm. Laundry is inexpensive at the Ural, so you can pack light and have them do your laundry.

There is a large department store across the street where you can buy anything. Down the street is another restaurant called Nostalgie and Café Carousel. The later is like a cafeteria where you point and place items on a tray. The Nostalgie is next door to the Baskin Robbins and has an English menu and a really good Chicken Fricassee. There is a restaurant called Metro located across the street on the side of the Ural Hotel where the market is located.

You can try a restaurant called Southern Fried Chicken, which is also on same street as Baskin Robbins. There are also other Southern Fried Chicken (SFC) places around town. They also carry good Tortilla Wraps with chicken, lettuce, tomato and cheese. Their fried mushrooms also come recommended. Some of them also have pizza, but go light on the sauce.Some parents really like the Southern Fried Chicken place by the "Tower of Death". It has a large variety of food, with a Baskin Robbins inside. It also has a large play area for children…and air conditioning!

Another good place to eat is Casa Mia, which is a very nice Italian restaurant a few blocks from the Ural Hotel. Also, in the Ural Hetel is Maxim Restaurant on the 7th Floor, which has their menu in English and Stroganoff's, which is in the basement and has an excellent breakfast buffet. If you feel like Mexican food, there is a good Mexican restaurant named Cactus, which is a short drive from the Ural Hotel.

For a nice grocery store try the largest "Family" market which is also a very short drive from the Ural Hotel. They accept Visa as long as you get in the correct lines that have a Visa indication over them. They have lots of brands that you see in your local market, plus a very nice little bakery in the middle. You have to pay for the bakery items separately and in Rubles.

The American Diner has pizza that is somewhat close to American pizza (no sauce on it—the Russians like to use ketchup). There is an art gallery near the American Diner. There is a very nice large supermarket near a church. Your facilitator will know which one it is. It has fresh fruit and other foods and a great bakery.

If you need to stay for the ten-day wait, consider upgrading to the **Perm Tourist Hotel**, 2 blocks from the Ural. The rooms are renovated, bathrooms are clean and the television has lots of channels. The cost is about $70 a night. Phone cards are sold in the lobby. There is an Italian restaurant near the Tourist.

There is also the **Kama Hotel**, which is right around the corner from the Ural Hotel. Not as nice, but cheaper in price. They do not have a restaurant, but there are two grocery stores within 5 blocks of the hotel with friendly counter ladies. Just outside the hotel are a small coffee shop and a pastry shop. The department store has a great deli with all sorts of great food. The Kama's address is 25B, Ul. Baumana; Tel: 7 (3422) 27-16-45, 27-00-82; Fax: 7 (3422) 90-27-40. It advertises that it has air conditioning, several bars and a pool table.

Another hotel is the **Mikos Hotel** at 10A, Ul. Stakhanovsk;Tel: 7 (3422) 24-21-49, 24-19-99; Fax: 7 (3422) 24-11-98. It advertises is has air conditioning, bars, poll table and a swimming pool. Also, the **Nikol Hotel** at 25, Ul. Sviyazeva; Tel: 7 (3422) 63-54-00, 28-88-58; Fax: 7 (3422) 63-54-00.

Internet cafes are not all that plentiful, but there is an Internet connection from the regular Post Office building. The Internet connection at the Ural does go down on occasions, but parents have been able to download their pictures onto a floppy and simply sent them that way. It is not clear whether the Ural or the one across the street has a USB connection. The Ural computer costs 80 rubles or about $3 an hour to use. There is an Internet Café across the street from the Ural, above Rock and Roll Pizza, but they do not speak English. They don't mind you using their computers, but they seem nervous about you hooking up your laptop or camera. They also don't have floppy drives. It is suggested that you practice with Cyrillic fonts in case you run into a computer that has the regular Windows icons, but does not have English fonts.

Do try the pastries when you are in Perm. They make huge apple tarts that can feed a family. There is also a photo album of the city that you must buy when you are there. It makes a wonderful keepsake.

You can look at a Perm trip adoption video called "A Passage to Parenthood." It is a 15 minute travelogue that follows an adoptive couple as they fly to Perm, meet their two babies with the Russian social worker, and then travel to Filatov medical clinic and US Embassy in Moscow. The Ural Hotel, shops, orphanage, history, and the children of the Perm region are shown. Contact Linda Brownlee at *lindbrownl@aol.com* of the Adoption Center of Washington.

There is a Perm adoption group on Yahoo! Here is a Perm oriented web site at *http://www.mgls.com/russia/russia.html* and a story of adopting from Perm at, *boltonfamily.org,* and for general history see *http://www.bisnis.doc.gov/bisnis/country/991221perm.htm* and *http://www.psu.ru/perm/index.html*

PSKOV

Pskov is about 200 miles south of St. Petersburg, very close to the border with Estonia. It is a city of about 200,000, and is located on the Veliskaya River. Parents have stayed at the **Hotel Rizhskaya**. It is old, but very cozy and has a very friendly staff. It costs about $20 per night. The food in the dining room is excellent and reasonably priced.

The Pskov regional "Baby House" orphanage (all children in orphanages in this region who are between 0 and 4 years old are here) is actually in the town of Pechory, which is about 30-45 minutes drive outside of Pskov, and is just about 1 km from the border with Estonia.

This is a two-trip process region. This region is fairly an adoption friendly. It used to waive the 10 days.

One of the Pskov orphanages has a web page at *http://www.roofnet.org/progs/bu-en.html* There is also a Yahoo! Group for the Pskov Oblast at *http://groups.yahoo.com/group/Pskov_Adopt*

ROSTOV

Rostov is the region and Rostov-on-Don is the major city. However, most people just say Rostov when referring to the city. Rostov is about and hour and half by air from Moscow. It is in southwest Russia. It is very hot during the summer, and the cars are not air-conditioned. It is a large city of a million people. You can get anything you want or need there. There are about 7 to 9 daily flights from Moscow to Rostov. Real Aeroflot flies only 1 or 2 times a day and ONLY from SVO-1 airport. These Aeroflot planes are clean and well maintained and the food is good. A few other airlines also fly to Rostov, some from the SVO-1 airport, some from VKO and DME. These are BAD. Try to avoid them if possible. Their planes are old and the food is bad. There are 20 or so domestic airlines in Russia and Aeroflot is just one of them. But it is the biggest air carrier and the safest among all of them. An example of one airline to avoid in going to Rostov is called Aeroflot-Don. It has nothing to do with the real Aeroflot, they have just misappropriated the name.

Another airline is called Donavia (a/k/a Don Air). On some flights, the pilots look too young to drive a car, let alone fly a commercial plane. They fly like they are flying fighter jets rather than rickety Soviet-built jetliners. However, even on Donavia the planes will get you there, although you may be more religious on arrival than when you first left.

In Rostov, families have stayed at a home stay although quite a few also stay at hotels like **Hotel Rostov** or the **Intourist**. The Intourist restaurant is not great, but there are three good ones within a couple blocks of the hotel. Make sure to go eat at the Babylon Restaurant and there is also a good Italian Restaurant. There is a refrigerator in the room so you can buy cereal, milk and fruit for breakfast. Try to get a room in the Executive or Business Section that will be cleaner (less dirty), quieter (less noisy), safer, in better shape, and heated/air conditioned. There are Internet cafes near both hotels and Internet access and ATMs in both hotels. The train is an overnight adventure, but might not be up to TranSiberian Railway standards. It would allow you to get over any jet lag.

If you plan to bring a doctor with you, check with your agency to be sure that your orphanage director will welcome the physician you select, as that is sometimes an issue in Rostov.

Rostov is generally a two-trip region, and although there are reports of a few families only having to make one trip that is now very rare. If you adopt independently, you will certainly have to make two trips. The ten-day appeal period used to be waived if you had a young child at home or if the children in the children's home were all getting sick, but now it is much harder to get the ten days waived by the Rostov Judges. They no longer seem willing to waive it even when you have young children at home or in one case, a grandparent die. This difficulty is not unique to Rostov, but rather in 2001, it became generally more difficult all across Russia. Nevertheless, the Department of Education officials, the judge, and even the prosecutor, who represents the state at the hearing, are very kind and supportive. The Judges have allowed Saturday and Sunday to count as part of the 10 days and have allowed parents to proceed with the paperwork during that period. They just had to stay in Rostov until the ten days was over. There seems to be one full time adoption Judge and one back up. Independent adoptions are allowed.

The procedure in Rostov is not unlike the rest of the country. You go to the Deputy Minister's office and present your translated dossier. She will ask you a few questions about the type of child you are looking for. If you have asked for a girl, she may remind you that there are a lot of baby boys. She will discuss the importance of post placement reports. This is a serious issue with the Russians and it should be to you. She will then write out her recommendation to the Social Services Director to refer a child to you as young and as healthy as possible, if that was your request. This visit will not take any longer than 20 minutes. You then leave and go directly to the Social Services office. She reads the request, asks a few questions and you leave. Later that day you are told about your referral. The next day you go to meet her. The Doctor/Director gives you her medical history and you spend an hour or more with her. If you are satisfied, you leave the children's home and go to the courthouse and signed and file your petition to adopt. The next day you may see the child again and play with her taking lots of pictures and measurements. You then fly home and wait for the court date. This part of the process usually takes a week.

Now after choosing your child and before flying home to complete your first trip, you will likely have an "interview" with the judge to present your dossier, and ask "permission" to file your adoption petition, and answer some "questions" from the judge. There are other regions that have this procedure, but not many.

There are about 40 children's homes in the Rostov Region. The children's homes in the city of Rostov (Rostov-On-the-Don) are numbered; those outside the city have names. It was reported in 1998 that Detsky Dom #10 was just terrific. The director was top notch. When a child was adopted, she would give each one their own little photo album and the parent a folder containing their complete, original medical records. You cannot ask for any better care than that!

Detsky Dom #2. is considered pretty good. Its director is strict and makes you wash your hands and wear a mask during each visit with your child. Because she is correctly strict about prevention, the children are pretty healthy. The kids are reportedly affectionate, bright and healthy. #2 is in central Rostov and very easy to get to.

Detsky Dom #3 in Rostov also appears to be a nice one. The home is clean although the building appears run down and there is a nice playroom with lots of toys in it. The children seem well taken care of by the caregivers. It is reported that one child adopted from here had a slight case of giardia, so that would something to check when you return to the States.

Detsky Dom #4 in Rostov is very clean and well kept even though run down in age. The caretakers seem to really take good care of the children. It is about one mile away from both Hotel Rostov and the Intourist Hotel off Red Army Street.

There is also a baby home in Novocherkassk, which is about a 40 minute drive from Rostov, but is in the Rostov Region. The building seems in good shape. The staff seems to care for the children.

About 60 miles outside the city of Rostov is the Kamensk orphanage. It is a two hour drive from Rostov. The children's home is small and relatively new. The children seem well cared for although there is not a lot of money. There is a nice playroom and the children seem well fed. The director appears to very competent. There have been no reported children with parasites or malnutrition from this children's home. The city of Kamensk is very accessible, and you will be able to buy whatever you need at the department store, camera store, and food store. Kamensk is the next city north of Shakhtinskiy, which is on the M4 highway between Rostov and Moscow.

Shakhtinskiy, which is only about an hour from Rostov, also has a baby home. It is the halfway point if you are traveling to Kamensk, which was two hours. If you do travel in that region during the summer, bring bottled water for the trip, and be sure to bring a video camera to capture the sights along the way, especially the people on the shoulder of the highway selling everything from fish to hubcaps to motor oil; and lots of sunflower fields. It is very hot in that part of Russia in the summer (90 in the shade), and the cars are not air-conditioned nor are homestays, so be prepared.

Here is a story of adopting from Rostov: *www.angelfire.com/co2/pattispage/rostov.html.* There is also a Yahoo! Group at *http://groups.yahoo.com/group/Rostov_on_Don*

ST. PETERSBURG

You can take a high speed train to St. Petersburg from Moscow. It is pretty safe. You can also fly from Moscow. St. Petersburg hotels range from cheap to very expensive. Some parents have stayed at the **Sheraton Nevskij Palace** and said it was great. Others have stayed at the **Oktybryskaya** and paid about $65-70 per night for a large room. Parents have stayed at the **Hotel Neptune**, which is nice and clean but not near the main street in St Petersburg (Nevsky Prospect). The walk to Nevsky Prospect is about 15 minutes from the hotel. Neptune is about $110 a night with breakfast. It is akin to a Best Western and is new with a great spa, pool and workout area.

Another one is the **Moscow Hotel**, which is nice and only costs about $80.00 per night. Breakfast is included. There is a convenience store and several restaurants located in the hotel. They also have a business center, although it is not very extensive. Other families have stayed at the **Hotel D'Angleterre** (attached to **Astoria**) and paid an adoption rate of $130. Families felt very safe there. Across the hotel on a side street is a restaurant called Koleso with great beef stroganoff. Hotel D'Angleterre has clean bathrooms (with soft toilet paper), bottled water and little shampoos. It is a small touch of home. It is also in a great location and you can walk to the Hermitage. Cafe Orient has a breakfast bar and coffee which is $3 for two people. You need to try their fried potato cakes.

There is a **Radisson** on Nevsky Prospekt at an adoption rate of from $175 to $200 depending on the room. The staff speaks some English. It is in the main section of the city and you are within walking distance of the Hermitage, St Isaacs, Church of the Spilled Blood, and Russian Museum. (IBM has done a great job placing some of the Hermitage collection on the web. It also set up a bank of Internet ready computers at the Hermitage for school children.) The business class rooms have a hot pot, hairdryer, shampoo, great towels, toilet paper, minibar, and two free bottles of water every day. It has a very good business center with easy access to email. There is a nice café and a restaurant in the hotel. Another hotel is **Hotel Pribaltiyskaya**. It is a beautiful hotel and large with 1600 rooms. It runs $100 per night. Do not use the room telephone to call the US unless you want a huge bill. Use a calling card instead.

The region of Leningrad (St. Petersburg) is far more relaxed about foreign adoptions than the City. The City of St. Petersburg has its own rules and procedures. The City is divided into wards and each ward has an adoption committee comprised of elected citizens, who must approve the adoption. They can be difficult or easy to deal with. Your facilitator should be able to handle them. The judge controls their ability to keep their job, so the judge should be advised immediately of any attempt to do this. She has the ability to straighten them up if she knows of the situation. There seems to be four judges that hear adoption cases. Two waive the 10 days and two do not. Independent adoptions are allowed.

Generally the number of children per caregiver is higher in urban institutions than in rural ones and this holds true in St. Petersburg. Children in a St. Petersburg home are likely not to wake up to the same caretaker on a daily basis due to shift changes as compared to a rural home. The infant rooms generally do not have anything on the walls or ceilings for the infants to look at and be stimulated. Infants are delayed and generally can only say one or two words at 18 months. Almost half of the infants are below 5% on the height, weight and head circumference growth charts. Most infants are delayed developmentally. Some of the baby houses seem to have exclusive relationships with certain agencies so that infants under 12 months are directed to those agencies. It is not known if this is true for all.

In 1999 in St. Petersburg, foreigners adopted 529 of the city's estimated 2,000 abandoned children. While the majority, 262, went to homes in the United States, many of the children were placed with families in other countries—including 126 in Italy, 36 in France, 34 in Israel and 33 in Finland.

St Petersburg has some amazing cultural sights. You can see where Tsar Nicholas II and his family (who were executed in Ekaterinburg in 1917) were recently re-buried. It is in the same magnificent cathedral as Peter the Great, Catherine the Great, and most all the other Romanovs. You can visit the log cabin Peter the Great lived in when he was first laying out the city. You can go on the battleship Aurora which played a key role in the 1917 Revolution and is now a museum. You can see the monument to the siege defenders during WWII.The city lost about a third of its population to the war (no thanks to Stalin).

The Russian Museum has a wonderful collection of paintings by Russian artists. Of course, there is the Hermitage, which exceeds the Louvre. There is a golden peacock clock that spreads its tail and crows the hour. You can see a ballet at the Mariinsky Theatre or go on a tour of the city on foot with Peter's Walks, which is an offbeat group that leads non-traditional tours. And on and on.

There is an interesting travel web site on St Petersburg at *http://www.finditlocal.com/stpetersburg/* and a Yahoo adopt list at *http://groups.yahoo.com/group/Adopt_StPetersburg.*

SAMARA

Samara is a 19 hour train ride from Moscow or an hour and half plane ride. The train is an interesting way to see a lot of the country. The train ride will also allow you to over come your jet lag. As with many Russian cities, the city of Samara is run down. In the summer the temperature climbs to over 100 degrees and can be very muggy. If you go in the summer, try to avoid a hotel without air conditioning. Samara is a very artsy city and is on the banks of the Volga River. It is a university city, home of Samara State University and the Samara Aerospace University. More importantly, it has a large chocolate factory and the famous Rodnik Vodka factory.

Samara is reportedly a favorite of some of the larger agencies.If you go with a smaller one, they may not be able to work here.The judges sometimes waive the ten days, even as recently as 2003.Second trips are usually scheduled fairly quickly as in within a month of you returning home from the first.

Many parents stay at the National Hotel. There is also the Moskva, which has been described as expensive and not very nice.

There are two orphanages in Samara. The children in children's home #1 seem to have a high incidence of giardia. Samara #2 seems clean and cheerful and a little bit better although incidences of giardia and the usual speech delys have been reported.The children do not seem as malnourished. It does not have a lot of resources. The staff is nice and helpful. Children's home #2 is very old and the outside grounds are a bit run down, but it is generally reported as being pretty well run. Originally, there were 3 orphanages, but orphanage number 3 closed down.Samara is an adoption friendly region.

There is a Samara listserv that you can sign on to and get lots of information. Go to Yahoogroups.com, sign up for Samarakids and you'll be part of the e-mail group

SARATOV

Saratov is the capital of the region and has a population of a million. Most parents fly Aeroflot from Moscow to Saratov. It takes about an hour and a half. The plane fare is about $100. There is a lot of poverty affecting the city and the children's homes. It is an industrial city and the air quality reflects that. If you have an asthmatic condition, you will use your inhaler constantly.

Saratov was under the one trip system in July 2000. This may have changed. In 2000 the ten-day appeal period was waived if you adopted a toddler, but not if you adopted an older child. This makes good sense actually.

Orphanage number 1 is poor but neat and clean. Some of the children are reported to have giardia so take the usual precautions. This home is for children ages one to three. The caregivers are kind and support foreign adoptions. You are usually allowed to visit up to 2 hours each day. Malnutrition does not seem to be a problem here. However, the home does need prescription medication, toddler shoes and very basic clothing for infants (not onesies), t-shirts, underwear and blankets. As is common the children's clothing has been washed and worn many, many times and would not even make it to a thrift shop in the US. The children's shoes are usually too small, but that is a common occurrence when you can't be picky about hand-me-downs as the alternative is none at all. Boys wear girl things and vice versa. They have plenty of toys.

There are other homes several hours outside the city.

Hotel Slovakia is the best in town. Most visitors stay there. The Hotel Slovakia is the largest hotel in the city of Saratov. It is nice but not plush. It is located on the embankment of the Volga River. The address is 30 Lermontova Street. (The phone number is (8452) 26-95-01. If you call, no one speaks any English. There is also a port in front of the hotel where cruise ships as well as boats for day trips stop. The Slovakia has no air conditioning and no screens on the windows but is clean and neat. If you go in the summer, take some screen material and duck tape. It is also suggested that you take a small ice tray and an insulated cup. The cost is around $30-45 a night depending on the size. Breakfast is included consisting of meat, potatoes, and tea. A four room suite ($45) has a living room, bedroom, bathroom and kitchen complete with microwave and refrigerator. It has a beautiful view of the river and the city. There are two restaurants, an outdoor cafe, a bar and a small grocery at the

Slovakia. You can also get out and walk around the area, which is filled with outdoor cafes. There is a path along the river. It is also within walking distance to German St. You must show your room pass to the security guard to take the elevator to get to different floors. There are also floor ladies (maids) on every floor. You can get same day service for laundry although anything too nice won't make it through the wash. You pay for the hotel and other things in rubles. It is reportedly cheaper to call the US from the room than using a calling card.

The Volga River is the largest in Europe and the longest bridge crossing it is outside your hotel window. The river is the heart of the city. The Adoption Center of Saratov, where the Department of Education is located is just around the corner from the Slovakia. The DoE is not the friendliest in regard to foreign adoption and several agencies have stopped working in the region.

Another hotel is the **Volga,** which is on German St., which is the main street of the city. It may not be as nice as the Slovakia.

German St is the main part of the City. It is filled with restaurants and shops. Souvenir shopping is much less expensive than in Moscow. Germain St also has a children's store where you can buy the donations to the home like diapers, clothes, etc.

You can do many things in Saratov such as visit the oldest circus in Russia. You can also take a short cruise down the Volga and go to the "beach on the Volga" for swimming and a picnic. (Do not try the dried fish with beer.) You can see a World War II memorial. The Radishchev Art gallery is known as the "Volga Hermitage.

The restaurants mainly serve meat and potatoes, even for breakfast. A nice restaurant is the Pandok—a Georgian restaurant. Other restaurants are the Barracuda and the Seahorse. You can get Pizza at the Barracuda. If you see a small stage in a corner of a restaurant that has a pole on it going form floor to ceiling, that means that at 11:00 it becomes a strip bar. You can buy and fresh fruits and vegetables in the market but you must clean them yourself with bottled water. Do not eat them in the restaurants as they have been cleaned with local water.

The adoption judge is very formal until after the ruling. The hearing takes about an hour.

One interesting story about Saratov is that when the first cosmonaut, Yuri Gagarin, returned after circling the Earth, he landed in a field near a military garrison in Saratov. The first person to see him was a soldier who asked for his documents, fearing he was an American spy.

There is a Yahoo group for families who adopted or are considering adopting from Saratov. It is *Saratov_adopt@yahoogroups.com*

SEROV

Serov is about 4 and half hours by car from the city of Ekaterinburg. It is also in the Sverdlovsk region. The road is new so it has not yet developed into the classic Russian potholed road from hell. Still, as on any long drive on a Russian road, a little Dramamine should be carried along just in case. There is a gas station stop along the way that has snacks and soft drinks. The outhouse is in the back. Bring your old toilet paper. If you go in the winter, nothing will quite prepare you for the outhouse experience at 30 below zero.

At the children's home in Serov, the Director gets produce from the surrounding farms so the children do not appear malnourished. They also get a lot of milk so their teeth are in very good shape. They are still low on the growth charts however, because it takes love as well as food, to grow a healthy child. The winters are harder than the summer, and as with all homes, vitamins are in short supply. The staff is very caring in the baby home and they support foreign adoption. Several children a month are adopted from the baby home and some of them are independent adoptions.

SMOLENSK

Smolensk is about a 6 hour train ride from Moscow. Overnight train from Moscow leaves at about 11pm.and arrives at 6:30am. It is 215 miles west of Moscow and is one of the oldest cities in Russia. It is 4 hours by car and the road is not bad. The police will pull your driver over at least once on the trip and negotiate a "fee" (roof). Try to stay in town, even if your agency doesn't want you to. Your will have more time to visit with your child and you don't want to have to do the long commute from Moscow the morning of the court hearing.

There are several baby homes in Smolensk. One is attached to the maternity hospital and is pretty nice. There is another for babies over 1, that is not so nice. Many children have been adopted from a baby home called Krasy Bor. Smolensk is a fairly smooth and quick process and seems adoption friendly. It is two trips. The 10 days is waived, although there is pressure on the Judges not to.

There is an eGroup of parents who have adopted from Smolensk and a Yahoo Group. Smolensk is a two trip city, but many agencies are able to give you a referral and video prior to traveling. Here is a web site with some general information on the city:
http://www.smolensk.ru/user/smolensk/index_eng.html

STAVROPOL

Stavropol is about a two hour plane ride from Moscow. It is near the border with Chechnya, however the fighting is not evident in the city. There is an email group for those who are adopting or have adopted from Stavropol at *http://groups.yahoo.com/group/stavropolkids/*, or *http://forums.delphiforums.com/stavropol/start* and at *http://www.greatwebpages.com/stavropol* just click on 'forum'.

There is a children's home for children 3-8 in the city. The outside looks terrible, but the inside is clean. The kids seem to be cared for and there are lots of toys.

There is only one hotel, the **Intourist**.

TOMSK

Tomsk is about 4 hours by plane from Moscow on Siberia Airlines. The Tomsk airport is about a half hour outside the city, surrounded by vast silver birch forests.

There is on baby home with approximately 30 children ranging from 0-4 years of age. The children's home is nice, but with few frills. There are also several orphanages for older children. It was reported in early 2001 that the Judge in Tomsk was nice, pro-adoption and would waive the ten days on occasion. Some parents report a pre-hearing meeting with the judge when they make the first trip. This is similar to what happens in Rostov. Independent adoption is allowed.

Tomsk is very inexpensive as it is suffering from considerable poverty. This makes the city a little depressing, although the people are very nice. A hotel costs around $30.00 per night and food costs are reasonable. There is not much to do. Electricity is generated by burning diesel fuel so you may notice the resulting air pollution.

Tomsk is a "university town" and has a population of between 600,000 and 1 million. It will celebrate its 400th anniversary as a city in 2004. It used to be the capital of Siberia but when the TransSiberian Railway was built, the railroad was routed through Novobristock, which therefore became the capital.

Tomsk is usually very sunny in the summer with the sun shining until 11:00 p.m. and then rising again around 2:30 a.m. In the winter it is very cold. The town is well laid out and relatively clean.

There is a Yahoo! adoption group from the Tomsk Oblast at *http://groups.yahoo.com/group/Tomsk_Adoption*

TVER

Tver is both a region and a city about 2 hours northwest of Moscow by car, on the road to St. Petersburg. Almost anyone who adopts from the Tver region will travel by private car from Moscow. You could take the train if you really wanted to (on the Moscow-St. Pete line), but car is the usually mode of travel. The city of Tver is the capital of the Tver region, so court would be held there if you adopt from either an orphanage in Tver or from another city in the region.

Tver has a few nice hotels. One is the **Hotel Osnabruck**, which is German-owned. There are only 19 rooms, and it is supposed to be comfortable. Some parents have stayed at the **Hotel Volga**, on the scenic Volga River. A nice suite costs about $100 a night, although you can get rooms for as low as $30 a night. A suite has a kitchen with microwave, hot pot, stove and small fridge, living room with TV, bedroom and large bath. The bathroom features a huge tub, but no shower curtain. Also, the hot water is temperamental. Towels are large and plentiful. The toilets are relatively new. A bar on the 2nd floor sells alcoholic drinks, water and sodas. There is an Internet salon on the 2nd floor. No one speaks much English, but it isn't a problem. There is also a nice gift shop attached to the hotel. There is a western-style supermarket a block or two away from the Hotel Volga. The supermarket allows you to fill your basket with food, and then pay instead of the traditional Russian way of paying first, then getting your items.

Tver is not a great looking place. It is home to a military base, so you will notice lots of soldiers and very large military aircraft flying overhead. The roads are terrible with potholes the size of Texas. There is a flea-market street sale that runs on weekend mornings outside the Hotel Volga. A great restaurant is called the Cafe Nadia-something. You can get salads, entrees, drinks and sometimes even dessert for $5-$10 (American) for two. The food is very good, especially their borscht, picante salad (like egg salad), chicken with nuts and veal stew in a pot.

The Tver region features 4 baby homes, in the cities of Kashin, Konakovo, Vizhny Volachek and Tver. Then there are numerous orphanages for older children. Reportedly the Konakovo baby home is only for special needs babies, and the Vizny Volachek home is only for local children. However, some have adopted children from Konakovo who were not special needs. The rest of the babies go to either Kashin or Tver. Young children are available.

Kashin is about 2 hours by car from Tver. You drive through the Russian countryside. Kashin is rather "provincial," and small. There really isn't a hotel there that is livable. The baby home is small. It was built to house about 50 kids from the age of birth to 5, but usually holds more like 60. The orphanage is two stories, and looks very run down from the outside, with peeling paint. When you walk in you go up a large staircase into the entry hall. Inside it looks like a very old home—high ceilings, dark wood, etc. It also smells like cats. There are lots of plants, lacy curtains, and a nice little entry hall with chairs, a table and telephone. They also have a nice bulletin board set up with pictures of their kids who have been adopted. The baby playroom has a large crib, toys, and a table where the babies are fed. They seemed to mostly have rattles for toys, although there are some walkers. The toddler playroom is furnished with many nice toys, and is kept very clean. Kashin is a very poor area, so their resources are few. However the caretakers seem to care greatly for the children. Most of the kids were small, mainly due to the lack of good food. They do not normally take the children outside. As is common throughout the FSU, the doctors believe that breezes cause illness.

One children's home in Tver is called Teremonk. Teremonk is a well run orphanage, but poor. The children are not hungry, but the food is not all that plentiful nor nutritionally great. There is a deficit in the calorie count. It is not unusual for orphanage children to eat a lot of starches, and little else.

After meeting your child on the first trip, you are sometimes taken to meet the Judge in Tver. She will meet with you individually, question you briefly and then perhaps give you a court date. This is similar to what happens in Rostov.

Court in Tver is not bad and usually lasts an hour. The 10-day wait is usually waived. The process had been one trip even as late as early 2002, but now it seems the region has gone to the two-trip process. Even so, some parents report the trips as being very short in duration at about 7 days each. Usually court will be on a Monday so you need to arrive by the previous Thursday in order to see your child for the requisite amount of time before court. Parents report different experiences with the Tver passport office. Some have had to wait 3 days before it was issued and others just 24 hours. Without the passport, your child cannot get the US Visa. If you have to wait the longer period, see if your agency is able to bring the passport to Moscow for you.

There is a Tver email group at *http://groups.yahoo.com/group/kashin/* and one family's journal of their trip to Tver and Kashin at *www.bylerbunch.com*

TYUMEN

Tyumen Oblast is the third largest oblast in area in Russia. Tyumen is an oil city of half a million people and is about 2 hours by flight from Moscow in southwestern Siberia. The planes are old.

There is only one baby home in Tyumen and it is pretty decent. The children seem to get above average care. The caregivers really care about the kids. The facilities, while not lavish, are clean. All the kids seem to be healthy and happy (they do have an infirmary) and there are plenty of toys. They are clean and well dressed, although still on the small side. In the summer it is not unusual for school-age children to help out so the babies got more individual attention. They get some massage and speech therapy. There is music play.

Your facilitator may be a woman named Irina. Parents report different experiences with the Court. With some, the female Judge seemed strict and asked a lot of questions. Other parents have been in and out in less than 40 minutes and had a pleasant time. They will sometimes waive the 10 days if you have an appointment letter from your pediatrician. Tyumen is a 2 trip process. It is friendly to single Dads.

Some parents have stayed at the **Quality Hotel**. The Quality Hotel is comfortable and has excellent food. It is a clean and recently built hotel. It s the most expensive in town. Its telephone number is 7 (3452) 49-40-40. If you travel in late fall or winter, bring lots of clothes and dress in layers as the temperature never goes much above 0 degrees F and the buildings are very hot and dry inside. There are mini-fridges in the rooms, 2 in-house restaurants with breakfast buffet, and a bar for the end of the day. There is TV, but only one channel in English, which is BBC News.

Tyumen was the home of Rasputin, who so mesmerized the Czarina. His grand daughter died, strangely enough in Los Angles in 1977.Lenin's coffin was kept in Tyumen for safekeeping during WWII.

Here are some web sites referencing Tyumen:
http://ourworld.compuserve.com/homepages/alfred_kuhn/S_TYUMEN.HTM
http://www.bisnis.doc.gov/bisnis/COUNTRY/000421tyumen.htm

UFA

Ufa is a two trip region. Some parents have flown to it on Bashkirian Airlines. The seats are close together, but the service is fine. Since it is a domestic flight, don't expect much English to be spoken.

Parents have reported receiving medicals and pictures on their referral, but no video. Baby home #2 has been described as being almost brand new. It was built in 2001. The kids appear to be in good shape and the orphanage seems to have a fair amount of staff. Bashkir enthnicity is not unusual in this region. Baby home #1 was also remodeled in 2002.

Some parents have stayed in Hotel Russia. It is simple and nice. The front desk speaks English.

There can be as much as a month between trips, although holidays can stretch that out to three.The prosecutor can be strict, but even so the ten day appeal period is sometimes waived.

ULYANOVSK

Ulyanovsk is the birthplace of Lenin and is located south of Moscow (about 2 hours by air) on the Volga River. A two mile bridge spans the Volga between the old and new cities.

Ulyanovsk has a very unique setup. In one children's home 10-15 children ranging in age from toddler to teens live in cottages. There are four large duplex type cottages totaling 8 homes. Each has a house mom and cook who work in twelve hour shifts with every other day off. There are a total of three Moms and three cooks who rotate, and also a tutor that comes in to teach the preschool age children and to help the older kids after school. There is also a baby home onsite with about 40 babies. The children attend the regular village schools. The cottages are very clean and the children are taught well. Everyone helps out and works as a family. You can actually live with the children for a short time. The kids are healthy, well adjusted, well taken care of, and mannerly. The cottages are located on the other side of the river from the city and are about a half hour drive from the city. There is a baby house in the city as well. It is described as being very nice.

This is a two-trip region. The wait between trips is about 5-8 weeks. Independent adoptions are allowed.

Some families have stayed at the Hotel Oktyabrskaya. It is fours stories and is just a block of concrete. It is about $50 a night including breakfast for a small room. Not much English is spoken. You can use the phone to make local calls, but you can only receive international ones. If your child is in the city orphanage rather than the cottages, this hotel is just 10 minutes away. It is 5 minutes from the Department of Education. Some have described as a 1970's Red Roof Inn. Comfortable, but not fancy. Here is the hotel's web site: *http://www.tourintel.ru/hotels/e_ru_uly_okb.html.*

VLADIVOSTOK

Vladivostok is home to the Russian Pacific Fleet, which is why it was closed to foreigners for so long. By the mid-1990's much of the Pacific fleet was obsolete.

This was already evident in the late 1980's. The disposal of ordinance was a major issue. One solution devised by the Pacific Fleet was to simply throw the ordinance into the Sea of Japan. Without a viable fleet, the Navy turned to importing second hand cars. Now Vladivostok is considered to be an attractive, lively city centered on hills overlooking the Golden Horn Bay.

Vladivostok is about a 9 hour flight from Moscow on Aero Air. The flight is usually full, so upgrade to business class. You may be the only English speakers on board, so take a phrase book.

Another way to travel is to take Korean Air from Seoul to Vladivostok. This is about a 2 ½ hour flight. Delta used to be a code-share partner with Korean Air so that frequent flyer points could be used. However, in 1999 Korean Air had safety problems so Delta suspended the arrangement and the FAA imposed certain restrictions. Delta has suggested that those safety issues have been resolved and they restarted the code-share arrangement in 2002. The FAA has also said that Korea now meets air safety standards. The flight from Los Angles to Seoul takes 13 hours. The flight from Seoul to Vladivostok is restricted to two days a week, Saturdays and Tuesdays. Korean Air flights are comfortable and flight attendants friendly and polite. Two other airlines that fly in from Seoul are Vladivostok Air (www.vladavia.ru) and Siberia Air.

The airport in Korea (Incheon) is reportedly very nice. They are used to international travelers with children. Bathrooms are spotless and have a courtesy bell, which you press while using the toilet to prevent anyone else from hearing any potty sounds. (Now, that's civilized!) Incheon airport has free internet access and the food is fairly good and fairly priced. There are many shops to wander around while waiting. You cannot gain access to checked luggage during the layover in Incheon airport, so take a change in your carry-on. You do need to get to the transit ticket booth prior to flight to have them transfer your bags and get your seat confirmation for the flight to Vlad.

There is a transit hotel in the airport. It charges by the 6 hour block and is comfortable and clean. After your long flight, there is nothing like a nice shower and sleep to prepare you for Russia. They take US currency in the Incheon airport so there is no need to change your money. Also, there is no need to get a visa for Korea if you are not leaving the airport, and are just laying over at the transit hotel. One problem is that if you do not want to go through customs, you will not have access to your luggage and will need to pack a change in your carry on. In the morning you go to a transit counter and they will book your flight to Vladivostok and make certain your luggage transfers as well.

The Moscow Aero flight is daily. Magadan Airlines used to fly direct from Seattle to Vladivostok. Some families prefer taking Singapore Air from San Francisco to Seoul then Seoul Airlines to Vladivostok.

The airport is about a 50 minute drive from the city. If the airport bathroom looks even passable, use it.

In Vladivostok, the U.S. Consulate will coordinate the issuance of the child's visa with the US Embassy in Moscow so that the parents are not required to make the 10 hour, 7 time zone trip to Moscow. It all depends on if the agency has made prior arrangements with the Consulate. If so, then the physical is done in Vladivostok at Children hospital #1, #35, Okeansky Prospect, Vladivostok 690090. Telephone number 25-9335, or 25-2426. The parents make a trip with the child to the Consulate. A Consular officer verifies the identity of each child, signing a document prepared by the agency according to Embassy specifications. The agency facilitator, using a power of attorney, makes the trip to Moscow while the passports are being processed. It is much less stressful and less expensive for the adopting parents. The parents then wait in Vladivostok for the facilitator's return from Moscow with the visa.

There is a children's home in the city. It is about 15 minutes from the center of town. There are several children's homes, which range from 1 to 3 hours outside the city. The conditions in the homes vary significantly. In 2001, it seemed the Court waived the 10 days more often than not. There are also children's homes in other surrounding towns such as Ussuriisk, which is about 1 1/2 hours from Vladivostok. Even so, all of the paperwork and court work is completed in Vladivostok.

Vladivostok generally functions under the "two-trip" system. There were some families in 2001 that traveled under the one trip system using an accredited agency, but it is not something to count on. On your first trip you will be taken to the a large white office building known as the "White House", to meet the Department of Education representative, Tatiana. You wait downstairs for about an hour or so before being taken to her office. She will ask you a few questions such as how do you like Russia? What do you like about Russia? She will then give you permission to visit one child. (You may want to give her a small gift at this time. Consult your facilitator over proper etiquette.) For some reason, Tatiana is difficult about allowing you to see another child, if you decide not to accept the first referral. This is contrary to the procedure in most regions. It does not mean it cannot be done, just that she is difficult about it. Keep your flight stubs and take photos of you and your child in case the Judge later wants proof that you actually came to Vladivostok on the first trip. Vladivostok is rumored to be closed to agencies that do not have the "right" connections. This should not concern you, even if true. It does mean the cost is higher since there are fewer players.

You have basically three choices of where to stay in Vladivostok. The least expensive is the **Hotel Vladivostok**, which has slowly been undergoing refurbishing. It is a bit rustic. It is said that along with your water you will also get your minerals. The Hotel Vladivostok overlooks the harbor and most rooms have a view. It has a laundry service. If you stay there, get a suite with double rooms as anything less is small. The hotel is clean and comfortable, but not fancy. You generally pay by the night and not at the end of your stay. There is a floor mistress who keeps your keys and is there if you need assistance. The hotel has a web site at *http://www.vladhotel.vl.ru/*.

Rooms with two twin beds cost about 1200 rubles or $40 per night. It is less expensive buying your personal items and souvenirs elsewhere as there is quite a markup at the hotel. The hotel takes rubles and Visa credit card. It also seems that different floors have different payment options. This, of course, makes no sense, but hey, it's Russia! The 5th floor has been remodeled and includes breakfast in the price. The 11th floor is ok as well. Each room has a small fridge. The second floor has the Internet center and there are several restaurants on various floors in the building.

You can exchange money at the hotel and get a good exchange rate. They also have email and fax service. It is about 100 rubles per hour ($3.33 per hour) for email. The hotel food is below average so you may want to go down the street to the pizza place. Also, there is a baby store (diapers, food) just down from the hotel (towards the train depot) and a grocery store across the street from the Hotel Versailles. There is another baby store north of the "Barbie" store. Take with you a cookie tin, or a sturdy Tupperware container, or something else that you can use to bring home fragile souvenirs such as tiny porcelain dolls for Christmas ornaments, which can be found at a store called Nostalgia. Nostalgia is down the hill, to the left, coming from the parking lot of the Hotel Vladivostok. It has a restaurant and a gift shop

The Nostalgia restaurant has good, inexpensive food. It opens around 9am and closes at 9pm. You can get eggs and ham for breakfast or Russian style "pancakes" which come with a honey or jelly topping. You can also get them filled with meat. The restaurant also serves dinner. Past Nostalgia and down the hill are the post office, the main train station, and the sea terminal. You can catch a tram by the statue of Lenin and go to the heart of downtown. Next door to the post office is a place where you can fax, email and make international phone calls. The calls are about $1 (29 rubles) per minute, which is much more reasonable than the hotel.

Moving up the hotel list is the **Versailles,** which is more expensive. Both the Vladivostok and Versailles are convenient to town. The most expensive, but also the least convenient, is the **Vlad Motor Inn.** It is close to American standards. It is outside the city and has only one floor. It is run by Canadians (everyone speaks English), has an attached restaurant, all of the bottled water you want, and cribs. It is a bit expensive, but some parents feel it is worth it. It is about $120 a night. They take most credit cards such as Visa and American Express. The hotel's website is *http://www.vlad-inn.ru/main.php?p=1.*

There is a fourth hotel that is also on the expensive end. It is **Hotel Hundi.** It is reportedly wonderful with a delicious, but expensive breakfast buffet. There is a bank right in the building and the Korean air office is there too in case you need to change your ticket. Rumor has it that it is mainly used by Korean businessmen looking for fun.

VORONEZH

Voronezh Oblast is often referred to as the heart of the Central Black Earth Region. It is locatedabout 300 miles to the south of Moscow along the banks of the Don, Usmanka, and Voronezh rivers.

Some parents have stayed at the **Hotel Don,** which is in downtown Voronezh. It has modern amenities (except for window screens or AC), and but furniture is from the 1960's.

The city has a baby home on Leningrad Street. There is another home 30 minutes outside of town called the Somovo orphanage. The city home is on a dirt road, pass some sheds. You go through a locked green gate to the orphanage. It is a large, very nice, well-kept building with flower gardens and playgrounds. The infants are on the third floor. The caregivers in the infant area care about the children but things move very quickly so there is not much bonding or attachment. The caregivers for the older children (4 and up) are there to take care of basic needs.There is little interaction between caregivers and children. Speech is greatly delayed as is social development.

The wait for a court date can be two months.

YAROSLAVL

Yaroslavl is about 150 miles north of Moscow.Most parents drive to it from Moscow. It's a beautiful region. Yaroslav the Wise founded Yaroslavl at the beginning of the 11th century at the confluence of the Volga and Kotorosl rivers. The city is approaching its 1000th anniversary as one of the great traditional centers of trade, culture and statecraft in the Russian heartland. Yaroslavl was a stronghold of resistance against the Mongol invasion; a temporary national capital during the 17th century Time of Troubles; the site of an outstanding ensemble of early Russian church and secular architecture; and the birthplace of Russian theater. Yaroslavl State University has long had an excellent reputation.

The children seem to have few developmental delays coming from this region. The officials are "adoption friendly." Some families are still able to make only one adoption trip in this region, although the in-country travel is about 3 weeks. The number of trips is not dependent on whether you use an accredited or unaccredited agency, but rather when the court date can be scheduled. As in Rostov, you meet with the judge during the first trip so he can go over your dossier and ask any pertinent questions. You just sit in his office with your coordinator. Independent adoptions are allowed.

There is a baby home of about 100 children from 0 to 4 years of age. They place a lot of children from this home. The older children's home is a pretty good home with well-nourished children, a ball pit, puppet shows, music room, birds as pets and gymnastics. It is a very well run place.

There is a McDonalds in town and a nice restaurant called Stary Zamok. Some parents have stayed in a guest house called Exeter or a hotel call Medvezhy Ugol.

CHAPTER XI

THE CHILDREN'S HOME

The Two Trip Process

Most regions in Russia, but not all, now require what is called a two-trip process. It is also known as the adopt-when-you-get-there process. The first visit to the children's home is similar to that described for Ukraine. Of course, there are a few regions that still allow pre-identified referrals while you are in the States and only require one trip. The number of these regions has declined and is likely to get even fewer now that the federal Ministry has officially come out and said that information on a child can only be released to adoptive parents at the time they visit the regional Department of Education. Still, because not all 89 regions follow everything Moscow says, there will still be a few regions that allow pre-travel information on referrals.

Actually, there isn't any requirement that you must make two trips. Just that the time between the first trip and the court date on the second is so long that most everyone comes home to wait out the time. Under the two-trip procedure, the first trip is used to identify a child and the second trip is used to complete the adoption at court. For example, on the first trip you visit the regional Department of Education (DoE) with your translator. Only one parent has to travel for this part of the process, if carrying a Power of Attorney from the other spouse. You do not need to have received your I-171H. The regional adoption official reviews your documents. If they are in order, she will go to the computer database or in some regions an actual photo album and give you a referral based on your parameters of age, sex, and acceptable health conditions. In some regions they will only give you one referral at a time and in others they will give you several. There is not a great deal of medical information. The official only knows if the child has something serious (cleft palate, missing a limb, etc). Otherwise they are all categorized as "healthy."

Now some officials may actually have quite a lot of information on the child's family history. It is not often the case, but it is worth asking. You can also ask the Department of Education Inspector.

Then the DoE person will give you an authorization to visit the children's home. It is basically a permission slip with your name and the child's name on it. Once the children's home director receives this document they are not suppose to show anyone the child, but you. Once you are given the permission slip you travel to the children's home to meet the child or children you have preliminarily chosen. After your children's home visit you may have the opportunity to fax or email medical information and your observations to your medical specialist in Moscow or the US before making a final decision. Since this is not as easy as it sounds, try to set this up with your agency beforehand. It is not difficult, if set up ahead of time. Make sure you write down or tape record everything that is said to you and you should ask a lot of questions. If the child had their birth parents' rights terminated, you should investigate the reasons as thoroughly as you can. Ask for court documents.

If you turn down the referral, you will be allowed to return to the Regional Department and go through their database or photo album again. This is how it is generally being done. The federal Ministry of Education in Moscow is applying pressure for all regions to adopt this procedure and to eliminate the former common pre-identification referral method. After accepting the referral, you will send an acceptance to the DoE by notarized letter and ask for the federal release letter. You will send another notarized letter to the court asking for a court date. This is all done while you are there and is not difficult. Your translator/facilitator will handle these matters. Meanwhile you return home to the US to await notification of the court date. The interval between trips is sometimes as short as 30 days or as long as several months. One part of the process driving the timing is the requirement that the petition to adopt be mailed (not couriered) to Moscow by the local jurisdiction to verify that the child's name is on the central registry of orphans, and then a registry release letter must be mailed back by Moscow and received by the Regional DoE. This can take 1 to 3 months to accomplish.

Sometimes an agency may have an idea before you travel as to how many children are available that match your criteria. If the DoE only has one or two, you might consider waiting a while to travel. If they have only one child available that matches your criteria and that child isn't the child for you, then you will have to return home without a referral. The more children they have available, the more likely you will find the child you are destined to adopt. Plan to be a bit flexible. Some parents go over searching for a daughter and come home with a son! If you are not that flexible, then make certain that your agency and DoE knows this as well.

If you decline all the referrals, then you return to the US and prepare to travel again to Russia, but to perhaps another region and do the whole process over. Some families have used the time before a court date to have a medical specialist in the States review the child's photo, video and medical records that they collected while on the first trip as a last check. Remember that the adoption is not final until there has been a court hearing. Some regions have gotten restrictive about taking photographs and giving you a lot of information. If you are in one of these regions, stand up for your rights. Under Russian law, they must give you adequate medical information.

It is always possible to accept a child, and then have the medical and video information you collected reviewed by medical specialists once you are back in the States and waiting to travel for the second trip. Since you have not yet gone through a court adoption hearing, you can change your mind and turn down the referral. It might not be easy for you or your agency, but this is your life and your family.

There are benefits if you have to make two trips, although saving money is not one of them. The benefits are that you get to see your kid(s), meet everyone, see the town, see the orphanage, take pictures, find out exactly what to bring for the orphanage, figure out appropriate gifts for your homestay, learn a little more Russian, figure out all your connections without having a baby in tow, and make friends. You are more relaxed the second time as you are now used to the travel and can focus on the child. You know what kind of clothes to wear, what to expect from the people, the weather, and from your child. You also do not need to carry any of the BCIS documents, as you will not be visiting the US Embassy on the first trip. Those documents will be needed for the second trip. In most regions, only one spouse needs to make the first trip. It is certainly better if both can do so, but it is not required in most regions. If one spouse needs to travel away from work as little as possible, consider having that spouse return to the States immediately after Court on the second trip.

The biggest change in Russia may be this process of choosing a child while you are in Russia, without any advance information. This is somewhat of a step backward as for years the agencies have been pressured to do a better job of providing more complete medical information. Yet, this other process seems to

have worked in Ukraine. It does place the burden of the medical review completely on your shoulders. It means that you must take with you the Russian
medical definitions as described by Drs. Jenista, Aronson, or Downing and a
range of appropriate height, weight, and head circumference chart points. In
addition, you should take with you a few educational toys and a milestone
cheat list. Just remember it will be normal for a child to be 3 or even 6 months
delayed developmentally, but the toys and milestone list will allow you to fax
these observations to your specialist for a better review. Be prepared. Have
your list of medical questions ready along with phone and fax numbers of your
stateside doctors. Prepare to send digital pictures or video. Try to have your
child's medical information translated by someone else other than your
agency, before you accept. Know what you can handle and what you cannot.
Do not be afraid to say no.

Try to conduct your observation privately if you can or with just your translator present. Some homes crowd you with the director, caretaker and other
personnel and try to hurry you. This can make the review difficult. One issue
you should address before you fly to Russia is how much time you will have to
assess a child. The problem is that some Directors of homes are very schedule
oriented and may not want you to stay any longer than necessary. You will have
to be your own advocate and try to make sure you have an adequate amount of
time. Try to see the child when nap time or lunchtime is not an issue. Make
sure your facilitator is not in such a hurry because of his schedule that he
rushes you. You may even need to reschedule your trip to a time when your
facilitator can devote his attention to your creation of a family. If the problem
is with the Director, then plan on bringing personal gifts to her, then ask if you
can return the next day. Bringing flowers and candy is not a bad idea. If the
orphanage schedule is the problem, then offer to assess the child at your hotel.
Schmoozing the system works in the US and in Russia!

Take along a few disposable cameras and leave them with the orphanage
staff. Ask them to take pictures of your child while you return home. Then,
when you return to Russia, you can pick up the cameras, bring them home and
get them developed. You'll have pictures of your children you would not otherwise have. You'll probably have some neat photos of his/her playmates and the
orphanage staff, too. Absolutely leave some items for your child. The wait for a
court date will seem like forever.

Some parents leave a photo album with pictures of family, friends, their
house (inside and out), her new room, grandparents, pets, her new school,
playground, and neighborhood. You can include photos of an airplane and a
map of the US in relation to Russia and pictures of her new home state. Kinko's
can laminate it all and make it into a book. You can also add a few photo

pocket pages in the back in which you can add Poloroid photos you took at the orphanage with her.You can someone back home write in Russian a description of each picture.

Some leave a little soft stuffed animal or play thing. If the Director doesn't want to create jealousy in your child's group, then offer to bring several of the same item. Leave some note cards for the caretakers so they can help fill in your child's early days or tell you funny things he has done. Always ask if there is a sibling or half sibling in the same orphanage or elsewhere. Some agencies and facilitators are reluctant to help you find a sibling. If you do, see if the children are attached to each other. You will know what to do next.

Another problem area with the two-trip process is the competition that can develop between families. This can occur if your agency has scheduled several families to go to Russia and they are looking for the same sort of child. A classic example is the search for a "young as possible, healthy as possible" infant girl. You need to tell your agency that you do not want to travel with a couple going to the same region with the same requirements. It is unfair to you even though it may be convenient for the agency.

Russia and its regions are always changing their foreign adoption procedures. Some regions still allow referrals with advanced medical and video information and others do not. The number of the former is getting smaller. Some regions will wait to give an agency a referral only when a family's dossier has been accepted and approved and not before.

This significantly lengthens the time frame between when a family submits their dossier and the referral. The two-trip process is becoming more and more the norm in Russia.

Independent adopters "theoretically" have a small advantage over families adopting through agencies. Usually "Indys" actually visit the judge on their first trip and (again theoretically) are given the court date immediately, i.e. they know when they will come next time. In contrast,families adopting through agencies fully depend on their facilitator. He can be slow or lazy or stupid OR quick and hardworking and smart. You never know. From this perspective, independent adoptions give a little more "peace of mind" since you know when your court date will be. One of the many reason for a delay in the court date might be that the judge is going on vacation soon and doesn't want to book court dates until after he returns. So not only do you have to wait for the judge to return before you can go to court, but you also do not know where you are in his court date book until then either.

There is one last, but important tip about the Two-Trip process. When you are returning to the States from the first trip, you will likely be on a plane with a dozen adopted children. Please offer to help the parents! You will forever be their fairy godmother and it also gives you a taste of what it will be like for you.

You Arrive at the Children's Home

As you enter the children's home, you will become very quiet and nervous. You will meet the home director and the home doctor. You will be taken to a waiting room, music room or perhaps a playroom. You will wait for a few minutes. It will be a moment that you will never forget. Then a caregiver will bring in your child. The caretaker will hand him to you. The years of waiting are over.

One of the neat things that will occur is that the husband will become the center of the child's attention. A lot of children, particularly infants, have never seen a man or heard a man's voice before. Women caretakers and doctors have surrounded them. This new creature with the whiskers will be brand new to them.

Start the cameras!

Do not be surprised if your child appears scared and is quiet. This is normal. After all, she has never met you before and there are all these people surrounding her. This may last for a few days while your child gets use to you and then suddenly he will blossom! They really do change once you get them home. Don't put expectations on yourself about how you or your child should react at that "first meeting." Let nature take its course. If you do have that instant bonding moment then you can say to the child (feminine form for a girl) 'Kraseevitsa'. It means beautiful little one. You can also say 'oom-nitsa' which means smart little one (feminine form). If you think the child is the one for you, then it will help you to build a bridge to the caregivers if you gush a little. It makes them feel good to know that a baby they took care of will be joining a loving family. It means they were successful.

At some point, you will be told that you can now discuss your child with the children's home doctor. It is a requirement of Russian law that they tell you about your child's medical condition. This is when you pull out your written questions and start to check them off. How much they are required to tell you is subject to interpretation. For example, a premature infant will likely have a medical record of at least 50 pages. The pages are handwritten. They may be located at the hospital and not at the home. There may be no copy machine available. You will likely be told that you cannot have a copy of it even though you will pay for the copy and translation. You can always ask though. Then you might ask yourself if this is necessary as the child might be months or years beyond his birth, thus the information might not be relevant and further once the child is tested and reviewed in the States, what is the point of the old record. Just know that there likely is more information, whether it is important to know and how hard you want to push for it is your decision and whether the Russians will give it to you is theirs.

Now if your child's parents had their rights terminated, then you need to push very hard to find out as much as you could. If abuse was the cause of the termination, that could have a lasting impact on your child and on your family.

Some parents have refused to meet with the child until his medical records have been translated and read to them. The orphanage doctor will have at least 8 to 10 pages of handwritten notes on each child. If you turn down a referral, ask if there are other children you might be able to see in the orphanage or in any nearby orphanages. Sometimes the Department of Education social worker is willing to work with you and make calls on your behalf. With her help you can return to the DoE and complete paperwork for the second referral.

While it is necessary to be as specific as possible about what you will and will not compromise on, you should also expect that there will be trade-offs and that you might accept a child older than you specified, but with better health and academic records.

Parents have also asked if they could make more than one visit to a potential referral. Children can be really surprised by your visit. They may have been woken from their nap or just be scared or off guard when you first see them. On another visit they may be more talkative and comfortable.

Parents have also asked that no one talk about adoption in front of the child. You might make try to make your comments and questions very general in nature and give the potential referral a gift when you leave—toys can ease lots of nervousness.

If you are going to a children's home and know of another couple who is adopting from there, you might arrange to take pictures or even video that couple's child. If the other couple is waiting for a court date they might like to see their child and read or hear a description from you. I have known people to play with and give toys to another couple's child.

Sometimes the regional Department of Education's Children's Inspector will accompany you to the children's home. She is usually a very nice woman who is there to observe how you react to the child. She will also be present at the court hearing and tell the judge how the meeting went. She is almost always on your side.

Some meetings are emotional and some are not. There is no right or wrong. Bonding doesn't have to happen in a nanosecond. Fireworks and bells don't have to go off. Nowhere is it written that the earth must move under your feet. Everyone is different. Just know that there are plenty of parents who have reacted just like you, whatever your reaction may be. You may feel a great amount of pressure to conform to the expected reaction. Be true to yourself. Parents have bonded instantly, in a week or at the end of a month or so after returning home from the court trip. It is common for that certain feeling to grow as the days and weeks go by and suddenly you look back and like a flower in full bloom, you can't imagine ever living without this child. You have to give both you and your child time. Remember that the family being created doesn't just start with you adopting this child, but also with this child adopting you.

With the advent of the two-trip process, the burden has grown on the parents to become instant child development experts. The Denver Developmental Screening Test is one place to start. You should be able to get a copy from your pediatrician. It covers all the developmental activities that children should be able to do at various ages 0-6 years old. You can order it from Denver Developmental Materials, Inc., PO Box 371075, Denver, CO 80237-5075; 303-355-4729; 800-419-4729.

Here are some things to check if you are able to have the infant unclothed. Look for deformities and birthmarks. Look for malformed genitals. Boys will not be circumcised, so be aware of that. Put the baby on its tummy and look at the back of the legs for creases where the knees bend and at the buttocks. The creases should be the same on both legs. If they are not, the baby might have a hip problem, which tends to make him favor one side. While the baby is on its tummy, run your thumbs up the spine checking for unusual curvature. Turn the baby over and see if he has painless full range of motion with arms and legs. Check the hands to see if she clenches and unclenches her fist. You want both. Give the child a rattle to hold and see how he grabs it. While he has one toy, give him another and watch how he figures out this dilemma. Does he reach equally with both hands? Can he pass the toy from one hand to the other? Can he find the toy if he drops it? It is normal for the toys to go into the mouth, and it would be abnormal if toys did not go into the mouth sometime.

If you have a flashlight, shine it into one eye and watch the pupil constrict; then do the other eye. The speed at which the pupil constricts and dilates should be the same for each eye. The baby should show some realization at having had a light shined in its eyes. Hold the light about 18 inches away from the baby and slowly move it across from left to right and back. The baby's eyes should track the light together without crossing or drifting relative to each other. While you're doing all this, listen for vocalizations and watch for smiling.

Both are good. Have your spouse stand on one side of the baby and clap hands one time. The baby should turn eyes and face toward the direction of the clapping. If not, try again and try doing it on the other side. If the child cannot find the source of the sound, he might have a hearing problem. Look closely at the face and head. The head should be perfectly symmetrical left to right. The hair, if there is any, will normally lack luster and body. After changing to an American diet the hair will completely change texture, body, and appearance. The eyes should be on the same level and same depth. The distance between the eyes across the nose should be about the same as the opening of the eye itself. If this distance is unusually wide between the eyes, it could indicate fetal alcohol syndrome. The white part of the eyes should be white, not red, pink, gray, or yellowish. The iris, the colored part of the eye, should be flecked with multiple colors if you look very closely, but there should not be a brown or yellow ring around the outside of iris.

Ears should be same height on the head and look the same left to right. Lobes might be attached or detached, but both should be the same. Make sure both ear canals are properly located inside the ear and they are unobstructed. You won't have the tools to examine the eardrums, so don't worry about that. The nose should look normal with two separate and distinct nostrils. Look for the ridge on the upper lip between the center part of the nose and top lip. Lack of a ridge is another indication of FAS. See if the baby will crawl or even stand up. Some stand even before coordinating the crawling motion. Can he do the push-up needed to get into crawling position? Do both legs cooperate equally? Does he turn his neck painlessly Can he sit up? Can he go from crawling position to sitting and back again? Pick the baby up and hold her in your arms. She should show curiosity about your face, jewelry, glasses or watch.

Questions for the Doctors

After meeting with your child, you will then be allowed to meet with the children's home doctors and ask questions. Prepare your questions ahead of time, as you will be so distracted by your child and the whole emotional experience that you will forget what to ask. Generally you want to find out as much about the child's living patterns as possible. This will make it easier to transition her to your home. You can find a question list translated in Russian at *http://groups.yahoo.com/group/Ind_Russian_Adopt/files/*.

Being in a foreign place is intimidating. You have the added stress of having just met your child, and you probably feel like you should not cause waves. You don't want to be the ugly American. However, in a way, by asking these questions at this time you are fighting for your child's personal history. It is your first advocate fight for your child. No one has as much interest in these questions and answers as you and your child. A lack of assertiveness will cost you the only chance you will ever have to have these many questions answered. Depending on how you feel about your facilitator/translator you may need to have a frank discussion with him beforehand. Some facilitators/translators have a tendency to think they know what is best for you and <u>will give you only the information they believe is necessary</u>. While it may turn out that you did not need the other information, there is a trust issue involved. You need to emphasize to the facilitator/translator prior to visiting the home that you want complete translations and complete histories. Tell him that you do not want, under any circumstances, for him to make any decision as to what information you should be given or not given. He is allowed no editing decisions. He may take no shortcuts. Now the truth is that your gut instinct will tell you a lot when you first see a child, however, you should still ask questions and obtain as much information as you can.

In truth, the orphanage doctor may not be able to help when it comes to a lot of these medical questions. These doctors are not well trained, are very poorly paid, and do not have much time to dwell on one child when they have 60 or 100 under their care. Orphanages barely have money for food so it is unrealistic to expect them to diagnose and treat children for RAD. The doctors and directors also have a bias when it comes to "Westerners." They believe that "Western" doctors can heal anything. They will ask the facilitator "…[w]hat do they want? They'll take him back to the US and take care of anything that might be wrong with the child." They don't connect with your fears, or understand that a child can have serious issues that are not subject to a "quick fix."

Still you must try and you will be surprised as to how much they do know.

Ask about your child's nap schedule and sleeping habits. How long and when does he sleep? What is his typical schedule for a 24-hour period? What type of bed does he sleep in? By himself?

What kind of foods does she like? What do you feed her? How much? When? Does she drink milk? How is the food prepared? Does she have a favorite food? Does she have a food she dislikes or reacts badly to? What is the feeding schedule?

Also, pay attention to the orphanage comments about eating, sleeping and moods. Generally, FAS kids don't sleep or eat well and are easily irritable. Of course, some kids are just like that so you have to look at the total picture before suspecting FAS.

When and how does she go to the bathroom" Does she have a crib mate? Does she have a favorite friend? What does she spend most of her time doing? What is she good at? What is hard for her? Has she had any prior illnesses, accidents or injuries? How does she act when sick?

How does she bathe? alone? With other children? tub? shower? Is the water hot, cold, warm? How long is the bath?

What makes her happy? What toys, games or songs does she like? What does she like to do most when playing outside? What makes her angry? upset? How does she react when she has done something wrong? Or when she is tired?

What is her story? Are there any baby pictures of her that I can have or get? Where and how was she brought to the children's home? Who named her? Does she have a pet name or nickname? What do you know about her biological parents? You might try to get the Director off to the side to answer these and other questions about your child's family history. She might know, but it might not be written down anywhere.

You may also want to ask if the child has (or previously had) any siblings or half-siblings anywhere in the orphanage system. Have they been adopted? By Americans? It can be difficult and expensive to attempt to acquire this information later, and your agency probably will not be interested in helping you, as it creates work and expense for them without generating revenue. Oftentimes the child's siblings have already been adopted, or are "unadoptable" for any number of reasons. But sometimes the siblings are simply in different orphanages due to differences in their ages or perceived "mental ability" or due to orphanage overcrowding. If you are unable to adopt the child's siblings yourself, try to take videos of the sibling and gather medical info, etc. so that you can attempt to locate an adoptive home for the siblings.

Are there any mementos of her life that I can keep? a favorite toy? shirt? You will be surprised at how much a young child will later want something of her past just to hold. Conversely, an older child may wish to forget.

Ask all about the time your child has spent in the children's home, how they arrived, with whom, and what they did on different milestone dates. You might try to fill in the gaps in their baby history, as these items become important to kids, as they grow older.

Take pictures of the caretakers and have them write their name, and if possible a small greeting to your child to be remembered by, or something they remember special about your child. One nice touch is to take some pretty writing paper and have the caregivers write a letter to your child. You can then give it to him when he is old enough. Give any left over paper to the caregivers as a gift.

If there is a caretaker your child is close to, ask to talk to her. She will probably be the greatest source of information about your child's daily life. Do you have any interesting/funny stories about my child? The social worker that you may not see until the court date is also an excellent source of information.

Ask to have the complete medical record on your child explained, even if you already have heard much of this when you accepted a referral. You may obtain more information regarding the child's medical conditions, which you can then pass on to your pediatrician when you return home. Ask about the medical history of the parents and any siblings. Ask why did they apply that diagnosis and what was the evidence. Look for how the child is similar/is different from others in the age group. Ask about the routine the child is used to. Take measurements yourself. Ask the primary caregiver for her impressions of the child and the personality. If child is fussy, look for reasons why—hungry, tired, shoes too tight (shoes rarely fit), etc. These things will help you evaluate the child.

Ask to see the child's play area and sleeping quarters and take pictures. This may not be allowed as they are protective of the other children, but some baby homes will give you a complete tour!

Ask what the orphanage needs such as supplies, medicine, and toys. You can always buy items in the town and give them to the baby home on your next visit.

You might gather some background information which may be of interest to your child later such as age of the facility, number of children there (average and right now), number of care givers, number of kids in their group, or in their room.

Ask where the birth parents were from if from another city. Does your child have a favorite caregiver, playmate, or toy? What treatments or tests would the orphanage doctor recommend for the child after you return home? Has the child been baptized and if so, are there any mementos?

Some homes maintain photo histories on children and will allow you to purchase or give you photos of your child when they were younger. This can be important to your child when she is older.

If you adopt an older child, make sure you ask the children's home what information have they told the child about you. In some cases, the child may be told that you are their biological parents and are returning to get them. This may be a symptom of the Russian idea that adoption should be kept secret. You will want to have the truth told as soon as possible, preferably before you arrive. You should ask if the child remembers her birthparents. Also, with older children you might want to know more about their mental state. Some of these questions can tip you off to attachment issues.

Therefore, you might ask:

Has the child ever bonded with a caregiver in the children's home?
How does your child treat the other children in her age group? This could be I important if you have other children at home.
Does she receive and give affection easily? Does she have good eye contact?
What is her temperament, and personality like? Is she easily disciplined?
How is her attention span?
Is she equal in language and physical development with the other children in her home age group? Just remember they will likely all be delayed somewhat.

Some developmental red flags might be poor eye contact, being socially withdrawn, engaging in self-stimulating behavior, self-injurious behavior, aggression, and hyperactivity.

Here are some other possible questions. You may not want all of this information nor may the Russians give it to you.

Birth Mother Information

Date of birth? City where she currently lives or used to live, of her birth? (Each Russian has an internal passport with a picture and vital information. Make sure you get the birthmother and birthfather's passport number.) Appearance and personality? General health? Education, specific schools? Career/work specifics? Any other information that would help to fill in your child's story…personal knowledge of birth mother's personal struggles, description of reasons for her decision, situation in life, education, health, family health history? Why the specific timing of entry into registry and relinquishment papers signed (or parental rights terminated)?

Relationship with birth father, circumstances of pregnancy and birth? Health during pregnancy? Full term? Pregnancy or delivery complications? Information regarding birth mother's parents, siblings, etc.? Any children living with birthmother? Ask for a copy of any order from court (which might provide details about siblings). Is the father of the siblings the same as your child? Talents, interests of birthmother

Try to get the heights of birthparents if possible. It's good to know, because you can calculate your child's future height.

Birth Father Information

First name? Last name? General appearance and personality? General health? Date of birth? City in which he currently lives, used to live? Education, specific schools? Career/work specifics? Any other information that would help to fill in your child's story…personal knowledge of birth

Father's personal struggles, description of reasons for his decision, situation in life, military background, education, health, family health history? Relationship with birth mother? Information regarding birth father's parents, siblings, etc.? Talents, interests.

Actual Birth History

Health information or general information regarding circumstances of pregnancy and birth? Health during pregnancy? Prenatal care information, or prenatal records? Original birth certificate or other medical records? Immunizations? Any drugs given to birthmother at birth or to child afterwards? Any allergies or reactions? Hospital records?

Orphanage Care-Givers, Director, and Doctor

Describe my child. Her favorite likes and dislikes…toys, food, games, sleeping and eating patterns, special relationship with any care-giver(s), personality, how she relates to other children and adults…any favorite stories or friends? Developmental milestones: roll over, crawl, smile, sit up, first tooth, solid food. Special events, celebrations, or memories? Any other visitors who inquired or visited my child? Original relinquishment papers or other documents?

Health Care at Orphanage

Health when arrived at orphanage and while at orphanage? Discuss specific diagnosis from referral medical and treatment—what, when, severity, when recovered? Names of doctors or nurses while in orphanage? Approximate ages in year of adoption? Health information or medical records while in orphanage? Original birth certificate or other records? Immunizations? Any drugs used? Any allergies or reactions? Growth records, weight records? Milestone records or memories? Ever in isolation or in hospital? Did she go directly from hospital to orphanage? When? Any medical records I can take with me? Other people special to my child

Baptized?

A Russian child who was baptized would have been "sprinkled" to be baptized into the Russian Orthodox Church. The child might have a cross to indicate this. If so, when, priest's name and his church affiliation (Russian Orthodox, Muslim for some families), location of church?), is there a certificate of baptism, cross or other memento of the baptism? Meet and thank priest; photo of him. Possible to see baptismal records? Possible to photograph them? Please describe their baptisms. Full immersion? Who performed them? Remember when? Get the church address(es) and priest's name(s).

You may receive puzzled looks from the caregivers when asking some of these questions. After all, the children eat what they are given and they eat everything/anything (i.e., they have no favorite foods because they have no choices and because they need to eat everything they are given just to survive). They sleep when they are told to sleep. One translator has even said:

"Tell your friends that they don't understand orphanage life. This is a job to these women, nothing else. All the children are the same to them. They might say to adoptive parents that one child or another is their favorite, but I see them on the times when there are no parents around, and it is not true. They don't care what your child likes to eat. The children eat whatever they are given. The bath is not a fun time. It is to get clean. You will know your son better than they do after a week of being with her."

Yet that is not a universal description. Another children's home is described as having caretakers in their 40s to 60s with most of them having already raised their own children and having grandchildren. Some are widowed or had invalid husbands. The pay is miniscule—a few dollars a month. For some of them, this is the only income their family has and they struggle to survive. Despite all this, they seem to genuinely like their work and cared what happened to the children in the orphanage. They speak of wanting to find more families to adopt those kids. They also want to help the oldest kids get the life skills they would need when they move out of the orphanage over the next couple of years.

Now it is true that whatever your child did/liked at the orphanage is likely irrelevant once he leaves because once his world expands and he has choices, he becomes a completely different person with different tastes. They might go from being quiet to being "a wild man." Your child will also change once he can express himself with English words (the frustration tantrums should subside).

Ask caregivers to write a letter to your child, about what she was like as a baby/young child and a message from you? See birth mother/parent's neighborhood and home; take photos. See some of the city where your child was born. Immediately write a description in your journal.

You may want to take a tape measure and measure the child's head circumference yourself. Try to use a paper tape not an elastic one. Make sure you ask your US doctor how he does it as the Russians tend to do it differently (not worse, just differently). You might start with the tape in a position in the middle of the forehead and rather level with the floor (same horizontal plane), then adjust the tape up or down NOT keeping it level with the floor to find the largest circumference. The most common Russian way to measure head circumference is to keep the tape always level with the floor, which can give a measure smaller than the method used by US doctors. See *http://128.248.232.56/mchbgrowthcharts/module5/text/page5a.htm* for guidance as to how to measure. As far as height goes, infants and young toddlers are usually measured lying down. They typically start to take a standing measure at two years old.

If you can, observe how your child interacts with the children in the children's home. Does she play quietly by herself or join in noisily with the others? Is she a chatter box with her friends? Outgoing or withdrawn?

Now you may observe that your child has green spots on her face and other places. This is a green ointment type medicine called Zelenka. It is used as a substitute for iodine in kids because it does not sting as much as iodine and stays on longer. It is used to prevent infection like antibiotic ointment or Betadine. It's an aniline-based dye, which happens to be a good antibiotic and disinfectant. The solution is alcohol-based. It is usually safe to use Zelenka externally, but it is very difficult to wash off clothes. If you see these green spots on your child, ask the doctor what symptoms the child had which required Zelenka, as you may need to continue with a substitute as you travel back to the States.

A list of other questions can be found at:
http://eeadopt.org/home/preparing/medical/referral/post/caregiver_questions.htm.

A few parents have been fortunate to have been able to hire an independent physician to examine the children's medical records and the children BEFORE they interacted with them. This is probably the best method of proceeding under the two trip process, however, it is not all that common since you first have to find a doctor who will do it and then obtain permission from the director to allow the physician to review the records. Directors can be very defensive about another doctor coming in to see her children. Yet some Directors also have no problem with a visit. A Doctor's visit is also no guarantee. If the child is very young, certain medical conditions are very hard to diagnose.

If you are planning to send information back to an IA doctor in the States before making your decision, find out from your agency or the facilitator where the best place is to fax or email that information. There are Internet cafes all over Russia and the local post office will normally have a fast Internet connection. Also, FedEx from Moscow to the US takes one day and mail will arrive by 10:30 the next morning. The price is usually half of what you pay from the States to Russia. It costs about $45 for a package of documents.

Court Hearing

You should always ask your facilitator about the court hearing and make him walk you through the actual process. Since he should have been to several adoption hearings in that region and before that very Judge, he should be able to describe the experience precisely. Some areas like Moscow and Stavropol want you to visit your child at least three times on the second trip. Make sure you ask your facilitator if there are a required number of visits, as the Judge will likely ask. Technically, your agency's facilitator is not supposed to be in the courtroom nor can he/she speak for you. Nevertheless, many times the Judge will allow the facilitator to observe.

Below is a list of possible questions that might be asked in Court. Some Courts only want the wife to answer and some divide the questions between spouses. Not all Courts ask all of these questions. Just go with the flow. While you are responding do not be surprised if the Judge is checking your answers against your home study. The appellate courts are very methodical and meticulous. In the past few years, the Courts have targeted for scrutiny whether the birth families have agreed in writing to a foreign adoption. Therefore, prior to any questions there may be a discussion among the Judge and Court personnel regarding who in the birth family has given such written approval and if it is enough to satisfy the Judge.

In answering the Judge's questions, long and complicated answers are not necessary. This is not a test. The hearing can take from 10 minutes to 2 hours. Usually the Judge is there to make sure the technical requirements of the law have been carried out. He or she really just checks that the proper papers are signed and in the file. Probably 99% of all adoptions are approved. But make no mistake; the Judge is the final arbiter of the adoption.

Usually present in the courtroom is the interpreter, baby house director, a representative from the regional Department of Education (usually the Inspector), prosecutor, your facilitator, court stenographer (no tape recorder or monkey mask) and of course the Judge. If your child is over 10 years old, she will attend as well. Your child's attendance may be painful to the extent she must hear a recitation of the reasons for the termination of her birthparents rights.

It will not be unusual for the husband to be the only man in the room although Regional Judges appear to be more evenly split between the genders. All will act deferential to the Judge and stand as the Judge enters the room. You should be respectful as well. It is a formal affair, although afterwards every one will be all smiles. The courtroom is likely not to be too large, but the Judge will be seated on a raised dais in front of a huge judicial bench, containing three large chairs. But only one judge will hear your case. Lying in front of the Judge will be your dossier. Prior to any questions, the baby home director and the Department of Education representative are likely to give a short statement supporting your adoption. If there are other people with you like a family member or agency representative then the Judge must give permission before they can attend the hearing. Otherwise they must stay outside the courtroom.

You should dress in business attire and look the same as if you were making a court appearance in the States. This is not a time for jeans and T-shirt. Always look and respond to the Judge, not your translator. The Judge and the court personnel take this proceeding seriously, and so should you. Do bring extra pictures of your home, city, neighborhood, and extended family. The Judge and other court personnel usually take a great deal of interest in these pictures and may want to make them a part of the court record.

Because the Russians view the woman as the primary caregiver, most of the Court's attention will be on the wife, but this is not always the case. Also, sometimes the Judge will ask a whole series of these questions in a row, which can make responding a little difficult since you don't know where to begin. Speak in a normal tone and remember that the translator is trying hard to keep up with you, so do not speak rapidly.

Here are some likely questions although certainly not all of them will be asked:

Do you recognize the authority of this court?
Your names, when and where born, occupation, address?
Place of employment
Your educational background
Describe your house, rooms, outside etc

Describe your neighborhood
Have you seen the baby/child?
Do you still want to adopt him after seeing him?
Why this age of child?
Why this child?
Are you aware of his medical record?
Are you prepared to do whatever is required for his medical needs?
What will you do if the child has unexpected medical needs?
Will you return him to Russia, if you decide you do not want him?
Do you have medical insurance?
Why are you adopting?

Why are you adopting from Russia? NEVER say you are adopting from Russia because it's easier. Instead, you might mention your Russian ancestors, love of the Russian people, Dr. Zhivago, or your best friend as a child was named Anastasia. You can say that you have friends who had adopted from there and you hope to have a similarly wonderful experience.

Why don't you adopt in the United States?
Why don't you have a biological child instead of adopting?
How will you raise him?
What are your hopes for this child?
Will adopting this child put a strain on your finances?
Who will take care of him, if you become sick?
How will you communicate until the child learns English? (older children.)
How many times have you met with your child?
How will you teach the child about his heritage?
What religion will you raise him in?
What do your other children think about this?
What does your family think about this?
You may be asked to describe your support system-family, friends etc
If you get her home and she is too sick, would you try to bring her back?
How many referrals did you see before her (rare question)?
How many times did you see her before court?
How do you and your spouse resolve arguments (rare question)?
What are the child care arrangements i.e. daycare; stay at home

Now an odd question that could pop up is one directed at who will take care of the child in case of your death. Usually families have discussed such things in general, but you might just be prepared to have a temporary answer. A few Judges, Irkutsk is one such region, ask whether you can have bio children.They find it hard to understand why someone would adopt, if they could have biological children. In Eastern European culture adoption is still viewed as second best and they wonder if you will treat your adopted children the same as your bio children. Some of these regions may even ask for a letter of *infertility* from your doctor.

If your child has Rom (Gypsy) ethnicity, the Judge may query you closely as to whether you understand this. Just remember that the Russians, as with most Eastern Europeans are prejudiced when it comes to Gypsies or Rom ethnicity.

Usually the prosecutor, Education Inspector and Home Director will make a short statement in support of the adoption. You may be given a chance to make a statement as well. If your facilitator says that it is usually requested, then practice it ahead of time.

You may be asked if you want the ten day waiting period waived and why. You may have even filed a petition asking for this. A good answer is that the child needs medical treatment or tests. If you use this answer, it helps if the orphanage director also tells the Judge that the child needs medical attention. You can also say that you have come a long way and that you have a small child back in the States that needs you, or older parents that depend on you, or a job which you must get back to as they have only given you a certain amount of time off.

The 10 days is the period of time within which the Judge's decision can be appealed. When the 10 days is "waived" all that is really happening is that the Judge has agreed to allow you to go forward with the process and obtain the child's new birth certificate, passport and visa while the 10 days runs contemporaneously. Technically, an appeal by the prosecutor could still occur, which is very rare.

(Asked of wife) Do you plan to continue working? How long will you take off from work? What are your childcare plans after you return to work? (The Russians are perfectly satisfied with a response that the child will be placed in daycare.)

If you are asked how your house is paid for, simply say that you have a mortgage. Going into details of a 15 or 30 year debt schedule will violate the rule against long and complicated answers.

Do you want the child's birth date changed?
Do you want the child's birthplace changed?
Do you want the child's name changed?

Statute 135 of the Russian Family Code states that an adopted child's place and date of birth may be changed by up to three months if the child is less than a year old at the time of adoption.

If the child is older, some parents keep the child's original name or a variation of it as a middle name or a first name to connect with the Russian heritage and identity. Some parents use two middle names, a Russian and an American one. Do not be surprised if the older child actually prefers a completely American name. If the child was placed in the baby home directly from birth, it may not matter and indeed the child's Russian name may have been given by the doctor or nurse and there may be no great familial significance. Most Russian children have formal names. The second name or patronymic name is the name of the birthfather. Most formal names have a child's or diminutive form, which are forms of affection. here is not one perfect answer to the question of how to name adopted older children. Here's a tip that may help though—imagine your child's name later in writing:in a recital program, in a school directory, on a business card, etc. Naming children is an adult decision, however getting the children's opinion is important when they are old enough to have feelings on the subject. But, soliciting opinions from family and close friends may just make the decision harder.

There is no right or wrong answer to this question of the name. It is whatever you wish to do. If you get back to the United States and change your mind, you can always correct it when filing for readoption. Indeed, your child can always change it later as well when he reaches adulthood by filing a name change.

Now some don'ts. Don't get into a political discussion or argument with the Judge over anything. Even in America, the Judge is always right. Also, don't spring a surprise in the courtroom. No one likes surprises. Don't announce a sudden job change, marital change, medical or gender change. It is best if you or your husband are not "active duty military" but rather listed as "government employees." Make sure this is what your home study says. Finally, there is that 1% of adoptions that are turned down. Russia has over 10,000 foreign adoptions a year and at least a couple of times a year, somewhere in all of Russia, some Judge will be a hard case and simply dislike foreign adoptions. You do have appeal rights.

Usually the Judge will not think crying is necessary, but crying after the decision allowing you to adopt this innocent child is not unusual. When the Judge comes back in the courtroom and announces his decision, it is a pretty special moment. If you feel like it, do it. It's your moment. You are creating a family.

10 Day Waiver

After your Court hearing there is a 10-day period before the Adoption Decree becomes final. During this period the prosecutor can appeal the decree. This is very, very rare. Some say that the 10 days is a period in which you can change your mind. That may have been the case pre-1995 when the process was less judicial and more an administrative one, however, once the Judge has issued the decree, even if the 10 days is not waived, that child is yours pending the prosecutor's right to appeal. Therefore, if for some reason you change your mind during that 10 days, you will more than likely have to go through another judicial proceeding to have the adoption dissolved.

Now some Judges will waive this period and allow you to proceed with getting your child's passport, birth certificate and US Visa. However, the Russians blow hot and cold about this so that sometimes it is generally waived, then sometimes an edict will be issued from Moscow and for a while it generally won't be. 2001 was one such year. Each region is different as to how they apply the waiver. Actually it is not a real waiver; just no one has come up with a better descriptive term. It really means that the appeal period proceeds contemporaneously with you going through the post-adoption paperwork and taking the child back to Moscow. However, some Judges do not waive this period. You will have an indication from your agency before you travel regarding the likelihood of a waiver based on other families' experience. Just be aware that you really will not know until the Court hearing.

Some reason parents have used in their request for a waiver are:

1) I have a young child at home

2) I have old parents at home that need me

3) This new child has this strange Russian diagnosis that needs immediate treatment

4) I have an appointment already with a pediatrician. "See here is the doctor's letter showing the appointment."

5) My job only gave me two weeks to complete this adoption.

6) My luggage got lost and I have nothing to wear during the ten days. (This actually worked once!)

If the Judge does not waive the period, also be aware that for some Regions it is 10 calendar days and others 10 business days. If the 10 days is not waived, then you have some choices. You can stay in town and visit with your child, go back to the States in which case only one spouse needs to return to get the visa from the Embassy, or go off on a tourist trip. The best choice is to stay with your child, if that is allowed. You may be allowed to keep your children during that time which will allow you to bond while you wait. This will be the decision of the orphanage director and possibly the Judge. Even if you are not allowed to take her back to your homestay or hotel, you will still be able to visit and play with her every day. This is also a nice way to slowly get to know your daughter and to get a deeper appreciation of her baby home life. You can gather pictures and names of her friends and caregivers, find out more about her likes and dislikes and habits. For an older child, this is the best option.

If you have a young child at home, then you may want to send one spouse back to the States, as the separation may be hard. The worst choice to make is to go off on a tourist junket if you are allowed to see the child during the 10 days. You will lose time to bond with the child before traveling to Moscow and taking the difficult flight home. You will also lose the opportunity to gain knowledge of your child's life before she became part of your family. This is something she will eventually ask you about. Of course, if you are not allowed to see your child, then the 10 days is yours to do with as you please.

If work or family does not permit either spouse staying, then both can return to the States and pay for an escort to bring your child to the US. You do have to make sure that the region you are in does not have a requirement that a parent must personally apply for the child's passport or register the decree or anything else. You have to make sure the Russians are ok with you leaving. Now the escort and the person who obtains your child's visa do not necessarily have to be the same person, but they can be. The escort can carry the child to America provided the escort has a US visa, if she is Russian. The escort should also have a power of attorney from you granting them the authority to escort your child and represent you and her before immigration when deplaning in the US. You can also simply have someone handle all of this paperwork and then one of you can fly back to Moscow for a quick turnaround and travel back with the child.

After the Court Hearing

After the Court hearing you will wait for the Judge's decision. Usually this is no more than a 30-minute to an hour wait at the very most. Then you have to wait while the Judge writes up the Decree. If the 10 day appeal period has been waived, you then take the Decree to OVIR and ZAGS (Zapis Aktov Grazhdanskogo Sostoyaniya), which are the Passport office and Bureau of Vital Statistics, respectively. ZAGS prepares the new birth certificate showing you as the parents. OVIR prepares your child's new Russian passport, which she will need in order to leave Russia and enter the United States. Somewhere in the process your child will have had her passport photo taken. A lot of times this is handled by the children's home and you reimburse them for the cost. The Russian passport will have your child's name rendered phonetically in French, not English. For example, "Alexander," which appears on the birth and adoption certificate might be spelled "Alexandre" on the passport.

Because ZAGS and the other departments are only open on certain days, and because you might get finished with your Court hearing late, there is always the possibility that you will be delayed in obtaining all of the these documents which will make you late in arriving in Moscow. This is why you should have a fudge factor of at least an extra day in your itinerary. In a few regions, even the payment of an expedite fee will not hurry the passport along. In these cases you might ask your facilitator if you can go on to Moscow and complete that part of the paperwork (medical exam, US visa) while waiting for the region to issue your child's Russian passport. The Komi Republic is one of these.

If your child is 14 years or older, he may be forced to obtain a propiska or Russian state passport (internal). The state passport forces Russians to register and work in their city of residence. It is used to prevent migration to the cities, i.e. Moscow. If your older child doesn't have one of these and the region makes you get one, it may delay you by a day or two. It is totally useless here in the States and would only be of value if he wanted to return to Russia to live. It is required for any travel inside Russia, even from city to city. They couldn't fly or travel by train without one.

If you adopt from a remote town like Solikamsk or Arkhangelsk, it is possible that the local ZAGS's office will have a small ceremony. It will be an incredible memory. Everyone will be dressed up, music will play on a small record player, and you might then be asked to sign your name in a large book. This wonderful ceremony has been lost, as the legal process has moved from the smaller towns to the large regional cities because of the changes in the law in 1998.

That night your facilitator/translator will be busy translating the Decree and the other Russian documents into English for the Embassy.

Usually the day after the court hearing you will pick up your child from the children's home and return to Moscow. One issue you may wish to discuss with the home director is the question of what mementos or keepsakes you can take with you. Some parents take the clothing their child wore in the referral picture, their "baby" shoes or other clothing or toys that is particular to their child. Of course, you should replace any items you take.

Other "heritage" ideas are:

1. Baby bottle or eating utensil used in home.
2. Blankets used. Replace if taken.
3. A list of the eating/ and daily routine of your child
4. A spoonful of "earth" from outside the home. Film canisters are good to use.
5. A leaf or two from a tree outside the home.
6. Any personal items used by child.
7. Have the caretakers write a goodbye note to your child.

Some parents have taken a small rock from outside the orphanage, which they then place in their curio cabinet. One parent collected some snow and had it blessed then used it to baptized her child.

Add pictures of all these items to your child's life book, they are priceless.

If you get the birthmother's/birthparents' address, you might want to drive by and take a photo of the neighborhood and the apartment for your child.

If you are leaving your translator/facilitator behind in the region as you travel back to Moscow, then you may want to ask him to help "prepare" your child for his new life. This is especially important if the child is older (3 years and up) Have someone explain to the child in RUSSIAN, as English means nothing to him at that point, what is happening to them, and what is going to happen to them. Have them show your child photos that you brought from home of your family, pointing out his sisters, brothers, dogs, cats, house, etc. It will make the transition so much easier. Explain the trip he is about to take to Moscow and the traveling on a train or airplane. Explaining to your child what is about to happen will help him successfully leave behind the children's home and all of his friends.

CHAPTER XII

BACK TO MOSCOW

Medical Exam in Moscow

Before your child can receive a visa she must have a medical clearance. The form is known as the "pink form" although it is white, not pink. This exam is usually done in Moscow at:

1) the **International Organization for Migration (IOM)**, No. 12 2nd Zvenigorodskaya; Metro: Ulitsa; 1905 Goda; phone (7-095) 797-8723 Appointment Hours: Monday-Thursday: 9AM-6PM, Friday: until 6:30PM Medical Examination for adopted orphans and other applicants: $70

2) The **Filatov Medical Clinic** (7) 095-254-9028, or 095-423-7780; e-mail: *drsevps@online.ru* (for adoption questions only). They are open on weekends. The Filatov Medical Clinic has been known to complete the exam in your hotel room when the child is sick. It is a two story building with a tree lined driveway and courtyard. It is not far from the US Embassy.

3) AO "MEDITCINA"
Metro Mayakovskaya; 2nd Tverskoy-Yamskoy Pereulok, bld. 10,
Room 420; Phone:(7-095) 250-9190, 250-9900, 250-9903;
fax:(7-095) 250-9180;
Appointment Hours: Monday-Friday: 8AM-8PM
Saturday-Sunday: 9AM-3PM
Medical Examination for adopted orphans and other applicants: $75

The American Medical Clinic (7) 095-956-3366, 933-7700 is no longer authorized to do the exam.

These clinics also have clean bathrooms, so take the opportunity. They have Russian doctors who speak English and have some Western training. The exam is not thorough, but rather a general look at the child. The evaluation is done for the purpose of preventing immigrants with infectious diseases from entering the country. They look for things like leprosy. They do not do a full medical screen. That is not the purpose. The evaluation should last about 30 minutes. If you know your child has some illness, point that out to the doctor and obtain medicine. Review with the doctor the list of medical conditions you were given when you first received the referral. It might shed some additional light, which you can then pass on to your pediatrician. The examination requirements can be found at *http://www.foia.state.gov/masterdocs/09fam/0940011N.pdf*. You can also ask the doctor for some medicine, if are feeling ill.

Sometimes children who have tested positive at least once for Hepatitis are asked to have a blood test for Hepatitis and HIV. Even if the child again tests positive (unlikely though that may be), the Embassy says it will not refuse a visa. Then you might ask, what is the point of testing in Moscow. After all, you no doubt plan on testing once you return to the States and the lab work is a whole lot more trustworthy here than there.

You should submit the expense to your insurance company when you return to the States. The medical clearance form is given to the US Embassy. Ask the doctor to make you a copy so you can keep it for the child's medical records. This is particularly important f you are adopting an older child and she had to have vaccinations like for Hepatitis B and Rubella. You will need proof once you are back in the States. Make a copy for your pediatrician as well.

The United States also requires certain vaccinations prior to the issuance of an immigrant visa for an adopted child. This is not a requirement for any child under 10 years of age as long as you promise to vaccinate them when you return to the States. Since you were planning to do this anyway, this is not a problem. The affidavit form can be found at *http://www.foia.state.gov/master-docs/09fam/0940011X2.pdf*. For older children, bringing the child's record from the home so that the panel physician can certify it may satisfy vaccination requirement. Of course, even for these children, you would want to reimmunize once you are back in the States (or at least do titers).

The following are the location of other medical clinics in Moscow. These are not authorized to conduct the required Visa medical review.

American Medical Center Moscow
Address: 1 Grokholsky Pereulok, 129010 Moscow
Phone:(7-095) 933-7700
Emergency Phone: (7-095) 933-7700
Fax: (7-095) 933-7700
Open: 24 hours a day, 365 days a year
Regular Office Hours:
Monday through Friday, 8:00 a.m. to 8:00 p.m.,
Saturday & Sunday 9:00 a.m. to 5:00 p.m.
Contact: Dr. Robert Young
E-mail: *moscow@amcenters.com*
http://www.amcenters.com/moscow_clinic.html

European Medical Center
Medical Center address: 10 2nd Tverskoi-Yamskoi Pereulok, 125047 Moscow,
Phone: 787-7000
Dentistry Center address: 34 Konushkovskaya Ul., 123242, Moscow,
Phone: 797-6767
http://www.emcmos.ru/services-e.cfm?CenterID=0

International SOS Clinic
Address: 10th Floor, Polyclinic No. 1, 31 Grokholsky Pereulok, 129010 Moscow
Phone: (7-095) 937-5760
Emergency Phone: (7-095) 937-6477
Contact: Maxine Ash, 937-5760
E-mail: *mow.marketing@internationalsos.com* to make an appointment or for free medical advice.
http://www.internationalsos.com/countries/Russia/
(There is also one in Kyiv.)

American Medical Center St. Petersburg
Address: 10 Serpukhovskaya St., 198013 St Petersburg
Phone: (7-812) 326-1730
Emergency Phone: (7-812) 326-1730
Fax: (7-812) 326-1731
Open: 24 hours a day, 365 days a year
Regular Office Hours: Monday through Friday, 9:00 a.m. to 6:00 p.m.
Contact: Alex Sokol
E-mail: *stpetersburg@amcenters.com*

US Embassy

By the time your Embassy visit arrives, you are in countdown mode. You are making the big push for the finish, knowing that the Flight From Hell is approaching. You are checking things off. You've had the Court hearing, gotten the child, created a family, returned to Moscow, done the medical visit and are headed for home. Emotionally you are wearing down. Physically, you and the child are likely a little sick. Just hang in there it will soon be over.

If for some reason you have a real problem with your stay in Russia, you can call the Embassy's Public Liaison Officer for advice. They cannot solve any adoption problem you might have, but they can assist in other ways. You first speak with the duty officer (Marine) who answers the telephone 24 hours a day and state the nature of your problem, and he will immediately transfer you to the liaison officer on call during that time. I cannot say enough how helpful the Embassy staff is to adoptive parents.

The Visa Unit is located at the old Embassy address at Novinskiy Bul'var 19/23 Moscow, Russia. The Embassy itself has actually moved to the new chancery building. This is the notorious building that the KGB had wiretapped from top to bottom in the 1980's. Presumably it is now been "de-bugged." The telephone number of the Visa Unit is (7)(095) 728-5058, or 728-5567, or the switchboard at 728-5000, ext.5804. Their fax number is 728-5247. You do not have to dial the (7) if in Russia and the (095) if in Moscow.

The Embassy visit is usually no big deal. You do need to check the holiday schedule as the Embassy closes for both US and Russian holidays and the Visa Unit is closed on the last Monday of the month for administrative duties. There is no need to dress up for it. The Embassy personnel are very happy for you. The purpose of the Embassy visit is to obtain an immigrant visa for your child to enter the United States. Without such a visa, your child cannot enter the US. Just because you have a Russian decree of adoption, which is recognized by the United States government, it does not automatically confer upon your child the right to enter the United States. You need to call the Visa Unit at 728-5567 a day or so ahead of time to schedule an appointment. If you need to, you can have your child's visa photos taken at the Embassy ($5). Don't forget to make two copies of your child's foreign passport for the Embassy.

A good summary of the process can be found at: *http://www.usembassy.ru/consular/wwwhci5.html.* Usually in the morning families will take their child to get her visa picture taken. You will need at least 3 photos. Then you can go and get the medical (pink sheet) checkup, unless this was done the day before. Then usually your facilitator or representative will go to the Embassy to file the required paperwork. They must file the paperwork between 9:30 and 11:00 am at Windows 10 and 11. (They need to pay the $335 Visa filing fee first.) If your papers are filed later than 11 am your Visa interview will have to wait until the next day. The paperwork is filed in the long room to the left of the main entrance on the first floor. If you don't know your way, just ask the marines. Your agency should supply you with the list of documents you need to bring. It is important that you review all of the documents with your facilitator the day before you go to the Embassy. Insist on it.

At 9 FAM (Foreign Affairs Manual) 42.21 you will find the requirements for submitting your paperwork at the US Consulate in order for your child to receive his new US immigrant Visa. You will need to submit the following documents:

American Documents

1.   Both adoptive parents' passports with a photocopy of the information page of each passport.

2.   Power of Attorney, if applicable. If one parent is not present, the remaining parent should provide photographic proof that they have met the child and a signed I-600. The Power of Attorney does not allow anyone else to sign the I-600 for the other spouse, but will allow the spouse that is staying to sign other documents on his behalf. You only need such a power of attorney if one spouse has returned to the States and will not be present for the interview. Otherwise, you can ignore this requirement.

3. <u>Form I-600</u> **Petition to Classify Orphan as an Immediate Relative** (the "blue" form) completed, signed and dated by both parents. The visa unit will now accept a downloaded copy of this form on white paper. A US citizen must sign this document in the presence of a consular officer. It does not have to be the same person who signed the I-600A. If the petitioner is married, the other spouse must also sign the petition once it has been completed, although he does not have to sign before the consular officer. Thus, if one spouse has to leave for home early, he just signs the I-600 after the court hearing and he goes on his way. The consular officer is supposed to verify that the other spouse did not sign it until all information relating to the child was entered on the form.

4. <u>Form DS-230</u> **The Application for Immigrant Visa** (the "white" form). This form should be completed from the perspective of the adopted child. You will fill out this form and file it in the morning, but only sign the application later that afternoon in front of the Consular Officer. Make sure the child's name and birthdate are correct, as the way it appears on this form is the way it will appear on the Visa.

5. You will need to pay the Visa fee of $335 ($332 for a second child) when you submit the application. Payment may be made in cash (dollars or rubles) or travelers' checks. They do not take credit cards or personal checks. The $335 visa fee is unrelated to the $460 you may have paid when you filed your I-600A. Keep the receipt. You will need to show it when you return that afternoon to actually pick up the Visa. If you are adopting children from different birthmothers, you will also have to pay an additional $460 for each unrelated child. For example, if you adopt 2 unrelated children, and paid $460 when you filed your I-600A back home, then you will pay $335 for each child's visa application and another $460 for the second child for a total of $1,120. If the children are siblings (birthmother is the same), then a second $460 is not paid.

6. <u>Form I-604</u> **Request for and Report on Overseas Orphan Investigation.** This form should be completed by you. This form contains information about the child before adoption. It used to be filled out by the Consular Officer, but they now want you to do it. Since it speeds up the process, it is an efficient change. Do not be afraid of the word "investigation." BCIS established your ability to furnish proper

care to an adopted child when it approved your I-600A, *Application for Advance Processing of Orphan Petition*. Consular officers have no authority to review this determination, unless they have a well-founded and substantive reason to believe that the I-600A approval was obtained on the basis of fraud or misrepresentation, or have knowledge of a change in material fact subsequent to the approval of the I-600A. If so, the consular officer must consult with BCIS. So this form has nothing to do with you, but rather has to do with whether the child meets the BCIS definition of an "orphan." This was the problem in Cambodia and Vietnam. This part of the form focuses on the "orphan" status and also the medical conditions of the child i.e. they ask you "were you told of this child's medical condition?" It is hard to say, "yes," if you haven't had the original medicals translated, but nevertheless, parents usually say, "yes" anyway. A further explanation of the I-604 can be found in the State Department's Foreign Affairs Manual at 9 FAM 42.21 N13.4 Orphan Investigations, et al. The form can be seen at *http://foia.state.gov/masterdocs/09fam/0942021X1.pdf*. To give you some idea of how to fill out the form, you might look at this sample filled out for China:

http://homepages.wwc.edu/staff/stirra/china/forms/i604p1.gif and
http://homepages.wwc.edu/staff/stirra/china/forms/i604p2.gif. Your form won't be filled out exactly like this, but it gives you an idea.

7.   I-864—**Affidavit of Support.** This is only required if one of the parents did not see the child before the court hearing or if parents reside outside the US. The result will be that your child will receive an IR-4 Visa. See the chapter on the I-864 for further information. If you are required to file it, then you need to attach photocopies of last 3 year's tax returns and proof of current employment. The tax returns do not have to be notarized, but you have to provide complete sets (all the schedules and forms you submit to the IRS). If you are adopting more than one child, you must submit a separate I-864 and set of financial documents for each child.

8.   A copy of your home study

9.   Your I-171H

10. The email or fax confirmation of your cable (Visa 37 cable). The Consulate should have received this from your local BCIS office in the States. You should email or fax the Visa Unit prior to traveling asking them if they have received the BCIS' cable regarding your I-171H approval and to verify how many children for which you have been approved. Take this confirmation with you when you go to the Embassy and give them a copy. It proves they have your file somewhere in the building.

11. Pre-visa physical report. This is the "Pink sheet," that is actually white, obtained in Moscow from the American Medical Clinic or Filatov. It is given to you in a sealed envelope. Do not open it. Give it to the Embassy, still sealed. Usually you can obtain a copy from the clinic at the time of the physical.

You may be asked to sign a waiver of immunizations. This form is just a promise by you that when you are back home you your child will be given all of the age appropriate immunization shots. Since this is what you plan to do anyway, it is an easy promise. Now if you adopt a child 10 or older, you cannot ask for a waiver except under certain circumstances. If you are adopting a child 10 or over, look into the exceptions to see if you can get this requirement waived.

Here are some web sites that are helpful in preparing for the Embassy visit:

For the current forms and fees of some of the BCIS necessary forms see:
http://www.immigration.gov/graphics/formsfee/forms/index.htm

For Department of State form (they begin with "DS") DS-230-Immigrant Visa Application; see
http://www.state.gov/documents/organization/7988.pdf

Russian Documents

1. The child's original birth certificate, i.e. the one with the birth parents listed, certified by ZAGS. Make sure you have a *certified* copy.

2.   Information on the resolution of the birth parents' rights: This could be in the form of death certificates of the parents, certificates certifying that the listed parents were not legally registered, letters of relinquishment, or court decrees removing parental rights, etc. If the parents can be located, there should be certified copies of documents of the search for such parents.

3.   The adoption decree issued by the local court.

4.   The letter from the Ministry of Education which indicates that the child has spent the required amount of time on the Federal Data Bank and has been released for adoption by foreigners.

5.   A letter from each children's home that the child has been in. This letter should include the dates of the child's stay in the institution, any information as to whether the child was visited and a statement of no objection to the adoption by the home's director.

6.   The adoption certificate.

7.   The amended birth certificate, showing you as the parents.

8.   The child's Russian passport and a photocopy of the information page.

Each official Russian document must be presented in the following way: the original document or a copy *certified* by the custodian of the document and an English translation, one photocopy of the original and a second translation. Translations from languages other than Russian must be notarized.

The copies and translations will become part of the child's immigrant visa. All originals presented to the Embassy are returned to you immediately following the interview with the Consular officer. Make sure you remind the Officer before you leave regarding the return of the originals.

If the paperwork is all in order, you will receive an appointment ticket to return that afternoon. If it is not in order, you will not get your child's Visa that day and will have to wait until the paperwork is fixed. In the afternoon you and your child will go to the Embassy for your 15-minute interview. You will need to bring with you the receipt for the $335 Visa application fee. Do not lose this receipt.

In order to get into the Embassy for your appointment, you need to be at the Novinskiy Bulvar entrance to the Embassy (the main entrance located on the right side) no more than fifteen minutes before the scheduled interview. If you are there too early, you will just have to wait outside. Just don't be later either. Only American citizens and their adopted children are admitted to the Embassy for the interview. Agency representatives, drivers etc. must wait outside.

Parents present their interview ticket and their U.S. passports to the Embassy guards. They may also ask to see your driver's license. The families should follow the signs to the Immigrant visa section on the second floor. (Take a dollar with you as there used to be a Coke machine in this room.) You take your appointment slip to window seven (near the cashier) and then take a seat in the waiting area.

The families will be called to one of four windows for the visa interview. The interview usually doesn't last more than 15 minutes. Parents will be asked about the adoption process, their financial status, and the health of the adopted child. They will also sign the Form 230 immigrant visa application on behalf of their child or children. This Application is submitted in the morning with your documents, but is actually signed by you at the interview, since a Consular Officer must witness it. At the interview the officer will likely raise with you any problems with the documents. Your facilitator's job is to make sure there are not any problems. The officer's job is to make sure that the adoption complies with all legal requirements of both Russian and American law.

If the Visa is approved, the officer will sign the appropriate forms and hand the entire visa package to an Immigrant Visa Unit employee who will complete the processing of the visa and hand the sealed immigrant visa envelope to you after the interview. If there is a problem with the documents, the consular officer will discuss with you what the remaining issues are, and suggestions as to how they might be resolved.

After you receive the Visa, and unless you are just too tired, you will have this huge grin on your face, as you will have finished with all official paperwork to adopt your child. (There is some follow up paperwork back in the States, but why ruin the moment.).

After the interview you will be given the sealed Visa package. Do NOT open this package and do NOT pack it in your luggage. It goes in your carry-on that is with you at all times to be delivered to immigration once you have landed in the United States. Once you have received the Visa package, you or your representative can then register your child at the Ministry of Foreign Affairs, if you would rather do that in Moscow than in the States.

Your child's immigrant visa is valid for six months, beginning with the date of issuance. Any visa issued to a child lawfully adopted by a U.S. citizen and spouse while such citizen is serving abroad in the U.S. Armed Forces, or is employed abroad by the U.S. Government, or is temporarily abroad on business is valid until the adoptive parent returns to the United States. In such cases the visa is valid for up to 3 years.

Almost all US Visas for adopted children from Russia are IR-3s. In 2000, only 22 out of 4,677 were IR-4s. If the child will receive an IR-3 Visa, then you do not have to file an **Affidavit of Support, Form I-864.** If your child will be receiving an IR-4 Visa, then you do. The difference is that an IR-3 means that both parents saw the child before the Court hearing. Usually an IR-4 is reserved for those adoptions in countries where the child was escorted to the United States or where only one married parent saw the child.

One surprise that occasionally happens is that you will have a Russian document that is not a certified original. It is your facilitator's job to see that all papers are in order. However, sometimes, even to the best facilitators, there is a slip up in the hurry to leave a region and get back to Moscow and a document will not get certified. The only solution is for you to spend an extra day in Moscow while your facilitator does whatever it takes to get that document certified. It means that someone in the region will be contacted and the document sent to Moscow by the next available plane or train.

If you are approved for more children on your I-171H, but are not adopting them all at one time then tell the officer to keep your file open. This may allow you to use your same I-171H the next year to adopt additional children.

If you decide to visit the US Embassy for some other reason, you will find that in front of the Embassy are Russian guards as well as American Marines. There will be a line of people. These are Russians. Go to the front of the line and tell them you are an American. You should be let right in. The Marine guard will inspect your bags and store your camera and camcorder. You will go through the usual metal detector. It is all very ordinary.

You used to be able to register your child with the Russians while you were in Moscow rather than do it back in the States. However, the process is now taking at least 2-3 days so you may want to insist to your agency that you will do it once you get home, rather than stay in Moscow. Your agency may ask you to pay them a refundable deposit to make sure you do it. The choice is entirely yours.

Leaving Moscow for Home

You will likely need to confirm your reservation a day or so before your flight. The phone number for Delta in Moscow is (095) 578-2939. If calling from Moscow, you do not need to dial (095). You should think about whether you want to buy a seat for your child. Some parents recommend a seat even for an infant as otherwise you will likely have to hold your child for the entire flight. Now on Aeroflot you may find empty seats available, but Delta is likely to be packed.

Make sure you have your child's visa document package in your carryon. You will need to give this to US immigration when you land. At the Moscow airport you will need to show the Russians your Russian exit visa, your customs declaration form that you filled out when you landed, your passport, and your child's Russian passport. The airline will want to see your ticket and your child's.

Beginning in 2003, you are allowed to export up to 3,000 U.S. dollars without providing a customs declaration or proof of how the money was obtained. You can also export up to 10,000 U.S. dollars by simply filling out a customs declaration upon exit. More than 10,000 U.S. dollars can be exported upon proof that it was imported into Russia legally (a stamped customs declaration or proof of a legal bank or wire transfer). Notwithstanding this liberalization of the customs rules, it is still recommended that you declare your funds when you first come through customs. It does mean that if one spouse is leaving before the other, you do not need to be so careful about splitting the money so one spouse doesn't have too much.

Get to the airport no later than 2 hours before your flight. Even earlier if you want a bulkhead seat. These seats are wonderful if you have adopted a young child and are reserved on a first come basis. Some airlines have a bassinet that attaches in bulkhead seating. It is really a plus. If you have older children, they have space to get down and play. It really is worth the extra trouble. The lines are usually much longer for Delta flights than for Aeroflot. You will have much to do. First, go to the airline counter and pay the change of flight penalty if applicable. Do not use a credit card but pay in cash. Then go to your airline. They will want to see everyone's passports and tickets. Then go through customs and give them your customs declaration form. Then get in line to go through passport control. This is what takes the longest time to go through. They will review your passport, exit visa, and anything else they want. They may wish to look at your child's sealed US visa package, but you will get instructions from the Embassy that they should not and if they try, for you to call for a supervisor and also call the Embassy. Russian passport control is so use to adoptive parents that this is really not an issue anymore. Some parents have experienced a wonderful courtesy, which is that a mother and baby can go to the front of any line! This courtesy is not always honored, however, I would certainly try it, if faced with any long line at the airport. This is particular helpful at the long passport control line (this is the one after security and baggage check-in). Just say "rebyonka pervaya" (children first)! A screaming child also seems to get you through the line fast! Now if there are 20 other kids in line with you, it probably won't work. The Delta 12:50 pm flight is considered a "baby flight" so this is one where you will have plenty of company.

The summer months are when most people travel so the airport can be a zoo during this time. You can have no lines, just a mob, and no air conditioning. If you are leaving Moscow during the summer, get to the airport even earlier than 2 hours before your flight and bring plenty of Cheerios if your child is with you. On the right hand side of customs is a money exchange place that will exchange rubles for dollars.

The passport control/border guard may ask for the Russian adoption decree. Just show it to them. All of your original Russian documents should be in your carryon in case they want to look at something. Do NOT pack them!

Once you are through the passport control/border guard station you are home free. A load will come off your shoulder and you will really feel like it is finally over, you are headed for home. On the other side of the border station are duty free shops and restaurants that take rubles and dollars. You can also make phone calls from there. Usually you end up sitting on the floor by your gate with dozens of other adoptive parents, some of whom you met at the Embassy.

If you are really dreading the airport lines, then you can pay for VIP service at $150 per person. Several travel agencies offer this service such as Peace at *http://www.go-russia.com/vinnetou.htm* and Allways Travel. There is also "VIP light" for departures—a cheaper option.

The flight time directly back to the States (JFK) is about 11 hours, which is an hour, or so longer than when you flew to Moscow. The reason is that westbound trips always take longer than eastbound because of the wind. In most of North America the prevailing winds are easterly, which is accentuated in the winter by the jet stream along the polar front. Since US-Europe jet traffic follows land as closely as possible as an emergency precaution, that route takes you over Canada, Greenland, Iceland, UK, to Europe and same in reverse for Europe to US. The tailwinds speed up the eastbound trip and headwinds slow down the westbound trip.

Now for the Flight From Hell!

Flight From Hell

Imagine being taken from the only home you know, surrounded by people you don't know, speaking a language you don't know, and then being placed in a flying machine, which you may never have seen. Add to this mix that you are hungry, sleepy, not feeling well and generally cranky. This is your child. It might also be you. This is why the return flight to the United States is called the Flight From Hell. Businessmen try to avoid it at all costs. On the flights are many parents and children. It can be very noisy. You will not sleep on the plane. Therefore, it is critical that you get a very good night's sleep the night before. It may be 20 hours or so before you are able to sleep again. Through it all just keep clicking your ruby slippers and repeating, "home, home, there's no place like home...."

You might take something to soothe your child on the flight like Benadryl or Dramamine. Ask your pediatrician regarding the correct dosage based on the child's weight. Test its effect in Moscow before flying as the pink kind may have the opposite effect because of the dye involved. Many children are affected by Red Dye 40 and will act like they have just had ten cups of coffee. I highly recommend the clear kind. Also, a child might have an ear infection or be congested which flying would aggravate. If you know that your child has an ear problem ask your pediatrician what you can give him to make the flight better. You can also ask the doctor at the American Medical Clinic or Filatov. Pack some Dimetapp just in case. You might give an infant something to drink while the plane takes off and lands. An older child should chew gum or also drink something to keep the ears open. Entertain them with some toys like a set of stacking cups, small cars, rattles, plastic keys, or small stuffed animals. Crayola makes markers that only write on the paper that comes with the markers. These are great. Also, take some snacks as the little creatures do quiet down at feeding time! Do not give your child a peanut butter or egg product until you get home, as you do not want him to have an allergic reaction while overseas. Also, be careful about too much fruit juice since their bodies may not be used to it and you may end up dealing with toddler diarrhea.

For a child under two you do not have to pay full price. Usually it is 10% of the adult fare. This does not provide your child with a seat, just breathing room on your lap. Of course, if there is an empty seat next to you then you are in luck, however, this is rare on Delta flights. Therefore, you should always try to get a bassinet or consider buying a full fare seat. Getting a bassinet on Delta is purely on a first come first serve basis at check-in. The argument against buying a seat is the cost. The argument in favor of it is that your child will be much more comfortable and happy in his seat. He will be able to sit up and play with his toys on the fold down tray and sleep in it also. You can change him there rather than in the tiny bathroom or on your fold down tray. Aeroflot does not charge the full adult price for a child's seat.If your flight is not direct, consider buying a seat for the longest leg.

Pack your carry-ons with at least 10 diapers per child, a box of baby wipes, two changes of clothes for each child, plastic bags for trash and extra T-shirts for you and your husband. Your clothes will look like a dumpster at the end of the flight.Take food for the kids, but make sure you eat or dispose all raw fruits and vegetables before going through the customs in the USA. If you think there is a remote possibility that you might miss a plane and stay in a hotel don't panic, it is not that bad. Pack some socks and underwear just in case. Take baby Tylenol and any medications you need on a plane. Don't hesitate to give Tylenol if you think your child is in pain. Give baby a bottle of formula or juice during takeoff and landings.

If you have a layover in Frankfurt, you will not need a visa, only a passport. However, Russian citizens do need a visa and your child will need a transit visa, which can be purchased and issued on site at the airport in Frankfurt. You just go to the "holding area" at the customs checkpoint. It should just take about 20 minutes. Telling them you've just adopted doesn't hurt either. There are lockers as well as a luggage hold in Frankfurt. For more information go to the airport's website: www.frankfurt-airport.de There is an English Language option in the upper left corner of the home page.

The trip itself will be something you will file purge when you get home. On a flight with 20 babies, you will see little heads popping up and down over the tops of seats like prairie dogs on speed. You can relax in the full knowledge that whenever your child is shrieking or throwing food, there is another child on board screaming even louder and chucking whole grocery stores down the aisle. You might want to change your child's diaper out on the wing, but they have a rule against that. Instead, you are allowed to use the changing table in the bathroom, which is the perfect size for your kid, but only if he's a hamster. I would say it all passes like a bad dream, but it doesn't, since no dreaming is allowed. You will be wide awake for every excruciating 36,000 seconds of the trip.

If your child really begins to scream and is unconsolable, then ask the flight attendants if they wouldn't mind speaking with him in Russia. Hearing a native language coupled with a mother's touch may be all it takes. Don't be embarrassed about asking for help.

When you land in the US, just follow the rest of your fellow passengers to the line for US citizens at immigration. You do not have to go through the non-citizen line. If you return on an Aeroflot flight, this means the line will be very short as many are Russian citizens. If you return on Delta, the line may be longer.

At JFK, there are usually about ten immigration booths so you get through it very quickly. Immigration is usually not very difficult. After they check your passports you will be directed to an immigration office where they will check your child's visa. Do not take any pictures of the BCIS personnel or office. This is a very bad idea and they do not like it. At immigration they will take that sealed package you received at the US Embassy in Moscow. (Remember, do not pack it in checked luggage or open it.) If you land at JFK, your whole customs and immigration experience will likely be 25 minutes tops.BCIS will stamp your child's Russian passport with "IR3" and give her a number. Double-check your child's passport that this is what they did. You will then be free to pick up your luggage, run it through customs and recheck it. If you are making a connecting flight, do not hesitate but go directly to the connecting gate. The reason for this is that JFK is not a small airport and getting to the other gate can take longer than you think. You do not want to spend any more time than necessary in an airport with your very tired family. You just want to get home as quickly as possible.

If you are lucky, your child's green card (which is not really green) showing her to be a Resident Alien will show up within 6 weeks to a year later with the same number as written in her passport. It really is an irrelevant document, as you do not need it to file for your child's citizenship if your child has an IR3 visa.

When you arrive home, you will be exhausted and probably a little sick. If you can have a relative or family friend stay with you for a week while you and the child adjust, it would be better for all. You may even have a meltdown yourself. Just know that this does happen and that it in no way reflects on your ability to parent. You are just running on empty and need to get home and recharge.

And most important of all............(drumroll)

Make a pledge to forget anything bad you said to your spouse during the flight once you come home.

CHAPTER XIII

HOME SWEET HOME

Insurance

The Health Insurance Portability and Accountability Act of 1996 helped remedy problems with health care coverage for adopted children. The Act mandates that all employers who provide *group* health coverage for their employees must extend the same coverage to adopted children as they do other dependents. Coverage may not be restricted because of "pre-existing conditions" and must take effect at the time of a child's placement. There are some exceptions and you should check with your plan administrator.

You have a period of 30 days in which to notify your insurance company/plan administrator of the adoption. If you do not notify them within 30 days, it is as if you are adding an existing family member to the policy and there will be pre-existing conditions limitations, as per your policy's description. To be on the safe side as far as when that 30 days begins to run, notify your insurance company as soon as you return to the States. You may wish to send the notification by certified mail in addition to sending it through your company.

Two important points to make. One, when you are notifying your insurance company, whether it is a group or individual plan, make sure you can track your paperwork. Send it FedEx or UPS or certified. You want to be able to prove it got there within the 30 days time limit, if the insurance company questions you.

Finally, individual plans have their own rules. If you have problems, file a complaint with your state's insurance commissioner. You can also file an appeal with your insurance company.

For persons with *individual* policies, coverage depends on the terms of the policy, which can vary based on your state's regulations.

Bathing

Bathing Russian children can be a problem when you first try it. Sometimes it is because they were only bathed in cold water, or simply hosed down, were washed with a brush or treated roughly. The soap may also have been very harsh and painful to their eyes. Also, some homes treat circulation problems with a shower of cold water. If your child shows anxiety regarding bathing, it will be a short-term problem.

Here are some techniques to reduce the anxiety.

1. Make the water warm before placing the child in the tub and then get into the bath with her. Just put in a little water at first. There is no need to fill up the tub.

2. Put a few familiar toys in the tub. Not a lot, just a few. You can let her play with them from the outside first.

3. Reduce the light in the bathroom so that it is not as bright.

4. Talk or sing softly to your child in a calming voice during the entire bathing experience.

5. Hold your child during the entire bath.

6. Do little actual washing the first couple of times to try to get the child used to the environment. You might even do sponge baths for a while.

7. Dry her in a warm towel and very gently.

8. Let the child set the pace of acclimation. She needs to learn to trust you and the tub.

Go through this experience a couple of times and the child should lose his anxiety.

Also, you will find that your child's skin is very, very dry. It is because of all the heat in the children's homes. Try to moisturize your child's skin after a bath. His skin will just soak it up.

Sleeping

In the 1960's we were all put to sleep in the traditional way. Your father would open the door and yell "...you're darn right there are monsters under the bed and if you don't be quiet and go to sleep, they'll get you." Unfortunately, this did not work, although it did make you keep your feet from dangling over the edge of the bed. There have been a few new ideas since then.

Children normally change their biological clocks at a rate of one hour per day. China is twelve hours ahead of Eastern Standard Time. Therefore nearly all children should be adjusted to U.S. time within two weeks of returning home. Getting the child outside in daylight will help the adjustment process. However, you need to be careful about exposing the child too fast to the outside world. Your child's immune system may not be too used to her new environment and your pediatrician may recommend that your child stay inside most of the time for the first two weeks.

Sometimes night time brings out fears that are not present during the day when you are around. You have to appreciate that you may be this child's fourth placement. There was her birthmother, an institution, possible foster parent, then you. This is a lot of transition in a child's first year of life. Some children are afraid to go to sleep and cry even when sleeping. While the Ferber book is excellent, it may not be the best guide for adopted children in their first year home. You may have to stay in the bedroom a little longer after the good-night book and kiss until they feel safe enough to fall asleep. Realize the stress this child has undergone from the sudden transition of leaving a long time foster parent to a strange hotel, then long flight to the US to living in a place where sounds and smells are completely unfamiliar. It may take a few months before trust and familiarity bring comfort.

Some children may never have been rocked in a chair or made eye contact with a caregiver. Activities that are normal for an infant-mother relationship may actually be new to the child. Allow the child to find her own comfort zone. Give her room to explore and let her open emotional doors at her own pace. Apply less structure and just sit on the floor and see which toys and games catch her interest. Eventually she will get comfortable with the sounds, sights and smells and learn to trust that you will always be there and she will become more relaxed at night.

Some parents have experimented with the amount of sleepwear or covers in case the child just naturally runs hot or cold. White noise like a fan is also an option.

There is another sleeping phenomenon that is not necessarily more prevalent in adoptive children and that is a night terror. This is not a nightmare and has nothing to do with nightmares.Nightmares occur during the end of the night when REM is most intense. Sleep terrors occur during the first few hours after your child has fallen asleep when non-REM is deepest-very deep non-dreaming sleep,.usually 1-4 hours after falling asleep.

A child having a night terror will scream and cry without opening her eyes.They do not want you to touch them and will arch and scream more, if you attempt to hold them or soothe them. They are sensitive to touch. As a parent it is terrifying. The event pretty much has to run its course.The child will have no memory of the event. There is not much you can do although some parents will try to gently distract the child and wake her up. This has limited success. Upon waking up, the child will not have a fear of going back to sleep like a nightmare.The child might.even be relaxed as the agitation has disappeared.

Do not try to wake him by holding him strongly or shaking him. Do not pester him with questions about what he was dreaming or what caused him to fear. He truly doesn't know and there is no answer. He may even make up a story for you.Do not remind him that he wa acting strange. That's the last thing a child wants to hear, that he is strange or something is wrong with him. If you become upset, then he will become upset. Try not to have an extended waking perod afterwards likewatching TV or playing games. The child will go right back to sleep quickly.

For some children it is related to stress or being over tired from the day. Their brains just are too hyoed up and can not relax. Children can have them because of a change in schools or other stress related event. Each child has a different stress triggering mechanism. In one child it might be having to go to the bathroom and being afraid to wet the bed. This subconscious conflict then triggers the night terror event. On rare occasions night terrors also occur in adoptive children and will stop a few weeks after returning home when their sleep pattern stabilizes.Children usually outgrow them after 3 years of age, but they can also go on for quite a while and in rare instances into the teenage years. It also seems to be an inherited trait.

Back to monsters for a moment. Some ideas that parents have used is giving the child a small flashlight or water pistol and telling the child he has protection and can zap the monsters away. It doesn't always work, but the child can also drink from the water pistol so it can serve two purposes.

Circumcision

There is no medical reason to circumcise a child, and for this reason most health insurance plans will not pay for it, unless your doctor recommends it as medically necessary (hint, hint). Instead, it is a cultural decision. If your child will not be circumcised, you have to teach your child to clean the area more thoroughly during a bath. You will also need to teach your son to pull back on the foreskin during tinkle time as otherwise the penis may get infected. The cost of a circumcision is roughly $600 to the surgeon, $1,400 to the hospital and then something for the anesthesia bill.

Check with your pediatrician, but generally you do not pull back the foreskin until the boy is older because by forcing it you can cause scarring and problems later. The foreskin with time becomes moveable away from the penis. When a child is younger it is tight and hurts to pull back. From the hygiene point of view, you don't need to worry about cleaning behind the foreskin until a boy is older.

Most European men are not circumcised and in the States it currently runs about 60/40 in favor. Contrary to what some may think, men do not check out each other's personal equipment in the locker room. So do not assume that there will be a "locker room" issue with "man land".It is always curious how Moms suddenly become experts on what goes on in a boys locker room!

One consideration is that the child will be under general anesthesia and will experience about 5 days of discomfort. Sometimes there is a problem with changing the diaper and then dealing with a bloody scab. If you're going to have a circumcision performed, do it in a hospital with a reputable pediatric urologist. Some places do not give anesthesia to a baby so this is a question you might ask. In an unofficial survey, Moms whose child did not have a lot of pain said they would do again, and those whose children did have a lot of pain said they would never do it again.

The way it usually works is that a bell like thing is placed over the foreskin to protect the head, and then WHACK! Ok, it's a little more scientific than that. The procedure itself takes about 15 minutes. The child is put under full anesthesia. He comes "fully" out of anesthesia just about 1 hr after the procedure and is in recovery for about 1/2 hour for continued observation. They observe him to make certain that he is taking in fluids and can pee. As soon as he can pee, they release him.

Some children are given Tylenol with codeine for pain. Others are fine with regular Tylenol. You be the judge. Popsicles and Blues Clues videos are important.Keep applying Neosporin or Vaseline to the area so the diaper or underwear does not stick. Change diapers quickly. Give the bandage plenty of time to fall off on its own. Don't pull it off! There is a very informative policy statement on the American Academy of Pediatrics website. The web address is: *http://www.aap.org/policy/re9850.html*

Some parents wait to circumcise little Johnny until he has to have his tonsils or adenoids taken out or PE tubes put in. The theory is that there is no sense having him undergo two operations when one will do. Boys have been circumcised at 4-1/2 years and even as late as nine years of age. You do not have to decide the minute you get back. Indeed, one consideration is that your child is already going through a lot of emotional changes and adding surgery on top of all his adjusting is just too much. Another consideration is to wait and see if your son develops repetitive infections under the foreskin. If you have to treat several, then you may want to circumcise.

Now there are some studies that conclude that circumcision reduces the risk of penile cancer (pretty low to begin with), AIDS, sexual transmitted diseases, urinary tract infections, and probably hairy palms. These studies are subject to a great deal of debate as evidenced by the Academy of Pediatrics' article cited above. The issue is not with circumcision itself, but with the fact that the foreskin needs to be kept clean. If you don't have a foreskin, then it isn't a problem. If you do have a foreskin, then it is another place for dirt, infection or a virus to find a foothold. Thus, older sons need to be taught to give the area a little more attention at bath time.

A detailed discussion of the procedure is at *http://www.cirp.org/*. This web site also links to pictures and even a video of the procedure! This web site argues against circumsicion, and is very informative.

Rocking

Many children rock themselves to sleep or when they are stressed or tired. It may even appear to be quite violent. If you do nothing, this behavior will most likely disappear after six months or so. The rocking is a symptom of a deep need for comfort through tactile stimulation. Your child had no one to hold or hug him, so he learned to hug himself. You may want to practice some techniques, which will fill this void and give him the comfort he so much desires during these times.

You should not try to stop a child from rocking. You should just let him rock and pick him up and rock with him, or try to get his attention focused on something else. Some parents gently rub their child's head or back when he goes down for his nap. They sometimes lie down next to their child so he feels their body against his. In one of Caroline Archer's books she suggests sitting down next to the child and rocking in rhythm together with her. This transforms the rocking from a self-contained, self-stimulating activity into a joint activity with the parent, and the child is drawn out of her self-contained world. You may end up laughing together as it slowly becomes a game. By the way, it comes as no surprise that "rockers" love swings.

These babies need a soothing routine at night, they need to build confidence in you as a parent that you will take care of their needs (hunger, calm, tender care and development needs) and they need to have their own rhythm respected (which is not the case in the orphanage). They have developed ways to tell you they are not comfortable with something.

Try singing or a music box. Rocking is about rhythm. Some parents place a loud ticking clock in the childs room on the theory that if the child focuses on the rhymic ticking he might lie still.Sometimes babies who do some rhythm exercises before bedtime quit rocking sooner. Also check for ear infections, as they are more painful when lying on the back.

Pediatrician Visit

When you return home your child should be given a thorough medical screening. It is best if both spouses are present to help with questioning the doctor. You may find that your child is the only Eastern European child the doctor has seen. If so, then you will need to educate the doctor on the necessary tests and immunizations. You may have to be insistent. If the doctor resists, change doctors. A pediatrician may hear you talk about your child's history in a children's home, but they may not really "understand" how that institutional experience MAY affect your child. It simply is not covered in medical school. All the local pediatrician sees is a very healthy child. You want someone who sees and understands the bigger picture or is willing to learn.

Come to the appointment with copies of medical articles on Eastern European adopted children and their medical issues. Leave these with him so that the next family can have an informed doctor. You might give him a copy of the American Academy of Pediatrics' article on the initial medical evaluation of an adopted child. See *http://www.aap.org/policy/04037.html* and also an article from Dr. Aronson at *http://www.adoptvietnam.org/adoption/infectious-disease.htm*. Suggest that she consult the 1997 Red Book, *Report of the Committee on Infectious Diseases*, American Academy of Pediatrics.

Dr. Gordina has developed a medical testing chart.While the chart is directed at Eastern European children, it has broad applicability. EEAC has created a special autoresponder that will send you the MS Word document. You can send a blank email message to *MedTests@eeadopt.org* and it will be sent to you as an attachment in a reply message.

Have the child checked for strabismus (eyes), giardia lamblia, anemia (both iron and B12 kind), rickets, salmonella, and scabies. The child should have vision and hearing tests by pediatric specialists. These tests are very important as vision and hearing problems can hinder language acquisition which can cause your child to be frustrated leading to behavior issues.

Correctable hearing problems are not uncommon in infants as they have had untreated respiratory and ear infections. Indeed, it is not uncommon for an American pediatrician to remedy the usual ear infection with the short 10-day program of treatment. The problem is that he is facing a child who may have had untreated ear/respiratory/bronchitis/sinus illnesses which can cause the bugs to be more numerous, hidden in unusual places (like the Eustachian tube where medicine doesn't reach) and just generally be of a tougher variety than your average middle class kid's ear infection bugs. Children in the orphanages are chronically overtreated with antibiotics for nothing and at the same time they are undertreated for persistent eat effusions (chronic ear and sinus infections) because there are no otoscopes in the orphanages and therefore no decent follow-up. Just be aware that your child might need a longer antiobiotic regimen, PE Tubes, or stronger drugs like Augmentin ES. Allergies are also very common among adoptees from larger cities because of significant pollution. Dr. Gordina even wrote a Phd thesis, arguing that only very healthy kids can live in Moscow. In summary, see a good ENT doctor, and do an OAE hearing test (not a booth!).

Every child born in the United States is getting the objective hearing test at birth, so called OAE—oto acoustic emissions. This test objectively evaluates the function of the middle ear, it does not evaluate the rest of the hearing pathway—acoustic nerve and brain itself. In 2003, the OAE test is considered the standard objective screening test for hearing loss in children with the BAER (brain auditory evoked response) or similar tests being the definite answers. In the BAER test, electrodes are connected to the forehead and behind each ear.Then a tube that emits sound is placed in each ear. Each ear is then tested at different levels of sounds and frequency and they look for brain activity. It is very definitive and is far better than the subjective old booth test. Sometimes a child, even after PE tubes come out, just learns to lip read and so you are unsure if there is a problem.

Check with your ENT and insist on an OAE test, as the booth is next to worthless for younger children. Here s the American Academy of Pediatrics (AAP) Statement on Hearing assessment beyond the neonatal screening: http://www.aap.org/policy/0121.html

HIV-1 and HIV-2 should be tested by ELISA (Western Blot) or if under 18 months of age by PCR or culture. Syphilis is not usually found in an infant and the Russian medical clinics treat syphilis in the population. Nevertheless, the VDRL for syphilis should be given and is another required test. Although Russian children's exposure to lead appears to be less than children in America, you might go ahead and have your child's lead levels checked just in case. You might find higher levels in school age children than in infants. Some studies indicate that Chinese adopted children have higher lead levels than children from other countries, but that all children have much lower levels after several weeks of being in the United States.

Also, test for Hepatitis A, C, and include a Hepatitis B profile, to include HbsAG, anti-HBs and anti-HBc. A second Hepatitis B profile screening is recommended after the maximum incubation period of 12 weeks passes. It is recommended by most IA doctors that a child be retested for Hepatitis B, C, and HIV 6 months later in order to cover any incubation period.

There is a new blood test for iron deficiency anemia (IDA), which allows for an earlier diagnosis. A test for reticulocyte hemoglobin content can spot IDA before your child shows signs. This is probably not that much of an issue with these children as any anemia they have will be well progressed. IDA causes your child to have pale skin, sensitivity to cold and to feel fatigued. It takes about 3 months of iron deficiency to show up in your child's blood as an abnormal red blood cell count. The cells called reticulocytes are the first ones sent into the blood stream and can indicate early stage iron deficiency.

Do not be surprised if your child has rickets. The children typically have a severe vitamin D deficiency, which may or may not be evident in the child's bone development and overall skin complexion. After about 2 months of being home and drinking good American milk, you will see a marked improvement in your child's overall health (complexion, strength, etc). Remember hearing about "fortified" milk on TV commercials? That means we add a lot of good vitamins (mostly D) to our milk. The Russians do not. The light from the sun activates Vitamin D. This is another reason the children are pale and often look sickly. When you get them home, expose them to natural sunlight as much as possible (make it a daily routine) and your child's health will benefit greatly.

Now rickets comes in two different varieties: Vitamin D deficient and vitamin D resistant. If deficient then it can be treated with sunlight, calcium and Vitamin D. If resistant, then there is a more concentrated vitamin D approach.

One effect of rickets can be bowed legs. With proper treatment, the legs should straighten out within a year. Another effect of rickets can be a temporarily enlarged head. This does not always occur in all children with rickets. If you are evaluating a child with this condition though, you will need at least two photographs to rule out hydrocephaly, a front face shot and a side shot. In hydrocephaly, as fluid accumulates in the head, the head expands at the expense of the face, which gets squished and smaller. In rickets, the head gets enlarged, mostly in the forehead, but the facial features remain normal in proportion.

If your child has a serious rickets problem, then you might want to discuss with your pediatrician or pediatric orthopedic whether your child should have a base line x-ray of his legs. That way they can compare the growth one year latter and determine if any orthopedic intervention is warranted. A discussion on rickets can be found at
http://www.orphandoctor.com/medical/4_2_5_4.html.

A stool examination should be conducted for ova and parasites. Giardia is usually treated using an awful tasting medicine called Flagyl or with Furoxone. If your child has giardia, there is a strong possibility that it has been passed on to you and you should be checked as well. Make sure your pediatrician and his lab know how to properly test for giardia. Query him on the specifics. The stool sample should be taken over three days and from different areas of the stool. Just taking one day's sample is not enough.

Also, have your child checked for head lice. Lice are not uncommon in any institutional setting. The way they work is they feed on scalp and the byproducts cause intense itching. The louse deposits its eggs (nits) on the base of the hair shaft. Nits are sometimes mistaken for dandruff, but are very different. Dandruff is flat and flaky and will easily slide off the hair with your fingers. Nits are tiny oval white shells that stick to the base of the hair shaft near the scalp. Lice do not travel through the air or jump from one head to another. They are caught only from direct contact with infected clothing. One cure is Nix. Be aware that Nix is not recommended for small children as it is a toxin and there are lice that are immune to Nix. It shouldn't be used to treat anyone more than 2 times and you should wash all clothing and bedding. Mayonnaise and Vaseline are home remedies that also work. Some over the counter medications do not really work. Also, fingernails are better than little combs at getting out the nits. Another home remedy is olive oil. You put it in the hair, top off with a shower cap and wash out the next morning. The lice suffocate and the oil is easier to wash out than mayonnaise. A diluted solution of white vinegar (one part vinegar to one part water) can also help loosen resistant nits. Remove the dead nits in bright sunlight, with hair wet, and look at each strand of hair. This is quite tedious and time consuming, but well worth the effort. Even if you think you got them all, check everyday for at least 2 weeks. Wash everything in hot water that has had contact with the infected person. Boil hairbrushes, combs, headbands, etc. If live lice are found, repeat the olive oil (you must have missed a nit that hatched). The good news is that lice can only survive a day or two away from a warm body.

Traditionally, lindane, malathions and natural permethrins, such as RID A200, have been used to treat lice. Newer agents such as 1% permethrin (Nix, Pfizer), anise and Hair Clear (Quantam), an herbal product, have proven effective. Ask your doctor about novel agents and reintroduced agents such as Malathion (Ovide lotion, Medicis), a rapid pediculicide and effective ovicide. One treatment is usually effective. However, the product contains only 5% active ingredient and 78% isopropyl alcohol—which is highly flammable.There is also Hair Clean 1-2-3, an herbal product containing oil of anise and Ylang Ylang oil.

There are also some rare parasites called Entamoeba Coli Cystus and Blastocytus Homoflous for which you could test if your child is not gaining weight, and eating poorly, but has no giardia type symptoms (diarrhea, very smelly stools, blood in the stool). You can also test for Helicobacter pylori, which is a bacterium that lives in the thin layer of mucus that lines the stomach. The symptoms are similar to that of giardia. If your child is not growing, I would rule out the other more obvious problems before testing for this. You can also test for lead levels and for hypothyroidism, which can retard growth. Interestingly, Russians have less risk for lead poisoning than do Chinese and American children.

If your child has an Asian, Rom or dark skinned background, he may have what is called a Mongolian spot on the lower back. It looks like a bruise, but it is not. It is completely benign and fades over time. You may wish to point it out to your doctor and take a picture of it so that you can explain to whomever that your child was born with it. The spot's name is actually a misnomer as all children have such a spot but it just shows up more prominently in non-Caucasian children. A good description is at
http://catalog.com/fwcfc/mongolianspot.htm.

As an alternative to re-immunizing your child (which is highly recommended), you can also have a blood titer test, which tests for antibodies and shows which childhood diseases your child has been immunized against. This test may reduce the number of shots that need to be given. The blood titer is not inexpensive though and you need to check if your insurance will cover it. Also, quite a bit of blood needs to be withdrawn which may be a problem in a child suffering from anemia. For all of these reasons, most people opt for simply re-immunizing. Be sure to avoid immunizing on a day your child is running a fever. If your child is sick, choose another day. For the recommended schedule of shots, see the CDC's web site at *http://www.cdc.gov/nip/recs/child-schedule.htm#Printable.*

Also, your pediatrician may find purple tattoo like marks on your child's buttocks. These are from vitamin and antibiotic shots. They are cheaper than pills. Also, in some children's homes, not all by any means, the children receive sedative shots (Aminazine) to maintain quiet in the home. The Russians are very free with their needles and since they don't always have alcohol wipes they will occasionally use vodka to clean the area and of course, re-use the needle! (Vodka is recommended a lot for sickness, and if you get a fever you may be given vodka in homemade raspberry jam. Works great!)

Balding on the back of the head probably indicates that the infant was lying on his back a lot. It's not necessarily neglect and is now commonly found in US babies due to infants sleeping on their backs to prevent Sudden Infant Death Syndrome (SIDS).

Some children are unfamiliar with milk and may not like the taste. This does not necessarily indicate lactose intolerance, simply unfamiliarity. However, children with an Asian ethnicity do tend to have a higher degree of lactose intolerance. Some families spike the milk with loads of cocoa, which usually never fails to entice a drink. Others have to resort to Pediasure. An alternative to Pediasure is Carnation Instant breakfast with a little canola oil in the bottle. Ask your pediatrician about these and other ways to increase your child's weight and overcome his malnutrition. Of course, if your child has chronic diarrhea, but no parasites, then lactose intolerance should certainly be tested.

There has been some discussion regarding testing internationally adopted children between six and twelve months of age with the full metabolic screen which is done on all newborns in your state. This test screens for some very rare conditions that need immediate treatment. Ask your pediatrician about whether this screen is recommended.

You should see a dramatic improvement in your child within the first six months. Malnourished children generally catch up with their weight first then height. If your child is not responding appropriately to his new healthy environment after a few months, you may wish to have him screened at an international adoption health clinic. Ask your pediatrician or local children's hospital for the one nearest you.

Other resources can be found at:
http://www.adoption-research.org/favorite.html

Scabies

Have your pediatrician check for scabies. A skin mite causes scabies. They look like small red bumps that are very itchy. The bumps typically occur on the face, head, belly button, hands or feet. Incubation period for scabies is about 2 weeks. It is extremely contagious and very hard to identify in a small and/or malnourished child. If the child's scabies were treated with corticosteroids, especially with fluorinated corticosteroids (very common in Russia) such as "Ftorocort", then the scabies may be resistant to treatment.

The usual cure is Elimite cream 5% (brand name). The Elimite cream is applied from head to toe and left on for 8 to 12 hours, then washed off. All bedding and clothing, including your clothes that have come in contact with the child should be washed thoroughly. If applying Elimite cream to an infant, apply it to yourself at the same time and leave it on for the night. Some infants should not use Elimite, as it is a poison. You need to check with your pediatrician first. One suggestion is to have a dermatologist make a salve from a vaseline base with sulfur in it and then "grease" up the child for a few days. Some children will seem to have scabies but in reality have infant actopustulosis. This is a condition that is an after-effect of scabies where the scabie mites are completely gone. It is not contagious. It is an allergic reaction to the dead scabies mites that are still under the skin. Once the dead mites have disappeared, the bumps will also disappear. The usual prescription is a strong hydrocortizone cream or Benadryl and anti-itch lotions such as Aveeno anti-itch lotion, Sarna lotion, or Calamine lotion. Do not use Caladryl due to its connection with Benedryl. Be careful if using these on an infant, as their skin is sensitive. Secondary bacterial infection is common in prolonged scabies and if this is a case—should be treated with topical and in severe cases—with oral antibiotics. Definitely see a doctor if your child has a serious case.

Be aware that it is a common practice for the children's home to hide any outbreak from the Regional Health Department (because it does not look nice on orphanage report and does not look nice on the Health Department report). Therefore, the odds of having it treated at the children's home are not good. Indeed, the home will sometimes try to pass it off as an allergy to red dye. (Of course, many children do have an allergy to Red Dye 40, but usually the rash is temporary.)

If you are able to treat your child for scabies as soon as she leaves the children's home, then apply Elimite cream all over her body from head to toe), not leaving any area non covered. The usual rule of thumb is a 60-gram tube is for one application for average adult, or 2 applications for school-age children or

3 applications for infants. Give your child a bath in the morning. Throw away all clothes she was in on the way from the children's home to the hotel/guest house (plastic garbage bags will come handy). Change bedding and wash it in the very hot water (boiling linens is usually sufficient). Think what to do with clothing, you were wearing to visit her in the home—those are contaminated too.

Do not reapply Elimite until 2 weeks after initial treatment and try not to use steroid creams, especially those, containing fluorinated hormones ("Ftorocort", for example). When you will return home you will have to re-treat everybody, who traveled, including disinfecting the luggage (washing in hot water or dry cleaning is sufficient). Ask your family doctor to check you several times if any itching lesion will appear.

Here is a pretty good link on the topic:

http://www.vh.org/pediatric/patient/pediatrics/cqqa/scabies.html and *http://www.orphandoctor.com/medical/4_2_1_5.html*

Tuberculosis

Tuberculosis is an ancient disease that was even mentioned by Hippocrates in 460 BC. In Russia, tuberculosis (TB) cases increased from 45,000 in 1991 to 125,000 in 1999. It is growing in prison and drug user populations. TB is not normally found in adoptive children, but all should be tested nevertheless.

Your child may have had a BCG vaccination for TB. BCG is made from the Calmette-Guerin bacillus. Look for the small scar on the left shoulder. BCG vaccine is routinely given in the countries of the former Soviet Union.Usually the vaccine is administered on the 5th day of life. Sometimes the vaccination is deferred because of the child's condition (sick and/or premature) and given later, at 6-12 months of age. You will need to have your child tested using the Mantoux/PPD with Candida control regardless. One consideration is that if the BCG was given recently then the reaction might very well make your child sick. Also, since the BCG may cause a reaction, your doctor must be competent to recognize when the reaction is from the BCG and when it is from an under-lying TB problem. Another problem is that your normal pediatrician will not know that he can test for TB where BCG was given. You will have to educate him. A skin reaction of <10 mm is usually due to the BCG. A result >10 mm should be interpreted as positive for exposure. Russian children are at a high risk for exposure. It doesn't mean they have the disease, but they were exposed to it at some time. BCG wanes, so never assume that a positive reaction is because of the vaccine. It has been suggested that PPD testing should be performed twice on all adoptive children—as soon after adoption as possible and, if the first test is negative or inconclusive, 6-9 months after adoption, at the same time with repeat testing for HIV, hepatitis B and C.PPD testing should be deferred if at the time of adoption the BCG scar is not healed completely and if your child recently did receive vaccination with the live vaccine (measles, mumps, rubella and/or chicken pox). Positive PPD test should not be explained by the previous BCG vaccination and should be considered indicative of TB infection (presence of the TB bacteria in the body without the disease) or even actual TB disease. Chest X-Rays usually can differentiate those two conditions.

If other children from the same home have tested positive but your child has not, then you may want to have your child retested in a year to cover any incubation period that may have been missed with the first test. If your child has a positive TB skin test (Mantoux), and a negative chest x-ray, the protocol is to treat with a daily dose of INH (isoniazid) as a prophylaxis for 9 months (some doctors do it for 6). The latest protocol is also to take rifampin with the INH. Rifampin will turn your child's bathroom experience the color orange! He may even think it's cool.

The liquid INH does have side affects such as diarrhea. An ingredient added for taste called sorbitol causes this diarrhea. Also, some children have a reaction to the sorbitol. They will vomit within a minute of taking the stuff. Also, you might notice your child begins to pick at his food rather than woofing it down as before. If you can get your pediatrician to agree, then have your pharmacist crush the INH pills and mix them in jam. That should stop the diarrhea. Some parents mix it with applesauce. Some pediatricians may not want to mix it with food, as the INH tends to bond with the food and not be completely absorbed. Some parents have switched to liquid INH and mixed it with a little water and then given it as a nighttime bottle. Some pharmacies will make the INH without sorbitol. In New York City, a pharmacy called Apthorp on the Upper West Side will make it and send it all over the country. If your doctor prescribes a two month regimen of rifampin and pyrazinamide rather than the INH, be sure to check with the CDC web site and get a second opinion. These drugs have been linked to severe liver damage.

Before starting this protocol when there is a positive skin test but negative x-ray, consult with a pediatric specialist. He may say that it is normal for her to show some reaction to the skin test due to her anemia and mild malnourished state. He may then suggest that the TB test be repeated in 1 year when she should be more nourished, anemia corrected and a stronger immune system developed, which would result in a negative skin test.

Here are websites with helpful information on TB:
http://catalog.com/fwcfc/TB_BCG.htm
http://members.aol.com/jaronmink/tb2.htm

Children's Dental Care

If you adopt an older child, you may face dental issues as soon as you return. One of your first stops should be to a dentist. Be aware that some of the children:

1. Have never had fluoridated water

2. Have rarely had milk

3. Have never taken vitamins

4. Were weaned from milk to sweetened tea

5. Drank sugary tea several times a day

6. Never saw a dentist in Russia, or did so only to have a tooth pulled

7. Never brushed their teeth before arriving in the children's home

The consequence is that the children may suffer from porous teeth, as they do not have enough calcium in the diet to support good bone growth. They may also have weak tooth enamel and lots of cavities or even gum disease. They may have had delayed development of adult teeth. Once the immediate work is completed, the good news is that after fluoride treatments, the establishment of good teeth brushing habits, vitamins, good diets, lots of calcium, and regular checkups, their teeth are remarkably improved.

If a lot of dental work is needed, yet your insurance will not cover it, consider having your child seen at a school of dentistry. They sometimes will provide free dental care as a teaching tool.

Not all children will have these problems. In some of the homes they do brush their teeth, but the problem is common enough that a dentist visit should be on your list.

Hepatitis

When you return from the United States it is recommended that your child be screened for Hepatitis A, B, and C. Until recently there were only limited treatments for Hepatitis B and C. At this time most treatments for chronic hepatitis involve the patient taking Interferon, which is rather expensive at $300 every 10 days. There are new drugs in the pipeline such as Pegintron and for Hepatitis B one called adefovir dipivoxil, which is made by Gilead Sciences. If your child does test positive, he should see a hepatologist as soon as possible and if you have not been vaccinated, you should be tested as well.

Hepatitis A is usually transmitted by drinking water or eating food that has been contaminated with fecal matter containing the virus. Symptoms only develop after the time when you are most infectious. It may cause flu-like symptoms such as fatigue, fever, poor appetite or nausea. Hepatitis A usually resolves itself in a few weeks and does not cause permanent liver damage.

Because the incubation period for hepatitis is up to 6 months, a child's hepatitis status is usually not clear until she has had two screening tests 6 months apart, or at least one test 6 months after leaving Eastern Europe. Apparent health is the normal condition of hepatitis B chronically infected children. Thus, every child must be fully evaluated.

Anyone who has either acute or chronic Hepatitis B is infectious. It is acquired mainly by bodily fluid contact and particularly blood to blood transmission, which is why you should always ask if your child has had transfusions if her medical records show a hospital visit. Hepatitis B is very contagious. If your child has Hepatitis B then all family members should have the vaccine and all caregivers should use "universal precautions" (latex gloves and a clean up solution of 1 part bleach to 9 parts water for example) for diaper changes and blood spills (i.e. bleeding nose, cuts, etc.). A person who converts to Hepatitis B anti-bodies will not be contagious. Basically they have the disease and develop natural immunity. Most children who actually have the disease do not convert, but remain chronic carriers. However, it's not uncommon when the birthmother has Hepatitis B for her Hepatitis B antibodies to circulate in the newborn child's bloodstream. They may not clear for 18 months. In that case, when and if they do clear, the child may then test negative for Hep B antibodies and be free of hepatitis (actually never had it, just the antibodies). Double check with your pediatrician regarding the type of test performed, since some are falsely told they have tested positive for Hep-B when what are actually detected are the Hep-B **anti-bodies** from a vaccine or from their birthmother's anti-bodies. It is a positive detection of Hep-B surface **antigens** that indicates the presence of an infection.

In a study by Dr. Aronson of 153 adopted Russian and 346 adopted Chinese adopted children, only 14 total, or 2.8% tested positive for the Hep B surface antigen. She also studied 495 children for Hepatitis C, and of those, 4 tested positive. Of the four children, one was from China, one from Moldova, and 2 from Russia. Two of these four children were under a year old and the antibodies disappeared by the time of re-testing. In summary, these studies are confirmation that foreign adopted children are not generally carriers of Hepatitis B and C.

At least six different genotypes and many more subtypes of Hepatitis C exist. In the United States, genotypes 1, 2 and 3 are most common. People with genotypes 2 and 3 are almost three times more likely to respond to therapy than those with genotype 1. The good news for Eastern European children is that most European strains are of genotypes 2 or 3. Genotyping can be used to determine the duration of treatment for many people. For those with genotype 2 or 3, a 24-week course of combination therapy is usually sufficient. Patients with genotype 1 who have responded at the end of 24 weeks of treatment may benefit from an additional 24 weeks of treatment.

Now if your child tests positive for Hepatitis C there is a small chance that the child will die from liver cancer in 20-30 years. But nevertheless there are treatments. Sometimes the disease never actually becomes "active," which means your child might never get sick from Hepatitis C at all. The medical world should be more advanced in treating Hepatitis C in the coming years. New treatments for chronic Hepatitis C are two peginterferon products. Schering-Plough has Pegintron and Roche has Pegasys.Ribavarin is also sometimes prescribed. Pegasys has been tested against another standard drug, Roferon-A, with a greater improvement in patients. The FDA recently cleared a more effective and longer-acting form of Rebetron for hepatitis C that has proven very popular. In 2002 an NIH panel said that the most effective treatment for chronic hepatitis C was combination therapy with pegylated interferon and ribavirin for a period of up to 48 weeks. The panel's conclusion was that combination therapy resulted in better treatment responses than monotherapy. See the NIH's statement at *http://www.consensus.nih.gov/cons/116/116cdc_intro.htm*. Also, see *http://www.fda.gov/fdac/features/2001/401_hepc.html*

A recent study reported in a 2002 issue of the American Journal of Epidemiology, downplays the risk of liver disease. Investigators discovered that the model that best matched what is seen in real HCV patients was one in which they had a relatively low rate of developing liver disease. "Because the disease progresses so slowly in some people, they are likely to reach an old age and die from something else before their hepatitis C infections ever progress to serious liver disease such as cirrhosis or cancer." For example, past studies have suggested that people infected with the virus in their 20s might develop cirrhosis anywhere from 20 to 38 years later. The new calculation suggested that half of men infected at age 25 would develop cirrhosis within the next 46 years and that fewer than 30% of women infected at this age "would ever develop cirrhosis," according to the report.

Two very good articles can be found at *http://catalog.com/fwcfc/hepatitisb.html* and *http://catalog.com/fwcfc/livingwithhepb.html*. A good website is *www.pkids.org* (click on the child, then look for the links for Hepatitis). The Hepatitis Foundation and CDC are also good resources. The Yahoo group for parents of adopted Hep B kids is *http://groups.yahoo.com/group/hbv-adoption/*.

Parasites

Giardiasis is a disease caused by the intestinal parasite, giardia lamblia. It is very common worldwide. You can get even get it from hiking in the back woods in America where it is found in streams contaminated with animal feces.

It is also common in children from institutions. Symptoms include those you would associate with gastrointestinal discomfort: diarrhea; cramps, bloating and gas; smelly stools; weakness, and weight loss. These are similar for Helicobacter pylori. Sometimes the disease exists even though no symptoms appear. Testing is usually done by detecting antigens in the stool samples (preferably 3 samples, collected on 3 separate days). Antigens are the immunological "signature" of the parasite. Relapses are common, especially in an immunocompromised host and newly adopted children are considered temporarily immunocompromised. Dr. Aronson has reported a study of 461 adopted children from various countries and 94 or 20.4% were positive. Out of the 94 children, 35 were from China, 38 from Russia, and 21 from other countries.

As a result of the disease your child's development will be delayed. He is also at risk of passing it on to other children and family members. It is very important that your pediatrician test for giardia. Symptoms range from diarrhea to weight loss to abdominal cramping. Giardia can block the absorption of major nutrients in the smaller intestines, including all fat-soluble vitamins, so a child may develop A and E vitamin deficiency.

The most common medicine given by doctors is called Flagyl (Metronidazole). The liquid version tastes just awful. Most adults hate it. Your dog will hate it. Your cat will sue you if you bring it into the house. But it is necessary in order to get rid of the disease. The trick to getting children to take liquid Flagyl (metronidazole) is to find a compounding pharmacy. These are few, but well worth a long drive to get to one. Any pharmacy can mix the meds with a flavored sugary syrup, but only a compounding pharmacy can truly mask the bitterness of the medicine. If Flagyl is mixed properly, your child may even ask for more! Some doctors prescribe Furoxone (furazolidone), which is easier to take and you may want to suggest this to your doctor. One problem with compounding the Flagyl is that some insurance companies have no clue as to why you have to and will refuse to pay for it. They insist on an NDC number of which none exists when mixing this type solution. If this is a problem then try submitting the NDC of the tablets used to make the compound or ask if a universal claim form will be accepted.

Another idea is to take Flagyl in pill form, rather than as a liquid. This is better tolerated. You could ask for small sugar coated pills.

Finally, there are other drugs just as effective as Flagyl. I would suggest recommending some of these to your doctor and see if he bites. Remember that your child may be the only child your pediatrician has ever treated for giardia, so it may be you that educates him and treats your child versus the other way around. Retesting is necessary after the cure has run its course.

There is another parasite called dientamoeba fragillis. If your child is having chronic diarrhea and it is not giardia, then have a test for this one as well as. You will also find that although a whole range of parasites were tested for the first time, that a second set of stool samples may reveal the little buggers. It is not unusual for parasites to get missed in a stool sample. If the stool sample is taken from a diaper, try to place cellophane inside so the stool does not come in contact with the diaper.

Treating giardia type symptoms that do not respond to the usual treatments can be very frustrating. You do not know if you should continue with further Flagyl or Furoxone, do a biopsy of GI tract for other pathogens (like Helicobacter pylori), look for presence of secondary infection, or test for lactose intolerance. All of these things can cause the same symptoms as giardia thereby masking the results of Flagyl treatment (since results of stool samples are often unreliable). It can be hard to tell sometimes if the Flagyl treatment was successful in eradicating giardia, if the loose stools remain, as these might be caused by other pathogens or the result of antibiotic treatment or food allergies.

Even after the infection is cleared you should be on the look out for consequences of the disease. For example, a child may suffer, post-giardia, from malabsorbtion and may need to be treated with an enzyme preparation (Ku-Zime, etc). Fat free, especially a milk-free diet can sometimes only add to the problem. Lack of fat—the building material for the intestinal wall, can predispose to delayed healing of the intestinal covering.

Subsequent to giardia treatment, the child may suffer from disbacteriosis, which is an imbalance of intestinal bacteria, which helps to digest food in the colon and an overgrowth of pathological flora, secondary to either intestinal disease or antibacterial treatment or both. If the child is taking an antibiotic you may want to ask your doctor about bacterial preparations together with any course of antibiotics. You can buy acidophilus or lactobacilli in any health food store and probably pharmacies. To a lesser degree, yogurt and other sour milk products such as buttermilk, cheese, and sour cream can also help.

Interestingly, it has been seen that in recently adopted children overeating can cause diarrhea. Their bodies cannot digest the amount of food. That condition is very common among adopted toddlers. Be sure not to limit their access to food, but provide them with easily digestible, high in fiber, healthy snacks such as bananas, applesauce, and bread.

There is also "toddlers diarrhea" caused by many factors, but mostly by apple juice. Sugars in apple juice are known to cause abnormal fermentation in the intestines and to predispose to diarrhea even in the absence of conditions. Toddler's diarrhea frequently is "treated" simply by normalizing their diet and especially their fat intake. One of the most frequent causes of constipation in pediatrics is excessive consumption of milk.

Useful web sites: *http://members.aol.com/jaronmink/giardias.htm*

Helicobacter Pylori

This is another parasite that can cause gastritis (i.e. giardia-like symptoms). If giardia is not found, then ask your pediatric GI to look for this bug. This bacterium is also associated with gastric antral inflammation and the infection is strongly associated with duodenal ulcers. Nevertheless, the bug causes a different reaction in different people and these disease outcomes are not always certain. Transmission seems to be the usual saliva and fecal route, so be careful changing those diapers.

The cure is easier than the diagnosis and a lot less painful. The usual method of diagnosis is to take an endoscopic biopsy test. This is not something most children enjoy. Almost as reliable, but not quite, is to test for the antigen. This can be done through a breath, blood or stool test. The cure is usually a treatment consisting of 3 medications: an acid suppression agent (i.e., proton pump inhibitor) and 2 antibiotics, given twice daily, for 1 to 2 weeks. The antibiotics are usually a combination of amoxycillin, tetracycline or clarithromycin. Metronidazole resistance occurs often enough so that this is not the optimum antibiotic (although doctors seem to prescribe it for giardia). Infected children who are asymptomatic are not thought to need treatment. Pediatric infection has not been studied as well as adult infection.

More than you wanted to know can be found at:
http://www.bioscience.org/2001/v6/e/lake/list.htm

Rare Food Absorption Problems

Remember the title above is "Rare" so only read this if all else fails. If you think your child is eating enough, but doesn't seem to be absorbing the nutrients then you should see a Pediatric GI. They will need to do a food absorption test (stool sample). There are some rare problems that children sometimes inherit. One is celiac disorder and another is called Alpha 1 anti-trypsin deficiency. Alpha 1 is an enzyme produced in the liver. When you have the deficiency your liver is unable to allow the enzyme into your bloodstream to do its work. One of the symptoms of the disease is malabsorption of vitamins A, D, E, and K and also fat. Your child can eat and eat yet always be skinny. There is more to it, but for the short story, ask your doctor to check for it. It is just a blood test. It is not well known in the medical community and even many doctors would not think to check for it. Most people who have it never know they do until they are in their 20's or 30's. It is genetic and passed on by both birth parents being carriers. With Alpha 1 their stools are frequent, loose, and a grayish color with a foul odor.

Sometimes they even test for cystic fibrosis since there is a very close correlation between the liver and the lungs. The Alpha 1 enzyme is what protects the lungs from harmful stuff and when you are deficient you have trouble with respiratory infections, and it can damage the lungs.

Sensory Integration Disorder (Dysfunction)

Sensory Integration Disorder is as a form of behavior by a child that is the logical reactive response to lack of early stimulation and which manifests itself to us as inappropriate or peculiar behavior. In general, early sensory stimulation enhances development of the central nervous system. If you consider that everything an infant touches, tastes or feels sends an information flow to her brain, then consider what happens when there is no such information flow. Notice that infants are interested in unusual textures like a bumpy ball, grit of a nail file, or soft ears on a stuffed bunny. Your child may not have had any of these sensory experiences in an orphanage.

A child with Sensory Integration Disorder has problems with tactile and auditory senses, as these have failed to develop properly because of this lack of sensory information flow. The child may exhibit difficulty with hearing, touching, sound or sight. A child may be overly sensitive to noise (hypersensitive) or not react normally to things that should hurt (hyposensitive). The child may be clumsy or give hugs that are too strong. The cause is not well understood. Some doctors believe that when children lack essential nutrients or human contact, or both, the links between different clusters of the brain do not work efficiently or are not formed at all. There is also a certain hierarchy in which these links are formed, so if you are trying to teach such a child, you need to return to basics and re-build weak or missing links, or otherwise there will be nothing but frustration. That frustration manifests itself in behavioral problems related to the sensory integration disorder. Luckily, occupational therapy has had very good success in re-integrating the senses. OT will use and train you to use such techniques as brushing, compressing, swinging, and playing "wheelbarrow."

Another form of therapy that has had a mixed review is Auditory Integration Training (AIT). Another is the Tomatis Listening Method. In rare cases some children may even have problems accepting solid foods, as the issue might be a severe oral aversion, which means they do not like food in the mouth. The book, The Out of Sync Child is excellent on this subject and is highly recommended.

Some behaviors may manifest themselves as a child having a very difficult time going to sleep, being very sensitive to smells and loud sounds, preferring to eat with his fingers (versus silverware), having a hard time sitting still during meals or when sleepy or nervous walk only on his tiptoes.

A proper diagnosis leads to a proper method of therapy. Brushing works for some kids but not others. Some therapy that helps is deep touch. Some OT starts with rolling a ball on the child or wrapping her in a blanket and rolling her. Some use a weighted vest to slow the child down and learn to focus. At first OT sessions can really overwhelm a child and lead to major meltdowns. You have to expect this since for kids with major SI issues, it's a huge amount of input that you're asking their brains to deal with in the beginning, and it's tough. But it should improve after a month. Both tolerance to SI input should increase as well as fine motor skills. There is an unknown, but discernable connection.

The EEadopt website has some good information at *http://eeadopt.org/home/parenting/development/sensory_integration/index.html* and also at *http://www.sinetwork.org/home/index.html.*

Post Adoption Education Issues

If you adopt an older child, one of your first questions upon returning to the United States, in addition to a medical evaluation, may be about education. Some of the children will pick up English at an incredible rate and within months be practically fluent. Others may have difficulties due to developmental delays and need help. There is a debate on whether it is better to put a Russian child immediately in school or hold him out until he is more culturally integrated. It all depends on the child. Some children respond very well to the stimulation of being in a school. Others may feel overwhelmed if they are not acquiring English fast enough.

Some basic questions are:

How quickly should I put him in school after coming home?
Should I place him in his age appropriate grade or his developmental one?
Should I keep him out and just do home tutoring for a few months?
How do I handle ESL (English as a second language)?
How should I handle objections of school officials?

A consideration in starting an older child in school is that they will likely make new friends quickly. These friends help in social and language development in a way no one else can. It helps them feel like they do belong here.

Don't be surprised if they have a slight accent. It will be part of their exotic charm.

By law school districts must provide ESL/LEP classes. LEP stands for "limited English proficiency," although some call it ELD (English Learning Development). The school districts don't want to provide LEP classes, but they must. These may meet from one to two times a week. Many ESL classes will have bilingual children where the home language is different than English. Their progress may be different than your child's although the ESL teacher may not recognize the reasons. Your child has a lot more on his plate than these children. He is trying to integrate into a new family where he must learn the family routine, family customs, how to handle new siblings and parents, trust and attachment issues, etc. The other children are not juggling all of these other issues and therefore your child's progress should not be compared to theirs. Another issue with ESL classes is that they are usually focused on Spanish or Asian speakers. This may mean that your child is better off with a private tutor or just learning at home.

Now what is interesting is that you may find that your child progressing faster than the usual ESL/LEP child. The reason is that your child's native language is not being spoken at home so he is undergoing total immersion. It is tougher for him at first, but eventually it will pay off in better English comprehension. Also, there can be a problem with the pullout ESL type of classes in that they focus on language alone while in mainstream classes they are learning actual subjects. You may have to supplement their learning by teaching them at night and on weekends until they are caught up in their subject matter knowledge.

One caveat to your child becoming fluent in English is that this fools the teachers into thinking that comprehension and social language acquisition are at the same level. Indeed, they may not even know they are separate pieces. Social language skills are obtained much more easily than academic comprehension. So your child's teachers may say that your child understands, but just doesn't get it. This is incorrect. Your child may take 2 or 3 years before he fully comprehends in a real sense, everything being said and its context, even though he was fluent in six months. Just be sensitive to that fact that fluency can mask a problem that his teachers do not appreciate. More on this difference can be found in this article at *http://www.ncela.gwu.edu/miscpubs/ncrcdsll/* click epr5.

Some older children have trouble "hearing" the difference between similar sounds "b" and "d" and "p" for instance. They may know the letter but not fully register the sounds of each letter. This may cause you to privately tutor him in this area using one of the private programs that are available. Some older children also may need help in learning English grammar and writing. It all depends on the child and whether he had any schooling before adoption. If he did have such schooling, then learning English may be easier. Dr. Boris Gindis has a very informative article on the web entitled "Language-Related Issues for International Adoptees and Adoptive Families." I highly recommend it. You can read it at *http://www.bgcenter.com/.* If you click on publications, you will see all of his articles. He has other information on this page such as what to ask the Russians when adopting an older child and how to obtain his schoolwork or teacher evaluations. Another language adoption site is *http://pages.towson.edu/sglennen/index.htm.*

All parents of older children are urged to have thorough assessments done on the child in the language of the child's country of origin to pinpoint present and future learning difficulties. Testing her as soon as she comes into the country will clarify what kind of difficulty she is having, how serious it is, and what kinds of therapy will be most effective in her treatment. Testing will also show any discrepancies in IQ vs. performance skills. If there are any discrepancies present in her base language, the assumption will be made that these discrepancies will also exist in the same subjects in English. This prevents your future kids from falling into "ESL Limbo."

"ESL Limbo" occurs as soon as your child loses her base language (often within a matter of a few months). The school personnel will start the "just wait until she has more English" litany. That wait can interfere with your child's ability to obtain services for the REAL issues of actual learning disabilities. This can inhibit you from seeking speech therapy for your child long before it is actually verified that there is a problem. Testing soon after arrival is just another way to save you possible problems in the future. It is no different from re-inoculating your kids or checking for parasites or testing for HIV, Hep B and C, and TB. If you're lucky, your children will never need services from the school system, and you can use the tests as a base line and file them away in your records.

Some children may need a school's special education services. Special education falls under the acronym of IDEA (Individuals with Disabilities Education Act), which is a federal law. Each State has its own special education regulations. Each State also has some kind of parent training education center. There is an organization that has state specific information called the National Parent Network for Disabilities (NPND). One recent change in IDEA is that the use of "developmental delay" now includes ages 3-9 whereas it was previously only for 3-5.

Getting "help" for your child obviously begins with a determination by an evaluation team that your child is "delayed". The outcome of such an evaluation should be an Individualized Education Plan (IEP)

Make sure that the child study team allows you to share your insights into the child's strengths, weaknesses and overall development. Evaluations should be non-discriminatory, which includes being done in the child's native language if necessary. This is tricky because after a few months the children are between Russian and English so it's hard to know which language to choose. Also, the written evaluation should reflect the child's strengths, not just weaknesses. The most important component of the resulting IEP should be goals and objectives. Also, the IEP must show strategies to deal with behavior problems. Remember that you are your child's only advocate. He has no one else. Don't let the school put him in a class or assign him a designation that you don't feel is appropriate.

You can also have your younger child seen for Early Intervention. This is a partially federally funded state program. It should be done by bi-lingual (Russian/English) therapists and psychologists. New York City has a good evaluation program. You can always have a formal MD evaluation, which can be completed in parallel.

If your child is about to enter elementary school you may find that a planned introduction is a great icebreaker. With the approval and assistance of the class teacher (And your child, of course) you might introduce their new classmate and show a bit of your Russian videotape. You can explain about Russia and give a brief version of your child's adoption and the obstacles he is facing such as a new country, new friends, new family and new language. A class exercise using a map of the world and letting the students find their city then your child's might be helpful. Then you might give out little flags or something indicating Russia. This exercise can be an icebreaker and the children will actually compete to help your child assimilate.

If you want your child to retain as much Russian as possible or feel that hearing Russian will help the child integrate in the family better, you may want to consider buying a satellite dish and subscribing to Russian programming. The Russian programming comes from a different satellite than the one that carries all the US stations. It is hard to aim at from the West Coast as it is barely over the eastern horizon, but it is not impossible to get a clear line of sight. For people on the East Coast this will not be a problem as the "bird" will be higher in the sky, but if you live on the West Coast, make sure you can see the eastern horizon from your roof or wherever your dish will go.

Some families buy a few Russian language videos and tapes. These are easily bought in Russia or from catalogs or websites. They have found that their child sometimes needs to hear his native language in the beginning and this can help with transition issues. They have also hired Russian speaking babysitters or teenagers to come over and play with their child, which also helps during the transition period. Finally, a Russian speaking therapist can ask your child how she is coping and allow her to fully express her feelings. These are just a few ideas of things that can help your older child make the transition into your family and to a new language.

Most of the above discussion relates to adopting the older child. However, it also applies to much younger children who were adopted with some of the risk factors as outlined by Dr. Dana Johnson. These children may manifest behavioral problems in school of which you were not aware. These issues may have always been there, but because they stayed in a family setting, they were more easily dealt with and not recognized as serious. Once these children are in a non-family environment where they are interacting with others all the time, their problems become more public. Now part of their behavior can also be related to being challenged by their schoolwork. They do fine in kindergarten and first grade, but in the third grade or fourth is when schoolwork becomes more abstract, more challenging and demanding more focus. Some of these risk factor children find themselves frustrated and begin to have developmental behavioral difficulties.

Finally, it is important to realize that these children come with significant learned survival skills, which must be un-learned for family and school success. It is not unlike de-programming.

Attachment

After the initial physical medical issues are taken care of, one of the most important psychological issues is "attachment." Attachment means bonding between a child and a parent. It happens very early with an infant and the more delayed the process the more difficult it can become. That being said, it is not impossible to have attachment at any age and if the child attached to caregivers at the children's home, or spent some time in a family setting, or is bonded with a sibling, then the groundwork has been laid.

Initial bonding by a child is not so unusual. Yet this bond can sometimes be an "insecure bond" and it may be longer before the attachment is deep and permanent. After all, you are a stranger to this child and he to you. The attachment process is something on which you should focus and work hard to nurture. Some signs of "insecure attachment" are that the child continues to be withdrawn or stiff or will show affection indiscriminately to strangers or just simply go off with anyone. Nancy Thomas has posted 21 red flags for attachment disorder on her web site at *www.attachment.org*. She believes children only need to have half to be considered at high risk and then should be diagnosed by a professional.

If it is possible to stay at home for a while, this will greatly help the bonding process. Also, try to limit social situations so that your child and your family spend as much time together as possible without outside distractions. It is also helpful if you can say some words in Russian so that your child can communicate basic needs and wants. You may also consider trying to be the sole provider of food and comfort to the child for a short time in order to establish dependence and trust. For a young toddler, you can augment bonding by holding the bottle for the child while cuddling and making lots of eye-to-eye contact and skin contact such as stroking your child's bare arms and legs while feeding. Skin-to-skin contact seems to help a lot. It's best not to let them hold the bottle or run around the house with a bottle like a typical toddler might. You want your child to give up control to you and trust you to provide for them.

Another idea that people have also used is to engage in deliberate holding, hugging and touching as much as possible. Some call this Holding Time (Dr. Welch) or baby time. You should carry an infant around as much as possible. Not in a car seat, but on your hip or in a pouch holder. If they are too heavy to carry, then sit and hold them a lot. If they are rocking, pick them up and rock them. Don't let them take care of themselves. You take care of them. You should try to make eye contact and talk softly to him. Lots and lots of eye contact. You can promote this by bending down and giving your child cookies or snacks at eye level. Let him follow you around the house or climb into your arms whenever he feels a need. Make faces, say silly words, and interact. Let him take a bath with you or spend time massaging his skin with lotion in order to promote close contact. Put the same lotion on you so you smell alike. Smells are very important to infants. Home should smell like home and mommy should smell like mommy. You might even wear the same color clothes once a week to promote how much you both are alike. Prominently place a picture of the whole family somewhere in the house. You have to recreate that early attachment time that was missed. You may even have to teach your child how to give hugs. Some parents have successfully used Theraplay, so this is another avenue to try.

Also, part of the normal integration process of a child into a new family is a process called "reparenting". It means that the child, no matter how old, may regress to a former developmental level in order to be "reparented" by the new family. This is an unconscious/subconscious effort to find his or her proper place in the fabric of the family. In many children, reparenting means rolling back to very young and immature levels because they have missed so many of the normal developmental milestones. For them, it's a double load to carry. For children who have spent entire lives within an institutional setting, they struggle with the lack of knowledge about normal family interactions.

You need to build trust and reciprocity. You can't break promises in the early stages. Their whole life has been a broken promise. Because of that these children view the world very concretely. They are black and white thinkers. They have no experience on which to base a proper response to the fuzziness of life. If you say, "we <u>might</u> go to the movies," they don't know what that means.

You will know you've succeeded when he loves to cuddle, seeks consolation from you when hurt, and is eager to see Mom and Dad when you return from the store or work. If he wants only you when other adults are around and his eye contact is good, then you should take this as a measure of success.

There are books on this subject and medical experts who specialize in the attachment field. One such book is <u>Facilitating Developmental Attachment:</u> <u>The Road to Emotional Recovery and Behavioral Change in Foster and</u> <u>Adopted Children</u> by Daniel A. Hughes. Try to avoid a traditional therapist or social worker. These professionals simply do not have the training to help a child with an attachment issue. It is like calling a plumber when you need an electrician. These professionals have been taught to look to the parents for fault, rather believe the parents about the child. This approach is completely counter-productive and tends to make the situation worse.

Other behavior to prepare for and which may or may not manifest itself is anger and grieving. Many things cause anger. Your child may have anger at his birth family for giving him up or for a lousy home life. He may be angry and grieving at leaving the only life (and friends) he has known. He may have anger and frustration at initially being unable to communicate in English or his native language with anyone. The symptoms will be tantrums, hitting, and crying. If they go on too long, seek professional help

Some early signs of serious attachment disorder can be the existence of "triangulation" after you return home. In this scenario, "mom" bears the brunt of the disorder since she is at home with the child. The child never takes to "mom" at all. He generally ignores her, disobeys, he may even hit her. "Dad", on the other hand, is the good guy and his time and attention are always sought. If you see this developing, read the books, but do not hesitate to call in the help of a therapist who specializes in attachment disorders. Do not wait too long if the behavior is serious or becomes dangerous. The Attachment center at Evergreen, P.O. Box 2764, Evergreen, CO 80437 (303-674-1910) has many good articles on the subject at *http://www.attachmentexperts.com/*. One aspect of attachment disorder that is counterintuitive is that children from physically abusive situations are in better shape than neglected ones. What these kids learn, even in a sick environment, is something about cause and effect. They learn they have some control over their environment. They are not completely powerless.

This attachment discussion should not scare you. It is the thin edge of the wedge. Many older children, who do not have a background of abuse, just breeze right through these stages without missing a beat. They have no attachment issues to speak of and the more stimulation the better. Their point of view is "World, bring it on, cause I'm ready for you." You will know the right approach to take with your child. Some children want to go to the Mall the day they come home. They want to visit people and see things and finally have some real fun. Just if you are aware of the possible behavioral reactions, even the negative, then you can be better prepared to help your child and that is what parenting is all about.

One book that many people read is Toddler Adoption: The Weaver's Craft by Mary Hopkins-Best. It is a good book and a scary one. It discusses all of the negative behaviors that could possibly happen. Do not view it as a prediction of what will occur. Some of her conclusions you may even disagree with such as that single people should avoid adopting a toddler because it's so difficult. In my opinion all parenting is hard work and the age doesn't really matter. Her book is a good place for starting discussions and to help you identify problem behaviors. Just don't rely on it as a roadmap of how your adoption will go. Indeed, her study of children does not include any children from Eastern Europe. The children she bases her research on had very different beginnings than the Eastern European children. Some had several placements. Some were domestic adoptions and others were from South America, which has a different system than Eastern Europe. Put it on the shelf as a resource book and hope you never have to pick it up again.

Transition Issues for Wobblers, Toddlers and Older Children

It is also perfectly normal to have other transition issues with your child. First, and foremost, is the fear and helplessness she might feel about being transitioned from everything and everyone she knew into an entirely new and different environment. This is culture shock to an extreme degree. All her underpinnings are gone, and it will take time and lots of patience on your part to wait for her new foundation to be built and for her to become part of your family.

Second, don't underestimate the language frustration she might go through. Even if you speak perfect Russian, she's hearing English all around her that she doesn't understand. Americans who travel to foreign countries feel the same thing. It's very disconcerting, especially if you are a verbal processor. She has all sorts of thoughts and feelings that she isn't able to express right now. The frustration of that is sometimes overwhelming. That is why an older child's transition anxiety is greatly reduced if there is someone she can speak with who knows Russian.

Now some parents have successfully used "baby signing." This doesn't have to be standard sign language, just some motions allowing for communication. This is becoming standard in regular baby classes. Parents say the English word, followed by whatever their sign might be for "please, more, thank you, all done, eat, sleep, more, bottle, milk, water, up, down, help etc." It really helps cut down on the whining, crying and overall frustration. It has also been shown to speed a child's acquisition of verbal skills.

Some other ideas to help with language acquisition are to talk to your child constantly. Describe what you are doing and what he is seeing. Just jabber away so he is undergoing immersion. Ask "Shtoh etta? What's this?" for everything, and give the English word until he starts saying it in English too. You can buy flash cards, which are used for teaching a second language. These have pictures of everyday things. There is a book called My First 1000 Words in Russian. Some parents have just used the book in reverse. It has pictures of things like the home, the doctor's office, the park, etc. and labels everything in Russian so that you can help your child make the connection. Also, you can make pictures of certain emotions like happy, sad, angry, scared, silly, etc. and allow him to communicate his feelings this way. You can buy a Russian baby bilingual video-tape at *http://store.yahoo.com/bigkids/bilingual.html*.

Transitioning an older child can take lots of time, but things do get better. The temper-tantrum/frustration stage of transition is very common for older kids. With improved English language skills this too passes. As suggested above, make some posters with different facial expressions on them like "angry" or "sad" so they can point and let you know how they are feeling. Let them listen to Russian language cassettes with songs on them. They may feel comfortable hearing familiar sounds. Just to illustrate the funny side of transitioning is a story about a family that was sending their Russian daughter to camp for the first time. She asked many questions and so they showed her pictures of the tents, cabins, activities and so forth. Then they came to a picture of a sleeping bag and she went into tantrum mode saying "no sleep in garbage bag." There will be many highs and lows, but you will get through it.

When you just return from Russia you are extremely tired. You've all had a very hard trip and will need to emotionally and physically recuperate. Be sure to eat well and get plenty of sleep. Transition work is HARD work and requires more sleep than normal. You are also extremely concerned about your new child's well being and peace of mind, but there are some rough spots she may have to work through on her own. Think about cutting down on stimulation and visits with friends and extended family for a while. Try to keep things real simple. Set a routine and stick with it. It is probably not a good idea to suddenly shower the kids with fifty new toys and then take them to Disneyland during their first week in America, or even make them the center of attention of many huge smiling strangers' faces, however well meaning. All things in due time.

Some older children fit in to a new family like a hand in a glove, but many need extra work. Provide comfort, calm, and quiet as well as some space and distance for all of you when she seems overwhelmed.

The message from professionals is to go younger on toys and games. Let them figure out the Fisher Price stuff before moving on to age appropriate toys. If they want to play baby, play baby with them. Before a child learned to run he had to learn to crawl. If he missed an early stage of development, he has to go back (with your help) and pick it up. Look at it as being akin to Pac Man, and having to go back and pick up the cherries you missed. What is interesting is that when he acquires a skill, he then will move on quickly. Many families describe going through these catch-up stages as watching a childhood video running at fast-forward. You can read some suggestions on transitioning at http://adoption.about.com/cs/understanding/a/chat_transition.htm.

You may find that alcohol was a factor in your older child being placed in the children's home. The parents' rights may have been terminated because of alcohol abuse. If this situation exists, you may wish to consider limiting alcohol in your home, as it may be a concern to your child.

Some parents also find that older children need to be transitioned to proper hygiene. Toilet paper may have only been used once a day. Nor are they are used to flushing it. You may not be able to get the point across to use it every time (for girls) so you might concentrate instead on daily baths with complete clothing changes.

They will not have taken baths frequently, nor changed clothing as often as we do. Oral hygiene will not be up to American standards, either. Get some cute toothbrushes and flavored toothpaste. Many children do not know how to bathe themselves and they might need a lesson. Try cute towels and wash clothes or sponges. It is likely that the boys are not circumcised and they may need some instruction on keeping the area clean in order to reduce infections. If the genital area is red, there is a likelihood of an infection, which you should bring to the attention of your pediatrician.

They may not be used to sleeping in pajamas. In the children's home they did not t have top sheets, just a duvet with a cover. Try having them sleep in oversize T-shirts. There will be many, many little differences that you will see. A thousand little things will amaze them, from how to buckle a seat belt to how to use a single lever faucet.

Institutionalized children have had less experience in making choices than children raised in a family. They do not know about food choices, clothing choices, activity choices, etc. Don't overwhelm them by presenting them with what to them are difficult choices. Don't send them to the closet to just "pick something." Let them choose between just two items instead. Be careful not to overdo anything. Reduce the amount of stimuli to which they are subjected. Going to the grocery store is like going to the circus for them. You also have to be very careful taking kids out in public who do not speak English and could not ask a stranger for help. You need to be sure they will stay with you and not run off before you do so. Give them structure by providing them with a schedule or a heads up on what you and they will be doing that day or that week. Don't just let them do anything in an open handed manner. They want and need guidance from you.

You may find your older child seems ungrateful or disinterested in the things you give her. It may be she is afraid to like anything too much, since it might be taken away from her. It's an instinctual protection mechanism that helped her cope in the orphanage. Reassure her and let her pick out things for herself as much as possible, so she understands that these are hers and you will not take them away. Within a few months, when she's built up more confidence that you are in this for the long haul, you will find a change in her attitudes. You can also have the other extreme where the child wants more and more. This could be the result of the caregivers having told them that once in America they could have anything they want!

With toddlers you may find that he needs and wants to be treated like a baby. This can be wonderful if you thought you might have missed out on his "baby time." Even a 12 year old will like an affectionate hug and maybe sitting next to you or on your lap during quiet time. A toddler may also want to stay in a crib longer than other children. He may consider it his private or safe place and enjoy "his crib." There is no urgency to moving a child to a bed. He'll get there before he goes off to college.

If your child needs to be near you and can not play in his room by himself, realize that he has never had anyone like you before. His emotional needs are like that of a 3 year old and he needs to be near you or within eyesight. He is simply not ready to move to self-play like a bio 6 year old might be. He'll get there eventually, but don't get frustrated if he doesn't want to leave you alone. He is just making up for years of lost emotional feelings.

The children will love being praised, as they have never had that before. They also like it when adults act silly and joke around. This will be new to them as well.

An older child will not know how to get in and out of a car (machina), and how not to ding other car's doors. So you might consider parking away from other cars until he learns. They won't know how to cross our streets or use a seat belt. They don't usually have seat belts in Russian cars. Also, be prepared for initial motion sickness. They may play with all the buttons, dials and switches they can get their little hands on so make sure the door locks can not be opened by them *while the car is moving!* Even if your child is 8 years old, childproof your home as if he were a toddler. He will figure out the rules pretty quickly, but during that transition stage he will try every dial on the stove, microwave, light switch, electric outlet and gas switch. Put the cleaning fluids away. Make sure to tell them that when they eat a muffin, not to eat the muffin paper and that melted cheese is not glue. They may have a problem with corn on the cob, since in Russia that's what you feed farm animals. Automatic doors and bathroom hand dryers can be scary, if you've never seen one before.

Here are some suggested foods to try at first: hot dogs and other cured meats, meatloaf, chicken, fish, vegetable soup, yogurt, white cheeses, oatmeal and other cooked cereals, fruits, crackers, and breads. They probably will not have ever eaten lettuce, peanut butter (be careful of any allergic reaction), cold cereal, colored cheese, broccoli, sweet corn, or steak. Fresh fruit is considered a treat in the orphanages and bananas in particular. So they are likely to revel in all the fresh fruit. Many families suggest keeping a large bowl of fruit on the table. Just be conscious of too much indulgence by children whose bodies are not used to it. Cold cereal with milk will be an unfamiliar item. Cream of Wheat or oatmeal will be something they are used to. Fried food is not a usual staple for them. While it should not take any longer than saying "McDonalds," to have them woofing down French fries, it still will be an unusual item at first. The children are not used to carbonated sodas or any drink with ice. Eastern Europe serves drinks warm. Tea is a regular staple of their diet. You may have to wean them from it depending on their age.

Sometimes you may see behavior such as gorging. This is usually a reaction to suddenly having lots of food available and three times a day at that! They have to learn that you will give them another meal as good as this one and soon. You have to find a balance between letting them eat a lot and not letting them eat so much they become sick. Usually this behavior does not last longer than a few months. Other manifestations of this behavior is to count the food in the cabinets to make sure there is plenty there and to eat any crumbs that fall on the floor. Just be understanding and this too will pass.

Hoarding is another behavior sometimes seen in toddlers and older children. It is for the same reason as the gorging phenomenon. Be understanding, as you would act the same if you were in their shoes. You might find food under beds, in sock draws, or in closets. This behavior can go on as long as six months, but eventually it slows down.

Many of these children have had nothing to call their own. What they did have, they shared with their "group." You may be surprised when something you bought your child ends up with a playmate. At the other extreme, some children react to this early experience by taking little things from you and hiding them. They can also be very sensitive to other children in the house taking items from them. All of these behaviors are normal reactions to their experience of which you need to be aware and gradually modify.

Try to find out before you leave the children's home, how the kids were disciplined. In some children's homes, children are placed in time-outs by being isolated in a room with the door shut. You may find that by repeating this response at home you are scaring the child and that a better time-out is just to place her on a couch in view of people. Some other places spank and yell at the children. If yelling was the method, then yelling at home may have little effect. You are the judge of what is appropriate; just realize that certain responses that mimic orphanage life will be frightening to her.

Older boys tend to play rough, as there wasn't anyone at the children's home to referee. It is like growing up in the Lord of the Flies pre-school and suddenly being told you have to play nice. There is an adjustment period before the new rules sink in. While this behavior could be a sensory issue, it could also just be that you need to modify the behavior by putting him on a short leash until he learns what is appropriate play. Dads understand this better than Moms. They were boys once too.

Children think in very concrete terms. Brothers and sisters are those children with whom the child lives. It is not a genetic term to a child. As children mature it changes and during adolescence many adopted people begin to feel intensely interested in the concept of genetic connection and what it might mean for them. Every child deserves to be wanted, loved, and valued for who he is rather than as a stopgap or replacement for a child one dreams of parenting. Nuture a sense of shared family culture. Highlight holiday traditions as a family. Share family mealtimes and bedtime rituals. Repeated games and visits to favorite places all contribute to each child's sense of "us" as a family unit. A common store of family based and sibling inclusive family experiences enhances the sense of family that each takes into adulthood.

Again, these are just general comments. Your child may have none of these questions or issues. Children are very much like snowflakes.

Adoption Disruption

Not every adoption is a success story. Sometimes an adoption, no matter how much effort is put forth to make it work, just doesn't. When an adoption fails after the decree, the term used to describe the event is "disruption." It describes adoptive parents cutting ties with a child and handing him back to the agency for placement, or placing him in state custody if the agency refuses to help. When an adoption fails before a final decree of adoption is issued, it is described has a "dissolution." Since most Eastern European adoptions are completed in the foreign country, most of these adoptions that fail are "disruptions." (Note that some professionals use the terms in the reverse.) Disruption is a hundred times worse than divorce. It is divorcing your child.

Starting in 1994 Tressler Lutheran Services began receiving calls from families asking for help with disrupting their adoption. These were mainly Eastern European adoptions. In the entire previous 10 years Tressler had only become called on 18 adoptions. From 1994 to 2002 they had been asked to become involved in 172 Eastern European adoptions with slightly more boys than girls. These were not Tressler families, but other families that had heard that Tressler worked with difficult situations. Tressler was able to place about 10% of these children. Russia led the numbers of children, but that made sense since Russia provides the bulk of Eastern European adoptions. Calls on Ukrainian children began to come in by 2000 as those adoption numbers rose. One theory regarding Ukraine has been that the pick-and-choose method places families at a great disadvantage at a time when they are most vulnerable and when they have few medical resources on which to call upon. At least with Russia, you can have the child's information reviewed between the two trips and you can also change your mind before the second trip. The importance of having the medical information translated before you decided cannot be overestimated.

The majority of disruptions happen with one year of the adoption. Some families have said that when they got home, they sort of knew right away that there was a problem. Yet many of these families give a tremendous effort over the years before calling for help from Tressler. The average age of the child Tressler was called about was 6 years old at adoption and 8 years old when the family called. The youngest child whose adoption was disrupted was 7 months. The oldest was a 17 year old, adopted at 15.

One comment you hear from adoption professionals is that the America culture of wanting everything done in a minute, with a no hassle home study, and no medical reviews of the child makes families vulnerable. The idea is just get it done, and give me my child now so I can have that perfect family and then get back to my life. I think this is a mischaracterization of most families, but it still paints a portrait of how moving too fast and wanting an instant family works against families when it comes to adoption. Adoption needs to be a carefully thought out process. It is for a lifetime, not until the next model.

There have always been disruptions in adoption. But the numbers seem to be growing. Yet no one actually tracks the numbers. There are no firm statistics. At the meeting on Hague intercountry regulations in 2001, parents pleaded for the US government to require agencies to report disruptions. The State Department, who doesn't really want to be involved in adoptions, but is being forced to by Congress, seemed surprised that it was an issue.

There haven't been any studies into the causes of disrupted international adoptions. Most studies have been of domestic adoptions, particularly those involving special needs. You can read a summary of such studies at *http://www.adoptiondisruption.com/disruption.html*. It is difficult to use the findings from domestic special needs adoptions and apply them directly to international adoptions.One unofficial survey of agencies placed disruptions at 2 percent of all international adoptions. Again, this isn't from any official source or study.

So what we are left with is anecdotal evidence of factors that might be called "red flags." Red flags do not mean that an adoption should not proceed, but rather that parents should recognize that this adoption under these circumstances poses a greater risk to their family, marriage and to the success of the adoption.

Some parents want to adopt two, unrelated children at one time so that they can save money and only travel overseas for one adoption process. That is a red flag. They have their instant family and they saved money in the process, but there is more to making everyone feel like they are part of a family than just a Decree.

Parents who want to adopt and have an instant family with two unrelated children may be looking at a very difficult time. Often one child is more delayed that the other and needs much more attention. So that child gets the attention and the one who is doing pretty well gets less attention. These kids have never been "filled up" and they all deserve their "own" time in a family where they are the only one special. Institutionalized children come with different backgrounds and situations and need to be able to be the "new" child. This is similar to when a family gives birth to a second child. The first one still gets attention, but the second one also needs to gain "their own place" in the family.

Now parents have good reasons, usually financial, for adopting two at once. Many parents have done so and it has all worked out, but red flags are meant as warnings that in some adoptions, it has not worked out and needs to be thoroughly thought through.

Where it has not worked out is when there is a wide difference in age between the two children, for example, a 4 year old and a 12 year old. Also, if the couple has had no other children, the parents are suddenly thrust into the learning curve of parenting a toddler and a teenager. Add to this is the extra attention one or both may need and the time involved with their medical appointments, and speech therapy appointments and you have one stressed out mom. You can have the same stress where you adopt two and they are close in age, but the children become "Irish" or virtual twins and can play with each other. That is a benefit to adopting two close in age that can help.

Here is another red flag situation. A couple with 3 children between the ages of 10 and 18 that wants to adopt two unrelated children between 5 and 7......*and both work full time!* Is this a family or a foster home? When are the parents going to have time for these new family members? They will need lots of attention. They may have speech, attachment and other developmental delays. Who is going to take them to the therapist while these parents juggle the needs of three older children and their full time jobs? This situation could work if there were supporting family members that could lend a hand. Perhaps the oldest child could carry some additional responsibilities. The question really is whether the family has thought through the whole scenario and made back up plans if certain situations or needs develop. This is the job of their home study social worker, but the ultimate responsibility for making this adoption work or not, lies with the parents.

If you want to adopt two at once, then consider siblings. Siblings who knew each other in their Russian family or the children's home have learned to create a family with each other. Sibling adoptions seem to do better. Just make sure that they are real siblings and not just siblings by birth. Some siblings are either too far apart in ages or live in different homes or simply never have been together to create that "family bond" that is the essence of being a real sibling. If you adopt an 8 and a 4-year-old sibling pair, it is possible that you are actually adopting two children that live in different homes, have no bond and for all intents and purposes are really unrelated. On the other hand, families have adopted a child and his unrelated, but best friend in the Destky Dom and have had a great experience. Again, where a child has had a previous bonding experience, even to an unrelated child, attachment issues are not as prevalent.

Another red flag for adoption is a child who has been sexually abused coming into a family that has younger children. These children need to be adopted by a family that has no other child living in the house. Not only will therapy be a long process, demanding time and attention from the parents, but also the other children in the house will be at risk.

Some of the descriptions from families where the child has serious reactive attachment disorder are chilling. "He is like a hollow soul. He is a like a Stepford child. He has nothing inside. There is no real child in there." RAD, with a lot of work, and the right **attachment** therapist, as opposed to the garden variety therapist who can do more harm than good, can be overcome in many cases over several years. Yet, the truth is that not every child can be saved.

Some domestic studies have also concluded that older parents have fewer disruptions and that the higher the educational level of the mother the greater the risk. The explanation of the first is that older parents have more patience and more time to spend. The theory on the second is that mothers with higher education levels have higher expectations. These expectations push against the reality of an adoptive child who not only does not have the same DNA, but also did not have the best pre-natal and post-natal care. When the expectations push too hard, the adoption breaks. Without adequate studies there is no way to tell if these same findings hold true for international adoption. You can find a discussion on disruption at *http://www.calib.com/naic/pubs/s_disrup.cfm* and *http://specialchildren.about.com/library/weekly/aa103000a.htm*, however, note that these discussions are only on domestic adoptions and focus more on special needs adoptions. Both discussions rely extensively on the work of Professor Barth at Chapel Hill.

Anecdotal evidence also suggests that the most vulnerable families to disruption are those with a high income and high education, who are used to succeeding and cannot imagine failing. They have no idea of what it is like to have a child in their home that doesn't do what they say (what child does). They begin to doubt their ability to parent. Having things not go their way is incredibly hard to deal with for a successful perfectionist. There are some very good life lessons to be learned from failure, as opposed to always succeeding. Failure early in life does not hurt as much and you can learn and grow. If you have them late, they hurt much more. This can rebound on the child and suddenly the parent's solution to parenting difficulties is simply to give up on that child.

Parents sometimes will say that they have a high income and a big home. "We have a lot to offer a child." But a child doesn't need a high income. The currency in childrearing is endless patience, silliness, laughing together and hugs. Family love is based on popcorn and movie watching in the family bed. Based on anecdotal evidence, the degree of disruptions among blue collar families is much less. The theory is that these families have more room in their hearts and lives for difference. They may not be looking for the "perfect" mini-me child and may have grown up in large families where difference and difficulty was the norm.

A factor that does seem to hold true for both domestic and international adoptions is that the older the child, the greater the risk of disruption. Again, this does not hold true for sibling adoptions and just means that with an older child adoption you must push for as much information as you can before making your decision. An older child adoption benefits the most from a two-trip process and from not having the appeal period waived as you have the opportunity to spend more time with the child in their original environment.

Here is a checklist for red flags:

1) The parents are divided about the child or adoption process. One parent is not completely onboard, but just going along for the ride.

2) One parent becomes the target of the child's behavior, while the child presents a completely different picture to the other. Usually it is the mother who bears the brunt of the behavior.

3) Parents begin to dread the inevitable call from day care or school about the child's behavior.

4) The marriage begins to resemble a negotiation session between parents and the marriage part is ignored.

5) Parents feel like psychiatric workers rather than mom and dad.

6) There is little joy or happiness in the house.

7) A parent begins to feel rage toward the child.

8) Previous multiple placements where the child has bounced around

9) The child was part of a previous disrupted adoption.

10) The child has serious reactive attachment disorder.

11) The child has a history of abuse or serious neglect.

12) Families who were given poor preparation by their agency or who opted for the No-Hassle-Adoption Agency. The family had a pie in the

sky view about adoption. They were enamored with idea of "saving" a child, rather than being focused on the actual child's needs and their family's need.

13) It's the second child. The first child was wonderful and then the second child comes along and has more needs and the family cannot stretch.

14) The child is viewed as a replacement for the perfect child the parent's couldn't have because of infertility. No one should ever ask a child to fill that role. That child doesn't exist. It is totally unfair to this adopted child who is an individual in her own right with her own genes, personality and emotions.

Finally, some disruptions occur through no fault of the child or children. The parents are just not able to give the child what she needs and vice versa. The adoption may have occurred because only one parent wanted it. Or it occurred because the parents thought it would save the marriage. There are also those rare cases, usually with older adoptions, where a child has been so damaged by her Russian family or institutionalization that she simply cannot meld normally into a family environment.

Agencies should also avoid contributing to the risk by giving the family multiple caseworkers. Just as the family gets comfortable with a caseworker and vice versa, she leaves them. Agencies also sometimes rush a family saying,…"You have 24 hours to make up your mine." You cannot do this to people. Another couple of days or a week won't hurt the child. He has been in foster care or an institution for a year, what s a couple of days. Agencies sometimes say…"if you don't adopt him now, then another family will get him." Fine. The child will get a forever family regardless. Wait for the next referral. These sorts of agency behaviors are simply wrong.

A major problem is who is there to help the family. Can the family turn to the home study agency or the placement agency? Many times the agencies do not help but say "sorry, our job ended with placement." Well, that's wrong. Maybe it doesn't extend for 20 years, but an agency has to help a family, even if it is there only to provide support or respite. A good agency will have a reserve of families in the wings who have special skills or special situations where they can take in disrupted children. Yet, some agencies have no resources at all. Most international adoptions work out just fine. For the small number that do not, a good agency should have a contingency plan.

Realize that many states DO NOT have ANY services available, particularly through social services, for kids who are adopted from foreign countries, even though they are now citizens. This is the way they disqualify for services, with the ever-shrinking state and federal budgets. Instead parents can face child endangerment charges if they keep a dangerous child in the home and child abandonment charges if they don't. If the state does take the dangerous child away, the parents can be financially charged for his/her care.

Children from disrupted international adoptions are available for adoption domestically and there are adoption agencies that assist in these placements. As an example, Tressler Lutheran Services has placed disrupted children and Global Adoption in Wyoming has a small camp/ranch where the children can go to heal. Other agencies have provided services as well. There have been many cases of successful forever families being formed from these placements. Adopting from a disruption still entails costs for a homestudy, lawyer's fees, and other items. If the child is moved from one state to another you MUST have approval from the Interstate Compact Coordinator for both states. Before even considering to adopt a child from a disruption, you must read Daniel Hughes' and Martha Welch's books. These children need a full time parent. You should not adopt a child from a disruption and think daycare will heal these children. It won't.

Here are helpful email groups:

http://groups.yahoo.com/group/adoptfromdisruptedadoptions,
http://groups.yahoo.com/group/adoptingfromdisruption/,
http://groups.yahoo.com/group/disruptedadoptions/,
http://groups.yahoo.com/group/HelpWithDisruptinganAdoption/
http://groups.yahoo.com/group/AdoptingHardToPlaceChildren

There is a news articles on the subject at *http://www.post-gazette.com/headlines/20000814russiadaytwo1.asp.* This article exaggerates the problem because the disruption numbers are small, but is worth reading because in the families in which it does occur the pain is immense.

There have been a few cases where the parents adopt a child and before leaving Russia and they discover that the child has issues that make the adoption impossible. These are not cases where the child is throwing tantrums or just being very difficult. It is not so unusual that occasionally a child is difficult. After all, he doesn't speak your language, doesn't know you from Adam, and doesn't know why he is with you or where he is being taken. You'll probably be told to hang in there and indeed in about 4 weeks of being home and a few trips to McDonalds things would have settled down. Situations where the adoption is in real trouble before leaving Russia is where the parents *know* there is a problem. I can't describe it any better than that. Remember parents want this adoption to succeed so it takes a lot for them to put the breaks on. A situation might be where the child exhibits evidence of having been sexually abused and the parents were never told and they might fear for a younger child in their house. Another might be where a child exhibits extreme RAD behavior, which the parents know is beyond their help. These cases are few and far between, but it has happened. Don't let the agency sugarcoat this for you and tell you to just come home. These are situations where you really do know this child has problems beyond your ability. Russian law allows for a reversal of an adoption. You go back to the Judge and in consultation with your translator, prosecutor, children's home director and DoE, the adoption is reversed. It is a sad day. The parents are always heartbroken. The law is at Statute 142 of the Russian Family Code. Here is a translation:

http://eeadopt.org/home//preparing/paperwork/laws/countries/russia/ russian_excerpts_1996.htm.

Finally, it is easy to be judgmental and tell a family what they should have done......when you haven't walked an inch in their shoes. Unless you have tried to parent a seriously RAD kid with soul destroying problems, you have absolutely no idea what a family goes through.

CHAPTER XIV

LAGNIAPPE

Social Security

Applying for your child's social security card is the easiest thing you can do. You should try to do it as soon after you return and have had a chance to settle down. You must go personally to the social security office. If you are in an urban area there will be several to choose from. Take all of your originals with you. You can fill out the form before you go or fill it out at the office while you wait. It's a short form so it won't take you but a minute to do. It is Form SS-5. You can call Social Security at 1-800-772-1213 and they might send it to you. You can also download the form from their web site at
http://www.ssa.gov/online/ss-5.html

Most social security personnel do not know that your IR-3 child is automatically a US citizen, nor do they care. Do not try to argue the law to these people. It is like talking to an orange. You can try a supervisor, but the odds are against you. If they do give you any trouble about anything, an alternative is to find another office where the IQ is above room temperature or wait until the person you spoke with is not there.

If you can wait until you have received your child's US Passport, then do so. Amazingly, the Social Security Office will actually honor an American Passport and allow your child to be entered on their computers as a US citizen. However, if you do not have the US Passport then they will want to see your child's green card. The odds of having such a card within a month or two of returning are astronomical so do not worry if you don't have it. If you do not have the US Passport, show them her Russian passport with the IR-3 number stamped inside. This proves that she is an authorized resident alien. Show them her Russian decree and the English translation. They will make a copy of both and tell you that they have Russian translators who will verify the translation. (Yeah, right!) They will give you back all originals once they have used their trusty copy machine.

Show them her amended birth certificate with translation. They will also want some identification as to who you are. A passport or driver's license will suffice.

The terrific thing is that you will receive the social security card within 2 weeks to a month later. The social security number will allow you to file your tax return and claim all child deductions and credits. You can do all that without the number, by using your child's A# stamped in his passport, but having it just makes life easier. The first three digits on the card refer to location and are determined by the zip code of the mailing address shown on your application. Each state is assigned a series of numbers, for example 318-361 for Illinois. More than you ever wanted to know can be found at *www.ssa.gov/foia/stateweb.html*.

If you did not have her US Passport when you applied, be sure to return to the Social Security office once your child has her BCIS citizenship certificate or United States Passport. The reason is that you will need to change your child's designation in their computers from "alien" to "citizen." It makes a difference as to available benefits. If they make an error on the spelling of the name or anything else, it is easy to change. Just takes another trip and filling out the same form again.

Here is a SSA memo in which the agency acknowledges the existence of the Child Citizenship Act and although it is a federal law, they say they will refuse to follow it. *http://www.ssa.gov/immigration/children.htm*.

The form itself is easy. First put in the full name of your child. Ignore the part about "full name at birth if other than above." This does not apply. At paragraph 3 mark the box for "Legal Alien Allowed to Work." If you don't believe it, just look at the IR3 stamp in her Russian passport. If you have already received her United States Passport you then check the citizen box. You can try to explain to the Social Security office that your child is a citizen automatically and does not need a US Passport to prove it, but they will not believe you. At paragraph 6, just put down whatever the information is shown on the amended birth certificate. If you have changed the date and place of birth, then use those. The answer to paragraph 10 is "no."

Green Card (Not green and not a card)

The famous "Green Card" has a dark secret, it's not green, it's sort of pink and its not a card, it's laminated plastic. The BCIS will automatically send it to you after you return, even if your child is a US citizen. When we talk the government wasting money, there is no better example than the BCIS manufacturing and sending an alien registration card to someone who is already a US citizen. The card will have on it your child's picture and the IR3 number. It usually arrives at your house between two months to a year after you return. You should place it in your safety deposit box as a memento of your trip. You will only need it if your child entered the US on an IR-4 visa and needs to apply for a citizenship certificate. At that time the BCIS will want you to send it in. There is really no point to having a "green card" at all for most Eastern European adoptions, since the Citizenship Act automatically makes all IR3 children citizens. It is now nothing more than a memento. You will need it though, if you are planning to take your child out of the country before you have received your child's US Passport. In order to be able to leave and return, your child will need his Green Card and one other document from the BCIS.

Tax Considerations

This is not meant to be tax advice, and you should consult your accountant, but here are some informational reminders. When you return you should obtain your child's social security number as soon as possible. It should not take more than a month to receive it. With this number, and barring a few exceptions, you may be able to receive the following benefits: dependent deduction, child tax credit, and adoption tax credit.

The Adoption Tax Credit is a wonderful gift from your government that was extended in 2001.It sunsets in 2010, however, Congress is working on extending it. It is also more complicated than it looks. In general it provides a tax credit (worth far more than a deduction) up to $10,000 per international adoption. It also has provisions relating to employer provided assistance. To take the credit you need to fill out and follow Form 8839 when you file your tax return. You should carefully read IRS Publication 968. Both of these can be downloaded from the IRS website at *http://www.irs.ustreas.gov* or you can call 1-800-TAX-FORM. The publication is located at *http://www.irs.gov/pub/irs-pdf/p968.pdf.*

The Economic Growth and Tax Relief Reconciliation Act of 2001 ("EGTRRA"), enacted on June 7, 2001, incorporated the provisions of the Hope for Children Act, previously passed by the House. These provisions extend the adoption credit for children and raise the maximum credit to $10,000 per eligible child. The beginning point of the income phase-out range is increased to $150,000 of modified adjusted gross income. This is double the previous amount. The phase out is complete at $190,000 of modified AGI. Finally, the adoption credit is exempt from the provisions of the alternative minimum tax. EGTERRA also extends the exclusion from an employee's taxable income of employer-provided adoption assistance and raises this amount to $10,000 per eligible child.

The Act left several provisions alone. It did not change the carry forward section, which allows you to carry the credit forward for up to five years. It also allows you to apply the credit against expenses incurred in the year prior to the adoption becoming final. You are still required to provide a tax identification number for your child in order to take the credit.

One idea to consider if you are close to your court date is whether you want to pay for your adoption by reducing the amount of your withholding. This would allow you to take advantage of the credit while the adoption is still a work-in-progress rather than having to front the expenses and wait for the refund. Obviously there is a risk here as well, but it is a thought.

For more information see Rep. DeMint's web site and also this one: *http://www.house.gov/jct/x-50-01.pdf.*

Also, do not forget to check into any state credits for which you may be eligible. For example, Missouri gives a $10,000 credit for special needs adoptions, including international adoption.

The Child Citizenship Act of 2000

Children who arrive in the United States on an IR-3 visa acquire US citizenship automatically upon admission to the United States. Children with IR-4 visas have to wait until they are adopted or re-adopted before they qualify under the Act. Readoption requirements may be waived by the State Department, if the state of residence of the United States citizen parent(s) recognizes the foreign adoption as full and final under that state's adoption laws. Michigan appears to be one of these. The Child Citizenship Act, public law 106-395, was signed in 2000 and amends the Immigration and

Nationality Act (INA) to permit foreign-born adopted children to acquire US citizenship automatically if they meet certain requirements.

To be eligible, a child must meet the following five requirements:

1)   The child has at least one United States citizen parent (by birth or naturalization);

2)   The child is <u>under</u> 18 years of age;

3)   The child is currently residing permanently in the United States in the legal and physical custody of the United States citizen parent;

4)   The child is a lawful permanent resident; and

5)   An adopted child meets the requirements applicable to adopted children under immigration law.

The new law applies retroactively to adopted children who are under the age of 18 on February 27, 2001. It is not retroactive as to those children over the age of 18 as of that date.

Your child will not receive automatic proof of citizenship. If you want a Certificate of Citizenship, you must a N-600 form and pay the fee of $145.00 and wait the usual long time. You will not be required to submit any evidence that is not already contained in the BCIS file, including translations of documents. (Your child's BCIS file is the material in the unopened visa envelope you give the BCIS when you reenter the US.) You only need to submit photographs and a check for $145.00. There will only be an interview if the BCIS has questions. In most cases BCIS will simply send you the COC and ask you to return the Alien Registration "Green" card.

An adopted child born and residing outside the United States cannot acquire citizenship under this new law, but must file a N-600K application with the regular supporting material. If a permanent US address is given, and the residence abroad is actually <u>temporary</u>, then a child can gain automatic citizenship by simply making an airplane stop in the US and getting the IR3 number (BCIS I-551 stamp) stamped into her passport.

When the Citizenship Act was enacted, the BCIS promised to work toward streamlining the process of obtaining a certificate of Citizenship. Almost everyone thought they would simply send you the Certificate in the mail, rather than the "Green" card. No such streamlining occurred. Rather, in 2003 the BCIS created a whole new form, the N-600, in which they ask a whole new set of intrusive questions about you, and this *after* your adoption. Even the BCIS suggests that if you need proof of citizenship, you should get a passport instead.You do not need a Certificate of Citizenship in order to obtain a passport. The BCIS' position is that a passport is both cheaper and quicker to obtain as a proof of citizenship.

More information on the Child Citizenship Act can be found at *http://travel.state.gov/childcitfaq.htm,*
http://www.immigration.gov/graphics/publicaffairs/backgrounds/cbground.htm
and *http://frwebgate.access.gpo.gov/cgi-bin/getdoc.cgi?dbname=2001_register&docid=01-14579-filed.pdf*

Passport

The best and easiest piece of paper to obtain in this whole journey is your child's US passport. The benefit of applying is that you will no longer have to use her original foreign passport or adoption certificate to prove she is an American citizen, but can use a derivative document like a US passport.

You can download the application at *http://travel.state.gov/download_applications.html.* You will need to file the forms DS-11 and DS-3053.

Once you have obtained your child's passport you can use that as proof of identity and citizenship for such things as school, job and future passports. It is also easier to replace if lost. Obtaining a passport is important as you can then safely put away all of the other documents.

To apply for your child's passport the passport office requires you to submit:

1) A certified copy of the final adoption decree. This will need to be translated, if from overseas. If it is from your state, then have the clerk give you a certified copy.

2) Either the child's foreign passport with the BCIS stamp (IR-3# or 4#) or the child's resident alien card;

3) Parent's identification.

4) A notarized letter from the non-filing parent stating he/she wants the passport.

5) Two photographs and a $70 fee.

If you re-adopt in your state, you can submit the state birth certificate and re-adoption decree, rather than the Russian documents. Some passport offices want the translation of the Russian Decree notarized. In other offices, this is not a requirement. If you do not have a notarized translation, just submit it to another office or to another person in the same office.

The passport office promises to treat these documents as carefully as they used to treat the Certificate of Citizenship and return them with the passport. You can avoid being nervous about your documents if you go to one of the 13 passport offices (not a post office or probate court) where they will make copies of your documents and hand them back to you. These offices are only in the largest cities. Be aware that these offices say they will only process passports for those who will be traveling within two weeks. The list of these offices is located at *http://travel.state.gov/agencies_list.html.*

Like the BCIS and Social Security, not every passport office has the same rules. Big surprise! Some offices will accept the Russian Adoption Decree as translated into English by your translator. Others will require you to have a "certified" translation. In some offices this means a cover letter notarized by your agency stating that the translations are true and correct. In other offices you have to pay a US translation service to put their seal of approval on it. Also, some offices require you to provide your child's amended birth certificate and others do not.

Your child does not need to have a social security number in order to obtain a US Passport. If you do not yet have your child's social security number, you can just put a string of zeros in box #6. If some post office clerk claims that you do need a social security number, first tell him he is wrong and second, show him a copy of the federal statute at 26 U.S.C. 6039E. Once you have the Passport, you can use it at the Social Security office to have your child designated a citizen, rather than an alien.

It takes about 6 weeks to receive the child's passport, if you do not pay for expedited service Some people have suggested paying the passport office for expedited service and enclosing an overnight envelope. Be aware that technically you are suppose to show an immediate need to travel before you can use the expedited service. This requirement is not strictly enforced during the off-season, but it is during the busy season like the summer. It is suggested that you take a copy of the State Department's fact sheet on the Act, located on their website, when you apply for the passport. Also, do ask for a supervisor if the entry personnel appear unaware of the Act.

Re-Adoption

Re-adoption is also called domestication of adoption. The federal government and all states recognize your child's adoption, if your child enters the country on an IR3 visa. This visa designation means that both parents saw the child prior to the adoption. Iowa used to make you file for a re-adoption before they would recognize the adoption even under an IR3 visa. Iowa finally changed its law in 2002 because one adoptive parent decided enough was enough. Never underestimate the power of one to make a change. About half the states make no provision at all regarding re-adoption. They simply have no law on it at all. Here is a web site containing a full review of all 50 States' requirements in regard to re-adoption: *http://www.calib.com/naic/pubs/l_abroad.cfm*

If your child entered the United States on an IR-4 visa, then you have to look to your states' laws to determine if you need to re-adopt. You will, in almost all cases, need to do so, but check with your states' laws. The State Department says that generally, where a child has an IR-4 visa, because only one married parent saw the child, then the child has entered the United States on a sort of "proxy" basis (even if it is final according to the sending country). The IRS calls this a "simple" adoption (although there was nothing simple about it). Whether both parents must re-adopt or just the one that did not see the child depends on your states' laws. The State Department will honor whatever your state says is a final adoption and let the Child Citizenship Act kick in and give your child a US passport. Michigan doesn't seem to like re-adoptions and appears to recognize the foreign decree regardless of whether the adoption is a proxy or not

Actually there are good reasons for filing for re-adoption even if your child enters on an IR3 visa. When your child has to show some school authority or employer his birth certificate it is better to use derivative documents like a states' Certificate of Foreign Birth than original Russian certificate. If you have to pull out the original amended Russian birth certificate or Decree from the safety deposit box, you will be fearful of losing it and you will have to deal with the Russian translation issue. It is far better to be able to use the Re-adoption Decree and the State's birth certificate for this purpose. Furthermore, if you lose the original birth certificate, it is practically impossible to get a replacement.

Further, there will be no question whatsoever of inheritance rights and if you ever move to another state that does not recognize the adoption then you have a state adoption decree that the other state must recognize.

The downside to re-adoption is that it may cost money. In some states it is a very simple process and you can do it yourself. In others, it is so complicated that you have to hire an attorney. Check with your county's adoption clerk, court clerk, or probate clerk as to the procedure. Another problem is that some clerks will ask you for your Russian originals. Do not give them to her, but instead insist on speaking to a supervisor. Most courts will allow you to file copies and the Judge will simply compare them with the originals in the courtroom.

As an example of how some states approach re-adoption, in New Hampshire there isn't any particular international re-adoption law. Instead, you have to fit the adoption into the domestic framework. This is not unusual and in some states you just have to shake your head at their requirements. In New Hampshire you file two forms (basic information) and provide copies of birth certificates, adoption certificate, and have a criminal records check done (no charge). There is a $50 filing fee. You do not really need an attorney. There is a 6 month supervisory period before a re-adoption can be final (Yes, the adoption is final but not the re-adoption. All you can do is shake your head and smile.) A social worker visits 3 times at 2 weeks, 3 months, and 6 months and then writes a report, which can double as a 6 months post placement. Court hearing is 5 minutes.

In New Jersey, you can just go to vital records with the adoption certificate, birth certificate, foreign court decree, proof of residency, and I-171H and for $6.00 you will receive a New Jersey birth certificate.

New York makes re-adoption very, very troublesome. It isn't worth it. The laws of New York are antiquated and do not work well in the international adoption field. The good news is that you can get a certificate of foreign birth easily by contacting the state office of vital records. It only costs $15 and is what you really wanted anyway. It is what you will need for the schools.

In Pennsylvania, re-adoption is virtually a free service. Usually you just file copies of your adoption documents at the county courthouse and they send them on to Vital Statistics. In a month or so you receive a Pennsylvania Birth Certificate and Pennsylvania adoption decree. You should check with your local county for the actual procedure, but re-adoption will not cost you much in time or money.

In Tennessee and Georgia re-adoption is a matter of drawing up a petition of re-adoption and having a 5 minute session with the judge in his chambers between his regular court sessions. The filing fee is about $100.

Texas is a little different. It doesn't have any state rules governing re-adoption so each Judge makes up his own. Friendly judges morph foreign re-adoption cases as best they can to fit regular old adoption law. What they wind up doing is winging it, making it up as they go along, and rubber-stamping the foreign adoption decree. Austin and Fort Worth (Tarrant County) seem to be reasonable in their practice, but Fort Bend County (Houston) is a disaster. Every county and every judge has their own rules. Some of the better judges are in counties where there are large agencies so they have been educated on foreign adoption. Definitely ask other adoptive families before filing in order to find the right judge. Now, to confuse the matter even further, there is a countervailing theory that re-adoption petitions can only be filed in the county where the child or parents reside. Now there are some bills that have been introduced in the Texas Legislature. One is Senate Bill 151. This bill will allow for the recognition of Foreign Adoption Decrees. Perhaps the Texas families can band together and get one of these bills passed.

In Virginia you do not need an attorney. The filing fee is about $29 and all you need are 3 post-placement reports within a year.

Citizenship Application

If your child does not qualify for citizenship under the Child Citizenship Act, then your child only becomes a citizen of the United States upon the issuance of a Certificate of Citizenship. Until then she is a Resident Alien. The Certificate of Citizenship is also another way to actually gain documentary "proof" that your child is a citizen even if she does qualify under the Act.

To apply, you used to fill out and file a very straightforward form N-643, *Application for Certificate of Citizenship on behalf of an Adopted Child.* However, the BCIS now wants you to file the N-600, *Application for Certificate of Citizenship.* The filing fee is still $145. If 4 months passes since you filed and the BCIS has not cashed your check or sent you a receipt, then that is bad sign. You will need to re-file the whole thing as the BCIS has lost the application. You may be able to find out the status of the application by calling 800-375-5283, but it won't be easy. You will need to include a copy of the full, final adoption decree and if the child immigrated as an IR-4 (orphans coming to the United States to be adopted by U.S. citizen parent(s)), evidence that the adoption is recognized by the state where the child is permanently residing. The form can be found at *http://www.immigration.gov/graphics/formsfee/forms/files/N-600.pdf.*

An explanation of the difference between the N-600 and N-600K can be found at *http://www.immigration.gov/graphics/lawsregs/handbook/PolMem95Pub.pdf*.

Some offices are quick to issue the Certificate, but most take a year to 2 years. California and Texas are the two states most backlogged. Also, the offices tend to process them in alphabetical order more so than the date when the application was filed. Usually you will receive a notice and receipt that they have received your Application. Then about a year later, you will receive an appointment notice giving you the date and time for the interview. Do not lose this notice, as you will have to show it to the BCIS as confirmation of your appointment. Other than these two pieces of paper, you will receive no other contact from the BCIS. On the date of the interview, you may take your child and meet with an overworked BCIS person. If your child is under age 14, you do not actually have to take him with you, although most do. The BCIS person will ask you a few questions and then hand you the Certificate of Citizenship to sign. He will also ask you take an oath that the answers on the application are true. Proofread the Certificate carefully. It is not unusual for it to have typos. It is far easier to change the Certificate right then, rather than after-wards. <u>Do not leave the room before proofreading the certificate</u>.

Now the BCIS will type your child's name exactly as your translator in the Russian Court Decree translated it. Therefore, you must make sure that your translator has done it correctly. The best time to do this is prior to your Embassy visit in Moscow. If your translator has made a mistake, he can correct it on the decree and then sign a statement at the bottom that he made a mis-take and write the correct name. One kind of mistake is placing a "K" rather than a "C" for Catherine. But really it can be any sort of typo. If you return to the States and there is an error, then the re-adoption Court Order will cure it. The BCIS will go by the re-adoption Court Order in that case and not by the Court Decree.

Some offices have a ceremony, but this is rare. Usually for children it is more of an administrative process. The certificate may say at the bottom that it is against the law to make copies of it. The law has now changed and you can and should make copies. If you get tired of waiting, call your Congressman. They are good for that sort of thing.

One very neat idea is to have your Congressman send you the flag that flew over the Capitol the day your child becomes a citizen. The cost is around $10. They run these flags up and down all day long every 5 minutes. You can also order a small flag set on a stand showing your child's heritage with flags of the US and Russia. These can be obtained from Gates Flag Co. at 1-800-US-1776.

Actually filing the form can be a troublesome process. The requirements state that the three photos must be identical, unglazed and taken within 30 days of the date of filing the citizenship application. Their regulations further state that the photos are to be in natural color and taken without a hat. The dimensions of the face should be about 1 inch from the top of the hair to the chin. The face should be a frontal view with the entire right ear visible. The photograph must be on thin paper with a light background.See the requirements at *http://www.bcis.gov/graphics/lawsregs/handbook/m-378.pdf.*

Most places that take passport photos cannot accommodate these requirements because their photos are on glazed paper. If you find that you cannot get anyone to follow the requirements, then go ahead and file regular passport photos. The BCIS is fairly reasonable when it comes to filing for a child's citizenship and will likely ignore the technical defect. There are few offices that will not waive this requirement.

Do not send any originals with your application. Just send copies. Bring the originals with you to the interview. Mail the application by certified or express mail so you have a record that it was received.

Since you will likely not yet have the "green" card or Alien Registration Card when you file your application, just put in the IR# number which was stamped in your child's Russian passport. That is all they want anyway. Include a copy of the amended birth certificate and final adoption decree, both the Russian and English translations, and a copy of the photo page from your passport, and a copy of your marriage certificate. Bring all originals with you to the interview. By the time you have your interview you will likely have the "green" card. Since you will have to turn it in to the interviewer, make a copy of it for your child's Lifebook.

The BCIS would like a statement from a Russian translator that he is competent to translate and that the translation of the Amended Birth Certificate and the Final Adoption Decree is accurate. Take this statement to Russia with you. Either have your Russian translator type and sign this statement on the English versions of these two documents or have a separate statement. The separate statement should say something to the effect "My name is _____, and I am a resident of _____, Russia. I accompanied the_____ when they adopted _____. I certify that I am competent to translate in both Russian and English and that the English translations of the Amended Birth Certificate and Final Adoption Decree are correct and accurate." Then have him sign and date it. If your translator does not give you such a statement, then just have someone in the States who is fluent in Russian sign one.

By the way, if you land in Hawaii from Russia (or from China, Korea) then on certain days of the week you can hand them your I-600 packet and your form for citizenship and get a citizenship certificate right then for your child.

This only makes sense since everything in your packet is the same stuff you have to file with your citizenship form.This is the only port of entry that lets you do this. If you intend to land in Hawaii, I would recommend asking the Honolulu office about this procedure before leaving.

Post Placements

The Russians require a certain number of post-placement reports after you return from Russia. They want to see that their children are being taken care of and are in good shape. It is a very reasonable request. Your agency will tell you how many reports you need and coordinate the filing of the reports. Usually your agency will ask you to fill out a form and write a letter describing how the child is doing. Photographs usually accompany the report. Your agency then translates everything and sends it on to the Regional Ministry of Education. The post placement report should be included in your fee to the agency. If the agency does not file these reports in a timely fashion, the Ministry will not be happy with them or you. So it is important for them, as well as for you and future Russian adoptive families, that they be timely filed. Indeed, at one time referrals in the Chuvash region, and in particular with orphanages in Cheboksary were placed on hold because the post-placement reports had not been coming in. You do not want to harm other American families and these children by failing to complete timely post placements.

The actual number of reports required has varied over the years and indeed can vary depending on the Region. Generally, you will need to file one 6 months after the adoption and then at a year, then one in each of the following two years. There is an indication that some regions are requiring more reports. Again, your agency will know. The reports are filed with the regional Department of Education so they have a good handle on who has filed and who has not.

The cost to you will likely be the cost of apostilling the form and the cost of an actual post placement visit by a social worker, if that is required. Some regions do not require either.

The post placement form may ask you what you have done to help maintain the child's connection to Russian culture. The funny thing is that it may actual mean more to you than to your child. It may come as a surprise but a lot of the children do not really want to celebrate an annual "Gotcha Day." Nor do they want to see the initial video that was sent to you or really discuss their Russian past. Their attitude is that they are American now and they want to be treated that way. Each child is different, but just make sure that any "heritage connection" you try to make is one the child wants, and not just you.

Some parents include such information as the date of the report, number of report (such as Post Placement Report #2), child's birth name, orphanage name, child's adopted name, date of birth, date of placement, and parent(s) name(s). There is usually a discussion regarding the child's physical development such as growth and weight gain, any illnesses and treatment, speech and other age related milestones. If a child has any delays you should discuss progress and therapy. You should not sugar coat the description of the delays. You are not a "bad" parent because your child has some. Indeed, the Russians assume that it is likely that there will be some issues related to the institutionalization of these children so it is important to let the Russians know that you are addressing them. Include the results of any physical exams, such as dentist and eye check-ups.

You may want to discuss the child's adjustments to life in America. This would include your child's emotional health. Speech therapy or your child's progress at speech acquisition should be mentioned. Of course, bonding and attachment progress or concerns and sibling interaction should be included. Paint a real picture. The Ministry of Education needs to know the effects of institutional life.

You can discuss the adjustments of parents, relatives, friends and neighbors (Dear MoE, Aunt Martha just loves that baby!). Tell them that the child attends pre-school a few times a week and that your child has good friends in neighborhood, school, story time and church and describe some little things that have happened in child's life since being in America.

Tell them that the child attends pre-school a few times a week and that your child has good friends in neighborhood, school, story time and describe some little things that have happened in child's life since being in America.

Then end it all with a gushy paragraph about how much you love this child and that you are grateful for having been allowed to make her a part of your family. Include 6-8 photos, usually covering the time since the last report. These should be body shots of your child and you having fun.

Registration

Russia, just like Ukraine and Kazakhstan, now requires that you register your child with the Russian Embassy in Washington, D.C. or with one of the Russian Consulates when you return. If you register when you return, then you must submit the registration card to the Consulate governing your state of residence. You can also do it in Moscow if you want. This used to be easy, however, the process is now taking at least 2-3 days so you may want to insist to your agency that you will do it once you get home, rather than hang around Moscow.

Registration at an Embassy or Consulate is a normal procedure for citizens living in a foreign country. The US even encourages its own citizens to do it. Since the Russians feel like these children are still Russian citizens until they are 18 years old, the registration requirement is just part of that. The registration form or card is one page and you must submit it to the Russian Embassy or to a Consulate with the child's Russian Passport, a copy of the parents' passports, a copy of the adoption certificate and a copy of the child's birth certificate, one passport photo of the child (same size as US passport photos) and $50 ($57 in New York). The copies do not have to be notarized. Always call the Consulate or check their web site to verify the requirements, before sending in your registration card.

If you send a self enclosed stamped envelope they will send the child's passport back, but not the copies of the adoption or birth certificate. If you pre-pay the return, then you do not have to include a separate $20 for the "return mail" fee. The form asks for the child's name and street address. It asks in section five for the name and address of the children's home. Of course, the Russians already have this information from your dossier and from the Russian passport application so it is really just duplicative information. The registration card also asks for the names of any of your child's known bio-siblings in the United States.

The registration card form can be downloaded from the foreign country's US Consulate. The Consulates are very fast about completing the registration and returning your child's Russian passport. If you are in the area covered by the Washington D.C. Consulate, the address is Russian Consulate, Attn: Passport Section, 2641 Tunlaw Rd, N.W., Washington, D.C. 20007.

Rude Comments

Prior to adopting, you may find that your relatives love to send you newspaper clippings about this or that adoption tragedy. First you get mad, then you realize they are clueless so you ignore them. Unfortunately, even after you return to the States you may be faced with rude comments from friends, family, and strangers about adopting a child from aborad.Here are some suggested replies:

Question: Which one of you is adopted?
Answer by the child: We were all adopted by one another.

Question: How much did it cost?
Response: You look them in the eyes for several seconds then respond, "Oh (long pause) Why do you ask? or "Why do you want to know? and just look at them, not responding to their question. Of course, if they say they are interested in adopting, then you can actually give them information. You could also explain that children do not cost anything, services are what costs. Just like when they gave birth in the hospital, there was a hospital bill which the insurance company paid. In your case it is the federal government (thru adoption credit) that paid. What's the difference.

Comment: What a good Samaritan you are for helping this poor orphan.
Response: I feel very blessed to finally be a parent. Parenthood is a lot more than a good deed. It is a lifelong commitment to love.

Or
Response: Actually, we're the lucky ones. We have a beautiful son/daughter who has added so much more to our lives than we could ever hope to give him/her.

Avoid agreeing with the savior concept. Your child didn't want a savior, he wanted a family.

Comment: What were her birthparents like?
Response: I consider that to be her personal information, so I don't discuss it. (Usually people apologize.)

Question: Why Russia-why not the US?"
Response: Because that's where my daughter (son) was. Why do you think a child in one nation is more or less important than another? Every loving adoption is a success. All children smile in the same language.

If the person is truly interested, then you could explain that it is difficult to adopt in the United States because so many parents are looking to adopt that birth mothers and agencies are selective. They may eliminate single parents, people of a certain age or race or income. They may prefer couples that have no other children or request a couple with a stay-at-home mother. Depending on who is asking, you could go on to explain that you wish to parent an infant and because of the pill and because many young girls now keep their children, infants are not very available in the United States. In the end, it is completely your choice as to what you say and to whom. You don't have to tell them that with 3 miscarriages, even thinking about that 1% chance of losing a child in a Baby M situation or within the 10 days a birthmother has to change her mind would be devastating. You don't have to discuss the stress and heartache in dealing with a domestic birthmother who can change her mind after you have spent thousands of dollars. You don't have to explain that you could wait years for an adoption waiting for a birthmother to pick your file out of the "beauty pageant," whereas with foreign adoption there is much more certainty that you will have a child (a family) within 12-15 months of your 171-H. You don't have to apologize for not being comfortable with a domestic "open adoption." How would they like to share their child? (that is not an accurate description, but...)

You don't have to defend yourself from racial comments that you just wanted a Caucasian child. Once you see a child or a picture of a child, more parents just say "he's my child and always has been" and do not dwell on whether he is part Tatar, Chuvash, Kazakh and on and on. Eastern Europe and Central Asia have hundreds of different ethnic groups and Russia is more of a melting pot than the US. Some people just assume the only reason you adopted from Eastern Europe was because you are a racist. You don't owe anyone an explanation as to what is a very personal decision. How dare they judge you when they haven't walked a foot in your shoes.

You can also throw their judgmental attitude back at them and ask "Oh, and since you are so concerned about children in the US, how many foster kids have you taken in?" You can also bombard them with the facts and figures about horrible orphanage life until they are the ones trying to get away!

It is always sad to me that people seem more negative about life than positive. They get a perverse thrill in tearing others down and wallow in *Schadenfreude*. Avoid these toxic people. That is why being around upbeat people, even when the chips are down, is so refreshing.

Question: Why are you going back for a second (or third) child?
Response: When I adopted my son, I promised that I wouldn't forget the children who were left behind.

Or
My family is not complete and when it is, I'll call you. (bit of sarcasm)

Question: "Is she yours?"

Response: "Yes she is."

"No, I mean is she REALLY yours?"
Response: "From the very first moment I held her."
       Or "why do you ask?

This last response sometimes works best as it puts the burden on them. You can determine if they have a real interest and proceed with more information, always keeping your child's personal history private. Of course, if they are just cluelessly curious, then just walk away.

Question: "Is her father Russian?"
Response: "Her Dad is right here, why don't you ask him." Then just walk away leaving them to deal with your husband.

Some singles respond by saying "I don't know, I never met him." This can leave them stopped dead in their tracks.

Question:"Does she speak Russian?
Response: "Yes, she is only one year old, but she's been teaching me everything she knows." Then just leave. There are just some people who should not be allowed to walk and think at the same time.

Comment: At least you didn't have to go thru labor
Response (if you want to): Excuuuuuuse Me!
6 months of BCIS and Russian paperwork nonsense, fingerprinted like you're a criminal, social worker asking questions about things not even your mother knows, second mortgage on your house, leaving your other children behind, flying 11 (or 27) hours straight, no sleep for 24 hours, Flight From Hell, etc etc etc

Transracial Adoption

There is a great song from the musical "South Pacific" by Rogers and Hammerstein called
       "You've Got to be Carefully Taught.
       You've got to be taught to be afraid

Of people whose eyes are oddly made
Or people whose skin is a different shade
You've got to be carefully taught!

You can read the rest of the lyrics at *http://www.turnofftheviolence.org/Carefullytaught.htm* or better yet, buy the soundtrack!

There are so many nationalities within the melting pot of Eastern Europe and Central Asia that it is entirely possible you might adopt a child that looks different than you. There are lots of books and articles on how to raise a child from a different race. If you have older bio kids, then tell them that people may stare at the family. Have an open discussion of why and how you and they might react; then progress to questions that people might ask and how you might respond. Each child can think up his or her own answer and you can role play. Questions range from curious to hostile and each question can have a varied response. Emphasize family privacy, rather than secrecy.

Only a handful of studies have been done on the success of transracial adoptions, but most show that the adopted children generally are well adjusted and comfortable with their families. In a recent study, the Search Institute found that a sample of 199 Korean-born adolescents scored as well as same-race adopted counterparts on 4 measures of mental health, and were more likely to be highly-attached to both adoptive parents. Sharma said 80% of Korean adoptees said they get along equally well with people of their own and different racial backgrounds, though 42% said they're occasionally ashamed of their race. Sharma noted that any family that adopts transracially "becomes inherently a transracial family, not a white family with a child of color."

An interesting point by one family was that in their travel through China to adopt, they experienced what it felt like to be a minority and from that experience could get a sense of what their daughter might later feel. There is no doubt that transracial adoption introduces a layer of complexity into the child's life, but so does illness, divorce, and everything else that goes along with living. It is also possible to emphasize adoption too much, creating a sense of differentness in the child. Teach your child that everybody is different. They have different hair, size, race, height, etc. While acknowledging the difference, also treat it the same as anything else. It's just there. Probably the wrong approach is for parent's to pretend that the transracial adoptee is not different. They are different. It's a difference that makes no difference, but it is still there. Once reality is acknowledged, then the child and the family can search honestly for the answer to the question of "who am I" and "who are we."

Now when a child is 3 or 4 that child is more into being 3 or 4 and not so concerned about anything else. Toys, sticks and popsicles dominate their lives.

But soon after that they begin to notice the little things like Mommy's hair isn't straight like theirs or they want to be blond like Mommy. Nevertheless, it is really during the angst of the teenage years that this question becomes more of a concern for the adoptee, as this is when children want the most to fit in. So you need to be particularly aware of the need for identity at this age. Yet, you may find that it is precisely at this age that your child really wants to "just fit in" and doesn't want any culture camps or anything dealing with Russia or Kazakhstan. A child can actually go in denial, not the parent. Instead, for many, it is only after 18 when they go off to the "big city" that they begin to seriously approach the identity question.

This search for identity is not just an adoption issue, but one with which many ethnic minorities in the United States grapple. Maya Lin, the American architect, once said that although she grew up in an all Chinese household all of her friends were Caucasian and she thought of herself as Caucasion.When she went to Yale, she even declined to join the Asian American students group because she didn't feel a connection.It wasn't until long after she graduated did she begin to explore that aspect of herself.

A parent should acknowledge that her child is Rom or Kazakh. She is still your child. It doesn't change that. The worse thing a family can do is never discuss their child's racial difference (or physical difference if it is a disability), but live in denial and allow the difference to just sit there, festering and eating away at your child. Avoidance creates its own adjustment issues.

It is sort of funny, but understandable, that sometimes a parent will simply not see the child's racial makeup at all, but view *her* child as *Caucasian*! The main goal is to instill in children enough self-confidence to deal with any problems, and to come to parents or others if they can't. There are as many approaches and theories on how to address the issue as there are grains of sand, but you know your child best. The child should learn that if they allow the opinions of others to influence their behavior, then they are in some part accepting those opinions and allowing them to limit their life. The worst prisons are those that we create.

The real problem for parents is matching the appropriate kinds of cultural information to the appropriate age of their child. Maybe not so much is needed when they are infants, but more so as they get to be 6 or 7.The child's home culture should be introduced at the child's pace. Culture shouldn't be forced on them. They go to school in America as American children and live in an American family. At the same time, there are many benefits to "culture camps" and time spent with other internationally adopted children can help the child become comfortable with herself and her background. Although some parents go overboard with the whole culture idea and forget that these children live in a non-Russian family, here are a few ideas for bringing their home culture into the home: (1) Go to Russian or Bulgarian cultural events or exhibits that come to your town; (2) Provide your daughter with books with her ethnicity; (3) include Russian language classes in your children's playgroup activities; (4) Buy Russian cassettes or Russian children's songs and play them as background music; (5) Show English-language videos featuring Russia or Kazakhstan; (6) Have "things Russian" around your home. You have to find the right balance. Too much emphasis on things Russian and being Russian is likely to create in the child, feelings of exclusion or being different; too little attention to things Russian (or any ethnicity) is likely to create the impression that this aspect of the child's identity is not valued nor an appropriate subject for discussion.

As parents you will have to be sensitive to racism and discuss it with your child. To some extent it will depend on where you live. There might be more instances in places where Central Asians are not so numerous like Minnesota versus New York, but it exists everywhere. The worst is "silent racism," such as where restaurant waiters are courteous to everyone else, but rude to someone who is Asian, or teachers who put your child in the back of the classroom. The child needs to be able talk about her experience as a *Kazakh American or Rom American or Chuvash American*, about the existence of racism in America and its effect on them. The ability and room for them to talk about their experience of being "raced" won't prevent painful experiences, but will allow them to understand and move on from those experiences. It will allow them to express the anger and pain such experiences cause and thus keep them from being mired in silence and denial.

Your daughter may encounter some prejudice as they go through life, but many people do. Your families may be gawked at or may encounter awkward comments and questions, but such is life. Don't worry, through it all you will survive. You may even be better people with stronger character, better insight and more compassion because of it.

Contacting Your Child's Birthfamily

After your child has been home awhile and blossomed into this incredible little person, it is not unusual for you to think about contacting your child's birthfamily to tell them what a great person this child has become and to obtain some family background for your child. It is perfectly legal under Russian law for you to do so. The only legal restriction is on the other parties in court to keep the proceedings confidential. This warning does not apply to you.

There is no right or wrong answer to the question of whether you should try to contact the birthfamily. You should ask yourself if you are you doing this for you or for the child. Some children simply have no interest at all. They could care less. If this is the case, then you really have to ask yourself why you feel this need, since contacting the birthfamily should only occur because it will help your child. Now there have been instances where an adopted older child was close to her grandmother and she is getting up there in years. That is a situation in which you might consider contact.

Also, while we may think that all birthmothers want to be contacted, this is not necessarily so. Birthmothers can become upset and want to know why you contacted her and what do you want. She might say that you opened up an old wound. Even in the United States it isn't a universal sentiment that birthmothers want their children to find them. It also is possible that the birthmother is very happy you found her. Just don't go into this thinking that it is going to be wonderful. You will not know that until contact is made. You may be cautioned that the Russian family will ask for money or try to use the situation. These are fears created by the unknown. Could it happen-of course. Is it likely-no. Remember too that the foreign family can not use the adoption for any immigration purpose as the BCIS does not recognize that there is any family relationship once the adoption is final.

One method of contact is to write a letter to the birthfamily in which you are circumspect about the adoption. Instead you discuss how you might be related because of old family emigration from Eastern Europe and just talk around the adoption. One suggested approach is to write that someone had suggested that she may have some information that she could provide on their child (using the Russian name) who was born X/X/X from AAA, Russia. You ask for some family background and provide a description of the child along with personality traits. You say your only interest is in providing information to the child. Enclose some baby and older photographs. Some parents send the letter through an intermediary (like your translator) so there is no return address except for that of the intermediary.

You cannot predict what the response will be. The family might be embarrassed that a child was raised by a children's home or the birthmother may have kept the birth a secret from her family. Or it might provide your child with the history to one of the roots of his family tree.

A story about contacting the birthfamily is here: *http://adoption.about.com/library/weekly/uc082001h.htm* and a Yahoo! Group

for people with (or exploring) birth family contact is at
http://groups.yahoo.com/group/Open_InternationalFamilies

CHAPTER XV

UKRAINE

Background

Ukraine is a former republic of the Soviet Union and has been an independent country since 1991. Other countries such as Russia, Poland and Lithuania have historically controlled Ukraine, a country of 49 million people.

It is economically tied to Russia and has suffered the same sort of financial meltdowns. It is still a country where even after independence the struggle is not over. There are two centers of power, and neither is strong enough to overcome the other. The totalitarian group is not strong enough to turn Ukraine back to the past or into a Belarus or a Central Asian dictatorship. But civil society is not strong enough to overcome the totalitarian state and build a democratic one as in the Baltics or Central Europe. The battle ebbs and flows, sometimes with top officers and strategists changing sides. President Kuchma manages it all. He scares the pro-Russian communists by cozying up to the pro-Western Ukrainian nationalists. He scares western Ukraine, with its Catholics and dominant Ukrainian speakers, by cozying up to eastern Ukraine with its Orthodox and dominant Russian speakers. Good maps of Ukraine and its cities can be found at this web site: *http://www.embassyworld.com/maps/Maps_Of_Ukraine.html*

Many people who are interested in adopting from Russia are also investigating Ukraine. Most of the chapters written in this book apply equally to adopting and traveling in Ukraine. The major procedural differences are described here.

The reform years of the 1990's saw an increase in the number of orphans and children deprived of parental care. According to the data provided by the Ministry of Education and Science of Ukraine, in 1999 their number was 103,400.This was almost twice as many as at the decade's onset. The numbers have increased because of greater family erosion due to economic stress.

In fiscal year 1999 (ends September 30), 323 visas were issued by the US to Ukrainian adopted children. It then doubled in 2000 to 659, possibly because of all the confusion in Russia when the April 2000 changes came into being. In 2001, the figure was 1,246 and in 2002, 1104. Many Italian, Israeli, German and French citizens adopt from Ukraine as well. The total for all foreign adoptions from Ukraine was 1,138 children in 1999, almost double the amount adopted in 1998 and up from a scant 14 in 1996, the year the government lifted a ban on foreign adoptions. Both single women and men can adopt from Ukraine. Generally, it seems that the average age of children adopted is between 18 to 48 months and boys out number girls about 55% to 45%.

Ukraine banned foreign adoptions in July 1994 following several cases of illegal adoptions. The moratorium was lifted in 1996. In the early 1990s, adoption in Ukraine was simple: Foreign and local parents alike needed only three documents and the approval of oblast authorities. Not only was it easy, it was also subject to fraud. For the right price, state adoption agents were more than willing to alter documents to enable the adoption of children legally ineligible for adoption. Investigators found two doctors and two officials guilty of falsifying documents in close to 135 adoptions between 1992 and 1994. Statistics such as the age of the children, the status of their health and other factors that could have nullified their eligibility for adoption were altered so that foreigners could take them. One type of common fraud was changing the date of birth to show that an infant was a four year old and thus eligible for adoption.

When the government lifted the ban in 1996, it introduced a number of measures designed to prevent abuse. It set up the National Adoption Center under the Ministry of Education and Science and introduced a more detailed accounting method. The Center keeps organized lists of children eligible to be adopted and parents wishing to adopt. The changes were designed to favor locals over foreigners. To be declared eligible for adoption by foreigners, children must first go through a 14-month period during which they are only available for adoption by Ukrainian parents. An exception exists if the children have health problems. Ukraine also banned foreign intermediaries, including non-profit agencies, from participating in the adoption process. Between

1996-1999 Ukrainian families adopted about 18,000 children, including 9,582 orphan children. Over the same period foreign families have adopted 2,044 children. Children are not necessarily placed on the registry at birth. Several children enter the orphanage at older ages after the parents are denied parental rights, or for other reasons. Even then, the orphanage director does not have to put the child on the registry for months or even years.

For more detailed information on the process see the State Department's bulletins on Ukrainian adoptions at
http://travel.state.gov/adoption_ukraine.html and
http://travel.state.gov/adoption_facilitators.html. For current information visit the Ukrainian list at the EEadopt web site and at the FRUA website. One of the very best web sites, which also include forms, is at
http://www.adopt-sense.com/fees&forms.htm. Templates for all dossier documents can be found in the "files" section at
http://groups.yahoo.com/group/Adoption_from_Ukraine/

The US Embassy in Kyiv has an excellent and very complete discussion of Ukrainian adoption requirements at
http://usembassy.kiev.ua/amcit_adoptions_eng.html#newpolicy.
You should read this discussion in its entirety. It also contains the 2002 list of serious medical conditions, which would allow you to adopt a child under 12 months. The New York Consulate also has a nice outline at
http://www.ukrconsul.org/consular/english/adoption_en.html
and in Washington at *http://www.ukremb.com/consular/adoption.html.*

Here are some other very helpful sites
http://www.adoptukraine.com
http://www.geocities.com/adoptukr
http://www.ukrainianangels.org/
http://www.geocities.com/adoptukr/UsefulLinks.htm

Here are 3 email lists that focus on specific regions in Ukraine:
http://groups.yahoo.com/group/kharkiv-adoption
http://groups.yahoo.com/group/mykolayiv
http://groups.yahoo.com/group/kyiv-adoption/

Ukrainian Process

The Ukrainian Consulate in Chicago has a very informative site on adopting from Ukraine. Their site is at *http://www.ukrchicago.com/inform/infgen_en.html*. Remember that if you plan to use the Chicago Consulate for your Visa and document authentications, you are supposed to be from one of those states, which is assigned to the Chicago Consulate. (Although the Chicago Consulate will unofficially take documents from all states.) Unfortunately, Chicago has changed its policy on allowing bundling of documents and does not allow it any more. Before sending your documents through the Washington, DC or New York Consulate, check to see if you can use Chicago. It is a lot easier to deal with.

One large difference from the Russian adoption process is that the American Embassy in Warsaw, Poland and not Moscow issues the child's visa. Indeed, it is to Warsaw that your I-171H (Visas 37) cable is sent. On your I-600A be sure to put down Warsaw, not Kyiv, as the Consulate. Adoptive parents visit the US Embassy in Kyiv, Ukraine to verify that they have followed all of the correct steps for a legal adoption in Ukraine and then travel to Warsaw, Poland to obtain the child's US immigrant visa.

You are not supposed to receive any pre-referral information on children available for adoption. Ukraine stopped pre-identification in 1994 because of a baby-selling scandal: there were allegations that doctors and orphanage directors conspired with overseas agencies to tell women their healthy babies had died, then would take the babies to the orphanages, and turn them over to foreigners for adoption. Ukraine's theory in stopping pre-identification was to minimize the chances of baby selling.

Therefore, families are not supposed to obtain photos, videos, medicals, names and birth dates of children or any other information about children until they actually arrive in Kyiv. Notwithstanding, there are some US agencies that say they pre-identify the children. This is against Ukrainian law. All identification is supposed to come through the Adoption Center of Ukraine a/k/a/ National Adoption Center (AC or NAC) or at a children's home when you are on site. Yet, some US agencies openly advertise that they can pre-identify because of some special relationship they have with a home director or Department of Education person.

Now the reality is that if a facilitator visits the same children's home many times a month, then he is going to know which children are eligible for adoption and which are not. If he supports the orphanage with money, he is going to be more welcomed than one who doesn't. Also, the truth is that some facilitators do have an "arrangement" with some orphanage directors so that there is some "hold-back" and some pre-selection going on. Pre-selection is not wrong in the sense that it probably helps parents more and is less stressful than the "blind" method. It also neither helps not hurts the children. You can also argue that it is more efficient for a "well-connected" facilitator to pre-select as it moves the parents through the adoption process faster. Yet it also risks been subverted by holding a child for the highest bidder. Regardless, everyone agrees that the cattle call system needed improvement, which is why Mrs. Parienko went to the appointment system. Indeed, the whole Ukrainian system as it now exists could use an overhaul.

There is an exception to the pre-selection prohibition and that is related to siblings. A family who learns of a sibling during their adoption is already properly registered with the NAC. The NAC understands that during your adoption you will receive information legally about your child. Sometimes this includes number of births to the mother or even specific information on siblings. It is not illegal to come into information on siblings during your legal adoption. It is also not illegal to inform the Adoption Center that during your child's adoption or during inquiries about your child after adoption that you came across information about a sibling. They are not cold hearted and you are a legally registered parent. Anyhow, if someone wishes to adopt a sibling after their first adoption, then they should notify the (NAC) of their request and if the NAC approves of this then you are set to go, from the Ukrainian side anyway. The US side depends on how many children you were originally approved for and whether your state allows additional adoptions without an entirely new home study. Now the Adoption Center is not likely to "hold" the sibling for you. Officially, they very much discourage any "holding" by any of their children's homes. However, if the child is available they will most likely approve your request.

Also, if you were to see a child while you were adopting another and wanted to come back and adopt that particular child, the Adoption Center would most likely accommodate you. Again, this would depend on if that child were still available. As in Russia, singles (including men) can adopt and the required age difference between a mother and a child does not have to be as great as in Russia.

You can use a US based agency and many do, however, their services are limited to the US side of the pond, and connecting you to a Ukrainian facilitator and translator. You will find that there is a sort of competitiveness between those who used an agency and those who adopted independently. Just as there is between those who pre-selected and those who did not. Each thinks theirs is the right way. The method actually makes no difference. The only thing that does make a difference is having a good, interested, and fairly honest facilitator. The question is what method feels right for you. Whatever method does, then that is the right approach to take. Adoptions from Ukraine are split evenly between agency and independent methods. One caveat to hiring a facilitator is not to go too cheap. A faciliatator that is charging you under the going rate may not be giving you all the services and you may find you are paying more by being charged a la carte. Also, a facilitator that only does a handful of adoptions a year, will not be as used to the NAC and them to him as one who does dozens. A facilitator's good reputation with the NAC is worth a lot.

Time spent in Ukraine is generally longer than in Russia, although this will not always be the case. It can depend on how long it takes you to find your "forever" child and whether the court waives the 30-day appeal period. The shortest period in country is probably 10 days and the longest 7 weeks. The average is about 20 days. As in Russia, there are regions that are very adoption friendly and some that are not. Some regions waive the 30 days, and some do not (Dnipropetrovsk, Ternopil). Some will only waive it if you pay an "expedite" fee, and some do not charge anything. Some families obtain passports for the child in one day, and some wait weeks.

The thirty-day wait, like Russia's 10 days, is the time period within which the adoption decree is pending to allow for objections to the decision by the prosecutor. The decree is final and automatically executable at thirty days. In order for it to come into effect any sooner an exception must be made in the judge's order and the judge must declare the order final early due to special circumstances. What is sufficient reason in each case varies by regional practice and individual judicial opinions. Along with Dnipropetrovsk and Ternopil, Kherson and Simferopol do not normally waive the period. Other regions like Donetsk, Kyiv, Kharkiv and Odessa used to be more inclined.

The cost to adopt is less than in Russia. Generally the cost to adopt independently is around $12,000-$16,000, which includes all travel costs, translations, and homestay, although some have completed the process for less. This also includes various "expedite" fees that might have to be paid depending on the region. If you use an agency, you will not see any of this, as it will be in the background between your facilitator and the payee. If you adopt independently, then you will. Some have reported that "expedite" fees in Kyiv and Kharkiv were in the $1,200 range. It was hoped that with the new NAC Director, the process would become more transparent. I did not say easier, just transparent. Ukrainian adoptions have increased in cost, as the Ukrainian Consulates no longer allow bundling of the dossier documents. Translators work for around $3,5000-$5000. That amount covers all translations, notaries, court filings, in country accommodations and train travel to the region where you adopt.

As in Russia, if one parent must return home after the court hearing then the other spouse can obtain the immigrant visa in Warsaw, Poland by power of attorney with the other parent simply signing the I-600 before leaving Ukraine. If both return home because of the thirty-day wait, then only one must return. The second trip will take 7 to 10 days to complete the child's Ukrainian paperwork and US immigration visa.

The databank wait is longer than in Russia. It is 1 month for the local registry, 1 month on the regional registry and 12 months on the national registry. This means that a child 15 months old is about the youngest you can adopt, as opposed to 7 months in Russia. Families have adopted children under the age of 12 months, but these infants must have a diagnosis that appears on a list authorized by the Ministry of Health. This list used to have several conditions that US parents found acceptable such as cleft lip/palate. However, in 2002 Ukraine reduced the list so that there are far fewer acceptable medical conditions. The complete list can be found at the US Consulate web site at *http://usembassy.kiev.ua/amcit_adoptions_eng.html#newpolicy.*

Ukraine is described as an "independent process" although there are agencies in the US that will help you on the US side. Many people find their own facilitator by word of mouth. A good facilitator is worth their weight in gold in this process. Invest a lot of time in choosing a facilitator. Ask reference families for their recent experience. An experience that is a year or so old is too far in the past. Use a facilitator that has a good relationship with the NAC.

When looking for an agency, you might ask the agency director and all references if information was available on children prior to the NAC meeting. Always ask the references if there are anyone else you should talk to. You would be surprised at the information you pick up from other families not on anyone's reference list. Look for signs that the agency is actually knowledgeable about Ukraine. You would be surprised at how many agencies do not know any more about it than you. They might be just one National Geographic magazine ahead. Have they traveled there? Have they actually met with the facilitators they use? Is their description of available children in Ukraine consistent with Ukrainian law and others experiences?

Ask references—What is the time line for dossier translation (prefer within one week), and how long did NAC approval take? Also find out how long from NAC approval to travel date; Find out what the foreign fee includes-translations in—country, hotel, train, or what? There is wide variation here.

Facilitators do not work for the NAC. There are a number of facilitation "companies" and agencies might hire one company or another. A company might consist of one or more "facilitators" who supervise a group of "translators" who actually help you at the NAC and in the region. These two terms (facilitator/translator) are often used interchangeably so it is a bit confusing. Persons who adopt independently hire a translator based on recommendations from other adoptive families. Many (although certainly not all) independent adoptions are usually the result of a parent working with the Independent Ukrainian Adoption Family Network or Sense Resource. There are other facilitators that parents have found through word of mouth or the Internet. Always obtain adoption family references for the person who is helping you in their adoption (be it agency or independent translator). You should ask as many questions as possible including what is and is not covered in the translation fee. Use the list of questions in the Russian Adoption section of this book and tailor them to Ukraine.

Generally translators work in teams and have partners working in Kyiv to complete the Kyiv portion of the adoption. Most families are in a region with a regional certified translator while another member of the team will be in Kyiv obtaining various stamps and approvals there.

Your dossier paperwork must be translated into Ukrainian, not Russian, although most Ukrainians speak Russian, and documents must be "authenticated" which is different than "apostilled." The notarized dossier documents are first stamped with your state's seal, which is the state's authentication of your notary, then sent to the US State Department where they get a federal stamp or seal of authentication and then these are authenticated by the Ukrainian Embassy where they receive an official Ukrainian stamp before being returned to you. There are fees. The State Department charges $5 per document, but call both to verify before sending any documents. If you have notaries from different states, you must have the state, which governs that particular notary do the authentication. If you want to adopt more than one child, then you must submit separate dossiers for each child. The NAC would prefer that parents adopt one child at a time.

The translator picks up the dossier at the Adoption Center for translation. Once you are registered with the NAC you will be sent a letter giving you a registration number and then you fax them your request for an appointment date. You usually work with two translators, one in Kyiv and the other in the region in which the children's home is located. In some adoptions, the Kyiv translator travels with you to the region as well. You can get a head start on the translation by faxing or emailing an unofficial copy to your translator ahead of when you send it to the NAC. The Kyiv portion of your adoption includes the Kyiv translator picking up the dossier, translating it, and redelivering it back to the NAC. He will also assist in picking you up at the airport, bringing you to the NAC, and obtaining the NAC's letter authorizing you to visit a children's home. While in the region you will likely send the request to adopt the child to the NAC by train or plane courier and the Kyiv translator will deliver it to the NAC. Then, the NAC's approval is sent back to you in the region in time for your court appearance. Afterwards, the court decree, child's passport, amended birth certificate and other documents are sent back to the translator in Kyiv for translation, notarization, and legalization with the NAC and other ministries. When you arrive, hopefully all of the Ukrainian government work is completed and all you have to do is go to the American Embassy for the Form 604 interview. Your return visit to Kyiv is usually one very long day or 2 days, depending on how long it takes for the translator to get the final stamps he needs on his translations from the ministries in Kyiv. It also depends on the American Embassy hours, holidays, etc.

Now the Ukrainian Embassy has become rather difficult and expensive about authentications. The Consulates in Chicago and New York will accept dossiers for authentication without obtaining the federal certification from the US State Department if the Secretary of State of the state where the document was notarized has certified the dossiers. This only applies to those states for which the Consulate has specific jurisdiction. Some families, after having their documents authenticated by the State Department in Washington, send them on to the Ukrainian Consulate in New York. The Ukrainian Consulate in New York is a little easier to deal with and will accept documents from any state, as long as they are first authenticated through the State Department. The same is true for Chicago. New York also used to accept bundled documents. This can save you quite a bit of money. Try to avoid using the Consulate in Washington, D.C. Since rules change frequently, always verify with the Consulates before using them. To avoid all of these headaches, many families use the courier services that are knowledgeable about the rules and keep updated. The couriers keep a pretty good eye on your dossier and can help you if there are mistakes. Usually they can tell you where your dossier is at any given time.

Some of your dossier documents may include: 1) Powers of Attorney for your facilitator and translator, 2) Commitment Letter or Petition To Adopt, 3) Application, 4) Affidavit for BCIS 171-H (and copy of 171H), 5) Home study, 6) Agency License, 7) Affidavit for Passport (and copies of passports), 8) Medical Forms for you and your spouse, 9) Criminal Record checks for you and your spouse, 10) social worker's license, 11) Letter from agency about social worker, 12) Certified Copy of Marriage Certificate or Divorce Decree, 13) employment letters, 14) self employed persons usually add a CPA letter on letterhead mentioning annual income and, 15) a Letter of Obligation stating that you promise to follow the laws of Ukraine when adopting and that your child will be raised by you, and then stating who your facilitator is. The NAC seems to have agreed to accept a notarized copy of the 171-H, by having you staple a cover sheet with a notarized statement from you that it is a true and correct copy. If you have trouble with this or any other document, you can always ask the US Consulate's office in Kyiv for advice.

The Home Study Agency license must include an expiration date. If the license does not have an expiration date, then a letter must accompany it from the Department of Social Services, indicating that the Agency is in good standing and that the license does not have an expiration date. The letter should be notarized and authenticated. Police, medical and income documents must be issued on the letterheads of respective agencies (e.g. sheriff's office, physician's office, employer) and signed by respective authorized officials. The NAC will not accept such documents printed on the letterhead of the U.S. adoption agency.

There is no particular format for the Ukrainian home study. If your home study agency follows the normal international format, as is done for Russia that will be fine. It can be just 4 or 5 pages. Here are just a few items of which to be aware. There needs to be a notarized copy of the license of the person(s) who signs your home study. Make sure that the agency license is current and will be valid for as long as it takes to complete your adoption. Meaning that their license cannot expire before the Adoption Center approves you. Sometimes where it is the agency not the social worker that is licensed, the agency provides its notarized license with a notarized letter stating the social worker is an employee. The notary needs to say that "the submitted copy of so and so's license is an exact photocopy of an unaltered original document." This is similar to what is described in the Russian paperchase.

You can bring documents that update your dossier. Very often the NAC will approve a dossier, but a document may expire before court (i.e.: a social worker license). Having the updated document to submit will save a lot of trouble in Ukraine. If your agency's license has expired and they are provisionally authorized to provide home studies during the re-licensing period, then obtain a letter from your state's licensing authority stating that the agency can continue to do home studies.

The home study can be just 5 pages long. Some social workers will attach an addendum to cover the BCIS requirements, but this doesn't have to go to Ukraine. Ukrainian document requirements change regularly, so you always need to check. Do avoid using the words "the Ukraine" in the home study. It is not proper and can be considered rude. The country name is Ukraine not "the Ukraine." Avoid placing information concerning adoption costs and household budget into the home study. They are not needed. Do not mention why these children are available for adoption i.e. "the circumstantial events that usually relate to adoption as poverty, unwed mothers and the presence of birth defects". Ukrainians would read this information and think they were being called whores and monsters. There is an extremely high intolerance for unwed mothers. This intolerance extends to talking about the issue. Ukrainians are highly sensitive to birth defects due to the nuclear accident in 1991 at Chernobyl. (See the discussion on Chernobyl in the Belarus section and in FAQ.) The name on the social worker license must match exactly the name on the home study. The address on the license and home study must also match. A Consulate authorized translation company must translate the home study in the US into Ukrainian. The translation must be sent to the Consulate to be certified by the Consular Office. The home study (with translation) is then returned to the applicants in a sealed envelope to be opened only by the NAC.

There should be a statement that the couple is approved for a certain number of children, age range, gender type, and with minor surgically correctable conditions or minor chronic medical conditions of any race. Your annual income must be stated in home study and the word "annual" must be used instead of per year. The home study must state adoptive parents are healthy and free of syphilis, TB and AIDS. The home study must state that adoptive parent have never been given an unfavorable home study and that they have cleared the state's child abuse registry (assuming your state has one).

Ukraine requires a statement that the adopted child will have the same civil rights as any American born child. The language is similar to the following:

> "Pursuant to (state's) law and the law of the United States of America, children that qualify as orphans and are legally adopted by an American citizen shall have equal rights as children originally born in the United States and his/her civil rights will not be restricted in any way."

One of your dossier documents to be sent to the NAC is a "Petition To Adopt." It might read as follows: "We, Barney and Betty Rubble, petition the Center for Adoption of Ukraine to register us as candidates for adoption of an orphan or abandoned child. We ask permission to visit orphanages and state-run children homes to select, make contact with, and get acquainted with children that we desire to adopt. We desire to adopt two children male or female between four months to six years old, with minor surgically correctable condition or a minor chronic medical condition of any race." The home study must have the address of the social worker that did it, not just name and copy of the license.

The NAC wants the police clearance letters done at the state level rather than the local level. It will not accept clearance on a local. In cases where the state does not issue such clearances, the NAC will accept locally issued documents if they clearly include a statement to the effect that the prospective adoptive parent has no criminal record in the state. Obtaining state clearances can be easy or difficult depending on where you live. For example, in Illinois you should call the State Police in Joliet. Tell them you need a state police clearance letter for an adoption. They will send the forms to you. If you're married, make sure to request two forms—there are tracking numbers on them so you can't just photocopy the form. The forms usually come in a few days and the actual letter can take up to three weeks before you receive it. There are two types of forms. One is for a fingerprint check and clearance and the other is just for a records search and clearance. You want the latter. In Missouri if you visit Jefferson City, they will do electronic fingerprints right there and you will have your letter within an hour. In Alaska, the State Police do it with or without fingerprints.

If you are divorced, but not remarried you need a copy of your divorce decree and not your marriage license. If you are divorced and remarried you only need your new marriage license.

It used to be that some of these documents could be bundled so that the cost of authentication was reduced. If you are using the Ukrainian Embassy in Washington you need to check with them for their latest bundling requirements prior to sending them to your State for authentication. As an example, they will now not allow bundling of the two police clearance reports for husband and wife.

Your Facilitator

Once your dossier documents are complete you will need to send them to the NAC. The NAC's address is 27 Taras Shevchenko Boulevard, Kiev, Ukraine 252032. Telephone number (380)(44) 246-54-31/32/37/49 and their fax number is (380)(44) 246-5452/62.

Try to translate them in the States before sending them. This will save you a few days. Express mail (UPS) to Ukraine takes about 3 to 5 days. Your translator then picks up your dossier from the NAC and translates. This should take 3 to 10 days. Once the NAC actually has the translated dossier documents, it takes them about 10 working days to approve you for adoption during the wintertime and around 20 days during the summer.

When working with an agency, it is likely that their facilitators probably only know certain regions of Ukraine and will lean toward adopting from those. One disadvantage of this is that it may actually limit you. For example, many parents adopt from Simferopol, as it is very adoption friendly. Yet, there are other regions which allow adoption but which few people visit such as Ivano Franko and Beregova. In Beregova the children's home is on a small estate with 3 houses, a small apple and peach orchard as well as a garden. The children are in small cottages with 10 other children. In interviewing an agency you should ask their references from which regions did they adopt. If it seems they all go to one or two regions, ask the agency why it's limited.

In contrast to the Russian process (the way it once was) you do not receive a "referral" of a child, but rather your dossier is first approved for adoption by the National Adoption Center (NAC) in Kyiv. This means you are now a registered family. Under the former Director, Mrs. Parienko, you were issued an invitation with a specific date. This appointment systen still seems to be in place, although there is a bit of a "cattle call" philosophy as well.

You then fly to Kyiv and meet your facilitator. Try to meet your facilitator by e-mail, or better by phone before you travel. Personalities can clash, and more important, lack of experience with the process or with English can be very detrimental to a happy adoption.

Now there are certain facilitators who have very good relationships with some of the children's homes and the NAC and they may be able to guide you as to which region you should travel based on information they may have on the available children. However, this is not always the case.

The NAC has some flexibility. For example, if the license of the notary on your documents has expired, normally you must have all your documents re-notarized. (This is why you should always have your documents notarized by someone whose license doesn't expire for years into the future.) The NAC might not raise this as an issue if you had recently adopted using those same documents and your facilitator had a good relationship with the NAC. In other words, if trust factor has been built up with the NAC, they are inclined to be flexible. It is only natural. Indeed, some are of the opinion that the key to getting the age and gender of child you request is not so much luck, but rather your facilitator's relationship with the NAC and his contacts in the region. Still, so many people feel blessed having adopted a child that was not within their original parameters, that you wonder if there isn't some guiding hand in all of this.

You will pay your facilitator for your housing, local transportation, legal fees and the services of the facilitators and translators. There are few hotels so you might stay in a homestay.

Traveling to Kyiv

Most of the discussion relating to preparing to travel to Russia applies equally to Ukraine. Most parents fly into Warsaw, Poland first, as that is where they will be leaving from eventually. They then take a plane from Warsaw to Kyiv. Delta does have a code share arrangement with Air France whereby you can fly from Paris to Kyiv direct. While I am not a fan of Air France, some parents have taken the Warsaw-Paris-Atlanta return flight. In Paris there is a time crunch getting from one terminal to the other. You should try to reserve your seat assignment when you are in Warsaw for the Paris—Atlanta leg, as this will help your time problem. When you get to Paris, you will more than likely take a shuttle bus to the terminal. Immediately look at the gate monitors (don't go upstairs yet, look at the ones downstairs where you come in) and see what terminal your Paris-Atlanta flight is leaving from, A, B, C, D, E, or F, then if need be get back on a shuttle bus and go to that terminal, and then to the gate. You won't know the gate until you get to Paris, and they frequently change the Paris—Atlanta gate. If your plane from Warsaw is late, you will want to notify the Air France people on the plane, and MAYBE they will hold the plane for you to Atlanta, but this is rare. Lufthansa seems to have better connections both flying to Kyiv and leaving Warsaw.

Now when you arrive in Kyiv, as with Russian customs, declare all of your money and keep your customs form. You will need a visa to go to Ukraine. Some types of travel like business and private do not require a letter of invitation. You should check with the Ukrainian Embassy or Consulate to verify whether you need an invitation for your adoption trip. Invitations generally come from a travel agency. They put a visa stamp in your passport and then send it back to you. No visa is required to travel to Poland whether flying from the United States or Ukraine.Poland is planning to require visas for Ukrainians, so that may be an additional document for your adopted child. An excellent website that explains how to fill out the Ukrainian visa application form is at: *http://www.adoptukraine.com/travelprep_visa.html* and at *http://www.ukremb.com/consular/visas.html.*

One airline that flies to Kyiv is the Polish airline LOT. Their website (www.LOT.com) lists their fares which can vary quite a bit, depending on when you travel, and which airport you fly out of. For example, before April 15 the cost is about $550 roundtrip (out of NY) after that it ranged between $550-$900. LOT charges about 10% of adult fare for a child under 2, and about 75% for a child 2-11. You can lay over in Warsaw for several days at no additional charge. There is VIP service available when you fly into Kyiv. This is similar to VIP described in Russia. Your agency or a good travel agency should be able to arrange this. The cost is around $50.00. Other parents have flown KLM from the US through Amsterdam and on to Kyiv.

As with any travel, go light. Kyiv is a big city and has shopping centers where you can pick up anything. You will likely have a long wait in the NAC hallway, so you might take a travel cup for coffee. Traveler's checks are useless. Cash is king. Take only one dress for Court. Otherwise jeans and capris are very common.

In Kyiv some families have stayed at the **Brataslova**. The rooms are clean and there is a nice breakfast every morning. The hotel is a very short walk to the metro, which you can use to quickly travel to downtown. Also there are several markets just outside, including a huge baby market. Some have also stayed in the renovated section at the **Libid Hotel** at Ploshad Pobedy (or Peromogi) meaning Victory Square (in Russian and Ukrainian). It is at the end of Shevchenko Blvd, just down from the Adoption Center on the same side of the street. It goes for just over $100.00 per night and it is less than a block away from the Adoption Center.

As in Russia, your laptop will work in Ukraine as long as your modem is compatible with their phone jacks. You can also use an Internet café. There are several in Kyiv such as one on Prorizna str., 21, up from the Kreshchatik metro stop; phone number is (+380-44) 2280548, http://www.cybercafe.com.ua and on the fourth floor of the Doetske Mir department store. There are at least two in Simferopol and at least one in Kramatorsk. As to US money, it should be the usual clean crisp variety. There are money exchangers located in every city.

National Adoption Center

Upon arriving in Kyiv, you travel to the National Adoption Center with your facilitator and translator and meet with the physician and Center Director. Tamara Kunko used to be the Director, but Mrs. Parienko replaced her in 2002 only to leave in 2003 and be replaced with Ms. Yevgeniya Chernyshova.The NAC is located at 27 Taras Schevchenko Blvd., Kyiv, Ukraine 252032; phone: 380-44-246-54-31/32/37/49;fax: 380-44-246-54-52/62. NAC personnel speak

Russian and Ukrainian, however officially they will likely only speak Ukrainian to your translator/facilitator.

Some have described the NAC visit as having an appointment at a doctor's office, where you sit and wait. In this case, everyone stands in a dark hallway. Your translator will position you along the wall. You will hear many languages and when one of the doors opens, there is silence with everyone watching to see who comes out.

The Ukrainian system has been in a constant flux for over a year and it does not look like that is going to change. There were allegations in 2002 that some NAC employees and children's home directors were engaged in back door dealing. In Eastern Europe, truth is a precious commodity and it is hard for anyone, but an insider to discover the real story. If a facilitator cannot get something done, then he might tell a parent "that it is because of corruption." This may be true or may be just a story to cover up his failure. I neither credit nor discredit these allegations, but simply point out that whether in the US or Eastern Europe, money attracts flies. Also note that some translators and facilitators work very hard and not for huge sums of money. So you have both sides. If one were cynical, you might say that Mrs. Parienko's reformist ideas stepped on too many toes, which is why she left. Again, there are plenty of theories, but few hard facts. What is true is that over the years the Ukrainian process has become harder, not easier.

Mrs. Parienko introduced some changes to the way things work. She employed interpreters/translators who participated in interactions with parents. Ms Parienko wanted to reduce the independent facilitators/translators' role in the NAC process. It is unknown how the process will work under this latest Director. NO gifts should be given to NAC staff. Save your money for buying things the orphanage needs.

The Director's office is up some steep stairs. You wait in a long, dark hallway along with French and Italian couples. The dress should be business casual. You are then brought into a room and discuss with the NAC the type of health problems you would accept. You are then recommended a number of children according to your parameters of health, gender, and age. Remember that the list of children you are shown will be only those who are available according to NAC's records. Once you get to a children's home there will likely be other available children whose paperwork has just not been updated at the NAC, but who are also off the database and are available. (Although at some orphanages the Director will not let you see any children not listed on your NAC permission slip.) The NAC is a busy place so don't be surprised to find a business type atmosphere when you are being shown children from the albums. The NAC employees will generally be pleasant and courteous. The atmosphere will be a little warmer at the children's home.

It is not uncommon for the NAC to try to guide you toward boys. They may even say "no girls available." Indeed, finding a young healthy girl is not as easy as it once was. If this is what you want, then your search will take longer. Also, appreciate that older children need families as well and will not necessarily come with medical issues. You should have a firm discussion with your facilitator about adopting a girl prior to traveling. The NAC says that inviting you to adopt does not guarantee that you will be able to adopt a child within your parameters. What seems to be happening is that at the NAC the children shown might have issues, but once you actually travel to several children's homes you might see other adoptable children who are healthier, younger or have correctable conditions. The NAC seems to have binders of children who have been available for some time, while at the actual orphanage you might see children who have recently come off the registry and whose paperwork is still making its very slow way up the chain to the NAC.

At the NAC you will see at least 27 binders with pictures of children from every orphanage across Ukraine. There is a separate binder of siblings. Some of these children have very real problems such as AIDS, Down syndrome, autism, FAS, hydrocephalic (real), hepatitis, microcephalia, missing limbs, misshapen heads, CP and other diagnoses. Also in these binders are children whose diagnoses are not true or have correctable problems. It is stressful reviewing these binders.

Never demand anything at the NAC, just keep reiterating what sort of child you want to adopt. If you become unhappy with the process, tell your facilitator, not the NAC, Judges or clerks. Let your facilitator be the sounding board, and chief flak catcher. If the NAC likes and trusts your facilitator, then you may be shown a picture of that toddler girl you've asked for. If you are rude or demanding to the NAC, you are likely to have an unhappy adoption experience. If you can, go early in the morning to the NAC and to the children's home. Like everywhere else in the world, the later in the day, the more tired people are.

Your experience at the NAC will also vary from that of someone else for a variety of reasons. You are likely to be shown lots of referrals, if you have no gender preference and are willing to adopt a child as old as the age of eight. Requesting a relatively healthy girl will likely limit the number of photographs and stretch out your time in Ukraine. An example of unrealistic expectations is to want an infant girl less than 15 months in age. Yet some parents have adopted such a child. A more realistic expectation, that still might take you 3 weeks to find, is to adopt a healthy girl at 3 years of age. One problem with discussing the age of available children is that it can vary widely and one family's experience may be completely different than another's.

Be wary of falling into a trap where you begin to feel desperate. You feel you have spent all of this money and traveled all this way and time is running out so you adopt a child whose medical information you haven't properly vetted. You must slow down and take a deep breath. This adoption is forever.

At the NAC you will be shown children's pictures and a brief abstract of their medical condition, description and family history. The information may be a lot if the child is older or less if an infant. It varies. Italians tend to adopt older children, as they are more comfortable with the greater medical information they receive. They feel that with an older child, any medical issues would already have manifested themselves.

Ukraine has also begun foster programs for young healthy children. These foster children are available for adoption, although there have been only a few adoptions. The Ukrainian families receive a stipend from the state and can have several children in their care. This is one reason for the change in the numbers of young healthy children. The foster care system is intended to do several things. First, the children have an opportunity to leave the orphanage and participate in a regular community and go to regular schools. They are hoping to give the children a more normal home life. They also hope that Ukrainians will adopt some more of these children. Because the families receive an income for foster parenting these children, they usually don't adopt the children. Once they are the child's official parents the foster income would cease. This used to be a problem in the United States as well. (Some states have changed their practice to allow an adopting foster family to continue to receive a stipend for some time after the adoption.)

Children are still available at younger ages, but with surgical needs or chronic medical conditions, or delays. Ukrainian families are not adopting children with such needs because they don't have the resources to correct the problems for these children. It has been true for sometime that more parents are coming to Ukraine who want young healthy children, than there are young healthy children available. However, for parents who are willing to accept children with surgical needs (especially boys) or with conditions that are manageable, there are still pre-school children available in Ukraine.

The information at the NAC is probably not as current as the information at the children's home itself. If you do not find any of these children suitable, then a phone call to the orphanage by the NAC can be made to determine if other children are available for adoption. You will likely see all of the available children in your age range that the NAC has on that particular day. On another day there might be more, or less. The more restrictive your criteria, the less children you will see. Be very polite and respectful and look and acknowledge each referral shown to you.

The NAC and your facilitator will probably try to steer you a little toward the more adoption friendly regions. If you are made of sterner stuff, then tell them you will go to any region. A difficult region (like Dnipro) means that the timeline could be longer as there will be less time periods waived and less service expedited. In general, southern Ukraine seems easier to adopt from than the western regions, although there is no difference in the care at the homes. Also, just because it might be a harder process in the west, that doesn't mean that adoptions don't occur. They happen all the time. The process is just more difficult. Traditionally, the south has always been a less conservative part of the country. Western Ukraine is different. It is poorer and its administration is much more conservative.

At the children's home itself you are likely to see additional available children that have not yet made it into the NAC photo albums. As in Russia, the anecdotal evidence is that there are more boys available then girls. Notwithstanding, many people have adopted girls. Ukrainian law requires both parents to meet the child and attend court. Although most parents prefer to meet the child and choose whom to adopt together, one parent can do that with the other spouse traveling over for court.

After narrowing down your search, the NAC sends you to a region and you travel to the children's home accompanied by the facilitator and translator. Which orphanage and the region you travel to depends entirely on the location of the child that you picked from the photo album shown to you in Kyiv. Make sure that your facilitator does not influence your choice. Some facilitators only want to go to certain regions to save themselves time and money. They may also want to go to a particular region because they are well liked (connected) there, which in and of itself may be helpful to you. (See how gray everything is—two explanations for the same thing.).

The Adoption Center will show a family many available children. Some are near your criteria and some are not. These children can be spread about the country depending on how proactive the orphanages have been during the year to register children. Translators should be ready to travel to any region of Ukraine to maximize a family's chances in finding their child. This is a subject that should be part of the interview before selecting your facilitator/translator or a topic you should at least discuss prior to going to the NAC. You do not want to be limited by your translator's reluctance to go to certain regions. If he is reluctant to visit certain regions, ask him for his reasons. You may agree or disagree, but at least it's your choice. After all, it's your adoption and your family you are creating, not his and not your agency's.

Children's Home

There are approximately 141 children's homes in Ukraine. The typical age ranges are from 0-3 or 4 from 3-7 or 3-17 or 7-17. It can vary greatly. There are a few homes that have children in age from 0-17, 6-17, 0-7, 0-5, 3-8, and 4-9. It varies across all the regions. Numbers of children in a home can be as little as 21 children and as many as three hundred. In 1999, it was reported that there were 4,467 children in the children's homes run by the Ministry of Education, 3,503 in those run by the Ministry of Health (baby homes), and 2,728 in those run by the Ministry of Labor. The status of the children depends on why they are there. You might find yourself in a home filled with children, but only a few are available according to the registry. This is because Ukrainian children's homes are also used for foster care. The Russians do the same thing. If a family is having a problem, they can place their children with their local children's home until they are better able to care for their children. In years past, these placements might be for abuse, drugs or alcohol, but more and more frequently it is because of the poor economic circumstances of Ukraine. Another reason children may not be available is because they simply haven't been registered. This could be because of lack of diligence on the part of the home director or in many cases because they are having trouble terminating parental rights. For example, perhaps there was a child who was placed for foster care, but the family never came to visit and they cannot be found. Therefore, there is no relinquishment letter in the child's file and the child must have the court terminate his parent's rights. Most of the homes have a director and a senior physician with whom you will meet to discuss the available children. You may also meet with a senior educator or a specialist like a speech pathologist.

You must have Adoption Center approval to see children and review their medical files. Once you decide which children you will go to see the Adoption Center issues a letter of approval. Most often the letters list specific children. But if there is a children's home that has a number of children who have come available within your criteria, then you will be issued a letter that is general and permits you to see all available children.

At the children's home you interview the recommended children. Present are probably their caretaker, your translator, the facilitator, and the home's pediatrician. Your translator may have translated the medical records and all history known about the child from the records. You ask questions of the director; the caretaker and the children based on the information in the file. If you have made arrangements, you can now have this information sent to the US for evaluation.

There are different ways of handling the interview process. Some parents have asked to see the children in their environment. They go into the room where the children are playing, and ask the director to go around to the available children and lay her hand on their heads. This way the children are not disturbed, and the parents can see the children without them feeling like they are 'on display'. The director just tells the children that the parents are there to visit the children's home, thereby removing any potential anxiety. The parents watch the children and interact with the ones who are available for adoption. This also gives parents a chance to see the children interact with one another. By this method, no one particular child feels the sting of rejection by you saying 'no' to he/she particularly, but that you say 'yes' to the one that you feel best will fit into your family. The problem with seeing one child at a time, and saying 'no', and then seeing another is that it may make a child feel so rejected. Seeing the children in a group setting eliminates that.

Of course, some directors have their own ideas about how it will be done. Indeed, sometimes all the available children are not in the same group. Also, in some homes the caretakers bathe and have the children's hair washed once a week. However, when you come they may bathe them specially and pick out nice outfits for them to be "presented" in. The caretakers want the children to have the best chance of being adopted.

It used to be that if you did not find "your" child, you could call the Adoption Center in Kyiv again and they will try to send you somewhere else. The NAC may also have a chat with the home director, and magically you may be shown other children from the same children's home. Was the director "holding" these children for some financial reason? Who knows? This problem of "holding" children seems to have been around Kyiv. Mrs. Parienko changed the procedure so that you had to explain why a child was not acceptable, before the NAC referred you another. Also, if you returned to the NAC to see another referral, you had to request another appointment. Previously, you would just come in and be moved to the front of the line. Whether the procedure will remain the same or revert to the old way, only time will tell.

You have the option in Ukraine of bringing a doctor with you to the orphanage to evaluate the children you have been referred. There are both western-trained doctors and locally trained doctors who will travel with you to the orphanage. Your facilitator will help you arrange for a doctor prior to your trip. For example, some parents have taken a pediatrician from the American Medical Center in Kyiv, 1 Berdichevskaya Str., Tel. 490-7600; e-mail: *kiev@amcenters.com*. The American Medical Clinic has a very informative web site at *http://www.amcenters.com/contact_kyiv.htm*. You may also be able to have the other medical establishment in Kyiv, the Clinic of the Oil and

Gas Industry, provide pre-adoption physicals (including blood tests, etc.) at their clinic in Kyiv. Their number in Kyiv is 380/44/277-4181, 244-8941. The doctors are all Ukrainian, but most of them speak basic English. Just in case, you might take your translator with you. The clinic doesn't look Western from the outside, but it has modern lab and x-ray equipment. It may also be cheaper than the AMC. The Clinic is located on a hill in a park-like setting. Blood tests can be done at a lab in Kyiv or flown to Germany to a better lab. You can also have your child's US visa medical evaluation completed at either the Clinic or at AMC prior to flying to Warsaw. The physical is about $26 US, which is cheaper than in Warsaw.

Another doctor is Dr. Yuri Bezdverny. He was employed for many years as a Designated Medical Provider for Canada Immigration and the Canadian Embassy and he is available for private medical consultations. Dr. Yuri will travel to the orphanages to meet with the children and the orphanage physicians. He is fluent in English, Ukrainian and Russian. He can prepare any medical abstracts on the child, and can ensure that medical tests are undertaken. His email address is *ybezdverny@freemail.ru*

In addition, a number of the US based adoption clinics as well as the usual adoption medical specialists will review medicals sent to them while you are in Ukraine, or consult with you by phone from there. You may be given a number of days to decide, and may be allowed to actually have blood testing done by the doctor you hire. One line of thinking is that conducting another blood test may actually increase the risk that the child will be exposed to infection from an unsanitary needle. If you want to run a blood test, you may want to bring your own needles. Also, there is always an issue as to whether the diagnostic results are accurate. Some families have foregone the whole medical evaluation and relied on their "gut" feeling when meeting their child. What these families say is that love is love and we chose the daughters that were meant to be ours. Others have taken actual tape measurements of a prospective child's head. One great advantage of the Ukrainian process is that you actually meet and interact with the child, which provides a lot of information that you just can't get from a medical record, picture or video. At the same time, emotionally it is probably more stressful. Even if you do not go through all of the medical evaluation when meeting your child, there is absolutely no reason not to be prepared to do so.

Here is a description of one Ukrainian children's home. The Stroganofski Orphanage in Simferopol, in the Crimea, is for children ages 5 to 8. It has a capacity of 80. The children are kept in groups of approximately 10 with three caretakers assigned to shifts to provide 24-hour coverage. These same caretakers usually stay with "the group" as long as they are there. The children are assigned to groups based on age, development and size. The children's home is clean, the caretakers friendly and warm people. Some caretakers have been there as long as 15 years with wages paid only intermittently. The home has no heat and electricity and water only part of each day. The children are fed cabbage, potato soup and a slice of bread with sugared tea several times a day. Milk and meat is not normally part of their diet.

Another pretty good older children's home is the Bilhorod-Dnistrovsky Children's Home in Odessa. It is for boys and girls between 4 and 8. It is clean and well run. Many Italian and French couples adopt from there. American couples are also turning up more often. Odessa is on the coast so it is sunny and has been described as being like Northern California. Anecdotally, Odessa seems to move through the adoption process pretty quickly.

Ukraine is no different than any other FSU country. Some regions and cities have no corruption (Donetsk) and others are rife with it (Kirovograd, Kremenchuk). Usually you will not know anything is going on, as it will be discussed behind closed doors and in Ukrainian. There is not much you can do about it if you don't know and if you did know, you would then have the dilemma of deciding what to do. The new NAC Director seems to be doing a lot to straighten out the system. The corruption is by officials who control the paperwork process. In these regions money greases the wheels of the administrative gatekeeper clerks. Now what I have described seems to happen more so in those regions that are unfriendly to foreign adoptions like the western regions rather than in ones that support the process like the south and southeast. It certainly is not in all regions or at all administrative levels. Your experience will likely be different, just know that sometimes, in some places, it occurs.

Ukraine requires a 30-day appeal period for all civil cases. It used to be that if the region had routinely waived this period when it was 10 days then the fact that it was now 30 did not make a difference. Technically, the Ukrainian law states that waivers can be given when there are circumstances that might cause a threat to the child's health (like treatment for a condition), or some obstacle to the adoptive parent. These same factors can be raised in order to obtain a quick adoption court hearing. In yet another change, Judges are waiving the appeal period less and less. If the 30 days is not waived, then your choice is to stay or return home and then go back for your child. You should decide in advance what you plan to do, if faced with this possibility. This is one reason why at least one of the parents should have a double-entry visa.

If you do decide that one parent will stay, consider renting an apartment. The cost is nominal. You should be able to rent one for 2 weeks for no more than $75.00 total. Kyiv might be more, but not by a whole lot. In Simferopol you can stay at a 'Red Cross' facility (somewhat like a hotel with a dining room) for less than $5 a day.

One interesting region is Dniproprotrovsk. There are children available from this region. Most parents do not adopt from there because the bureaucracy places additional obstacles in your way that other regions do not. For example, they never waive the 30 days. Most parents just leave and then one returns to travel with the child. It takes 2 to 3 court sessions to finalize the adoption and more documents are requested than is really required by law. This is why no one wants to go there, but there are children there if you have the patience to wait out the long process and stay the 30 days or make two trips. This region could take 3-4 weeks for your first trip and then the wait in country or a second trip of approximately another two weeks. You really need a facilitator that understands what this region's officials want. Now after saying all of this, realize that if most parents do not want to endure the hassles that could very well leave a larger population of adoptable children waiting for families. It is sort of like adopting from Siberia in the winter. This is just something to think about.

In the Dniproprotrovsk region Americans and Canadians have adopted from Orphanage #1. The orphanage is very poor, but the workers are very dedicated and show much love and affection for the children. The children eat fairly well and they get to be outside a lot. They have music classes and daily massages.

After choosing your child, and with the recommendations of the home director, you submit your adoption petition to the court and the hearing is placed on the judge's calendar. At the same time the papers are sent back to the National Adoption Center in Kyiv for approval. When that approval returns from the NAC, you can go to court. It's taking an average of 3 days to get the permission letter the NAC sends to the court stating they are in favor of your adoption. It is also taking about 1 business day to get the permission letter to visit the region AFTER your appointment. So be sure to plan enough time.

As you might expect, since Ukraine was part of Russia for so long, its courts run pretty similar to those in Russia. Present in court are normally your facilitator, translator, the Inspector representing the Ministry of Education, the Prosecuting Attorney representing the State and the court reporter. This is very similar to the way the Russian court hearing is handled. The judge and Prosecuting Attorney ask you questions to make sure you know your responsibilities under Ukrainian law toward the child and the Ukrainian government. (The child keeps Ukrainian citizenship until age 18 and you must send annual letters on how she is doing in school and her health.)

The prosecutor will ask you about childcare provisions you have made and about school. They will ask about your ability to provide the child medical care. The questions are similar to the Russian Courts. You may also request a waiver of the 30-day wait. After the decision, you have it recorded in the jurisdiction's records at the "Notary's." This is the equivalent to the county clerk where all official records are kept of municipal government transactions. You then may have to travel to the regional city to get a new birth certificate with you named as the new parents. You will need this to get the child a Ukrainian passport. The information you receive (original birth certificate copy, court decree, mother's refusal and medical history summary) is the only information you may legally obtain. It is certainly possible to try to track down the birth mother informally through unofficial means, and this is not prohibited. A new adoption law was recently passed, which allows adopted children to have access to their files once they turn age 14. These files are kept in the orphanage permanently.

Make sure the local passport office (OVIR) issues your child an international passport (red book), and not the child's travel document (blue book). Local passport (OVIR) agencies are not always able to issue international passports. If local OVIRs do not have the required passport books, contact the oblast OVIR office and inform them about the problem. If your child leaves Ukraine with a child's "blue" passport, there is a small possibility that the border guard at the airport and a larger possibility at the border itself may stop you, if you drive or go by train. If the OVIR office does not have the red passport books, obtain the child's travel document (blue passport book) and ask OVIR to issue you a letter stating that OVIR cannot issue an international passport to the adopted child and therefore the child's travel passport with the same validity has been issued. If the border guard stops you, contact the Embassy's American Citizens Services Unit at (044) 490-4422. In case of an emergency outside business hours, American citizens may reach the Embassy duty officer by calling 044-490-4000.

You then travel back to Kyiv with your child, his new Ukrainian passport and amended birth certificate. You then take the final adoption decree to the National Adoption Center, then to the Ministry of Education, and Ministry of Foreign Affairs. Your facilitator should take care of all of that. If one parent needs to leave early, then the leaving parent should go to the US Embassy in Kyiv and sign the I-600 in the presence of a consular official. The Consular section of the Embassy has asked parents to make an appointment with them prior to showing up to complete the Form I-604 report. The Embassy is closed the last working day of he month and on US and Ukrainian holidays. The Embassy's holiday schedule is located on their web site. Since, the Embassy in

Kyiv does not issue immigrant visas, but rather Warsaw, you must put Warsaw, not Kyiv on your I-600A.The spouse remaining with the child must also go to the US Embassy's Consular Section so they can complete *Form I-604, Report of Overseas Orphan Investigation*. This will become part of your visa package that you take to Warsaw. The Embassy in Warsaw will ask you some general questions about the child and your knowledge of what was told to you. The Consular officer will also inspect the adoption papers. Since the I-864 Form is no longer required for IR3 adoptions, you will be asked for a copy your previous year's tax return or your last two month's pay stubs.

The US Embassy in Ukraine is located at Kozubinskoho 10, 254053, Kyiv, Ukraine Phone: 380-44-490-4000. The Consular office is at 6 Mykoly Pymonenka St., Phone: 38-044-490-4422; Fax: 38-044-236-4892.

As with the Russian process, you will need to have your child medically examined before you can receive a US visa. This can be done in Kyiv or in Warsaw. The US Embassy in Warsaw will need the same sort of medical review "pink" sheet as is described in the Russian process. You leave Kyiv with your child and fly to Warsaw, Poland to get the child's American visa from the US Embassy there. Immigrant visas are not issued in Kyiv, which is why you put "Warsaw" on your I-600A as the consulate office. It is to Warsaw that the BCIS will send the cable confirming that they have issued the I-171H. The Embassy web site in Warsaw has a list of approved doctors. Some have used a Dr. Wanda Korulska, whose fees appear reasonable. Next to the waiting room at the Embassy in Kyiv is a telephone, which you can use to call the US Embassy in Warsaw and make your visa appointment. The phone number is on a sheet of paper near the telephone. You may have to call several times before you can get through.

For those living in Illinois, things are a little different in relation to how the I-171H is handled. There is a state requirement in Illinois that you identify your child before they will permit BCIS to send your cable onto Warsaw (or Moscow or anywhere else). Thus, your 171H notice reads that you are approved but that BCIS is holding your cable. Obviously, you cannot pre-identify for Ukraine, so families have been contacting the DCFS intercountry coordinator, Muriel Shennan, to work out a solution. This solution consists of notifying her that you will fax identification information from Ukraine to her and request that she contact Jennifer West at Chicago BCIS as soon as possible after receipt of your identifying information. Then, Jennifer West cables Warsaw and if all works well, your cable has been received in Warsaw before you arrive from Ukraine. The National Adoption Center of Ukraine requires a letter explaining why your 171H is being held. You can ask for a letter of explanation from Jennifer West, or from Landon Taylor, the vice-consul at the American Embassy in Kyiv. Here is the contact information: Muriel Shennan: phone-217 785 2692; Jennifer West phone: 312-385-1819, fax: 312-385-3404; Landon Taylor at TaylorLR1@state.gov, phone Consular Section (380) (44) 246-8048. 380 is the country code for Ukraine.

US Embassy in Warsaw

Poland is the most western of all the Eastern European countries, except for Hungary. You will feel you are back in Europe. The US Embassy is in the center of Warsaw. The Embassy in Warsaw opens at 8am and although you should make an appointment you can also just show up. You should be able to leave by late morning and then return in the afternoon for the visa. The email address for the Warsaw Embassy is ADOPTWRW@state.gov. The Embassy operator is (48-22) 504-2000 and Consular phone number (for scheduling adoptions and adoption inquiries): (48-22) 625-1401 Consular fax number: (48-22) 625-4734 A good explanation of the US Embassy procedure is at *http://www.usinfo.pl/consular/iv/adoptions.htm.*

Poland is moving toward requiring all Ukrainians to have a Polish visa, including your adopted child. Look into this before you leave Kyiv. US citizens do not need one. People travel from Kyiv to Warsaw by planes, trains and automobilesTraveling by car with your new child will be a disastrous experience. The train is only slightly better. Taking a quick plane flight is really the best answer. Tickets on Aerosvet (local airlines) are about $140 per person one way Kyiv-Warsaw. There are 1 or 2 flights per day on this airline and it is a 1 1/2 hour flight non-stop. You can buy the tickets a couple of days before by visiting a travel agency in Kyiv. There are other airlines. The flights are full and cramped, but quick. The train leaves Kiev in the evening, and travels through the night to the train station in Warsaw where you then take a taxi to your hotel or the embassy. The cost is $35 per person for a sleeper car. Be sure to lock your sleeper car. The train ride is about 12 hours with a 4 hour stop at the border so they can adjust the wheels to the different width of Western rails.

Some parents have used *http://www.hotelspoland.com* to book their hotel in Warsaw. In Warsaw, families have stayed at the **Hotel Polonium**; ph.—011-48-22-628-72-41; FAX 011-48-22-628-66-22. The rooms are generally about $78.00 per night and include a huge international breakfast buffet. The hotel is very centrally located. There is a McDonalds and Pizza Hut near by. The metro station is less than 1/2 block away. This hotel is within about a 7 block walking distance from the US Embassy. Some parents have stayed at the **Forum Hotel**. It is about $140 a night and is a short 15 minute walk to the U.S. Embassy.

Others like the **Sheraton**, which is just a 10 minute walk to the US Embassy. It is very nice and luxurious. The adoption rate is around $140 a night. You can book the Sheraton from the States or from Ukraine. It has a toddler playroom and will provide a crib upon request. They have a house doctor that speaks Russian and English. They have very good room service and the rooms come with a mini bar. You can simply relax in your room, have cheeseburgers delivered and watch television. It is almost like home. The address is Sheraton Warsaw Hotel & Towers, 2 B. Prusa Street, 00-493 Warszawa Poland Tel.: (+48 22) 657 61 00

There is also a very nice **Marriott**. It has a pool. Always ask for the adoption discount when checking in or buying an airline ticket. If you don't ask, you don't get!

Another hotel is the **Hotel Metropol**. It is less expensive than the Sheraton or Marriott. It is located at 99a Marszalkowska Street, 00-693 Warszawa, Poland Tel.: (+48 22) 629 40 01, 621 43 54; Tel.: (+48 22) 621 10 93 (rezerwacja) Fax: (+48 22) 625 30 14 Also, you can try the **Warszawa Hotel** at 9 Plac Powstancow Warszawy, 00-039 Warsaw, Poland; Tel.: (+48 22) 826 94 21; Tel.: (+48 22) 827 18 73 (rezerwacja); Fax: (+48 22) 827 18 73

When exiting the airport in Warsaw just keep going straight until you hit the line of Mercedes outside. Avoid the swarms of the private drivers on your way. There will be a dispatcher assigning the jobs to the first in a line driver. Just explain to him where you'd like to go in English. The average ride fee is about $15 from the airport to the hotel. If you like your driver he may be able to help you with several matters such as exchanging currency (he might stop at the local market to exchange the dollars to zlotys), or being a tour guide until your departure from Warsaw.

When you arrive at the Embassy just walk straight to the consular section doors and bypass the people waiting on the street. Just show the guards your American passport and they will let you in. It shouldn't take more than 10 minutes to see a clerk. You file your papers at the "special" window on the far left side of the room. She will check your papers to make sure you have everything (packet from American Embassy in Kyiv, I-600 form, etc.). If your child will be receiving an IR3 visa, the Warsaw Embassy Visa Unit only requires a copy of your most recent tax return (it will be returned after the interview) or your most recent pay stubs. They do not require the last 3 years as some Embassy Visa Units arbitrarily do. In an hour you will be called for the interview with the Consular Officer. There is a small play area for the children. It should all take just 5 minutes, assuming all paperwork is in order. (This was actually the same procedure used in Moscow before they changed it in December 2000.) You will then be directed to the cashier line to pay $335 for the Visa. Make sure you save the receipt as you will need to show it when you pick up your Visa at 3pm in the afternoon. The Visa will be in a sealed packet of information, which you should not open. You should pack it in your carry on and give it to the Immigration Officer when you land in the States.

When you return to the States your child must be registered with the Ukrainian Embassy in Washington within 3 months. This is not an unreasonable request if you follow their line of thinking that since the child has Ukrainian citizenship until they are 18, and then they should be registered, as they would be if they were adult Ukrainians. Russia now has such a rule as well. This registration requirement does not stop your child from becoming an American citizen, or give Ukraine any rights over your child. You register your child by filling out a form and attaching a color passport photo of the child. Send this form to the Ukrainian Embassy along with the child's passport. The Embassy will stamp the passport and return it to you. Once the passport is returned to you, you will need to make a photocopy of the stamped page and fax or mail it to The National Adoption Center. The NAC is getting stricter about making sure you have registered. It is important to them, so it should be important to you. The NAC has a serious concern with the failure by parents to register their adoptive children and send in annual reports. If this continues, look for repercussions.

You will need to submit annual reports to the Ukraine Embassy until your child turns 18. This will keep your child's Ukrainian citizenship up to date. The form for the report is at *http://ukraineinfo.us/consular/adoption-report.html.* Ukraine does not require post-placement reports, just this yearly letter detailing the child's progress with some photos is all that is required. Neither your agency nor a social worker needs to be involved unless your state has some extra requirement. The registration requirements are at the Ukrainian Embassy web site at *http://ukraineinfo.us/consular/adoption-registration.html.*

More Ukrainian adoption links are as follows:

http://adoption.about.com/parenting/adoption/library/writes/blaw_post01.htm
http://diettmeier.tripod.com/Lostlamb/
http://www.zooid.com/valente/
http://ukrainianadopt.tripod.com/start.html
http://www.geocities.com/rmlegv/index.html
http://williamsfamily_4.tripod.com/independentukrainianadoption/
http://members.aol.com/pupchek/
http://hometown.aol.com/jlt413/Adoption.html

http://joyjeffers.tripod.com/OurUkraineAdoption/index.html
http://www.beardens.homestead.com/first.html
http://www.geocities.com/tonia_cce/ukraine_adoption.html
http://members.aol.com/_ht_a/trcfill/myhomepage/
http://www.e-bragg.com/ukraine%20adoption/we_are_adopting.htm
http://www.paulandjulie.homestead.com/Ukraine.html
http://user.tninet.se/~gdr662s/indexb.htm
http://pages.prodigy.net/a_jharrell/index.html
http://www.worldadopt.org/index2.html
http://ruth.oppedahl.com/
http://groups.yahoo.com/group/Adoption_from_Ukraine/
http://groups.yahoo.com/group/UkrainianPostAdoptiveParentsGroup/
http://groups.yahoo.com/group/olderchildukraineadoption/?yguid=78437358

If you want to help, there are several groups that take donations. Here are just a few:
http://rod.rakes.com/orphans.html
http://www.cry.org.uk/fathers_house.html
http://www.geocities.com/Heartland/Valley/7607/Main_eng.html

CHAPTER XVI

KAZAKHSTAN

After Ukraine, Kazakhstan is probably the next most popular former Soviet Republic from which to adopt. Kazakhstan has the second-largest landmass in the former Soviet Union, yet its population of 17 million makes it one of the most sparsely populated regions in the world. It is four times the size of Texas. More than 100 nationalities live in Kazakhstan, with Kazaks and Slavs (about 40 percent of the population each) constituting the two largest ethnic groups. There used to be a large group of Germans thanks to Stalin moving them away from Russia's border, but many repatriated to Germany when Kazakhstan became independent.

Americans adopted 672 children from Kazakhstan in fiscal year 2001. It was the eighth most popular country from which to adopt. This was more than double from the previous year. In FY 2002, Americans adopted 799 children who received IR3 visas and 20 children that received IR4s.

Kazakhstan became independent from Russia on December 16, 1991. As to be expected, the President of Kazakhstan is Nursultan Nazarbayev, the former Communist boss. It is the usual totalitarian government with the usual repression of opposition parties and individuals. The strongest opposition came in 2002. The United States has frequently criticized his repressive moves, but without visible effect. The situation in Kazakhstan is sensitive for the United States, which has long considered this country an important future source of oil and more recently a key ally in the war on terrorism. The United States signed an agreement with Kazakhstan allowing use of the country's major airport for emergency landings by U.S. warplanes operating over Afghanistan, whose northern border is just 300 miles away.

Although the country has rich oil revenues from the Caspian, the children's homes do not receive as much support as the country can afford. Instead, Kazakhstan has followed the all too familiar road of personal wealth for the family elite with allegations of Swiss bank accounts. However, the President and his wife are supportive of foreign adoption and for that the children can be thankful.

There are several American enclaves in the larger cities supporting the major oil companies and their employees. ChevronTexaco, ExxonMobil and other companies even support an American Little League team in Almaty. There are American styled grocery stores that take Visa cards. ChevronTexaco is head of a consortium, which has built a pipeline through which Kazakhstan oil is exported to a Russian port. If you are a ChevronTexaco employee, you will have resources in-country that others do not have. The Kazakhstan oil field of Tengiz is one of the world's ten largest and the newly discovered Kashagan field 50 miles offshore in the Caspian could have twice as much oil. The Tengiz project is the largest Western-run oil producer anywhere in the former Soviet Union, producing 286,000 barrels a day. After some financial brinkmanship, the government and the oil companies have agreed to an expansion that will lift output to 460,000 barrels a day by 2006.

Kazakhstan is notably different from the other four Central Asian republics of the CIS in that a majority of its citizens are Russian speakers. The Kazak language is spoken by over 40% of population, but Russian is the language spoken by two-thirds of the population and is used in everyday business. Your dossier is actually translated into Russian. The country is composed of Kazak 46%, Russian 34.7%, Ukrainian 4.9%, German 3.1%, Uzbek 2.3%, Tatar 1.9%, other 7.1% (1996). Because of its large Russian population in the north, there is always some underlying tension between the two countries. The country is religiously divided between Muslim 47%, Russian Orthodox 44%, Protestant 2%, other 7%. It has a very high literacy rate with some 98% of the population able to read and write. Kazakhstan relies on commodity exports, particularly oil, for its hard currency. Many of its manufacturing industries have closed. It has 14 regions with a geography ranging from mountains to steppes to desert.

Many adoption agencies started Kazakhstan programs after a law allowing foreign adoption was passed in Kazakhstan in December 1998. Generally, the age limit for parents wanting an infant is 45 years old for the mother and 50 for the father, although there is quite a bit of flexibility so this is not a real rule at all. Single women can adopt either gender, although some regions have placed restrictions and are not allowing single women to adopt infant girls, only infant boys or older girls. There is no rule on how many other children you can have in your home, but rather this is a regional preference. Some regions are also imposing a prohibition on adopting two unrelated children at one time as well.

Foreign adoptions used fall under the Ministry of Education's international adoption committee with the regions really running things. Kazahkstan started to impose stricter controls in 2002.The Education and Science Ministry was given the responsibility of maintaining a database of all the children with information about the state of their health and possible relatives. Parents have to register with the migration police once they arrive in Kazakhstan. This is similar to what Russia requires.

Newborns remain in a maternity hospital until they are 5 months old, then they are transferred to a baby house. Waiting time for a referral used to be minimal although the time is beginning to lengthen. Reports indicate that there are some 14,000 children living in the children's homes. Not all of these may be available for adoption. There are at least 30 US based agencies working in the country. Generally the cost is between $15,000 to $23,000. The usual length of time on the registry database is 5 months. Children cannot be adopted until after they are off the registry. Foreign adoption is permitted throughout the country.

As with Russia, your notarized dossier documents are apostilled. Some states, like New York and Kentucky, require that the notaries be 'certified' at the county level before they can be apostilled. The dossier documents are similar to those needed for Russia (birth certificates, marriage certificates, medicals, employment verification, bank reference, passport information, home study, post placement agreement, agency license). In addition to the dossier documents, an adopting family must also be registered as an adoption family with the Republic of Kazakhstan. This entails filing a "Registration Letter" along with the dossier. Your dossier first is sent to the Kazakhstan Consulate in the US then it is filed and approved by the Ministry of Foreign Affairs and then it is passed on to the Ministry of Education for approval and processing. Once the Ministry of Education has approved your dossier you will be issued an "invitation to travel." The actual pipeline of dossier processing is as follows: the Kazakhstan Embassy in the U.S then it is released to the Ministry of Foreign Affairs in Astana; then passed to the Ministry of Education; then the Guardianship Board in the city where the child resides. There can be a problem with the Kasakhstan Embassy in that they sometimes hold on to the dossiers for up to 3 months or so before sending them on and also create new bundling/ unbundling requirements when it suits them. The Washington D.C Consulate seems to be the slowest. Avoid them if you can and don't call them as they might just move your dossier to the bottom. Of course, part of the problem could be that your agency has not had all of their returning families registered with the Consulate. You can find a detailed outline of the dossier procedure at *http://www.asststork.com/pages/kazdw.html*. After your dossier has passed through the Ministries, you will be sent a Letter of Invitation and then Confirmation Numbers which you use to apply for your Kazakhstan Adoption Visa.

Generally, both parents must attend court. The length of time you must spend in country can vary. Kazakhstan requires a 14-day visitation before you can go to court and then a 14-day appeal period before the decree is final and you can pick up your child's passport and exit visa. Families who adopted soon after the Kazakhstan law was revised in December 1998 experienced more delays in their process as the regions worked their way through the new process. Notwithstanding the mandatory 14-day period before court, some adoptions have been completed in as short a time as 8 days. The average appears to range from 10 days to 3 weeks. The shorter time frames are occurring less and less though and even in the larger cities like Almaty, Karaganda or Astana the courts are reluctant to waive time. As in Russia, there seems to be some variety in how each region handles adoptions. Some regions apply the 14-day appeal period strictly and at least one parent must wait out this time after the court hearing before the court decree is final.There is judicial discretion in reducing the appeal period. As in Russia, the waiver is determined on a case by case basis and is solely up to the judge. There are cases where the prosecutor has requested verification of some of the documents presented to the court such as the child being born outside a major city and the mother's letter of abandonment being legalized by a notary unknown to that particular court. The judge may well then enforce the waiting in that case. In 2003 there was a trend of not reducing the waiting times, and the average time in-country was 3-4 weeks with the Kyzylorda region topping the list at 5 weeks.

You should always ask the agency you are considering using regarding the length of stay in the region in which they work. The reference families should verify this. Both parents do not have to be there the entire time, although they both must attend court.Some regions allow you to wait with your child and in others the child must stay at the children's home.

You may receive a referral with medical information and a video while still in the United States although some families have received very minimal information. It varies by region and children's home. Some allow pre-identification material and some do not. Karaganda is one city that does not allow pre-identification although it does allow children to come to the United States on summer camp programs. Technically, the official Kazakhstan position is that there is no referral system and the child is not your son or daughter until the adoption decree is final. They view the referral system as treating the children as items in a catalog. Nevertheless, there are some agencies that can obtain a referral for you very quickly, although the wait for a girl is longer. In another trend in 2003, many regions were prohibiting the adoption of two unrelated children at the same time.

If only one of you is a US citizen, the other spouse will be required to obtain a letter from their country of origin stating that the child will be allowed into that country as well.

With some directors you can call and ask additional questions of the children's home doctor before accepting the referral. Once at the children's home, you may receive additional information regarding the background of your child. If the city is relatively small, the director may know quite a bit about the details of the lives of the birth parents. This information is always very helpful and can be passed on to your child when the proper time comes.

The children's homes seem generally to be in better shape than the Russian ones. The caretaker to child ratio seems to be lower. Generally children from infant to age 3 are housed together and older children are housed according to age as well. The children seem to be within their average for weight and look to be healthy. They eat a lot of "Kasha" which is like cream of wheat and borscht soup. The diet is mainly starches so you need to pump them full of proteins, fruits, and vegetables once they get home. If you are a vegetarian, discuss with a doctor about your child's protein deficiency and how to handle it. Children process nutrients differently than adults so placing these children on a strict vegetarian diet at this stage may be unhealthy. Also, the same sort of medical evaluation with an IA specialist should be performed. Just because this is Kasakhstan doesn't mean that some of the same sort of medical questions are not present.

Here is a description of a children's home in Atyrau, Kazakhstan. The children's home consists of a row of white buildings, in a nice secluded area near a park with a lot of trees. Outside there is playground equipment. The entrance is at the top of a skinny, metal row of stairs. There are several long, thin rooms, all connected by doors to other rooms. It is like a maze. The place is very clean, and every room had hard wood floors covered by bright rugs. There are about 50 children, age's birth to three in this baby house. It is very quiet. Inside one room are about 15 little children, about 2 to 3 years old. They are sitting in little chairs around the edge of the room.

Conditions in the institutions will vary from home to home, city to city. Children's homes in Karaganda and Almaty seem better than in Aqtobe. Generally the conditions overall are better than in Russia. However, do not read into the cleanliness of a children's home that they are receiving great care. This is an orphanage after all. The children are neither getting the best nutrition nor loving attention. Their emotional needs are not being met. If a child is a caregiver's favorite, then she or he will be emotionally stronger. There are still bad children's homes where babies are fed huge bowls of porridge using large spoons with their heads tilted back and are fed as quickly as possible. Sweetened tea is all they have to drink. Most caregivers do the best they can and most Directors work miracles on a slim budget. Generally the children are resilient and turn out fine. Most of the children do not have major behavioral issues. Just know that some Kazakhstan adoptees do come home with SID or attachment issues and prepare yourself as you would for an adoption from any other country.

While FAS/FAE is always a concern, because Kazakhstan has a large Muslim population, generally there is less alcohol consumed. Indeed, there is a huge difference in the amount of alcohol consumed between the Russian population within Kazakhstan and native Kazaks. Notwithstanding, the country practices a more secular form of religion so it might not be rare for a pregnant Kazak woman to have a few drinks. In all FSU countries the population's general medical knowledge is lacking and the connection between alcohol and birth defects is not well appreciated. You should always prepare for a Kazakhstani adoption just like you would for any country where the children are living in an institution. The same behavioral problems can appear.

The number of foreign airlines flying to Almaty, Kazakhstan has grown from 3 in 1993 to more than 12 in 1998. Today you can take direct flights to Almaty from Amsterdam (KLM), London (British Airways), Frankfurt (Lufthansa), Vienna (Austrian Airlines), Moscow (Aeroflot, Transaero), and Istanbul (Turkish Airlines). Kazakhstan also has a national airline, which is cheaper. A lot of parents fly into Moscow first as you can fly from Moscow's domestic airport to the city in Kazakhstan nearest your children's home bypassing Almaty. Air Kazakhstan flies from on of Moscow's domestic airports, Domodedovo, which is about 50 miles away from Sheremetyevo II and Air Astana and Transaero flies from Sheremetyevo I, which is about 5 miles away.

Remember that the Kazakhstan customs declaration form will be in Russian. A suggestion is to copy the English language one you filled out for Russia. The forms should be very similar. Do not lose your Russian or your Kazakhstani forms. You will need them when you leave. Both Russia and Kazakhstan require visas so you will need two for your trip. If you travel through Moscow, your Russian visa will have to be double entry.Some families have paid for VIP service at the Almaty airport. This basically means your facilitator will meet you and walk you through customs. The airport is not that large so this service is really not needed when you fly in. However, if you a single woman flying out with a newly adopted child, you need all the help you can get. In that instance, you might ask your facilitator about it.

Internet cafes abound in Kazakhstan. In Almaty there is one located on the first floor in the same mall as the RAM store and also at Stalker café in Panfilov Park (other side of town from RAM store. Most of the post offices in the cities have access as well.

After spending some time at the children's home, you then go to court. Court may be a local civil court or a regional court. Joining you will be your translator. You are asked the same sort of questions as in a Russian court. There is generally a 2 week delay before the adoption decree is final. This is supposed to be used as your "bonding" period. It is very useful for older children and not so useful for infants. You may be allowed two visits a day at the children's home. After this two week period runs its course, you then follow the same steps as in Russia in that you apply at ZAGS and OVIR for your child's amended Kazakhstani birth certificate and passport.

Some families have stayed throughout the period and some have made two short trips. It all depends on your situation.

There are at least 4 baby homes in Almaty. Baby Home #1 in Almaty is 3 stories high and very well maintained. The walls are generally white, but have beautiful murals, and even decorative tile in some places. The windows are covered with white lacey curtains and all the floors are covered with large rugs. Philip Morris has a huge plant outside of Almaty and supports the children's home. They have donated beautiful new cribs, toys, and tumbling mats for the children. The children are typically small and most suffer from giardia. The kids seem to have plenty of food, unfortunately, the nutrition of the food isn't too good. Most of the kids are fed potatoes, rice, bread, brothy soups, and tea. They receive very little milk, fruit, or veggies. The babies are fed kefir. It's a dairy based product similar to runny cottage cheese in consistency. It's filling, but not too nutritious. There have been reports that the caregiver to children ratio is like 2 to 20, and that because of this discipline is harsh. Other parents describe it as a ratio of 2 to 12 with the children on a strict schedule. So there is a variation in description. The children are given lessons in music and speech.

Baby Home #3 (Internat) in Almaty is reputedly run by a very caring woman. The director is dynamic and knows all 300+ kids by name and she is Mama to them all. If you adopt in Almaty you may be shocked by the appearance of the courthouse. In 2001 it resided in an old concrete building that was crumbling and in serious disrepair. The hallways were dark, dingy, and damp

Many families adopt from the city of Karaganda. The process can be long. In Karaganda there is a baby home by the name of Malyutka. It is clean and well run. The caretakers are kind and have a genuine affection for the children. This home has about 150 children under the age of 4 years. Parasites are a concern and in 2002 the Malyutka Baby House in Karaganda reported several cases of giardia. (In 2003, it was chicken pox.) Usually you can take your child around the orphanage grounds during the waiting time, but not outside of them. The babies are dressed in the usual heavy layered fashion and are never taken outside without a hat. Because of the number of children, the caretakers can not spend much time with each child and none of them get as much cuddle time as they need. Breakfast is a bowl of warm porridge, or rice cereal, and sometimes a bit of grated boiled egg sprinkled on top. Each baby has a cup of juice, warm chocolate milk, or warm weak coffee. The babies at Malutka wear a large cotton blanket for a diaper, and when it is time to go outside a plastic, wrap is wound around their diapers and legs. As a result of this layered binding the children are delayed in crawling and walking. Malutka is in the middle of a large complex that looks like soviet style public housing. Blocks and blocks of it. Yet, the orphanage building is quite lovely with its marble staircase and bright painted colors inside.

There is another children's home by the name of Iskorka.The children at Iskorka seem to range from about 4 to 15 years in age. They are well cared for although they have the normal orphanage speech delays.The director's name is Botagoz Kalievna. Iskorka has a music and program which the children enjoy.

Karaganda is a great city. There are two nice hotels by Kazakhstani standards: The Chyka and The Cosmonaut. The Chyka cost about $45 dollars a night for a 2 room plus bath suite. The water smells, but is clear. Internet hookup is very reliable at the Chyka and runs at 50 bps. You can ask the local computer store to hook up your laptop for a small fee. There are also three Internet cafes, which charge a reasonable rate. The rooms at the Cosmonaut are a little bigger and the laundry service is cheaper. However, the Internet service at the Cosmonaut is slow. There are 2 new European grocery stores in town. Two restaurants that are not bad are the "Aladdin" and the "Ascarte." If you are thinking about bringing your laptop, remember the phone lines are pulse, not tone, and you will likely need a device to connect the pre-modern wiring to your RJ-45 connection. It may not be worth all the trouble, if you don't plan to use it much.

Karaganda has a department store pronounced "Zoom" or "Tsum." It is a cross between an indoor flea market and a department store with each department an independant separate little shop. There is also a place called "Fantasy

Bowling" with a great bowling alley,billiard tables, and bar. All the comforts of home.

Many parents have also adopted from Astana. It has a great baby home run by Dr. Alma. Parents stay at the Alten Dara Hotel, which is old but clean. You can use the Internet to send pictures and reports to your IA doctor at the Nursat Internet Café, which was in the "Press Club" building on the Astana square. It is cheap and convenient. Court is usually brief with the usual Court questions. The judge will sometimes waive the remainder of the waiting period, if you have children waiting back home.

After obtaining your child's amended birth certificate and passport, you must travel with your child to the US Embassy in Almaty.The US Embassy web site is at: *http://www.usembassy-kazakhstan.freenet.kz/consular/index.html* The US Embassy in Almaty now issues immigrant visas, so you do not have to travel to Moscow as in the past. You will need to complete your child's medical evaluation (pink form). The Embassy will complete Form I-604, *Report of Overseas Orphan Investigation.* The Consulate's business hours are from 9 am to 6 pm. (Almaty is 11 hours ahead of the US EST.) The Consulate's address is 97 Zholdasbekova, Samal-2, 16th Floor Mailroom, Almaty, Kazakhstan 480099; Phone: (7 3272) 50-48-02; Fax (7 3272) 50-48-84. Email: *AdoptionsAlmaty @state.gov* The Consulate is in the Samal towers, near the huge Ramstore and not at the older building in the center of town. They like you to file the I-600 and related documents the day before your brief interview. The Consulate's visa services are run very well by Sara Craig. She is top-notch.

Information about the medical examination can be found at *http://www.usembassy-kazakhstan.freenet.kz/consular/medical-exam.html.* A review of the whole process can be found at *http://travel.state.gov/adoption_kazakhstan.html.* Unless your child is receiving an IR4 visa and you are filing the I-864 form plus tax returns, you do not have to submit any financial information. Still, I always recommend taking last year's tax return just in case.

Almaty is a fairly modern city. It has pollution. It even has a Hyatt Regency with a yurt hanging over the atrium bar. It is a large and lovely city. If you have a few days, you might take a short tour into the surrounding snow-capped Altai Mountains. Almaty is the former capital of the country. Astana was officially named the new capital in December 1997, however most foreign missions are still based in Almaty. The city has a few tourist sites to visit if you have the time, such as Panfilov Park, Zenkov Cathedral, Arasan Bath, Central State Museum, Kasteyev Museum of Fine Arts and Tsum. There's also a gondola that runs from Almaty (near Hotel Kazakhstan) up to Kok-Tobe (Green Top) that overlooks the city. At the top of the mountain overlooking the city are a zoo and circus and a great barbecue restaurant. About a 30 minute drive into the mountains is the Medeo Skating Rink. Its web site is _http://www.kz/eng/goroda/almaty/medeo/medeoeng.html_. Some families have stayed at hotel Kazjol which is small and is located behind a chicken place on a side street. It has clean comfy rooms (an older building) with good breakfasts. It is reasonably prices, which can be helful if you have to stay the whole 3 or 4 weeks.They have 2-room "suites" and smaller rooms.

The number of post placement reports is about the same as for Russia. They are usually due at 6, 12, 24 and 36 months after the adoption. Some areas require one at 18 months as well. Check with your agency if these post placements need to be by a social worker as that increases the cost.

Before leaving Kazahkstan you are required to register your child with the Ministry in Astana.Your agency will handle sending in the papers.This adds at least a day to your trip.This is a better process than having you do it when you return to the States. By having you do it before you leave, Kasahkstan doesn't have revert to the previous practice of slowing down adoptions until all families are registered. To register your agency has you sign a power of attorney for them to do the registration. You complete an application.to register each child.and send in their new Kazakh pappsoprts. The passports are returned to you with the registration stamps. The cost is about $35.

Your child has dual citizenship until she is 18 years old. Kazakhstan believes each child should have the right to choose whether or not to renounce its Kazakhstan citizenship. At 18, if your child wishes to no longer be a Kazakhstan citizen, they simply write a letter to the Embassy stating such and include their original passport. The Embassy will keep the passport and that's the end of it. That is the only time they keep the passport. If the child wishes to keep their citizenship, they send in their passport with a new photo and state that they wish to keep their Kazakhstan citizenship and the Embassy will issue them a new "adult" passport.

More information on Kazakhstan adoption can be found on the Kazakhstan email list at the EEAC web site. There is another email list at _http://groups.yahoo.com/group/Kazakhstan_Adoption_. If you look in the "files" section you can read some great family stories and a pretty good list of travel tips. A great web site for information is at _http://www.geocities.com/kazakhstan_adopt/_. Some adoption links can also be found at _http://www.karensadoptionlinks.com/_. A video of one families' Kasakhstan adoption can be purchased at _http://www.littlemiracles.org/bookstore/journey.html_.

Yahoo also has a list serve for particular cities such as Pavlodar. If you go to the GROUPS section and put Pavlodar in the search bar, it will appear. Many

Kazakhstan adoption resources are listed at *http://www.geocities.com/kazakhstan_adopt/resources.html.* This site has hyperlinks to parents who have adopted from the cities of Pavlodar, Uralsk, Petropavlovsk, Semipalatinsk, Karaganda, Almaty, and Zhezkazgan. Another Kazakhstan resource list is *http://adoption.about.com/gi/dynamic/offsite.htm?site=http%3A%2F%2Fwww.geocities.com%2Fkazakhstan_adopt%2Findex.html.* A family that adopted from Petropavlovsk is at *http://www.baileydoginc.com/journey.*

A great map of Kazakhstan is in the May 1999 National Geographic.An index card with all the important phone numbers can be printed off at *http://www.geocities.com/kazakhstan_adopt/emergency.html*

Information on Kazakhstan generally can be obtained from these web sites:
http://www.president.kz/main/mainframe.asp?lng=en
http://www.kazakhstannews.com/
http://www.kazakinfo.com/
http://www.virtualtourist.com/vt/672/
http://www.virtualtourist.com/m/2475a/672/
http://www.virtualtourist.com/m/2f1a9/672/
http://www.virtualtourist.com/Asia/Kazakhstan
http://expat.nursat.kz/?section_id=81

Books on Kazakhstan:
Journey into Kazakhstan—The True Face of the Nazarbayev Regime
Kazakhstan (Cultures of the World), by Guek-Cheng Pang.
The Soul of Kazakhstan by Wayne Eastep

CHAPTER XVII

BULGARIA

Bulgaria is a small country on the Black Sea. Romania and Turkey border it. It is on the same latitude as Cleveland Ohio, but the Black Sea changes the weather somewhat. The Danube River is Bulgaria's only major inland water-way and is used for both domestic and international traffic. In 2001 its old king returned to the country after five decades in exile and became Prime Minister Simeon Saxe-Coburg—former King Simeon II. However, there have been too many scandals and too little prosperity to view Bulgaria as a success story. 12 years of political reforms have not convinced the people of the advantages of democracy and a market economy. The average monthly wage in this Balkan country of 8 million is little more than $100, while the average old age pension is not enough to cover heating and electricity bills. About 22 000 children, 3 000 of them infants, are in institutional care. This represents a staggering segment of a population of only 8 million. Some 65 per cent are Roma, far disproportionate to the Bulgarian Roma population.

Since Bulgaria was never part of the Soviet Union the adoption process is a little different. Bulgaria requires you to make two trips with the option of having your child escorted to the US on the second trip. There is also the option of obtaining a waiver. The waiver is more commonly used when adopting children over seven years of age. Prospective parents adopting children over 7 are required to stay 2 weeks in-country visiting with the child they wish to adopt. If a family is unable to stay in Bulgaria for 2 weeks, they can sign a "waiver" form requesting the Ministry of Justice waive the 2 week stay requirement.

Parents still must visit the child, but not for the entire 2 weeks. Now a new law was passed in July, 2003 that makes some significant changes to Bulgarian adoption law. Therefore, there may be changes to the time spent in-country.

Now parents who have their child escorted have very good reasons for doing so. Sometimes it is because they have other children at home they do not want to leave. Or sometimes they feel that having someone who speaks the child's language can help the child get through the exhausting trip home.

In the past, most Bulgarian children came into the U.S. on IR-4 visas, meaning both parents had not seen the child prior to the court decree approving the adoption. With the passage of the Child Citizenship Act in 2000, however, more and more parents have chosen to make the first trip together, as it results in the child receiving an IR-3 visa and thus automatically gaining citizenship once the plane touches down in the US, as the following table demonstrates:

FY-1996: IR-3 visas—53, IR-4 visas—107
FY-1997: IR-3 visas—58, IR-4 visas—90
FY-1998: IR-3 visas—50, IR-4 visas—101
FY-1999: IR-3 visas—129, IR-4 visas—91
FY-2000: IR-3 visas—173, IR-4 visas—40
FY-2001: IR-3 visas—261, IR-4 visas—36

There were 260 adoptions in FY 2002. Children available for adoption from Bulgaria are over one year in age. Because of the time it takes for the Bulgarian process, most children are not home with you until they are 2 years old. Most of the available children will be of Roma (Gypsy) or Turkic heritage, although some older Bulgarian (Slavic) children may also be available. About 65% of the children in children's homes are Roma.The Roma suffer and have suffered tremendous prejudice throughout Eastern Europe. The children of Bulgaria are often of mixed ancestry and many times are of Gypsy heritage with beautiful dark olive skin, brown eyes, and dark hair. Because of the Roma ancestry, you should become educated on transracial adoption. Children are separated by age. Infants and toddlers reside in the mother and child orphanages (Baby Homes). Children aged three to six live in Pre-School homes. Children over age seven live in live in orphanages for school age children and go to public school. Healthy children are generally separated from those with special needs.

The conditions in the orphanages seem to be a mixed, as in other countries. The physical condition of the homes is no different than what you might see in Russia. Some are in a state of decay and others are nicer. There doesn't seem to be much malnutrition, but deprivation does exist, with conditions in children's homes varying greatly. If there is a generally sense, it is that older children are not in very good homes. The children available to foreigners are mostly Roma (Gypsy). The Roma children are beautiful with their lovely complexion, dark hair and big dark eyes. Bulgarians tend to adopt young ethnic Bulgarian children. There are many older ethnic Bulgarian children available. Adoption is considered a very private matter and if a child is old enough to know he is being adopted, then Bulgarians consider the child too old to be adopted. Their attitude toward orphans and disabled children is no different than elsewhere in the FSU.

Per Bulgarian law (and Russian and Belarusian etc), all children are offered to three Bulgarian families before becoming available for international adoption. Referrals are typically made shortly after submission of your dossier to Bulgaria. Photolists are no longer permitted. The adoption process has become longer because of reluctance by the Ministry of Justice to process international adoptions. Notwithstanding what your agency may tell you, an adoption now takes ten to 12 months to complete after the first trip. Nevertheless, the Bulgarian adoption process is very stable. It just takes longer.

Bulgaria enacted changes to its adoption laws in July, 2003. There is a very good chance that these changes may really speed up the process. The new law creates the usual national registry on which a child must be placed for 6 months before he is available for international adoption.He must be over 1 year old before a foreign adoption can take place, although there is an exception if the child has certain medical conditions. Bulgarian families have first priority, of course, and the child must be offered to three Bulgarian families.The Ministry of Justice (MoJ) will become the Central Authority as that term is used in the Hague Convention and will control the registry. There is an accreditation process for US adoption agencies. Within the Ministry of Justice there will be a Committee that approves a parent's application and dossier and matches the parent with a child. Once you have accepted the referral and met the child you send in your consent to the MoJ. The court case should be filed within a month of sending in your consent. The Judge will hear the case within 14 days and issue a written order within 7 days of ruling. Theoretically, you should only have to wait about 3 months from the time you accept your child to the time you are parents.This is in contrast to the current 10 months.The details of exactly how the new law will function are still a work in progress. Essentially everything will run through the MoJ rather than be delegated to the local officials. Your dossier and post placement reports will all go to the MoJ.

Both agency and independent adoption is available. Both usually work through local Bulgarian attorneys. Because your US agency is so dependent on

Bulgarian facilitators, it is those facilitators/attorneys you have to research. The object is to find a relatively honest one (by Eastern European standards) and one that can get the job done.

The age restrictions for adoptions from Bulgaria are very lenient. In general, couples and/or single women should be under the age of 55 to adopt. Many agencies list 49 years of age as a cutoff for infants. The age difference between parent and child should not exceed 45 years of age. Couples should be married at least two years, and childless couples are preferred for infant adoptions although there are some exceptions for special needs children. Adopted children must be at least a year old before they are eligible. Parents who had other children used to be restricted from adopting a child under 3 years of age. That restriction has been removed. In practice, most children adopted in Bulgaria by U.S. citizens are at least two years of age or older although special needs children such as cleft palate children are generally younger. Sibling adoptions appear to be easy to find.

It is possible to receive health histories, photographs and videotape on each child referred. Agencies and orphanages differ as to the amount and type of information. Some provide just a half page medical and still photos and others provide photos and a 3 page medical report. In general the children are no different than other institutionalized children. Some come home with giardia, ringworm, respiratory illness, ear infections (need PE tubes), and language delays. Some come home with none of these. Some have sensory issues, rocking, and the usually attachment behavior. Some need OT and PT and some do not. The prior Russian discussion regarding medical history applies to Bulgaria. You may receive a complete medical history or be surprised with additional information once the adoption is completed. Push your agency to acquire all such information before the court hearing. Phoning the children's home doctor in order to get updated medical information and answers to additional questions does not seem to be the norm. Updated information during the long wait period is usually not given to you, although some parents report that they have received updated emails and even a video. There does not seem to be any western trained doctor in Sofia that parents can request to visit their child. That option appears to unique to Russia and Ukraine.

There have been a few cases of parents asking for a "babushka" or "granny program" to be set up for their child. This is not common. There are organizations that place babushkas in orphanages for children. Babushka programs are useful in helping to minimize attachment problems. It costs about $100 a month to have a nanny visit your baby 5 days each week for 3 hours each day. This needs to be organized by an agency, however, not directly by parents. The Varna Mother and Child Orphanage is one place where the "granny" program has been implemented. You will need to inquire as to whether it is provided based on the child's need or based on a fee arrangement. Parents have said that the children's home in the city of Varna is decent, befitting its status as a resort town. The orphanage in Varna is described as very bright and colorful, with a lot of toys, and outdoor play equipment. Another town from which parents have adopted is Bourgas on the Black Sea. It is about 6 hours by car from Sofia. Parents have stayed at Hotel Bourgas for $100 a night. The Baby Home in Bourgas gets mixed reviews. The former director was investigated and replaced. The Bourgas Mother and Child Home also seems to have children who are reportedly well cared for and medically healthy (no reported parasites etc.), however other parents have reported that their children from Bourgas were not as well taken care of and that the "granny" program did not really exist. This may have been related to problems with the former director. So the Bourgas home gets a mixed review. Some parents have been able to actually have their children moved from the orphanage and placed in a "foster care" like situation. Obviously the children benefit tremendously from this arrangement. Explore all options with your agency or facilitator on the ground. Use your first trip to make these arrangements.

There are many children's homes in Bulgaria, but not all children are available for adoption. There is no central registry for identifying available children. Regional committees of supervising physicians and officials, together with the directors of each orphanage, determine whether a child may be placed with an adoptive family. It is really the home director that has most of the authority. Adoption agencies assist in identifying available children, often through videos or photographs. You can see pictures of some homes at *www.bulgarianchild.org.*

Bulgaria actually requires no paperwork in order to start the process. (This may all change once the MoJ issues its regulations based on the new law.) Your agency may have its own requirements, but Bulgarian law does not require any documentation to be completed before you make the first trip to visit the child. Indeed, many parents report that they did not pay their agency any money (except for an application fee) until they had visited and accepted the child. On the first trip you will likely not be able to take your child outside the children's home. This is particularly true if the child is an infant or toddler. There are exceptions so ask your agency about the procedure at that particular home.

One important paperwork change in 2001 was Bulgaria's acceptance of the Hague Convention Abolishing the Requirement of Legalization for Foreign Public Documents. This means that your dossier documents need only be apostilled, not authenticated, saving you much time and expense. Note that some prosecutors regularly ask for additional documents such as a medical form/letter on your children in the US. You also have to be HIV tested and have a FBI criminal record check every 6 months until your adoption is approved (FBI keeps your fingerprints on file for 15 months). Given that the adoption process is taking over 9 months to complete, families have to be prepared to incur the inconvenience and expense of getting this done more than once.

On the first trip one or both of the prospective adoptive parents (see the above discussion on IR-3 vs. IR-4) meet the orphanage director, visit with the child for one or two days, and sign the papers to begin the process and accept the referral. You have the option of declining the referral on this trip or any time up to the date of the court hearing. It won't make your agency very happy, but it is your family and your life. When you sign the paperwork in Bulgaria, you must be prepared to provide the new name you intend to give the child. Parent(s) first submit an application and dossier to the Ministry of Justice for a determination whether the child is legally free for adoption. After the Ministry of Justice approves, then the age of the child determines if the paperwork is sent to the Ministry of Education or the Ministry of Health for signature. The homes for children under 7 are under the Ministry of Health and the Ministry of Education has jurisdiction over the homes for children 7-18 yrs. It can take a few months for the paperwork to make its way through these two Ministries. You do not need a visa to visit Bulgaria for stays of less than 30 days. This first trip lasts between 5 and 8 days. You do not have to obtain a visa for your travel to Bulgaria as long as you are not staying beyond 30 days.

The second trip occurs after the Bulgarian Court has granted you the adoption (you are represented in abstentia by a Bulgarian attorney) and is for the purpose of collecting the post-adoption documents and applying for an US immigrant visa for the child. This trip also lasts 5 to 8 days. It occurs about nine months after your first trip depending on Bulgarian governmental delays (elections, vacations, etc), or almost anything. Sometimes the court hearing will be delayed because of a phoned in bomb threat. This occurs because the court employees want a day off or because there is a divorce hearing and one party objects so he calls in a bomb threat.

You can have your child escorted rather than make this second trip. However, most parents now seem to lean toward making the second trip in order to be able to share the Bulgarian cultural experience with their child as well as speeding up their child's citizenship.

The cost of a Bulgarian adoption is around $16,000, excluding in-country travel cost if you use a US agency. If you adopt independently and use a *reputable* Bulgarian attorney/agency, the cost is likely to be $10,000 to $12,000 including travel costs.

Most parents find it very hard to meet their child and then return months later. But in some cases updated photos and videos are provided and you should send regular gifts and packages if the child is older. Some parents even go over for a visit while they wait. The child will love to keep a picture book of their new family, relatives and neighborhood. Remember that while this delay is hard for you, it is practically life and death for them.

The delay is caused by the judge taking a few weeks to write the decision or he wants another piece of paper. Some judges have asked to see your actual fingerprints or have a psychological test (usually you just get your doctor to say you are in good mental health, although some want the letterhead to have psychology/psychiatry in it.). Then there are the many holidays. Remember that August is an entire holiday in itself. Then your lawyer has to arrange and gather your child's travel documents. That can take six weeks or so. The general outline is 1) Court date; 2) Decree is signed (5 to 30 days); 3) Decree becomes effective 14 days after it is signed; 4) Apply for new birth certificate and have it entered on police system (20 days); 5) Apply for child's Bulgarian passport (3 weeks). Before you leave for the second trip make sure the US Embassy in Sofia has received the BCIS cable regarding your I-171H approval. You can email consular assistant Emanuil Georgiev at *GeorgievEK@state.gov*. The US Embassy in Sofia Immigrant Visa Unit Phone number is 011 359 2 980 5241, ext: 191 or Immigrant Visa Unit direct line at (359-2) 963-1250.

The Bulgarian process is very linear. One step follows the next. There doesn't seem to be paralleling tracking where numerous pieces of paper and signatures are gathered simultaneously. One glitch that sometimes happens which can slow things up is that the birthmother cannot be found to sign off on the release paper. Many times this is resolved by placing an ad in the paper and the police in her hometown giving a statement that she has moved. Under Article 61 of the Bulgarian Family Code, a birth parent can sign a declaration stating their willingness for their child to be adopted. Or in accordance with Article 57 of the Bulgarian Family Code, if a child has been left in an orphanage, and has not been contacted by a family member for at least a year, the law allows the Director of the orphanage to consent to the adoption. When this is the case, the court tries to publicly summons the parent through the official newspaper (most often no parents are found). Unfortunately, the court does not summons the birth parent until after the perspective adoptive family's documents have cleared both ministries and are submitted to the court. Additionally, the current laws have no advance method of depriving the birth parent of his/her rights prior to the adoption being finalized. Rather, once the adoption takes effect, the parent's rights are automatically deprived. If the birth parents do not respond to the summons (or the parents consent is on file) and all of the adoptive parents documents have been approved by both ministries and the prosecutor in court accepts them (it is not uncommon for the prosecutor to ask for some additional documentation or to have a document re-done) the case will go before the judge. The judge then, hears the case (and if he/she doesn't ask for anything else) the adoption will be verbally approved. When the judge does ask for more paperwork, you usually have only 2-3 weeks to obtain the necessary document and forward it to Bulgaria for the next court date. The judge may then take up to 4 to 6 weeks before putting the formal approval in writing. Once the written decision is in hand, a new birth certificate is issued and a new passport. Finally, the child is ready to emigrate. When you pick up your child at the children's home you must bring a complete set of clothes and shoes for them. The children are not allowed to take anything that belongs to the orphanage and this includes the children's clothing. See the packing list in the previous Russian section.

On the second trip you will visit the US Embassy in Sofia and go through the same procedures as in Moscow or Warsaw in obtaining your child's immigrant visa. They process adoption visas on Wednesday mornings and sometimes on Fridays, but beware of delays due to US and Bulgarian holidays. You must also factor in getting your child's medical screening and passport photos. Because of all of this, most parents arrange for the photos and medical screening on Tuesday. Ask to be taken to the 'public clinic" that charges around $20 as otherwise you might get taken to the $150 one for the same cursory exam. The address for the Consular Section is U.S. Embassy, Sofia, No. 1 Kapitan Andreev Street, Sofia, Bulgaria. The phone numbers are [011] (359 2) 980-5241 through 5248 (through the Embassy's main switchboard) and (359 2) 963-1250 (direct line to Immigrant Visa Section) Fax: [011] (359) (2) 963-2859. There will be a line of Bulgarians in front. Just go to the front and tell the Marine you are an American and you can go right in. After filing the usual paperwork (see the Moscow Embassy section), handing over two passport photos of your child, the Form I-604 interview and paying the usual fees, your child's visa should be ready by 5 pm for pick up. The Sofia Embassy does not want you to bring any tax returns, if your child is receiving an IR3 visa. Nevertheless, I would still bring your last years, just in case. The interview room is up about 3 flights of stairs. There is a little couch next to the two desks. After you leave the first interview room, you are directed downstairs to pay your fees. You are asked a few questions during the process of paying your fees. There is a couch in the waiting room for mothers with small children. When you go to the Embassy in Bulgaria, it is staffed mostly with Bulgarians. The first stop after payment is with a Bulgarian staffer. The next stop is with the Department of State officer.

By Bulgarian law, parents need to submit post-placement reports after 3 months, 6 months and 18 months. These reports can be prepared by the parent and do not have to be prepared by a social worker or agency. There are some agencies that ask for reports for several years. I would do the required number and then choose whether you wish to continue.

Travel to Bulgaria

Most parents fly on airlines requiring a stop in Europe. London seems to be a popular stop over. British Airways has a flight that leaves at 10:15 am and arrives at 3:30 pmin Sofia (there's a 2 hour time difference between London & Bulgaria). Olympic Airlines also flied direct to Sofia from Athens, Greece. Air France (code share with Delta), Lufthansa and Austrian Air also fly into Sofia. Many families have used the same travel agencies mentioned in the Russian airfares section. Specific Bulgarian travel agencies include Sofia Travel and BTC 2000. BTC is a travel agency in New York that is ran by Bulgarians. Their web address is *www.btc2000.com*.

The Sofia airport terminal has been significantly renovated and is new and clean. The people are friendly at passport control and customs. There is also a nice duty free shop there. Once through passport control you are likely to be confronted with a mob a predatory taxi cab drivers. Try to arrange for your agency to pick you up.

In Sofia some parents have stayed in the hotel **Maria Louise**. They report it as being nice with adequate security. It's very small, only 15 rooms and 5 suites. Privately owned, and they deal with a lot of Americans. The rooms vary in size, from comfortable, to "smallish" but the bathroom is great.It is close to everything. The mall Tzum is right across the street and a half block up and the indoor market is to the right. The Pizza Hut is with in a 5 minute walk, and McDonalds is next to the indoor market. The prices of the better hotels (**Marriott**) can range were from $100 to $350 per night. You can sometimes negotiate a lower rate.

Others like the newer **Hotel Rotasar**. It is very reasonably priced at about $50 a night. The staff is friendly and it is only about a $2 cab fare to the city center.It is a small, quiet sort of place located in a very nice neighborhood. It is not downtown, but has all sorts of shops within walking distance (likely due to the presence of the nearby Hotel Pliska). The Rotasar is very pleasant though not as fancy (or as expensive) as the Princess. It is smaller, more homey, more personal staff (English speaking), there is free Internet for email at a computer behind the desk, although it doesn't always work. There is an Internet Café around the corner for 50 cents an hour. They served continental breakfast in the room. There is also the **Grande Hotel Bulgaria**. The rooms are small, and the bathrooms tiny.

Another hotel is the **Sofia Princess Hotel** in downtown Sofia. It costs about $70-$90 a night and children stay for free. It is located near the railway station, and about 20 minutes walking from the **Sheraton**. You can make reservations on the Internet at: *http://www.sofia.com/accommodation/hotels.html#Central%20Sofia.* It is located at 131, Maria Luisa Blvd. (Tel. 317151 Fax: 320011 It is sometimes listed under its former name Novoltel Evropa. All of the employees speak English. There is a breakfast and dinner buffet in the restaurant as well as all day service. There is also a pharmacy just blocks away. The hotel has a gym, spa and hair salon. Dinner is around $5 US. There is a casino attached. There is a money exchange right across the street. The hotel has an Internet accessible business center in the lobby. Charge is per minute.

Another hotel that has changed its name is the the Grand Hotel Sofia, which has been renovated and renamed the **Radisson SAS Sofia**. The lobby of the Radisson is just beautiful and the rooms are large and very comfortable. The bathrooms have floor to ceiling marble with a separate tub and shower. The price is $180 a night. The Radisson has a great view across the street towards the parlament and towards the Cathedral. It is a beautiful hotel. If you want the view, ask in advance, the other side of the hotel is not so nice. There is also a **Hilton** that is just like home.The **Sheraton** has nice bathrooms with a bathtub. You can ask for a room with terrace doors that look out toward the old church.There is a McDonalds across the street. It is cheaper to make reservations through Sheraton in the US than calling the hotel direct.

If you stay in a homestay, make sure you ask the usual questions of your agency so you can decide if a hotel is better. See the homestay chapter in the Russian section. Some agency apartments have cable (CNN, Animal Planet) and others look like a homeless shelter. It is also possible and not too much trouble to rent an apartment yourself (without a host), with all the amenities, for a daily rate of $25 per person. Sofia is easier to manage than Moscow.

The train has become the cheapest (lowest cost) of transportation in Bulgaria. The tracks and equipment are in dire need of maintenance. If you like trains, then you will enjoy the ride. Otherwise, gird thyself. Air travel is relatively inexpensive in country. The planes are not new and the best that can be said is that it is always a short flight. A car is the most expensive mode of transportation at $75 per day for a driver/translator. Yet it gives you a lot of flexibility as far as sightseeing, or traveling to markets, as well as having a translator along to get you through those times when speaking Bulgarian is required. If you are an asthmatic, you will definitely use your inhaler due to the lack of emission controls. A Bulgarian taxi is usually a Russian made Lada and is a good way of getting around in Sofia.

Most Bulgarians dress in dark colored clothing as the Russians used to do. But even in Bulgaria, colors are making an appearance and you can get away with blue jeans to some extent. Also like the women in Moscow the Sofia women wear very, very short skirts. Buy a pair of black shoes, wear dark colored clothing, and you will fit in better. Keep in mind that Bulgarians shake their heads up and down for "No" and side to side for 'Yes." (Maybe we've been doing it wrong all these years!)

Only drink bottled water. The food is inexpensive. Children are not usually seen in restaurants, so tip a little more than usual. MacDonald's, KFC, Dunkin' Donuts, Pizza Hut, and other fast food restaurants are available in the larger cities. If you are buying your own food remember to cut out the front panel from what ever you like. You can just use the picture and/or the cyrillic writing as flash cards for future purchases.

If you have time to shop, the wine in Bulgaria is pretty good and Bulgarian rose oil is the best in the world. As in a lot of countries there is a two-tiered pricing system at the hotels, shops and museums that cater to foreigners. Some places even post separate prices for Bulgarians and foreigners and these are not conversion rates but actually separate prices. If you want to take donations to the children's homes remember that you can buy foodstuffs in Bulgaria from such stores called Metro that are sort of like a Sam's. They are in several cities including Rousse and Sofia. You can probably load up there. The children are not starving but they are undernourished and miss out on fruits and vegetables. Food, juice, vitamins, shoes, and underwear are also needed.

Phone service is available in most hotels and private homes. Making calls in Bulgaria can be a problem at times. The telephone booths accept "smart cards" as payment. These cards are available in many shops. Calls to the US are not that expensive and the usual international phone cards (see Russian section) work very well. Computer connections are available, but limited. Cell phones are common using GSM. ATMs are available in Sofia and Rousse that will give you Levs. Do not bring Traveler's Checks and do bring an amount of the usual crisp American dollars. See the previous Russian section on money. That section is applicable in Bulgaria as well. Once you leave Bulgaria (or Russia) no one will accept your lev (or rubles) so never exchange more than is necessary or you may be stuck not being able to change it once you leave the country.

Learning a little Bulgarian can go a long way. There are two language sites that help: *www.travlang.com/languages* and *www.sowards.net/BGphz.html.* Also, you can buy a $12 Bulgarian language CD directed at adopting parents by emailing *frederick.d.deschenes@intel.com* or go to his web site at *www.cybermesa.com/~fdd.* There is a travel language CD called Transparent Language's Bulgarian CD, which is travel-oriented vocabulary. Their web site is *www.transparent.com* What really helps in studying Bulgarian is already having learned Russian since they use the same Cyrillic alphabet (a few letters are pronounced differently, that's all). The grammar is somewhere between Russian and English.

You will see a large number of homeless people, mostly gypsies. It is very hard to extricate yourself from their begging. The best advice is to avoid any interaction with street gypsies.

Some informative web sites:

http://travel.state.gov/adoption_bulgaria.html
http://www.usembassy.bg/visa/adoption.html
http://www.bulgaria-embassy.org/Consular%20Information/adoption.htm
http://www.netwurx.net/~tsh/bulgaria/silistra.html
http://www.bulgariaadoption.com/adoption.htm

This is an excellent resource:
http://groups.yahoo.com/group/FaCAB1/files/Orphanages/orphanages.txt
http://groups.yahoo.com/group/FaCAB1/links

For stories see
http://groups.yahoo.com/group/FaCAB1/links/Adoption_Stories_000991839339/
http://hometown.aol.com/kimber143/myhomepage/diary.html
http://www.rainbowkids.com/Articles/1098Kalina.htm
http://news.mpr.org/features/200010/09_nymanl_adoption/adoptiondiary.shtml
http://heatherlende.com/lende/stojanka.html
http://www.iaradopt.com/old%20site/www/Orlewecz.shtml
www.TruthInAdoption.org

About Bulgaria in general:
www.onlinebg.com
http://www.bulgaria-embassy.org/ and then click on "About Bulgaria." Links to a map as well.

CHAPTER XVIII

BELARUS

Belarus is the former Byelorussia Republic. It became independent of Russia in 1991. It has only 10 million people and is the size of Kansas. Ethnically the country is composed of Byelorussian 81.2%, Russian 11.4%, Polish, Ukrainian, and other 7.4%. The country is divided into 6 regions centered on the regional capitals of Minsk, Grodno, Brest, Mogilev, Gomel, and Vitebsk. The country is landlocked and bordered by Russia, Ukraine, Latvia, Poland and Lithuania.

One third of the population is retired. Its claim to fame is that it was the home of Olympian Olga Korbut (now living in Atlanta). It is a land of flat fields, birch groves and green marshes. Belarus has been the stomping ground of invaders for centuries, from Lithuanians and Poles to Germans and Russians. During World War II, the Germans leveled its capital and a quarter of its population was killed. Today it serves as the buffer between Russia and NATO.

Belarus—the name means "White Russia"—is culturally, ethnically and linguistically about as close as can be found to Mother Russia. The two countries have a loosely defined "union" allowing visa-free travel across the border. On New Year's Eve, many Belarusians set off fireworks at 11 p.m. because that is when Russian television, based one time zone to the east, marks the turning of the calendar. Russian television dominates the market.

In the capital, Minsk, the roads are wide and clean, but bereft of traffic, as few residents can afford cars. Other than the occasional McDonalds, Western businesses are absent. Soviet symbols remain everywhere including the hammer and sickle.

It is a land with the bloodiest history in all of the former Soviet Union. You cannot look anywhere in Belarus and not see a place where some atrocity by Stalin or Hitler did not occur. Between 1937-1939 more than 300,000 innocents were killed on Stalin's orders. President Clinton placed a memorial bench near the village of Kurapaty, outside Minsk, the capital, to commemorate the victims. As a sign that some things have not changed, there is no other memorial to the victims by the official government and instead it paved a road over the graves.

The Belarusian government is completely dependent on Moscow for its survival. If Putin gets tired of Belarusian President Alexander Lukashenko, he will be gone overnight. In the meantime the people have to endure this throwback to harsh Soviet times. They live in the last true Soviet-style state. It is like a bad spy movie from the sixties. What is interesting is that Belarus has a lot of potential, if it was run in a more Western way like its neighbor Poland.

Lukashenko, a former collective farm boss, won the presidency in 1994. He quickly set about renationalizing key industries and establishing an authoritarian state. His claim to fame is that he always pays pensioners on time. That is where his support lies, not in the younger generation. Those who oppose Lukashenko have been executed and their supporters suppressed by his security forces, which are still called the KGB. He is Europe's (although not the FSU's) lone dictator. There is still an opposition but he is in open undeclared warfare with them. In a political move copied from Russia, he has made Russian Orthodox the official government religion and thus co-opted that possible source of opposition.

Since taking power in 1994, Lukashenko has wrecked the country's economy. He wants to rejoin Belarus with Russia in a reconstituted Moscow-led empire. What is funny is that Putin is not so inclined to rush in and acquire another region with a host of economic and political problems. For example, Belarus had 197% inflation in 1999 and subsequently devalued its currency. The real reason for falling living standards is the fact that Belarus does not produce any goods that can compete on world markets. Most production is shipped to Russia, often at prices that are below cost. As the government prints more money, inflation grows, and the economy sinks deeper into crisis. Lukashenko's answer has been to arrest the heads of the factories and claim the economy is bad because they were stealing.

Now for the surprising good news, Belarus is adoption friendly!

Belarus imposed a moratorium on foreign adoption in late 1997, but lifted it in the summer of 1998. There are now about a half dozen US based agencies working in Belarus. Belarus tries to limit foreign adoptions so they do not exceed domestic ones. Therefore, it is better to try to adopt earlier in the year rather than later as there could be a cut-off. The cut-off was October in 2001 and September in 2002, so you can see the trend. There were 60 adoptions in 2000 and 129 in 2001. There were 169 adoptions by US families in FY 2002. The children all received IR3 visas, as parents must attend court. There is no escorting. The ten-day appeal period is almost always waived (unless you live in Belarus) and the trip takes about a week. The process takes 6 to 8 months start to finish. The age requirement for an adoptive parent is flexible with some parents 48 years of age when adopting an infant. Agencies seem to have their own rules about age. Singles may adopt. The wait for a boy is shorter than for a girl. The process might take 12 months, if you wish to adopt a girl.

The children must be on the registry at the National Adoption Center for 6 months. Therefore, the youngest a child can be adopted is usually around 10 months in age. The Adoption Center in Minsk provides a centralized data registry for available orphans and registers potential adoptive parents. The Center also refers children according to the desires of adoptive parents. Currently, the Director of the Adoption Center is Ms. Olga Karaban. Some parents have adopted a child as young as 9 months old, although toddlers are more common.

After adoption is completed, adoptive parents forward their required post placement reports through their adoption agencies to the Center. Post-placement reports are required every 6-months for a 3-year period. Post-placements are very important as agencies and entire countries can be suspended from adopting, if these are not completed. Belarus suspended Ireland for a time because post-placements were not completed. The children's homes seem much better organized than in other countries as adoptable children are placed on the registry soon after arriving at a children's home. You may or may not receive a referral video. Belarus does not encourage photos or videos. Medical information can be a lot or a little. Sometimes you are told you have to wait until you get there. The same discussion relating to pressuring your agency for more information applies to the Belarusian process. Because of procedural requirements, the youngest an infant that can be adopted is usually 8 months. Most Americans adopt from baby homes in Minsk. There are at least two (Baby Home #1 and #2) and they seem in good shape. There have been adoptions from Brest, Pinsk and Gomel. Generally travel outside of Minsk is a little harder than if you adopted from Minsk. Accommodations outside Minsk are also more rustic. The children in the homes are like those in the other FSU countries. They eat lots of starch and do not get enough protein, fresh fruits and vegetables. They lack human stimulation as well. Now some homes are better than others and provide for a great deal of caring from the caretakers and stimulating toys and activities. The home in Soligorsk is of this type. The conditions in the homes vary as in all countries.

Your dossier must first be apostilled, translated into Russian and sent to the Ministry of Education (National Adoption Center) in Minsk, Belarus. After the Adoption Center approves the dossier, it then matches you with a child and a referral is generated with videotape and sent to you through your agency for consideration. Referrals have come as soon as a month and a half after your dossier is filed. Referrals of one-year-old infant girls have been reported. It is possible to visit the child prior to accepting the referral, if your agency is able to make such arrangements with the Adoption Center. Normally an adoptive parent will simply accept or decline a referral after an IA doctor has reviewed the material. If you accept the referral, you then send an application to the Belarusian National Center of Adoption addressed to the District Court at the child's place of residence, or in Minsk to the Minsk Municipal Court. The application must state the surname, first name and other names, which are to be given to the child following adoption. You are also asked to specify in this application whether or not you plan to alter the child's time and place of birth. Belarusian law provides that the child's date of birth and place of birth may be altered by the adoptive parents. After you accept a referral, you may travel within 4-8 weeks for your court date. Delays can occur if officials go on vacation. If their signature is needed, there is not usually a backup to provide it. All you can do is continue to wait until they return.

You travel to Belarus where you first visit the regional administration and receive permission to visit with the child. Then you attend court. The adoption of children by foreign citizens is approved by District Courts in Belarus except in Minsk where the Minsk Municipal Court approves adoptions. Similarly with the Russian process, when you appear in court, a social worker testifies that she saw you interacting with your child. This is why you must arrive a few days prior to court to allow you to meet with your child.

After court you will be issued an adoption certificate and also the child's new birth certificate. You will then obtain your child's Belarusian passport from OVIR, just as in Russia. As in adopting from Ukraine, parents must go through the US Embassy in Warsaw, Poland to get their child's immigrant visa. Warsaw is the Embassy that must be notified by the BCIS of your advance approval so that is what you put on your I-600A. See the discussion in the Ukraine chapter on visiting the US Embassy in Warsaw with your child. Within a month of returning to the United States you must register your child with the Belarusian Consulate as is done with other adoptions from Russia and the FSU. Now you do have to complete Form I-604, *Report of Overseas Orphan*

Investigation in Minsk. This will become part of your visa package that you take to Warsaw. The Embassy in Minsk will ask you some general questions about the child and your knowledge of what was told to you. The Consular officer will also inspect the adoption papers to be sure the child meets the definition of an orphan as contained in the INA. These documents include: a court decree terminating parental rights (if natural parents are living) or parental consent, the adoption decree, birth certificates (original and new), permission from the child's legal guardian (usually the head of the orphanage) and health documents. The I-604 interview takes about 10 minutes then you travel to the Embassy in Warsaw to finalize the paperwork that allows your child to enter the US. Although the I-864 Form is no longer required for IR3 adoptions, you will still be asked in Warsaw for a copy of your last year's tax return. The medical screening exam is also completed in Warsaw, not Minsk.

Belarus requires one post placement report/visit every 6 months for three years for a total of six reports.

Chernobyl always comes up in discussions of Belarus. The disaster occurred in 1986 in northern Ukraine and the immediate effects were limited to southern Belarus (Gomel and Brest) and to children born soon after. There have been a lot of studies on this subject. Europeans in the path of the radiation cloud have a statistically higher degree of cancer. Some studies say there is no effect on children born 16 years after and others say that there is higher thyroid cancer among children in the regions around Chernobyl. One of the problems is that people have moved back to the radioactive areas around Chernobyl and are farming and catching fish. Certainly your newly adopted child should have a thyroid test when he arrives home with you. This test will rule out thyroid deficiency as a cause for failure to thrive and developmental delays. The general consensus, both in American and post-Soviet (Russian, Ukrainian and so on), literature and clinical practice is that there is no reason to repeatedly screen children from those areas for thyroid cancer. Manual evaluation (palpation) of the thyroid gland during routine check-ups is usually more than enough. Do your own research and reach a comfort level, as your extended family is certain to bring up the subject.

Telephone, cellular and Internet service is poor outside Minsk. However, since it is such a short trip, communication is not as important. There are no direct flights from the United States to Belarus. Many parents fly from the US on Lufthansa into Minsk, with a connection in Frankfort or LOT Polish airlines and British Airways from the US with a connection. You can also fly into Warsaw, Poland and from there fly on Belarus National Airlines to Minsk. This is a very short flight. As elsewhere in Russia and the FSU, Traveler's Checks are not accepted and with credit cards you have the same issues as described in the

Russian section. You should bring some bottled water with you, if you travel outside Minsk. If you travel in the summer, bring some bug spray and a screen.

Parents have stayed at Orbita in Minsk, but some say Hotel Belarus is nicer. The Orbita is fine. The bathrooms have been upgraded. There are two kinds of rooms: standard and business. A standard room is small, but clean with two single beds, a TV, a chair and a table. The business rooms are larger so you might ask for an upgrade if your agency places you in a standard room. The hotel has a web site. The Orbita's restaurant is pretty good with a delicious beef stroganoff.

A visa is required prior to arrival and can be obtained from the Belarus Embassy located at 1619 New Hampshire Ave, N.W. Washington, D.C. 20009, tel. (202) 986-1606; Internet: *http://www.belarusembassy.org* or the Belarus Consulate in New York at 708 Third Avenue, 21st floor, New York, NY, 10017, tel. (212) 682-5392.

The U.S. Embassy is located in Minsk at 46 Starovilenskaya Ulitsa; telephone (375) 172-10-12-83 or 172-17-73-47 or 172-17-73-48; fax: 375 17 234-78-53. The after hours number is 375 17 226-16-01

The actual Belarusian adoption law outlining all of the steps that need to be taken can be found in English at *http://ncpi.gov.by/eng/indexeng.htm*. Click on the hyperlink for "English translations of the most important Belarus legal acts," then on the hyperlink for "Social Law," then on the last document, which deals with adoption.

For more information there is an adoption group at
http://groups.yahoo.com/group/Adoption_From_Belarus

Other information on Belarus and adoption can be found at:
http://travel.state.gov/adoption_belarus.html
http://www.usis.minsk.by/html/adoptions.html

Map of Belarus:
http://www.friends-partners.org/oldfriends/geography/BELARU.GIF

General information on Belarus can be found here:
http://www.eurohot100.com/belarus/
and *http://www.undp.org/missions/belarus/eng_pg01.htm*

CHAPTER XIX

GEORGIA

Georgia is a small country lying next to the Black and Caspian Seas and is bordered by Russia, Turkey, Armenia, and Azerbaijan. It gained its independence from the former Soviet Union in 1991. The capital of Georgia is Tbilisi. Georgia is slightly smaller than South Carolina and contains 5 million people. Ethnically it is divided into Georgian 70.1%, Armenian 8.1%, Russian 6.3%, Azeri 5.7%, Ossetian 3%, Abkhaz 1.8%, other 5%. The official language is Georgian although most people also speak Russian. Georgia is primarily an agricultural country noted for its food and wine throughout Eastern Europe.

Georgia has always been against foreign adoption on any large scale. President Eduard Shevardnadze's wife and others in government would rather have the children grow up without a family than leave Georgia.Therefore, there are few adoptions from the state run orphanages.You can read more about the otphanges at

http://www.eurasianet.org/departments/culture/articles/eav031403.shtml.

There were either 16 or 26 (depending on which State Department web site you look at) IR3 visas issued by the US in FY 2001. There were probably double those numbers in FY 2002. It is an unusual system as the process can take two tracks, private or public. The private track does not involve a national Adoption Center or other government agency. Instead, it is akin to a US domestic adoption whereby it is a private adoption between you and a Georgian birthmother. Under Georgian law, the biological father has no rights unless he is married to the mother. Georgian law permits the birthmother to give consent for a specific person to adopt the child or she can simply relinquish the child for adoption. The first scenario does not meet the requirements of U.S. immigration law. An agency is not supposed to assist a birthmother in seeking an attorney, but rather she is supposed to find one by herself, relinquish the child and then the child goes into a foster care arrangement. In the adoption you are represented by a US agency and it is facilitated by a Georgian attorney. It is possible to hire your own facilitator and bypass an agency. Reportedly, the birthmothers are usually single women.

A private adoption is tricky as the circumstances of the child's adoption must meet the BCIS' definition of an "orphan" or else the child will not be given an US immigrant visa. The cost to adopt privately using a US agency seems to range from $23,000 to $25,000, exclusive of in-country travel. Because of the opportunity to adopt a very young infant, agency's Georgia programs are very popular and there can be a waiting list. While the cost to adopt in Georgia is higher than almost any other country, if one factors in the cost of two trips to Russia, the cost isn't look that out of line. The risk to a Georgia adoption is that there is a lot of money involved and no one and no government adoption center is really checking to see that the money is properly applied. There is a higher risk that Georgian adoptions will have problems in the future than any other Eastern European country. This is not to discourage you, just a reminder of the risk.

The public track is the familiar process where a child is on the National Data Base for 6 months and you adopt from a children's home with the consent of the regional authorities. Usually these are toddlers or older children. There are three orphanages for infants (until age three). The largest is in Tbilisi. Georgian couples usually adopt infants, which is why infants adopted by Americans are through the private adoption process. Adoption requires the consent of the child being adopted if he/she has reached the age of 10 years.

In Georgia there are at present 72 children's homes, in which 8,000 children are housed. In general, they are not in the best of shape and the children suffer the usually maladies of institutional life including malnutrition, lack of heat during the winter, and illnesses which could be cured by antibiotics. All of the children have their hair cut very short to prevent lice. These homes are under the administration of the Ministry of Education (63), the Ministry of Health (3), the Ministry of Social Welfare, Labour and Employment and the Ministry of the Interior (4). The ages of the children in these homes range from 3 to 18 years.

There are three infants' homes, two for babies from birth to the age of 3 and one for infants from birth to the age of 6. These homes are intended for partially or completely orphaned children, healthy children abandoned by their parents, and children with physical or mental deficiencies. The average number of children in each home is between 100 and 110. The infants' homes are placed under the control of the Ministry of Health.

Most of the children's homes are controlled by the Ministry of Education (total number of children: approximately 3,800). They care for children with impaired hearing or eyesight, children suffering from chronic diseases, those suffering from "moderate" mental deficiencies, partially or completely orphaned children, children left without parental care, children from poor families or families with five or more children, children living in areas where there are no ordinary schools, and "problem" children. The age range is 3 to 18 years.

The homes have the usual problems, including almost complete dependence on humanitarian aid; the treatment of the children, which is punitive rather than educational in character; lack of an external monitoring mechanism; poor teaching staff, etc.

Where a foreign adoption occurs, the decision is made by the Ministry of Education and is then referred to the court for a final decision.

In the period from 1994 to 1997, 171 children between 6 months and 10 years of age, 97 of who were girls, left the country as a result of foreign adoption. Of these, 109 were adopted directly from maternity homes or medical establishments and 62 from children's or infants' homes. One hundred and forty-one children were adopted in the United States, 23 in Canada, 5 in Spain, 2 in Belgium and 1 in Cyprus.

As in Ukraine your dossier documents must go through the authentication process. See the Ukraine section for details on authentication. Your documents are first authenticated at the state level, then by the U.S. Department of State and finally by the Georgian Embassy in Washington. They are translated into Georgian. A courier service is recommended for the Washington D.C part.

Single women and couples can adopt from Georgia. The age range of parents is very liberal. Infants from 2 to 6 months can be adopted in the private adoption process. You can adopt more than one child. The usually scenario in a private adoption is that your dossier and other documents are submitted to the Ministry of Education for review. This review takes about 3 weeks. Once the Ministry approves you, your agency sends you a referral with a medical history, still photos and sometimes a video. Because the child is under the care of an agency's foster family, medical information and follow-up questions are easily obtained. After you accept the referral, a court hearing takes place within a few weeks, which both parents must attend. In most adoptions the 30-day appeal period is waived so that the Adoption Decree is effective immediately.

In the event it is not, then you have the option of staying, returning, or having the child escorted home.

After the Court hearing, you receive the Adoption Decree, amended birth certificate, and the child's Georgian passport. You then visit the US Embassy in Tbilisi with the usual list of documents. This is where the I-604 *Request For and Report on Overseas Adoption Investigation* interview is conducted. Since May 1, 2003, the Embassy has issued US immigrant visas for adopted children. This is a welcomed change as before parents had to travel to Moscow to obtain the visa. Prior to visiting the Embassy your child will need to be seen at an approved clinic to obtain the "pink" medical clearance form. Although the process is similar to visitng the Moscow Consulate, the US Consulate in Georgia does not issue the visa all in one day. Rather, you or your representative file the papers in the afternoon, then the Consulate conducts the brief 15 minute interview the next day (assuming your papers are in order).

The U.S. Embassy in Georgia is located on 25 Atoneli Street, Tbilisi, Georgia, 380005; Phone number (995 32) 98-99-67/68, Ext: 4137 for adoption information. Fax: (995 32) 92-29-53; *http://web.sanet.ge/usembassy/consular.htm*. The Embassy's email is *consulate-tbilisi@state.gov*. It has a specific web site relating to adoption requirements at *http://web.sanet.ge/usembassy/consulate/adoptvis.htm*. Because the Georgian process is more akin to a private adoption in the United States, the Consulate's suggestiod I-604 questionnaire mimics US domestic adoption concerns. You can see the I-604 form at *http://foia.state.gov/masterdocs/09fam/0942021X1.pdf*.

There is a Marriott Hotel in Tbilisi and that is where most Americans stay when they visit. It is not unusual to see US military personnel staying at the hotel. The hotel has a web page. There is also a Sheraton and families have stayed there. Both of these have a business center with Internet access.

You need a visa to enter Georgia. You can obtain a Georgia one at the Tbilisi airport on your arrival or from the Consular section of the Georgian Embassy at 1615 New Hampshire Ave., NW Suite 300, Washington, DC 20009; Phone number (202) 387-23-90; Fax: (202) 393-45-37. For details, see the Georgian web site at *http://www.georgiaemb.org/Home.asp*. It may be that your Georgia visa obtained at the airport will expire before you are through, so be sure to renew it before it expires. The airport visa is usually good for 2 weeks. A good list of travel sites can be found on the Georgian Embassy web page at *http://www.georgiaemb.org/links.asp*.

There are at least 5 US adoption agencies working in Georgia. There is also a Georgia email list available on Yahoo! and on EEadopt. Here is a website with information on Georgian adoptions:

http://travel.state.gov/adoption_georgia.html and one family's trip is at *http://www.geocities.com/maryanns01/index.html.*

Other informational sites are at
http://www.eurasianet.org/departments/culture/articles/eav031403.shtml
http://www.eeadopt.org/index.html
http://groups.yahoo.com/group/repgeorgiaadopt/
http://web.sanet.ge/usembassy/consular.htm (This is the Embassy site in Tbilisi, Georgia) and *http://www.geocities.com/georgianchildren* (Describes orphanage conditions)

CHAPTER XX

AZERBAIJAN

Azerbaijan has recently become a popular country from which to adopt. The first Americans adopted from there in 2000. There were a total of 16 adoptions in FY 2001 and 49 in 2002.

Azerbaijan is a small, former Soviet republic of 8 million, mostly Muslim people. It lies at the point where Asia meets Europe, in the southeastern part of the Transcaucasian region, bordering Russia in the north, Iran in the south, Turkey, Georgia and Armenia in the west and Kazakhstan and Turkmenistan in the east, along the Caspian Sea. It is divided into 62 districts, with Baku as the capital containing some 2 million people. Ethnically the country breaks down into Azeri 90%, Dagestani 3.2%, Russian 2.5%, Armenian 2%, other 2.3%. 93.4% of the population is Muslim, Russian Orthodox 2.5%, Armenian Orthodox 2.3%, and other 1.8%. Its President, Heydar Aliyev, controls the country. Oil and gas count for 90% of its exports. BP-Amoco, Chevron and ExxonMobil all have a presence in Azerbaijan.

From 1918 to 1920 Azerbaijan enjoyed independence, but after Red Army units moved in, it ceased to be independent and became one of the Republics of the former Soviet Union (1920-1991).Since 1992, the Azerbaijani Republic has been a member of the United Nations.

After the collapse of the Soviet Union in 1991, Azerbaijan went through a difficult period of civil strife and lost a war with neighboring Armenia over an ethnic Armenian enclave. A cease-fire in effect since 1994 continues to contain the conflict with Armenia over Nagorno-Karabakh; however, minor outbreaks of fighting still occur. The active phase of the conflict lasted from 1988-1994, claimed over 35,000 lives, and displaced over one million people. Despite the cease-fire that has been in place since 1994, hundreds of people are killed each year along the Line of Contact by sniper fire and landmines. Armenian forces occupy an estimated 16 percent of Azerbaijan's territory (including Nagorno-Karabakh).

The capital is the ancient city of Baku. Located on the shores of the Caspian Sea, Baku traces its roots back to the seventh century B.C. The baroque apartment and office buildings that line its wide boulevards date to the early 20th century and the city's first oil boom. The first oil boom came to Baku a century ago and built fine mansions, museums and theaters in the city's first golden age. The Soviets added a distinctive, if uninspiring layer of architecture during more than 70 years of ruling Baku and Azerbaijan. Even when the second oil boom started in the middle 1990's, signs of prosperity were restricted to a few fancy restaurants and new office buildings occupied by foreign companies.

While Tbilisi, the once elegant capital of neighboring Georgia, seems dowdy and frayed, Baku's parks and plazas are filled with people strolling and children splashing in the fountains, and its skyline is dotted with at least 20 high-rise buildings under construction. Dozens of older buildings are being restored. Times are good, when oil is high.

In 2001, Azerbaijan switched back to the Latin alphabet from the Cyrillic. Another vestige of the Soviet yoke was thrown off. According to a decree by President Geidar Aliev, all official documents as well as Azerbaijani-language newspapers, magazines and books, must change to the Latin alphabet.

Alphabet switches aren't new to this part of Asia. Turkish, to which Azerbaijani is closely related, changed from the Arabic alphabet to Latin letters in 1928. In the past decade, the former Soviet republics of Turkmenistan and Uzbekistan, whose languages are also part of the Turkic family, have adopted the Latin alphabet. Soviet policies and ethnic diversity also led to the widespread use of Russian across Azerbaijan. Those who did not speak Russian fluently were considered ignorant.

Russian remains widely spoken in Azerbaijan, not only among Russians and other minorities, but also among ethnic Azerbaijanis in urban areas.

Generally, you must be under 50 years of age to adopt from Azerbaijan, although it is flexible. Couples and single women may adopt. You can have other children in your family. It does not appear that single men can adopt. While it is not clear, there may be a cutoff age of 42 for a woman to adopt an infant. You can adopt independently, but be very careful on choosing whom you rely upon locally. Azerbaijani children have fair or olive complexions, with brown or black hair and brown eyes. You can adopt infants under one year of age as well as older and special needs children. Infants as young as 6 months have been referred with most at least 10 months of age at the time of adoption. The medical information you receive is a medical form and still photos. Sometimes there is a video. Because it is a predominantly Muslim country, alcohol abuse is not as widespread. A centralized registration has been established by the Ministry of Health for children ages 0-3. After the age of three, the Ministry of Education coordinates their registration and supervision. Children can be released for international adoption after three months of being registered in the Central Database.

There are several baby houses in Baku. Americans have adopted from Baby House No. 1. It has a playroom up stairs. The hall is immaculate and lined with large, bright windows. The playroom is cheerful, furnished with two large playpens, high chairs and changing tables. Toys hang from the ceiling above the playpens and around the walls. The Director of the orphanage is Gulshan Aghayeva.

Your dossier is notarized, state authenticated, then authenticated at the Department of State in Washington, DC and finally (with an application letter) authenticated at the Azerbaijan Embassy in Washington, DC. Azerbaijan does not seem to allow for bundling of documents. Unless you live in Washington, D.C a courier service is essential. One required document is evidence of home ownership. You should be able to satisfy this with a certified copy of your deed. Your dossier is translated into Azerbaijani.

Your dossier and application are then sent to the Ministry of Foreign Affairs in Azerbaijan who then sends it on to the Ministry of Health (MoH). For children under 3 years of age, the MOH sends it on to the Baku City Health Department. After the submission of your dossier, you usually receive a referral from your agency within a month or so. After your acceptance, the case winds its way through the Azerbaijan bureaucracy. This process can take 5 months.

Both parents are required to travel to attend court in Baku for the final decision. This trip usually occurs 5 months after you accept the referral. The stay is very short on the first trip lasting just a couple of days. The court decision is not final until 30 days later. You can stay and bond during those 30 days or leave and one parent can return(with power of attorney from the other spouse) to pick up your child, her Azerbaijan passport, Court Decree, amended birth certificate and going through the usually US immigrant procedures. Your child's medical screening and immigrant visa is completed at the US Embassy in Moscow, Russia. That will change in the later part of 2003 and it will be issued in Tblisis, Georgia. So it is Moscow (or Tblisi) that you put down on your I-600A and who you check with regarding your I-717H cable.

The Form I-604 *Report on Overseas Orphan Investigation* interview is conducted by the US Embassy in Baku. Because both parents saw the child before the adoption was final, your child usually receives an IR3 visa and obtains automatic citizenship as soon as the plane touches down in the US. In FY 2001, there were 14 IR3s issued and 2 IR4s.

You will need a visa to enter Azerbaijan. Here is the application form: *http://www.traveldocs.com/az/visa.pdf* and more information can be found from the Azerbaijan Embassy's Consular section at 2741 34th Street, N.W., Washington, DC 20008; phone number 202-337-5912; Fax: 1-202-337-5913 Website: *http://www.azembassy.com/* and at *http://www.usembassybaku.org/consul/azvisa.html*. You will also need a visa to enter Russia (or Georgia). You may be able to just use a transit visa for Russia on the first trip. You just have to check.

The US Embassy in Baku is at 83 Azadlig Prospekt, Baku, 370007; Phone number (9-9412)-980-335, 36 or 37 and Fax number is (9-9412)-906-671; Email: *consularbaku@state.gov*; Web site: *http://www.usembassybaku.org/*

It has been noted that the US Consulate in Baku is beginning to take a stricter approach to the I-604 review and making sure that the child meets the "orphan" definition. Make sure the agency you are about to hire has not had any problems by emailing the Consulate.

Cost to adopt in Azerbaijan is about $15,000 to $18,000. Parents have done it for less and others for more. Some agencies are asking $22,000-$25,000, although there doesn't seem to be any reason for such a high cost. These costs are exclusive of travel. Airfare can be quite expensive, as you have to fly twice. There is a western style medical clinic in Baku, which can review your child's medical records.

Azerbaijan requires post-placement reports at 6, 12, 24, and 36 months after returning home. This is no different than other countries. There does not seem to be a registration requirement although that is likely to happen as adoptions increase.

When in Baku be sure to climb Maiden's Tower and look out over the city. It has a beautiful medieval charm including the amazing medieval 15th century Shirvanshah Palace. Take a walk along Nizami Street, Fountain Square and the Boulevard by the bay. Place a little water from the Caspian in a vial to give to your child when she is older. You may even visit Shahidlar Khiyabani (Martyr's Alley, where victims of Black January and the Karabakh War are buried) and the eternal flame high above Baku. Take pictures of the fountains and the many statues immortalizing Azerbaijani poets erected throughout Baku. For the adventuresome at heart, take a two hour drive outside of Baku to the world renowned

Gobustan where ten thousand year old petroglyphs and mud volcanoes spew continuously. Internet cafes exist in Baku and in some of the larger cities.

The Embassy of Azerbaijan in the States is located at 2741 34th Street, N.W. Washington, D.C. 20008; Tel: 202-337-3500; e-*mail azerbaijan@tidalwave.net*; Web site: *http://www.azembassy.com*

Here are some links on Azerbaijan adoption.

http://travel.state.gov/adoption_azerbaijan.html
http://hometown.aol.com/soniabee/page4.html
http://groups.yahoo.com/group/azerbaijanadopt
http://www.azer.com/aiweb/categories/magazine/93_folder/93_articles/93_kimi _guidelines.html
http://adoption.about.com/library/weekly/aa082701a.htm
http://www.wiaa.org/azerbaijan.asp
http://www.usembassybaku.org/
http://www.elinaadoption.org/AzerbaijanianProgram.html
http://www.azer.com/aiweb/categories/magazine/93_folder/93_articles/93_kimi _inara.html
http://www.eeadopt.org/home/services/mlists/index.html
(Listserv on Azerbaijan adoptions.)

http://www.angelfire.com/ab/adopt/
(Great pictures of Baby Home #1 and of Baku)

http://www.babyasa.com/images/sandraparty/thumbs1.shtml
(Another set f adoption pictures)

On Azerbaijan in general:
http://www.azer.com/
http://www.president.az/azerbaijan/azerbaijan.htm
http://resources.net.az/

Books:
http://www.trailblazer-guides.com
Azerbaijan with Excursions to Georgia *by Mark Elliot,* and
Azerbaijan: Land of Fire *by Azerbaijan International*

CHAPTER XXI

MOLDOVA

Moldova is a small country with an agricultural economy. There is not much industry. It is also very poor with the average salary of $21 a month. It periodically suffers from droughts and storms, which devastate its agriculture. The capital is Chisnau, which is famous for its wine cellars with its huge casks of wine. It is a pleasant country and was the site of a 1997 session of the heads of the CIS (Commonwealth of Independent States) when Yeltsin was President of Russia. It has a large Russian-speaking minority, particularly in the Transdniester region.

Moldova is an "artificial" country, meaning that it is really an old province of Romania that in the recent past was carved out as a separate unit. It was part of Romania (the principality of Moldova) until June 1940, when this area (Bessarabia and northern Bukovina) was taken over by the USSR. The territory became one of the Soviet republics until 1989 when it became an independent republic. Under the communist regime, and especially during Stalin's era, huge replacements of population took place, with Romanians being moved far away to Siberia and replaced by Russians in an attempt to have the Russians as the majority—a warped ethnic exchange. This was a common pacification scheme devised and used by Stalin in all the Soviet republics. Moldova is now comprised of Romanian, Ukrainian and Russian ethnic groups along with a smattering of Turks

Soon after independence in 1989, the Moldovans suffered a war with the breakaway republic of Transdniester in the country's east, sparked largely because its Russian speaking majority believed the Moldovan government planned to join Romania. But the war has long been over and with it went the plans for reunification with Romania. The Moldovans speak Romanian, since that is what they really are. They call it Modovan, but the two are indistinguishable. Two-thirds of Moldova's 4.3 million people are ethnic Romanians.

Moldova has two baby homes in Chisinau: Mama Lisa and Botanica. The children are a combination of Russian, Romanian and Gypsy background. Many parents have been impressed with the Mama Lisa home and slightly less so with Botanica. Mama Lisa is described as clean, bright and cheerful with caring caregivers. There are other children's homes as well, but they are in other parts of the country such as in Balti (pronounced Beltz). Mama Lisa herself gets quite a bit of praise from parents for running a loving and well run home. The adopted children seem to be just slightly delayed and attach well. The caregivers at Mama Lisa's really love the children there. They worry about them getting sick or eating their meals. The babies even get massages. Many of the adoptions from Mama Lisa prior to the moratorium were by Americans. In 2000, 79 children were adopted by Americans and another 200 by other countries.

Moldova is still going through foreign adoption law growing pains. There was a moratorium in 2000 between March and June. Then on February 25, 2001, general elections were held and Moldova's old communist party won a majority of seats in the Parliament. This was probably a reaction to the lack of economic progress that had occurred since becoming independent from Russia. Since Parliament elects the President of Moldova, an old communist leader, Vronin, became President of Moldova. Prime Minister Braghis remained Prime Minister and he is a Centrist. Subsequent to this election, in March 2001, Moldova halted all foreign adoptions. Moldova claimed there had been irregularities and raised the well-worn specter of children being adopted for their body organs. This is a common urban legend in these countries trotted out by their governments, press, and politicians when it suits them. As proof, the Moldovian government pointed out that doctors in the United States had adopted some of the children.

Throughout 2001 this "investigation" continued. Families who had been waiting for children, slowly moved on to other countries. The US had the FBI interview several families, including the doctors. Moldova sent investigators to come over to the United States and investigate. As everyone knew, nothing wrong about any of the adoptions was ever found. Nevertheless, the government's television reported that body organ trafficking had been discovered.

The Moldovan investigation included a review as to whether Moldovan law was being followed. Under Moldovan law, a non-Moldovan citizen may adopt an orphan only if he or she cannot be placed in a Moldovan home, or if the child requires medical treatment not available in Moldova. In practice, this has meant that Moldovan authorities must offer the child to three different Moldovan couples or parents before making the child eligible for adoption by U.S. parents. Investigators believe that in some of the cases they are reviewing none of the children were offered to Moldovan couples. Also, investigators believe that in some cases, Moldovan officials falsified medical documents in order to indicate that some children had medical conditions that could not be treated in Moldova. Whether any of this is actually true is unknown.

In late 2001, the Moldovan Ambassador asked families to send in reports on how their children were doing. Apparently, Moldova had no way of accessing its post-placement records.

A few cases were completed in 2002, however these were "pipeline" cases where the adoption was almost completed when the moratorium first took place. Michael Sears, the Vice Counsel in the Commercial Section in the U.S. Embassy in Chisinau, worked diligently in trying to get to the root of the investigation, satisfy Moldova, and get foreign adoptions started again. He has rotated to the Ukrainian desk in Washington, but he was great.

Finally, in late 2002 Moldova said foreign adoptions could begin again. It instituted a new agency accreditation policy and about a half dozen US agencies have been authorized to place Moldovan children. Children must be on a national registry for six months before they are eligible for foreign adoption. During these 6 months, only Moldovans can adopt. Parents must work through an accredited agency Many of the rules remain the same. Single women and older parents may adopt. The age cutoff is 50.There is only agency directed adoption, not independent.

First, your dossier is submitted to the Moldova Adoption Committee (MAC) in Chisinau for acceptance and a referral. Your documents must be authenticated, not apostilled. This means it must go through the authentication process at your Secretary of State, US State Department and finally Moldova Embassy. After it is returned to you from the Moldova Embassy you send it to the MAC. The MAC sends it to the regional Department of Education. The children's home Director, home physician and welfare inspector match your dossier with a child subject to your parameters for gender and age. You get a pre-identified referral with the medicals being similar to what you might see on a Russian referral. You review the medical information with your specialist and you can ask more questions.

You send an acceptance (or rejection) letter to the MAC. The regional Department of Education then sends a Notice to Approval of Adoption back to the MAC who then decides to approve or disapprove the adoption. You will

need a visa to enter Moldova and while you can obtain one at the Chisniau airport, you should try to get one from the Modovan Consulate in the States
before you travel.You then travel to Moldova for a court hearing. You can fly
direct to Chisinau from Germany on Air Moldova. Both parents do not have to
attend Court (see IR3 vs IR4 discussion). After court, you must wait out the
appeal period of 14 days. This period is rarely waived. You should be allowed to
visit your child for several hours each day during this time. He will greatly benefit from you playing with him and feeding him. The one on one time with you
will result in immediately gains in development. You will have uninterrupted
time to get to know each other and do some bonding before arriving home.
You will also have time to explore Moldova and learn about your child's birth
culture. One or both of you can also return home. There are three options
regarding Moldova. You can spend 3 weeks in country and complete everything in one trip. You may also fly over for court (3-5 days) and return to pick
up your child (7-10 days). The third option is rather rare but you can fly over
for court (3-5 days) and then arrange to have your child escorted home.
Moldova requires post placement reports for 3 years after the adoption

After the adoption is final your child will need a Moldovan passport and
you will need to visit the US Embassy in Chisinau for the *Form I-604 Report on
Overseas Orphan Investigation* interview. The 30 minute I-604 examination
takes place in Chisnau then you travel to Bucharest, Romania for the medical
exam and the US visa for your child. The Consular Section of the US Embassy
in Moldova does not issue immigrant visas. The Embassy's phone number is
(011) 373-2-40-83-00, and email is *searsmj@state.gov*. The address is 103
Strada Mateevici, MD-2009 Chisinau, Moldova.

The Embassy has a list of documents they want to see for the exam:

1. Your US passport
2. A certified copy of the child's original Moldovan birth certificate
3. The child's new birth certificate
4. The letter of recommendation on the adoption from the MAC
5. The adoption decree
6. The child's Moldovan medical report
7. Proof that the child has been abandoned by his/her birth parents (usual relinquishment document)
8. A statement from the children's home Director that no one has visited the child for 6 months.

The Embassy is open from 9 am to 6 pm Monday through Friday except for US and Moldovan holidays (so you need to check their holiday schedules).

After the quick I-604review you are off to Bucharest, Romania for your child's immigrant visa. The US Embassy in Bucharest is located at Filipescu 26. The Consular Section is located behind the Hotel Intercontinental on a street running parallel to Magheru Boulevard. Email: *adoptionsbucharest@state.gov;* *Telephone*: +40 1 210-4042; *Fax*: 01-211-3360. You will need to check on their holiday schedule as well, since they are closed on Romanian and US holidays. It is on their web site.

The Moldovan Embassy is at 2101 S Street, NW, Washington, DC 20008; Phone: (202) 667-1130, ext. 15; Fax: (202) 667-1204; Email: moldova@dgs.dgsys.com; Web page: *http://www.moldova.org*

See these web sites for more information:
http://www.usembassy.md/en-consulateado.htm,
http://travel.state.gov/adoption_moldova.html
and *http://www.usembassy.ro/InfoA/AdoptionMoldova.html*

AFTER THOUGHTS

Having a child that comes from a children's home environment is a walk into the unknown. But then that is the way it is with all children. You never really know what their personality will be like or how they will be when they reach adulthood. There are certain traits that come with the DNA like personality, which can be considered a template, but it is a child's character that fills that template and which you have been given the gift of responsibility to mold.

In one sense you have a head start. Like a child who comes from a family with a history of an hereditary disease, you know that your child may be at risk for certain issues. Because you are aware of the possibility, you are more in tune to your child and more likely to get help if such a situation occurs.

You will be more sensitive to your child's development and take action if it is necessary. The action may be to hire a tutor one summer to help them with a subject, or to get medical help if that is the issue. You will be more tolerant, more accepting, and more knowledgeable. Enjoy the journey!

I once read a fable about a beachcomber who was observed picking starfish off the sand and throwing them in the water before they dried out and died. The beach was littered with thousands of starfish so the observer told the beachcomber that his actions made no real difference. At that moment the beachcomber picked up a starfish and tossed him in the water to safety and replied, "it made a difference to him."

All children have the right to be loved, to be nurtured and to reach for a dream. A chance is all they ask.

I'll leave you with this imaginary discourse from a toddler taken from one of the adoption books:

"Please learn as much as you can about me before you decide to be my Mom or Dad, so you won't be surprised about me. Don't think of me as a helpless infant, even though I may not yet be able to do all the things most kids my age can do. Don't treat me as if I'm older than I really am just because I act as if I don't need you to take care of me, however. When I push you away is when I need you to hold me and tell me that you will never let me go. I had to learn to do many things for myself before you came into my life, and it's hard for me to learn to depend on you as much as I should. Please recognize and help me with my special needs, but remember that I am still a lot more like other kids than I am different. See me first as your child, not as your adopted child or a child with special needs. Sometimes I feel really sad and really mad. Don't pretend that I don't have these feelings, and don't get discouraged when I take out my strong feelings on you. Most of the time I am not really mad at you, but you're the one who's here now and the one I can safely show my feelings to. I know in my heart that you didn't do anything to hurt me, but I get all mixed up. My memories of other moms and other places where I've lived are all in my mind, but they're stored in pictures, sounds, feelings, and even smells. I don't have the words to talk about these things. I can't figure out why that other Mom disappeared, and I'm worried that you might go away, too. I often have to test you because it's hard for me to believe that you won't leave me, too. In fact, it's pretty scary for me to love you and trust you, so I might have to test your love the most when you start to become important to me. Sometimes I just want to curl up in a ball and be a little baby again so someone will take care of me. Other times I want to do everything by myself and I feel like running away from you. Please be patient. We have a long time together. After all, the really worthwhile things in life usually aren't very easy and they don't happen overnight."

FREQUENTLY ASKED QUESTIONS

1. What if my child wants to find his Russian birth parents?

The Russians are not too keen on the American idea of open adoption. Indeed, the Russians have strict privacy laws regarding keeping the adoption proceedings sealed. You and your child can always try to contact the birthfamily, but all others are prohibited from revealing the confidential adoption proceedings. When your child is older, he may wish to visit his birth city or perhaps even find his birth relatives. This is only natural. Neither your child's birth parents nor siblings gain any special access to an American visa simply because your child was adopted by you. As far as the BCIS is concerned, the connection is broken once you've adopted. The Russians treat adoption like we did many decades ago. Russian women often feign pregnancy and adoptions are handled in utmost secrecy and privacy. Physical looks are carefully matched and the child may never be told he/she is adopted.

2. How tall will my child be?

If you can find out the birthparent's height, you might be able to tell. For boys, add five inches to the birthmother's height, then add that number to the birthfather's height and now divide by two. You might add an inch or two for good old American nutrition. For a daughter, subtract five inches from the birthfather's height, add that number to the birthmother's, and then divide by two. Of course, insult due to environmental conditions also plays a part.

3. I've heard it is difficult to get information from Russians?

Russians, like a lot of Europeans, have difficulty at first with the American style of frank and blunt questioning. While we perceive it as the most efficient method of obtaining information, they may perceive as being rude. They will often not respond to direct questions if they do not know you. You may have to ask several times to get an answer to a question and may have to ask it a different way each time. Be polite but persistent. Once a friendly and personable relationship is established, then they are more likely to respond with a lot more information. Just don't be surprised if they are reserved and not as forthcoming at first. It's the European way.

4. Must both Spouses travel to Russia?

Generally yes, although the Judge can allow only one. It is in her discretion. At least one spouse must appear at the Embassy to apply for the child's visa, unless a representative has a power of attorney. Both parents must see the child prior to the court hearing, if that child is to receive an IR-3 visa. Notwithstanding this rule, the US Embassy has issued a small number of IR-4 visas each year, which indicates that there are exceptions.

5. How can my spouse return to the States early?

Your agency will know the rules. Generally, if a spouse has to leave after the Court hearing to return to the States, then the leaving spouse must sign a completed (no blanks or incompletes) I-600 form and give you a Power of Attorney authorizing you to act in his place. The Embassy needs proof the absent parent has met the child, such as a photo of them together. The remaining parent cannot sign the I-600 for the leaving spouse; and the Power of Attorney does not extend to the signing of the I-600 petition. You should check the requirements with the Consulate before you travel Sometimes they have asked to see airplane tickets.

6. How can I find out what was in the Visa package?

Some parents want to see what was in that Visa package (for the most part nothing you do not already have). You file a G-884, which is mailed to the BCIS office that processed your I-171H or a G-639, which is mailed to Mesquite TX. You can find these at

http://www.visalaw.com/forms/g-884.pdf
and *http://www.visalaw.com/forms/g-639.pdf.*

7. What do I do if I have no crib in Russia?

Here are some ideas if you find yourself in need of a crib. You can push your twin beds together and put the child between you. Be very careful about rolling over if the child is an infant. You can place the baby in an empty suitcase with a blanket. Or you can pull an empty drawer out, put a blanket it in then the baby. What also works is to place the baby on a soft blanket on the floor and surround her with suitcases so she can't go anywhere.

8. I've heard Moscow is different than the Regions?

If you have ever worked in a federal agency you will notice that rules that apply outside Washington, do not apply at headquarters. So it is if you are adopting from Moscow. Everything in Moscow seems to be a little different. One of the new requirements is a letter from your mortgage company stating your loan amount, how much you have paid, and the balance. They also seem to want a medical review on you that is not any older than three months (Vladivostok is the same). Also, generally Moscow does not waive the 10 days. Moscow seems to make up new little rules as they go along. The other Regions seem to stick with a list. You agency should be on top of any changes, just be aware that Moscow is different than the Regions.

9. How do I handle all the vodka toasts since I don't drink?

The best thing to do is to let them pour you a drink of whatever and take part in the toasts, but only sip your drink or don't really drink it (depending on how much you want to drink). If you do it this way, you won't offend anyone. It's very easy for women to refuse hard liquor. They usually offer women wine or champagne anyway. Be prepared to say some toasts. They WILL call on you to say one!

Other parents have handled it by putting something else in their glass, but still participate in the toasting. What also works is to pat your stomach and explain that your doctor won't allow it, or that you cannot for a religious reason. Try to redirect by blaming a nonexistent third party like a doctor and then asking for fruit juice or mineral water. If there is a server, you can quietly ask him or her to put the alternative liquid in your wine glass without making a fuss in front of your hosts. Be tactful with this option.

Always accept and savor the little biscuits and sweets offered. This is a good way to redirect: "I can't partake of alcohol, but I would love one of those delightful little cakes I see there. Are they particular to this region?"

Try not to refuse a cup of coffee or tea. The sharing of a cup of java demonstrates mutual good will and civility. You are sharing your time. One added note, sometimes Russians will add a dollop of ice cream to their coffee. It is really good!

10. What is the difference between internal and external passports?

Russian internal passports are given to persons who become legally of age, which happens when a person reaches 16 years old. So the kids going abroad cannot receive internal passports. In fact, if they cross a frontier, they should not be given passports, but they must be registered in the passports of their parents. Russians have special pages in their foreign passports for their children's information.

As adoptive parents are not Russian citizens and the kids still continue to be Russian citizens, they are given Russian "foreign" passports with which they can use to travel abroad.

11. What is the difference between Krai, Region, and a Republic?

It is in the autonomy they get from the federal government in Moscow. A Region is a unit of the Russian State. It is a territorial division of Russia just like our states in the US. A Krai is an historical autonomous area with local self-governing, like Krasnodar Krai (where Kossaks (Cosacks) lived), still belonging to the Russian nation, but relatively independent of the central power.

Autonomous republics (do not mix them up with national republics which are separate formations) have a different national structure and the basic nation is not Russian. Accordingly, they have maximum autonomy to solve local matters.

12. Where can I get a good map of Russia?

If you can find a February, 1976 National Geographic, it contains a map that details how different nationalities populate the former Soviet Union. Michelin, of course, has wonderfully detailed maps, which can be found in any large bookstore. There are also maps you can download from the web. See this web site: *http://plasma.nationalgeographic.com/mapmachine/*

13. Are there summer programs where potential adoptive children are brought to the United States for a few weeks?

There are many such programs. The children generally stay with a host family and there is a high success rate in adopting these kids. You get to spend a few weeks with them and see them as they really are. These children can keep up a façade for a while, but eventually you should see them as the kind of people they can become. You still must research the organizations thoroughly to make sure that these children are really off the database and available for adoption and that they have been screened.

You can read about these sorts of programs on the Nightlight, KidSave, Bridge of Hope, and Camp Hope web sites. There are many others as well.

14. Will my being Jewish be a problem?

There is a pattern of anti-Semitism that runs through Russia's history and exists today. The largest groups of émigrés to Israel are those from Russia. Nevertheless, there does not appear to be any anti-Semitism in the adoption process. Here is a web site on Jewish orphans:
http://interconnection.org/yeladim/organizations/

15. What is Russian Orthodox?

It is the official religion of Russia. The story goes that in somewhere around 988, Vladimir, prince of Kiev, brought Eastern Christianity to what was then known as Rus. Possibly he preferred the Byzantine liturgy, and maybe Islam's prohibition of alcohol ruled that religion out as a possibility. But whatever the reason, Vladimir did it in a serious way, warning Kievans that "Whoever does not turn up at the river tomorrow [for baptism by immersion], be he rich, poor, lowly or slave, he shall be my enemy." When Byzantium—the Second Rome—fell to the Islamic Ottoman Empire nearly 500 years later, and Moscow, which had replaced Kiev as the Russian political center, won its independence from the Tatars shortly thereafter, many came to view it as the Third Rome.

16. Does our adopted child need a Russian visa to visit Russia?

Adopted children are Russian citizens until they are 18. They must travel to Russia on their Russian passport, not on their American passport and a Russian Visa. When they return to the United States, they travel on their American passport. If you do go, remember that you can go through the much shorter Russian line at the Moscow airport upon arrival, rather than the longer foreign one. Just have your child go first and claim to be just one big Russian/American family.

17. Why doesn't the US have orphanages?

It still does. The oldest orphanage in the United States, Bethesda, is still operating. John Wesley founded it in 1743 in Savannah, Georgia. The residents are now troubled youths rather than true orphans. The reason the US doesn't use orphanages anymore is because of studies in the 1940's that found a connection between caregiver-child disruption and later psychopathology. Three responses were theorized as derived from that disruption: protest, despair and detachment. Other studies found that institutionalism caused not just physical delays but also cognitive, emotional, social and language delays. These studies started the movement in the US away from orphanages for young children and toward foster care.

18. How safe is the water?

Russian public water can cause problems with American stomachs. Russians generally think their water is just fine, but it all depends on what you are used to. To avoid any difficulties, you should only drink bottled water while in

Russia. This is widely available. Both Coca-Cola and the Russian Orthodox Church sell water. Saint Springs or Vera are good brands. Even seltzer water is better than taking a chance with a faucet. Of course, it is hard to tell when a bottle has gas in it or not. The only way you can reliably tell is to squeeze the bottle. A bottle with gas is almost solid when you squeeze it. A bottle without gas dents in quite a bit.

You might drink bottled water but brush your teeth with seltzer. You can always boil water using a small hot plate. If you plan to stay a few weeks, then take a water distiller or pump. They will cost around $165 from Magellans. Anything costing under $100 probably won't really help you get rid of the giardia organisms and heavy metals although some swear by filter bottles at ww.safewateranywhere.com. Iodine tablets also work. If you drink the public water, the odds are you will make it home without Stalin's Revenge. However, pack some antibiotics just in case.

19. Can I choose a child from a photolist?

Agencies used to post photos of adoptable children on the Internet. However, the Russian Ministry and many other countries frown on doing that. Indeed, when you are at a Children's home the Russians will not want you to intentionally take pictures of other children. This is not to say that you cannot find such a photolisting, just that it is no longer common practice. Bulgaria has also decided not to allow photolists.

There are also many abuses with photolisting sites. Bait and switch occurs all the time. Ukrainian children have been place on a photolist, which is illegal—no pre-selection is allowed. Multiple agencies have listed the same child. Some agencies even advertise children who are not legal orphans, but if you pick those kids, they'll get a relinquishment by the parents.

Photolistings are also a useful tool for an agency with a new program, and are especially helpful in finding families for older and other hard to place children. One recommended site is *http://www.welcomegarden.com/*.

20. Will my child be drafted into the Russian Army?

No, you have to reside in Russia. For those that do reside in Russia the rule is that all healthy Russian males are subject to the draft, but the reality is that not all of them are drafted. For those enrolled into vocational schools or colleges, the draft is postponed upon graduation. If they graduate from a college, which has a military division (most engineering schools do), they become lieutenants and need to attend boot camp just for few months to finish their military training.

The youngest age at which men can be drafted is 18. The obligatory draft ends at age 28. There are a lot of exceptions and excuses from the draft. Most Russians try to avoid conscription at all costs. They pay doctors to write up phony injuries and diseases. The reason is that a conscript is subject to a great deal of brutality at the hands of the NCO and officer corp. Also, there is not enough money for food or decent accommodations. The list for the draft is compiled based on one's registration at a permanent address. (All Russian residents are supposed to get registered). Adopted children, living abroad permanently, are not registered in Russia and are not a subject for the draft, unless they volunteer to serve in Russian forces or come to live in Russia permanently. They cannot be drafted while just visiting Russia.

So as far as adopted children are concerned, it's not going to happen. Persons must reside in Russia permanently in order to be drafted. Besides, as soon as the Chechnya business is finished, Russia is very likely to go to a professional model for their military and quit using conscripts. It will not only make the Russian military more competent, but also more economical. Putin is slowly trying to get the Russian military to modernize, but he is having a difficult time.

21. What happens to the orphanage children after age 16?

Russian children are enrolled in regular school at age 7. The school week was changed from 6 to 5 days so they added an extra year to the curriculum. Thus school is now 11 years instead of 10. Kids should graduate therefore at 18, but since the enrollment age requirements are not as strict as in the US, some of them start school earlier and graduate from high school at 17. At 16, children are allowed to get out of school for vocational training—and this often happens with orphans, but it gives them only a middle-school education. Since high-school education is mandatory in Russia, it is assumed that they get high school diploma along with their vocational degree, although the quality of such education is somewhat doubtful.

However, not every orphan goes on to vocational school and instead they simply move out into the world. They move out without any money or much in the way of possessions. The boys, if they are really lucky, have been taught a trade. This is probably a minority. A lot of the boys are conscripted into the army. In the Russian military, conscripts are treated very harshly. After the army, their life is on the streets. For the girls the prognosis is equally grim.

Prostitution and begging are not uncommon. This description does not cover every child, but it occurs often enough. Some statistics show that one third of the children become homeless, fifth criminals and ten percent commit suicide.

It is virtually impossible for a child to go on to a university in a major town. The high schools do not provide for a top-notch education, although surprisingly many children will have learned some English. If any student wants to get into Moscow State, the preeminent university in Russia, then he must pay thousands of dollars to take tutoring lessons from well-connected grad students and professors and sit for an all or nothing entrance exam.

22. Should I take a car seat?

Russians do not use car seats. Nor do they use seat belts. After you put your luggage and yourselves in the car there is simply no room. Add in another family and there really isn't any room. Normally you just hold your child on your lap. Now don't forget that whoever picks you up at the airport when you return to the States should have a car seat. But since your child has never been in one, expect some crying. A few parents have taken car seats for use on the airplane due to fear of turbulence. If the plane crashes, it will not help much, so you have to balance lugging the seat all over Eastern Europe versus the fear that if there is turbulence your child will only be safe if locked into a car seat on the plane. It also means you must buy a separate plane seat for the child. Most planes have seat belts that you can tie you and your child together. Just ask.

23. Do I send out baby announcements?

When you return from your adoption, you may want to send out an adoption announcement similar to a birth announcement. Some people buy cards from a store on which they place their child's photo. On the front you might write, "Please help us welcome (or are thrilled to announce, or placed in our loving arms) the newest addition to our family." Then her name, birth date (birth city) and adoption date. There are lots of variations, which are limited only by your imagination. Other parents place the announcement on vellum and then on card stock with a ribbon. Here are two ideas:

In our hearts he was already our son.
We simply had to bring him home.
With hearts full of praise

and thanksgiving,
we joyfully announce God's gift to us.

We welcome with love...
(name of child)
Born on
in Kirov, Russia
Placed in our arms forever
April 27, 2002

OR

Once upon a time in the town
Of Murmansk, Russia
A special baby girl was born
on December 21, 1998
She embraced the hearts of
The so and so Family
on June 14, 2000
Her proud parents named her
Alexandra the Great
And she was loved from that day forward.
The Beginning.

24. How can I give money to the children's home?

Some homes have a special bank account to receive humanitarian aid. This account is most likely to be held at SBERBANK, which is Russia's largest savings bank and perhaps the only solvent one. It is government controlled. Whether the money is actually used for the children is another story. A better alternative is for someone to hand deliver rubles or donated goods (bought here or there) to the children's home director. Insist on a receipt. Sometimes adoptive parents even go with the home director and let her pick things out with them that the children need. Now that is fun!

There are many organizations that help children's homes. One is *http://www.fireflykids.org/engl/*.

25. *What is a toddler's daily routine?*

This is a general description of a standard day. Keep in mind that each children's home is different. All children who are not infants sleep in their own little toddler beds. The beds have sheets, blankets, and pillows on them. They are lined up in rows, much like military dorms. Each child sleeps in only a diaper or underwear with their clothes draped at the foot of their beds. Toddlers eat at child size tables with child size chairs. It looks like a toddler Sunday school class. The children feed themselves as best they can using large adult spoons. They eat soup, mashed potatoes, bread and occasionally a little sausage. They are given tea to drink. The children eat very fast, little gets spilled, and they guard their plates. The children are placed on potties after each meal and certain other times during the day regardless of whether they need to go or not.

They then might be put down for a nap from about 1:00-3:00 p.m. each day after lunch. Bathing might consist of being hosed down with cold water from one of those European hand-held shower attachments.

The children are not allowed to touch the light switches at the children's home so the children have a tendency to flick the lights on and off over and over again once you have them home. It is a novelty. The children's toilet (if not just an actual pot) probably did not have a flushing mechanism so they will need some training in remembering to flush. Older children are required to always ask permission before doing anything, so it will take them a little while to get out of that habit. They may be obsessive about cleanliness.

If you give an older toddler some food, he will share it with his group. Group consciousness is very strong. Nothing belongs to individual children. Clothes are rotated around and shoes are used as needed (for going outside) and not for everyday wear. Hair is kept very short to cut down on the need for grooming. Even the girls have "bowl" haircuts.

Discipline might vary from time outs where the children must stand against a wall with their hands up beside their head as if being frisked to more physical punishment such as slapping. The children are not read to. Older children might see puppet shows dealing with fairy tales.

Here is what a general schedule for a 4 to 5 year old group might look like:

6:30-7:30 am—Potty time, Play
7:30—Breakfast
8-8:30—Play/Lessons [music, etc.]
8:30-11:30—Walk [to playground, walk to watch a nearby construction site, etc.]
11:30—Lunch

12-12:30—Play
12:30-3—Nap
3-3:30—Play
3:30—Snack
4-4:30—Play/Lessons
4:30-7:30—Walk
7:30—Dinner
8-9—Walk
9pm-6:30am—Sleep

26. What is an infant's (under 18 months) routine?

They have three meals a day and one snack. They are not given baths but rather pitchers of water are poured on them and they receive a sponge bath. They take two naps a day and are put to bed for the night by 7:00.

The babies spend a lot of time in their cribs. The room might have a dozen cribs and the back of their heads might be almost bald from lying in the crib so much.

27. How can I change my I-600A to another country?

Try to change countries before you receive the I-171H. You can do so by simply mailing in a letter to your local BCIS amending the I-600A. If you have already received the I-171H, then you must file form I-824 (Application for Action on an Approved Application or Petition) at a cost of $140.00 to have your approval sent from your old country to the US Embassy issuing the child's US visa. If you designated a country in your homestudy, then you will need an updated one reflecting the change. If you just said Eastern Europe, then update the home study and take that with you to Russia or wherever. The BCIS does not need it. Include an overnight envelope with your form so the BCIS can overnight your new I-171H to you.

The BCIS will send a Visa 37 cable to the old and the newly designated post. In the cable to the old post it will say, "Pursuant to the petitioner's request, the Visa 37 cable previously sent to your post/office in this matter is hereby invalidated. The approval is being transferred to the other post/office addressed in this telegram. Please forward the approved advanced processing application to that destination." After awhile you should email the adoption unit in the new Embassy's adoption office and ask them if they have received your file. When you file your I-824 to change countries, make sure you tell them in a cover sheet that it is for an adoption. If BCIS knows it is for an adoption they will process within 30 days, otherwise it will sit for months on a desk.

Be aware that if you want approval to adopt in two countries rather than simply transferring approval, it is likely to cost you another $460 and a second I-600A. Just you won't have to be fingerprinted again. Also, some people have actually received their I-171H approval even though they left line 16 blank on their I-600A. In that case all they did was to send or fax a letter to the BCIS telling them which country they wanted the approval sent to. No additional fee was required.

28. How do I notify the BCIS if I change Agencies?

Have your new agency write a letter on their letterhead stating they are now your agency for all adoption proceedings. Then write a cover letter to the BCIS enclosing the letter from your agency and informing the BCIS to make the change in their files. Enclose a copy of your I-171H with your cover letter.

29. Are my children Russian or American?

Your children are Russian until they are 18 or even beyond if they want. They are also American pursuant to the provisions of the Child Citizenship Act. They can travel under either passport although in leaving and entering the United States they must use the US Passport and when entering or leaving Russia, their Russian passport. So your child should bring both if you are going back to Russia for another child. There is a provision in Russian law for your child to renounce his Russian citizenship, but why.

Some of the Russian passports will show that they expire in 5 or 10 years. Even if you do not renew their Russian passport, your child still has the right to claim Russian citizenship, as long as the Russian government allows him to. Most countries have an artificial cutoff at 18 when your child is supposed to declare his citizenship. This is usually artificial, as most countries (such as France) will allow you to submit documentation later to prove and reclaim your dual citizenship. Even the State Department now recognizes dual citizenship. See more at the State Department site:
http://travel.state.gov/dualnationality.html and at
http://www.richw.org/dualcit/?from=.

30. How do I adopt if I live overseas?

The BCIS regulations at 8 CFR 204.3 cover this. You can find them at
http://www.access.gpo.gov/nara/cfr/waisidx_99/8cfr204_99.html Your I-600A
can be filed with the BCIS office in the country you reside. You can have your
home study prepared by anyone that is licensed or authorized by the foreign
country's adoption authorities to conduct home studies under the laws of the
foreign country. There is an indication that if you are fingerprinted at a United
States Embassy or consulate then you do not need to be fingerprinted by the
BCIS and are exempt from the $50 fingerprint fee. You would then file your
completed fingerprint card when you file your I-600A. See the regulations for
further details. If you live overseas and adopt there, then if the child is with you
for two years you may be able to file a Family Petition, Form I-130, rather than
go the I-600 orphan route. You should check with an immigration attorney to
see if this is available to you.

31. How does the Bulgarian naming system work?

Bulgarians have three names (the given name could be hyphenated, e.g. Anna-
Maria or Ivan-Asen). The first one is chosen by the birthparents by the following tradition. The first-born has to be named after the paternal grandparents;
if a girl usually after the grandmother, and if a boy usually after the grandfather. Luckily, a majority of names in Bulgarian have both female and male ana-
logues, and this gives one a limited choice. (For example, Radoslav and
Radoslava, Ivan and Ivana, Penyo and Pen(k)a.) Then the following children
have to be named after the maternal grandparents following the same scheme;
then one moves to the best man and the maid of honor (who typically are an
older, more-established family to whom the young couple can turn for advice).

Nowadays, this tradition is modified in the following ways. First, if one happens to like the names of one set of grandparents more, one just goes with
those names. Also, a very popular modification is the "first-letter-rule". Also,
the best man rule is usually thrown out, and perhaps more and more people
just choose names that they like!

The middle name is not chosen randomly; in fact it is fixed. If the father is
known, the middle name is the -ov(a), -ev(a) derivation of it. If the father is
unknown, then one does the same thing with the name of the mother. With
the Turkish and Jewish and Armenian names of Bulgarian citizens, one just
sticks for the middle name the exact name of the father (or mother if
unknown).

The third name is the family name, and sometimes your father's middle name (this is getting pretty uncommon!) and thus in this rare case, it is most often your grandfather's name.

The gender differences in nouns in Bulgarian carry over to family names. Thus, a woman's name almost always ends in "a". Thus, if a father's name was Gargov, then his daughter is Gargova.

32. How long is my I-171H valid?

Just to review the time lines again. You have one year within which to file your home study after filing your I-600A. The home study or the most recent update must not be any older than six months at the time you submit it to the BCIS. Once you receive your approved advanced processing (the I-171H), the I-600 must be filed within 18 months of the date of such advanced approval. Now if you do adopt, it may be possible to use that very same I-171H to adopt again within that 18 months. Whether you can or not depends on your local BCIS office and your state's home study requirements. Some states will allow you to simply send in a two-page update and you are off to Russia again. Other states require a completely new home study. Some BCIS offices are satisfied with using your old FBI fingerprints to run a check on you although they are only valid for 15 months. The FBI actually keeps them on their system longer. Other BCIS offices make you do the whole fingerprint ordeal over again. It really all depends. The first step is to check with the US Embassy in Moscow by fax or email and ask them if you are approved for more children than you have already adopted and if your file is still open. If it is, then find out from your home study agency what the rules are about updating the home study. Even if your file is not open, some BCIS offices will allow you to piggyback on your old I-171H and using the home study update, amend your I-171H. You just have to check.

33. Should I adopt one child or two at a time?

There are pros and cons. The pros are that you get all this adoption stuff over with at one time. You don't have to go through the whole thing again. This makes sense if you are older and want to complete your family quickly. You also save money. Normally agencies only charge a third or quarter more for an additional child plus you get an additional Adoption Tax Credit and Title IV reimbursement check. The children stimulate and play with each other. They grow up as best friends. They will always be there for each other. Displacement issues may be nonexistent. Somehow, two babies together are even cuter than one and you will find yourself an instant celebrity and everyone will want to come over and play with your babies. You've given one more child a home. They also realize that they are not the only adopted Russian child in the family and can take comfort in the similar experience of their sibling.

Now the cons. It's hard to travel home from Russia with two children. Sometimes they both want to be fed, cuddled and played with at the same time! It takes lots of paraphernalia (diaper bag, car seats, stroller) to go any-where. You spend a fortune on formula and diapers. If you adopt unrelated children and one is older, it could add stress in the home, which could nega-tively affect the older child. You also are unable to give one child your full attention, which he may need in order to happily integrate into your family.

If you are planning to adopt two at once and/or 'artificial twinning,' you must think through the 'what-ifs'. What if one or both of the children have attachment issues? What if one or both are more delayed than you anticipate? Do you have a support system and a 'game plan' to deal with these types of 'what-ifs'? Hopefully they won't happen, but you must think through 'what-ifs' and decide what you will do if it does happen because coming up with a game plan after the kids are home is much more difficult. The children are likely to be more developmentally delayed than you anticipate. If you adopt young tod-dlers, then you really have 2 infants on your hands and not toddlers. 'Infants' involve a lot more 'hands on' care than toddlers. Also, both kids may very well need some Early Intervention, speech, or OT/PT. While many families who adopt two at once close in age say they made the right choice, they don't say it until the first year is over as they are too tired to say anything! You really need a reality check on your support system. Still, the children will likely bond well and be the best of friends. They will spur each other on in their development.

Artificial twining (adopting two whose ages are within 9 months of each other) does have its critics and the points raised are worthy of consideration. See *http://www.eeadopt.org/home/preparing/process/issues/twinning.htm* and *http://www.perspectivespress.com/notwinning.html.*

34. Is there adoption financial assistance?

The National Adoption Foundation in Danbury, CT can provide such assis-tance. The National Adoption Foundation Loan Program offers unsecured loans and home equity line of credit loans of up to $25,000 to adopting par-ents. The annual percentage rate (APR) is usually very competitive compared to other unsecured loans. NAF can be contacted at (203) 791-3811 for loan applications. Also, you can call 800-448-7061 to apply for a loan over the phone. Usually, you will hear something within a week. The loans are usually below credit card rates. The loans are funded by MBNA America of Wilmington, DE. There is some confusion as MBNA claims they really do not offer a special adoption rate. The number for MBNA is (800) 626-2760. Credit unions may also offer a special adoption loan program. NAF also offers grants that are not based on income. Call them for that information as well.

There is also a foundation called "A Child Waits Foundation" at *http://www.achildwaits.org*. A Child Waits is a non-profit charitable foundation, which provides loans to parents needing funds to complete their adoption. There is also the DOMOI Foundation, which promotes international adoptions and may provide loans. Its address is The DOMOI Foundation (Shayna Billings, Ex. Dir.), 1915 Polk Court, Mountain View, CA 94040 (650) 969-1980.

Other groups that offer assistance are **Project Oz Adoptions, Inc,** Website: *http://www.projectoz.com* or phone: (410) 286-5454; **His Kids Too!;** Website: *http://www.hiskidstoo.org* or phone: (850) 524-5437, **JSW Adoption Foundation;** Website: *www.jsw-adoption.org* or phone:1-877-905-2367; **Bright Futures;** Website:*http://www.homestead.com/brightfutures/*; **Adopt$hare;** Website: *http://www.adoptshare.org/*; **Ibsen Adoption Network;** Phone (360) 866-7036; **Love Knows No Borders;** Website: *www.loveknowsnoborders.com*; **God's Grace Adoption Ministry;** 203) 572-4539; **Jacob Free Loan Foundation;** Website: *http://www.jfslink.org/freeloan.html* or (413) 737-2601; **Hebrew Free Loan Association/DOMOI Foundation;** Website: *http://www.hflasf.org/adopt-loans.html* or (415) 546-9902; **His Kids Too Adoption Bank;** Website*: http://www.hiskidstoo.org/* or (850) 524-KIDS (5437);

Also, The Dave Thomas Act of 2003, H.R. 584, was introduced by Representative Peter King (R-NY), and if enacted will amend the Internal Revenue Code of 1986 to allow penalty-free withdrawals from individual retirement plans for adoption expenses.

Some families have also received donations from fundraisers held by their church.

A web site with some information is at *http://www.kids4us.org/cost.html* and at *http://adoption.about.com/cs/financesintl/*.

35. At what age are children not allowed to be adopted?

The current US law does not permit children 16 or over from being adopted. There is an exception if you have adopted a younger sibling and the older sibling is between 16 and 18. In 1999, Public Law 106-139 was signed amending the Immigration and Nationality Act to provide that an adopted alien who is less than 18 years of age may be considered a child under such Act if adopted with or after a sibling who is a child under such Act. The details of this exception can be found at *http://www.immigration.gov/graphics/lawsregs/handbook/adoptchi.pdf.*

36. How does the Russian naming system work?

In Russia, the child is given a patronymic name. The term patronymic refers to a naming system that incorporates the name of the father into the name of the child. In Russia, the patronymic is used as a second given name (a middle name, if you will), with the suffix "ich", "vich" or "ovich" (for boys) and "ovna" or "evna" (for girls) being added to the father's given name. So, if your child's patronymic (middle) name is Vladimirovich that means that his birth father's name is Vladimir.

A Russian-born child is given a first name just like children in other cultures. The Russian child is also given a middle name, but unlike their Western cousins whose middle names, if given at all, are similar to a first name or perhaps a family name, Russian babies take on a special version of their father's first name, known as a patronymic, or otchestvo."

Ivan Alexandrovich is translated—Ivan, son of Alexander. If the child is a daughter of Alexander, she will receive a first name (such as Maria) and she will be known as Maria Alexandrevna, or "daughter of Alexander." So, the boys attach "ovich" or "evich" and girls attach "ovna" or "evna" depending on which works better with their father's first name.

As for boys who are named for their fathers, well, there are no "Juniors" in Russia. If a boy child is named for his father Pavel, then his name will be Pavel Pavlovich, or Pavel, son of Pavel. There is also Alexander Alexandrovich, Mikhail Mikhailovich etc.

Russians change the way they call each depending upon the person and the circumstances. If the relationship is a formal one, such as employer/employee, then both names are used upon greeting and in conversation. The use of both first and patronymic together is also used as a mark of respect or affection, whether to older people, people one does not know well, or even little children.

There are also cases where someone may refer to another person *only* by their patronymic. In other words, to her close family and friends, Tatiana Ivanovna may be referred to only as "Ivanovna" or, daughter of Ivan. There are even Russian married couples that will refer to one another in this manner. In the case of good acquaintances, friends, co-workers and family, chances are good that only the first name is used, although that name will most certainly be shortened and altered in various ways. Russians love word play, especially with names and nicknames. Some examples include: Sergei = Seriozha, Maria = Masha, Mashka, Tatiana = Tasha, Tatya, Ivan = Ivanushka and so many, many more. It is a sign of affection.

Another unusual aspect of Russian names concerns the surname, or "familiya." Anyone who has studied a Romance language is familiar with feminine and masculine endings for words. In Russia, a woman who is married to a man with the surname of Chekov, is addressed as Chekova. An unmarried woman also adds an "a" to her father's surname.

Since Soviet times there has been no such title as "Mr." or "Mrs." Prior to the Revolution, men were referred to as Gaspadeen (or Mister) and his wife would be Gaspazha. Since the fall of the Soviet Union, these titles have resurfaced, much like the return of old city and street names.

37. Why is my child's head shaved in the video?

Some Russians believe that shaving children's heads makes their hair grow faster. (This appears to be based more on myth than reality.) It could also have to do with lice control in the children's home or in a minority of cases emotional problems of children, which would cause hair twisting, etc.

38. What is PAD?

PAD is post adoption depression. It is very similar to post pregnancy depression and occurs for the same reasons. It is not uncommon. Probably more than 50% of adoptive mothers get some sort of situational depression. You cry and are depressed and you don't know why because you are so happy. You cry because parenting is so hard and you want things back the way they used to be. Yet you are so in love with your new children you wouldn't change a thing. Eventually everyone gradually adjusts to the changes in the family and in time as the stress disappears, the depression will too. If it becomes too serious, then you may want to get help from a professional.

Physicians and the mental health community expect new birth mothers to go through a transition period after the birth of a child. Many articles about the birth mother experience attribute the depression to hormonal changes. Others relate it to the stress of being a new parent (which probably triggers hormonal changes). Just know that post-adoption stress is real—and it can lead to post-adoption depression. Factors that can effect the depression are your support system and your goal of trying to be "Super-Mom" or the "Perfect Parent." If you have a good support system of family and friends so you can catch a break every now and then and go off by yourself or with your spouse that will help you. Do not feel "guilty" for doing something for you for a change. If you pressure yourself so you feel you must be the perfect mom (just like a bio mom), this can trigger the depression. Also, it can be very difficult at first transitioning from working full time to suddenly being at home full-time and away from daily contact with adults. You have to plan for you to get a required dose of "adult reality" on a regular basis.

Even fathers can feel depression. The baby's nighttime feedings and your loss of independence to come and go as you please all have an impact all your emotional being. This depression is not the same as unhappiness. You can feel overwhelmed with your new child, but that does not mean that you do not love your child or believe that this child is not right for your family. Just accept that it is normal to feel down after the trip to Russia and to permit yourself to have these feelings and to recognize that they are perfectly all right.

39. Why do Russian women have so many abortions?

The Soviet Union first legalized abortion during a widespread famine in 1920.They were banned under Josef Stalin in 1936 in hopes of encouraging births, then legalized again in 1955 after his death. With no access to decent contraceptives, Russian women came to view abortion as a routine procedure comparable almost to a tooth extraction

On average, a Russian woman will have 7 abortions during her lifetime. Some have many more. Russian health care emphasizes medical cures over prevention or education, the mantras of Western health care. The government offers no funds for contraceptives and leaves sex education up to individual schools, most of which offer little or none of it. Citing public opposition, Russian federal officials in 1997 scrapped a U.N-funded project to introduce sex education in Russian schools.

In contrast, state-funded clinics provide free first-trimester abortions upon request and second-trimester abortions up to the 22nd week of pregnancy for medical or social reasons that include lack of a husband, housing or adequate financial support.

It is typical of Russian attitudes about sex that young people are left to discover the options and risks on their own. A common expression among Russian health officials is that Russians have abortions but not sex. As one health official said…"[I]t's just that we were not supposed to talk about it.

Everyone would watch sex on TV with pleasure, but to talk about it would be bad manners."

There is some slight progress. Contraceptives are slowly being introduced. The number of Russian women who have died from abortions has also dropped by one-half in the 1990s, according to a Rand study. However, the "Pill" is still not readily available in Russia despite its synthesis in 1951 by a Bulgarian named Carl Djerassi. Where the Pill is available in Russia, the cost is prohibitive.

More about the "Pill." It was first synthesized in 1951 in Mexico City. 80% of all American women born after 1945 have used the Pill. It is available in more than 78 countries. Japan first allowed it in 1999 and only then because that is when it also approved Viagra. Japan, for cultural reasons, ranks at the bottom in health care for women. Even Russia probably provides better health care. Japan's doctors are predominately men and they make money from providing abortions, not contraceptives.

Carl Djerassi is now a leading organic chemist, art collector, novelist and playwright.

40. Is there a problem if I have a hyphenated name?

The only problem is if your passport is in your maiden name. It is recommended in general, not just in adoption, to change your passport if your name changes. Whatever is your passport name is what you travel under. You really do not want to have inconsistent documents. Simplify your life and your adoption. You can find information on passports at *http://travel.state.gov/passport_services.html* and for expedited service at *http://travel.state.gov/passport_expedite.html*.

41. How many ethnic groups are there in Russia?

There are hundreds. Here are some sites with lots of information. *http://src-h.slav.hokudai.ac.jp/eng/Russia/minority-e.html*, Red Book of Peoples of Soviet Empire at *http://julia.eki.ee/books/redbook/introduction.shtml* and Peoples of Siberia at *http://www.nmnh.si.edu/arctic/features/croads/siberia.html*

42. Should I take my US child along on the adoption trip?

The answer varies by family. Is there a reliable caregiver at home? Sometimes grandparents are not physically up to the task of taking care of children for a whole month. Does your US child travel well or does he have problems with food, different situations, timetables etc.? Would it make bonding as a family easier? Will there be a lot of waiting and downtime or will you always be on the go? Will there be room in the car or train or will you have to pay for two drivers or two train compartments? Some schools consider trips to different countries great educational experiences and are willing to work out some kind of arrangement about their schoolwork. It is a once-in-a-lifetime opportunity for them to see other cultures at a young age. It will stay with them forever. You can always ask your agency to get a van, rather than a car. Remember though that this trip is 99% business and sleep doesn't always come when expected and there is lots of running around. Also, your attention and focus should be on your new child.

43. What sort of schooling would my child have had?

Prior to 1989 school started at 7 years of age and continued for 10 years (finishing at 17-18 years). There was an option to finish at 8th grade and study in vocational school for 2-4 years (depending on trade). In 1989 this system was changed and a grade was added so that 1st Grade began at age 6 bringing total number of school years to 11 (or 9 with vocational school option). They still finish school at 17-18 years. This is generally how it is done in the urban Russian Federation schools. There is no clear distinction between elementary middle and high school so it is not unusual for a child to attend the same school and even be in the same class from grade 1 through 11. Now, as with everything in Russia, it is not a uniform system and some children might still begin 1st Grade at age 7.

Also, if the child has been labeled with a low mental ability classification, her education will be limited. The Russians have long embraced the "Brave New World" concept of classifying children as Alphas, Betas etc., although they use different terminology, and then slotting them in defined educational and work categories for life. For example, a child might be given a debil diagnosis, which roughly translates as mild mental retardation. In Russia, the children are evaluated at specific times and if they are thought to be impaired, they are separated from the "regular" children and sent to a "specialized" internat. Here, education ends at a fourth grade level and then the children are sent to vocational school for two years. After that they can do menial jobs but can never hold a drivers license. The children actually go to school for 9 years, but since they have a much slower program than in a regular school, they get an equivalent of a 4-year (or elementary school) education. They do not mainstream children with learning disabilities or mental retardation. They separate and isolate them.

These labels are placed on a child after minimal testing according to western standards and after a very quick review. Further, the child is likely to never be tested again! The sad fact is that it was very possible that a child did not test as well as her peers simply because of severe neglect and because she was never placed in school until she went to the orphanage. It may have nothing to do with her ability or potential.

44. Are international adoptive children at a higher risk for ADD?

I do not believe that there has been any statistical study on that. However, once you have given a child enough time to learn English so language acquisition is not the source of any frustration, had his eyes and ears checked, reviewed any allergies in his diet, then you may need to look into that subject. The same as you would with any child. Remember that food allergies to Casein and Gluten can play a role.

One theory about domestic adoptions is that if you assume the children come from young mothers who were involved in risky behavior and perhaps lacked appreciation of cause-and-effect, then you would expect a higher incidence of such behavior in these children. There has been no study to validate that theory.

45. How do I change to Cyrillic fonts on my computer?

Starting from Win98, all versions of Windows come with Cyrillic support. For WinXP go to Control Panel-Regional & Language Options. Click on tab Languages, then Details. Click add, then scroll down and choose Russian, click OK. After that all you need to do is configure the keyboard to switch from English to Russian and that's it. You'll also need Russian keyboard stickers that normally can be bought in big computer superstores

For earlier operating systems you might:
Click your start button and go to settings

click on control panel
click on keyboard
click the language tab
click on "Add" and on the drop down menu choose Russian
Click on OK

Once this is done you will have a small icon on the bottom of your screen with En. Open up MS Word and pick Russian or English with this small icon and when you type it will be whatever you selected. You can also switch back and forth on the same page if you might want to type something in English and then type the Russian translation.

46. Can I breastfeed my adoptive child?

If you're a guy, this could be difficult. Otherwise, the best overall source of information about adoptive breastfeeding is the book *Breastfeeding the Adopted Baby* by Debra Stewart Peterson. The La Leche League sells this book in its catalogue, but it is also available through other sources. This book is fairly short (140 pages), but it is packed with information. You probably should contact your local La Leche League for additional information and check out their web site. There was also an article on the subject in Mothering Magazine a few years back. You need not have ever been pregnant in order to breastfeed.

47. Is there an adoptive single parent organization?

According to the Census Bureau, 82 million people over the age of 18 are single. Thus, it comes as no surprise that a sizeable number of adoptive parents are single as well. There are several organizations for adopting singles. There is The Association of Single Adoptive Parents (ASAP) based in the metro DC area. It can be contacted by phone at 703-521-0632 and its email address is *ASAP-metroDC@yahoogroups.com*. There is also SPACE (Single Parents for Adoption of Children Everywhere and its web site is *http://www.geocities.com/odsspace.*

Robert Klose's book, *Adopting Aylosha,* on adopting as a single man from Russia is a great read. He has also adopted again. Both Ukraine and Russia allow single men to adopt, although certain regions may have restrictions.The key in Ukraine is to have a great facilitator.

People seem to find it fascinating that a single man (versus a woman) would give up freedom and independence to adopt. What they don't realize is that single men know that if all they can say at the end of their life is that they got a lot of sleep, saw some good movies, played golf and went on vacation when they wanted too, then they've missed a big wonderful part of life—having a family.

Single people adopt for the very reasons that couples do. They want to be parents. They want to make a difference in the world that doesn't have to do with careers or financial portfolios. They want to know that somehow they have contributed to the bigger picture of life in some significant way. When you look at it like that, it isn't so strange. Singles are out there just looking to live their life. Like everyone else.

See these *stories http://catalog.com/fwcfc/HuaJunGetsDaddy.html,* and *http://www.csmonitor.com/2001/1031/p22s1-hfes.html,*

A great resource for adoptive singles is at *http://www.calib.com/naic/parents/single.cfm.*

48. Why don't more Russians adopt these children?

Russian nationals still adopt more Russian children than foreigners. But as a growing number of people find they cannot afford to raise a child, the number of domestic adoptions has been declining, from 13,942 in 1992 to 8,799 in 1996. Moreover, an estimated two-thirds of the children available for adoption are labeled with some sort of medical diagnosis at birth, which gives them a stigma and renders them unadoptable according to Russian culture. In a sense, Russian society is still frozen in time in the 1930's where Stalin traumatized it. It is has been difficult for Russian men to accept that they can parent someone else's child.

49. What is the general medical health of the Russian population?

It could be a lot better. In 1999, outside of Africa, only Haiti reported higher male mortality rates than Russia. The life expectancy of Russian men is 59 years, shorter than that of men in three-fourths of the world's countries and shorter also than Russians lived in 1965. The leading cause of death for Russian and American men is the same: circulatory, heart or cerebrovascular disease. But the risk of death is far greater for Russian men, largely because of their lifestyles: three times higher for heart or circulatory failure, and seven times higher for cerebrovascular disease.

Almost two-thirds of Russian men smoke, compared to one-fourth of U.S. men. The typical Russian man drinks a pint of pure alcohol every two days, compared to less than two pints a month for the average American man or woman. Only 6 percent of Russians exercise regularly. Next to heart disease, violence and accidents claim the most Russian men. More of them die every year of accidents, poisonings, drownings, homicides and suicides than die of cancer. About 40,000 Russians die every year of alcohol poisoning contrasting with just 300 in the United States, with nearly twice Russia's population. About 17,000 Russians drown annually, most of them drunken men, a rate nine times higher than in the United States, where most drowning victims are children.

Surprisingly, the principal reason Russian men die so young is not poor medical care, although many of Russia's hospitals are antiquated and spending on health care is just a fraction of that in the US. More significant is the dreadful lifestyle of Russian men and the failure of doctors and the government to stress preventive health care. Of course, solving the problem is not easy. Gorbachev tried to reign in the alcohol abuse by greatly increasing taxation on vodka. All this did, as our own history can testify, is to increase homebrew and smuggling and in the end failed because of the political backlash. There is little taxation on cigarettes and a Western brand pack can be had for as little as 50 cents in Moscow. A half-liter of vodka goes for a $1 and beer is seen as a breakfast drink.

Of the more than 2 million Russians who die every year, 600,000 are of working age, according to the Health Ministry. The death rate surpasses the birth rate by 70 percent. It is predicted that Russia's population will drop from 144.5 million to 104 million in the next 50 years. That would make Russia the world's 17th-most populous nation, instead of the sixth. But the real drain on population is a steep decline in the birth rate, one of the lowest in the world. About 5 million—or 13 percent—of Russian married couples are infertile, and doctors report that diagnoses of infertility are on the rise. In nearly three out of four cases, infertility is attributed to the woman, typically because of complications from one or more abortions. Abortion-related infertility is one piece of a much bigger health care crisis that has yet to command much of the Kremlin's attention. Russia's health care system is in a state of collapse, and with it, the public's health, by almost any measure, whether heart disease or HIV

The abortion rate has been declining rapidly for 15 years because of the availability of contraceptives. Still, it remains five times higher than that of the United States. The Health Ministry reports that for every live birth there are

1.7 abortions, compared with more than three births for every abortion in the United States. A study of mid-1990s data by a group of health researchers showed Russia's abortion rate was the fourth highest of 57 countries, after only Vietnam, Cuba and Romania.

Russia spends 2 to 3 percent of its gross domestic product on health care, compared to 7 to 9 percent in Europe as a whole. The public health system is ancient, inefficient and increasingly financed by under-the-table payments. The World Health Organization recently ranked it 130th in the world. A good book on the subject is called <u>Russia's Torn Safety Nets: Health and Social Welfare During the Transition</u>, by Mark Field and Judyth Twigg. St Martin's Press published it in 2000.

50. What is the difference between an "expedite" fee and a bribe?

Only a lawyer would love this discussion. Remember that you will not always face this dilemma. Corruption is not present on every level and in every place. The less you need something from an official gatekeeper, the less opportunity there is for the pinch. No Westerner can truly appreciate the Russian (or FSU) cultural basis for doing things po-chelovechesky (like a human being). You have to be Russian and have lived under a system where laws were written to create obstacles and protect the elite.

The difference between paying an "expedite" fee and a "bribe" is in the amount and your tolerance level. For some people, the issue is very black and white. If it is not listed on a government fee list, then it must be a bribe. Other people see the word "bribe" as being an arrogant western moral judgment on another country's economic system. If a Ukrainian official mentioned to your facilitator that for $50, your sick child's passport could be issued within one day versus 30 days, the answer as to what to do is obvious. If a children home's director said she was short of children's shoes and food, is there really a question? If a Judge mentions that she could get your order out quicker if she just had some computer paper, where does this request fall? How about paying $1000 to a Department of Education person? My suggestion is to view the problem as being one created by both sides and to view requests that relate directly to the health and welfare of your child as being within your parental role of protecting your child. For all others, let your facilitator guide you as to the norm within the country and reject those requests that are outside those parameters.

Remember also that in Eastern Europe there hasn't ever been any other way to get things done other than the system of service/payment/gift. We are not used to it, but they are. It is their culture, not ours. Just as one example, they don't have a system of paying UPS or FedEx to move documents across their country. That system, thanks to Communism, never got created. Instead, they have an alternate, but entirely workable system of payment or favors to a pilot to carry the documents on a regular passenger flight. Both countries have the same idea that one pays more for expedited service. The only difference is that in the US those fees are written down, but in the FSU they are not. It is not illegal in those countries to pay such fees. It is only when the amount is rather large that you get into a gray area where your conscience and your facilitator should be your guide.

51. What is the Intercountry Adoption Act of 2000?

In 2000, Public Law 106-279 was signed providing for implementation by the United States of the Hague Convention on Protection of Children and Cooperation in Respect of Intercountry Adoption. The Hague Convention will impose intercountry adoptions rules on countries that have ratified and implemented the Hague Convention. The Hague Convention has been ratified by Albania (2000), Bulgaria (2002), Czech Republic (2000), Estonia (2002), Georgia (1999), Latvia (2002), Lithuania (1998), Moldova (1998), Poland (1995), Romania (1994), Slovakia (2001) and Slovenia (2002). Belarus and Russia have signed, but not ratified. Kazakhstan has not signed.At this time the Convention has not significantly impacted the Eastern European process.However, that will change when the regulations are implemented in the United States some time in late 2004.

When they are implemented four things may happen:

1)   A few agencies will go through the expensive process of being accredited by the State Department (this accreditation will have no impact on the actual quality of adopting).The cost to adopt will rise as only the largest agencies will be able to fund the accreditation process. Smaller agencies will simply quit working in countries that adopt The Hague or joint venture with an agency that does.Parents will also be charged between $100-$200 in fees to pay for the extra State Department employees.

2)   Parents will pursue more independent adoptions as these are not covered by the Hague,

3)   The children will wait longer to be adopted and parents will wait longer as they have to file more paperwork with the United States Government under the regulations.

4)   There will still be no protection for parents in receiving adequate medical information. This is the worst problem in foreign adoptions and it is ignored. It would be nice if there were a standard medical form for the kids. Foreign countries won't do anything they don't have to do. They will continue to get by with sloppy and inaccurate reporting of medical information, while requiring ridiculous amounts of paperwork by the adopting families.

The reason that accreditation will not solve the problems is that many international agencies (which do not have to be licensed in most states) are licensed to place domestic adoptions. In other words, some of the same agencies that have had problems with international adoptions have already gone through a licensing process and we still have problems.

The State Department's proposed regulations have many inconsistencies. They acknowledge that parents adopting independently are exempt from the IAA, yet at the same time say they must comply with it. While most of the Hague requirements are simply delegated to agencies, you are not allowed to adopt a child until the State Department gives you a Certificate. This is like the Russian Databank Release letter. How long parents will have to wait to receive this Certificate, and what paperwork you must file is unknown. There is no provision addressing the likelihood that your 15 month FBI fingerprint check and 18 month I-171H timeline will expire while you wait for your Certificate. The State Department's solution to complaints by parents is for parents to send their complaint to a "Convention Complaint Registry." There is no description of this Registry or what it is supposed to do.

Support for the Hague Convention as a cure for the problems of foreign adoption has diminished. However, it is all we have.

The goal of the Intercountry Adoption Act of 2000 (IAA) and of the regulations and procedures promulgated there under is two-fold: first, to provide some accountability in an industry that has had none and two, *to do no harm* to Americans who are seeking to create a family. The State Department does not recognize that there is tension between these two goals. Indeed, it is my opinion that the time delay caused by the additional paperwork required by The Hague Convention, particularly Articles 16 and 17, will result in

Americans greatly reducing adoptions from those countries who are full parties to the Convention.

The State Department needs to recognize that the goal of the IAA was not to slavishly follow the 1993 Hague Convention, but rather to remedy three (3) problems, to-wit:

(1) Give parent(s) better education and preparation.

(2) Give parents a more complete medical and social history on a child

(3) Give parents a forum to voice complaints

The proposed regulations do not appear to address these issues. A good summary of the problems that will be caused by these regulations can be found at *http://www.chinaseasadopt.org/statement.html*. The State Department should try to streamline the adoption process and make it more efficient. If the procedures promulgated under the IAA do not actually solve these three issues, but simply add to the adopting parents' bureaucratic burden, then nothing has been accomplished. My reservations can best be described by quoting Senator Brownback when he said "…: [w]*hile the treaty will provide significant benefits, I had serious concerns that the proposed method of implementation would have caused more harm than good.*"

One suggestion that was made at the public forum on the regulations was that the State Department should get involved diplomatically in resolving the problems of inadequate medical information. It was suggested that the State Department meet with the Russian Ministry of Education and some of the regional departments and persuade them that it is in the best interest of all parties that parents be given all the medical and social information on a child that is extant. For older children in particular, the documents supporting the termination of the parental rights should be made available at the earliest opportunity. The State Department ignored this suggestion.

More on the Hague project can be found here:

http://hagueregs.org./images/AccreditationProcedures-Dec0501.pdf

52. How can the BCIS process be improved?

Currently the BCIS and State Department share responsibility over foreign adoptions. Everyone agrees that it should fall under one authority.

BCIS offices are currently inconsistent as how they process I-600A Orphan Petitions. It makes little sense to have each field office handle these petitions.

Instead:

a)   Either one or no more than 3 offices should handle all of the petitions in the country. There is no geographic reason for numerous locations when FedEx, UPS and the US Mail can get to the same place, regardless of location, within a day or two. It's not like a parent needs or wants to visit the local field office. There is no interview requirement.

b)   This office should issue a tracking number and parents should be able to check the status on a web site like a UPS, FedEx or US mail package.

c)   There should be an ombudsman in the office that actually answers the phone, is trained and knowledgeable, can answer questions and can find out status etc.

d)   Because of country delays, the I-171H and FBI fingerprint checks should be valid for 24 months, not 18 or 15 months. Parents are running out of time and having to redo all their I-600A paperwork simply because of sending country delays. The US government should help, not hinder, its citizens in building a family.

e)   Parents should have the option of letting the FBI keep their fingerprints on file for up to 5 years. BCIS fingerprinting causes the biggest delay on the petitions. Many parents adopt another child within a year or two after the first. Why should they have to redo their prints when they can just authorize the BCIS to run the check on the prints already on file? The fingerprint and re-fingerprint procedure is utterly absurd.

f)   The BCIS should automatically send an IR3 visa child a Certificate of Citizenship and not a pointless Green Card. This would save the BCIS and the parents a lot of time and money.

g)   The BCIS should view adoptive parents with a rebuttal presumption that they will be approved. Too many BCIS offices treat adopting US citizens as the enemy. This should stop.

h)   Many parents adopt several times. The BCIS should keep their records on file so parents do not have repeatedly submit the same supporting documents time after time. Having a previous approved I-171H, should mean that you only have to submit documents created after the first I-600A was submitted i.e. a new divorce or marriage. This will allow the I-600A to be electronically filed.

i)   The BCIS should only consider felonies and misdemeanors that occurred in the last 10 years unless related to child or spousal abuse.

The BCIS seems preoccupied with misdemeanors that occurred 20 years before when the parent was a teenager or college kid.

j)   BCIS should work with states to standardize their procedures relating to international adoption. For example, in North Carolina a parent can use an old I-171H by filing an amended home study, but in Georgia, a parent can-not use their old I-171H until they submit a brand new home study by which time the old I-171H has expired. Since the I-171H is the BCIS' approval, the BCIS should be the one to make the rules regarding how it can be used or extended.

53. Can I travel overseas with my adopted child?

If you are planning to travel to a European country with a child who only has a Russian passport and US green card, then you will likely need to obtain a visa for your child. Most western European countries do not require this of Americans, but they do of Russians, and until your child becomes a US citizen, she is completely Russian. Visas can be obtained in advance from Embassies or consulates. It can be expensive and time consuming if you are planning to visit several countries. If your child is a US citizen, then she can travel on her US passport and does not need a visa. If you plan to visit Russia, note that you may have to register your child with the Russian Embassy. Sometimes the Russians refuse to give visas to adoptive children who want to travel on the US passport. The Russians idea is that the children are still their citizens and should travel on a Russian passport to Russia.

54. My pediatrician thinks my child is younger than her age?

Be careful about labeling your child a different age. A Russian child first starts school in the September after her 7th birthday. So if she has started school, then that is a way of checking her age. Malnutrition and deprivation (as well as chronic illnesses) can delay growth and make determination of the age (bone age, dental assessment and so on) very inconclusive. As far as school goes, this should be a matter of developmental age coupled with other factors, not just birth age.

Giving HGH shots should be carefully considered and only after a full series of endocrine tests. These shots are three times a week, very expensive, and come with their own psychological issues.

55. How can I translate something into Russian?

There are many services in the United States that will do so. If you live near a university, it will have a language department with this service. Also, with the large numbers of Russian and FSU immigrants, there are Russian speakers everywhere. If you just want to send a letter, then you might check out the translation services of Victor Sluczewski in Bryansk, Russia. You can email him at *victor@wrestling.bitmcnit.bryansk.su.*

The New England Language Center at 603-332-2255 also offers translation services. They will also act as an interpreter to help you with your international conference call to the orphanage doctor. Hudson-Neva Translation Service is in the U.S at *http://www.hudson-neva.com/translation/index.html.* These last two have experience with translating adoption documents for the Russian courts. Another one University Language Services, Inc. 15 Maiden Lane, Suite 300, New York NY 10038 Call them at (212) 766-4111.They will translate, certify the translation and notarize if asked. You can also obtain translations of Russian medical records and general translations from Kevin Matthews at 801-982-0896, email: *kevin.matthews@juno.com.*

One way to read Russian web pages is to:

1) Open up http://babelfish.altavista.com (or http://translate.ru)

2) Copy and paste the link into the appropriate place on the on-line translator (in babelfish it's in the middle of the page, in translate.ru you have to go one page forward—look for the "translate the www" on the left hand side of the page.

3) Hit enter.

4) You can get really bad English, or sometimes very good English.

5) It helps to open up two windows on your computer so you can go back and forth. Open one window and then "minimize it." Then open another window for babelfish...then you just go back and forth.

56. Is there a Russian Barbie?

There have been two Russian Barbies. One is the 1996 version and the other one is older (1980's?). There is an entire series of international Barbies and the Moroccan ones look the closest to Bashkir children. (Dark brown hair, dark almond eyes)

57. Does the adoption give the birthfamily immigration rights?

No. The restriction on birth parents is found at 101(b)(1)(F) of the INA. It reads: "That no natural parent or prior adoptive parent of any such child shall thereafter, by virtue of such parentage, be accorded any right, privilege, or status under this Act." There is a 1997 9th Circuit case that also limits bio sibling immigration rights. Plaintiff was an adopted child trying to get her natural siblings into the country. She tried to get them visas. BCIS opposed the effort and 9th Circuit supported the BCIS. The case is <u>Young v. Reno</u> and can be found at *http://caselaw.lp.findlaw.com/scripts/getcase.pl?navby=search&case= /data2/circs/9th/9616663.html*

58. What is the risk of adopting from Chernobyl?

The Chernobyl disaster occurred in 1986 in northern Ukraine. The greatest radiation exposure was in that area and in southern Belarus. Very short-lived iodine isotopes that disappeared within months of the Chernobyl accident did cause an increase in thyroid cancer risk in children living near Chernobyl. However, studies have shown that there is no known medical reason for a child born after 1986 to be at increased risk for thyroid cancer because of the Chernobyl accident.

The estimated risk is greatest for children born between 1983-86. According to reports at an international conference in 1996, children in the heavily contaminated Gomel, Belarus region have something less than a 1% chance of developing thyroid cancer over 70 years. Most of the so-called contaminated regions have a rate much smaller than this. For children born after 1986, the risk of thyroid cancer is nearly the same as for children born in the West.

59. Can I adopt from Poland?

Poland allows foreign adoptions. Since the birth rate in Poland is not very high, fewer newborns are available. In Poland, foreign adoptions represent 10-15 percent of all adoptions. Every year only 50 percent of children awaiting adoption are placed in Polish and foreign families. Domestic adoptions take priority over foreign adoptions. Priority goes to Polish residents or to people of Polish ancestry. Their regulations provide that the mother cannot be more than 40 years older than the child. Most Polish couples are interested in adopting babies. Older children, even if completely healthy, are less likely to find a new family, thus a foreign family has a better chance at adopting if they want an older child. In Poland the National Adoption Center (KOA) has all the information on the child. Prospective adoptive parents receive full information about the health of the child and as much information as the KOA can collect on the genetic family.

Adoptions can probably be arranged at a much lower cost than the typical U.S. adoption agency rate if you use a Polish attorney to handle all the paperwork. There is a good web site called "FAQ about Adopting in Poland" that can be found at *http://www.polish.org/en/frames/faq_main.html* and at http://www.polish.org/ which gives a lot of detailed information on what is needed for adopting in Poland as well as a list of agencies helping expedite Polish adoptions. The US Embassy also has a good review at *http://www.usinfo.pl/consular/iv/adoptions.htm#Locate%20a%20Child%20in%20Poland*

Other web sites with information can be found at:
http://www.caritasforchildren.org/index.html
http://www.catholiccharities.net/workingadoption.htm
http://groups.yahoo.com/group/adopters
http://www.npimall.com/angels/
http://www.polish.org/en/no_frames/adoption.html

60. What is Failure to Thrive (FTT)?

This is a nonsense label that American doctors sometimes give to a child. It is not a diagnosis. All it means is that your child is significantly below the average in height or weight. The real diagnosis could be a parasite problem, a GI problem, thyroid or human growth hormone problem, prematurity, or genetics i.e. the biological parents were on the small side. It could even be that the child was so long in the institution that the psychosocial dwarfism condition that is usually cured through catch-up growth cannot be completely overcome. Since the FTT label doesn't actually help parents or doctors analyze the issue, it is as much a useless word as the Russians' "perinatal encephalopathy."

61. Are there special military programs for military couples?

The military will reimburse active-duty personnel for most one-time adoption costs up to $2,000 per child. Travel costs, foreign or domestic, are not covered. There is a maximum of $5,000 in a given year, even if both parents are in the military. Reimbursement is made only after the adoption is finalized and only if the adoption was completed through a state adoption agency or a non-profit private agency. Fees that can be reimbursed include adoption fees; placement fees, legal fees and court costs; and medical expenses. The DoD Instruction reference number is DODI-1341.9, dated 29 July 93 and can be found at
http://www.dtic.mil/whs/directives/corres/pdf/i13419wch1_072993/i13419p.pdf.
The reimbursement form is DD 2675. Go to
http://web1.whs.osd.mil/icdhome/DD2500-.htm and scroll down looking for "DD2675". An excellent article on the obstacles military couples face is at
http://www.adopting.org/military.html

Other articles are at:
http://www.calib.com/naic/pubs/militarybulletin.cfm
http://www.calib.com/naic/pubs/f_milita.cfm.
http://www.anewarrival.com/military.html

If you are in the military, then you should downplay the military connection in your home study. Say the spouse is a "government employee" and absolutely NO PICTURES IN UNIFORM. You do not lie to the Judge if asked, but in the home study the social worker should not emphasize it. Some parents have even traveled under civilian passports, not military ones and left their military identification at home.

62. Is there a problem bringing donated medicines into Russia?

If it is just over the counter items like vitamins and Tylenol, then usually there is not any issue at customs. However, if you are bringing in prescription medicines then you might want to do the following:

1. Pack medications separately from your luggage and mark it clearly "humanitarian aid". Pack it in such way, that you will be able to open and close it easily—or at least have additional packing tape to secure your package after customs.

2. Have a disclaimer ready (preferably in Russian) with the names of medications, expiration dates and were those medications are going (detski dom, dom rebenka, etc.) It has to be stated that all medications were given to you as a donation—that can help you to avoid customs fees. If you can have an actual letter (fax is enough) from your orphanage with the request for those medications—it will help a lot.

3. Be calm, cool and collected during customs control. If they want to detain the medicines or charge customs fees, try to convince them that this is a very small shipment, not intended for sale and that you did not pay anything for those medications.

63. Can I go for a jog in Russia?

You will not see many Russian runners. It has not caught on yet. However, you can still run if you take some precautions. In Moscow, try to run early in the morning. Otherwise, the traffic, lights and congestion make it no fun. Use your street smarts, be careful, don't get lost, dress in muted colors, stay away from drunk Russians and you should be fine. Always carry copies of your passport and visa, enough money for cab fare and a note written in Russian that could be given to a cab driver to take you back to where you are staying and the number to the US Consulate or Embassy. The streets often have many of the same landmarks and it is very easy to get disoriented. There are no street signs, for one thing. Addresses and street names are written on buildings. Many buildings are alike and identical buildings can appear in clusters or strips all over the place. In Moscow one of the best places to run is along the Moscow River. Another good choice is around a park. The idea is to find a route with little cross traffic.

If staying in Moscow, Yekaterinburg or Vladivostok, call the Regional Security Officer (RSO) at the US Consulate or Embassy and get his opinion as to a safe place to run. Monitoring the safety and security for Americans is his job.

If you are staying at one of the nice hotels in Moscow that has a gym, the better policy is to work out there rather than take any chances. Some just run up and down the stairs in the hotel.

64. If I adopt a toddler, will he be potty trained?

Not likely. Remember that potty time in a children's home is a group thing at a specific time. They are on a schedule and after they eat are held over the pot until they go. When they are a little older they are all in the potty room sitting on their pots, which in some homes are these orange plastic pots, which they use like race cars scooting along while sitting on them! If they don't sit on the pots, they are strapped in.

Do not expect the infants to have diapers. Only the babies have cloth diapers, everyone else has a plastic pot within reach. They are made to stay on them a looooong time until by luck something happens. This isn't potty training, it's lottery time!

One thing that you may want to inquire about, if the kids seem unusually "potty-trained" (especially with regard to night dryness), is how much the kids get to drink during a day. In some homes, they intentionally withhold fluids to control the need to urinate. As soon as your child gets to your home, he will immediately lost his ability to sleep through the night dry. In other homes they are awakened three times during the night just to go potty.

Some children are even afraid of bathrooms for the first couple of weeks you have them home. They may be frightened about sitting so high off the ground, as they are used to these little bucket type things. If you are adopting a toddler, bring some diapers just in case. In a larger town you should be able to buy them. Do not bring Pull-Ups. Look at it this way, if he really is potty trained what a pleasant surprise. Just don't count on it. With all of the confusion, difference in foods he will be receiving on the trip home, and being pulled out of the only environment he's ever known and being dragged from one place to another (airports, embassy, hotels, etc.), there are bound to be a lot of accidents.

65. Will my infant have to relearn the sucking instinct?

Most likely. Sucking is very important for the development of facial muscles used for speech. Speech therapists recommended heavy sucking. You can obtain medium flow nipples and make your child really work for those calories. Frozen popsicles and a candy called "war heads" are also a good tool for older toddlers. There will be a tremendous difference in your child's face and speech after she starts pursing those lips and begins sucking again. Her earlobes might even begin to grow!

The reason children in these homes lose that instinct is that the bottles are often propped up on the pillow and because things are so old and worn out, the holes in the nipples are big and the formula or milk just runs down their throats…assuming the bottle didn't slip off the pillow. Going back to a bottle, even for a toddler, can be a great tool to facilitate bonding and attachment and when she asks "baby time" remember that she missed her baby years and so did you and it really is fine to give you both a cuddle and a bottle.

66. Is there racial prejudice in Russia?

Absolutely. Even in some children's homes you will find some caregivers do not like dark skinned children who might be Rom or even Uzbek. If a child has a Tatar name, then she might be teased by the other children and told she is not a real Russian. It is the same the world over, if you are not one of us, then you are one of them. There have been reports of Moscow skinheads attacking black Marines. Fortunately, this sort of stuff does not happen often. But you can not have the sort of pogrom history Russia has without there still being an undercurrent of us versus them.

67. What happens if my child fails her visa medical exam?

This is very rare and usually involves TB. The law is that any person applying for a permanent residency visa must undergo a physical examination by a medical officer approved by the US. The absurdity is that for IR3 children, they are citizens immediately upon entering the United States and the law does not apply to them. Yet because there is a brief period between when they leave the foreign country and land on US soil and are residing at 35,000 feet you must go through this bureaucratic hoop.

The examination must look for these excludable conditions: Sexually transmitted diseases including chancroid, gonorrhea, granuloma inguinale, lymphogranuloma venereum and syphilis. Also, active leprosy. HIV infection, active tuberculosis, mental retardation, insanity, narcotic or alcohol addiction or sexual deviation. Serious or permanent physical defects, diseases or disabilities. In addition, persons 15 years and over must have blood tests for syphilis and HIV infection and a chest x-ray looking for signs of tuberculosis. Children under 15 are not required to have these tests unless the examining physician feels the history or physical examination indicates a possibility of exposure. Notice that many contagious diseases such as hepatitis B, chicken pox, measles, intestinal parasites and malaria are not on this list. They are missing because: the conditions are already very common in the US, they are not spread by casual physical contact or the conditions needed to spread the diseases are not found or are rare in the US.

You might think based on this list that special needs children cannot immigrate. The real answer is that it is not strictly applied and except for children with active TB, there usually are not any problems.

Most children just have a brief physical examination including a medical history (if there is any information). If the child does not have any obvious abnormalities and there is no reason to particularly suspect one of the listed infectious diseases, no other tests or examinations are required. The officer will fill out the medical form that is then sealed into an envelope to be delivered to the US Consulate. There, after all other documents have been approved, the medical examination is reviewed and the visa usually granted. The actual medical report goes into a sealed packet that is left with the Immigration Officer at the point of entry into the US.

If the examining officer were to issue an unfavorable report because he found a condition on the excludable list, you have the right to appeal. If the child has active tuberculosis or another untreated infectious disease, the condition can be reclassified after the child has begun treatment. If the condition is a mental or physical disability, the orphan visa officer may interview the parents, if they are present, to assure himself that they realize the extent of the condition and that they are capable of caring for the child. However, for most severe disabling conditions and for HIV infection, the parents will have to undertake a "waiver process." To obtain a waiver, the embassy or consulate forwards the visa medical report and any supporting evaluations or tests to the Centers for Disease Control (CDC) in Atlanta. There, the Office of Quarantine contacts the family who must then provide:

• an affidavit explaining that they understand the extent and severity of the condition and giving a compelling reason to allow the child to enter the US. (Adoption is considered compelling for most children!)

• proof that they have adequate financial resources to care for the child. This may include proof of health insurance and sometimes even an advance approval from the insurance company guaranteeing that the child's condition will be covered.

- an affidavit from a physician stating that he will provide care to the child after arrival in the US.

This information is forwarded to the CDC where a panel of physicians reviews the material and makes a determination that the child will not likely not be a threat to the health of others or become a public charge. This determination is then sent back to the embassy or consulate. The material is again reviewed and, if all appears appropriate, an orphan visa granted. The waiver process typically takes 3 to 6 months to complete; however, it can be accomplished in as short a time as a week if the medical condition is life threatening or there is some other compelling reason to move quickly. Most waivers applied for by adoptive parents are approved, probably because the parents have already had plenty of opportunity to review the child's condition and their own financial resources.

RUSSIAN READING LIST

For travel information see the Lonely Planet guides as well as their phrase-book. They cover a lot of cities in Russia. Eyewitness and Fodor's also offer decent guides to Moscow and St. Petersburg.

If you want to know more about the Russian Mafia than you ever cared about, read <u>Comrade Criminal: Russia's New Mafiya</u> by Stephen Handelman.

For the Gorbachev era there are several from which to choose. You can try David Remnick's <u>Lenin's Tomb</u> or his <u>Resurrection; The Struggle to Build a New Russia</u>, or Dobbs' <u>Down With Big Brother: The Fall of the Soviet Empire</u> or Hedrick Smith's <u>The New Russians.</u>

Books on the Yeltsin era include, <u>The Oligarchs: Wealth & Power in the New Russia</u>—by David E. Hoffman

For books on current life there are many such as <u>Waking the Tempests: Ordinary Life in the New Russia</u> by Eleanor Randolph<u>, Moscow Days: Life and Hard Times in the New Russia</u> by Galina Dutkina, or for a funny one <u>read Moscow Madness: Crime, Corruption, and One Man's Pursuit of Profit in the New Russia</u> by Timothy Harper.

For more on the economic disaster that was Yeltsin's tenure, see <u>The Tragedy of Russia's Reforms: Market Bolshevism Against Democracy, by Peter Reddaway and Dmitri Glinski</u>, 769 pages. United States Institute of Peace.

See also <u>Please to the Table: The Russian Cookbook</u> by Anya Von Bremzen and <u>First Thousand Words in Russian</u> by Heather Amery & Katrina Kirilenko.

If you want to read the daily Russian news, you could try "Russia Today" at *http://www.russiatoday.com/* or "Moscow Times" at *http://www.moscowtimes.ru/*

If you want to read about your particular Region or city, all of the Regions and most of the major cities have websites.

ADOPTION READING LIST

For Russian adoption stories see <u>Adopting Alyosha: A Single Man Finds a Son in Russia</u> by Robert Klose and <u>The Russian Word for Snow: An Adoption Story</u> by Janis Cooke Newman. Do realize that these books describe just one person's trip and it is unlikely that your story will be like these except in the most general way.

Two recent Russian adoption books are <u>Adopting a Toddler: What Size Shoes Does She Wear?</u> by Denise H. Hoppenhauer and <u>Adopting In Russia: Your Rights and the Law</u> by Irina M O'Rear.

For general adoption issues read <u>Twenty Things Adopted Kids Wish Their Adopted Parents Knew</u> by Sherrie Eldridge. This is a good laymen's outline of adoption issues. Others include <u>Being Adopted: The Lifelong Search for Self</u> by David Brodzinsky; <u>Talking With Young Children About Adoption</u> by Susan Fisher and Mary Watkins; and <u>Journey of the Adopted Self: A Quest for Wholeness</u> by Betty Jean Lifton.

For attachment issues, read Caroline Archer's books, <u>First Steps in Parenting the Child Who Hurts: Tiddlers and Toddlers</u> and <u>Next Steps in Parenting the Child Who Hurts: Tykes and Teens, Toddler Adoption: The Weaver's Craft</u> by Mary Hopkins-Best, <u>Facilitating Developmental Attachment: The Road to Emotional Recovery and Behavioral Change in Foster and Adopted Children</u> by Daniel Hughes; <u>Holding Time: How to Eliminate Conflict, Temper Tantrums, and Sibling Rivalry and Raise Happy, Loving, and Successful Children</u> by Dr. Martha Welch; <u>Give them Roots, Then Let them Fly: Understanding Attachment Therapy</u> by The Attachment Center at Evergreen. Their web site is at *http://www.attachmentcenter.org.* <u>The</u>

<u>Handbook of Attachment Interventions</u>, published 1999 by Academic Press. <u>Attaching in Adoption</u> by Deborah D. Gray was published in 2002 and has had good reviews.

For sensory issues, good books are <u>The Out of Sync Child</u> and <u>Teaching Children to Love</u>. Also, see <u>Raising a Spirited Child</u>, which concerns children who have some of the behaviors, but do not actually have sensory issues and are just considered wonderfully "spirited."

Printed in the United States
25187LVS00004B/28-45